Hugh Gough, 1st Viscount Gough, is an interesting and controversial figure of the late Georgian and early Victorian British Army. It is said he commanded in more battles than any other British soldier of this period, save for the Duke of Wellington. Despite this there are many who have questioned his command capability and his competence, particularly where the two Sikh Wars are concerned. In this, the first major account of his life for over one hundred years, the author seeks not to defend Gough but to better understand him. This is done by attempting to draw out the other periods of his life. By so doing we gain a greater understanding of his background, experiences and influences. Gough, like so many British officers, was part of the Anglo-Irish community. However unlike many he wore his Irish heritage with pride, and would always refer to himself as an Irishman. Yet he was a 'Unionist' and fiercely proud of the British Empire. Born into a military tradition he first wore the King's uniform at the age of thirteen. He saw extensive service during the French Revolutionary and Napoleonic Wars of the late eighteenth and early nineteenth century. He fought in Southern Africa and the Caribbean. During the Peninsular War he commanded the 87th Foot and was said to have been the most experienced battalion commander of the conflict. After the war he served in southern Ireland during the counterinsurgency response to the 'Rockite' movement. After a lengthy period on half-pay and promotion to major general he was appointed to command a division in the Madras Army. It was from here that he was despatched to command British forces fighting in China. He worked closely and effectively with his civilian and naval counterparts and was considered to have been an extremely effective commander. Returning to India he was overlooked for command of the Madras Army but was instead rewarded with the appointment of Commander-in-Chief in India. In this capacity he conquered the Gwalior State and the Sikh Empire and greatly enhanced British India. However his victories came at a high price in terms of casualties, and he was much criticised for this. Despite this he never lost a battle. He was loved by his men, largely because he suffered with them and was always willing to share in the danger. In battle he wore a white fighting coat, which made him easily identifiable to both his men and the enemy. Whilst his command ability was sometimes questioned, his courage never was. His life is an interesting tale of a career soldier, a fighting soldier, who was, as an officer who served under him remarked, "as brave as a lion".

Dr Christopher Brice was born and raised in Leicestershire, where he has lived all his life except for two years in Suffolk. He read History and Politics at undergraduate level before embarking on a PhD thesis, initially as part of a joint research agreement between the War Studies Department of the Royal Military Academy, Sandhurst and De Montfort University. The thesis was entitled 'The Military career of General Sir Henry Brackenbury 1856 1904'. Dr Brice has given lectures at the Royal Military Academy Sandhurst and the National Army Museum on Henry Brackenbury and elements of his career. He is an early stage career historian and his first book, a biography of General Sir Henry Brackenbury entitled *The Thinking Man's Soldier*, was published in January 2013. This biography of Field Marshal Hugh Gough, 1st Viscount Gough is his second book. He is presently acting as editor and as a contributor to a forthcoming book entitled *Forgotten Victorian Generals*. He is also writing a brief history of the Abyssinian Campaign, 1867–68, and is currently researching a history of the British Army from 1815–1868. Dr Brice is also editor of the Helion & Co Warfare in the Victorian Age Series.

BRAVE AS A LION

War and Military Culture in South Asia, 1757-1947

www.helion.co.uk/warandmilitarycultureinsouthasia

Series Editors

Professor Emeritus Raymond Callahan, University of Delaware
Alan Jeffreys, Imperial War Museum
Professor Daniel Marston, Australian National University

Editorial Advisory Board

Squadron Leader (Retired) Rana Chhina, Centre of Armed Forces Historical Research, United Service Institution of India
Professor Anirudh Deshpande, University of Delhi
Professor Ashley Jackson, King's College London
Dr Robert Johnson, Oxford University
Lieutenant Commander Dr Kalesh Mohanan, Naval History Division, Ministry of Defence, India
Dr Tim Moreman
Dr David Omissi, University of Hull
Professor Peter Stanley, University of New South Wales, Canberra
Dr Erica Wald, Goldsmiths, University of London

Submissions

The publishers would be pleased to receive submissions for this series. Please contact us via email (info@ helion.co.uk), or in writing to Helion & Company Limited, 26 Willow Road, Solihull, West Midlands, B91 1UE

Titles

No 1   *'Swords Trembling In Their Scabbards'. The Changing Status of Indian Officers in the Indian Army 1757-1947* Michael Creese (ISBN 978-1-909982-81-9)

No 2   *'Discipline, System and Style'. The Sixteenth Lancers and British Soldiering in India 1822-1846* John H. Rumsby (ISBN 978-1-909982-91-8)

No 3   *Die in Battle, Do not Despair. The Indians on Gallipoli, 1915* Peter Stanley (ISBN 978-1-910294-67-3)

No 4   *Brave as a Lion. The Life and Times of Field Marshal Hugh Gough, 1st Viscount Gough* Christopher Brice (ISBN 978-1-910294-61-1)

No 5   *Approach to Battle. Training the Indian Army during the Second World War* Alan Jeffreys (ISBN 978-1-911096-51-1)

BRAVE AS A LION

The Life and Times of Field Marshal Hugh Gough,
1st Viscount Gough

War and Military Culture in South Asia, 1757–1947 No. 4

Christopher Brice

 Helion & Company

Helion & Company Limited
26 Willow Road
Solihull
West Midlands
B91 1UE
England
Tel. 0121 705 3393
Fax 0121 711 4075
Email: info@helion.co.uk
Website: www.helion.co.uk
Twitter: @helionbooks
Visit our blog http://blog.helion.co.uk/

Published by Helion & Company 2017
Designed and typeset by Mach 3 Solutions Ltd (www.mach3solutions.co.uk)
Cover designed by Paul Hewitt, Battlefield Design (www.battlefield-design.co.uk)
Printed by Lightning Source Limited, Milton Keynes, Buckinghamshire

Text © Christopher Brice 2017
Images open source unless individually credited
Maps drawn by George Anderson © Helion & Company 2017

ISBN 978-1-910294-61-1

British Library Cataloguing-in-Publication Data.
A catalogue record for this book is available from the British Library.

For details of other military history titles published by Helion & Company
Limited contact the above address, or visit our website: http://www.helion.co.uk.

We always welcome receiving book proposals from prospective authors.

Contents

List of Illustrations

In plate section from page 260

Early Life
Colonel George Gough, the father of Hugh Gough. (Private collection)
Gough's brother William, the third son of George and Letitia Gough. William was a major in the 6th Foot and served extensively in the Peninsular War. He was drowned off Kinsale in 1822 when returning from Canada with his regiment. (Private collection)
Hugh Gough's mother Letitia Gough, née Bunbury. (Private collection)
Sir James Henry Craig. Commander of the expedition to Cape Colony in which the young Gough got his first taste of action.

Peninsular War
General Sir Thomas Graham, 1st Baron Lynedoch. An underrated general whose victory at Barrosa deserves greater praise than it receives.
Arthur Wellesley, 1st Duke of Wellington, was the dominant force in the British army for the first half of the 19th century. His relationship with Gough was often strained.
The Battle of Barrosa, 5 March 1811.
General Graham directing his troops at the Battle of Barrosa.
Siege of Tarifa. The painting depicts the French attack on 31 December 1811.

China
The Daoguang Emperor was a curious individual. The version of events his 'courtiers' reported to him often meant that he was a deluded individual.
This image is very hard to date. Although Gough looks quite old, the absence of the whiskers that were a constant feature of his old age makes one wonder. There is a similar engraving from 1842 on which the painting might have been based. It might be that the painting is set a little later, and there is a suggestion that Gough's uniform is that of a Colonel of the Horse Guards and thus after 1855. (Private collection)
Nemesis in battle against Chinese warships on 7 January 1841.
Negotiations on board HMS *Wellesley* on 4 July 1840, the day before the capture of Chusan.
The destruction of Opium being overseen by Commissioner Lin in 1839.
On the right of the painting the steam powered iron warship *Nemesis* can be seen.
Made by John Gilbert of Tower Hill, London circa 1840, this telescope accompanied Gough to India, and was presumably used during his campaigns both there and in China. (National Army Museum, NAM 1966-05-14)
British troops being unloaded before the advance on Canton 24 May 1841.
The British bombardment of Canton from the surrounding heights, 29 May 1841.
Sir William Parker developed a good working relationship with Gough, providing great logistical and firepower support for the campaign on land.
Brigadier General Armine Mountain. His support for Gough during the First Anglo-China War was greatly appreciated by the former.
A Chinese scroll recording the *Nemesis* and another British ship.
Sir Henry Pottinger, who managed to work well with Gough and Parker, and was reluctant to overrule them.
Boats loaded with soldiers being towed by a steamer ready for the attack on Amoy, August 1841.

Medals and Portraits

Gough in triumphant mode at the end of the Second Anglo-Sikh War, painted c 1850 by an unknown artist. A copy of this portrait hangs today in the entrance hall of the Radisson Blu St Helens hotel that was once Hugh Gough's home. (National Army Museum, NAM 1999-02-24-1).

Awarded to staff and field officers largely, although not exclusively, for service in the Peninsular War. Gough received clasps for Vittoria, Nivelle, Barrosa and Talavera. (National Army Museum, NAM 1966-10-27)

Sometimes incorrectly called the Mahrajpoor Star, but was awarded to those who also fought at Punniar. The only difference is the inscription on the silver disk in the middle of the medal which has the name of either of the battles. (National Army Museum, NAM 1966-10-27)

The medal for the First China War, although obviously it was just called the China War Medal at the time. Originally the medal was to have been issued only by the EIC to its officers and men. However it was issued by the British Government on the orders of Queen Victoria to all ranks of the army and navy. No clasp was ever issued for the First China War, so it is unclear why one appears to be missing. (National Army Museum, NAM 1966-10-27)

The Punjab Medal was issued for the Second Anglo-Sikh War. In a first for a British campaign medal it was issued to those troops who had been present in the Punjab but not taken part in any fighting. In this case it was obviously issued without claps. (National Army Museum, NAM 1966-10-27)

'Miniature Medals' of the Army Gold Cross and the Knight's Cross. (National Army Museum, NAM 1966-10-27)

The gold leaf in the centre of the broach is said to be taken from the eagle that was captured at Barossa by the 87th Foot under Gough's command. (National Army Museum, NAM 1966-10-27)

This portrait of Hugh Gough's wife, Frances, shows her at around 56 years of age, painted c.1844 by an unknown artist. She is wearing the Mahrajpore Star, which she was awarded for coming under enemy fire whilst accompanying the army during the Gwalior Campaign. (National Army Museum, NAM 1997-08-20-1).

Retirement

Miniature, watercolour on ivory, of Gough by unknown artist. Although listed as circa 1850 this does not look like the face of a seventy year old man, and might perhaps be earlier than that. (National Army Museum, NAM 1979-09-23).

Portrait of Hugh Gough by Sir Francis Grant, PRA. Although it depicts Gough commanding during the Second Anglo-Sikh War, Gough actually sat for the portrait in 1852.

Hugh Gough in civilian clothing wearing his Army Gold Cross. (Private collection)

An 1850 daguerreotype of Hugh Gough, illustrating that he was still a physically impressive looking man at the age of seventy. (Private collection)

Whilst the modern addition to the property either side can clearly be seen, the main house is much as it would have been in Gough's day. The author was informed by the management that it was apparently the first property in Ireland to have a preservation order placed on both the exterior and interior. (Courtesy of Radisson Blu Group)

The front of St Helen's, now a hotel in the Radisson Blu chain, once owned by Hugh Gough. Taken by the author on his 2013 visit to Ireland.

Lough Cutra Castle, County Galway, purchased by Hugh Gough in 1854. He seldom visited it and his son George seems to have had more to do with than he ever did.

The Coat of Arms of Viscount Gough of Goojerat and of Limerick. (Private collection)

This image appeared in the *Illustrated London* News on 6 March 1880. It gives some sense of the significance that was placed on the unveiling of the statue.

The statue of Lord Gough by John Henry Foley as it stands today in the grounds of Chillingham Castle, Northumberland.

List of Maps

War and Military Culture in South Asia, 1757–1947
Series Editor's Preface

The aim of this new academic historical series is to produce well-researched monographs on the armed forces of South Asia, concentrating mainly on the East India Company and the Indian armed forces from 1757 until 1947. Books in the series will examine the military history of the period as well as social, cultural, political and economic factors, although inevitably the armies of the East India Company and the Indian Army will dominate the series. In addition, edited volumes of conference papers, memoirs and campaign histories will also be published. It is hoped this series will be of interest to both serious historians and the general military history reader.

The foundation of the series coincides with the rise of academic interest in Indian military history over the last few years. In particular the series will contribute to the 'new military history' of South Asia. This came to prominence at an academic conference held in Cambridge in 1997 that was reinvigorated at two recent conferences held at the University of Greenwich and Jadavpur University, Kolkata in 2013–2014 with aim of 'Re-newing the Military History of Colonial South Asia'. The aim of this series is to harness this explosion of interest and channel it into a series of groundbreaking volumes that add to the growing historiography of the period. For example in the field of Second World War studies and the period until Partition, Daniel Marston and Tim Moreman have spearheaded this historical research with their volumes: *Phoenix from the Ashes: The Indian Army in the Burma Campaign* (2003) and *The Jungle, the Japanese and the Commonwealth Armies at War* (2005). These are complemented by Raymond Callahan's *Churchill and His Generals* (2007), a seminal work published in the United States that should be better known in the United Kingdom, and the wider study by Ashley Jackson on *The British Empire and the Second World War* (2006). Similarly there have been a number of relevant conferences such as one held at the Imperial War Museum in 2009, the papers of which were published as *The Indian Army, 1939–1947: Experience and Development* (2012). Daniel Marston's *The Indian Army and the End of the Raj* (2014) has also recently been published.

This interest has been mirrored in India as eight volumes of the official histories of the Indian Armed Forces during the Second World War were reprinted in India in 2012 and another four in 2014. They were originally published between 1954 and 1960. As Squadron Leader Rana Chhina stated at the launch of the reprints: 'As a resurgent India seeks to be a major player on the world stage, it behoves it to discard its narrow post-colonial world view, and to step up to reclaim the role that its armed forces played out on a global scale' during the Second World War. Anirudh Deshpande's *A Spring of Despair: Mutiny, Rebellion and Death in India, 1946* will be published in 2015. Similarly Rana Chhina and the United Service Institution of India are organising a number of events for the centenary of 'India and the Great War', including a number of detailed academic studies in partnership with this series. It is envisaged that monographs will be published on the role of the Indian Army in all the major First World War theatres as well as other aspects of the war such as the Indian State Forces and an edited volume of essays.

The series editors, members of the editorial advisory board and our publisher, Duncan Rogers of Helion, are all delighted to be involved in this series and we hope it will be of interest not only in the UK and India but globally, too.

Alan Jeffreys

Foreword

I suspect one's most famous forbear is bound to appear to be an icon if he was considered to be as brave as a lion, have a high moral outlook and live into his 90th year.

That is what my great-great-grandfather proved to be. In his teens he was at the Capture of Simon's Town in 1795 with a Scottish Regiment, 78th Highlanders. He returned to his Irish roots by going with the 87th to the West Indies and he fought through much of the Peninsular War leading the 2nd Battalion of the 87th Foot, gaining a Peninsular Gold Cross and a Spanish Knighthood. The Channel Islands and Ireland called him. Half-pay featured until he went to India in 1837.

He had not expected the considerable active service that was to follow. The first China War came next followed by three campaigns in India, the Gwalior Campaign, the First Anglo–Sikh War, and the Second Anglo–Sikh War, finishing in 1849 when he was 70! Wounds and fever had featured throughout his career, largely because he had never spared himself any of the danger or hardships that his men endured.

In retirement honours and rewards periodically came his way. He was sent by the Queen as her representative to the Crimea to dub knights and give out other decorations. He was a pall-bearer at the funeral of the Duke of Wellington and as a result an original Governor of Wellington College.

He also had a happy marriage, that appears to have been a true 'love-match', and he had a generally happy family life with his children and grandchildren. So in that regard life was good to him.

In the modern age it is now hard to imagine how difficult it was to successfully move an army in the tropics with basic transportation and infrastructure, particularly before the building of rail networks. One also forgets how basic the medical cover was, and how slowly this changed. Even in September 1914 my father had an arm amputated without anaesthetic, which goes to illustrate that change could be slow in this direction.

Although the 1st Viscount was not a great user of clever tactics he was greatly loved by all ranks through his long service. His personal bravery was never doubted, and this goes a long way to explain why the ranks felt the way they did about him.

This bravery continued in the family and he was the great-uncle of two recipients of the Victoria Cross. They were brothers and the son of one was also awarded a Victoria Cross in the 20th century.

Read on and I hope you enjoy the biography of an eminent Georgian/Victorian soldier.

5th Viscount Gough

Acknowledgements

I am grateful to many people for their assistance in the researching, writing, and production of this book. Two people in particular deserved special thanks. Firstly, Duncan Rogers, managing director of Helion & Co, who had long felt that an updated biography of Field Marshal Hugh Gough, 1st Viscount Gough, has been required. I am grateful that he had the confidence in me to, 'put his money where his mouth is' and commission me to write this book. Throughout this project Duncan's generosity, both financial and otherwise, and his continued support, understanding, and encouragement have been of inestimable help.

Secondly, I am deeply grateful to the present Viscount Gough, the great-great-grandson of the 1st Viscount, for his considerable assistance throughout. Lord Gough has kindly provided the author with access to privately held family correspondence, provided many photographs of items from his private collection, and been extremely helpful throughout. His assistance has made the research and writing of this book far smoother than it might otherwise have been. Yet at no time has he sought to influence or sway the author in the writing of the book. For all this I am deeply grateful.

I am grateful to the many academics and writers who have assisted my research. I am grateful to John Hawkins for his introduction to the present Viscount Gough and his kind interest throughout my work. The Irish writer and historian, Turtle Bunbury, himself a distant relative of the subject of this work, has been helpful throughout the process, particularly in terms of his contacts in the Republic of Ireland. Also in Ireland, I am grateful to Karen D'Alton of St Brigid's Church, Stillorgan for information regarding the funeral and burial of Hugh Gough. Thanks are also due to the management and staff of the Radisson Blu St Helen's Hotel, for allowing me to look round the former residence of Hugh Gough, and for their assistance with the book.

Although mention has already been made of Helion & Co it is only right that I should thank all those associated with that company for their assistance in bringing this book to completion. My thanks are also due to Alan Jeffreys, Professor Ray Callahan, and Dr Andrew Bamford for reading through the manuscript and offering their advice. I am grateful to my friend Anna Coombs (or to use her Chinese name, Qing Wang) for the translation of several letters written in Chinese found in the National Archives. Her assistance in what I understand was not an easy job of translation is much appreciated. Thanks also to Dr Edward Gosling for his assistance in accessing material held at the Bodleian Library, Oxford. I am also grateful to Christopher Normand for his assistance regarding the history of the Gough family.

Thanks must also go to the various archives that I have visited and had contact with. This includes the National Archives at Kew, the British Library, the National Library of Ireland, the National Archives of Ireland, and the National Library of Scotland. Particular thanks are due to the National Army Museum, Chelsea for their kind assistance with regards to the Gough papers. They made great efforts to facilitate the use of this archive. I also wish to express my gratitude to Mr Andrew Orgill and the staff of the Central Library at the Royal Military Academy, Sandhurst for help during the early days of my research.

My thanks are also due to Bill Whitburn author of *Bright Eyes of Danger: An Account of the Anglo-Sikh Wars*, our regular 'lively' discussions over the years of my research and his alternative view point has been extremely helpful.

My thanks are also due to my parents and my partner Jane for their help and support during my studies.

Introduction

The title of this book borrows from the words of an officer who served under the future Field Marshal Hugh Gough, 1st Viscount Gough. The full quotation, referring to Gough, is that "He is brave as a Lion but has no headpiece".[1] The fact that only the opening part of this quotation is used in the title should not be taken as an indication that this is an uncritical biography. The quote does in many ways demonstrate the popular conception of Gough as a military commander: brave but lacking in intelligence. Having said that, 'popular' is perhaps the wrong word to use given that like the majority of Victorian military commanders Gough remains largely unknown. Sadly what is generally known tends to concentrate on the negative. However the intention of this biography is not to defend Gough but to attempt to better understand him. By illustrating the whole of his career it is hoped to enable a better understanding of a general whose long and devoted service to the Crown deserves to be better known.

Yet Gough even by Victorian standards appears 'old-fashioned'; particularly in regard to his notions of warfare. In many ways he was an unlikely commander-in-chief, and his assumption of such an office says much about that perennial problem of the British Army; higher command leadership. Gough was very much a 'fighting' general rather than a 'planner'. Gough's career was best summed up by Professor Sir Hew Strachan when alluding to the point that Gough was a Blucher who never found his Gneisenau. "On innumerable occasions in the Sikh Wars, a Gneisenau to match his Blucher would have saved Gough from planning mistakes which had to be recovered by hard fighting".[2]

Field Marshal Gough was undoubtedly one of the most significant British soldiers of the 19th century. His career spanned the period from the French Revolutionary Wars to the early Victorian era. He fought against the Dutch in southern Africa, and against the French, Dutch, and Spanish in the Caribbean and South America, and against the French in Portugal and Spain and indeed into France itself. He was part of a now largely forgotten counterinsurgency campaign in the south of Ireland and then after a period of semi-retirement he led the campaign against the Empire of China during the First Anglo–China War. There followed a brief war against the Mahrattas during the Gwalior Campaign, before he commanded an army in two wars against the Sikhs.

It has been said that no British soldier of the 19th century, except for the Duke of Wellington, took part in more battles than Gough did. Although Gough was a successful general, who never lost a battle, he was – and indeed remains – a controversial figure. He was an active officer for over 56 years, but his career is defined somewhat unfairly by the two wars he fought against the Sikhs from December 1845 to March 1846 and then from April 1848 to March 1849. For such a short period of command to define his career is to an extent unfortunate. Indeed it is the intention of this work to draw out the other periods of his career and not to concentrate solely on this short period. There is so much more that deserves attention in his career.

There has been a previous attempt to chronicle the life and career of Hugh Gough. In 1903 a two volume biography of Gough was published, written by Sir Robert Rait. Yet in many ways

---

1   National Records of Scotland (NRS) RH2/8/69: Folio 26 W.M. Stewart to the Lindesay Family, undated.
2   Strachan, Hew, *The Reform of the British Army 1830–54* (Manchester: Manchester University Press, 1984), p. 147.

this illustrates the previously made point that there has been an over-concentration upon the Sikh Wars. Almost the entire second volume, save a few chapters on his years of retirement, is devoted to the Sikh Wars. Indeed a number of the closing chapters of the first volume are an introduction to the Sikh Wars. Whilst no one would deny for a moment the significance of the two wars against the Sikhs, there is far more to the life and career of Gough. It is inevitable that such significant campaigns deserve a great deal of comment and space in any biography. However the present author has tried to make more of the other periods of his life. This is not only because of their significance, but because to understand Gough's behaviour and attitudes during the Sikh Wars one has to understand and appreciate his past experiences. To that end, events in Gough's life and career that were either given scant mention or not mentioned at all in the previous biography, have been placed in better context. Many events were deserving of a chapter unto themselves and now have one.

His previous biographer, Sir Robert Rait, attempted a defence of Hugh Gough.[3] Indeed in the preface he makes it quite clear that this was his intention stating that, "the present work is an attempt to present at once a record of Lord Gough s career, and a vindication of his military policy from the charges which are most frequently brought against it".[4] To an extent this was required at the time to redress the balance. Much had been written that was deeply critical of Gough, the majority of it presenting the point of view of other significant figures during the Sikh Wars, such as Dalhousie, Hardinge, Napier, Smith, and Havelock. Often the praise showered upon such figures was at the expense of Gough. Much of what was written was factually inaccurate, or at the very least one-sided and biased, and Rait attempted to expose it as such. However Rait's otherwise excellent biography consequently does have something of a 'crusading' feel to it, and can therefore equally be accused of bias. This was not just because he attempted to praise Gough, without really examining his faults and failings, but also because he became rather obsessed with putting the record straight. One particular target in this regard is Colonel George Bruce Malleson. Malleson's 1883 book *The Decisive Battles of India from 1746 to 1849* had been extremely critical of Gough. That, in and of itself, was not a problem. The problem was Malleson's overreliance on 'camp' gossip, the opinions of people as witnesses who had either not been present or had not been privy to the plans and thoughts of Gough, and a general reliance of legends rather than fact.

By comparison, Rait had access to all the papers of Hugh Gough, made available by the 3rd Viscount Gough, but had also been able to 'interview' several of Gough's staff, including the by then Field Marshal Frederick Haines, as well as numerous officers who had served under Gough, many of whom had retired with general rank. The current Viscount Gough has allowed the present author access to many of the papers in his possession and has assisted in access to papers held on his behalf at the National Army Museum. However at some point some of the collection has been broken up and thus not all the papers Rait had access to have been available to the present author. Rait also had the assistance of Lord Wolseley, who read his manuscript before publication. According to Rait, Wolseley made many suggestions concerning the chapters of the book

---

3   There is a quirk of fate in that Lord Gough's two biographers, Sir Robert Rait and the present author, were born in the same county, Leicestershire. Although often called a Scottish historian, as the family moved to Aberdeen when he was very young, Rait had been born in Narborough in Leicestershire. Rait was educated at the University of Aberdeen, and indeed taught there for a time, before moving to New College Oxford. From Oxford he achieved First Class Honours, won the coveted Stanhope Prize, and became a Fellow of the college. He worked as a lecturer at New College for a number of years. In 1913 he became Professor of Scottish History and Literature at the University of Glasgow. This was interrupted by the First World War during which he worked from 1915–1918 in the War Trade Intelligence Department. In 1929 Rait was made Principal of the University of Glasgow and in 1933 he was knighted. He died in May 1936.

4   Rait, Robert S. *The Life and Campaigns of Hugh Gough First Viscount Gough Field-Marshal*, Two Volumes (London: Archibald Constable & Co, Ltd, 1903), p. vi.

that focused upon China. Amongst the others who read Rait's manuscript before publication was Professor Sir Charles Oman, perhaps best remembered for his seven volume history of the Peninsular War. All of this allowed Rait to produce a well-researched and well-supported piece of work, if somewhat uncritical in its nature.

In one sense this has been helpful to the present author, as he has not been required to attempt to redress the balance himself. Indeed, more often than not it has been necessary to add the critical voice to comments made by Rait. Rait's biography was also part of an academic 'duel' he was engaged in with Sir William Lee-Warner. Indeed Lee-Warner launched a thinly veiled attack on Rait in his biography of Lord Dalhousie.[5] Rait is not mentioned by name, but is clearly the target of Lee-Warner's comment that, "Biographers who have thrown themselves into the controversy with an eagerness of offence, would have shown greater wisdom had they imitated the dignified reserve of the man [Gough] whose cause they championed."[6]

This does however touch upon a relevant point, in that as regards the controversies concerning his role in the two wars against the Sikhs, Gough did keep a 'dignified silence' in public. When accusations against his conduct, his ability, even his sanity, were made Gough did not respond publicly. It was a difficult situation, and a highly political one. If he had responded and publicly defended himself it would have been a very messy situation, one which Gough had no desire to become embroiled in. However, not responding could also be interpreted as acceptance of the validity of the adverse statements. Yet when one reads Gough's private correspondence he does not hold back in his criticism. Many of the most highly critical letters are written to his son, George, later 2nd Viscount Gough, or his nephew, John Bloomfield Gough, later a full general. He knew he could rely on the discretion of the two men. Indeed at one point in his private correspondence Gough does threaten to go public, saying "were I inclined I have a tale to unfold which would be very unpalatable to my honourable masters", but we shall look at that in more detail later.[7]

The letters to his son and his nephew were equivalent to a safety valve. They allowed him to blow off steam without having to defend himself, or explain himself, in public. Gough was not equipped for political games either intellectually or temperamentally. Yet by confiding his opinion, thoughts, and feelings to close family members he was able to express such feelings in a safe environment. Whilst not public knowledge during his lifetime, this correspondence is a valuable source to historians and perhaps deserves greater research.

Yet Gough remains a largely maligned figure. As recently as 2000 he was branded as a military incompetent by an author who repeats, and appears to give credence to one of the wilder 'fantasies' that after the Battle of Chillianwala there were proceedings planned to court-martial Gough and execute him if found guilty on charges of incompetence. The story is fanciful to say the least and comes from battlefield rumours and the misreading separately of the correspondence of Lord Dalhousie and the future Field Marshal Sir Neville Chamberlain.[8] Although many would not go to this extreme, the general view that Gough was incompetent is widely held. We will look at this in more detail in the conclusion, using the excellent framework on the psychology of military incompetence constructed by Professor Norman Dixon.

However whether or not there is a case to answer in regard to military incompetence, two things are certain, firstly that Gough was an unimaginative general, and secondly he was very much a

---

5   It is interesting to note that Rait actually acknowledges Lee-Warner's help. However Lee-Warner's reaction to the finished article, after publication, was not positive.

6   Lee-Warner, William, *The Life of the Marquis of Dalhousie* Vol. I (London: Macmillan & Co Ltd, 1904), p. 217.

7   The National Army Museum (NAM), 8303–105, Gough Papers, Gough to unknown, 19 March 1849.

8   Allen, Charles, *Soldier Sahibs* (London: John Murray, 2000), p. 191. The first point to make concerning this would be to question who sits in judgement at a court martial of a commander-in-chief?

product of his time and his experiences. As a subaltern, Gough saw considerable service outside of Europe. As a battalion commander he led his men with distinction during the Peninsular War. In Ireland in the 1820s he led a mixed force of infantry, cavalry, and militia in a counterinsurgency war against the 'Rockites'. The period of unparalleled success in China was important in developing him as a general. Indeed all this experience is important in understanding the man, and in turn understanding his conduct during the Sikh Wars.

Gough also suffers from the fact that he was not one of the 'elite' set of early 19th century Britain. Gough was unfortunate that the two governor generals during the Sikh Wars, Lords Hardinge and Dalhousie, were both close personal friends of the Duke of Wellington. The Duke of Wellington was commander-in-chief of the British Army for most of this period, and even when not holding that office he inevitably had a strong influence over military affairs. This close personal relationship with Wellington was something that Gough never enjoyed. Indeed Wellington had been deeply critical, in an unfair manner, about the battalion Gough had commanded during the Peninsular War, and one cannot help but wonder if this coloured Wellington's thinking in the years that followed. Hardinge by comparison had worked on Wellington's staff and had been an important ally at the War Office in the years since the Napoleonic Wars. As for Dalhousie, he was almost akin to adopted son of the Duke of Wellington.

Another factor that meant Gough was something of an outsider was his nationality, or to be more accurate the fact that he embraced it. The British Army has a long list of general officers of Irish background. However, unlike most of them, Gough proudly declared his nationality. He was both an Irishman and a proud servant of British Crown, and saw no contradiction in the two. There is little hard evidence to support the theory, but it is possible that much of the contemporary criticism of Gough had an undertone connected to him being Irish. Criticism of him using such terms as referring to his excited 'Irish blood', or 'Tipperary tactics' are partly evidence of this but one gets the feeling that there was an undercurrent against Gough being proud of his nationality. Gough is also said to have had a strong Irish brogue and to have made no attempt to hide it. It would perhaps be wrong to make too much of this but it is difficult to discount it completely. This was of course during a very difficult period in the Anglo-Irish relationship.

Gough also suffered from the rather bizarre attitude towards the reporting of military success. When one reads the press of the time, or the parliamentary debates, one is struck by the fact that when things are going wrong Gough as commander-in-chief takes sole blame, but when they go well the governor general and other officers share equal praise. Indeed one can go further and point to the fact that when Wellington gave thanks in the House of Lords at the end of the First Sikh War he inexplicably did not mention Gough by name.

It would be wrong, however, to paint the picture of Gough simply as a victim. His unimaginative mind and tactics, added to a dislike of logistics and administration, do open him to justifiable criticism. In this work the author has not hesitated to criticise Gough where necessary and appropriate. Gough's tactical mind might have been limited, but he was in many ways a product of his time. Firepower was still a rather secondary consideration. Particularly, that is, for the infantryman. Throughout the era in which Gough commanded the musket remained the firearm of the infantry. Towards the end of his era of command the flintlock was replaced by the percussion cap as the means of igniting the weapon, but it remained to all intents and purposes the weapon commonly referred to as Brown Bess.[9] This was inaccurate and unwieldy, and indeed only really had effect when firing in mass volleys. Many commanders of the era, including those who were considered to be Gough's betters, considered that firing was a tactic of defence not offence. Indeed one can argue that the British infantryman in

---

9   Brown Bess is a rather generic term that was applied to several patterns of weapon during this period that were similar in many ways.

general was better suited to the defence rather than the offence. Gough was therefore unfortunate in having to command in two campaigns that required him to act on the offensive.

To say that Gough was a simple man might be misconstrued, so it is perhaps better to say that he was straightforward in his approach. He spoke his mind and appreciated those who did likewise. Indeed he had little time for 'politics'. What he certainly had was a big heart. Although this was best seen in his love for his family and for the men who served under his command, it was not reserved for them. A story exists, that might be apocryphal but certainly fits his character, and tells of an incident in a hotel in Athlone in September 1855.[10] Four commercial travellers, three Irish and the other a Yorkshireman, were having dinner, when in walked a tall, be whiskered man who had a martial bearing. The man proceeded to pace up and down as if waiting for someone. The Yorkshireman discerned from his complexion that he had spent many years in India. Yet rather than the general that he turned out to be he had mistaken him for an NCO. The soldier was heard to mutter something about 'commercials' that sounded derogatory to the Yorkshireman's ears – it appears the comment had something to do with the habit of commercial travellers to have dinner at around 5:00–6:00 p.m. rather than later in the evening as was the preference of 'gentlemen'. The three Irishmen however simply smiled and carried on with their dinner, for they knew who the soldier was. The Yorkshireman was however fuming, and when the remark was made yet again he could restrain himself no longer. Getting up from the table he confronted the taller man, saying that yes, he was a commercial, and that it was a respectable trade and that he was as good a man as any sergeant in a barrack room. What looked a tense situation was eased as the tall soldier smiled, held out his hand, and was reported to say:

> Give me your hand old fellow, for I see you are a regular brick. I love a fellow who will stand up for his class and order against all comers; and to assure you that I had no idea or intention of insulting either you or this company, I would stop and dine with you, although I am particularly engaged to dine out this evening with an old friend, and would not like to break my agreement.

It was only when he summoned the wine waiter and ordered drinks for the commercial travellers, that the Yorkshireman discovered who he had challenged when the waiter responded 'Yes, my Lord Gough'. Gough left £1 (over £55 in modern money) to pay for the drinks he ordered which included four bottles of the best wine, two of port, and two of sherry.

As previously stated, the story may not be true. However the character traits of Gough that come through this story are most certainly accurate. He was a strong, blunt, and determined man. Yet he was not without humour, discretion, heart, and of course great generosity. Now it may well be that £1 was an investment to get him out of an unfortunate argument of his own making, and there are no doubt those who have studied Lord Gough's career who might suggest that interpretation. However if that were the case one wonders if there would have been such humour and such admiration in the way in which he did it. The story gives us a good insight into Gough as a man, but is also an insight into the attributes he brought as a general. The fact that he also appreciated the Yorkshireman's determination and tenacity was also in keeping with his own spirit and emotions.

Gough had not only the temperament of a soldier but also the look of one. He was tall – around six feet in an era when that was rare – slim, and handsome. Indeed he was once described as the 'beau ideal' of a soldier.[11] The uniform suited him well. Yet these characteristics were somewhat at odds with his reported character as a soldier. Whilst he might look like the 'beau ideal' his behaviour did not always match. We have already seen something of the character traits that he

---

10   *The Times*, Thursday, 27 September, 1855.
11   *The Times*, Wednesday, 25 June 1856.

exhibited. Yet his ability to share the hardship of his men in equal measure was not in keeping with his appearance. He was not a 'beau' aloof from his men.

Gough had never lacked courage. As one historian stated, even his "worst critics never accused him of a lack of courage or lack of loyalty to the Crown".[12] Both points are valid but we will concentrate on the courage element for now. Gough had never been afraid to place himself in harm's way. As a subaltern he had pushed himself forward, as a battalion commander he had led from the front, and even as a general he was never far from the front line. In battle, in later years, he wore a distinctive white coat that he called his 'fighting coat'. It made him easily identifiable to the men under his command and the sight of it could send his men into frenzied cheering. On the other hand it also made him easily identifiable to the enemy. Yet Gough, with consummate bravery, used this to his advantage. He did on occasions deliberately ride forward to draw the fire of the enemy so as to save his troops. This not only gave respite to his men, it gave them a great deal of added respect for his qualities as a soldier, if not necessarily a general. His movements to the front in his white coat however should not be construed as vainglorious or reckless; they were in fact thoroughly practical.

It is hoped that the following is a balanced account of the life of an extremely significant late Georgian and early Victorian soldier. The fact that Gough's career crossed this divide is in some ways unfortunate. It is unfair, as some have done, to view Gough's battles by the standards of the later Victorian period. The technology was still largely that of the Georgian era, or the era of the Napoleonic wars at least, as were the tactics. Indeed Gough was perhaps more a Georgian in outlook, instinct, and behaviour than he was a Victorian. Thus by looking at the career of Gough we get an insight into that crossover period in British Imperial and military history from one era to the next. The career of Gough also gives us a further insight into that perennial problem within the British Army: higher command leadership. It is far easier to point to Gough's leadership in later years and say that he was out of his depth or unsuited to higher command, than to point to any credible alternatives amongst his contemporaries on the list of general officers. It is easy to say Gough should have been replaced in command, but far harder to name a suitable replacement. Thus, Gough's career needs to be placed in context. Whilst there are clearly faults and failures in his leadership they also need to be placed in context.

To do this his career is examined for the most part in chronological order. Occasionally it has been felt necessary to move away from this approach to help to explain events and to further the aim of placing Gough's career into context by so doing. Sometimes it has been necessary to place correspondence out of chronological order so that it can be better understood. The reason for doing this is due partly to the the length of time communication took between Britain and India or China. This often meant that letters were two or three months behind events on the ground. A good example of this is seen regarding the Battle of Chillianwala, fought on the 13 January 1849. By the time details became public in Britain it was early March, by which time Gough had fought and won the Battle of Gujrat and the war was virtually at an end. It was therefore the case that the press, public, and politicians were reacting to something that had already been overtaken by events. Given this problem regarding the time taken for correspondence occasionally it has been felt appropriate to place such correspondence all together to better understand the debate.

Other than that, this biography progresses through the life of Hugh Gough from his childhood to his retirement. His was a significant, if often controversial, career and one that it is important to reconsider when looking at the period of development in the British Army that it encompassed. By examining his career in more detail, placing it in its proper context, and by a fair and critical analysis of his life and times, this study enhances our understanding not only of the man but the wider issues of the British Army's development, tactical and technological change, and the expansion of the British Empire throughout this era.

---

12   Farwell, Byron, *Eminent Victorian Generals: Seekers of Glory* (New York, W. W. Norton & Co, 1985), p. 60.

Part 1

Early Life and Career

1

The Gough Family

Before entering in to our narrative, it will be helpful to look briefly at the background of the Gough family. This will help us to understand not only where Hugh Gough was coming from but also the circumstances into which he was born. This is not intended to be a detailed account of the Gough family, but merely to provide some helpful context for the life of the man we will look at in more detail later on.[1]

The name of Gough appears to be Welsh in origin, and is considered to be a derivation of either the Welsh word *Coch*, which means Red, or *Gof*, which means blacksmith. The name Goch was used in Wales and this is an early form of the name we now know as Gough. History records a Welsh archer called 'Sir' John Goch who commanded a company of archers at the Battle of Hastings in support of King Harold. There was also a 14th century Welsh poet called Iolo Goch. In the late 14th and early 15th centuries Sir Matthew Gough commanded in many of the actions of the later period of the Hundred Years War, particularly at the Battle of Formigny in 1450. Matthew Gough was from the Welsh line and some sources do refer to him as Goch rather than Gough. After his death, during the Cade Rebellion of 1450 whilst defending London Bridge for the King, his descendants settled largely in the area around Wiltshire. The family developed great wealth, particularly through the wool trade. During the English Civil War the family divided, the Royalist side using the spelling Gough and the Parliamentarians Goffe. William Goffe was a captain in the New Model Army and later one of the Regicides. During the Republic, William was Cromwell's Major General for Berkshire, Hampshire and Sussex. After the restoration he fled to America where he is thought to have lived out his remaining days. His brother was Stephen Gough, a military chaplain in the Low Countries in the late 1620s and early 1630s. He worked as an agent for the exiled Charles II, and was later chaplain to the widowed Henrietta Maria. Although primarily from Welsh ancestry it was after members of the family had moved to Ireland that our story, and that of the 'modern' line of the Gough family, really begins.

The Gough family were part of the Anglo-Irish community that for many generations supplied a very important part of the British Army officer corps. The Goughs, Wellesleys, Napiers, Lord Roberts, Lord Wolseley, Lord Alanbrooke, Lord Alexander, and even Viscount Montgomery, were amongst the many distinguished soldiers that came from this cultural group. Indeed it can be argued that this was the closest that Britain came to having a military caste similar to the Prussian Junkers. Although this might be to take it too far, it is surprising how many senior British generals

---

1   When it comes to looking at the background of the Gough family I am indebted to the current Viscount Gough for his assistance. Equally valuable has been the assistance of Mr Christopher Normand. He is currently preparing a history of the entire Gough family, and despite the great demand on his time of such a work he has always been extremely helpful when it comes to matters concerning the family. I am also grateful to the Irish historian and broadcaster Turtle Bunbury, a distant relative of the Goughs, for his assistance and for his introduction to Christopher Normand. Rait's biography of Gough also contains considerable information of the background of the Gough family.

of the 19th and 20th centuries have come from such roots. When one looks at the number of members of the Gough family who entered the Army it is tempting to view it as the 'family business', although for a time being the same could be said of the Church. The family would go on to earn three Victoria Crosses and it can easily be argued that several other Goughs, including Hugh Gough, would probably have earned such an award had it been constituted during the French Revolutionary and Napoleonic Wars.

The Goughs had first come to Ireland during the early days of the reign of James I. Three brothers – Robert, Francis, and Hugh – had left England for Ireland. They were the sons of Hugh Gough, Rector of All Cannings in Wiltshire, so already we see that the name Hugh was something of a family tradition. They were all in Holy Orders and had all graduated from Oxford University. The Hugh Gough that we are concerned with is thought to be a direct descendant of Francis Gough, Bishop of Limerick from 1626 until his death in 1634. However it gets a little confusing and records for that period are not the best. It has been suggested that in actual fact he might have been descended from the youngest brother, Hugh.[2] The line becomes a little clearer from our subject's Great-great-great-great grandfather. This was the Reverend Hugh Gough who was born in 1599. Even here the records are conflicting, some recording his death as 1682 others as 1670. The fact that there are so many family members either called George or Hugh makes this all very confusing for historians. The Reverend Hugh Gough was the Rector of Rathkeale and Chancellor of Limerick Cathedral. His son was George Gough who would also be Rector of Rathkeale. The ecclesiastical traditional was continued with his son the Rev Hugh Gough who was Rector of Kilfinny in county Limerick and a graduate of Trinity College Dublin. His son, also Hugh Gough, is not recorded as having entered the Church, and indeed the only employment we know of is as a 'Cornet of Horse'. The family took a break from the name Hugh, and his son and grandson were both named George. The George Gough born 1720 was our subject's grandfather, and the George Gough born either 1750 or 1751 was his father. The latter was himself a military man and his career somewhat overlapped with that of his son.

Lieutenant Colonel George Gough, as he became, had married Letitia Bunbury, a member of another distinguished Anglo-Irish family, in January 1775.[3] By the time of his marriage he had already made a military career for himself. He was first commissioned as a cornet in the 4th Regiment of Horse. History somewhat losses touch with him until 1793 when we have record of him being appointed Deputy Governor of the city of Limerick. Another term for this position would have been military magistrate, as his main job was to organise the Militia Ballot and to make sure it was enforced. The main prerequisite for this job was that the individual should have authority within the district. In this age that meant property, and this appears to have been the main qualification for the position. So we get a clear picture that the Goughs had developed considerable wealth and prestige in the Limerick area. He had taken on this appointment in April 1793 and a month later he was promoted to captain having transferred from the cavalry to a militia regiment. Shortly after this he was promoted to major and in 1797 he was given a brevet lieutenant colonelcy. This was the time of the Irish rebellion usually referred to as the Rebellion of 1798.

The truth was that the rebellion had been going on since 1793. However it was in 1798 that it really came to a head. Whilst to go into detail of the various rebellions and uprisings in Ireland is not necessary for our purpose, it is useful to look briefly at the growing problems that George Gough faced. The main group behind the rebellion were called the United Irishmen, founded in Belfast in 1791. Originally this had been a liberal group concerned with political reform, particularly in the aftermath of the Catholic relief legislation between 1778 and 1784. This had lifted

2   Rait, *Gough*, Vol. I, p. 4.
3   For information on the Bunbury connection I am indebted to the Irish historian Turtle Bunbury.

some of the restrictions placed upon Catholics in the Popery Act of 1698. Yet this was not enough for many in Ireland and the desire was to move to full emancipation. The term United Irishmen was apt as the group comprised both Protestants and Catholics who had joined together for the benefit of Ireland. However there was a clear split as elements of the group started to favour more revolutionary action, influenced by events in America and France and by the recently published work of Thomas Paine the *Rights of Man*. The outbreak of war between Britain and France in 1793 forced the group underground and it became an organisation dedicated to revolution in Ireland. Its leader, Theobald Wolfe Tone, travelled to France to negotiate for a French invasion of Ireland to support their cause. This led to the launching of the *Expedition d'Irlande* by the French where an army of approximately 14,000 French soldiers and a fleet of 17 ships of the line, 13 Frigates and 14 other vessels were dispatched for Ireland. Whilst the fleet managed to evade the Royal Navy and indeed reached Bantry Bay, a number of factors, not least of all the weather, prevented a landing and the expedition was forced to return home. Wolfe Tone was later attributed as saying, "England has had its luckiest escape since the Armada". For a time the government response was a mixture of attempts to deal with the causes of rebellion whilst brutally putting down any such movements towards that. However the imposition of martial law meant that the United Irishmen came to be dominated by those in favour of rebellion, leading to open rebellion in 1798.

In the response to this George Gough was to play an active role. As a lieutenant colonel, his seniority often meant that he was in command of more than just the Limerick Militia. There were two particular occasions when his prompt action helped to prevent the growth of the rebellion, particularly around the area of Edenderry, in County Offaly. In June 1798 George Gough moved quickly when rebels occupied the house and land of Irish politician Lord Harbertson. Upon hearing the news that the rebels had occupied Harbertson's property, Gough paraded his battalion of Limerick Militia and started for the area in question. By early the next morning he was ready to attack and succeeded in driving the rebels not only from the house but the surrounding land, killing 14 of them and suffering no losses. The rebel force, which is recorded as being a large one although no accurate figure survives, was virtually destroyed as all their stores and many of their weapons were taken. By quick action George Gough had struck a major blow and the residents of Edenderry were extremely grateful for his prompt action which probably saved the town, as it is clear that the occupation and concentration at Lord Harbertson's residence was a prelude to an attack on the town itself.

About a month later George Gough was in action again. In July a force of 4,000 Irish rebels "were laying waste the county in the neighbourhood of Edenderry".[4] Gough set out with 400 men of his own Limerick Militia, 30 dragoons and 35 mounted yeomanry, to attempt to deal with the rebels. It says much for the disorganised and ill-trained nature of the rebels that this force of less than 500 men dealt with a force many times their superior in numbers. Gough completely defeated the rebels at Johnstown, capturing their leaders in to the bargain. During the engagement Gough had his horse killed, shot through the neck, and had the cockade of his hat shot off. Whether this was simply the risk of being an officer, and an easy target on horseback, or similar to the disregard for personal safety that his son would later exhibit, is unclear. It does however illustrate that this was real combat with real risks, no matter how superior British forces might be in terms of training and equipment to their Irish counterparts.

In August 1798, the French General Jean Humbert landed in Kilcummin harbour near Killala in County Mayo, with a little over 1,000 troops. This 'invasion' also met with initial success and Humbert was successful when his force of about 2,000 Frenchmen and Irishmen defeated a British force of 6,000 militia, in what became known as the Battle of Castlebar. Humbert, using local

---

4   Rait, *Gough*, Vol. I, p. 8.

knowledge, managed to move through an area the British had thought impassable and appeared from a different direction to that anticipated. The British under Lieutenant General Gerald Lake, who had in June 1798 brutally put down a rebellion in Wexford, hurriedly had to change their deployment and were still doing so as the French attacked. British artillery caused many casualties to the advance force, but the bayonet charge of the French infantry was so ferocious that much of the militia turned and ran, and not a few joined the enemy. The few British regulars made a fight of it but were quickly overwhelmed and the numerically-superior British were soon in full retreat. Franco-Irish success was short-lived and the French were disappointed that the Irish never rebelled in the numbers they had hoped and expected. The French and Irish were later defeated at Ballinamuck on 8 September and Killala on 23 September, and the rebellion was largely at an end.

Of interest to us is that between the Battles of Castlebar and Ballinamuck there was an action involving George Gough at a place called Coloomey near Sligo. Humbert was attempting to avoid the large British Army being gathered by Lord Cornwallis and to this end he decided to try and ignite a revolt in Ulster. He headed there by way of Sligo, where Colonel Charles Vereker commanded the garrison and George Gough commanded the Limerick Militia. On hearing of the advance of Humbert's force, Vereker moved out of Sligo with the intention of stopping what he believed was an advanced guard at the village of Coloomey. Exact figures for the number of men he commanded vary but it was between 300 and 500 at most, the majority of which were Gough's militia battalion. He also had 30 light dragoons and two guns. He placed his guns on Union Rock above Coloomey and the artillery pieces did much to slow the advance of about 2,000 French and Irish troops. However once they were put out of action it was only a matter of time before the British would have to withdraw or be defeated. Vereker lost both his guns and about 60 to 100 men killed or captured.

Yet his action had halted Humbert who believing the force before him to only be an advanced guard, decided against a further movement into Sligo and ultimately Ulster. For his part in this Vereker was awarded a peerage and received the thanks of Parliament. George Gough seems to have got little out of it other than a specially struck medal and a bit of prestige. His Limerick Militia had borne the brunt of the casualties, about 35 out of 300, one of whom was Gough himself. Exactly what was the nature of his wound is unclear; however it does appear that he received it by leading from the front. On the signing of the Peace of Amiens in 1801, George Gough's battalion was disbanded, and he returned to the life of a landowner and local figure of authority. However by this stage his son Hugh had already entered the regular army and had embarked of what would be a remarkable career.

2

Early Years

It will be useful for a moment to consider Hugh Gough's siblings. This will not only help to confirm the military tradition of the family, but also provide a degree of background for when they or their descendants appear later in our text. The eldest son of George and Letitia Gough was also named George, born on 26 December 1775.[1] He was commissioned into the Limerick City Militia regiment that was commanded by his father. By 1797 he was a major and very likely served in the action at Coloney mentioned in the previous chapter. Even before the disbandment of the Limerick City Militia, George Gough had transferred into the regular army, joining the 28th (North Gloucestershire) Regiment of Foot. He saw service with this regiment in Egypt in 1800 and in the Peninsular War from 1810–1814. He was married on his return from the war to Sarah Croker of Ballynagarde, County Limerick. Later they had four sons. The eldest, another George, was born in 1814 and later inherited his father's estate at Woodsdown. The second son was Edward born in 1815 and who later served in the 58th (Rutlandshire) Regiment of Foot and died, unmarried, in India in 1838 whilst with his regiment. The third son was Thomas Gough, born around 1815, who married Elizabeth William of Clonmel. He died in 1885. The fourth son Hugh was born in 1816, and later entered the 1st Royal Regiment of Dragoons and died unmarried.

The second son of George and Letitia was the future Reverend Thomas Bunbury Gough, born 13 June 1777. He attended Trinity College Dublin and graduated as a Doctor of Divinity. Entering the Church he later became the Dean of Derry and on 19 March 1800 he married Charlotte Bloomfield of Redwood, County Tipperary. It is perhaps a little surprising that it was from a man of the Church that some of the most prestigious soldiers of the Gough family sprang. In 1804 his son John Bloomfield Gough was born, later General Sir John. He went through training at the Royal Military College, by this stage already moved to Sandhurst, and was commissioned into the 22nd (Cheshire) Regiment of Foot in February 1820, before later transferring to the 23rd Royal Welch Fusiliers, and then exchanging into the 3rd Light Dragoons with the rank of captain. He will return to our narrative later, as he subsequently served on the staff of his uncle during the First China War, the Gwailor campaign, and the Sikh Wars.

Another of the Reverend Thomas Bunbury Gough's sons was George Gough, a judge for the East India Company, who married three times. It was two of the judge's sons, by his third wife Charlotte Margaret Gough, nee Becher, who contributed one of the most extraordinary achievements in the long history of the Victoria Cross. Both sons, Hugh Henry Gough and Charles John Stanley Gough were awarded the VC for service during the Indian Mutiny. Later Charles Gough's son John, better known as Johnnie, was awarded the VC for service during the Third Somaliland campaign in 1903. This ranks as a unique 'hat-trick', and when taken alongside the career of the

---

1   As with the background of the Gough family, I am grateful to Christopher Normand and Turtle
     Bunbury for their assistance in filling in some of the gaps.

subject of this work shows what an honourable military tradition the Gough family holds in the annals of the British Army.

The third son of George and Letitia Gough was William Gough born in 1778. He joined the 68th (Durham) Regiment of Foot, later the famous Durham Light Infantry. William Gough served in the Peninsular War, seeing action at Salamanca and Vitoria. At the latter he was severely wounded and missed the rest of the campaign. He remained in the Army after the peace and achieved the rank of major. In 1822 whilst returning with his regiment from North America the ship was wrecked and William drowned off Kinsale in Ireland. Although dying unmarried it is said that he left behind a child in Canada. The likelihood is that William was the father of Alexander Gough born 1819 or 1820 who later owned a cooperage and stave manufacturer in York County, Ontario. He rose to be a distinguished citizen and a justice of the peace. He briefly carried on the military tradition serving in the Canadian Militia during the revolts of the late 1830s.

George and Letitia Gough had two daughters. The eldest, Jane Catherine Gough, was born in 1776. She later married Lieutenant Colonel Richard Lloyd of the 84th (York and Lancaster) Regiment of Foot who fought in the Peninsular War and was killed on 11 December 1813 during the Battle of the Nive. They had one daughter, Letitia, who died unmarried. The youngest daughter, and indeed the youngest child of George and Letitia Gough, was Elizabeth Gough. She was born in 1788 and in March 1810 she married Benjamin Frend of Boskill, County Limerick. They would go on to have five sons and six daughters, one of whom, Colonel George Frend, would serve on the staff of Hugh Gough in India.

All of which brings us to Hugh Gough the youngest son of George and Letitia Gough and the second youngest child. Hugh Gough was born on 3 November 1779 at Woodsdown House, County Limerick.[2] The legend exists, encouraged by Hugh Gough in later years, that he was in many ways an unwanted child, although that is not to say unloved. The family already consisted of three sons and a daughter and thus it is perhaps understandable that his parents desired another girl, if for no other reason than a sense of balance. Whether his parents' relationship towards Hugh altered when they had their second girl in 1788 is unknown. The fact that the family had yet another son would have placed a further burden on the family. This may explain the story, again one that Hugh Gough would delight in telling in future years, that his own education was informal to say the least. The story goes that Hugh's schooling consisted of what he picked up from listening to the teaching of his brothers by a private tutor. It was a good story, which no doubt explained Gough's desire to tell it over and over again. However one cannot help but wonder how accurate it is, or whether perhaps it has been taken a little out of context. No doubt the tutor would have been employed to teach his elder brother, but the story rather suggests that the young Hugh listened somewhat surreptitiously to his brother's tutor. A simple explanation might be that the family did not want the expense of providing a tutor specifically for yet another younger son and might simply have placed him in the room with his brother. Whatever the nature of this teaching he was sufficiently schooled so as to be able to read and write: there are no glaring errors in his correspondence, and by the standards of the day his handwriting is remarkably legible. In later years he would exhibit a dislike of paperwork and administrative matters, but whether or not this had much to do with his lack of formal education can only be conjecture. He would hardly be unique as a general of this era who disliked the administrative side of his work.

We have already seen a little of the military heritage of the Gough family. Perhaps, in light of this, it would seem extremely likely, if not inevitable, that Hugh Gough was destined for the army. He was of course a younger son, and from a family of military background. Thus a career in the

---

2   Woodsdown House is not only in County Limerick but is not far from Limerick itself. Only the ruins of the house remain today.

Army would have seemed logical. Interestingly he was not the only one of the children of George and Letitia Gough's to enter the Army and have a military career. So perhaps the heritage of the family had more to do with his career path than simply following the traditional path of a younger son of the gentry. One must also remember that this was a time of global war, and thus it is not surprising that a family of military tradition was sending more than its 'normal' share off to war. This goes beyond the scope of this work but it could be argued that in such an age of warfare there was an obligation for a family such as the Goughs to provide officers for the army. To an extent a parallel can be made with the two world wars of the 20th century. Although there was never conscription on the large-scale of the 20th century conflicts, there was certainly a sense that there was a need to do one's duty particularly during the years that there appeared to be a direct threat of invasion from France. Indeed the Goughs were well aware of this having recently helped to repel the rather half-hearted French invasion of Ireland.

Although the question as to whether or not Hugh Gough was destined to be a soldier is difficult to answer conclusively, many factors point to this being the case. Not only was there the family military tradition and the fact that Great Britain was involved in a global war, there was also the question of what else he was to do. The social status of the family meant that there were only a limited number of professions open to him. The obvious ones were the Church, the legal profession, the Royal Navy, or the Army. One might also add politics, but that was normally best achieved after service, however brief, in one of the aforementioned professions, and Gough's later life would suggest a general disinterest in politics. He is only recorded as having spoken twice during his time in the House of Lords. On each occasion it was to add his voice to the vote of thanks for the efforts of the Army. His temperament would likely not have suited either the Church or the law, and, if we believe the story regarding his schooling, his lack of formal education would have hampered him in seeking to further his career in either.

It is possible therefore to suggest certain inevitability about him becoming a soldier. His early entry into the military was also less than surprising as his first taste of military life came when he was appointed to his father's battalion of the Limerick City Militia. This was at the age of only 13 in 1793. Strange as it may seem to the modern reader to have such a young officer, it was not uncommon for the times, particularly in the militia and particularly when there was a family connection to the colonel of the regiment. This was an age when the regiment was very much the property of its colonel. This was the case in the regular army as much as the militia. However the militia units were a special case, raised as they were by a local figure of importance, normally a major landowner. The militia was unique amongst the British military of this period in that there was in theory an element of compulsory service. The usual course was to try and fill the ranks through voluntary enlistment but through the Militia Act there was the power to complete the established strength through a ballot of all men of the locality aged between 18 and 50.

Gough's time in the Limerick City Militia was short-lived and he soon transferred to the regular army and one of the many newly raised regiments of foot that the war against France necessitated. He was commissioned as an ensign in the Hon. Robert Ward's Regiment of Foot on 7 August 1794 and on 11 October that same year he was transferred to the 119th Regiment of Foot.[3] Gough served with this regiment for just less than eight months. The only interesting thing to note of his service with the 119th is the fact that at the age of just 15 he was serving as the regimental adjutant.

This is interesting for several reasons, not least of all his age. He was still only an ensign and it was unusual for such a junior officer to hold the post. It also raises more questions with regards

---

3   The 119th had existed from 1761 to 1766 as the 119th (Prince's Own) Regiment of Foot, through the amalgamation of previously independent companies. In 1794 a new regiment, with no noticeable link to the previous unit other than the number, was raised and served until disbandment in 1796.

to the education of Hugh Gough. The adjutant, charged as he was with the maintenance of unit records and accounts, duty rosters, daily orders, and general staff work, needed to have a good head for figures, a good and steady pen, and more than a degree of administrative know-how. It is possible that his appointment was based upon his previous service with the Militia, and although no record of it exists it is also possible that his father chose to use him in such a way and thus Gough had previous experience of acting as an adjutant. The other possibility is that it says much about the quality, or approach, of many of the other officers of the regiment. It might simply be that nobody else wanted the job and that Gough was appointed by default.

In June 1795 Gough was transferred to the 78th Regiment of Foot with the rank of lieutenant, on the formation of their second battalion.[4] It was here that Gough's long active service career would begin and with them he saw the first of his many battles. Although few details of his actual involvement are known, we do know that he was present with the 78th at the capture of the Cape of Good Hope from the Dutch in 1795. Although Britain and the Dutch Republic had enjoyed relatively good relations since the Glorious Revolution of 1688–89, in recent years relations had become strained. There had even been an outbreak of war, the Fourth Anglo-Dutch War 1780–1784. The latter had weakened the Dutch state and with the loss of commercial power the disaffected middle classes had looked to the example of the United States and sought to remove hereditary power. They organised themselves into militias and at times there was open revolt, such as 1787 when it required Prussian military intervention to defeat the 'Patriots' as they called themselves. When two years later the French Revolution occurred it had a profound impact on the Netherlands. The 'Patriots' took heart from events in France and it was inevitable that sooner or later the conflict would spread into the Dutch Republic, particularly as Britain, Russia, Prussia and several other German States had placed troops on the French border. The Flanders Campaign of 1793–1795 was disastrous for the nations that opposed Revolutionary France, not least of all the forces of the Dutch Republic commanded by the Stadtholder William V. Many of the 'Patriots' who had fled to France were returning with the French forces thus giving them less of the feel of an invader and more of a liberator from the 'dictatorship' of the Stadtholder and the control of foreign powers. On 18 January 1795 the situation had deteriorated to the point that William V fled to England, where many of his family had already escaped. The following day the Batavian Revolution occurred in Amsterdam and the Batavian Republic was declared.

This placed the Dutch East India Company, the *Vereenigde Oost-Indische Compagnie* (VOC), in a difficult position. Technically it had a charter from the Dutch Republic but it could not ignore the fact that the Batavian Republic was very much in control of Holland and therefore their base of operation. They also faced potential problems in terms of their relationship with their British counterpart. Britain's Honourable East India Company regularly used the Dutch East India Company port at Cape Town as a stopover on the route to India, both for water and repairs. It was likely, with a government back home friendly towards the French, that pressure would be placed upon the VOC to deny the British access. The British were thinking along similar lines. Considerable pressure for a pre-emptive operation against the Cape had been placed upon Sir Henry Dundas, the Secretary of State for War, largely by the East India Company, and in particular one of its most prominent directors Sir Francis Baring of the famous merchant banking family. A fleet of warships and a small force of infantry were prepared to sail to the Cape of Good Hope. The fleet was commanded by Vice Admiral George Elphinstone, who had experience both of sailing for the East India Company and of successfully fighting the Dutch during the Fourth Anglo-Dutch War.

---

4   The regiment was raised between March and July 1793 as the 78th (Highland) Regiment of Foot. In 1796 they became the 78th (Ross-shire Buffs) Regiment of Foot. In 1881 they merged with the 72nd (Duke of Albany's Own) to form the Seaforth Highlanders.

Initially it was hoped to persuade the authorities at the Cape to declare for the Stadtholder, now in exile in Britain. The fleet consisted of seven warships and one merchant ship, including three 74 gunners and two 64 gunners.[5] Given the demands placed on the Royal Navy at this time this was a considerable force and demonstrates the seriousness with which the operation was viewed. It was also an appreciation of the quality of the Dutch squadron on station at the Cape.

The second battalion of the 78th Foot, about 500 strong, were reinforced by around 400 Royal Marines. The land forces were commanded by Major General James Henry Craig, an officer of some experience who had a good reputation for leading light infantry and skirmishers. He had seen action both in the American Revolutionary War and the operations in the Netherlands during the Flanders Campaign. The fleet left England on 1 March 1795, arriving off the Cape in early June 1795 and anchoring in Simon's Bay.[6] On arrival Vice Admiral Elphinstone, in overall command of the expedition, 'suggested' to the Dutch Governor, Abraham Josias Sluysken, that he placed the colony under British protection. To support this, Elphinstone had a letter from the Stadtholder but this seems to have the opposite effect to that desired. Sluysken was reluctant to fight, being both ill and indeed due for replacement, and was largely persuaded to resist by the military commander Colonel Robert Jacob Gordon, who as the name would suggest was not Dutch but of Scots ancestry. Gordon was the son of a Dutch mother and a Scottish soldier who had joined the Dutch service. His second in command was Lieutenant Colonel Carel de Lille, who would not only be accused of cowardice but ultimately of collusion to deliver Cape Colony into the hands of the British.[7]

The British took Simon's Town without resistance, but the Dutch still held the position at Muizenberg about six miles to the south of Cape Town. The British continued to try to negotiate surrender without having to commit troops in an assault of a reasonably strong position. Much of the negotiation was carried out by Colonel Mackenzie of the 78th. The British position was simply that they wanted to protect the colony, or more importantly British access to it, and a guarantee was given that there would be no interference with Dutch laws or government. There were those amongst the Cape Colony Council who were prepared to accept British protection if they could be certain that it would be in the name of the Stadtholder. However the suspicion existed, with some justification, that the British and in particular the East India Company wanted to take over the colony.

Sluysken and the Dutch continued to play for time. Whether they hoped that Dutch or French reinforcements were on the way or were simply hoping that something would happen to make the British withdraw is unclear. By July the 78th and the Royal Marines had been augmented by 800 sailors from the various ships in the harbour to form a makeshift naval brigade under the command of Commander Temple Hardy of HMS *Echo* and Commander John William Spranger of HMS *Rattlesnake*. This gave Major General Craig a force of around 1,600 men to assault the Dutch position, an option that now seemed inevitable. The Dutch force amounted to about 1,100 men. Although outnumbered, they held a strong position on a rocky outcrop at Muizenberg, a suburb to the east of Cape Town, and also possessed 11 artillery pieces of various calibres. The British on the

5   James, William, *Naval History of Great Britain* (London: Harding, Lepard & Co, 1826), Vol.I, p. 300, names the ships as follows: HMS *Monarch* (74 guns & Flagship), HMS *Victorious* (74 guns), HMS *Arrogant* (74 guns), HMS *America* (64 guns), HMS *Stately* (64 guns), HMS *Echo* (16 guns) and HMS *Rattlesnake* (16 guns).
6   Simon's Bay is better known as the naval base at Simon's Town. For many years this was home to a Royal Navy squadron and today is the headquarters of the South African Navy. It is named in honour of Simon Van der Stel the first governor of Cape Colony. Given the future racial complexity of South Africa it is interesting to note that Van der Stel was of mixed race, being in the terminology of the day a Eurasian.
7   A good account of the political side of the conflict between the British and Dutch and the personalities involved can be found in Barnard, Madeline, *Cape Town Stories* (Cape Town: Struik Publishers, 2007). Barnard also suggests that Gordon committed suicide in the wake of the capture of Cape Town.

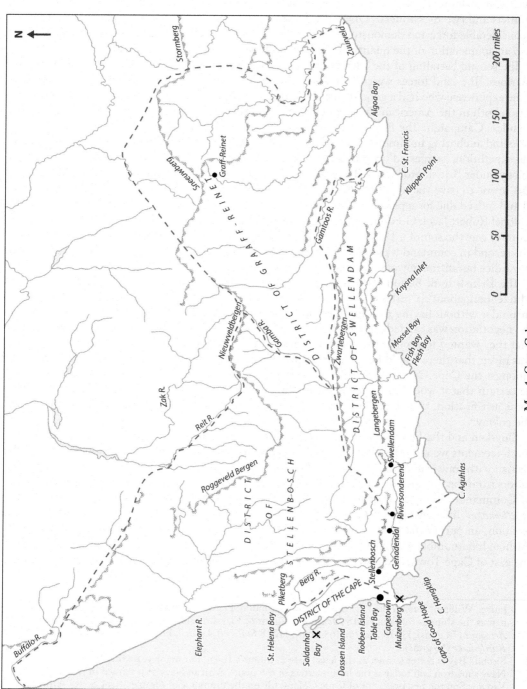

Map 1 Cape Colony.

other hand had no field guns. However the ships of the squadron were able to bring their guns to bear on the Dutch position. The launches of the various ships of the squadron were also used, and mounted a carronade on the bows.

On 7 August, the ships in the bay opened fire on the Dutch position with devastating effect. The Dutch were forced to abandon their position and retreat into the rocks. However due to the naval bombardment the movement of the British infantry had been limited, thus the Dutch were able to take some of their guns with them and were able to put up greater resistance than should have been the case after such a ferocious naval bombardment. The coordinating of artillery and infantry movement was one that would continue to confound future generations with more modern forms of communication, so one should not be too critical of the naval and military commanders of 1795.

The same day the British infantry advanced and cleared the enemy from the rocks, the 78th bearing the brunt of the attack. This was an important moment as it marks the first time that the young Hugh Gough had seen action and come under fire. The British casualties were relatively light. The 78th suffered one officer, Captain Scott, and seven men wounded, but remarkably no fatalities. Other than this, British casualties were two killed and five wounded. The Dutch now retreated into the town itself.

On 8 August, the Dutch attempted to retake the position lost the previous day. Exact numbers for the Dutch are unclear however they are believed to have outnumbered the British force and possessed eight pieces of field artillery. The British stood steady on their defensive position, even using two guns captured the previous day against their former owners. The action of the eighth is remembered for the steadiness shown by the Naval Brigade in seeing off the Dutch attack. Major General Craig noted of the Naval Brigade that, "They manoeuvred with a regularity which would not have discredited veteran troops".[8] The British again sought to negotiate with the Dutch but to no avail. An assault of the Dutch town was felt inadvisable with the forces at their disposal and the British decided to wait for the reinforcements that they knew were on their way.

On 2 April 1795, a fleet of 14 ships of the East India Company had set sail from England on route to India, carrying with it a large number of troops and supplies ostensibly for the defence of the sub-continent. This force of approximately 2,500 soldiers was commanded by Major General Alured Clarke, later to become a field marshal and a knight. Clarke had been given secret instructions that his first duty was to land on the Cape and, if Elphinstone and Craig had yet to take the colony, to capture it before continuing his journey to India. Clarke arrived on 3 September 1795. Whether or not the Dutch were aware of his imminent arrived is unknown but it may explain why on the first three days of September they attempted to break the British siege. On 1 September, the 78th had been attacked by a force sallying forth from the town, but had beaten them back with relative ease. On the third, the Dutch were prepared to attack with everything they had including 18 artillery pieces. However the arrival of British reinforcements led to the attack being called off.

The British now prepared for the attack. Up to this point casualties had been relatively light and, not for the first or last time, the majority had fallen to disease rather than the enemy. Of 34 deaths only eight had been as the result of wounds inflicted by the enemy. However it was now expected that the assault on the town would cause large-scale casualties. It took until 14 September for men and stores to be disembarked and readied for the attack. When the advance began, the Dutch governor Sluysken realised that the game was up and sent out a flag of truce to negotiate the terms of the surrender. Two days later the colony surrendered and the British forces took possession. Along with the colony, seven ships of the VOC were also captured and either sold or transferred to the Royal Navy. Cape Colony remained under British control until 1802 when it was returned to the Batavian Republic under the Treaty of Amiens.

---

8   James, *Naval History*, Vol. I, p. 301.

Although little more than a footnote in the wars of this period, the capture of Cape Colony is an important part of our narrative of the life of Hugh Gough. As previously mentioned, it was his first taste of action and his first experience under fire. Not yet 16 he had taken part in the first of what would prove to be so many campaigns. He had also had the experience of travelling to the other end of the planet and of seeing southern Africa, and surely that in and of itself would have been a notable experience in his development. The campaign he had taken part in had been successful and well led and was a useful pointer to a young officer learning his profession. Gough made little mention of the campaign in future years but it is to be hoped that he was already learning the art of command. This was of course what in modern military parlance would be called a combined operation, and the coordination of naval gunfire and infantry was one which we shall see Hugh Gough put to good effect later in his career.

3

War in the Caribbean

There are periods of Hugh Gough's life that, whilst not necessarily unaccounted for, raise questions about his exact movements. We are now faced with one of them. The *Army List* tells us that in December 1795 Gough was transferred from the 78th to the 87th (Prince of Wales Irish) Regiment of Foot, still with the rank of lieutenant. However in August 1796 Gough was still in Cape Colony and was present at the capture of a Dutch Fleet in Saldanha Bay. A Dutch fleet of eight ships, including two 66-, one 54-, two 40-, one 26-, one 24-, and one 18-gunner, was sighted off Saldanha Bay 65 miles north west of Cape Town on 3 August 1796. Major General Craig, with a force including Gough and the 78th, marched off towards the bay to oppose any attempted landing. However the Dutch fleet was completely outnumbered and outgunned by the Royal Navy squadron at Cape Town, still commanded by Vice Admiral Elphinstone. Amongst his ships were two 74- and five 64-gunners, outclassing anything the Dutch had. The Dutch had been promised French support, which never materialised, and had entered Saldanha Bay to await them. However rather than French support they awoke on 16 August to see the British squadron drawn up in line of battle. Elphinstone asked for their surrender which was obtained on the 17th.

Gough later recalled witnessing this event so despite his appointment to the 87th we know that he is still in Africa as late as August 1796. There is a suggestion that Gough was not actually serving with the 78th at this stage and may have been acting in some other capacity. He is recorded as having witnessed the surrender of the Dutch fleet, but not from what point of view. The possibility exists that he was actually on board one of the ships commanded by Elphinstone that may have been on its way either home or directly to the West Indies. This is supported by the fact that he arrived in the West Indies before the end of 1796, which suggests he left shortly after the Dutch fleet surrendered in August of that year.[1] Again, like so much of this period of his life, this is unclear.

The reason for the move to a new regiment is also unclear. It might be explained by the fact that in June 1796 the 2nd battalion was to be disbanded, although that would not necessarily have meant he would have left the regiment. It may also have had to do with prospects for further active service. The 78th was destined to spend much of its future service in India, something of a backwater in terms of the global war with France and her allies. As the 87th was earmarked for intervention in Europe this would undoubtedly have been more appealing, especially to a young subaltern who wanted to make his mark in his new profession. The only real way to do this during the era in question was through active service. Europe was always considered to be the main theatre of operation and distinguishing himself in battle in this theatre would certainly have given him a higher profile. That said it might simply have been that Gough preferred the opportunity to serve in an Irish regiment rather than a Scottish one, although the 87th would spend little time in Ireland

---

1   Rait, *Gough*, Vol. I, p. 19–20.

in the future years. Also, the fact that almost a year after his transfer he had not joined up with his new regiment might simply have been down to a lack of transport and opportunity.

The 87th Foot had been raised in 1793 by John Doyle, later Sir John Doyle 1st Baronet. It was therefore a reasonably new regiment but had already seen plenty of active service. Doyle had studied law at Trinity College Dublin, but shortly before his studies ended he had to leave on the death of his father and instead of returning he entered the Army in 1771. By the 1790s Doyle was a veteran soldier having served with distinction during the American Revolutionary War. On his return he commenced a political career and in 1783 entered the Irish House of Commons as MP for Mullingar. In September 1793 he raised the 87th with the title Prince of Wales Irish.[2] The connection with the Prince of Wales was due to the fact that Doyle was, for a number of years, one of his private secretaries.

Doyle commanded the regiment in Flanders from 1793 to 1795. By 1796, although officially the regiment's colonel, he was also serving as Secretary at War in the Irish House of Commons. This proved helpful when in 1796 he needed to refill the ranks of the 87th. In early 1795 the regiment had been stationed at Bergen-op-Zoom when the Dutch changed sides. The regiment, surrounded, was forced to surrender and was taken prisoner almost to a man. Doyle had happened to be in England when this event took place and was spared their fate. He wasted no time in raising what was in effect a completely new regiment and by August 1796 the re-formed 87th were earmarked for service in support of Admiral Duncan's operations in the North Sea and Northern Europe. Doyle did not forget his men who were prisoners. He provided 500 guineas out of his own pocket to provide for the wives and children of the imprisoned men. The majority were released at some point in 1796. Doyle went to meet the men on their return to England and many were later enlisted in the 1st Battalion of the 87th Foot.

However, with the entry of Spain into the war on the side of France a number of operations were planned against Spanish colonies, particularly in the West Indies. It was for this purpose that the 87th were despatched to the Caribbean as part of a force of almost 8,000 reinforcements under Lieutenant General Sir Ralph Abercromby. Due to various delays, probably due to the problems of refilling the ranks, bringing in new officers, and general administrational matters, the 87th did not sail for the West Indies until October 1796. This also provides a possible reason for Gough's delay in Cape Colony, as there was no point in him sailing to join his new regiment until they were actually on their way to the Caribbean.

The West Indies, the Caribbean, and South America were never more than a sideshow in the wars of this era, at least in terms of numbers of men and the size of engagements fought. However the commercial value of the West Indies, through sugar, spice, tobacco, and so forth, was sufficient to ensure that pressure was placed upon the British government to undertake operations in this area. This was both to protect British interests but also to disrupt the interests of other powers whether that be France, Spain or the Dutch. There was at the time, and remains to this day, a question as to whether or not such operations were worth the cost. This is particularly so in terms of manpower. There is a staggering statistic associated with the operations in this area from 1794 to 1796, the period just before Gough's arrival, which illustrates that the total number of fatalities

---

2   This would later change to Prince of Wales Own Irish, and on the Prince of Wales ascent to the throne in 1820 would be renamed the Royal Irish Fusiliers, although this did not officially occur until 1827. In May 1881 the regiment merged with the 89th (Princess Victoria's) Regiment of Foot, to become The Royal Irish Fusiliers (Princess Victoria's) Regiment. However in August 1881 the title was reversed and became Princess Victoria's (The Royal Irish Fusiliers) Regiment, until 1920 when it went back to the title first used in May 1881. Cunliffe, Marcus, *The Royal Irish Fusiliers 1793–1950* (London: Oxford University Press, 1952).

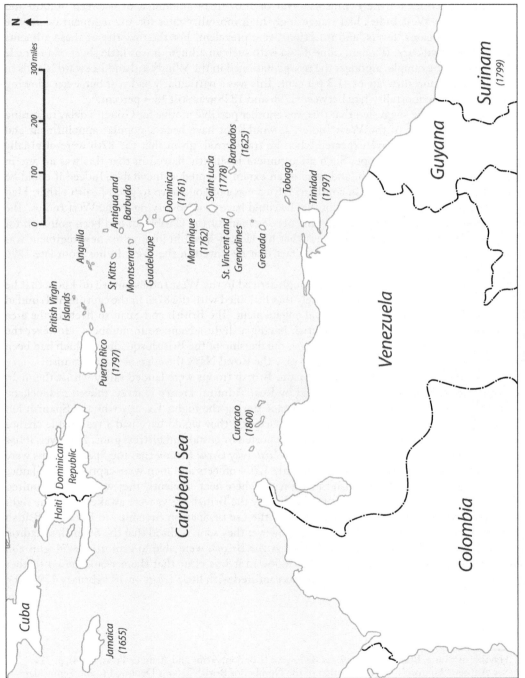

Map 2 The Caribbean.

and those invalided out through ill health reached 80,000 men.[3] Over half of this number were fatalities, the large majority the result of disease rather than enemy action. To place this in context, total British casualties for the Peninsular War of 1807–1814 amounted to between 40,000 and 60,000 men.[4] The West Indies had staggeringly high mortality rates for any regiment on service there. Tropical diseases, fevers, and infections were prevalent. For the majority of these ailments there was no known cure. If a man came down with such an ailment it was little short of a miracle if he survived. For example, amongst the troops stationed in the Windward and Leeward islands in 1796 there was a mortality rate of 41.3 per cent. This was a particularly bad year but, even allowing for this, the average mortality rate between 1796 and 1828 was still 13.4 percent.[5]

It could therefore be suggested that this was another possible motive for Gough's delay in joining with his new regiment in the West Indies. It would not have been a popular appointment and one which he would not have expected when he transferred, given that the 87th were originally earmarked for service in Europe. Such an argument is slightly flawed in that this was an age in which mortality rates were high, and were to an extent accepted as inevitable. Indeed it could be argued that where he had been in southern Africa was not conducive to good health either. Had he really wanted to, there is little doubt that he could have avoided serving in the West Indies. The practice of officers transferring from regiments destined for the Caribbean had been going on for many years and would continue. The idea that his lack of speed in joining his new regiment was connected to this is also repudiated by the fact that he stayed in the West Indies from late 1796 until 1800.

We do not know exactly when Hugh Gough arrived in the West Indies but we do know that he had arrived by early 1797. It is thought likely that he joined with the 87th in the capture of Trinidad in February 1797. This was mainly a naval engagement. The British and Spanish fleets in the area were fairly evenly matched, with the British having a slight advantage in numbers. However the decisive factor was the 98-gun *Prince of Wales*, the flagship of the British squadron, which had been especially despatched to the West Indies to give the Royal Navy the edge over the Spanish.

The Spanish fleet remained in Port of Spain. British troops were landed safely whilst the main ships of the British Squadron, commanded by Rear Admiral Henry Harvey, moved to blockade the Spanish in fear that they might try to escape during the night. Exactly why the Spanish felt their position was so dire is unclear, as on the face of it they would have had a reasonable chance against the British squadron especially when supported by costal and fortress guns. However, it has been suggested by William James in his *Naval History of Great Britain* that the Spanish ships were woefully undermanned. Records show that only 1,704 officers and men were captured, and James calculates that to operate the Spanish squadron anywhere near efficiently they would have required 2,704 officers and men.[6] At 0200hrs on 17 February the British crews were awakened by the sight of fire in the harbour. Originally they expected the use of Spanish fire ships to force the British squadron from anchor so as to allow escape. However they soon realised that the Spanish squadron was in fact on fire. Such was the confusion that the British were able to capture the 74-gun *San Damaso* without resistance. In the day that followed it was clear that there would be no further resistance from the Spanish, and Trinidad was captured with little effort on 18 February 1797. The

---

3   Haythornthwaite, Phillip, *The Armies of Wellington* (London: Arms and Armour Press, 1994), p. 214.
4   See Andrew Bamford's 'A Computation of the Number of British Troops Deployed to the Peninsular Theatre, 1808–1814', <http://www.napoleon-series.org/military/organization/Britain/Strength/c_Strength1814.html>.
5   Haythornthwaite, *Armies of Wellington*, pp. 214–217.
6   James, *Naval History*, Vol. II, p. 98.

exact role of the 87th is unclear. Some sources suggest they were not even present with the fleet. It is however more likely that although on board the fleet they were not landed, being kept as a reserve.[7]

The ease of the capture of Trinidad was not replicated at the next operation in which the 78th and Gough took part. Attention turned towards the Spanish colony of Puerto Rico. This was always going to be a harder target. Over the years the colony had been the target of other European powers and as such strong defences had been built up especially around the port of San Juan. San Juan had been attacked previously by the English in 1595 and 1598 and by the Dutch in 1625. None had been successful. The British squadron arrived off the coast of Puerto Rico on 17 April 1797. As on Trinidad the land forces were under the direct command of Sir Ralph Abercromby. The next day a successful landing was made in the face of little opposition. However as the British force, of about 6,000 men, advanced upon the fortress of San Juan they encountered fierce resistance. Exact figures for both sides are debatable, and vary wildly; however it is likely that they were fairly evenly matched. Sources from the Puerto Rican/Spanish point of view give a surely inflated number for British forces, arguing that it may have been over 13,000. This seems almost impossible. It is the author's opinion that 6,000 soldiers would be the maximum likely to have taken part, given the levels of disease and the various garrisons and commitments elsewhere in the West Indies. It has been suggested that German mercenaries were used, although this is hard to verify. However even this is unlikely to have increased the available force much beyond 6,000 men. Cunliffe's history of the 87th Foot puts the British force at only 4,000 men. This may refer only to the number of regular soldiers, the rest of the roughly 6,000 being made up by Marines and sailors.

Unlike Trinidad, this time the Spanish decided to fight, and were led by a determined and skilful commander Brigadier General Ramon de Castro. They were supported by a small force of French soldiers and a large number of civilians who formed an ad hoc, but effective, militia. Even in the attempt to force his way to San Juan itself, Abercromby found the Spanish resistance to be fierce and suffered over 230 casualties. Matters were not helped by the fact that Abercromby himself was in bad health and would shortly be forced to return to England. By 22 April Abercromby had commenced a siege of San Juan. The Spanish continued to raid British positions, and had some success but were always driven off. Both sides suffered casualties and it must have been a very different siege for Gough to have experienced relative to that he had witnessed in Cape Colony. On 30 April Abercromby lifted the siege and started to withdraw his forces from the island. The 87th had lost two men killed, three wounded and 13 missing.[8]

Although the attack on Puerto Rico had ended in failure, it had not been a disaster. Abercromby took a command decision, possible influenced by his ill health, that he did not have the means at his disposal to take a well-fortified position held by a determined and organised force. This seems to have been understood at home and there was no criticism of him for his effort. It is to be hoped that Gough learnt from the experience. He had been fortunate thus far in his career to have been under the overall command of two of the better British generals of this era: Sir Ralph Abercromby and the now Sir James Craig. Although only a subaltern he would have been aware of the higher command elements of the force of which he was part. In the aftermath of Abercromby's departure, operations ceased. The 87th remained in garrison on the island of St Lucia for the remainder of 1797 and indeed until late July 1799. St Lucia had an unusual history in that French, English, and at one time Dutch, settlements had been present side by side, although the official control of the

---

7   Cunliffe in his history of the 87th Foot suggests that they were present with the fleet but did not take part in the action. However William James's *Naval History of Great Britain* makes no mention of the 87th as part of the military force. See also, Alonso, Mariá M. and Milagros Flores *The Eighteenth Century Caribbean and the British Attack on Puerto Rico in 1797* (San Juan, Puerto Rico: National Park Service, Department of the Interior, 1997), Cunliffe, *Royal Irish Fusiliers*, p. 10.

8   Cunliffe, *Royal Irish Fusiliers*, p. 10.

island changed hands many times. The French influence led to a slave uprising in the wake of the French Revolution, and with little alternative the French Revolutionary governor of the island, Victor Hugues, declared that all the slaves were free. This coincided with a British invasion of the island in April 1794, so it can be inferred that the governor's 'benevolence' in freeing the slaves may have had an ulterior motive, and indeed the former slaves, or brigands as they were generally called by the British, would cause problems for several years.

The initial British invasion had been led by Sir Charles Grey, and whilst he had some success the level of insurgency and the inadequacy of his own force compelled him to evacuate the island in June 1795.[9] In April 1796, Sir Ralph Abercromby had landed on St Lucia and after some hard fighting had subjugated most of the island by June of that year. We know little of what the 87th did during this period and there appears to have been little trouble for them to deal with. Gough must surely have found this a tedious interlude, and was no doubt relieved when in 1799 he had a chance for further active service, although once again there was to be little fighting. On 31 July 1799 a British squadron under the command of Vice Admiral Lord Hugh Seymour carried a British force of several thousand men under the command of Lieutenant General Thomas Trigge to invade the Dutch colony of Surinam. Although often treated somewhat like a Caribbean colony Surinam is, like Guyana, actually in South America. The British arrived off the coast of Surinam on 11 August. On the 16th the squadron drew up in line of battle off the coast and demanded that the Dutch governor surrender. The Dutch offered little resistance and agreed to the capitulation on the 18th. The rest of the colony followed soon after and by 22 August the British were in total control. The 87th had landed in Surinam but had found there was little call on their services. Although Gough had seen no fighting he was no doubt relived for the temporary respite from garrison duty in St Lucia.

From here we once again briefly lose track of Gough's career. It is unclear whether or not he even returned with his regiment to St Lucia. In December the 87th moved to Martinique, and again Gough's whereabouts are unknown. He may have returned with the regiment to St Lucia but whether he left them before that point, or after the move to Martinique, is unknown. We do know that the 87th continued to serve in the West Indies, moving on Dominica in April 1800, and then Barbados the year after that. In August 1801 they sailed for Curacao, another Dutch colony, which had been occupied by the British. In March 1802 the Treaty of Amiens was signed and the war against France and her allies was halted, albeit temporarily as events would turn out. It was not until January 1803 that the 87th set off for home on board a Dutch ship, but bad weather forced them to seek shelter in Jamaica, then Antigua, and finally St Kitts. However by the time this had happened, around the end of June 1803, war had broken out again. It was not until July 1804 that the 87th finally sailed home, and arrived in Plymouth on 28 September 1804.[10]

During the eight years that the 87th Foot had been stationed in the West Indies they had lost somewhere in the region of 700 to 800 men through disease.[11] This again emphasises the point made earlier as to the risk under which Gough served at this time. It also adds another dimension to the unknown period of his life from mid 1800 until June 1803. There is no mention of his service during this period and we know nothing of him until 24 June 1803 when he was promoted to captain. There is no doubt that his health had suffered during his service in the West Indies however we do not know for sure that this was the reason for his departure. Rait suggests that

---

9   Sir Charles Grey became Baron Grey in 1801 and Earl Grey in 1806. His eldest son, the 2nd Earl Grey was British Prime Minister between November 1830 and July 1834. The latter is best remembered in modern times for the tea that is thought to be named in his honour.

10   Cunliffe, *Royal Irish Fusiliers*, p. 11.

11   Cunliffe, *Royal Irish Fusiliers*, p 11. The confusion comes because not all those with disease necessarily died, as some were invalided home, yet the record does not differentiate between the two.

Gough returned home in late 1800, quoting from some private papers that do not appear to have survived. Yet despite this now unavailable source Rait is still unable to explain Gough's movement from his return home until June 1803.[12]

This period of regimental service in the West Indies had been an important part in Gough's development as a soldier. In the years that lay ahead he would have an aversion to fighting in extremely hot weather, and this may have been due to his experiences in the West Indies. Although medical care in general was not great during this period, Gough would in future years take the care and treatment of his men seriously, and it may well be that this was borne of the suffering he had witnessed, and perhaps endured himself, during this period. Whatever the case, Gough had seen further service, seen more of the world, and had continued his development as a soldier. Although Britain had technically been at peace for a time, this would not last and there were to be further periods of overseas service. What he had experienced up to now was a preliminary compared to what was to come.

---

12   Rait, *Gough*, Vol. I, pp. 20–21.

4

A Brief Interlude of Peace and Duties in England

We know that Hugh Gough returned from the Caribbean in 1800, presumably through ill health, but the next few years are something of a mystery. He would not have returned home until late 1800. How long it took him to recover we do not know. The fact that so little is recorded about the circumstances of Gough's return rings true to the reputation of the man in future years. If indeed it was ill health that caused his premature return then it is unsurprising that Gough, in the manner with which he faced such matters, would not have complained and would have played down the whole matter.

In March 1802 there was a brief respite in the war with France and her allies due to the signing of the Treaty of Amiens. The Peace of Amiens that this created lasted a little over a year and war recommenced in May 1803. When peace came it was initially generally welcomed, although perhaps not by young officers such as Gough who wanted to make a name for themselves, and to whom the war brought adventure and the chance to earn distinction and promotion. However to most people after nine years of war it was a relief. With the peace much of what had been captured by the British was restored either to the French or the Batavian Republic. It must have appeared to Gough and many others that all their effort had been in vain as, with the exception of Trinidad, all the colonies he had been fighting for were returned. The peace was generally unfavourable towards Britain and soon became the source of much criticism within Parliament and the nation at large. There was for a time a tendency amongst historians to view Prime Minister Henry Addington, who negotiated the treaty, in analogous terms to Neville Chamberlain and appeasement in the 1930s. This is unfair and ignores the fact that the peace gave Britain much needed time to regroup, particularly from a financial point of view, and prepare for what even Addington saw as an inevitable resumption of hostilities.[1]

Britain had suffered economically from the war with great expenditure being required for the Army and Navy whilst British trade had been diminished by the war and the loss of markets on the continent. As so often was the case Britain had been unprepared for war in 1793 and had spent the nine years of war playing catch-up, trying to implement in war what should have been done in peace. The Peace of Amiens gave a brief but valuable breathing space for the military and allowed Addington to commence the construction of costal defences, a large number of Martello towers

---

1   For more on Addington and now he has been treated by historians see: Fedorak, Charles John, *Henry Addington, Prime Minister, 1801–1804: Peace, War and Parliamentary Politics* (Akron, Ohio: University of Akron Press, 2002). This is an excellent reassessment of Addington. An example of now the analogy with appeasement in the 1930s seeped into popular culture can be seen in the 1942 British film *The Young Mr Pitt*. This wartime film aligns Pitt with Churchill, Napoleon with Hitler, and Addington with Chamberlain. The actor Henry Hewitt who plays Addington even seems to be attempting to mimic the style of Neville Chamberlain during the House of Commons scenes.

being built under his orders.[2] In the 18 months from the signing of the peace, between 500,000 and 600,000 men were placed under arms in preparation for the renewed conflict, many of them militia and volunteers designed for home defence. When war came again in 1803 Britain was in a position to fight on much better terms.

We know little of Gough's movements until the resumption of the war in 1803 when in June of that year he is appointed Superintending Officer of the Army of Defence for Oxfordshire and Buckinghamshire. Much of what he had to do was supervise training, and as a regular officer who now had the credit of having seen combat he was ideal for this role. If he was still suffering the effect of his ill health this would have been a less demanding role than returning to regimental duties overseas. Some of his work also entailed a degree of administration and bookkeeping, which is probably not something he enjoyed. There is an incident documented during this period which gives an early insight into some of the traits that would appear to characterise Gough's later career. Correspondence exists between Hugh Gough and the paymaster for the Bedford District, M. Wilson. The first of the correspondence sees Wilson 'telling off' Gough for being too generous with his financial allowances for his men. The nub of the matter seems to be that when they travelled home, as many of the men in question were volunteers and militia, Gough was allowing them three days' pay for travel, as opposed to one, plus a halfpenny for accommodation and a penny for beer money. Gough's reaction was simply to say that if the paymaster objected so much that he would refund the money himself out of his own pocket.[3] It is a pointer to the future care that Gough would show for his men. Whether or not he knew he was breaking the rules does not matter in one sense. It illustrates that he did what he thought was best for the men he was responsible for. This sense of care and concern would be evident in his later career and is strangely at odds with his battle tactics that appeared to necessitate large numbers of casualties. Although we are perhaps getting a little ahead of ourselves it is interesting to note that this character trait had already started to emerge. The concern is rather paternalistic in nature and is not contrary to the understanding of the men as soldiers. We start to see that he cares for them like a father, but has no delusion as to the fact that they are soldiers.

If there had been an error in the way he did things it would appear that Gough learnt from this. The following year, in July 1804, Gough took exception to a complaint from the paymaster over the recording of his accounts.[4] Whereas last time he had freely admitted his error this time he strenuously denied it. Later correspondence does seem to indicate that this time it was the paymaster who was in error. Although Gough might not have been expert at such work he does appear to have been better at it than most. In October 1803 Wilson, the same paymaster who questioned some of his work, wrote of Gough that, "I wish that every other officer on the duty of the Army of Reserve had been equally correct as yourself in making out the paylists. I should not have experienced the trouble and vexation which I do at the present".[5] At the same time Gough found himself frustrated by the accounting system. For instance he had understandably claimed for the cost of postage and stationary involved with his work. He was told that he was not able to claim for such things. "You must recollect that it [postage and stationary] can never be inserted in the accounts without

---

2   The Martello towers were round stone fortresses of thick walls and with a considerable range and viewing position for guns. They were based on the defences the British had encountered at Mortella in Corsica in 1794. Testament to their strength is the fact that a surprising number can still be seen today. Of the 103 built in England 47 still exist today, many how converted to other purposes. They can also be seen throughout the world in former British colonies.
3   The National Army Museum (NAM) Gough Papers 8303–105. Gough to Wilson, 31 August 1803. Wilson to Gough, 12 Sept 1803. Gough to Wilson, 2 October 1803.
4   NAM: Gough Papers, Wilson to Gough 26 August 1804.
5   NAM: Gough Papers, Wilson to Gough 2 October 1803.

a certificate signed by the Inspector General, as a voucher accompanying the paylist in which the charge appears".[6] Gough was frustrated by this and asked now he should proceed. The official answer no doubt failed to improve his humour, stating as it did that "I am at a loss how to advise you respecting the charge which you wish to make for postage and stationary".[7] Although such complaints from a soldier against bureaucracy are not new, one does see in this correspondence a more administratively able Gough than one might expect based on his future reputation.

Another element of his duty at this time was the supervising of the Militia Ballot, a duty he may have been familiar with due to his father's responsibility in this direction for the city of Limerick. As mentioned in a previous chapter the Militia was unique in having this degree of compulsory service. If the ranks could not be filled by volunteers then the ballot was called. Even then a man did not have to serve if he could find a substitute, and this was a common practice. To take an example from Gough's time responsible for the ballot, of the 17 men balloted for the subdivision of Wootton in Oxfordshire on 9 September 1803, only two men chose to serve. The other 15 found substitutes, some coming from as far away as Manchester.[8]

There is a suggestion that some time during 1804 Gough returned to the West Indies to rejoin the 87th shortly before their return from the Caribbean. If he did, he cannot have been back in the Caribbean for long. The idea that Gough returned briefly to the West Indies is based upon a letter written in October 1859. This letter from Gough to Mr E. Blakeney, states that Gough did briefly rejoin his regiment, and suggests that this might have happened in the West Indies. The passage of time might have confused the by-then Lord Gough.[9] We know that he was still performing his duties in England until at least 31 July 1804, meaning he would not have left England until at least August 1804. Since and the 87th returned in mid September of that year, this makes it unlikely, but not impossible.

After a short period in Southampton the regiment sailed for Guernsey where their colonel, John Doyle, was appointed governor. Gough served in the position of brigade major, in modern terms a chief of staff, to the forces on the island. This series of more administratively-focussed appointments might be at odds with the later reputation Gough earned for neglecting staff work and organisation. It perhaps illustrates that later criticism should not be taken at face value. Gough had clearly showed something in his nature and his ability at this work that earned him the continuance of such appointments. Whilst his earliest appointment, as adjutant of a battalion might have been down to the fact that nobody else wanted the job and that as the youngest officer he was selected for the task, this cannot surely be the case for his later appointments. There was obviously something in his work that was admired. He clearly had ability, as proved by his work in Oxfordshire and Buckinghamshire, if accompanied by a disregard for some of the red tape that accompanied such work.

In July 1804 an Act of Parliament called for a strengthening of the army by the creation of second battalions for a number of regiments. Consequently in July 1804 a second battalion of the 87th was formed from men recruited from the counties of Tipperary, Galway and Clare.[10] The initial intake of 600 Irishmen were formed up in Frome, Somerset in late 1804 and came onto the strength of the Army on Christmas Day 1804. The command of the second battalion was taken on by another member of the Doyle family, this time Lieutenant Colonel Charles William Doyle. Later Lieutenant General Sir Charles, this Doyle had first joined the regiment in 1795, but had

6   NAM: Gough Papers, Wilson to Gough 26 August 1804.
7   NAM: Gough Papers, Wilson to Gough 26 August 1804.
8   NAM: Gough Papers, Ballot List 9 September 1803.
9   Rait, *Gough*, Vol. I, p. 22.
10   For further information on the formation and training of the second battalion, see Cunliffe, *Royal Irish Fusiliers*, pp. 62–65.

spent much time away from it on other duties and left altogether in 1803. However he returned in 1804 to command the second battalion, but even now he continued to spend a great deal of time on other appointments away from his regiment.

In March 1805 the second battalion sailed for Ireland where further recruiting raised the strength of the battalion to 800 men. Gough initially remained with the first battalion and continued to act as brigade major in Guernsey until at least 8 August 1805. On that date Gough succeeded to a majority within the regiment. This was due to Major E. Blakeney selling out before he had planned in order to help Gough, in what the latter later referred to as "an act of almost brotherly kindness".[11] Gough did not join the second battalion immediately upon his promotion, but when in November 1805 the first battalion left Guernsey for Portsmouth it is clear that Gough did not accompany them and shortly after that he joined the second battalion in Ireland where it was continuing its recruitment and training. The second battalion remained in Ireland until October 1806 when it was transferred to Plymouth, whilst the first battalion had been despatched ultimately to take part in the abortive campaign in South America. Due to the need to reinforce the first battalion before it sailed, the second battalion had been somewhat denuded of manpower and thus reduced to just over 600 men.

Whilst the second battalion continued its training in Plymouth an event happened that would have a lasting effect on Hugh Gough's life. He met, fell in love with – for it was truly a 'love-match' – and ultimately married Miss Frances Maria Stephens. A story exists about their first meeting and whilst seeming to be overly romanticised in nature it does appear to be true. Sir Robert Rait, Hugh Gough's first biographer, was able to verify the story with many family members and acquaintances of the Goughs when researching his book and was convinced of the veracity of the story.[12] The future husband and wife first met at a military ball held in Plymouth. However the story starts the night before when Frances dreamt of the man she knew she would marry. He was dressed as a soldier and his uniform had green facings on it, the same colour as that of the 87th Foot. The following evening at the ball Major Gough entered the ballroom accompanied by two fellow officers of the 87th. Frances, who was standing by her father, turned to him and informed him that this was the officer she had seen in her dream. The story continues that they danced together twice that evening and that in the weeks that followed a courtship developed that within a year would culminate in marriage. The 87th left Plymouth to take up garrison duties in Guernsey in April 1807 and although Gough accompanied them he returned to Plymouth in July of that year to marry Frances.

Frances Gough was the daughter of Lieutenant General Edward Stephens of the Royal Artillery who at that time was serving in the garrison artillery in Plymouth. Very little has been written about her before. Even Rait in his biography of Gough mentions her in passing a number of times without really considering her. In better understanding Frances Gough, née Stephens, the present author is indebted to the 5th Viscount Gough for access to some of her private correspondence with her husband. In her letters to her husband we get the picture of a woman strong in character and mind, although from time to time her health does not enjoy the same status. Being the daughter of a soldier she seems to have entered the marriage already aware of how to behave as an officer's wife, particularly one who even during the early years of their marriage is growing in stature and reputation. Their marriage came at a 'suitable' time for both of them. Frances was 20 years old and would have been considered the right age for an army wife. Much younger and she may not have been able to understand her responsibilities and carry out the duties of an officer's wife correctly; much older and she might not have wished the upheaval that a soldiers wife might have to face.

---

11   Rait, *Gough*, Vol. I, pp. 22–23, quoting from Gough's letter to Blakeney dated 27 October 1859.
12   Rait, *Gough*, Vol. I, pp. 23–24.

It was much easier if a wife had time to grow into her responsibilities and get used to them before children and age came upon her.

At times her relationship with her father seems to have been somewhat strained, particularly when she was living with him during the period when Hugh Gough was in the Spanish Peninsular. However at other times the good advice of her father probably helped her, and consequently her husband. During the long absence there were undoubtedly times when Frances longed for her husband's return, even if only on leave. Yet she made it quite clear that although she desperately wanted this she did not wish for Hugh Gough to obtain such leave. The source of this decision appears to have been her father who seems to have convinced her that it was not the 'done thing'.[13] This decision, and level of understanding from his wife, was wise. The commander in the Peninsula, Sir Arthur Wellesley, later Lord Wellington, would complain bitterly about the number of officers, many far senior to Gough, who would take the slightest opportunity to return home on leave. This would be a constant problem for Wellington. For example in July 1811, a time of the year when he would wish to be actively campaigning, he was hindered by the fact that five of his eight divisional commanders were absent, along with six brigade commanders, a cavalry brigade commander, and the commander of the Royal Artillery. That Hugh Gough did not take such a course of action, and just as importantly had an understanding and intelligent wife in this regard, certainly did his reputation no harm at all. Thus the only time Gough returned to England was when he had been wounded, and was not recovering as well as he ought: even then, he took advantage of this opportunity to deal with regimental business, most importantly recruiting.

As previously alluded to it no doubt helped that Frances would have had her own mother to look up to as an example of an officer's wife. As for Hugh Gough, there existed an old maxim within the military fraternity that 'subalterns shouldn't marry, majors may marry, and colonels must marry'. He was reaching that point in his career, and his life – for he was now nearly 28 – when a wife was becoming 'necessary' for keeping up appearances and from a social point of view. Senior officers' wives played an important part in the social life of a regiment. The officer whose wife could join this social circle was always better placed and better informed. We see clearly from Frances's letters to her husband that this was true in their case. This was particularly important during the long period he spent overseas during the Peninsular War, where she was able to manage not only his affairs in England but to keep him up to date with events – military, political, and social – that were occurring in Britain. In so doing Frances shows herself to be an educated and intelligent woman, and a devoted and loving wife who is anxious to help her husband succeed.

However, at the same time one does not get the feeling that she was a 'social climber' and that her main interest at all times appears to have been the welfare of her husband. This is borne out by the way in which she addressed her letters to him referring to him as "my best beloved", "my best friend", "my dearest love" and "my blessing" at various times. We also see her frustration at delays in ships to and from the Spanish Peninsular that delayed letters both to and from her husband. There are also times when this results in her fearing the worst from having had to rely on news from other quarters. These were particularly anxious times, reinforced by the fact that she records in the letters to her husband details of friends and acquaintances of theirs who have been hit by the tragedy she fears.

Frances clearly felt the separation greatly. This sadness at their separation is particularly acute on what should normally be times of celebration. For example on 2 November 1811 she writes "Tis your Birth day, and I am ready to cry!!!".[14] The genuine feelings of distress at the absence from the

---

13   Private Collection, Frances Gough to Hugh Gough, 2 November 1811.
14   Private Collection, Frances Gough to Hugh Gough, 2 November 1811. The eagle-eyed reader will have
      noted that Hugh Gough's birthday was actually the following day the 3 November.

man she loves appear throughout the correspondence of this era. The feelings expressed in the letter of 2 November are particularly acute due to the fact that their daughter Letitia was recovering from a serious illness. All of this added to the stress and strain under which Frances Gough was to be found during this period.

There is the usual news one would expect about family matters, and, as time went on, reports on the activities and health of the children. Altogether the Goughs had six children, the first two being born during the war with France and the others after the peace. The eldest, Letitia Mary Gough, was born on the 17 July 1809. The second child, and the first son, was Edward William Ord Gough born on 9 December 1810. Edward tragically died young, shortly before his third birthday, in September 1813. Unsurprisingly the illness and ultimately death of their son put a strain upon the marriage and it is the only time when there is recorded evidence of harsh words between the two. Frances' correspondence during the period shortly after the death of her son clearly illustrate this strain, which was not helped by the separation from her husband and the continued fear that she might also lose him before too long. In time this tension passed.

The Goughs faced not only the common problems of any married couple, but also the added ones created by the fact that he was a soldier in time of war. Despite this, theirs was a long and happy marriage. Perhaps it is simply because this period is so well documented in their remaining correspondence, but it seems that at no point was greater strain placed upon their relationship than the time Gough spent in Portugal and Spain during the Peninsular War, and it is to this extremely important early career experience that we now turn our attention.

Part 2

Peninsular War

5

Hugh Gough and the Peninsular War

The Peninsular War of 1807–1814 was the first time that Britain was really able to fight back on land against the French during the wars of this era. Up until this point the warfare had largely been naval in nature and included small amphibious operations, which varied in degree and quality. As the poet Sheridan, also an MP at that time, is said to have commented, up to that point the war had consisted of 'filching sugar islands'. There were obvious exceptions to this such as the operations in the Low Countries and Egypt but neither had been a sustained operation such as the British campaign in the Spanish Peninsular would become. For Britain, this became the main theatre of war, especially for the fortunes of the Army, but after Trafalgar and with Royal Navy supremacy assured, the Peninsular War became the focus of the whole nation during the war with France.

It was during this campaign that Hugh Gough first came to prominence and in many ways this marks the start of his prestigious military career. Although the campaigning he had seen up to this point had been useful, it cannot be compared with facing the French army in Portugal and Spain. It could be argued that the minor operations he had seen against the Dutch and the Spanish had been a 'comfortable' baptism of fire. This cannot be said of the Peninsular War and it would mark some of the hardest fighting he would see in his career. The Peninsular War, as the British have always called it, was fought from 1807–1814 and the battles ranged from Portugal, through Spain and culminated in France itself. Although a detailed history of the Peninsular War is beyond the scope of this work it will be useful for a moment to consider the conflict in a little detail.[1] As we have already seen, Spain and France had become allied during the war and thus a large number of French troops were now present in Spain. In 1807 they launched an opportunistic attack on Portugal. The main reason for this was to do with what has become known as the Continental System. The system was an attempt by Napoleon to place economic pressure on Britain by closing all continental ports to British goods and trade. Such a system was, in theory, a sound tactic by the French and had it been truly successful it could have severely damaged Britain's ability to fight the war. The British Empire had always been one based on trade and without the ability to access

---

1   There are many fine books on the Peninsular War that can provide further reading. Sir Charles Oman's seven volume *History of the Peninsular War* (Oxford: Clarendon Press, 1911) although now somewhat dated remains a very impressive account of the campaign. Of the older works William Napier's six volume *The History of the War In the Peninsular* (London: G. Routledge, 1828–1840) remains interesting. Ian Fletcher's *Peninsular War: Aspects of the struggle for the Iberian Peninsula* (Staplehurst: Spellmount, 1998) is an interesting modern account. Michael Glover's *The Peninsular War, 1807–1914* (Newton Abbot: David and Charles, 1974) is an interesting introductory book. David Gates *The Spanish Ulcer: A History of the Peninsular War* (London: Pimlico, 2002) is a modern work that attempts to look beyond the purely British perspective of the conflict. As a consequence it often questions our established understanding of the conflict. Andrew Bamford's *Sickness, Suffering, and the Sword: The British Regiment on Campaign 1805–1815* (Norman, Oklahoma: University of Oklahoma Press, 2013) although not specifically about the Peninsular War contains much useful information on the campaign and gives a good insight into regimental life, often mentioning Gough and the 87th Foot.

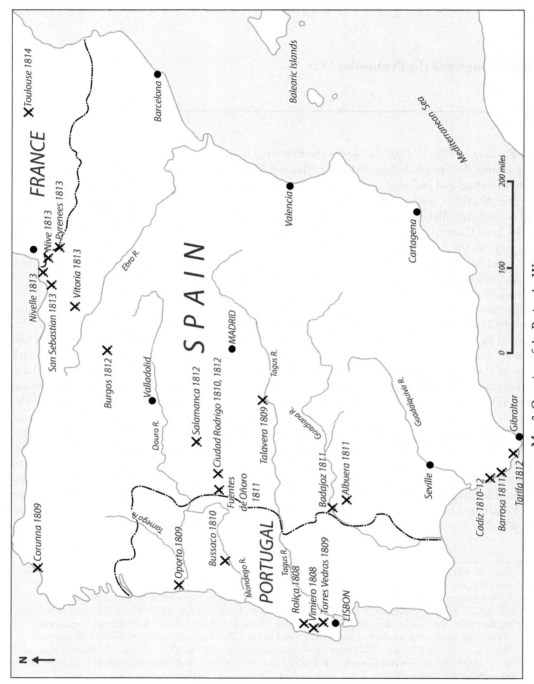

Map 3 Overview of the Peninsular War.

European markets that trade was severely restricted. French ports were not really the issue, as the Royal Navy had been doing its best to blockade French ports for several years. What really started to hurt British trade was the fact that as the French armies advanced through Europe more and more ports became closed under the Continental System. France also placed diplomatic pressure, and the threat of military action, on neutral countries to close their ports to British ships. To begin with it was easier for such neutral states to comply with French demands. However as years rolled on, and the impact of the loss of such trade started to hit home, many neutral states started to look for ways around this.

Caught up in this was the country of Portugal. For centuries Portugal had been an ally and trading partner of England and later Britain. The origins of this were the Anglo-Portuguese Treaty of 1373, although the alliance was reinforced by various treaties throughout the centuries. The friendship between the two countries had been maintained largely due to financial expediency, trade being an important part of the relationship, and the fact that they shared a common enemy: namely Spain. In many ways it was simply a case of following the old proverb 'my enemy's enemy is my friend'. Once Spain and France were allied, Portugal's position deteriorated. However before that, in 1793, Portugal had joined Spain in a war against Revolutionary France. This temporary alliance with Spain collapsed in July 1795 when the Spanish signed a separate peace. At this time Portugal received its first military support from Britain as an expeditionary force under the command of Lieutenant General Sir Charles Stuart was dispatched. This force remained until November 1798 when it was transferred for operations in the Mediterranean. In 1801 a Franco-Spanish force invaded Portugal in an effort to force the closure of Portuguese ports to the British. This conflict, sometimes called the War of Oranges because of an anecdote associated with the Spanish chief minister Manuel de Godoy, ended in humiliation for Portugal with the Treaty of Badajoz in 1801. Portugal was forced to close its ports to British ships, give trade concessions to the French, and to cede the region of Olivenca to Spain. After the Peace of Amiens ended Portugal, who had during the peace restored trade with Britain, once again found herself under pressure to adhere to the Continental System. However, after Trafalgar Portugal felt secure enough to reopen all her ports to British ships.

Throughout 1806 and 1807, France and Spain attempted to create a *casus belli* for war with Portugal through a series of increasingly severe demands. Ultimately on 19 November 1807 General Junot invaded Portugal with a French army of 24,000 men. There was little the Portuguese could do by way of resistance, even had their army not been weak, corrupt, and divided. On 30 November Junot marched into Lisbon. However he found that the Royal Family, and just as importantly most of the state treasury, had boarded a Royal Navy wquadron and had set sail for the Portuguese colonies in South America. Under an agreement signed in October 1807, France and Spain had agreed to partition Portugal. Although this firmly shut Portuguese ports to British ships, the effect on British trade was not as severe as it might otherwise have been as much of the trade was continued with the Portuguese colonies and the government-in-exile.

However, this period of Franco-Spanish harmony was always likely to be short-lived, and so it proved. Napoleon had intended all along to bring Spain fully into the war on his side rather than allow a continuation of the vacillating policy they had taken up to that point. Spain had aided France only when there was something in it for them: the invasion of Portugal being a case in point. Indeed in 1806 there was even talk that Spain was considering supporting Prussia against France. In many ways the alliance between the two nations had been a good excuse for Napoleon to station thousands of French troops in Spain. Thus in February 1808 Napoleon was able to use these troops to secure the main fortresses, defensive positions, and most importantly the route through the Pyrenees. The French commander Joachim Murat then led 118,000 men into Spain, and by the end of March 1808 he was in control of Madrid. At first the French had been welcomed, due to the unpopularity of the Spanish government and Royal Family. However this very quickly changed with anti-French riots in early April. These became more serious once Napoleon had manoeuvred his brother Joseph onto the Spanish throne, and in May 1808 riots in Madrid were brutally put down.

This had the reverse effect of that desired by the French, and within the month such anti-French riots had spread throughout Spain. In June 1808 Spain was preparing what forces were left for war with France, and on the tenth of that month the Junta in Seville sent an appeal to the British authorities in Gibraltar for assistance. Despite this appeal for support the Spanish were always somewhat reluctant allies to the British and were suspicious of their motives. The Spanish regular forces, numbering over 100,000, were badly organised, dispersed over a wide area, and poorly led. The Spanish delayed the French advance, but that was about all.

In early August 1808 a British force arrived off the coast of Portugal, under the command of the young, but surprisingly experienced, Lieutenant General Sir Arthur Wellesley. Wellesley had initially gone ashore in Corunna, Spain on 20 July to discuss the state of things with the Junta in that city. He was not only a member of parliament but was also serving as Chief Secretary for Ireland. The force had been put together in some haste and troops and been called in from various locations. Over 10,000 troops came from Ireland, a battalion was despatched from the garrison in Gibraltar, and another battalion came from Madeira. There is a certain irony in the fact that the majority of the troops used to support Spain had initially been earmarked for attacks on various Spanish colonies around the world. Even this force, whilst small by the standards of the other combatants, had been difficult to assemble given the British Army's other commitments. Thus from the very outset it was made clear to all commanders that this was, as Wellesley would later say, 'England's only army'. If the aim had simply been to support the Spanish in resisting the French invasion this force might have been adequate. However it soon became clear that the state of the Spanish Army was such that a larger British force would be necessary. A force of 10,000 men under Sir John Moore was diverted from proposed operations in Sweden. Again other troops were dispatched from garrisons and proposed expeditions, which would now have to play second fiddle to what would become known as the Peninsular War.[2]

Whilst further troops, and a more senior general to command them, were being organised Wellesley's force started to disembark at Mondego Bay, in Portugal. This bay was partly chosen because it was a suitable location at which to unload an army but also because students from the local university had seized the fort that commanded the bay. Once the force was landed they were replaced by Royal Marines from the squadron that protected the transportation of the troops. On the first day of the landing, 1 August, 8,500 troops and three batteries of artillery were landed successfully. This was not without loss of life, but by the standards of the day the loss was small. The success of landing so many troops and guns in such a short space of time was remarkable. By the eighth some 13,500 men and 30 guns had been taken ashore. The following day part of Wellesley's force set out to find the enemy.

Wellesley's orders were deliberately vague, as the exact purpose of the force had not yet been determined, and included the wonderful phrase, "His Majesty is graciously pleased to confide to you the fullest discretion to act according to circumstances, for the benefit of his service". Wellesley, who had already used such discretion by deciding to land in Portugal rather than Spain, met with almost immediate success, defeating the French at Obidos on 16 August, at Rolica on 17 August and at Vimiero on 21 August. At the first two encounters the British had clearly had the advantage

---

2   Moore had initially been suggested as the commander of the force to go to the Spanish Peninsular, however he was a political opponent of the incumbent Tory government, indeed he had spent six years as a Whig MP, and was thus overlooked. However he was widely considered to be the best general in the army at that time.

in numbers whereas at the latter the sides were more evenly matched. Vimiero was an important victory in that it demonstrated the way forward for British forces. As would prove the case time and time again, a British battalion drawn up in line formation proved a match for any French unit attacking in column. The action of the 29th (Worcestershire) Regiment of Foot in resisting two French battalions was a demonstration of this. It also demonstrated the lack of control shown by British cavalry that would continue throughout the war, and beyond. The 20th Light Dragoons had routed a unit of retreating French Grenadiers, but as was so often the case continued to charge again and again, lost discipline and organisation and were easy prey for the French cavalry who killed 45 men, including the commanding officer, and captured 11 men, out of a total force of 240.

Vimiero could have been an even greater success had Wellesley been left to his own devices. The French had lost over 2,000 casualties and 13 guns. However at the moment of victory Wellesley was superseded by the arrival of Lieutenant General Sir Harry Burrard. Although both Burrard and Wellesley were lieutenant generals, Burrard was senior by length of service. Indeed with Wellesley having only been made a lieutenant general in April 1808 he was one of the most junior officers of that rank in the army. Burrard refused to allow Wellesley to pursue the enemy, and given the state of disarray the French were in after the battle this would appear to have been a grave mistake. As it happened this was the only order Burrard gave as he himself was superseded by the arrival of Lieutenant General Sir Hew Dalrymple on 22 August. Dalrymple was an unusual man who seems unsuited to the task. More importantly he undertook his mission rather half-heartedly to say the least.

On the same day as his arrival, Dalrymple signed the Convention of Cintra (or Sintra), which was surely one of the most disastrous documents ever signed by a British officer. The convention threw away all of what Wellesley and his army had achieved at Vimiero. It allowed the 26,000 French troops in Portugal to leave with their arms, baggage, and indeed the booty they had gathered in Portugal, still intact. What was even more unusual was that the evacuation was to be undertaken by the Royal Navy! This perfectly illustrates the half-hearted nature with which some were fighting the war with France. It is a bizarre chapter in the war and would seem inconceivable in many respects that anyone would help to evacuate so many of the enemy in good order. The Convention, unsurprisingly, caused uproar in Britain and Wellesley, Burrard, and Dalrymple were all recalled to face an inquiry. It had done very little good for Britain's relationship with her Portuguese and Spanish allies, and understandably made them question British intentions. The Portuguese in particular were disappointed and naturally started to question Britain's commitment to the war. The subsequent enquiry was held at the Royal Hospital, Chelsea from 14 November to 27 December 1808. The three lieutenant generals were exonerated, although Dalrymple and Burrard never held active commands again. Wellesley alone received the thanks of Parliament for the victory at Vimiero. Although Dalrymple had acted foolishly, and worse than that had tried to pass the blame onto his subordinates, he did have some justification in the wording of his orders from the Secretary of State for War, Lord Castlereagh, which had stated that he was to exercise his own discretion to expel the French from Portugal. This he could claim he had done, albeit not in the conventional manner in which the orders had intended.

In the meantime, operations in Portugal had continued with the forces now under the command of Sir John Moore. Despite the rather unusual way in which he had extricated himself, it should not be forgotten that General Junot had in effect lost Portugal. This, and the Spanish victory at Bailen on 19 July, had an effect on other French forces who lifted a number of sieges and retreated beyond the Ebro River. In an attempt to finish operations in the Spanish Peninsula once and for all, Napoleon himself marched an army of 200,000 men into Spain to deal with matters personally. The Spanish had organised three armies to meet this new invasion. Even if all frontline, reservists, garrisons, and the famous 'guerrillas', were added together they amounted to barely 230,000 men. Nor was there any cohesion to this force. Napoleon's forces defeated the Spanish at Espinosa,

Reynosa, Tudela, and Somosierra, and the route to Madrid was once again opened. This broke the back of the Spanish armies and what was left fled either southwards or towards the Portuguese border.

This placed Moore in a difficult position as there was now little between him and the whole of Napoleon's army. On 23 December 1808, Moore's cavalry led by Lord Paget gained a victory at Sahagun, but it did not disguise the fact that Moore faced with overwhelming odds had no choice but to retreat to the coast, where he could if necessary be evacuated by the Royal Navy.[3] Moore managed to keep his army of 30,000 men just ahead of the French who were now in pursuit of him. To this end he was aided by the minor rear-guard actions fought at Benavente, Cacabelos, and Villafranca.

When Moore reached Corunna he was forced to fight another action whilst waiting for the Navy to return from having evacuated his advanced force from Vigo. On 16 January 1809 Moore fought the Battle of Corunna. Moore's force stood at 15,000 men, and nine guns. He faced slightly over 16,000 French troops, of which about 3,000 were cavalry, and around 40 guns. This was, from Moore's point of view, simply a holding action designed to give time for the ships to return so that his army could be evacuated by sea. That said, Moore was a clever enough commander to appreciate the opportunity to counter-attack and at one point he had some success. Yet the battle remained largely a defensive engagement and ultimately a British victory. British casualties were about 900 dead and wounded whereas the French had only suffered slightly more than 1,000 dead and wounded. However the great advantage had been that the battle gave time for Moore's army to be evacuated by sea largely intact. The retreat to Corunna had been costly for Britain. Spain had been lost, although there was probably little that Moore's force of 30,000 could have done about that, and the campaign had cost the British 7,000 men. Unfortunately amongst those 7,000 men was Moore himself.

The question now remained as to what should be the next step. Moore had questioned the possibility of continuing the war and holding Portugal once Spain was lost. However Wellesley, appointed as Moore's successor, took a different view. It was his belief that, with the aid of a reorganised Portuguese Army, Portugal could be held and, in time, form a base for operations into Spain. This gives us a little background into the course of events in Spain up to this point. Under Wellesley's command the army in Portugal and later Spain would become the main focus of the war effort against France. It was into this arena that Gough and the 87th would now be deployed. The second battalion of the 87th would play an important part in the army of Wellesley as he sought first to hold Portugal and then to march into Spain and defeat the French. Gough would be at the forefront of his battalion's action, and it is to this period of Gough's career that we now turn our attention.

---

3   Some have been critical of Moore for continuing the retreat rather than turning and fighting from a defensive position. This is perhaps harsh and ignores the fact that he was not in the best place geographically to make a stand against the French. To withdraw and be landed in Portugal made much more sense. Moore, like Wellesley, was only too aware that he had "England's only army" under his command. Whilst with the benefit of hindsight we might criticise him for not being more adventurous, he took what at the time appeared a prudent command decision.

6

Command of the 87th Foot

Before briefly looking at the origins of the Peninsular War, we left Gough and the 2nd Battalion of the 87th Foot undertaking garrison duties in Guernsey. For a new battalion this had been valuable experience. It had given them time to train, to get used to the regiment, its traditions and its methods, and by all accounts to become a disciplined unit. A demonstration of this is seen that in one week in July 1807, for example, 35 soldiers of the garrison in Guernsey received corporal punishment for various offences but none of these was a soldier of the 87th, and the battalion had the lowest number of disciplinary offences of the garrison during its stay.[1]

This was further supported by the testimony of Brigadier General Fraser who, after inspecting the garrison in June 1807, remarked that he found:

> everything in a state of perfection that would have done credit to an old established regiment, and which could not have been expected in a battalion so lately formed ... I am of opinion that the second battalion of the Eighty-Seventh is fit for any service, and very likely to be distinguished.[2]

The words had a somewhat prophetic nature: as we have seen in the previous chapter, the expedition to the Spanish Peninsula saw a demand for battalions from where ever they could be spared. Therefore it is not surprising that a battalion on garrison duties in Guernsey was from the very start intended for service in Spain, particularly as with the Royal Navy having supremacy of the seas the likelihood of an invasion of Guernsey was now remote. In May 1808 the 87th were ordered to prepare for active service in the Spanish Peninsula.

They were to be ready to sail on 4 June. However the initial destination was not Spain but Harwich. The reason for this was that they were to form part of a new brigade. This demonstrates that there was some serious planning given to the deployment of troops to Spain. Too often the fact that battalions were drawn from so many different locations gives the impression of a rather chaotic organisation, and perhaps this was true for the initial deployment. However even from this early stage we see that there was thought being given to proper organisation in sending brigade formations rather than piecemeal battalions. It also points to the size of the operations that were planned in the Spanish Peninsula as there was a need for large formations rather than a handful of battalions.

From Harwich, Gough and the 87th marched to Danbury in Essex, not far from Colchester, where the brigade was to form. The movement of the battalion was somewhat delayed by the outbreak amongst the garrison in Guernsey of ophthalmia, a type of eye infection, and a number of soldiers were not transported to the mainland until they had fully recovered. The movement

---

1   Cunliffe, *Royal Irish Fusiliers*, pp. 63–65.
2   Cunliffe, *Royal Irish Fusiliers*, p. 65.

of the troops was done with caution towards the possible spreading of the infection amongst the army. On the recommendation of the Medical Department, all the bedding and blankets were to be boiled with potash before they could again be issued. Although most of the preparations seem to have been the work of John Doyle, it would have proved a useful lesson to Gough in how to deal with such infections. As a man who was noted for his care of soldiers, he no doubt took note and remembered the event for future reference.[3]

There was however a little confusion over exactly what use the new brigade would be put to. It must be remembered that at this stage there were still a number of other proposed expeditions being planned and it appears that this clouded matters for the battalion. For example, on 3 December 1808 they were told they would not be going overseas. On the fourth they were told they would be posted overseas, but not to Spain. Finally on 5 December they received orders to pack as they would be going to Spain in three or four days. The latter proved to be the case, although due to a lack of shipping, poor winds, and tides the battalion did not embark at Ramsgate until 27 December. It appears that the decision was made to keep the regiment at home until after Christmas. This was probably done for the advantage of the officers rather than the men.[4]

The final days in England were no doubt a busy time for Gough, not simply because the battalion was due to go overseas, but because he was to command it. The colonel of the regiment, Sir John Doyle, who held the rank of major general in the army, was employed as Lieutenant-Governor of Guernsey and by all accounts doing a fine job in reclaiming land, building roads and generally improving the Bailiwick. His nephew Lieutenant Colonel Charles Doyle had been commanding the second battalion. However he was on loan to the Spanish army as a military commissioner. Thus Gough as senior major was to command in the forthcoming campaign. Whether there was any thought to placing someone else in command is unknown. Cunliffe's history of the regiment suggests that the fact that Gough was, "a young and active commander whom [the battalion] all liked", was sufficient to ensure that he was not replaced.[5] After all, Gough could claim to be an experienced soldier, not only with the army but in particular the regiment. It is important to remember that although our narrative has moved quite quickly Gough had been an officer in the 87th for almost 13 years. He had risen from lieutenant to major during this period, and whilst he might have spent most of that time in the first battalion he was certainly accustomed to the regiment and very much part of its traditions. So, despite the fact that he was only 30 years of age, seemingly somewhat young to command a battalion, the fact that he was liked by the battalion and just as importantly well-known to them, meant that the 87th embarked in good spirits.[6]

The battalion split into three for embarkation and transport to Spain. The initial plan was that the 87th would be part of a force of about 3,000 men sent to Cadiz to be commanded by Major General John Coape Sherbrooke. This proposed force was made up of the 1st Battalion Coldstream Guards, 1st Battalion 3rd (Scots) Guards, 1st Battalion 88th Foot, 2nd Battalion 87th Foot and two batteries of light artillery. Wellington called Sherbrooke "a very good officer", however he had neither the temperament or intellect to hold an independent command. However the Spanish, still

---

3   Cunliffe, *Royal Irish Fusiliers*, p. 67.

4   Cunliffe, *Royal Irish Fusiliers*, p. 67–68. The delay until after Christmas was possibly not even for the benefit of the 87th as at this time they were brigaded with the 1st Battalion the Coldstream Guards. No doubt the Guards officers had many social commitments during this season.

5   Cunliffe, *Royal Irish Fusiliers*, p. 68.

6   Although the age of 30 was young to command a battalion under normal circumstances there was a surprising number of young colonels and senior officers during the Peninsular War. Twenty-eight was the average age of a lieutenant colonel in the peninsula at one point, and the average age of a major general was just 40. See Glover, Michael, *Wellington As Military Commander* (London: Penguin Group, 2001 reprint) pp. 197–198.

suspicious of the motives of the British, particularly when it came to their largest port, refused the troops permission to land. The crossing to Spain had been a very difficult one made in bad weather. As a consequence, having left England on 27 December 1808 it was not until 12 March 1809 that the men of the 87th finally landed, in Lisbon rather than Cadiz. Indeed, having gone from Ramsgate to Portsmouth, the attempted sailing had to be aborted due to severe weather and the ships of the convoy were ordered to make port, with the majority finding safe haven in Cork in early February. After a few days they set off for Cadiz but, as noted, ultimately had to land in Lisbon. Whilst the battalion had left England in fine order it arrived in the Peninsula somewhat the worse for its journey.

The 87th was now formed up into a new brigade, commanded by Major General Christopher Tilson, with the 1st Battalion 88th (Connaught Rangers) Regiment of Foot, the 1st Portuguese Grenadiers, five companies of the 60th Rifles, and a detachment of the 14th Light Dragoons. The brigade also had a unit of Portuguese cavalry attached to it from time to time. Indeed the brigade, although largely British in composition, served under the command of William Carr Beresford who had assumed command of the newly-reconstituted Portuguese Army which was now commanded by a combination of British and Portuguese officers. In the following April and May 1809 the brigade was part of a movement to try and secure a crossing of the Douro River. This would lead to the Second Battle of Oporto on 12 May 1809. However Gough's brigade was not engaged in this battle and indeed saw no action during this movement. Wellesley split his Anglo-Portuguese force, save for a smaller force left behind in Portugal, in two. Wellesley took a predominantly British force north on the Oporto road, whilst a predominantly Portuguese force commanded by Beresford and including the 87th, moved further inland to try and turn the left flank of the French forces, commanded by Marshal Soult. This required the 87th to undertake a lot of marching in wet and cold weather, which added to an already difficult march, often through mountainous regions.

This march included a rather treacherous river crossing of the Tamega, a tributary of the Douro. This would have proved a valuable experience for Gough, given that much later in life he would hold command in an area, the Punjab, often called the Land of the Five Rivers. The difficulty was exacerbated by the fact that the 87th were the last regiment to cross. Due to the other units taking longer than expected, when it came time for Gough to lead his men across the river it had risen considerably and was running fast. With a fast current, the men had to ford in Indian file with the water above their waists. At one point an officer and 14 men were swept down the river but were saved by the efforts of the mounted officers. Amazingly it appears that the regiment lost no men during this hazardous enterprise. As Gough took personal command of this river crossing it is to his credit that there was remarkably no loss of life. However, what they did lose was all of their bread, a few muskets, caps and shoes, along with several thousand rounds of ammunition. Thus they spent the night already cold and wet, which was added to by torrential rain, and a lack of food. Whilst this was the case for the whole brigade, Gough alone amongst the regimental commanders took it upon himself to try to alleviate his men's suffering by helping to organised fires and shelter for them.[7]

All of this movement took its toll on the battalion. Despite the intentions of Beresford to engage the enemy, this never happened. On at least three occasions Gough records that the 87th prepared to engage the enemy who simply retreated rather than accept battle.[8] The battalion however was suffering casualties from sickness if not from battle, and fever was sweeping through the brigade.

---

7   Cunliffe, *Royal Irish Fusiliers*, pp. 72–72. Rait, *Gough*, Vol. I, pp. 32–33. The latter quotes from a description of the movements of the 87th placed in a long since lost letter from Hugh Gough to his father. The entire letter is recorded in the text.

8   Rait, *Gough*, Vol. I, pp. 32–36. This is from the aforementioned letter written by Hugh Gough to his father.

In the 87th, nine officers and 47 men went down with fever. At first Gough avoided catching it, putting it down to the fact that he drank a glass of mulled wine every evening. Eventually he succumbed and spent a month away from the command of his battalion. Indeed, when the battalion moved on to Castello Branco on 12 June, Gough remained behind at Guarda for at least a month, of which he later told his father he had to spend a fortnight confined to his bed.[9] For Gough this must have been doubly galling. He was not the sort to sit still, but worse than this he might miss his opportunity to lead the battalion in battle. The latter point would have concerned him. He would surely have appreciated that he had a wonderful opportunity to make a name for himself. A young officer given chance to lead a battalion in battle would understandably have been eager to take advantage of this opportunity, for advancement, glory, and to make a name for himself that could last beyond the war in the Peninsula.

As it happened, the 87th did little during Gough's absence, and by June 1809 he had rejoined them at Castello Branco. There are reports that with Gough absent, and having endured a tiresome and difficult march, discipline amongst the 87th broke down. Exact details are hard to come by and it is possible that the 87th were tarred with the same brush as the 88th, where discipline certainly did break down, partly because they were in the same brigade but also because they were also an Irish regiment. Wellesley, who had a strained relationship with the Irish in general despite – or perhaps because of – his own heritage, had threatened to send both regiments into garrison and report them as unfit for service.[10] This was a hollow threat as Wellesley could not afford to lose regiments so easily: he needed every man he could get. It also seems strange that a battalion that had been praised for its discipline when inspected in Guernsey could fall so fast. It is of course possible that the duress of campaigning had created such a situation. It is also likely that with Gough absent that there naturally appeared, at least for a time, to be a lack of authority. It is often difficult for a second in command to immediately stamp his authority, particularly when he knows he will only temporarily be in command. If the battalion fell into ill-discipline when Gough was absent it speaks both to his credit as a stern, disciplined, and commanding leader, but also perhaps to his lack of ability to delegate and the fact that control was maintained merely by his presence rather than any system put in place by him.

---

9   Rait, *Gough*, Vol. I, p. 75. The events are corroborated by the account of Ensign William Knox, which can be found in Cunliffe, *Royal Irish Fusiliers*, p. 75.

10   Cunliffe, *Royal Irish Fusiliers*, p. 76.

7

The Battle of Talavera

The brigade that the 87th was part of now had a new commander, with Tilson having resigned. Tilson was a somewhat strange soldier, who seemed to have no inclination towards his profession. He had been upset to be placed under Beresford's command as Beresford was actually below him on the list of major generals but superior because he was acting as a Marshal of Portugal. He asked to be removed from Beresford's command but later withdrew the request. Tilson and Beresford's relationship never recovered from this, and the former reacted angrily to the latter's criticism of his lack of activity and alacrity during their recent advance. Tilson was transferred to General Hill's command but fared no better there and was eventually recalled to England. The new commander was the wonderfully named Colonel Rufane Shaw Donkin. Donkin and Gough might have known each other before this point as they had both served in St Lucia at the same time. However Donkin was seriously ill during this period, so much so that he was invalided home, so their paths might not have crossed. Donkin's health would continue to bedevil him for the rest of his life, so much so that at the age of 68 he could stand it no longer and hanged himself.

In June 1809 the army was reorganised into divisions, and Donkin's brigade, now consisting of the 2nd Battalion 87th, 1st Battalion 88th, and the 5th Battalion 60th Rifles, was part of the 3rd Division commanded by Major General John Randoll Mackenzie, once a lieutenant of marines but better known as an officer of the 78th Foot. It will be remembered that Gough had previously served in the 78th and this is the same Mackenzie who led the 2nd Battalion 78th Foot in South Africa during that earlier expedition. The link would no doubt have helped both men, with Gough being known to the commander of the division and the commander of division already knowing, and having seen in action, the commander of one of his battalions. With the army reorganised it now set off to enter Spain to engage the French. The difficult relationship with the Spanish, previously alluded to, was to cause many problems during this campaign, none more so than in the movements that led to the battle of Talavera in July 1809. Wellesley was finding it increasingly difficult to work with the Spanish and particularly their commander General Gregorio Garcia de la Cuesta. Cuesta was by the time of the Peninsular War 67 years old and although an experienced soldier his talent for command was limited to say the least. In fairness it does have to be added that he was operating in extremely difficult circumstances, with various political factions fighting for control of the army, with a ramshackle organisation and an army both defeated and nervous. Despite this, Cuesta was determined to fight the French before the British arrived to support him. This was largely due to the fact that like most Spaniards at the time he was as suspicious of the British as he was of the enemy. There has also been a suggestion that as he had lost his last two battles he was somewhat jealous of the younger and victorious allied commander Wellesley.[1]

Thus Cuesta went forward alone to engage what he thought was just the corps led by Marshal Victor of some 23,000 men. On the evening of 26 July he returned with his army to Wellesley's

---

1   Glover, Michael, *Wellington As Military Commander* (London: Penguin Books, 2001), p. 74.

position behind the River Alberche near to the town of Talavera with his force in some disarray and quickly followed by a combined French force of 46,000 men. Even now, largely out of devilment and to prove his independence, he camped on the eastern side of the Alberche at the mercy of the French advance in a poor defensive position with his back to the river. The following day Cuesta consented to fall back to the defensive position held by Wellesley's British troops.[2]

Talavera is widely regarded as the hardest fought of Wellesley's victories in Spain. When combined, the British and Spanish allies had superior numbers to the French forces facing them with Joseph Bonaparte and Marshal Jourdan in overall command. The British contingent amounted to 20,641 and the Spanish brought over 34,000 men to the field. Against this the French fielded 46,100, although they had an almost two to one superiority in artillery. Wellesley had constant problems in getting agreement from the Spanish. Although a detailed account of the battle is not necessary it is important to understand a little of the movement that led to the confrontation in which Gough and his battalion would get their first taste of battle in the Peninsula.

By the afternoon of 27 July the British and Spanish allies were holding a line almost two miles long. If Wellesley had ever had any illusions about the quality of his allies they were shattered on that morning when the sight of French cavalry sent some Spanish troops fleeing from the battle-field in disarray, and requiring that the British troops nearby also had to withdraw. To cover this withdrawal Wellesley sent forward the 3rd Division, commanded by Mackenzie, and his cavalry. It was this force that spotted the French columns advancing around noon. For whatever reason, Mackenzie did not expect the French to press their advance. He allowed his men to sit down in leisure whilst organising for some huts nearby to be burnt to the ground so as to avoid giving a defensive position to the enemy. Unfortunately the smoke from the burning huts covered the continued advance of the French column and the men of the division had to quickly reform when the French started to appear through the smoke. As Donkin's brigade were the nearest to the enemy they bore the brunt of the attack. The 87th in particular suffered heavy casualties. There appears to have been some level of resistance put up by the 87th but details are few and what role Gough played in this is unclear, however it brought the army and the rest of the division the time it needed to get reorganised.

Donkin's brigade found itself facing the French division commanded by General Pierre Belon Lapisse. Wellesley had galloped over to the position, almost being captured by the French in the process, and ordered the withdrawal of the rest of Mackenzie's division to a position where they could cover the retreat of Donkin's brigade. In this way Donkin's brigade was able to retreat and re-form behind the rest of the division. With the support of British cavalry the situation was recovered. This part of the action on 27 July lasted barely two hours but the 87th had paid a heavy price. The failure lay outside the regiment, with Donkin, Mackenzie, and even Wellesley taking a share in it. It was to the credit of the 87th that they did not panic and retreat in disorder. Had they done so it is likely that they would have suffered far more casualties. As it was they sustained almost 200 casualties including 34 taken prisoners, and one officer killed and 10 officers wounded.[3] Cunliffe's history of the 87th concludes that the fact they sustained far more casualties than the other line regiment in the brigade – the 88th only having a third of their casualties – demonstrates that the 87th kept better order and bore the brunt of the French assault and put up the majority of the resistance. This might be to take it too far. However it is clear that the 87th had in general performed well, under the eyes of the same commander who had been critical of their discipline the previous month.

---

2   The term British troops is used because at this stage the Portuguese Army was still going through its reorganisation and was consequently left behind to complete this.

3   Cunliffe, *Royal Irish Fusiliers*, p. 78.

Once the allied withdrawal was complete, Donkin's brigade was now holding a position on the Cerro de Medellin. This elevated position was perhaps the key to the allied left flank. Again, through lack of orders from higher up the chain of command, Donkin had placed himself slightly in advance of the rest of the line, but he was clearly occupying a key position. This position was being held by a brigade that had already had a harrowing day and was a little the worse for its experience. At 2100, the French again attempted an attack, trying to outflank the British and Spanish. The exact detail remains unclear but there was clearly an attack upon the British position and some accounts give the 87th the credit for charging and clearing the French from the hill. If this is so then it is testament to the ability of Gough and his battalion. One imagines that Gough would have used the earlier experiences of the day as motivation for the charge. It was a chance for revenge, to give the French back some of what they had received earlier in the day. Several cries of 'Faugh a Ballagh', the war cry of the regiment which loosely translated means 'Clear the Way', would have heralded the advance of a group of determined and angry Irishmen, keen not only to prove themselves but to make up for the events of earlier in the day.[4]

After the losses sustained by being heavily involved twice on the 27th the brigade commanded by Donkin was moved behind Major General Rowland Hill's 2nd Division. In effect they now made up the second line of defence in anticipation for the action on 28 July. The remainder of the night was a restless one for all the soldiers. Supply problems meant there was little food, and every now and again a nervous sentry caused an alarm and a flurry of musket fire, but there was no further attack. There was some debate amongst the French high command as to whether they should attack on the 28th or wait for further reinforcements.

It appeared that Wellesley was not going to move from his position, notwithstanding that Soult's French corps was on the march to cut him off from Portugal. However at 0500 on 28 July the French artillery opened up a ferocious bombardment of the British and Spanish troops as a prelude to an attack. The French not only had superiority in terms of number of guns but also calibre. Although in a slightly withdrawn position, the 87th suffered under this barrage. When the bombardment slackened the French columns attacked and were beaten off several times throughout the day until at 1800 the French, having failed to break the British defensive line to any great degree called off their attack. Exact figures for the battle are uncertain however the British lost between 5,000 and 6,000 casualties over the two days, with the Spanish sustaining a little over 1,000. The French had suffered close to 7,500 casualties. The great difference was in the percentage of the force. Wellesley had lost 25 percent of his force, the French only 16 percent. The following day the Light Brigade under Brigadier General Robert Craufurd, consisting of three battalions, arrived to reinforce Wellesley after a forced march. Craufurd's brigade was allotted to the 3rd Division and the 1st Battalion 45th Foot was attached to Donkin's brigade to bring it back up to strength after the losses of the two days which had severely affected the ability of the brigade to operate as such. The division had been at the forefront of the battle, so much so that the divisional commander Mackenzie had been killed on the 28th.

The 87th had consisted of 826 officers and men before the two days of battle. They had sustained 354 casualties of which 111 had been killed. One officer had been killed and another 13 wounded,

---

4   Exactly who cleared the French from the hill at Cerro de Medellin is debated by historians. What was for many years considered the greatest authority on the campaign, William Napier's *History of the War in the Peninsular*, held the view that it was Donkin's brigade and in particular the 87th who did in fact 'clear the way'. However Sir Charles Oman's *History of the Peninsular War* and Sir John Fortescue's *A History of the British Army*, give the credit to the 29th (Worcestershire) Foot for the decisive engagement. Whatever the exact role of the 87th Foot is clear that they were heavily involved in the fighting. For further details on the battle in general Andrew Field's *Talavera: Wellington's First Victory in Spain* (Barnsley: Pen & Sword, 2006) for a modern interpretation of the battle.

of which two would subsequently die of their wounds and another would have to have his arm amputated. Amongst the officers wounded on 28 July was Gough, who received a cannon wound to his right side. Exactly when Gough received his wound is unclear. The possibility exists that Gough was wounded during the artillery bombardment that commenced the action on the 28th, and that despite his injury Gough continued to command the battalion until which time he was obliged to leave the field. This theory is supported by Cunliffe who quotes from a letter from Donkin to Gough, without giving a reference for the correspondence. The letter includes the lines, "permit me on this occasion … to repeat the assurances of the high sense I entertain of your personal exertions and gallantry at Talavera, until the moment when I was deprived of your assistance by your being wounded and taken off the field". [5] If so it is again typical of the man that he remained in command despite his own personal injury, until such time as he could safely leave the field.

The battalion had stood up well to its first major fight and was justly rewarded with the battle honour 'Talavera'. However, given the state of the battalion, particularly its shortage of officers which necessitated the promotion of the acting sergeant major to an ensigncy, the 87th could not continue to operate in the field after the battle. It was thus decided shortly after the battle that the battalion would have to go into garrison, at least until it could build its strength up.

---

5   Cunliffe, *Royal Irish Fusiliers*, p. 81.

8

After Talavera

Despite what appeared a British victory, and was indeed treated as one, it was Wellesley who had to withdraw and retreat towards Portugal. Wellesley was now down to 18,000 men and had behind him Soult's force now consisting of around 50,000 men. It was clear that he would have to move quickly if he was to return safely to Portugal. Portugal guaranteed a sound defensive position and, just as importantly, supplies. Due to the failure of the Spanish to deliver on their promises, the British had never received the promised supplies from their allies. The Spanish initially agreed to cover the retreat by continuing to hold Talavera. It appears that Cuesta's motivation was that he hoped the French would attack him again and he could thus win a great victory for himself and Spain without the British. This was wishful thinking to say the least.

On 3 August Wellesley moved, and was shortly followed by Cuesta who was now worried that he might be surrounded by superior numbers. This caused great problems for the British who had understandably left many of their wounded behind at Talavera, to come on later when transportation could be obtained. Albeit understandable under the circumstances, the withdrawal by the Spanish now left the wounded at the mercy of the French. Amongst those left behind in Talavera was Gough.

He was in a difficult position. His wound made it difficult for him to walk. However had he stayed in Talavera after the Spanish had withdrawn he was certain to be taken prisoner. As a major there was a possibility that he might be involved in a prisoner exchange, which was not uncommon at this time, and his value as a commander of a battalion might have increased the likelihood of this. However given the character of the man it is unlikely that he ever considered this. Despite great difficulty, and undoubtedly considerable pain, he managed to leave Talavera. One account claims he literally had to crawl away, and managed to hide in a nearby farm with Captain James Poole Oates of the 88th who had been badly wounded in the head. The two men hid for a while in a wood, maybe for as long as a fortnight, before managing to return to the British position at Almaraz. Unfortunately few details of the extraordinary adventure remain but it undoubtedly added to Gough's reputation both within the regiment and the army at large. It was a typical display of his tenacity and courage. It is also typical of the man that he made no mention of this great feat of courage in any account of his time in the army. It is likely that he told the story in private, but as usual he was reluctant to discuss such a matter in public. Indeed our account of this event comes not from Gough or even from the 87th Foot, but from Captain Oates.[1]

---

1   Although this story does not appear in Rait's biography of Gough it is told by Cunliffe and in Jourdain's history of the Connaught Rangers. The story seems to be authentic and the failure of Rait to record this event is not that surprising when one considers that he goes into little detail about Gough's career in the Peninsular War. Cunliffe, *Royal Irish Fusiliers*, p. 82. Jourdain, Lt. Col. H.F.N., *The Connaught Rangers* Vol. I (London, Royal United Service Institution, 1924), p. 39.

The 87th had suffered during the Talavera campaign and were now considered a weak battalion, that is under strength and not able to operate in the field as part of a brigade. Thus it was decided to send them into garrison at Lisbon. That the battalion had a wounded commander might also have played a part in this decision. It also appears that Wellesley continued in his poor opinion of the battalion, and of the 88th Foot, as emphasised by his order to the garrison commander at Lisbon to keep a careful eye on the "discipline and drill" of the two battalions.[2] This appears to have been based on pre-conceived ideas and second-hand information from people who were not well placed to express such opinions. The brigade commander, who had surely seen them closer that any but their own officers, wrote to Gough in praise of his battalion and his regret at its loss from his command. Donkin wrote, "I trust that the reinforcements you seem to expect from England will enable you soon to join us again".[3] The tone of this letter intimates that Donkin is anxious they should return to his command as soon as possible. Also the conduct of the battalion at Talavera would suggest that discipline was strong where it mattered, in terms of holding the line of battle. Had discipline been as bad as Wellesley seemed to believe then surely the 87th would not have reformed so quickly to meet the French attack on 27 July, nor held so firm, despite being depleted, on the 28th.

It is worth taking a moment to consider the contemporary view taken of Talavera, particularly since we will consider how Gough's Indian battles were viewed by those back in Britain. At home, Talavera was officially viewed as a victory and certainly celebrated as one; indeed the guns of the Tower of London were fired in salute. It was thus a bitter blow when Wellesley was forced to withdraw to Portugal. Questions were raised in the press as to whether it was really a victory.[4] There was also criticism in Parliament, particularly for the loss of 25 percent of his force in one battle. There were those, mainly his political opponents on the opposition benches, who were convinced that he had fallen into a trap set by the French and persisted in the belief that Wellesley was an adventurer who would fritter away the army. Indeed when the vote of thanks to Wellesley for the victory at Talavera was proposed in the House of Lords, Earl Grey, the future Prime Minister, responded that he saw no evidence of a victory and went further claiming that Wellesley had demonstrated "want of capacity and want of skill".[5]

This was not the end of the matter, as there was criticism from within the House of Commons over Wellesley's despatches, which were felt to be one sided and vainglorious, and when a vote of a pension to go with Wellesley's being created a Viscount was discussed, many thought it unwarranted. This is mentioned not to suggest that Talavera was not a victory, but to show that even the future Duke of Wellington, arguably the greatest British general of all time, was not immune to the criticism of press and Parliament. This will be worth remembering when we come to look at the similar treatment metered out to Hugh Gough later in his career, in remarkably similar circumstances.

---

2   Cunliffe, *Royal Irish Fusiliers*, p. 83.
3   Cunliffe, *Royal Irish Fusiliers*, p. 83.
4   The view of the battle has almost come full circle. At the time it was questioned, but then as the legend of Wellington took hold, it was accepted as a victory. In one of the most recent, and well respected, histories of the conflict, Dr David Gates book *The Spanish Ulcer: A History of the Peninsular War*, suggests that if Talavera was a victory it was a pyric one.
5   Glover, *Wellington As Military Commander*, pp. 77–78. Hansard, House of Lords Debate, 26 January 1810. Objections to the vote of thanks and rewards given to Wellington for Talavera were also made by the Earl of Suffolk (a retired General), and the Earl Grosvenor.

9

Lisbon, Home, and Cadiz

Whether or not garrison duty was popular, it was a needed break for the battalion, and indeed in many ways was inevitable. It gave them time for their wounded to recuperate but also for reinforcements to arrive from home. Some reinforcements arrived in Lisbon on 24 September 1809, and it is clear that they had been earmarked for the battalion even before the losses at Talavera were sustained. Shortly after this, a further number of men arrived from the British Isles. However they were also men who had been destined for the battalion before the losses at Talavera. Although no exact number for the reinforcements exists it is likely that combined they amounted to a little more than 150 men. Whilst this was a welcome addition and did increase the strength of the battalion it was not sufficient to allow them to take the field again. After reinforcement the battalion had a strength of 568 officers and men by October 1809. Of this number 144 were listed as sick but many would recover and swell the number of 'effectives'.[1]

Gough remained with the battalion in Lisbon until late November 1809. Despite it having been almost four months since he received his wounds at Talavera it appears that Gough had not recuperated as well as he should and was still in some discomfort. Obviously the daring nature of his escape and the trials and tribulations of his journey back to British lines had not aided his recovery. It is likely that Gough had not taken care of himself properly since his return: no doubt his desire to get his battalion in a state where it could get back in the war meant that he pushed himself harder than was wise. At the end of November he was forced to return to England, and then on to Ireland, to aid his recovery. However even now there was a secondary motive and he spent some of his time helping to recruit extra men for the battalion and organise their transport to Portugal.

With the British having retreated to Portugal the French now had free rein to attack throughout Spain. Spanish troops, though numerous, were dispersed over large areas, and with different regions and locations controlling them there was no single command that could coordinate and concentrate Spanish forces. Thus the French were able to defeat them in detail. By the end of January 1810 much of Spain had fallen back under French control and the decision was made to attack Cadiz, the most important port in Spain. However this was easier said than done as the defences of that city were strong.

The Spanish, having been reluctant to allow the British to land in March 1809, now appealed for British help to defend Cadiz. Wellesley, who since 26 August 1809 had become Viscount Wellington, immediately organised the despatch of a force to assist with the defence of Cadiz consisting of the 1st Battalion 79th Foot, 94th Foot, 2nd Battalion of 88th Foot, the 20th Portuguese Regiment, and some artillery, all under the command of Major General William Stewart. To this force was added the 2nd Battalion 87th Foot, now up to strength but lacking its commander with Gough

---

1 <http://www.napoleonseries.org/military/organization/Britain/Strength/Bamford/c_
BritishArmyStrengthStudyPeninsular.html>. This is Andrew Bamford's 'British Army Unit Strengths: 1808–1815 The Peninsular War'.

still in Ireland. This composite force arrived in Cadiz in February 1810. In March it received a new commander, Lieutenant General Thomas Graham, later Lord Lynedoch.

Gough's exact movements are unclear after he returned home in November 1809. It is possible that he returned to Portugal at some point in the New Year, but then returned home again before returning fully in June 1810. The absence until June 1810 is based on the fact that there was no recorded correspondence between him and Mrs Gough during this period.[2] In late December 1810 he is again absent from the battalion. Indeed the regimental history records in April 1811 that in the past six months the battalion had successively been commanded by Gough, Captains James Jones and Anthony William Sommersall, and then by Major Archibald Maclaine before Gough returned in early 1811.[3]

Why Gough was again absent is unclear. Whether it was his wound still causing him pain, official business connected with the regiment, or simply a desire to see his son Edward William Ord Gough who was born on 9 December 1810, is unclear. If the latter is the case it may well have been the only time he met his son who would die in September 1813 whilst he was still in Spain. Again we do not know when he left but a regimental inspection report leads one to believe that it was November 1810 at the earliest and his correspondence with Mrs Gough recommences with a letter dated 7 February 1811. So this second visit was a brief one, when one accounts for the time spent travelling back and forth.[4]

After Lieutenant General Graham took command of the British troops at Cadiz, the force at his disposal was increased from 3,000 to 9,000 British troops by the end of July 1810. The fact that this happened whilst the city was being besieged by the French, which had been ongoing since 5 February, is important to note as it shows the strength of the allied position at Cadiz. With the Royal Navy in command of the seas there was nothing to stop fresh troops and supplies being ferried in on a constant basis. Warships also assisted in the bombardment of the French artillery positions, so much so that it was said that the French only dared relieve their gun crews under cover of darkness.

Towards the end of 1810, Graham planned an attack on what he viewed as the weakened force besieging Cadiz, as many of the troops once besieging the city had moved north with Marshal Soult in an attempt to engage Wellington. The plan was to make use of the naval assets available to land behind the French lines and attack them from the rear, whilst leaving minimal forces to defend Cadiz, and hopefully support an attack on the French. Unfortunately, this meant cooperating with the local Spanish forces under the command of General Manuel Lapena. Lapena commanded some 10,000 Spaniards. At the same time it was planned that 4,000 Spanish troops would sally forth from Cadiz and attack the besiegers. The plan was that the force would sail 50 miles along the coast to Tarifa, which would form a base for the operation.

Altogether Graham had a force of a little over 5,000 men split into two brigades, and accompanied by two squadrons of from the 2nd Hussars of the King's German Legion (KGL). Brigadier General William Dilkes commanded one of the brigades consisting of 2nd Battalion 1st Foot Guards, two companies of the Coldstream Guards, three companies of the 3rd (Scots) Foot Guards and a detachment of the 2nd Battalion 95th Rifles. The other brigade was commanded by Colonel William Wheatley, consisting of the 1st Battalion 28th (North Gloucestershire), 2nd Battalion 67th (South Hampshire) and 2nd Battalion 87th. Alongside some artillery were two composite

2   The exact location of the correspondence for these years is unclear. Rait had access to it when writing his biography, but the correspondence held by the 5th Viscount Gough, to which the author has been granted access, starts in 1811.
3   Cunliffe, *Royal Irish Fusiliers*, pp. 87–88.
4   Cunliffe quotes the inspection report on p. 88. Letter from Private Collection, Frances Gough to Hugh Gough, 7 February 1811.

flank battalions: the first under Major John Browne consisting of two companies of the 28th detached from the main battalion, and companies from the 1st Battalion 9th (East Norfolk) and 2nd Battalion 82nd (Prince of Wales Volunteers); the second commanded by Lieutenant Colonel Andrew Barnard consisting of four companies of the 3rd Battalion 95th Rifles, two companies of the 2nd Battalion 47th (Lancashire), and four companies of the 20th Portuguese Regiment.

The British force started to embark on 19 February and two days later were ready to sail for Tarifa. As it was, bad weather made it impossible for them to land at Tarifa. It might have been possible for Graham to land some of his infantry, but not his artillery and it was therefore impossible to land his entire force. Rather than divide his command Graham decided to land a little further down the coast at Algeciras. Having started to land on the 22nd, it took them until the 26th to assemble outside the original destination of Tarifa. On 27 February the Spanish arrived at Tarifa, they also having been delayed by bad weather. Lapena brought with him 7,000 men split into two divisions. Graham had agreed to give up command to Lapena, who – not fully trusting either the British Army or Graham himself – designated the British force as a reserve. Although Graham had agreed to serve under the Spanish commander he had been given secret orders by the British government to disobey Spanish commands if he felt it endangered the British force.

There was some difference of opinion between the commanders, and, other than the movement along the coast the exact purpose of the expedition did not appear clear. Lapena presumably hoped that he could win a Spanish victory, rather than an allied one, but exactly how he saw this happening is unclear. Gough recorded at the time that "the object of the expedition, I hardly know", and it points to a lack of direction if even a battalion commander was unclear of the purpose of the mission.[5] It appears that the intention was simply to relieve the siege of Cadiz, but exactly what they were to do about the sizeable French forces elsewhere in the area remains a mystery. Lapena made a series of marches that did little good and seemed to serve little purpose. All they achieved was to tire his men, deplete his supplies, infuriate his subordinates (both British and Spanish), and give the French valuable time to move to meet him. On the evening of 4 March, Lapena decided upon another night march, a precipitous manoeuvre at the best of times. Graham, arguing that battle was now probable, tried to persuade Lapena to allow the men time to rest. However his protests went unheeded and Graham did not feel that this was an opportune time to take advantage of his special orders.

---

5   Rait, *Gough*, Vol. I, p. 46. Rait is quoting from a letter from Gough to an unnamed person dated 6 March 1811. This appears to be a lost letter.

10

The Battle of Barrosa

On the morning of 5 March 1811 the advance guard of Marshal Victor's French army was sighted. Victor had with him a little over 10,000 men, although he was expecting 3,000 reinforcements. The Anglo-Spanish force in front of him was about 14,000 strong. However they were not in a strong position and due to the previous night's march were strung out in lose order. The Spanish and KGL cavalry had gone forward and had found the French troops at a place called Bermeja; a fierce fight ensued and the Spanish were eventually victorious, thanks to the advance from Cadiz of General Zayas, who had made a boat bridge across the river that led back to Cadiz. Rather than continue his advance, Lapena decided that it was safer to return to Cadiz. Again this makes one wonder what the purpose of the expedition had been as having lifted the siege they would now return to Cadiz, simply to be besieged once again.

The British had occupied Barrosa Hill, as they called it, known to the Spanish as Cerro de Puerco. However Lapena now ordered Graham to withdraw. Despite strong protests Graham was overruled but he managed to persuade Lapena to hold Barrosa Hill, at least while the withdrawal took place, with the composite battalion commanded by Major Browne, along with two Spanish battalions and the Spanish and KGL cavalry. The cavalry was commanded by an Englishman in Spanish service, Samuel Whittingham, who held the Spanish rank of Major General. Whittingham had been the commander of a troop in the 13th Light Dragoons, however before joining the army he had travelled throughout Spain as agent for his brother-in-law's mercantile house. He therefore knew the Spanish language and customs well. Graham reluctantly withdrew the rest of his force through the woods towards Cadiz.

The 87th, as part of Wheatley's brigade, were in the lead. However shortly after this the French forces started to emerge and threaten Barrosa Hill. Graham knew that he had a strong defensive point under his command and wanted to hold it, no doubt hoping that if he could place sufficient forces on the hill he would either halt the French advance or inflict severe casualties upon them if they decided to attack him. Also, with the enemy now present, he feared the effect of retreating. As Graham himself remarked,

> A retreat in the face of the enemy, who was already in reach of the easy communication by the sea-beach, must have involved the whole allied army in the danger of being attacked during the unavoidable confusion, while the different corps would be arriving on narrow ridge of Bermeja at the same time.[1]

In short, the whole allied army would be trying to move across the same narrow piece of ground at the same time. This necessarily slow movement would have made them an easy target for the French.

---

1   Oman, *Peninsular War*, Vol. IV, p. 110.

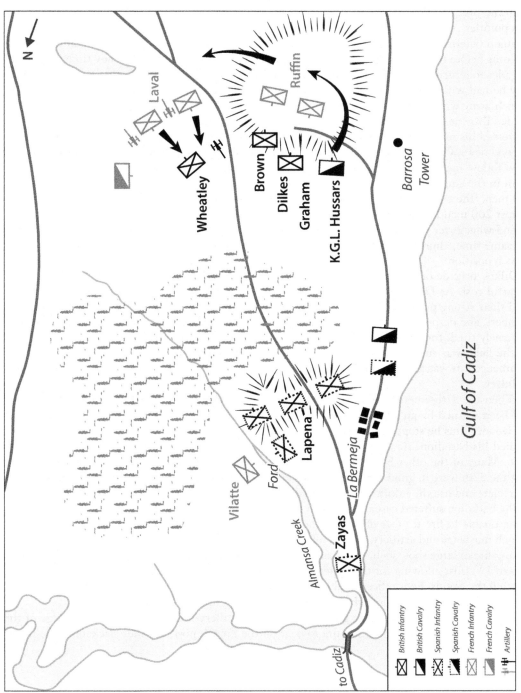

Map 4 The Battle of Barrosa.

Graham turned his force around and started to head back towards the hill. When Graham emerged from the wood ahead of his troops it was to find the Spanish had unilaterally withdrawn from the hill. Faced by two French divisions marching in column, Major Browne decided that it was pointless to remain on the hill alone and was starting to withdraw in good order. However Graham determined that he needed to secure the hill in order to launch an attack on the French columns before they could unite and overwhelm his force. To do this, and to buy time for his two brigades to return to the field, he approached Major Browne. The story goes that he asked Browne why he had withdrawn. Browne is said to have replied, "You would not have me fight the whole French army with four hundred and seventy men?" Unfortunately that was exactly what Graham needed Browne and his men to do: so as to buy time for the rest of his force. Browne is said to have addressed his men in a tone that was typical of the age "Gentlemen, I am happy to be the bearer of good news. General Graham has done you the honour of being the first to attack those fellows. Now follow me you rascals!" Browne then led his troops forward in their forlorn hope, leading them in the singing of 'Hearts of Oak'.[2] The composite battalion was made up of 22 officers and 470 men. The entire French force now on the hill opened fire. In the first volley 11 officers and almost 200 men fell. Remarkably the battalion did not disintegrate and run away. The men tried to find what cover they could, behind trees or mounds, and remained on the route to the hill. At the same time, almost in a skirmish style, they started to lay down whatever fire they could on the French position.

Dilkes' brigade of Guards was now in sight. Browne and his men had bought time for them at a fearful cost. As Dilkes' brigade started to climb the hill the four French battalions, rather than hold their strong position, inexplicably moved to attack them. Although the French had superior numbers, and despite the fact that the British line was rather ragged through marching and its men extremely tired, the fire of the Guards battalions and of the 67th, the first of Wheatley's brigade on the field, was such as to halt their advance. The French returned fire and a duel of musketry commenced. It was the superior firepower of the British infantry that won the day and the French withdrew.

When the 87th entered the field of battle they did so in close column and good order. Gough had been warned by an artillery officer that the French columns were advancing on the edge of the wood.[3] Thus he stopped his men before they exited the wood, and under its cover formed and readied his battalion. As a consequence they emerged in good order ready to meet the enemy at once. Many of the other battalions were still reforming after emerging from the wood. The fact that the 87th were in good order speaks not only to their discipline but to the ability of Gough to appreciate and use the information provided to him.

The battalion suffered casualties whilst the skirmishers of other battalions were ahead of them, being unable to fire for fear of hitting them. At the same time they came under heavy fire from French musketry and artillery. As one officer of the 87th later recalled, it was "the hottest and most galling fire of large shot, shell, grape, canister and musketry that was ever seen or felt in the annals of war".[4] Whilst allowing for the hyperbole, it does give an idea of the reception they received on clearing the woods. Four officers and over 50 men were hit in this barrage, and given the supposed ferocity of the attack it is somewhat surprising that the figure is not greater.

To the right of the 87th, some guns of the Royal Artillery had unlimbered on the edge of the wood and were now bringing their fire to bear on the French position, thus slackening the fire of

---

2   Haythornthwaite, *The Armies of Wellington*, pp. 241–242.
3   Cunliffe, *Royal Irish Fusiliers*, p. 94.
4   Cunliffe, *Royal Irish Fusiliers*, p. 94. This is taken from a letter by Lieutenant Thomas Dowling to his brother that was reprinted in the Dublin *Freeman's Journal*.

the French infantry. The French were continuing to advance. As would happen time after time in the Peninsular the French attacked in column, and the British met them in line. This meant that the British could maximise the number of men who could fire, whereas the French column minimised the number who could shoot whilst at the same time providing a denser target for the British.

The second battalion of the French *8e Ligne* had not stopped to fire as the other French battalions had. In many ways this was sensible as it was felt that stopping to fire slowed momentum, a theory we shall return to later. However it did mean that the *8e* got slightly ahead of the other French battalions and were now marching directly for the 87th. At roughly 60 yards from the 87th, the French battalion stopped to fire a volley. Whilst it is recorded that this did some damage to the 87th, it was nothing to what happened when the Gough ordered his regiment to return fire. The accuracy and ferocity of the 87th's volley brought down almost the entire front rank of the French battalion.[5]

This in turn caused those of the second rank who had not themselves been hit to stumble over their fallen comrades. The volley had momentarily stopped the French, and caused them to veer to the right where they got tangled up with their first battalion, which had also suffered from the 87th's volley. The two French battalions slowed almost to a halt and the tangled nature of the battalions meant that few men had the opportunity to open fire on the British.

Seeing his opportunity, Gough ordered his battalion to advance with bayonets to the front. The steady march forward of the 87th added to the confusion in the French battalions. When the 87th were within 25 yards of them, the French battalions broke and ran. At this point General Graham, now on foot and at the head of the Coldstream Guards, ordered them to charge. The 87th were ahead of him and with the cry of 'Faugh a Ballagh' charged with bayonets.

Vigo-Roussillon, commanding the second battalion of the *8e Ligne*, recorded what happened next. He called it, "the most terrible bayonet fight I have ever seen".

> I continued to shout encouragements to my men, but the noise of the fight often drowned my voice. Every man was fighting for himself; in vain I shouted for someone to come and hold me up (for he had been shot in the foot); at last two soldiers came and took me up by the arms, but almost at the same moment one of them was shot dead, and the other fell down beside me wounded. The remnants of my battalion, seeing themselves nearly surrounded, gave way, and a further vigorous charge by the 87th British Regiment, completed its overthrow.[6]

That the 87th had broken a French column spoke not only to their discipline and training but to wider strength of the British soldier who had once again proved more than a match for the soldiers of a French army that had hitherto seemed almost invincible. However it was not just that the British regiments were disciplined, both in order and fire, but also that they had a fearsome reputation with the bayonet. Research has shown that on fewer occasions than would be expected did soldiers actually engage in a bayonet fight during this era. Often what happened was that the determined and disciplined advance of troops, with bayonets to the front, continued, either until the attacker was stopped by defensive fire, or the defender broke and ran away rather than standing to face a charge.[7]

---

5   Cunliffe, *Royal Irish Fusiliers*, p. 95.
6   Cunliffe, *Royal Irish Fusiliers*, pp. 95–96. This is based on a translation of Vigo-Roussillon's memoirs that appeared in the Regimental Gazette *Faugh a Ballagh* 51/77/14. The memoirs had first appeared in French in the July-August edition of *Revue des Deux Mondes*.
7   Haythornthwaite, *The Armies of Wellington*, p. 91.

At this moment of triumph Gough demonstrated a side to his character that whilst always present was shown on the surface few times. He later wrote

> The scene in this charge was even distressing to my feelings. The French waited until we came within about 25 paces of them before they broke, and as they were in column when they did, they could not get away. It was therefore a scene of most dreadful carnage. I will own to you my weakness. As of course I was in front of the regiment, therefore in the middle of them, I could not, confused and flying as they were, cut down anyone, although I might have had twenty; they seemed so confused and so frightened. They made, while we were amongst them, little or no opposition.[8]

This personal confession to his wife shows a side that does not chime with his public image. Indeed it is quite strange to compare this with the public image that led to a legend that Gough had decapitated the French colonel of the *8e Ligne* in a personal duel on the battlefield.[9] Whilst the latter might have fitted the public image of the man, we see here a glimpse that Hugh Gough was a more sensitive and considered man than might be first thought. Attributed to another man the comments might unfairly be interpreted as 'cowardice', yet it would be wrong to say this of Gough. Perhaps it speaks more to an understanding and sensitivity that one would not necessarily attribute to the common image of Gough, or indeed to an officer of that era. It speaks to an officer only too aware of the horrors of war and who saw no reason to needless add to the slaughter, as the enemy were beaten and running for their lives.

We also see that Gough was not a detached officer, who saw little of the real cut and thrust of battle. Barrosa had been one of the toughest battles of the Peninsular War. An outnumbered British force had triumphed through tenacity, determination, and discipline. The British soldier that day stood firm against the onslaught and then replied with aggression and defeated a superior force. On the face of it, Barrosa was clearly a battle that should have been a French victory. That it was not spoke to the quality of the British soldier on that day. This was certainly the case when it comes to the 87th. The French battalion lost over half its strength during the battle with the 87th. However after the French column had broken the day was far from over for them or Gough.

The men of the 87th now had the Imperial Standard, the Eagle, of the French battalion as its target. The French Imperial Eagle was based upon that of the Roman Empire. A Bronze statue of an Eagle, 12 inches high and 10 inches wide, stood on a plinth that bore the regimental number. The whole was attached to a blue flag pole. Added to the eagle of the *8e Ligne* was a laurel wreath attached by Napoleon himself. The Eagle held the same significance to the French soldier as the regimental colours did to the British soldier. The same tenacity and determination would be shown in defending it. There would have been an added determination at Barrosa as the British had yet to capture a French Eagle. The Austrians, Prussians, and Russians had all done so, and the Spanish had captured three Eagles after the battle of Bailen in 1808 although the French had recaptured them from the Spanish in 1810.

A party of men from the 87th, led by Ensign Edward Keogh of the grenadier company and Sergeant Patrick Masterson, were attempting to fight through to the Eagle. They faced fierce resistance and the French colour party died almost to a man in defending it. Eventually Ensign

---

8   Rait, Gough, pp. 52–53. This is an extract from a now missing letter from Hugh Gough to Frances Gough, 6 March 1811.

9   Cunliffe, *Royal Irish Fusiliers*, p. 100. Rait, *Gough*, Vol. I, p. 52, also mentions the story. Rait also records Gough as saying, "I was once the white headed boy who cut off the head of the French Colonel at Barosa". Gough is said to have made this remark many years later during his time in India as an example of how newspapers exaggerate and embellish events.

Keogh got a hand on the standard but was killed instantly by a shot through the heart. Now Sergeant Masterson went for the Eagle which was being defended by *Sous-Lieutenant* Guillemain. In response to the shot that killed Ensign Keogh someone from the 87th had returned fire and hit Guillemain. Masterson took advantage and captured the Eagle and staunchly defended it. The legend goes that in his Irish brogue he then cried out "Be Jabers, boys, I have the Cuckoo!" Due to the fact that Barrosa was such an important battle for the 87th many legends and myths have been raised around it. Indeed we have already mentioned the supposed decapitation of the French Colonel Autie by Gough, and although Autie died there is no evidence to show it was Gough who killed him; indeed there is evidence to the contrary. Masterson is also subject to some legends. Firstly it is said he captured and defended the Eagle with a broken musket that he was using as a club. As a sergeant he would have carried a short sword and a pike, thus if he used a musket it was not his own, and what had happened to his pike and sword? Indeed Gough himself recorded that when Masterson captured the Eagle he 'ran through' the French officer with his sword. There is also no corroboration for the quote by Masterson, but it is such a fitting exclamation that one likes to believe it is true.

The capture of the Eagle was not the end of the battle for the 87th. As this was being achieved, the French *45e Ligne* was starting to move to the left of Gough's men and was attempting to get behind them. Whether or not Gough had spotted this is unclear; however Sir Thomas Graham had. He rode over to Gough and asked him to move to confront them. That Gough was able to turn his men around in the chaos of battle and reform them to face another enemy not only gives credit to him but also to his men. It once again makes one question Wellington's poor opinion of the 87th's discipline. That said, it does have to be pointed out that Gough was in amongst his men and one account suggests that he had to physically push some of his men to reform. Even so, the achievement is one that should not be underestimated. There were probably few battalions, or commanders for that matter, within the British Army who could have achieved this so quickly or in such good order.

Gough had gathered together about half of his battalion, at most 300–400 men, and rather than lining up in defence to face the French, he decided to charge. This obviously speaks to Gough's believe in the power of the bayonet and his confidence in his men. It was probably also supported by the evidence of the day thus far. The *45e* continued to fire until the 87th were within 50 paces of them. At that point they broke and ran, obviously recalling what these same men had done to the *8e Ligne*. Half the 87th drove a full French battalion from the field and in the process captured a gun. Although the capture of the Eagle was what the battalion would be remembered for that day, it was perhaps this latter engagement that was the greater achievement.

Gough also suggested, in a letter written to Colonel Wheatley two days after the battle, that one of his men captured another Eagle, that of the *45e*, but being wounded was not able to hold on to it and it was recaptured.[10] The defeat of the *45e* was virtually the end of the battle and it is fitting that given their dramatic work on the day that it should be the 87th under Gough's command that concluded the battle. The battle had lasted around two hours. Ensign Knox, an officer with the 87th, recalled some years later that at the end of the battle Sir Thomas Graham came over to the battalion, warmly shook hands with Gough and then thanked the 87th for, according to Knox, "deciding the fate of the day".[11] It could be argued with some justification that they had indeed been the decisive factor in the battle. Largely by their efforts alone, three French battalions had been stopped and routed. Given the severity of the fight the 87th's losses were remarkably small. One

10 Cunliffe, *Royal Irish Fusiliers*, p. 97.
11 Cunliffe, *Royal Irish Fusiliers*, p. 97.

officer and 45 men were killed, four officers and 124 men were wounded, meaning a total of 154 casualties out of 722 men who took the field.[12]

Having broken the French, Graham would no doubt have wanted to pursue them. However there were two problems with this. Firstly Graham's men were tired and in no condition to pursue the enemy. This was partly due to the exertions of the day but also of the last few days: the series of forced marches that Lapena had undertaken were now telling. Secondly, Graham had no fresh troops, as despite numerous requests for Lapena to join him on the field of battle the latter had refused. Indeed with the exception of their cavalry the Spanish had largely been spectators. The two battalions that had withdrawn from the hill under Lapena's orders returned during the battle and strengthened Graham's right, and Whittingham and the Spanish cavalry also played an important role in keeping some of the French Army away from the main field of battle, but this was little enough from so large a force. The editorial in *The Times* on 3 April 1811 went so far as to say,

> It is unquestionable that the conduct of our allies, or rather their officers, at the glorious battle of Barrosa, has excited considerable pain in the people of this country; and we must in candour confess, that it would be no sufficient defence of the suspected parties to say that they had conceived disgust at the conduct of the English on any previous occasion. For it was their cause, not ours, which we were defending; and in such a quarrel, all selfish and personal feeling should have been buried, and the Spaniards should have been the first to tread the paths of danger.

Whilst this did ignore the legitimate concerns of the Spanish as to exactly what 'game' the British were playing, it had more than a degree of truth to it. In fairness it must be said that the problem was largely Lapena. Many Spanish officers, most notably General Zayas, urged him to move to support the British. However Lapena refused. He may genuinely have felt that Graham was doomed and that he had to save his force so as to be able to defend Cadiz. However when hearing that the British had won a victory he still refused to release his troops to complete the rout of the French. His reasoning was that the light was fading, although there was still time before it failed, and that his men were too tired to fight. If the latter was true he only had himself to blame.

Whilst arguably mistaken, they are understandable excuses. However it is indefensible that at no point did he send as much as a staff officer to check on the battle or enquire of what Lapena's nominal subordinate was doing. Graham's patience had been exhausted, particularly when reports emerged, that may or may not have been true, stating that although they had not taken part in the battle stragglers from Lapena's force were now killing wounded French soldiers and plundering the battlefield and baggage of both friend and foe. It is reported that men of the 95th Rifles were ordered to guard French prisoners as much to protect them from the Spanish as to prevent their escape. Graham was angry at the turn of events. Partly out of petulance, and also because supplies were low, he decided to withdraw from the field of battle and return to Cadiz. Unlike his ally, he had the good manners to let Lapena know what he was doing. Lapena took this as a further excuse to justify his withdrawal: he could not stay if the British were withdrawing. As it was, the French were in such disarray that he could have swept them away with the forces at his disposal. The fact that this did not happen allowed Marshal Victor to claim a strategic victory, since shortly after the battle he was able to recommence the siege of Cadiz. Barrosa had been a tactical British victory, but strategically it had been indecisive.

---

12   There is a minor discrepancy with the numbers killed. Gough recorded one officer and 45 men, whereas the official regimental history records one officer and 44 men. It may be that Gough was in error and had added Ensign Keogh twice in his calculations. Amongst the wounded officers were Major Maclaine, and Captain Somersall who had both temporarily commanded the battalion during Gough's absence.

11

The Captured Eagle

The relationship between the two allied commanders, Graham and Lapena, had collapsed and a bitter war of words ensued. Graham refused to serve under the Spanish again and asked to be removed to join Wellington's main force. As for Lapena, he was called before a court martial for his actions, and whilst acquitted he was removed from command and never held military office again. Graham left Cadiz in early July 1811 bitter at what had happened. During the war of words with Lapena the Spanish government had attempted to mollify him by offering him various awards, all of which Graham declined fearing that to accept would somehow vindicate the actions of the Spanish.

Before Graham left he had many offers to dine as a farewell gesture. He declined them all with one exception, that from the officers and men of the 87th Foot. This demonstrates not only the fondness Graham had for Gough and his battalion, but is a mark of the growing stature of the battalion. This was an emotional occasion and Gough recorded in a letter to his wife that as he and Graham spoke to one another there were tears in their eyes. Barrosa had bound them in a comradeship that is hard to comprehend for those who have not witnessed battle.[1]

Graham made special mention of the 87th in his despatch. The battalion was now well known both at home and abroad. The captured French Eagle was sent to England, where it arrived on 24 March and then spent two weeks in the Earl of Liverpool's office at the War Department, before being presented to the Prince Regent. On 8 May 1811 a parade, a 'Royal Depositum' as it was called, was held on Horse Guards Parade where all the trophies captured in Spain were paraded. Naturally the Eagle took centre stage. The parade ground was flanked by men of the 1st and Coldstream Foot Guards and a large crowd of the public gathered behind them. The Dukes of York, Cambridge and Gloucester rode on the parade ground. Behind them processed the trophies captured in Spain, at the sight of which the cheer of the crowd grew louder. The Eagle was then moved to the Chapel Royal where it was to be housed for a considerable time. In 1835 the Eagle was moved to the Royal Hospital, Chelsea, until it was stolen on the 16th April 1852. The theory was that the thief believed it was solid gold, a common misapprehension. If that was the case one cannot held but imagine his reaction when he discovered it was bronze!

The arrival of the Eagle led to a renewed interest in Gough and the 87th. Various toasts and thanks were proposed and loudly seconded up and down the British Isles. The Secretary of State for War, the Earl of Liverpool, wrote to Graham that, "The memory of those who conquered and of those who fell in the hour of victory upon the height of Barrosa will be ever cherished by the British nation, and their names will hold a conspicuous rank amongst the bravest and worthiest

---

1   Cunliffe, *Royal Irish Fusiliers*, p. 102. See also Rait, *Gough*, Vol. I, p. 63, which tells of the emotional nature of the dinner and speeches given afterwards. This quotes from a letter dated 29 June from Gough to his wife which records that as he gave the speech Graham had tears in his eyes. Gough records that "I own I could not avoid shedding some".

of our heroes".[2] There were even popular songs written about the battle, including references to Gough and the 87th. Perhaps the best known was written by the English dramatist Thomas John Dibden and simply entitled *General Graham*. Indeed one verse mentioned Gough, "Full tilt at the boys, led by bold Major Gough, determined to cut, hack and slay 'em".[3] When reading this public exhalation of Gough's character it is interesting to recall the private confessions of that day written to Mrs Gough.

Graham himself continued to give credit to the 87th. He wrote to the colonel of the regiment Sir John Doyle that, "Your Regiment has covered itself with glory; recommend it and its commander (Gough) to their illustrious patron the Prince Regent: Too much cannot be done for it".[4] The regiment was distinguished by being restyled as the Prince of Wales Own Irish Regiment, and with additions to its regimental colour of an Eagle and laurel wreath and the coat of arms of the Prince of Wales. It is interesting to note that this regimental honour was due to the exertions of the relatively recently raised, and as it would prove, short-lived second battalion. Yet it was all added to the regimental history and tradition of the 87th Foot and later still the Royal Irish Fusiliers.

There were also individual honours. After the battle Gough had promoted Sergeant Masterson to sergeant major. Later on, Masterson, for capturing the Eagle, was given an ensigncy in the Royal York Light Infantry, although he would later return to the 87th as an officer. As for Gough he was immediately promoted to brevet lieutenant colonel. Brevet rank existed due to the peculiar nature of the British regimental system whereby an officer could not achieve his next rank until there was a vacancy in the regiment, or by transferring to another regiment with a vacancy at that rank. To get around this brevet rank Gough carried the rank of lieutenant colonel in the army, but only the rank of major within the 87th. At the personal request of Wellington the rank was later antedated, rather strangely, to the date of the Battle of Talavera. Gough was the first officer ever to be awarded a brevet promotion for leading a battalion in battle. Gough was also awarded the freedom of the cities of Dublin and Limerick. His name was becoming widely known and his reputation grew. This was perhaps felt more by Mrs Gough at home than by Hugh himself. She wrote to him that she had gained lots of new 'friends' since the triumph at Barrosa, and rather pointedly remarks on there being no such thing, "as disinterested friendship".[5] The Goughs had moved up in the world thanks largely to the capture of that French Eagle at Barrosa. Though the fame would pass a little it would be recalled from time to time by those talking of or discussing Gough.

The accomplishment is still remembered and Barrosa Day is still marked on 5 March, particularly by the modern descendents of the 87th, the Royal Irish Regiment. On that day the Barrosa song is sung at dinner, believed to have been written by an unnamed private of the 87th who had been at the battle. It includes the verse:

> Here a health to Gough and Graham and the soldiers on that field.
> Who, though they fought them ten to one, soon taught their foes to yield;
> who put them in confusion, and their Eagle took away,
> Long live our Irish lads to cheer, on each Barrosa Day.[6]

There were also celebrations in Spain particularly, when news of the despatches to home reached the battalion. A dinner was given for the officers and friends at which, Gough recalled, 104 bottles

2   Rait, *Gough*, Vol. I, p. 56.
3   The whole of this song is reproduced in Cunliffe, *Royal Irish Fusiliers*, pp. 99–100. It also contains a reference to the decapitated French colonel and may be a source of the story regarding him and Gough.
4   Cunliffe, *Royal Irish Fusiliers*, p. 101.
5   Private Collection, Frances Gough to Hugh Gough, 20 May, 1811.
6   Cunliffe, *Royal Irish Fusiliers*, pp. 449–450.

of wine were drunk. Most of the financial burden for this fell upon Gough, although it interesting to note that one of his junior officers recorded that, "a general rejoicing on the glorious Victory and the distinguished share our Regt. had in it, together with two or three public entertainments Col. Gough brought on us, threw myself and many others in debt".[7]

The second battalion of the 87th under Gough's command had grown in stature with the opportunity of active service. Barrosa and the capture of the Eagle had done much for the reputation of not only the battalion but also its commander. However the activities of the 87th were far from over and there was shortly to be a further call upon its services.

---

7   Rait, *Gough*, p. 60. Cunliffe, *Royal Irish Fusiliers*, p. 102.

12

Tarifa

After Barrosa the 87th were stationed on the Isla de Leon a few miles outside Cadiz itself. Once again the battalion found itself almost reduced to garrison duties due to the losses sustained not only through battle but also sickness. By March 1811 they were reduced to 522 officers and men, of which 159 were listed as sick.[1] Added to which reinforcements were unlikely as every recruit was required for the first battalion in Mauritius. Some officers even thought that the battalion might be returned to England, and then possibly Ireland, whilst they tried to recruit more men, but also to take the plaudits for their triumph at Barrosa.[2] However the battalion remained in Spain.

After the great 'excitement' of Barrosa, there was always likely to be something of an anticlimax. Indeed the major complaint was boredom. The area around Cadiz was under siege again, and there was occasional bombardment by the French but this had little effect, with the legend arising that the only casualty was a cat! At one stage there had been the suggestion, from Graham himself, that he wanted to take the 87th with him when he rejoined the main army under Wellington. However this never occurred and until the end of the summer the battalion continued in a mundane routine.

This is attested to by a letter from Gough to his wife in which he gave the outline of a typical day.

> I get up at five, walk about two miles to the sea to bathe: after returning, I have just time to dress for my Parade at eight, which I dismiss at ten, breakfast, and read till twelve, from which hour to one I give up to the interior of the Regiment, at my desk. I now lie down for an hour and a half, get up and dress for dinner at three. I generally take the first allowance, a pint, which, with chatting to, I believe, an attached set of brother officers, brings me to five, at which hour my horse is at the door, and from which I ride until half-past seven. It is by this time getting dark. I then devote one hour to contemplation, strolling on an eminence near my quarters. You may well conceive where my thoughts wander. I transport myself to Plymouth, and almost in idea then feel all the joys I should there experience. From nine to ten I read, when I look round to see everything quiet, and retire to a solitary bed … In this account of one day and night, you nearly perceive how I pass my time.[3]

Although it does not necessarily sound an unpleasant existence, the daily routine would have proved anticlimactic to say the least after the recent activity. However that has been the way of the soldier throughout history, the brief moments of 'excitement' and danger interrupting what is otherwise largely a routine and dreary experience on campaign. Towards the end of the year, Gough proposed

---

1   <http://www.napoleonseries.org/military/organization/Britain/Strength/Bamford/c_
    BritishArmyStrengthStudyCadiz.html>.
2   Cunliffe, *Royal Irish Fusiliers*, p. 102. Ensign Knox certainly felt that this might happen, and his comments, quoted by Cunliffe, suggest that this view was prevalent amongst the officers of the battalion.
3   Rait, *Gough*, Vol. I, pp. 64–65. The letter quoted is from the 9 August 1811.

coming home on leave, partly because of the lack of opportunity of further action. However there was also a very real sense that Gough felt he could be of more use at home.[4] His growing reputation and that of his battalion could be put to good use in terms of recruitment. Yet as it turned out the chance for further 'adventure' was not far away.

1811 had been a mixed year for British fortunes in Spain. Whilst Graham had won the victory at Barrosa, Wellington a victory at Fuentes de Onoro, and Beresford a victory at Albuera, the position was far from advantageous. The battlefield success had achieved little. The French for their part had resolved to finish off Spanish resistance and there was a deliberate targeting of Spanish forces as time went on. Perhaps this was a backhanded compliment to the way in which the British had fought. Rather than attempting to destroy the British army they would destroy their allies and leave them isolated. A Spanish force under General Francisco Ballesteros had been harassing the French forces in Andalusia for some time and it was here that Marshal Soult turned his attention. Ballesteros was not without talent as a military commander and his harassing of Soult's forces was useful to the allied war effort. However he was a political intriguer and fell afoul of such actions. In October 1812 he would mutiny rather than accept a foreigner, Wellington, as supreme commander, for which he was arrested and imprisoned in the Spanish possession of Ceuta on the North African coast. The Spanish had developed what might be styled 'hit and run' tactics, where after an attack they would retreat to one of the well-defended bases, whether Cadiz, Gibraltar or Tarifa.

It will be remembered that Tarifa was where the British army under Graham's command had intended to land prior to Barrosa. Tarifa was a small fortified coastal town on the edge of the Strait of Gibraltar facing across the sea to modern day Morocco. At the time of the siege it consisted of about 6,000 people, save the garrison. The town had first been fortified by the Moors in the 10th century and the fortification had periodically been continued and improved over the years. Yet it was not really suited to defence against siege warfare of the 19th century. During the period we are concerned with the fortifications, and particularly the gun towers, had been improved under the auspices of Charles Holloway, an engineering officer perhaps best known for his role in the defence of Gibraltar during the Great Siege. Soult, however, saw Tarifa as the weak point – which when compared to Cadiz and Gibraltar it undeniably was – and decided to launch his attack there.

When it became clear that this was what the French intended, the 87th were readied for deployment to Tarifa. The departure was a little hurried, and the urgency required was obviously impressed upon Gough. For his part he responded by embarking his men and their baggage in only three minutes on the morning of the 10 October 1811. Gough two days later recorded that this had been done, "to the astonishment of every person present". Even the ship's captain was said to have declared that in all his years in the Navy, "he never saw a regiment embark in the enthusiastic style the 87th did".[5] Someone had obviously done some good staff work. If it had not been Gough himself, he had at least had the good sense to pick the right man for the job. The captain had very kindly made this comment at a dinner when all the other officers of the force for Tarifa were present.

Once again the fickle nature of sea transportation meant that although they left Cadiz on 10 October and were off Tarifa by the 12th, it was not until the 16th that the weather allowed them to land. Eight companies of the 87th, totalling 525 officers and men, formed part of a force of a little over 1,200 British soldiers sent to Tarifa. This force included eight companies of the 2nd

---

4   Rait, *Gough*, Vol. I, p. 64. There is also a suggestion that Gough wanted the appointment of Adjutant at Limerick. This is made by Gough's previous biographer. His present biographer has not seen any reference to this in any of the remaining correspondence.

5   Rait, *Gough*, Vol. I, p. 68. The letter quoted is dated 12 October 1811 and was written at sea. The Royal Navy Captain was called Bruce, and apparently knew Mrs Gough well, no doubt from their time in Plymouth.

Battalion 47th (Lancashire), the 1st Battalion 82nd (Prince of Wales Volunteers) Foot, two companies of the 2nd Battalion 11th (North Devonshire), and a company of the 95th Rifles. Added to
this were a half squadron of the 2nd KGL Hussars, and a battery of artillery. This British brigade
was commanded by Colonel John Skerrett of the 47th. Skerrett appears to have been a cautious
but not necessarily untalented commander. His second in command was Lieutenant Colonel Lord
Proby, later 2nd Earl of Carysfort, and by seniority Gough was third in command. In truth this
mattered very little as the entire British and Spanish force within Tarifa was under the command
of Brigadier General Francisco Copons. Copons was a 47-year-old officer of some experience and
ability. There were some British troops already in Tarifa and with the arrival of the reinforcements
Skerrett commanded some 1,800 soldiers. To this were added Copons' 1,300 Spanish troops.

Gough recounts an interesting event on 1 November 1811 when he had the opportunity of
making the crossing to Tangier on what appears to have been akin to a 24-hour leave. Whether
there was any official purpose to the trip is not recorded, but given that some supplies were coming
from this city it is quite possible that Gough's visit was not entirely recreational. He made the
crossing in three hours, although the vagaries of travelling by sea during this age meant that the
return journey took five hours. Gough enjoyed his visit and it obviously did him good to get away
from the frustrations of the campaign and command for a few hours. He was also impressed by
the people, and in the common language of the time he referred to them as Moors, later writing
that "They are an uncommon fine race of men, and in my humble opinion deserve the name of
savages quite as little as the lower order of Spaniards, or I will add, my own countrymen".[6] It is to
be presumed that the last remark refers to 'Irish' rather than 'British', as there was still a tendency
to view the lower echelons of Irish society as 'savages'. If so it is interested to note that Gough
clearly saw himself as Irish rather than British. Whilst in Tangier, Gough had a good look round
the city and was impressed by the Bazaars, and amazed at the low prices, particularly for eating
and drinking.

However this was a brief sojourn from the trial of the campaign, the nature of which he disliked.
The main intention of Skerrett was to try and draw some of the pressure away from General
Ballesteros. This he attempted to do by making a series of marches from Tarifa in an attempt to
draw off some soldiers and to confuse the French as to his exact purpose. Unfortunately it also
appears that Skerrett confused his own officers as to the exact purpose of his movement. On one
of these marches Skerrett had moved towards, and indeed occupied, the town of Vejer to the
north-west of Tarifa. This occurred on 6 November 1811, with the troops subsequently retiring to
Tarifa on the ninth. By the 12th, they were back in the vicinity of Vejer. On both occasions they
threatened the French lines and would fire a few shots before retiring. Gough found this extremely
frustrating and did not care for this sort of warfare. On 17 November, he attempted to engage in a
more conventional battle, taking advantage of being temporarily in command due to the absence of
both Skerrett and Proby. Gough was commanding 1,100 men at Vejer when three French columns,
amounting to around 2,500 men, appeared before them. The French arrival on the scene had been
spotted by Gough himself and in a letter home he was critical of the lack of reconnaissance and
sentries that Skerrett had put in place.[7] Given the later criticism of Gough for a lack of reconnaissance, it is interesting that he makes this comment. It clearly shows that he appreciated the necessity of such tasks.

Gough immediately ordered his troops to prepare for battle and had decided to attack. He had
deployed his light company in skirmish order to engage the French, and it is likely that this is what

6   Rait, *Gough*, Vol. I, pp. 71–72, quoting a letter to Frances Gough dated 11 November 1811.
7   Rait, *Gough*, Vol. I, pp. 72–74. The letter Rait quotes from regarding the action at Vejer is to his wife and
     is dated 23 November 1811.

Map 5 Tarifa.

Gough meant by attack rather than a massed charge. He held a small hill just outside the town, from which it would have been foolish to move, unless the French were starting to break ranks and lose discipline. The skirmishers, and then a volley from his men, may well have achieved this, and then he could have unleashed his men in a bayonet charge. However there is also a possibility, implied in a letter to his wife, that he might have considered charging the enemy as they were still forming up as in his view, and that of the senior engineering officer (according to Gough), they were some way from being organised to resist such a charge.[8] One might call Gough's proposed course of action reckless, others courageous. It is on such small margins, and indeed fortune, that the difference between military genius and failure is decided.

However despite Gough's preparations, and the fact that his skirmishers were already engaging the enemy, when Skerrett arrived on the scene he ordered a withdrawal. There was a clear clash between Gough and Skerrett. Both men held honourable positions. Gough accepted that Skerrett as senior man had the right to act in this way, and whilst annoyed, Gough made no great argument about it. He even conceded that he understood that Skerrett had orders not to engage any force that outnumbered him. Added to this, the French lines at Cadiz were only a few miles away where some 14,000 troops were stationed. It was quite conceivable that what faced the British at Vejer was only an advanced guard and that yet greater numbers of French soldiers were on their way which could have seen the odds against the British turn from two to one to three, four or five to one quite easily. Perhaps Skerrett better appreciated the situation than Gough did. Caution was perhaps called for but as Gough recorded, "if a man does not venture, he will never win". He continued that:

> We would have beaten them back with very little loss, and we could then have fallen back. Those who wish to vindicate the propriety of not fighting say: What object would you have gained? My answer and I think the answer of every British Soldier would be: We would have supported the character of British Arms, which by falling back before a force but double our numbers is in a measure injured.[9]

Whilst seeing the propriety of Skerrett's position, there is some sense to what Gough was proposing. There was a danger, which Gough perceived because he also felt it, that British soldiers would get disheartened and lose morale due to the consistent 'running away'. Though they might not have longed for the horrors of battle, the constant effort of movement towards an enemy only to fall back when he approached, time and time again, would sap not only morale but the physical condition of the troops. It could also lead to a carelessness which could prove fatal if they did ever have to fight for their lives.

However this was the nature of operations in this region. Losses were to be avoided at almost all costs. The aim was to harass the enemy and force him into some indiscretion. In a sense this worked, as we shall see, but equally so might Gough's idea of fighting and then withdrawing. If this had been attempted good control of the army would have been essential so as to avoid a trap. In this the British always had the advantage that they were operating near the coast and could always be reinforced, resupplied, or if necessary withdrawn, by sea.

However this is part of a much wider concern about the manpower limits of the British army. In short Britain could not afford to lose even one soldier for two French, because the manpower reserve at this time was most definitely in favour of France. However this was not Gough's idea of war and he had for some time been disillusioned by the task he and his battalion were being asked to perform. Back in October Gough had confided in his wife that, "It really is a sin they [Gough

---

8   Rait, *Gough*, Vol. I, p. 73.
9   Rait, *Gough*, Vol. I, pp. 73–74.

and the 87th] are not in Portugal and not employed in this dirty little peddling warfare".[10] Skerrett was over-cautious and took his orders too literally. Gough was perhaps too aggressive and a middle ground was required. Gough himself, in a thinly veiled reference to Skerrett, actually had the solution when he wrote that "Oh for a Graham! This is the country for such characters".[11] Perhaps someone of Graham's ability would have been able to follow and direct a course that would have kept all parties happy.

Regardless of the difference of opinion between Skerrett and Gough as to the choice of tactics, the movements of the British force did have an effect. Skerrett had been planning another movement with the hope of linking up with General Ballesteros, when his plans were interrupted by the arrival of several thousand French soldiers in the vicinity around Tarifa. This was the advanced guard of around 8,000 French soldiers under the command of General Laval. The hit and run raids of both Skerrett and Ballesteros were diverting French troops from the siege of Cadiz, but Soult also hoped that the taking of Tarifa would discourage the allies and assist in the siege. At first Skerrett doubted that they intended a siege, as the weather conditions were not really ideal. This was despite the fact that *The Times* had reported on 31 December information that the French were preparing roads to transport their heavy guns to Tarifa. *The Times* had received this information in a report from Spain dated 4 December 1811.[12] Where this report came from, and whether anyone in Tarifa or the British Army in the Peninsular, were let in on this intelligence is unknown.

However by 22 December it was clear to the garrison that the French were preparing for an assault. This was not going to be like Cadiz where the siege had become little more than a blockade. Any siege of Tarifa would be prelude to an assault. The French were by now in the process of bringing up heavy guns and their numbers had grown to 15,000 men. To defend Tarifa, the British and Spanish between them could call upon around 3,000 men. Somewhat surprisingly they had superiority in the number of guns, 26 to 16, not something one would normally expect in a siege. To this number could also be added the firepower of the ships in the harbour. However the French guns were heavy siege pieces. They also had the advantage that there were positions around Tarifa in which they could be placed where they could bombard the town out of the range of all allied artillery.

At this point Skerrett, no doubt recalling his orders with regards to fighting against the odds, was ready to give up Tarifa and withdraw by sea. However, this time he was clearly making an incorrect decision. The damage that this would have done to relations with the Spanish would have been obvious, but to give up a defensive position that could be reinforced and supplied by sea was clearly an error of judgement. Skerrett seems to have been unclear as to what was expected of him, and a curious chain of command did not help matters. Technically he was under the overall authority of Major General George Cooke at Cadiz, who had assumed Graham's old command. Cooke accepted Skerrett's advice that evacuation was perhaps the best option. However matters were confused by the fact that Skerrett's artillery, engineers and some of his infantry had come to Tarifa from the garrison at Gibraltar and were therefore under the overall command of Lieutenant General Colin Campbell then Lieutenant Governor of Gibraltar. Campbell was adamant that Tarifa must be held and made his views known. If Tarifa were to be in French hands it would create a safe harbour for the French which could be used to bring in supplies from North Africa. It could in turn prove a threat to Cadiz and perhaps even Gibraltar. Campbell was said to be furious and although there was a question mark over whether he had the authority to stop the withdrawal he

10   Rait, *Gough*, Vol. I, p. 68. This also appears in Cunliffe, *Royal Irish Fusiliers*, p. 104.
11   Rait, *Gough*, Vol. I, p. 70. This quotes a letter to Mrs Gough dated 19th October 1811. This is another letter that appears to be lost.
12   *The Times*, Tuesday 31 December 1811.

did have the practical means by which to prevent it. Thus he ordered the shipping that could have lifted the garrison from Tarifa returned to Gibraltar. There was now no alternative to Skerrett other than defending Tarifa.[13]

---

13   For the decisions regarding the defence of Tarifa see Cunliffe, *Royal Irish Fusiliers*, pp. 105–107, Chandler, David, *Dictionary of the Napoleonic Wars*, (New York: Simon & Schuster, 1993) pp. 436–437, Gates, David, *The Spanish Ulcer*, pp. 277–281.

13

The Defence of Tarifa

It appears that Gough had not been reticent in expressing his opinions, and equally unsurprisingly he had been strongly in favour of remaining and defending Tarifa.[1] Although the walls and gun towers were not designed to meet assaults by modern weapons they were greatly assisted by the fact that they had been crenellated, that is there were apertures and loopholes through which defenders could fire. Captain C.F. Smith, an engineering officer, had done all he could to improve the defences in the days before the siege. The walls were also six feet thick and flanked by gun towers. Although the defences of Tarifa were not ideal there were many factors in their favour. To the south and part of the west of the town it was covered by the sea, and there was nothing to fear from that direction. Indeed any French positions near the sea were untenable as the British ships off the coast could bombard them. The danger came from the north and east of the town. To the north there were hills that made good positions for artillery and which were out of range of naval gunfire. To the east there was a ravine and fast-flowing stream which led into the town. Where it entered the town was defended by a portcullis. The problem was that the ravine covered the advance of an enemy almost to the very edge of the town. Initial French preparations to the west of the town, that was accessible by land, were disrupted on 21 December. Three times French troops were attacked by British raiding parties from the town, meaning that any attack on the western side was unworkable.

On 22 December, a French *picquet* had been established to the west of the town. Although the position became untenable due to artillery fire, not only from the town but also the ships in the harbour, it was felt necessary to charge the French position to clear them completely. Though this was probably the idea of the Spanish commander Copons, it was Skerrett who asked Gough to see to it, no doubt confident that Gough would welcome the opportunity to attack.[2] Gough replied by sending one of his flank companies, although we do not know whether it was either his grenadier or light company, to see to the task. It was achieved in emphatic fashion and there are no records of any British casualties. There is also a possibility that Gough himself led the attack.[3] If this is true it might be considered reckless for the commander of a battalion to lead such an attack. Indeed in many ways it was, but in others it would be no more than the norm for a battalion commander in this era, when he would have been expected to lead from the front.

---

1   Despite his opinions expressed to Skerrett there were letters home in which Gough expressed doubt as to the desire of the French to attack and the unlikely possibility of any fighting. Rait in his biography of Gough concludes that the letters should be read in the context of reassuring Mrs Gough of his safety and wellbeing rather than having any military value. This is a view with which the present author concurs. Rait, *Gough*, Vol. I, pp. 82 & 74–75. See also Cunliffe, *Royal Irish Fusiliers*, p. 106, and Gates, *The Spanish Ulcer*, p. 278.
2   Rait, *Gough*, Vol. I, p. 81. This includes a reproduction of Skerrett's handwritten, and barely legible, note to Gough.
3   Rait, *Gough*, Vol. I, p. 81.

With the failure of French preparations on the west this left the eastern side of the town and in particular the ravine and river. Unsurprisingly, this was where the French decided to make their preparations. At first they were aided by the weather. On 23 December a gale forced the British ships to put out to sea, to avoid being forced aground. This reduced dramatically the fire-power of the defenders. Despite this, the French suffered casualties throughout the siege due to the defenders' land-based artillery, and in particular two 10 inch mortars. By 24 December the French had dug their way to within 400 yards of the walls on the eastern side of the town, using the ravine as cover. There was no attack on Christmas Day as the defenders had feared, and no doubt as the besiegers later regretted.

On the 26th the weather turned against the besiegers and heavy rain descended which in the course of the next few days flooded the French positions and required a withdrawal. By the 29th the weather improved sufficiently for the French to be able to use their 10 heavy guns, targeting the wall near the portcullis. Within a day the French guns had opened a breach in the town's walls which, by the time the light failed on 30 December, was some 60 feet wide. General Laval, under a flag of truce, demanded the surrender. The Spanish commander refused, replying that "When the breach shall be absolutely practicable, you will find me upon it, at the head of my troops to defend it..."[4] Whilst these were stirring words, Copons was never to be found standing on the breach, nor indeed were Spanish troops: it was to be British troops, and specifically Gough and the 87th, who would undertake this dangerous task.[5]

After the refusal to surrender, Laval determined to attack on 31 December. Despite the breach in Tarifa's wall and his superior numbers, Laval was in a somewhat desperate position. His preparations had taken far longer than he had planned, his supplies had been disrupted, and the severe weather had not only delayed his action but had also led to widespread sickness throughout his besieging force. Indeed, even the opening and widening of the breach on the 30th had been delayed by torrential rain. In short he had to attack on the 31st and he had to succeed. However, what Laval did not know was that although the breach looked serviceable it was in fact hiding a myriad of trouble for anyone who managed to reach it. The other side of it was a 14 foot drop, which then led into a narrow street at the end of which a barricade of iron gratings had been formed. In short it would be a deathtrap for any attacker who was unfortunate enough to make the breach.

In Tarifa preparations were made for the expected assault. The 87th were given the 'honour' of defending the breach. Whether this was due to Gough's criticism of Skerrett and the former's desire to fight, or simply that they were an experienced regiment is unclear. The latter viewpoint is perhaps supported by the fact that the assaulting division commanded by Laval was the same unit that the 87th had done such damage to at Barrosa. Perhaps there was a hope that their reputation would go before them and that the presence of the 87th in the breach would unnerve the French. Whatever motivated Skerrett's choice, it is known that Gough had offered the services of his battalion for this task.[6] The heavy rain caused the 87th problems during the night, as the stream flooded and brought down from the French camp all manner of baggage, waste, and even corpses. This debris pushed against the portcullis and started to bend it inwards. Gough and his men laboured to repair the defences as best they could during the night. Gough split his battalion in half, keeping one half sheltered from the rain in a nearby church, whilst the remainder were at

---

4   Rait, *Gough*, Vol. I, p. 83.
5   In one of the most famous histories of the Peninsular War, that by Sir William Napier, his first edition erroneously recorded that it was the 47th not the 87th that defended the breach at Tarifa, and that the latter merely defended the portcullis. When the first edition appeared Gough wrote to Napier to highlight his error, and the mistake was rectified in future editions. See Bodleian Library, Oxford, MS Eng Letters c. 251. Napier (William) Papers, Gough to William Napier 14 July 1836.
6   Rait, *Gough*, Vol. I, p. 88.

the defences repairing and manning them as best they could. At various intervals during the night the two halves of the battalion switched. Thus Gough ensured that the work was done whilst saving his battalion from having been at work all night. In short the men were fresher for the morning's battle than might otherwise have been the case. Whilst appearing to be common sense, it would not necessarily have been every officer's approach.[7]

At 0800 on 31 December the French were sighted making their advance. According to Ensign Knox of the 87th, the first the defenders saw of the French was their bayonets sticking up over the top of the entrenchments.[8] Whilst the attack was expected it was a little careless of the French, if Knox's story is true, not to better shield their exact movements. Indeed the French attack was somewhat chaotic. When they left the trench and started their advance towards Tarifa, they lost their way and rather than head for the breach they headed towards the portcullis, this despite exiting their entrenchments only 300 yards from the walls. It has been suggested that the movement towards the portcullis was due to the fierce nature of the 87th's volleys from the breach.[9] Although their fire was no doubt fierce this might be to give too much credit to the battalion, rather than simply to admit that the French attack was confused and ill-led.

The French force of 2,000 men, largely made up of grenadiers, was slowed by the mud and their misdirection. They were an easy target for Gough's waiting men and the guns of the flanking towers. As the French tried to force their way to the breach Gough's men laid down a vicious fire. Despite the fury of the 87th's firepower a few French soldiers actually made it to the breach, but no further. Some of the French attackers managed to find what cover there was and attempted to fire back. However the French could not hold on to their position for long. The attack had become confused and many had become trapped against the portcullis, whilst the others could not dislodge the 87th from the breach.

After barely half an hour the French attack was forced to withdraw. The gruesome nature of the events was slightly masked by the fifes and drums of the 87th who at Gough's request had been asked to play the tune 'Garryowen'. This stirring air is said to have urged on his men. Gough had drawn his sword and was in the thick of the action, encouraging his men to use the bayonet wherever possible. Gough was wounded by splinters that hit him both above the eye and in the hand. The cut above the eye, although slight, bled prodigiously and Gough later claimed that the sight of his face covered with blood as he urged his men on led to the vigour with which they engaged the enemy. So much so that when the French began to withdraw Gough had to physically restrain his men from charging after them. The story is told that one of Gough's men implored him in his Irish brogue that, "Colonel, I only want to tache 'em what it is to attack the aiglers", referring to one of the nicknames for the battalion that had developed since Barrosa: 'the aiglers' or 'eagle-catchers'. Gough refused the request and responded that, "next time they come, we'll give them *Garry-Owen to glory* again". Another story was told that Gough actually led a charge after the French. This did not happen and perhaps is inspired by Gough's later 'reputation' rather than any evidence.[10]

However, there was not to be a next time at Tarifa. The French had lost over 200 casualties in the assault, and the whole exercise had cost them over 500 dead, many through disease, and over 180 wounded and around 30 men captured. The allies, although in fairness mostly the British, had suffered 36 casualties. The 87th accounted for 28 of them. They had 23 wounded, including two officers, and five men killed out of a total of nine fatalities suffered by the garrison. Many of the officers and men of the 87th, including Gough himself, were commended for their bravery. That

7   Cunliffe, *Royal Irish Fusiliers*, p. 107.
8   Cunliffe, *Royal Irish Fusiliers*, p. 107.
9   Cunliffe, *Royal Irish Fusiliers*, pp. 107–8.
10   Cunliffe, *Royal Irish Fusiliers*, p. 108. Rait, *Gough*, Vol. I, p. 85.

evening Skerrett wrote, "Two thousand of the enemy's best troops attacked the breach, and were totally defeated with immense loss. On our side all behaved nobly; but the conduct of Lieutenant Colonel Gough and the 87th Regiment surpasses praise".[11] From a man who had clearly had issues with the 87th's commander, if not necessarily the battalion, this was high praise. The second in command, Lord Proby, added his voice to the praise, and concluded that the 87th had "under their truly gallant and able commander, completed the splendid military reputation they have acquired at Barrosa, by gaining fresh laurels of a description not recently worn by British arms, by showing, in a breach opposed to the most formidable assaults, the same individual courage with which they carried dismay into the ranks of the enemy".[12]

Although not wishing to diminish in any way the achievements of the 87th, it must be remembered that the French had faced a difficult task, and it would perhaps have been more surprising if they had been successful. The assault of a breach was never an easy task and with so much in the defenders' favour, in particular the difficult nature of the breach, it was always going to be difficult. Perhaps praise was heaped upon the 87th partly because of their previous reputation but also because there were those, notably Skerrett, who wanted to detract from the fact that they had argued against holding Tarifa. By praising the 87th this fact paled further into the background. Indeed had it not been for Campbell ordering the transports away Tarifa would have been abandoned. Major General Campbell at Gibraltar also offered his praise for "the eminent services of that distinguished corps on this day … when the bravery and discipline of the 87th was so conspicuously displayed in the defence of the breach".[13]

Gough seems to have appreciated that these were 'special times' for him and his battalion, strange as that might sound. As he confided to his wife:

> How productive of fortunate events was the last year to me. I can hardly hope that this will, or indeed can, be equally so, and the conclusion, if properly stated in the despatches, will add lustre to the British arms by the conduct of our Corps; not a man of any other having shared in the defence of the breach which was solely entrusted to me. Indeed such a degree of respect are we now in, that I, in fact, command, as no one is allowed to interfere with any orders of arrangements of mine, not alone with regards to my own gallant corps, but likewise the 95th, and the Detachments, together with the whole line of defence.[14]

Gough was clearly not only enjoying the success but also the authority and respect that clearly came with it. Had the incident at Vejer taken place after the defence of Tarifa, one wonders if Skerrett would still have countermanded Gough's orders.

Tarifa and Barrosa were on the face of it small engagements in the Peninsular War and have suffered from the fact that neither are directly associated with Wellington. Though largely forgotten now, they were significant at the time and the fame and reputation of Gough was based upon such exploits. At the same time, the physical and mental strain was starting to tell a little. To his wife he confided, "The enemy are deserting by hundreds, and we hourly expect them to take themselves off. I will own I shall not be sorry, as everything being left to me, my mind and body are day and night on the alert".[15] Gough's more humane side came through again when he confessed to his wife that his greatest "pride and self-congratulation", was due to the fact that he had suffered so

11   Cunliffe, *Royal Irish Fusiliers*, p. 108.
12   Rait, *Gough*, Vol. I, p. 86.
13   Rait, *Gough*, Vol. I, p. 85.
14   Rait, *Gough*, Vol. I, p. 86–87. Rait quotes from a now-missing letter from Gough to his wife, dated 4 January 1812.
15   Rait, *Gough*, Vol. I, p. 87. This is taken from the same letter of the 4 January 1812.

few casualties. He saw this as a vindication of his arrangements, and there is clearly relief that he 'got it right'. This perhaps deserves further comment as in future years there would be criticism of his approach to casualties amongst the men he commanded. The comment above illustrates that he was clearly mindful of such, and not careless in that sense. However, at the same time, he saw casualties as inevitable, and appreciated that sometimes the nature of the battle would necessitate them being quite high.

Yet Gough had clearly been proud, almost boastful, about the achievements of his men. To his wife he expressed this by saying,

> How glorious is all this, after all our grumbling; never did British courage and discipline over-come more difficulties, a garrison of less than one thousand firelocks to drive off with disgrace ten times their numbers, from a town the walls of which were breached in six hours, and which is commanded from all the heights round it, in several places within fifty yards.[16]

Whilst there is a little exaggeration, this is clearly due to the pride he felt in what had been achieved.

Although the casualties had been light the rigours of the campaign were now starting to tell, not only upon the battalion but also upon Gough. Gough even felt that it might be in the best interests of the battalion if they were returned home, even if only for the short term. Indeed the battalion had been in Spain far longer than had originally been intended, and throughout the Peninsular War there was an attempt to rotate weakened battalions so that they were not constantly in Spain or Portugal. Obviously the fortunes of war made the practicalities of this difficult. The 2nd Battalion 87th Foot had been in Spain since March 1809. Perhaps Gough also wanted to take advantage of his new found fame at home. The Spanish had conferred upon him the Grand Cross of the Order of Charles III of Spain. In later years Gough would be granted permission to augment his coat of arms with symbolism of Tarifa. The battle honour Tarifa was justly added to the colours of the regiment.

After the attack the French high command were split over what to do next. Marshal Victor wanted to continue the siege and renew the attack. However Laval better knew the condition of his men and could better judge the likelihood of success. Not only had the weather and a lack of supplies, taken their toll but the events of 31 December had weakened their morale, which had not been high to begin with. For the rest of the 31st, there had been a flag of truce as the French had carried their wounded from the field. It was not until 3 January that the French command agreed to abandon the siege. The weather had made the roads impassable and much of their siege equipment, including seven of their heavy guns and much of their ammunition and stores, had to be left behind, where it was gratefully seized by the British and Spanish. The French had attempted to set much of their stores and equipment on fire before leaving. The weather had made this difficult and indeed what they did manage to set alight was soon rescued from the fire by the British who came out from Tarifa as soon as the French started to withdraw.

By 5 January 1812, Gough was making preparations for the battalion to leave Tarifa, with the expected destination being Cadiz. Exactly when the battalion left Tarifa is unclear, and yet again they had an eventful journey being forced by bad weather and a broken cable to put in to Gibraltar first of all. When they reached Cadiz, most likely in late January, they were given a warm welcome and the praise for Tarifa was renewed. At this point Gough and many of his officers received their medals for Talavera and Barrosa. This period in Cadiz gave the battalion chance to rest but also to reorganise. A number of new men joined the battalion, many coming as volunteers from the Dublin, Tipperary, Tyrone and Mayo militia. At the same time the burden of being a second battalion meant that they lost around 20 men who were drafted to the first battalion to bring them

---

16   Rait, *Gough*, Vol. I, p. 88–89.

up to strength. The battalion remained in Cadiz until April 1812. By this time the battalion had a strength of exactly 700 men.[17]

At the end of March 1812, Gough had been given command of the garrison at Tarifa. The confusion in the chain of command that had been present the previous year was now ended. The garrison and the town were now under the control of Major General Cooke's command, and ultimately Wellington's command. It is quite strange to think that the man who had been willing to abandon Tarifa had now been given overall control, as opposed to Campbell who by his actions and urgings had assured that it would be defended. It was not until the beginning of May that Gough actually returned to Tarifa. Whilst this might seem strange, there was no apparent threat to Tarifa, and he was not far away should there be an emergency. There was also little for him command until this point.[18] He took with him six companies of the 87th, the remainder staying at Cadiz under the command of Major Maclaine, three companies of what was called a Battalion of Foreign Recruits, a part company of Royal Artillery and a detachment of engineers.

A reason for the delay of despatching the men of the 87th might have been the want of equipment and clothing. The regimental history records that the companies left behind were want of equipment and that the men were 'almost naked' due to the need to fully supply the companies in Tarifa.[19] There appears to have been little left to command at Tarifa. How many Spaniards remained is unclear, but other than the six companies of the 87th, there were three companies of the Battalion of Foreign Recruits and about 50 artillerymen to man the guns in the towers. Although in truth Gough found the appointment somewhat boring, it is important to record that this was his first independent command and therefore marks an important landmark in the development of his career. The success he had had on the battlefield had not only increased his profile but his reputation to an extent where he was considered for such postings, albeit that Tarifa was now lacking in its former significance. As Gough himself recorded, whereas Tarifa had last year been, "the most important fortress" in Europe it was now "the most wretched little village in Europe". In somewhat mocking tones, he would head his letters to his wife during this period, "The important Fortress of Tarifa".[20]

Indeed it appears that Gough was busiest by way of entertaining. The fame of Tarifa meant that many officers and tourists wanted to visit it. The attraction was only added to when they discovered that the hero of the defence of the breach would be their host. One notable visitor was Major General Cooke himself. The day of his visit turned out to be an eventful one. This was in late May 1812, and Marshal Soult had despatched two regiments of infantry and one of cavalry to within nine miles of Tarifa. Their exact intentions were unclear, and it is unlikely they represented anything more than a feint against Tarifa. However their arrival was so unexpected that the very place where they rested had been visited by Cooke and Gough only three hours earlier![21] By a narrow margin the French missed the opportunity of capturing the two of them and a host of other officers. The French raided the area around Vacinos and Vejer; at the latter they demanded a 'contribution' from the town in return for not plundering, which was duly paid. The rest of Cooke's visit passed off without anything so dramatic, although Gough did note that many of the preparations and measures Gough had put in place met with his approval.

17   Cunliffe, *Royal Irish Fusiliers*, pp. 109–110. See also, <http://www.napoleon-series.org/military/organisation/Britain/Strength/Cadiz/c_Cadiz4.html>.
18   Again I am indebted to Andrew Bamford for his assistance. See <http://www.napoleon-series.org/military/organisation/Britain/Strength/Cadiz/c_Cadiz4.html>.
19   Cunliffe, *Royal Irish Fusiliers*, p. 110.
20   Rait, *Gough*, Vol. I, pp. 90–92.
21   Rait, *Gough*, Vol. I, pp. 92 & 94.

Although Gough had little to do other than entertaining, he does appear to have rather enjoyed the opportunity for this independent command. His men also seemed to enjoy Tarifa. His officers were delighted that he allowed them to visit Gibraltar regularly. Whilst this was probably due to the fact that Gibraltar was British and therefore it housed many of the social trappings of life in Britain, many of his men seemed to make an attachment to the people of Tarifa. Gough told of an occasion, which he repeated with pride, when the men of his battalion sent the NCOs to see him as a deputation. Such a move normally spelt trouble. However the grievance they felt was not theirs but that of the poor of the town. As Gough recalled the story, his men had been moved by the poverty they saw amongst them and had asked the NCOs to approach Gough to ask permission for each man – no mention is made of the officers following suit – to donate a day's pay to a fund for the relief of the poor of the town.[22]

As always in any siege it was the poor who had suffered most, for as many of their houses had been outside the walls the majority had been destroyed by the French during the siege. Due to the lack of supplies in the town, mainly due to the failure of the Spanish supply system, prices had risen to an extent where the poor of the town could not even afford a loaf of bread. This act of humanity by Gough's soldiers raises many points. It is perhaps no coincidence that the majority of his men were Irish peasants and could perhaps better appreciate the poverty and suffering of the Spanish poor than, say, their English counterparts. The uncaring Spanish leadership and the fact that the rich continued to live relatively well partly at the expense of the poor, would have spoken to feeling that many of the soldiers had about the situation in their own country. That the "scum of the earth", as Wellington, is said to have once called his soldiers, could be capable of such an act speaks volumes. It perhaps also goes some way to reflect the compassion that Gough had shown to his men. Gough had several times shown a level of care, which would seem quite normal today, but for the time was unusual. That night in May 1809, previously mentioned, when Gough alone, amongst the battalion commanders, made sure that his men had shelter and firewood for the night is symptomatic of this. Equally so was his care of the men in Tarifa, "They have better bread and meat than any soldiers even in England, I make my commissary answerable for that".[23] This was despite the problems of supply. It clearly shows Gough's care, but also speaks to his confidence in his staff arrangements that despite the difficulties of the area they would be able to accomplish what he wanted. Exactly who was responsible for this, whether it was within the regiment or another officer especially appointed, they were clearly doing a good job.

Gough was convinced that the idea of helping the poor had come from the men themselves and not been prompted by any officer. Indeed the officers seemed ambivalent to all around them. No doubt the soldiery of the 87th had gotten to know the locals reasonably well, and it is interesting that they were obviously shown a degree of kindness by the locals to prompt such a return of affection. It perhaps helped that these were the men who had defended the breach and had thus saved the local population from the ravages of the French. Also, it points to the discipline and behaviour of the 87th. There had clearly been few if any incidents between the men of the 87th and the locals as so often occur when soldiers and civilians, particularly of different nations, are in close proximity on so regular a basis. Indeed the behaviour of the men was such that Gough wrote that, "I may abolish the Guard Room, and talk of the Cat of Nine Tails as an obsolete term".[24] It is difficult not to ascribe such good and caring behaviour to the attitude and actions of the commander of the battalion. Thus, just as ill-discipline reflects on the commander, so does good discipline, and clearly high morale despite all they had been through.

---

22   Rait, *Gough*, Vol.I, pp. 92–93.
23   Rait, *Gough*, Vol. I, p. 93. This is a quote from a letter to his wife, dated 28 May 1812.
24   Rait, *Gough*, Vol. I, p. 110.

14

The Tide Turns

1812 was the beginning of the end for the French and not only in Spain for the year also saw the start of Napoleon's ultimately disastrous invasion of Russia. The need to support such a large campaign obviously had an effect on the French capability in Spain. By the middle of the year, Soult's campaign in Andalusia was all but finished. Early in the year both the large French fortresses near the Portuguese border, Ciudad Rodrigo and Badajoz, fell to the allies and in July Wellington defeated Marshal Marmont at Salamanca. This opened the road to Madrid and Soult withdrew from Andalusia as a consequence of this victory, lifting the siege of Cadiz for the last time in August 1812. Soult had not wished to withdraw from Andalusia, and had indeed urged Joseph Bonaparte to allow him to continue the fight in that area. Soult had 60,000 men under his command and wished to attack and take both Cadiz and Tarifa. This would keep the allied forces separate, and would indeed threaten Gibraltar. Whether or not this was possible is open to debate, but it was sound in theory. Joseph however wanted all available manpower before Madrid. He had to issue the order to withdraw twice before Soult reluctantly obeyed.

After the French withdrawal there was no longer any great need for Gough and the 87th to remain in the region, and Tarifa had now lost its importance to the allied war effort. At the end of August Gough and the six companies of the 87th that were with him left Tarifa and marched for Cadiz. From there they would march on to Seville, where the remainder of the battalion was already stationed, having played a role in the capture of that city after the French had lifted the siege of Cadiz. On 6 September Gough formally resigned as garrison commander at Tarifa, having actually left Tarifa on 31 August. Indeed Gough was anxious to reunite his command as there was clearly going to be further action in the not too distant future. Wellington had ordered the concentration of all available manpower in central Spain, with the intention of threatening Madrid. Whilst from a strategic point of view he would have been better attacking in the north of Spain, political considerations swayed his judgement. When Gough reunited his battalion he found that the 87th were to form part of a force of 3,500 men under the command of Colonel Skerrett. One wonders whether Gough was pleased at the idea of having to serve under a man who he had thought was tactically timid. Skerrett's force was ordered to march to Truxillo on the main road between Lisbon and Madrid to become part of the detached corps commanded by Lieutenant General Sir Rowland Hill. Hill is widely considered to be the best of Wellington's officers and amongst the few that Wellington would trust in an independent command. Curiously when rumour emerged that the 87th would be either part of Hill's command or Maitland's command Gough expressed a preference for the latter without giving any further explanation.[1] The aim of Hill was to move the majority of the forces that

---

1   Rait, *Gough*, Vol. I, p. 96–97. This quotes from a letter Hugh Gough wrote to his wife dated 6 September 1812. Gough gives no Christian name for Maitland, and it is unlikely that he is referring to Brevet Colonel Peregrine Maitland of the 1st Foot Guards (Grenadier Guards) as he did hold a command at this time. It is possible that he might have meant Lieutenant General Frederick Maitland who at that

had been pinned down in the south by Soult's campaign to a point where they could join up with the rest of Wellington's army. Although the British position appeared to be in the ascendance, there were two major problems. Firstly finance, and by association supplies, were increasingly becoming problematic after years of war. Secondly, the perennial problem of manpower was becoming even more pressing, particularly as during this year war broke out with the United States of America and the demand for troops initially to defend Canada, meant that Wellington would receive little in the way of additions from home. The war with the United States also affected the supply system as the majority of the corn used to supply Wellington's army in Spain had been coming from the Americas.

Skerrett's force, now including the reunited 87th, arrived at Truxillo on 14 October 1812. At some point during September, the 87th were transferred to a brigade commanded by Lord Proby, who Gough stated was "not a little proud of us".[2] Gough suggested that the pride might also have been relief that he now had a reliable and battle-hardened unit under his command, as Gough questioned the state of the rest of the brigade. However, Gough had himself been shocked by the state of the four companies of the 87th that had not been under his command, commenting that "I have found the detachment in shocking order, but am making every exertion to fit them out".[3]

By the end of September things seemed to be back to normal and Gough boastfully wrote that

> My men have astonished the Division in marching; I never saw such a set of fellows. I came yesterday seven and twenty miles over a most wretched road, and it raining all the time, in eight hours and a half, without one man out of his section an inch. The Guards saw us come in to their astonishment. Skerrett, who was present, cried out 'God damn me, my Brigade, let them look at that Regiment, and be ashamed of themselves.[4]

Whilst no doubt a slight exaggeration, influenced by the pride he felt in his battalion, it does appear that the 87th were in good order, with high morale and good discipline. Once again one must give Gough some of the credit for this. He was clearly a motivator of men. On 25 October 1812 Skerrett's men joined up with the 4th Division south of Madrid at a place called Aranjuez. Hill commanded 31,000 Anglo-Portuguese soldiers, facing 60,000 French soldiers commanded by Soult. Wellington had 24,000 Anglo-Portuguese Soldiers and 11,000 Spaniards, facing 53,000 French under General Souham, who had taken over from the wounded Marmont. Wellington had been attempting to take the castle at Burgos. Burgos was not only important due to its history, being the ancient capital of Castile, but also due to its strategic location, on the main road back to France. It also housed an important French supply centre and arsenal. However, with superior French forces massing against him it was no longer practical for Wellington to continue this siege. Debate has continued amongst historians as to whether Wellington was unwise to venture into central Spain at this point. The combined French forces were far greater than his even if he could muster every British and Portuguese soldier. He had learnt from bitter experience that he could not rely upon the Spanish. Perhaps such a debate is beyond the scope of this work, however one has to note that Wellington realised that he would have to venture this far from the safety of Portugal if he were ever to defeat the French and drive them from Spain. However the fates had conspired against him. The siege of Burgos had been badly handled. Had it fallen the French would have been forced to regroup and their supply situation might have necessitated withdrawal.

time was commanding in Alicante a rather desolate force of mainly foreign troops (Germans, Swiss, Neapolitans and Sicilians) who had been serving in Sicily. Why Gough might have had a preference for Alicante is unclear.
2 Rait, *Gough*, Vol. I, p. 100.
3 Rait, *Gough*, Vol. I, p. 100.
4 Rait, *Gough*, Vol. I, p. 101. This quotes from a letter to his wife dated 15 September 1812.

However it was Wellington who was forced to withdraw. He decided to winter around the defensive position of Ciudad Rodrigo whilst he planned for next year's campaign and waited what reinforcements he would get. The withdrawal was not easy and saw the 87th in action once again. As the army attempted to cross the Tagus on 30–31 October 1812, the 87th and the 47th Foot were tasked with defending a bridge at a place called Puente Larga. They faced a large force of French cavalry and infantry along with six guns. The bridge had been mined and on the 31 October it was destroyed. In the defence the two battalions only lost one man killed, an officer of the 47th. The 87th had 23 men wounded. They continued to hold the river bank all day, until withdrawing at 2000 under cover of darkness. Wellington and Hill's forces finally joined up on 8 November, and this was no doubt a relief to all concerned. Not only were they being harassed by strong French forces, but the weather had turned bad and their march was made all the harder for it. It was an ignominious end to a year which had on the whole been very successful for British arms in the Peninsular.

The withdrawal and the harsh winter took its toll upon the entire army. There was a breakdown in discipline across the board, not confined to the rank and file by any means, and even the 87th which had showed such good discipline throughout the year was not immune to this. Gough's letters take on a more sombre tone during this period. The pride in the battalion that he had so happily expressed only a month ago was gone. The supply service had broken down; added to which, in the withdrawal much of the army's baggage had been lost. The men were hungry, lacking in clothing, and an army forced to withdraw after being in such high spirits was always likely to face a loss of discipline. For a while, after Salamanca and the ending of Soult's campaign in Andalusia, it had appeared that the war would soon be over. Indeed officers had talked of reaching the Pyrenees before the end of the year. This when added to the conditions made many a man wonder if the war would ever end and question what they were doing there.

The winter quarters for the 87th did not help matters as they were in what Gough called "a most wretched little village".[5] It didn't help that there was overcrowding, and perhaps more importantly that pay had been delayed. Gough recorded in mid December that the battalion had not been paid since 24 October, and that the majority of the army had not received their pay since 24 July. It appears that Gough had used not only his influence but his strength of character to successfully demand the pay for his men from the appropriate authority. Once again this points to Gough's not inconsiderable care for his men, and more importantly his willingness to make that extra effort. Indeed paying for the war in Spain was stretching the British exchequer to the extreme. It needs to be remembered that despite a short interlude Britain had been in an ongoing war since 1792, with all the disruption to British commerce and trade that this had included.

One can understand Gough's sadness at what he saw before him, and how quickly the fortunes of war had disrupted the discipline of his battalion, and in fairness that of the whole army. It would also seem strange after what had been a successful year for British arms, and the 87th in particular, to finish the year in such a bad state. Furthermore, in March 1813 the 87th suffered a severe rebuke from Wellington over the conduct of a detachment of the battalion that had been bringing stores from Lisbon. Exact details are unclear but Gough felt the remarks were harsh given that they were no worse than the actions of any regiment in the army in Spain at that stage when discipline was collapsing throughout the army. Gough also felt that there was a certain prejudice against the battalion over discipline based on Wellington's previous opinion of the battalion. Robert Rait suggested that Wellington wished to make an example of a unit and the 87th were the unfortunate target.[6] All of this left Gough feeling that he would have to start again, both in terms of equipment, and establishing discipline and spirit. However this would be the last time that the British would be forced into a major withdrawal.

5   Rait, *Gough*, Vol. I, p. 103.
6   Rait, *Gough*, Vol. I, p. 104.

15

The Road to Vitoria

1813 was to be a decisive year for the British in Spain. It took some time however for the 87th to recover its strength. In early January 1813, the battalion had been reduced, largely by sickness, to only 324 men. In January the battalion received 80 men by way of reinforcements, 23 of them volunteers from various militia units in Ireland, but this was offset by 78 deaths suffered in Spain through illness and disease between December 1812 and February 1813. The situation did not improve quickly, and by the start of May 1813, Gough commanded only 456 men fit for action, still having over 160 men in the hospital.[1] The 87th was no better or worse than many regiments in the army who had endured a long and active 1812, only to be forced to withdraw to winter quarters that had not been properly prepared, and where sickness and disease soon spread. So it was not just the 87th but the entire army that steadily improved and increased in size throughout the early part of 1813 so as to be ready for the coming campaign of that year. By April there were encouraging signs that the army was starting to recover, and the worst of the sickness brought on by the winter was clearing. In the new year's campaigning Wellington would have the advantage in numbers for the first time. Despite the demands for manpower from the conflict in North America, Wellington had been reinforced to a strength of around 58,000 British soldiers, added to which he had with him the entire Portuguese army of over 27,000 men. Also in 1813 for the first time Wellington was able to use his new power as Generalissimo of the Spanish army. Although technically he had 40,000 Spaniards under his direct command, for the forthcoming campaign he would call on around 8,000. Whilst the bulk of his army was to be the tried and tested Anglo-Portuguese force, he now no longer had to 'waste' such experienced and trusted men on garrison duties or defending his lines of communication. This could be left to the Spanish. His supply situation was greatly improved and saw the welcome return of his excellent Quartermaster General George Murray, now a Major General. Wellington was also able to deploy his force for the first time with two trusted officers commanding large forces on his left and right; namely Sir Thomas Graham and Sir Rowland Hill respectively.

On the other side, the French forces had been reduced in the aftermath of the disastrous Russian campaign, as Napoleon attempted to strengthen his position in Germany. The four French armies facing Wellington had been reduced to around 60,000 men. Despite the deficit in numbers they still had the advantage in artillery by about 60 guns. They also had the advantage of being predominantly of one nationality, whereas Wellington commanded a mixture of British, Portuguese, Germans and Spaniards. Napoleon had long called the campaign the 'Spanish Ulcer' and it is possible that he underestimated not only the strength and ability of Wellington but how dangerous the French position was in Spain. Not only did he recall many of his best troops, but also Soult, his

---

1 Cunliffe, *Royal Irish Fusiliers*, pp. 113–114. Andrew Bamford's research has shown that during the month of May this rose to 501 effectives and 174 sick. <http://napoleon-series.org>. British Army Individual Unit Strengths: 1808–1815 The Infantry Part III.

best commander in Spain. This left command under the tactically inept King Joseph, with Marshal Jourdan as his chief of staff. Jourdan was a tactically astute officer, who urged that the French, now that their forces were reduced, should attempt to contain and delay Wellington in Spain. He urged against fighting a major battle, but was overruled by King Joseph, with disastrous consequences.

In late May 1813, Wellington began to move against the French. His plan was to outflank the French position so that he could force their withdrawal and avoid having to face them on his side of the Douro River. By a series of such flanking movements he was able to make prepared French defensive positions untenable. These movements were carried out by the left wing under Sir Thomas Graham. Amongst Graham's command were the 87th under Gough. They were part of Major General Charles Colville's brigade, which formed part of the 3rd Division commanded by Lieutenant General Thomas Picton. Colville's Brigade also consisted of the 1st Battalion 5th (Northumberland) Foot, 2nd Battalion 83rd Foot, and the 94th Regiment of Foot. The 87th stood at just over 500 men when they started their journey as part of Graham's command through the Tras-os-Montes towards Zamora. Whilst this movement was ongoing Wellington forced the French backwards, and when Graham's force appeared on the banks of the River Esla on their right flank they were taken by surprise and forced to abandon their position.

During this march the 87th were in good order, although Gough recalls an inspection of the brigade by Wellington where he states that the latter never took his eyes off the battalion. Gough declared, "I never saw so minute an inspection".[2] It is clear that for some reason Wellington still doubted the battalion, despite all it had achieved. Yet it appears he could find no fault. The fact that the 87th had been restored to good order after the falling off of discipline during the previous winter speaks to the good work of Gough and his officers. Perhaps it also confirms that the weakening of discipline was part of a wider issue throughout the army rather than any particular failing in the battalion.

Gough concluded his account by saying, "We were marching in prime order; he [Wellington] said not a word".[3] Graham's flanking march had been a tough assignment, through difficult country, and one which he and his men had achieved with great success: the sheer surprise felt by the French at their presence points to that. Such was the confusion and amazement felt by the French that they abandoned their strong positions, including the defences around the important centre of Burgos, and withdrew beyond the Ebro River. Indeed such had been the speed of this flanking movement that many of the defences had yet to be manned.

---

2   Rait, *Gough*, Vol. I, p. 107. This is taken from a letter from Gough to his wife, dated 8 June 1813.
3   Rait, *Gough*, Vol. I, p. 107.

16

The Battle of Vitoria

Graham's success in turning the French flank was such that he was asked to undertake a similar movement, this time through the Cantabrian Mountains through rough terrain. This would bring him out to the north of the French position around Vitoria, where King Joseph had, against Jourdan's advice, decided to give battle behind the line of the River Zadorra. Indeed the French had chosen a poor site for battle. Firstly, they did not properly defend all the crossing points of the river. Secondly, they were spread out too thinly for the forces at their disposal. Thirdly, the roads were such that any attempt to withdraw from the battlefield would soon turn into a rout. King Joseph clearly felt he had to make a stand somewhere but had chosen the wrong place and time. Indeed a more skilful commander, such as Soult, would undoubtedly have tried to engineer a battle in which he had faced only part of Wellington's numerically superior army. As it was on 21 June around 50,000 French faced over 70,000 allies.

Although they had acted under Graham's command until now, the 3rd Division, still commanded by Picton, in which the 87th were placed, were now the left of the two centre columns. The left-centre column was nominally commanded by Lieutenant General George Ramsay, 9th Earl of Dalhousie, although in truth Wellington exercised command over the centre columns of Dalhousie and Lieutenant General Lowry Cole. On the morning of the 21st, Gough lined the men of the 87th up for what would become known as the Battle of Vitoria.[1] Despite all that had happened he was confident in their ability and discipline. Wellington spent some time waiting for Graham to arrive on the left and threaten the right flank of the enemy. Graham was, perhaps unsurprisingly, delayed given the difficult of his task. Wellington, in anticipation of this, ordered Hill to attack the French left, his aim being to keep the enemy tied down and distracted from Graham's movement. At the same time the ferocity of Hill's attack forced the French to commit a division that had been held in reserve, and, as a consequence, when Graham finally did arrive on the other flank there were no reinforcements that could be sent to meet him. Wellington had made good use of his numerical superiority and his flanking movements had deceived the French.

When it became clear that Graham was starting to engage the enemy, Wellington advanced with his centre columns. The 3rd Division were able to find an undefended ford at which to cross the Zadorra. Indeed it was not until they were safely across and reformed that a French brigade was sent to confront them. The 87th had to force their way up a hill under fire from two French battalions and several French artillery pieces. It appears that they had become separated from the rest of the brigade due to the topography; a village blocked the movement of the whole brigade meaning that they were ordered in a different direction. This meant the 87th charged up the hill alone, which makes the events that followed all the more remarkable. Gough with around 600 men dislodged an enemy of close to 2,000 men who were supported by artillery. It was no surprise that after the

---

1   Some older sources give the name of the battle as Vittoria rather than the more common Vitoria.

battle Colville declared, "Gough you and your corps have done wonders."[2] As Gough pointed out, Colville had only seen the result not the action itself. This they had achieved, despite fearful loss. Gough as ever led from the front and after having his horse shot from under him continued on foot and was shot three times, although on no occasion did the bullet find its way through his coat sufficiently to break the skin. Once on top of the hill, the work of the 87th was far from over. The French were defending a small village called Hermandad and Gough's men swept them from it. Once again their achievements were testament not only to the courage and bravely of all concerned, but also the leadership and discipline of Gough. Whilst Wellington might have had his concerns about their discipline away from the battlefield no one could doubt their discipline on it.

The onslaught by the centre columns cracked the French line. As had been previously noted, the route to retreat by was narrow and crowded and the battle soon turned into a rout. The French could have been utterly destroyed. There were however two problems. Firstly Graham's column had been so bitterly engaged that it had not been able to block the path of retreat of the French. Secondly the pursuit of the enemy was stopped by the discovery of the French baggage train, which was looted, with many officers joining their men rather than attempting to stop them. Whilst there were strategic assets, such as all but one of the 153 French artillery pieces, many of the men descended upon the personal baggage. Indeed, it is said that King Joseph himself was almost captured in his coach, and was able to escape because the men were more concerned about the wealth rather than him. Wellington deplored the looting, but was powerless to prevent it given the number of men involved. The soldiers helped themselves to what Wellington estimated at one million pounds worth of loot. This was probably a conservative estimate and the real figure was likely double that. For men who had been willing to sign their lives away for the King's Shilling, such treasure was irresistible. This was in effect the wealth of six years of occupation by the French forces, and it had now fallen into British hands. It was this battle, and particularly this event, that gave rise to Wellington's oft quoted reference to the soldiers of the British Army being "the scum of the earth..."[3]

The 87th were not immune from such looting. Gough wrote to his wife, "Some of my fellows have made fortunes."[4] Gough appears to have turned a blind eye to such looting, partly due to the severity of the battle his men had faced. One almost gets the sense that he felt it was the 'prize' for those who had been fortunate enough to survive a tough day's fighting. He had at least 250 casualties out of a little over 600 men. One hundred and fifty seven of these were wounded including at least nine officers, two of whom would subsequently die from their wounds. This number does not include Gough, and it says much of the man that he did not class himself as wounded but did class Ensign Knox amongst the wounded, who had very similar injuries to his; little more than cuts and bruises.

There was also a famous incident at this battle where a soldier of the 87th, said to be Paddy Shannon, found amongst the baggage the marshal's baton of the French commander Jourdan. Gough wrote to his wife that,

> I found one of my sergeants got the Batonner (sic) of Marshal Jourdan, who commanded the French, carried, I should think by one of his staff who was killed. I shall present it tomorrow to General Colville for Lord Wellington. Unfortunately no officer saw the fellow take it, I should therefore fear our action shall not appear".[5]

2   Cunliffe, *Royal Irish Fusiliers*, p. 116.
3   Chandler, *Dictionary of the Napoleonic Wars*, p. 469.
4   Rait, *Gough*, Vol. I, p. 111. This quotes from a letter from Hugh Gough to his wife dated 22 June 1813.
5   Rait, *Gough*, Vol. I, p. 111. This also quotes from the letter to his wife mentioned previously. The story is also told in Cunliffe, *Royal Irish Fusiliers*, p. 118.

The baton was two foot long covered in dark blue velvet, decorated with gold eagles, and gold caps on either end, which by the time Gough saw it were missing. Gough believed that Shannon had stolen them, writing to his wife that Paddy Shannon, "pretends he has lost them". However, there does appear to be another possibility. According to Phillip Haythornthwaite, the baton was original captured by Corporal Fox of the 18th Hussars, a unit that was notable for its looting on that day.[6] Not realising what it was Fox pocketed the gold. It is then suggested that the baton was then stolen from him, presumably by Shannon, although Fox may simply have thrown it away after pocketing the gold. For reasons that are not clear, some months later Fox surrendered the gold caps to his commanding officer, and they were ultimately reunited with the baton. This captured marshal's baton was ultimately presented to the Prince Regent in London. On its receipt the Prince despatched a British version of a marshal's baton to confirm Wellington's promotion to Field Marshal with the words, "You have sent me, among the trophies of your unrivalled fame, the staff of a French Marshal; and I send you in return that of England. The British army will hail it with enthusiasm, while the whole universe will acknowledge these valorous efforts which had so imperiously called for it".[7] Certainly Gough and the 87th had taken a full part in whatever valorous efforts there had been that day, although they got little credit for it. The original baton presented to the Prince of Wales remains to this day in the Royal Collection at Windsor. The once blue velvet of the baton now appears rather brown in colour due to its age. An exact replica of the baton was produced for display by the regiment and can today be found in the regimental museum of the Royal Irish Regiment.

Although the Baton received a great deal of attention it is also worth remembering that the 87th also captured the colour of *4e Battalion* of the *100e Ligne*.[8] Perhaps somewhat surprisingly, given the chaos that followed the battle, this was the only French colour recorded as having been captured at Vitoria. It appears that this was also found with the baggage rather than captured on the field of battle. Both trophies added to the impressive haul of the 87th Foot. There does not appear to be any suggestion that Gough sent his men out deliberately looking for such trophies during the battles they fought in the Peninsular. It perhaps speaks more to the fact that the 87th were usually to be found right at the heart of the action in any given battle. Much of this had to do with the battalion's commander.

Vitoria is a prime example of the way in which Gough pushed his men forward. At Vitoria their action in attacking a numerically superior force in a strong defensive position, supported by artillery, is testament not only to Gough's nature and aggression, but to the faith he had in his men and consequently that they had in him. When one looks at what the battalion did at Vitoria the casualties are surprising, from the point of view that one would have expected them to be far greater. To lose less than 100 men, even if one calculates those who subsequently died of their wounds, is remarkable. In similar circumstances another regiment might have been decimated. This surely speaks to the discipline of the battalion where it really mattered; on the battlefield. It also is testament to the confidence and belief that the men had in Gough. They charged against superior odds at Vitoria not simply because it was an order, but because they had faith in Gough. Gough was one of the most experienced battalion commanders in the army in Spain by this stage. The fact that he was not personally mentioned in despatches, despite the efforts of his battalion, was down to a new directive from Wellington. In an attempt to end jealousy amongst his officers Wellington had resolved not to mention by name in his despatches any officer commanding a battalion, other than

6   Haythornthwaite, *Armies of Wellington*, p. 251.
7   Haythornthwaite, *Armies of Wellington*, p. 251.
8   Cunliffe, *Royal Irish Fusiliers*, p. 118. The battalion in question had actually been disbanded, and thus the 'colour' was in storage. Also, the 'colour' was a 'Fanion' rather than a full colour, and therefore there was no Eagle attached. I am once again grateful to Andrew Bamford for clarification.

those who had been killed in action. This was unfortunate as brigade and divisional commanders who had in fact done less to bring about victory than Gough did receive a mention.

The Battle of Vitoria forced the French very much on the defensive. In its aftermath Marshal Soult returned and attempted to gather the remaining French soldiers together to delay Wellington's advance to the border with France. Wellington now started to besiege San Sebastian and Pamplona, for until they had fallen he could not risk an invasion of France. The fact that he had to take time in doing this, and the fact that the ill-discipline of the British Army had meant that he had not been able to make the victory at Vitoria the rout it should have been, all meant that the French position, whilst bleak, was not hopeless. It also gave Soult time to prepare. French strength was such that they were able to threaten the siege of Pamplona to the extent that Wellington chose to withdraw from the siege and merely blockade it whilst he concentrated on San Sebastian. Soult showed great skill in manoeuvring and continued to threaten Wellington. It was only after the First and Second Battles of Sorauren, in which Soult lost over 7,500 men, that he was compelled to withdraw across the French frontier in early August 1813. The 87th took no major part in the battles of this period, although present on the field at Sorauren, but were engaged in a lot of marching back and forth to counter the manoeuvres of Soult.

17

The Invasion of France

The French had by now all but abandoned Spain, and Wellington would now have to venture into France to complete the war. However he was cautious about actually venturing into France itself at this stage. He chose to continue the sieges of the remaining French garrisons in Spain whilst holding the Roncesvalles and Maya passes through the Pyrenees. It was in defence of the latter position that the 87th were to find themselves employed. San Sebastian fell on 8 September, followed by some of the worst atrocities allegedly committed by British troops in the Peninsular. The town was ransacked, and having found a large supply of brandy and wine the British troops allegedly committed drunken acts of murder, rape, pillage and looting. Exactly what happened has long been disputed, with Wellington believing that much of what the British were accused of, and being asked to pay compensation for, had actually been committed by the French. Part of the problem was that so bad were the relations on the ground between the British and Spanish, and such was the distrust that neither believed the testimony of the other. However the fall of San Sebastian marks virtually the end of the fighting in Spain.

Wellington now had to turn to the invasion of France, which was always going to be a difficult prospect. Wellington planned a series of attacks across the border, rather than concentrating on one point. The 87th, still part of the 3rd Division which was now commanded by their old brigade commander Colville, were to attack through the Maya Pass to the valley of the Nivelle and seize the bridge at Amots. This was the centre of Wellington's attack, whilst Hill commanded two divisions on the right, and Sir John Hope two divisions on the left. In the centre Beresford was in command leading the 3rd, 4th, 7th and Light Divisions. Once again the allies had numerical supremacy standing at around 90,000 men to the 70,000 French commanded by Soult. The battle that the centre fought on 10 November 1813 is generally known as the Battle of the Nivelle. The day was a busy one for the 87th, who started the day attacking the redoubt east of Amots around the village of Sare and finished further down the River Nivelle at St Pee. It was a tough day as the battle raged from first light until darkness fell. The 87th behaved with the bravery that had become expected of it. Gough wrote to his wife that, "The old corps behaved as usual … Nothing could withstand the Prince's Own. Old Colville cried out, "Royal 87th, Glorious 87th", and well he might."[1]

Wellington had been understandable in his reluctance to cross the frontier and attack the French defences. They were strong and Soult had organised them as best he could in the short space of time. Although the battle of the Nivelle itself cost Wellington about 2,500 casualties, the entire campaign attacking across the frontier cost him somewhere in the region of 10,000 casualties.

---

1   Rait, *Gough*, Vol. I, p. 120. Rait quotes from a letter from Gough to his wife dated 9 November 1813. This is said to have been written the evening of the battle. Gough's speed in writing was due to the fact that he did not wish his wife to worry as his name had been listed amongst the wounded. He was perhaps more concerned than usual as to how she would receive this news given the recent death of their son Edward, on 9 September 1813.

The Battle of Nivelle was one of the worst days that the 87th had in terms of casualties, and certainly the worst in percentage terms. Already reduced through sickness and the losses of Vitoria, only around 386 men took the field. Of that number 216 were casualties, including one officer and 75 men killed. Gough was amongst the wounded, and we do not know whether it was the attack on the redoubt or the action at St Pee that caused this. Gough had been shot through the hip, but fortunately it had missed the bone. There was therefore a good chance of recovery. However Gough remained in hospital until the end of the year.

Gough's recovery was slow and painful, but by mid December he was able to move about with the use of crutches. At the end of December Gough was pleased to read Colville's despatch on the Battle of the Nivelle. Unlike Wellington, Colville had no reticence in mentioning officers by name. "The Major General [Colville] is happy to communicate the latest information received from the Medical Officers in the rear, that the severe wound of Lt. Colonel Gough of the 87th, does not threaten more than the temporary loss of his very valuable services."[2] Gough was said to have been delighted by these words, and one can imagine why. Whatever others would say of him or make of his service, the words most valuable to him were from those who had seen what he achieved, knew what he had been through, and could report with their own eyes rather than second or third hand reports.

The 87th had been reduced to a shell of its former self. In a strange way this brought relief to Gough during his recovery as he did not have to suffer watching someone else lead the battalion during his absence. Although the battalion did not take part officially in the Battles of the Nive or St Pierre, it has been suggested that what was left of the battalion was used to form two flank companies that did take part in the action. This is based largely on the fact that we know that members of the battalion were awarded the clasp for the Battle of the Nive on their Military General Service Medal. As such medals were awarded some years afterwards, being introduced only in 1847 and backdated, it is possible that there was an error. However it is equally likely that Wellington's desire to use every available man had led to the temporary consolidation of such effective manpower as remained in the 87th.[3]

Gough's recovery was not helped by the fact that he was moved from the hospital at Zugarramurdi to a new hospital called Restoria. This required an uncomfortable journey in a bullock cart that did not help aid his recovery. Yet it was necessary as the war was moving forward, deeper into France. Although the 87th would take part in two more major engagements before the abdication of the Emperor Napoleon, the Battle of Orthez on 27 February 1814 and the Battle of Toulouse on 10 April, they would do so without Gough. Whilst the wound he had suffered had not been life threatening it had incapacitated him. At Orthez, the 87th once again suffered heavy losses: out of 551 men who took the field 264 became casualties, out of which number 93 were killed. The Battle of Toulouse, whilst technically an allied victory, was a bloody one in which the British lost many more men than the French. Figures vary but the Allies lost over 4,500 men to the French figure of 3,236. However the war ended the next day when news of Napoleon's abdication reached them. At Toulouse the 87th suffered 100 casualties out of a strength of 464, of whom 28 were killed. Gough clearly felt regret at having missed the battle, not simply because he had missed one last chance for distinction in the war, but because his men suffered such heavy casualties. It is almost as if he felt a certain guilt that he had not been with his men.

With the war against Napoleon seemingly at an end the 87th left France on 7 July 1814. They arrived at Cork on 20 July, and, after a month in Ireland, were ordered to Portsmouth in late August, which they did not reach until 14 September 1814. From there they marched to Horsham,

2   Rait, *Gough*, Vol. I, p. 120.
3   Cunliffe, *Royal Irish Fusiliers*, pp. 121–122.

and spent some time there before transferring to Plymouth in November. Gough's exact movements are a little harder to trace. We do not know exactly when he came back home, and whether that home was Ireland or England. It is possible that he was back by late March or early April 1814, and it is quite conceivable that with the end of the war in sight he had been sent home slightly earlier. It would have been clear, despite his perhaps hoping otherwise, that he was to see no further part in the fighting.[4]

We do know that by June of 1814 the wound he received at the Nivelle was still such as to require him to use crutches. There is a letter from his wife written in early September 1814, addressed to him in Aylesbury, and the tone suggests that he has only recently returned from a difficult journey.[5] However whether this is the crossing from Continental Europe, or the journey to Aylesbury is unclear. It is also unclear why he was in Aylesbury, as it does not appear that the 87th were. However this letter does illustrate his wife's concern for his 'constitution' after the journey, although he assures her that a certain Dr Bailey has told him that it is not permanently 'shaken' by his injuries or travelling. The remainder of this letter deals with family matters, largely of a financial nature. Hugh Gough's father is anxious to find out who the agent is for his daughter's widow's pension: Jane Gough, the eldest sister of Hugh, was the widow of Lieutenant Colonel Richard Lloyd of the 84th Foot who was killed in France in 1813. However, a later letter, dated 18 September 1814, seems less concerned with Hugh Gough's health. It is therefore to be presumed that the ill-effects of the journey have worn off and in general his health is improving.

At some point after the 87th returned to England, Gough joined them, and given his family connections with the area it is likely that this was when they reached Plymouth. We know for certain that when the battalion was inspected in November 1814 that Gough was present and in command.[6]

Thus after almost six years of tough fighting and campaigning his war was over. The significance of the Peninsular War to Gough's career should never be overlooked. From a military point of view it was the making of him. His continual service at the head of a battalion made him one of the most experienced men, for his rank, in the Army. He had faced up to the hitherto invincible French army that had defeated the armies of the great European powers of the day. The 87th, under Gough's leadership, had played an important part. They had distinguished themselves in battle after battle. Gough had experienced one of the major campaigns of British military history, and had seen the good and the bad, the highs and the lows, of the campaign. He had witnessed commanders such as Wellington, Hill and Graham at close quarters. The experience clearly influenced his future career: it would be impossible for it not to have done. Although for a time it would appear that the days of the Peninsular War would be his most intense campaigning, it was only a part of his long career. At that stage he could not have known what lay before him. Indeed one wonders what Gough envisaged for himself now that the war was over. One thing was clear from his last letter to his wife during this campaign; he longed to see his family again.[7]

---

4   Cunliffe, *Royal Irish Fusiliers*, pp. 124–125.
5   Private Collection, Hugh Gough to Frances Gough, 6 September 1814.
6   Cunliffe, *Royal Irish Fusiliers*, p. 124.
7   Rait, *Gough*, Vol. I, p. 121. This last letter to his wife was dated 28 February 1814.

Part 3

Ireland and the wilderness

18

After the War and Command of the 22nd Foot

Since his return to England Gough had received various rewards and honours for his service in the Peninsular. However this did not include, as he had hoped, either his promotion to colonel, or his application for a company of Guards, the latter bringing with it a level of social standing. Sir John Doyle had written to Wellington in the summer of 1814 suggesting that Gough deserved to be breveted colonel in the Army. Despite Wellington replying that, "I should be very ungrateful if I was not ready to apply for promotion for the gallant officers who have served under my command, and will forward Colonel Gough's Memorial", there was to be no promotion.[1] However in August he was awarded a pension of £250 a year, later increased to £300, along with a medal for Talavera. It was at this point that Wellington moved to have Gough's lieutenant colonelcy antedated to the date of the Battle of Talavera. In short this meant that his seniority as lieutenant colonel dated back to July 1809. Perhaps this was Wellington's compensation for not being able to secure for him a colonel's brevet. In June 1815 Gough was knighted for his services in the Peninsular War and allowed the special privilege of adorning his coat of arms with representations of some of his achievements in Spain. Thus he was allowed to add the Portcullis at Tarifa, the Cross of the Order of Charles III of Spain, the Eagle captured at Barrosa, and a banner bearing the number of his regiment; the 87th.[2]

Throughout the rest of 1814 Gough's battalion continued garrison duty in Plymouth, which also included providing a detachment to guard American prisoners of war being held at Dartmoor. On 6 December 1814 the battalion sailed for Guernsey. The Governor of this island was still Sir John Doyle, and he was no doubt delighted to welcome back his second battalion from their success in Spain. Undertaking garrison duties on the island, the battalion was reduced from a paper establishment strength of 1,000 to 800 in late December, followed by a further reduction to 600 the following December.[3]

Somewhat surprisingly, given their proximity to France and the fact that Guernsey did not appear to be under imminent threat, the battalion was not called upon during the 100 days of Napoleon's return to power in 1815 that culminated in his defeat at Waterloo. One wonders why when they were a battalion of Peninsular War veterans, and still commanded by one of, if not the most, distinguished battalion commander of the campaign they were not dispatched to France. There does not appear to be any known reason to account for it. Even at a reduced strength of 600, or even 400, they could have been a useful addition to Wellington's command. During the Hundred Days the battalion carried on as normal. On the 21 June 1815, the anniversary of the Battle of Vitoria, and incidentally the day before Napoleon abdicated for the final time, the battalion was reviewed by its

---

1 Rait, *Gough*, Vol. I, p. 122.
2 NAM: Gough Papers, 8303–105. Throughout the papers there occur pictures of the updated coat of arms, as additional items were added to this throughout his career.
3 Cunliffe, *Royal Irish Fusiliers*, pp. 124–125.

regimental colonel, Sir John Doyle. Afterwards in the officers mess a silver cup was presented to Gough, subscribed to by all the officers of the battalion, in remembrance of Vitoria. Gough replied in thanks that:

> This mark of affection I will hand down to my children as a proof of my exertions in the cause of my country, and if they inherit one spark of my feelings, they will estimate its value as I do, and will preserve it with heartfelt pride and honest exultation.[4]

Later that evening they held a dinner in remembrance of Vitoria. It marked not only the bravery of the battalion but a conflict that would end for good the following day.

With the war over, a spirit of military retrenchment overcame the political and military powers at be. In some sense this was inevitable. The Army did not need to be the same size for peacetime duties. Although over half a century later the idea of dual battalion regiments would be introduced, there appeared little sense at the time of having two battalions for a regiment such as the 87th. In December 1815 the establishment of the second battalion had been reduced to 600 men, and it became little more than a garrison unit for Guernsey. In April 1816 the battalion left the island for Portsmouth, and later that year it moved on to Colchester. It therefore came as little surprise when in January 1817 the 2nd Battalion of the 87th Foot was told it would be disbanded. It had been in existence for only 13 years. However during the majority of that time, for about eight years, it had been constantly at the seat of war involved in a gruelling campaign. It was no doubt a sad day for Gough when he had to issue his final orders as battalion commander. He took the occasion to record their achievements but also their contribution.

> The Prince's Own Irish bled prodigally and nobly; they have sealed their duty to their King and country by the sacrifice of nearly two thousand of their comrades ... In parting with the remains of that corps, in which Sir Hugh Gough has served twenty-two years, at the head of which, and by whose valour and discipline, he has obtained those marks of distinction with which he has been honoured by his Royal master, he cannot too emphatically express the most heartfelt acknowledgements and his deep regret. From all classes of his officers he has uniformly experienced the most cordial and ready support. Their conduct in the field, while it called for the entire approbation of their Commanding Officer, acquired for them the best stay to military enterprise and military renown, the confidence of their men, and led to the accomplishment of their wishes, the Approbation of their Prince, the Honour of their Country, and the character of their Corps. Every non-commissioned officer and man is equally entitled to the thanks of their commanding officer. To all he feels greatly indebted, and he begs to assure all, that their prosperity as individuals, or as a corps, will ever be the first wish of his heart, and to promote which he will consider no sacrifice or exertion too great.[5]

His final thoughts were not merely words. When news reached Gough that an administrative error meant that by late 1818 many of his men had still not received their certificates of honourable discharge, he took up the cause. From his correspondence it appears that this was the first he had heard of it and wrote to the Secretary at War, Viscount Palmerston, regarding this matter. The main problem for those who had not received such certificates was that without them they could not claim their pension rights of 5d per day. That the situation took so long to resolve, and require the intervention of the former commanding officer, probably spoke to the fact that as a disbanded

4   Cunliffe, *Royal Irish Fusiliers*, p. 125. This is in turn a quote from the *Evening Star*.
5   Cunliffe, *Royal Irish Fusiliers*, pp. 125–126.

unit they were hardly a priority. The correspondence continued until January 1819 when the situation was finally resolved.[6] Gough had used similar emotive language in his correspondence with the War Office, writing that, "I therefore confidently look forward to your Lordships favourable decision in favour of those gallant and deserving men all of whom served for years on the Peninsular where many of them bled in the service of their country."[7]

The battalion officially disbanded on the 1st February 1817. As previously alluded to, many of the men took their discharge. However 330 men and many of the officers transferred to the first battalion, now simply the 87th, who were serving in India having just finished campaigning in Nepal. The extra officers and men were most welcome, as before the year was out the 87th would see action in the Pindari War. For Gough however the situation was not so simple. He was now a lieutenant colonel without a battalion. For a little over two years he remained on half-pay. One wonders whether there might have been the perception of Gough as a wartime leader rather than peacetime battalion commander. If so this period on half-pay would be understandable. However there were many conflicts going on throughout the empire, in India, Arabia, Southern Africa, and elsewhere where his talents could have been put to good use. It may simply have been that there was no vacancy for him. However an officer with such a distinguished record could not with any justification be kept out of command for any length of time. In the great scheme of things two years was not very long, and no doubt in some ways Gough would have appreciated the break after the long years of campaigning. It certainly would have done his health no harm to have had such a break. His exact movements during this period are unclear but no doubt he spent considerable time with his family both in Plymouth and Limerick.

On 12 August 1819 his period of unemployment came to an end and he was appointed commander of the 22nd Foot, whilst at the same time being promoted to full colonel. The 22nd (Cheshire) Regiment of Foot was one of the oldest in the British Army. Having originally been raised in 1689, it continued to serve as an independent regiment until 2007: the regiment lives on today as the 1st Battalion of the Mercian Regiment. It had not served in the Peninsular War, instead being deployed to the West Indies, Southern Africa, and India during the wars with France, where it saw considerable fighting. It was a regiment with a distinguished reputation and tradition. Whilst it did not have the glamour or social status of the Guards it was a county regiment of great standing. The 22nd had just returned from Mauritius where it had spent the last nine years, having been part of the force that had initially captured the island from the French in November 1810. A battalion that had been stationed overseas for that length of time had understandably become somewhat weakened during that period. In a sense they had been little more than a garrison for the island. In the last few years, particularly since any French threat to retake the island had passed, the battalion had little to do and led a rather mundane existence. Returning to England they found they had a new commander.

Little is known of the reaction to the appointment of Gough, but given his reputation from the Peninsular War it is likely that there was some excitement. The regimental colonel since 1809 had been Lieutenant General Edward Finch, fourth son of the Earl of Aylesford. Although an experienced officer, it is unclear how much control he had over his regiment's only battalion for he had not been with the 22nd in Mauritius. The other lieutenant colonel on the strength of the 22nd was

6   After his correspondence with Palmerston there followed several letters to and from Richard Neave, the Deputy Paymaster at the War Office. NAM: 8303–105: Gough Papers, Neave to Gough, 27 November 1818 & Gough to Neave, 11 January 1819. There is also one letter from the Deputy Secretary at the War Office, Mr William Merry in the same collection dated 7 December 1818, which also discusses the lost certificates.
7   NAM: 8303–105: Gough Papers, Gough to Secretary at War, 16 November 1818. For some reason the certificates were lost, either in the post or misplaced somewhere in the War Office.

Sir John Hamilton-Dalrymple, M.P., not to be confused with John Hamilton Dalrymple, later 8th Earl of Stair, who was also an army officer. The Army List does not help as it just lists him as J. Dalrymple, leaving out the other part of his surname and hyphen. He seems to have taken little active interest in the regiment during this period.

For the majority of the next two years the 22nd were stationed in Northampton. At some point before 25 March 1821 the battalion moved to Newcastle-upon-Tyne. The exact purpose for this is unclear. In late August or early September 1821 the battalion marched to Liverpool. There, on 9 October, it embarked for Ireland, arriving in Dublin the following day. There was growing unrest in the south of Ireland particularly in Munster. Although a police force, or more correctly a peace preservation force, had been created in Ireland in 1814 it was not considered sufficient to deal with the rising disturbances.[8] Nor were the troop levels already deployed to Ireland deemed sufficient. Thus a number of extra battalions were sent to Ireland, including the 22nd and their relatively new commander.

---

8   The police force in Ireland had been created when the 'father' of modern policing Robert Peel had been Chief Secretary. In 1822, partly in response to the disturbances in Munster, a system of county constabularies was established. In 1836 a national police force, the Royal Irish Constabulary, was formed.

19

Ireland: Fighting 'Captain Rock'

The earlier chapters of this book looked briefly at the revolts and uprisings in Ireland in the late 18th century, and the role that Hugh Gough's father had played in helping to supress them. Although these had passed, the 'troubles' had not. The period in the 1820s is an often overlooked one in the agrarian and religious turmoil of Ireland. As we are largely concerned with part that Hugh Gough played in them we will not go into much detail.[1] The problems were largely confined to the province of Muster and in particular the counties of Cork and Limerick. Gough's role in fighting them was slightly different from that of his father. After all, the younger Gough was a regular officer who had been deployed with his battalion. His father had been a local landowner and magistrate and had served in the militia as an extension of this. Whilst the younger Gough clearly had a connection to the local community, he was deployed as a professional soldier rather than a local landowner. The problems in affected areas were mainly to do with agriculture, the collection of rents and tithes, and the large number of absentee landlords.

The rebels had links to the 'Whiteboys' of the previous era, and were occasionally called such. However increasingly they became identified as 'Rockites'. This was the name given to those who were the supporters of Captain, sometimes self-promoted to General, Rock. It has never been entirely clear exactly who Captain Rock was. Many things done in his name were not directly linked to one individual. More often each area had its own 'Captain Rock'.[2] However the definitive work on this era in Irish history identifies the original Captain Rock as Patrick Dillane, the son of a blacksmith from Shanagolden in County Limerick. He followed his father into the trade and became a blacksmith's apprentice in Newcastle West (often simply referred to as Newcastle), about ten miles south of Shanagolden. The irony was that this man would later become an informer and give evidence in the trial of several of his former followers.[3] Dillane's betrayal in 1822 severely damaged the cause of the Rockites, as did the similar actions of David Nagle who had acted as 'Captain Rock' in the north of the county, and John Dundon, also a 'Captain Rock' in the area around Castletownroche. However the fact that these betrayals did not end the insurgency demonstrates that this was a lose organisation without the need for any individual leader. In many ways this made it much harder to combat for the authorities.

Rather than open warfare, the unrest was now expressed through an insurgency. There was also a change in the nature of the people engaged in the struggle. Whereas in the past many of those fighting had been involved in the egalitarian pursuit of freedom as a political ideal, encouraged by

---

1   The outstanding work on this era is that of James S. Donnelly Jr, and in particular his book *Captain Rock: The Irish Agrarian Rebellion 1821–1824* (Cork: The Collins Press, 2009). For further background the aforementioned is certainly the work that is most accessible.

2   The identity and use of the title Captain Rock is a recurring theme in James Donnelly's book. For information on the earliest use of the term see Donnelly, *Captain Rock*, pp. 37–38, 51, & 369–70.

3   Donnelly, *Captain Rock*, pp. 38–39 & 316–317.

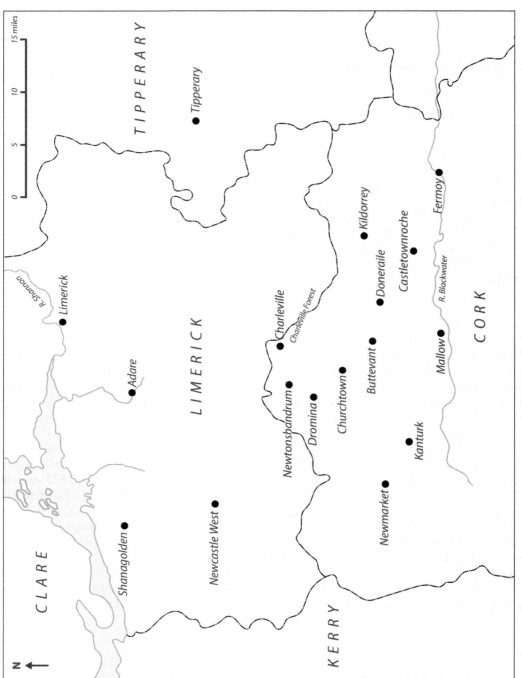

Map 6 Ireland.

the revolutionary ideas of France and the United States, the current problems had their roots in more practical concerns. Whilst a detailed history of this period is beyond the scope of this work, it is interesting and helpful to look at the background and causes of the problems Gough faced whilst commanding the troops in Ireland. The main cause of the trouble was land reform. During the recent wars with France, prices had risen and, whilst never having great wealth, the Irish peasant farmers had experienced better times due to this increased demand for their agricultural products. With the end of the conflict demand fell and prices fell. Indeed a large part of this was due to no longer needing to feed a large army either for home defence, in the Spanish Peninsular, or in other areas where the fight against France and her allies was being conducted. This great drop in demand had a negative effect upon Irish farmers who found little call for their products; particularly to the extent they had been producing them. As a consequence of this the issues of high rents and absentee landlords also became more pressing.

There was also a wider issue at the heart of the struggle to do with Catholic emancipation. Under various penal laws, Catholics had been barred from public office, owning land, serving in the Army, and endured various other restrictions. In 1766 there was a step forward when the Papacy finally recognised the Hanoverian succession in England. This removed one of the major concerns to allowing Catholics responsibility or authority. In 1778, what was called the Papist Act was passed which withdrew a great number of the restrictions, allowing the right to own land or inherit it, and to join the Army, in return for the swearing of an oath renouncing the claims of the Stuarts to the throne. Further reform was perhaps stalled by the response to this Act which had seen anti-Catholic riots in Britain, most notably the Gordon Riots of 1780. In 1800 at the Act of Union there was the hope, possibly even the promise, that Catholic emancipation would follow. It did not. The cause of Catholic emancipation had been going on for many years but it was particularly after the campaign started by Daniel O'Connell in 1823 that it became an increasingly popular cause.

Gough certainly had more than a little sympathy for the cause of Catholic emancipation, if not necessarily for land reform, although even with respect to the latter he was not without concern and was critical of many of the landowners. It is clear from his letters that he felt the former would help reduce the protests at the lack of the latter. Gough was a deeply religious man who held more to his private interpretation of God than a formal one. Whilst he had been brought up in the teaching of the Protestant Church of Ireland he was not as anti-Catholic as many of his contemporaries. Indeed one gets the feeling, from a general reading of his letters that deal with religious matters, that he was only anti-Catholic when the latter manifested itself in either an anti-British or anti-Monarchy guise. Gough had expressed his support for Catholic emancipation as early as 1812, writing "I wish to God the Prince [the future George IV] had declared for Catholic Emancipation. This measure in the end he must give way to, and every hour injures his popularity".[4] Whilst Hugh Gough had some sympathy over this matter he could not defend the acts of violence against land-owners that had led to the deployment of extra troops to Ireland, including the 22nd. Gough was a man who unlike many of the Anglo-Irish gentry was not afraid to express his belief that he was an 'Irishman'. It was therefore something of a difficult task which he had to undertake. Although clear in his duty, he clearly had more than a little sympathy for the difficulties of the local populace, if not necessarily for their actions.

It was indeed an extremely difficult and complicated situation in which Gough and his new battalion found themselves placed. There was clearly an element of sectarianism to the situation. This in one sense was inevitable, as the majority of the peasantry were Catholics and the majority of the landowners, magistrates, police and army commanders, were Protestant. From the 'Rockite' point of view, it is difficult to ascertain how much of the violence was sectarian in nature. Certainly

---

4   Rait, *Gough*, Vol. I, p. 124.

from the point of view of Protestant landowners and clergymen there was no doubt that they interpreted the atrocities committed by the 'Rockites' as the beginning of a general uprising by Catholics throughout Ireland. Although the latter sounds simply like propaganda, it should not be dismissed out of hand. In a sense this was what Gough was saying. The longer the Government waited to enact Catholic emancipation, the more likely it became that what was an isolated revolt about agriculture could become a national revolt about the rights of Catholics.

20

Fighting the Insurgency

Like so many insurgencies throughout history it was often difficult for the military to distinguish friend from foe. Indeed such was the nature of things in rural Ireland at this time that many of the farmers found it safer to side with the 'Rockites' than become informers. The latter term of derision was reserved for all those who were thought to be cooperating in any way with the authorities. Even to be seen talking to a soldier or policeman could gain one this dubious distinction. This made it very difficult for men like Gough to obtain reliable intelligence. It was also difficult for Gough to know whether or not the reports of atrocities he received were genuine or not. There were many farmers who took advantage of the offered compensation for 'Rockite' attacks. It was not unknown for a farmer to deliberately burn his own stored crops to obtain compensation from the Government rather than risk attempting to sell such goods in a volatile and depressed market. There were reportedly other incidents where farmers would burn their hay and then claim that all their crops had also be burnt. With clear evidence of a burning it was difficult for the authorities to claim otherwise. Farmers were then known to secretly sell their crops at a reduced price, which when added to the compensation they received from the government meant that they made a considerable profit.[1]

Indeed there was further motivation to almost encourage such atrocities. As Gough recorded every "outrage" committed helped the farmers to press their case for the abolition of tithes, and gave them a good reason for not being able to pay their taxes on time. Gough's language was its usual forceful nature and on occasions he described many of the local farmers as "bigoted", "selfish", and "ignorant". One can understand why at times he saw such farmers as a bigger problem than the 'Rockites' themselves.[2] At the same time it was very difficult to get local farmers, and for that matter anyone, to give evidence against their attackers. Many farmers who had been robbed or had their crops burnt knew that if they pressed charges there was little to stop the accused's accomplices from returning and either burning down their houses or murdering them and their families. For some there might have been other concerns. As Gough recorded:

> Though the farmers evidently know them, still such is their dislike to prosecute, either through fear of personal danger, or what I consider much more likely, an apprehension if they should come forward their own former insurrectionary acts would be divulged, that it is with difficulty I can ever bring them to acknowledge their having been attacked.[3]

---

1   Donnelly, *Captain Rock*, pp. 281–282.
2   National Archives of Ireland (NAI), State of the Country Papers (SCOP) 1, 2614/11 Gough to Lt. Col. Finch, 10 January 1824 & 2516/25 Gough to Major J Finch 22 November 1823. Finch was the military secretary of Lieutenant General Sir Stapleton Cotton, at that time carrying the title Baron Combermere, the Commander-in-Chief, Ireland.
3   NAI: SCOP 1, 2614/37. See also, Donnelly, *Captain Rock*, p. 297.

In such a situation it was not surprising that as Gough recorded not only that many farmers would refuse to identify the men they knew had carried out the attack, but often that they even refused to admit that such attacks had even taken place. In such a situation it was incredibly difficult to fight an insurgency, without the support of the local community and without people prepared to take a courageous stand and give evidence. In the accounts that Gough gives of those who did stand up to the 'Rockites' and did give evidence, they can appear to be rather arrogant and bigoted. However such character traits probably helped them to stand against the threatened repercussions of their actions. One such example amongst the Gough papers is that of Dr Edward Ring. Ring believed there was a general conspiracy amongst the population of the village against him. He might have been right but this produced a rather hate filled statement, found amongst the Gough papers, as regards the people of the village in North Cork where he lived.[4]

Although the government at one point was willing to pay to protect property, including having many of the thatched roofs replaced with slates to make them harder to burn, the burning of property was only part of the atrocities. Murder became common place, as did mutilation – the cutting off of the noses of informers was a not uncommon practice – and in several well publicised cases, rape. Reports vary somewhat but it is clear that some gang rape did take place. As so often in these cases when the reports appeared in the press the number of men involved, and the exact details, were somewhat exaggerated. Yet that should not detract from the severity of the crime. There are also suggestions that there was a sectarian nature to the attacks as Protestant women were separated from Catholics.[5]

In February 1822 a group of women whose husbands were soldiers in 1st Battalion the Rifle Brigade were moving through Kildorrey on their way to new quarters. The convoy was attacked by a group of 'Rockites' and a number of women were gang raped. This unsurprisingly led to a hardening of the attitude of soldiers towards the 'Rockites'. In March 1822 there was also the abduction and subsequent rape of the 14-year-old Honora Goold. Although rape was acknowledged to have taken place seven men were actually charged with abduction, a charge considered more serious under the law at that time. They were defended by the celebrated Daniel O'Connell, and although all were convicted O'Connell managed to get three released on a technicality due to an error in the original indictment.[6]

Indeed such a technical dismissal was just one of many problems the authorities found with trying the 'Rockites' through the normal courts. The usual assizes only took place twice a year, and it was impractical to keep those suspected of crimes imprisoned for so long. Thus they were often released and free to abscond or intimidate witnesses. There was also a further problem with witnesses. Often they were unwilling to give evidence in the first place. Even if initially wiling they were often 'encouraged' to change their minds by the time the trial came. An example of this is the court case involving the Hassett sisters. Catherine Hassett had agreed to give evidence against some 'Rockites'. Her sister Ellen had been 'encouraged' to contradict her evidence, and when she refused she was raped in February 1822 outside the farmhouse of her employer. What made the court case remarkable was that her employers, the Neligans, contradicted the evidence and claimed that she had not been raped, nor had she been outside their house at that time, nor had she been coerced to give evidence against her sister. In short such were the Neligans fear of reprisals against themselves and their property that they committed perjury, despite the strong evidence supporting Ellen's story. The jury believed Ellen and three men were convicted. Indeed it seems they dismissed

---

4   NAM: 8303–105 Gough papers, 19 March 1823.
5   Donnelly, *Captain Rock*, pp. 144–145
6   Technically the crime of abduction could carry the death penalty, whereas rape could not. Indeed seven men were condemned to death for the abduction of Honora Goold but sentence was never carried out. Donnelly, *Captain Rock*, p. 186.

the Neligans evidence out of hand. The Neligans were fortunate not to be prosecuted for perjury, which carried the penalty of transportation. However such was the pressure placed upon such witnesses that the possibility transportation was perceived as the lesser of two evils.[7] This goes to demonstrate the problems that Gough and others like him had in even getting 'victims' to admit a crime had taken place let alone give evidence.

The problems of intimidation, corruption, and a slow legal process, meant that new legislation was needed. The Insurrection Act of 1822 was designed to make it easier to secure a prosecution under the difficult circumstances concerning witnesses, coercion, and the inefficient court system. Although originally intended to run for eight months to deal with the initial outbreak of violence, it was continually extended and was not finally repealed until 1825. In many ways it placed the areas affected under martial law. A curfew from sunset to sunrise was put in place, with the maximum penalty for breaking it being transportation to a penal colony for seven years. Although the hangings under the Insurrection Act received the most attention the large majority of offences were punishable by transportation, including threatening behaviour, coercion, illegal oaths, illegal assemblies, and unlawful possession of firearms. The Act removed the right to trial by jury, replacing it with a bench of magistrates. The magistrates only had to give a majority verdict. Many of the traditional values of justice remained, with defence and prosecution council; there was still the right to cross examination when witnesses appeared in person. However, given the intimidation, and indeed murdering of witnesses before trial, written evidence was allowed to be presented to the court. Courts also met to deal with cases as they arose rather than the six monthly assizes courts. The Insurrection Act was only enacted in certain counties or baronies by the Lord Lieutenant, and never covered the whole of Munster let alone Ireland.[8]

---

7   Donnelly, *Captain Rock*, pp. 295–297.
8   Donnelly, *Captain Rock*, pp. 303–314, discusses the provisions, implementation and usefulness of the Insurrection Act of 1822.

21

Protection and Reaction

The inability to protect landowners was a problem for the army. Gough was certainly one of the more active commanders during this period and dispersed his men as widely as he could. The problem was that by the time the nearest troops responded to an attack it was usually over and the rebels had withdrawn to safety. This was exacerbated by the lack of local intelligence, and the lack of mobility. It was therefore understandable that landowners would sometimes turn a blind eye to atrocities against their estate. Thus it was not surprising that such burnings became common place for a time, to an extent that in April 1823 Gough recorded that such incidents were inevitable under the present system.[1]

Gough deployed the 22nd in what today would be referred to as a counterinsurgency operation. This meant deploying small detachments of his battalion throughout the area around Buttevant in County Cork. His responsibility was the area of County Cork north of the River Blackwater, or Munster Blackwater as it is also known. Given his seniority Gough not only commanded the 22nd but all the British troops in the area. His main responsibility was for regular troops: technically his control of militia units was questionable, but due to the nature of events in Ireland his orders to militia troops were never questioned. At times Gough commanded a considerable force. In 1823 he had under his command the 22nd, the 11th, and 40th Foot, along with the 6th Dragoon Guards and the 3rd Light Dragoons. At other times both the 57th Foot and the 42nd Highlanders were also under his command.

Gough's own battalion was split into small detachments and spread over quite a large area. He was able to ensure that each detachment, at a strength of between 25 and 30 men, was commanded by two officers and two sergeants. For example in early July 1822 he had nine detachments in nine separate towns and villages in the area around Buttevant. In Newmarket he had 60 men, and in Kanturk 40 men. The remaining detachments consisted of three of 30 men, and four of 25 men.[2] There were also eight similar sized detachments made up of soldiers of the 40th Foot placed in eight different towns and villages in the area, that were also under Gough's overall command. The remainder of the 22nd were held under Gough's command in Buttevant to act as a mobile reserve to support each detachment if trouble should occur.

Although that was the theory, it was often difficult to put into practice, and often the garrison detachments were on their own. For example early in 1822 the 'Rockites', or 'Whiteboys', launched an attack on Newmarket, about 15 miles to the west of Buttevant. It was later claimed that some 3,000 such rebels attempted to attack the town and were forced back by 30 men of the 22nd Foot, who inflicted severe loss on the enemy. The two officers commanding, Captain Keappock and Lieutenant Green, received the thanks of the commander-in-chief, and were presented with

---

1   NAI: SCOP 1, 2512/5, Gough to Major John Finch 11 April 1823.
2   NAM: 8303–105, Gough Papers, hand written lists of the deployment of the 22nd and 40th Foot, dated 1 July 1822.

a silver cup by the inhabitants of the town.[3] However by the time reinforcements arrived, the rebels had dispersed. In this sense it was vital that the technological superiority of the British soldiers remained in force: this simply being that they were armed with reasonably modern muskets whereas what few firearms the rebels had were extremely dated and in poor condition. Although consistently outnumbered, the British had the advantage of firepower and discipline.

Indeed as time went on many of the attacks on property were aimed at capturing firearms. Gough points to several incidents where the 'Rockites' ignored the family silver and just stole firearms and ammunition. Whilst the silver would have allowed them to buy such weapons, both the purchasing of weapons, and the selling of silver, were far more difficult exercises.[4] Gough spent much time making sure that local landowners made sure their weapons were secure against such attacks. A lot of the protection money that was collected by the 'Rockites' from farmers who feared attack was used to purchase weapons, gunpowder, or bullets. The 'Rockites' also improvised weapons, making good use of farm implements. At other times they made their own, or where possible bought professionally made ones. The latter was difficult due to tight regulations. Attempting to make them was not as difficult as might be thought: rudimentary weapons, such as 'polearms', could be made quite easily, but metal was hard to come by, especially lead. Supplies of this were found by stripping the roofs of churches, preferably Protestant ones, and public buildings. In one incident that was extremely embarrassing to the Army lead was stripped from the roof of the artillery barracks in Limerick.[5]

Over time the British gained some support amongst the local population, not confined to the gentry by any means. In this the attitude of Gough helped by demonstrating genuine concern for the local population. Indeed it is clear that he was extremely approachable. To this end it also helped that Gough was not only the military commander but also a local magistrate. Such an attitude helped in the winning of hearts and minds. As is so often the case in any insurgency, it was the poorest who suffered most. In the pursuit of their aims the 'Rockites' often inadvertently destroyed the livelihood of those whose cause they championed. On at least one occasion the attacks by the insurgents left such devastation and hunger in their wake that Gough ordered that emergency supplies of food to be brought in from Dublin and distributed amongst the poor.[6] Whilst to Gough this would have been an act of paternalistic concern or Christian care, the modern commander would recognise it as an act attempting to win over 'hearts and minds'. It is one of those strange occurrences that often happen in such insurgencies where the fighter for 'freedom' commits acts against the oppressor that lead to such a humanitarian crisis that the 'oppressors' acts in the role of kind guardian against those they are accused of oppressing. This helps to demonstrate the difficult and confusing nature of an insurgency style conflict that modern military commanders will appreciate as much as Gough and his men did.

For the first 18 months or so of the 22nd's deployment to Ireland, they acted largely on the defensive. The detachments occupied villages and towns and would provide escorts to those who required it, such as land agents, revenue men, or prominent landowners.[7] However, commencing in 1823, Gough attempted to be proactive and sought to engage the insurgents. He had sensibly taken

---

3   Unfortunately little record remains of this event and the only one we have is that of the Cannon, Richard, *Historical Record of the 22nd Foot* (London: Parker, Furnivall and Parker, 1849), pp. 25–26.

4   NAM: 8303–105, Gough Papers, Gough to Lt. Col. Scovell, 31 October 1822. Although no Christian name is given by Gough it is likely that this was Henry Scovell, the younger brother of George Scovell the famous code breaker and intelligence officer of Peninsular War fame.

5   Donnelly, *Captain Rock*, p. 283.

6   NAM: 8303–105, Gough Papers, Gough statement, 22 June 1822.

7   NAM: 8303–105, Gough Papers, Gough to Lt. Col. Scovell, 31 June 1822. Through this and other letters it is clear that Gough himself used to regularly accompany the local magistrates.

time to get used to the area and appreciate the circumstances of his locality. This action was also prompted by a number of "outrages", as Gough called them in his letters, against local landowners, that had occurred in the latter part of 1822. By the end of June 1822 Gough had prepared a report, an assessment of the situation in his area of responsibility, on the nature of the insurrection. He was aware of where much of the trouble was coming from, but the insurgents were taking advantage of the geography. For instance, in the report Gough records a gang who are operating in the area between Churchtown and Newtown (Newtownshandrum), not far from Dromina. He knew that the gang consisted of only seven men. They were making hit and run raids on local farms and their local knowledge made them difficult to deal with. They were hiding in the Charleville Forrest and in the area known as the Red Bog. It was dangerous, to say the least, for anyone to attempt to follow them in without similar local knowledge.[8]

Gough's report contains accounts of various acts of vandalism and destruction such as the burning of wheat stacks, the burning of cow sheds, and the stealing of farm equipment, some of which was also being used as improvised weaponry. Gough estimated that in the month of September 1822 this amounted to £1,000 worth of damage (over £42,000 in modern money).[9] Towards the end of that year a number of kidnappings and attempted kidnappings took place. Although such attempts had occurred before during the insurgency, this was the first experience that Gough had of it. The targets were usually landowners or officials, and the attempt was to prevent tithes and taxes from being collected. Kidnapping was far from the only violence meted out to individuals by the insurgents. The most recent work on this subject records that during 1822 to 1824 over 93 people were murdered by the 'rebels' in the southern counties, the majority in County Cork.[10] There were also over 1,000 beatings and often many of the arson attacks trapped innocent victims who perished in the blaze. Given the impact that this had on society it is perhaps not surprising that during the 1820s over 50,000 people left Ireland on an assisted immigration scheme to Canada alone.

Although Gough continued to attempt to make it difficult for the 'Rockites' to operate in the area, there was only so much he could do in this regard. Whilst attempting to protect property there was little he could do to attack the rebels. The latter was also problematic due to the lack of informers and local intelligence. It was ultimately the latter that would bring the insurgency down. As time went on there was greater success in gaining informers. This was not simply achieved by the winning of 'hearts and minds'. Indeed it owed much to the Insurrection Act which made it harder for the 'Rockites' to operate. The punishment of transportation or being sent to a convict ship helped to reduce the 'Rockites' effectiveness. It should not be thought that such punishment was merely directed at the poor, or those directly involved in violence. Indeed two apparently-respectable farmers were sent to a prison ship after being caught out after curfew. It became clear that their reasons for being out were unscrupulous and that they were guilty of hiding a crop of corn. The suspicion was that they were carrying out the previously mentioned practice of burning hay and claiming compensation for all their crops.[11] There were also other 'respectable' farmers, gentry, and indeed a headmaster who were similarly punished for being party to 'Rockite' conspiracies. This 'rough justice', as one historian has called it, was an important factor in tightening the screw on the 'Rockites'. Under these circumstances it was far easier to turn informers against their former co-conspirators. Transportation was to many a particularly unpopular punishment and as a consequence it was used more frequently by the authorities. Surprisingly it was found to have a

8   NAM: 8303–105, Gough Papers, Gough to Lt. Col. Scovell, 31 June 1822.
9   NAM: 8303–105, Gough Papers, Gough to Lt. Col. Scovell, 15 September 1822.
10   Donnelly, *Captain Rock*, p. 253.
11   Donnelly, *Captain Rock*, pp. 163–164.

greater deterrent effect than hanging. There were also cases of individuals who after being sentenced to transportation were prepared to turn King's Evidence in return for a pardon.[12]

Hanging had its place, and was the ultimate punishment for 'Rockite' crimes. However the deterrent value was not what the authorities had hoped for. Even when the condemned were persuaded to give a final speech on the gallows repenting and urging others not to commit the same errors, the results were often not what was hoped for. When John Hickey gave an impassioned speech on the scaffold of that nature Gough recorded that he believed it would have a profound effect on those who heard it. The problem was that because Hickey had urged people to surrender their arms whilst in jail, through the auspices of a Priest from Doneraile, only around 80 people attended his execution. For a 'Rockite' execution this was remarkable small as often large crowds of thousands were seen. Thus Hickey's execution did little good for the authorities by way of deterrent. This was because he was perceived as an informer for urging his confederates to surrender their arms. In actuality Hickey had rejected offers of clemency as they were conditional upon him naming his confederates.[13]

The use of such informants could be a two-edged sword. It was not unknown for juries or magistrates to dismiss such evidence as being unreliable. However on the whole a great deal of use was made of such informants. The one that most concerns us is David Nagle, one of the men to bear the name of 'Captain Rock'. Exactly how he was captured is unclear but it is likely that the 22nd had some role in this. In an incident around Buttevant in early February 1823 a party of the 22nd led by Gough in person engaged with some 20 'Rockites'. After a brief fight they ran away however the 22nd did capture one man, a certain Philip Nagle. Exactly who he was and whether or not he was related to David Nagle we do not know. However it is possible that Philip Nagle led Gough to David Nagle. It is clear that David Nagle was somehow betrayed and once captured in July 1823 he was persuaded to turn King's Evidence. Gough's evidence suggests that this was achieved rather easily, but that may just be propaganda. However there is a letter written by Nagle to Gough from prison that seems to shed some light on events. The letter commences by thanking Gough for intervention which has saved him from the death penalty. This was clearly in return for cooperation and Nagle promises further assistance if he can be spared transportation.[14]

Gough was certainly fully aware of the prize they had and used Nagle's capture and 'cooperation' to good effect. Gough even went so far as to parade him through his former haunts under military escort. The effect on the morale of the 'Rockites', witnessing one of their former leaders acting in collusion with the authorities, can be imagined. Gough recorded that the action had more tangible results. Arms were surrendered and many came forward acknowledging their criminal action and claiming, for the most part, that they had been forced into such behaviour. Of those who remained loyal to the cause, Gough claimed that there had been a noticeable sense of disillusionment and that there work was visibly disorganised now, "that all their proceedings have been disclosed, so much so that most respectable [people] – respectable from their situations – have come forward and

---

12 Donnelly, *Captain Rock*, pp. 309–312, specifically deals with the issue of transportation both from the point of view of the public and the authorities. Donnelly gives evidence that is contradictory and suggests transportation was both feared by some and considered a light punishment by others. However the authorities clearly believed that the former was the case, and the sentence became the main course of action. After the sentence of transportation had been made, the individual had the right of appeal to the Lord Lieutenant. Such an appeal had greater chance of success if the individual in question had 'cooperated' with the authorities.

13 NAM: 8303–105, Gough Papers, 'Hand written statement of the last words of John Hickey, April 1823'. Gough kept this amongst his private papers. See also Donnelly, *Captain Rock*, p. 319, & NAM: 8303–105, Gough Papers, 'Report by Colonel Gough', 19 March 1823.

14 NAM: 8303–105, Gough Papers, 'Letter from David Nagle to Gough' undated but likely written in June or July 1823.

acknowledged the part they acted or, as they say, were obliged to act, and the correctness of David Nagle's information."[15]

Amongst the papers of Hugh Gough for this period, we find an interesting letter from Major J. Finch, the military secretary of the Commander-in-Chief, Ireland, Lord Combermere, written in August 1823. This is in response to a letter from Gough and mentions some of Nagle's evidence. What stands out is that Nagle has implicated, without naming, a British officer of colluding with the 'Rockites'. Finch seems to have presumed that this was a serving officer, although a later comment by Gough suggests that it might be a retired officer or one on half-pay. Obviously details are light for reasons of security, and little of this continued correspondence survives. Indeed what we have are snippets in letters that largely deal with other matters. Finch, in a letter that is extremely hard to read, states that:

> I am directed by Lieutenant General Lord Combermere to request you will be pleased to endeavour to ascertain more circumstantially all the information you can possibly collect from Nagle, respecting the officer he represents to be connected with the disturbances, especially his name, the Regiment he belongs to, his connexions [connections], where they reside … and if possible where he is likely to be found or any other circumstances that may throw light on the subject.[16]

Sadly there are few details regarding this incident, and for obvious reasons of security and also prestige the matter was not publicised. It does go to demonstrate once again the confused nature of the situation that Gough found himself in. On both sides it became difficult to know who to trust.

Gough seems also to have obtained for himself a useful spy. There are a series of letters which survive in Gough's papers from an anonymous informant. These begin in March 1823. Exactly how he obtained this source is unclear, but the fact that he wrote to Gough personally strongly suggests that he was 'his man' rather than a general intelligence source. The identity of this informer is unknown and we do not know whether he was a former 'Rockite' cooperating to avoid prosecution or if he had purer motives. The tone of the letters might suggest the latter, but we do not know.[17] What we do know is that he was able to provide Gough with valuable information regarding the movements of the 'Rockites', or 'incendiaries' as he called them. He was able to pass on details of hideouts, secret meetings and names of people involved. This individual also kept Gough informed in regards to the conduct of his officers and men. Indeed one letter laments the conduct of one detachment of officers and men who according to the informant spent their time "laying at ease drinking wine and tea with their neighbour ladies and suffering the incendiaries to blast the country."[18] Perhaps the fact that the informer also felt able to comment on the actions of soldiers suggests that he was more than simply a former 'Rockite'.

Late 1823 appears to have been the turning point in the fight against the 'Rockites'. The use of former 'Rockites' like Dillane, Dundon, and of course Nagle, as informants no doubt had a great impact. It created distrust and disheartened those still loyal to the cause. This in turn provided good intelligence for the authorities and enabled them to be more effective. In late 1823 Gough records

15   Donnelly, *Captain Rock*, pp. 164–165. This a quotation from a letter written by Gough to William Gregory dated 22 May 1824.
16   NAM: 8303–105, Gough Papers, Maj. Finch to Gough, 25th August 1823.
17   NAM: 8303–105, Gough Papers, informant's letter of 8 March 1823. The latter is the date of the first letter from this informant that survives amongst the Gough papers.
18   NAM: 8303–105, Gough Papers, informant's letter of 19 March 1823.

an increased success in capturing weapons, or in many cases recapturing them.[19] The dramatic reduction in offences committed under the Insurrection Act was such that by July 1824 no one was being held under its provisions. Such was the confidence of the authorities that the worse had passed that in August of that year the Insurrection Act was lifted in most of the country. There were still some who wanted to maintain it indefinitely as an aid to better controlling the local population, but Gough was certainly not one of them and he was delighted that the Act was lifted.[20]

The decline of the 'Rockites' had not simply been due to the increased efficiency of the courts, intelligence, the police and the Army. The external factors of economic improvement and large-scale migration also helped to quell disillusionment. Gough had clearly played a part in the 'defeat' of the 'Rockites'. In late 1823, largely due to the delight at the turning of Nagle, the Lord Lieutenant of Ireland, the Marquess Wellesley, had his Secretary write to Gough that "I am commanded by his Excellency to express his approbation and thanks for your exertions." The tone of this letter makes it clear that this was for the wider efforts he had made rather than simply the capture of Nagle.[21]

Indeed, Gough had been extremely active. As always he had been prepared to take the lead and had placed himself at the head of his troops whenever possible. One instance of this is on 7 February 1823 when he personally led a detachment of the 22nd in a brief action against some 20 'Rockites' in the hills around Buttevant. Gough himself is recorded as challenging them to stand and then ordering the charge, no doubt leading from the front.[22] At the same time as being a military commander Gough was also a local magistrate and this gave him extra authority and made his movement throughout the country more than simple adventuring. He was also known to accompany other magistrates as protection, and there does seem to be the suggestion that the mere presence of the red coat was sufficient to prevent an attack under some circumstances. What lasting effect Gough's service in Ireland had upon his reputation is difficult to estimate. This is largely because the period in question has been so little researched. Had he been fighting the 'Whiteboys' a generation before, or dealing with the land war a generation later, the impact that Gough's service had on his career would be easier to judge. However we do know that his employment seems to have remained in the memory of some. In 1886 when Major General Redvers Buller's deployment to Ireland was debated in the House of Commons, mention was made of the successful deployment of Gough in a combined magistrate and soldier role; or civil and military role. Although long since forgotten, his work had clearly had some impact on the contemporary mind.[23]

---

19   NAM: 8303–105, Gough Papers, 'Returns for Weapons taken from 'insurgents' by 22nd Regiment between 23rd Nov 1821 and 4th October 1824'.
20   Donnelly, *Captain Rock*, pp. 323–324. In July 1824 the Act was lifted in the whole of County Kerry and Northern County Limerick. In August it was lifted in King's County. Yet it was not until 1825 that it was finally repealed.
21   NAM: 8303–105, Gough Papers, William Gregory to Gough, 25 August 1823.
22   NAM: 8303–105, Gough Papers, 'Report by Colonel Gough dated February 1823'.
23   Rait, *Gough*, Vol. I, p. 139. This was during some quite excitable debates in the House of Commons over the instructions and actions of Buller. Whilst this might not have placed Gough in the best possible light it does show that the work he had done had been remembered and appreciated at least by officials.

Leadership of the 22nd and a Court of Enquiry

The 22nd remained in the southern part of Ireland until October 1824. By this time there was little more than the usual rate of crime in the area, and what problems remained could be handled by the local police. Thus the battalion was redeployed to Dublin. It had been a difficult few years fighting the insurgency for Gough. Whilst many of his men had simply been placed in various village and town garrison where they conducted the occasional patrol and never saw sight of a 'Rockite', this had not been the case for Gough. He had actively been involved, not only in the command of the 22nd and the other troops in the area, but with policing, intelligence, local government, and the law.

His fellow magistrates sent him a collective letter in which they stated that:

> We gratefully acknowledge that through your Prudence, Zeal, Activity, and Example, have we been enabled hitherto to avert those evils which were impending over us. In you, Sir, have we seen combined the prudent foresight of the commander, the upright spirit of the magistrate, (and) the humane heart and courteous demeanour of the gentleman.[1]

Similar thoughts were expressed at a meeting in Mallow in October 1824. In a farewell address to Gough at a meeting of magistrates, noblemen, and landowners the president of the meeting Viscount Doneraile stated that:

> On your first appointment to the command of this district, you were placed in a situation, arduous and critical, a situation which required the most active and increasing energy, joined to the most cool and deliberate judgement, and never was the union of these rare and essential qualifications more fully and uniformly exemplified, than in your conduct on every occasion, whilst every evil passion of a misguided and infatuated population was let loose in the land, while the murderer and incendiary were destroying the lives and properties of innocent, unsuspecting and defenceless families, while social order and security were shaken to their very foundation, your persevering activity and judicious arrangements interposed a barrier against miscreant outrage.[2]

Whilst allowing for the somewhat colourful prose, and the slightly offensive and biased language of the tribute, it does illustrate that once again Gough had proved sufficient for the task presented to him.

This period in Gough's career, though quite minor in the grand scheme of his life, does give us an insight into another side of Gough. It shows his ability and tact in a difficult situation, and

---

1   Rait, *Gough*, Vol. I, p. 140.
2   Rait, *Gough*, Vol. I, p. 141.

his ability to show kindness and firmness in juxtaposition where needed. They are not necessarily character traits for which he is remembered. So by examining this little known period of his career it is hoped that we have helped to not only widen our understanding of his life but also the man.

For the next two years the 22nd remained in Ireland. At some point during this period they left Dublin and were stationed in Galway for a time. In August 1826 Gough's command of the 22nd came to an end. Six companies of the 22nd were to be sent to the West Indies, and Gough chose not to accompany them. This was partly due to family commitments, which largely revolved around his wife's ill health. No doubt Gough was also reminded of the years he had spent in the West Indies as a young man, and the effect it had on his health. There was also the fact that the 22nd was destined to be little more than garrison troops, and a long spell in a distant garrison, in conditions not conducive to good health, was not an attractive prospect to a 46-year-old family man. So as a consequence Gough's time with the 22nd came to an end. He had led them through some difficult service. Garrison duty in Ireland was never easy at the best of times, and the past five years had certainly not been the best of times. Yet there is no record of the battalion losing its discipline or any record of any crimes or outrages committed by the men. Once again discipline seems to have been high, despite the suggestion by Gough's spy that some of his officers and men were perhaps over-indulging in drinking and womanising during their garrison duties. This perhaps spoke more to their boredom rather than ill discipline, as, if true, there is no evidence to suggest that it affected the performance of their duty. Indeed, more often than not it was simply the presence of the redcoats that was required as a deterrent. There are only a handful of recorded incidents during this period where the troops actually had to fire on any enemy.

Gough had reintroduced a system of regimental good conduct awards. Originally introduced into the 22nd in 1785, such a system had fallen out of use in the years since the end of the Napoleonic Wars. Indeed it was something of a rarity for such a system to be used in peacetime, until the introduction of a service-wide good conduct medal in 1830. Lady Gough seems to have played a part in its reintroduction, for we know that the badge awarded to soldiers who were eligible was designed and stitched by her.[3]

On the whole Gough appeared to have left a good impression on the 22nd when he left. However there was to be some unfinished business connected with Gough's time commanding the battalion. In December 1828 a court of enquiry was held at Limerick to look into financial irregularities in the accounts of the 22nd Regiment. The President of the Court was Major General Sir Edward Blakeney, later to become Commander-in-Chief, Ireland in 1836. However the findings of the Court were issued in the name of Major General Sir Fitzroy Somerset, better known to history as Lord Raglan of the Crimean War, who was military secretary at the Horse Guards in London. The main concern of the court was in regards to incorrect dates of enlistment being given for some of the men. Given that the regiment had been overseas for many years and had seen many men released from its service and others join the regiment during that period, there is some mitigation for the irregularities in the accounting system.[4]

The problems appear to have come to light because some of the former soldiers with incorrect dates of enlistment were at the Royal Hospital, Chelsea. Exactly when this matter came to light is unclear, but it was discovered that the ages of the soldiers and their supposed length of service did not tally up. For example it was calculated that for Private Joseph Vaughan to have served for the time that his discharge claimed, he would have had to have joined the 22nd Regiment when he was

---

3   Rait, *Gough*, Vol. I, pp. 141–142.
4   The Report of the Court of Enquiry is found amongst the Gough Papers at the National Army Museum. NAM: 8303–105, 'Report of Court of Enquiry held at Limerick from December 1828 to January 1829', 26 October 1829.

six years and 11 months old! In some cases the discrepancy of service being claimed was an extra year or two. However in the case of Private John Quick he was receiving a pension based on eight years more than he was entitled to. At the same time there were found to be further discrepancies in the length of service that had been done at various ranks, for example Sergeant Church was paid two years extra pension at the rate for a corporal and one year extra for the rank of sergeant.[5]

There also appears to have been more than simply falsifying enlistment records. A wider practice of submitting what the court of enquiry called "false bills" appears to have taken place. An example of this was for the varnishing of muskets that was done 'in house', but was estimated to have been incorrectly claimed to the tune of £117–9–2. There were also repairs to barracks that never took place, and various other services that suggest someone in the regiment had come to an arrangement with local merchants and tradesmen to charge more than the actual cost and split the surplus between them. There was also a suggestion that the regiment had overcharged for oil and fuel but this could not be proved. The question that the Court of Enquiry never really got to the bottom of was who was responsible for this and all the other fraudulent behaviour. However the Court of Enquiry criticised the arrangements within the regiment.

Many suspects were put forward. One gets a strong impression from reading the findings of the Court of Enquiry that they were confident that the acting second in command of the regiment, Major Jasper Craster, had been a party to much of what went on. However there was little that the Court of Enquiry could prove. Sir Edward Blakeney adds to the suspicion surrounding Major Craster by defending all the other officers involved, including Gough but excluding Craster, in a hand written amendment to the Report of the Court of Enquiry. What role Craster had in the corruption is unclear, however given that during this period Gough was actively involved in a hands-on capacity with fighting the insurgency in Ireland he understandably delegated much of the day to day business of the regiment to others.

Unsurprisingly the adjutant, Captain Thomas Edwards, also received much criticism from the enquiry. However he chose to blame his assistant Sergeant Church. Indeed somewhat unsurprisingly there does appear to have been a tendency on the part of the Court of Enquiry to lay most of the blame at the door of the NCOs rather than the officers. However, passing the buck was not confined to the officer class. Indeed Sergeant Church had laid the blame on Private John Duckworth. Duckworth, a duty room clerk, had been asked to make out the account book due to his having 'good' handwriting, which in itself is somewhat surprising for an enlisted man of this era. Edwards seemed to suggest that what he told Church was altered or misunderstood and therefore incorrectly entered in the book by Duckworth. This seems a rather poor excuse and one which the Court of Enquiry dismissed. Whilst stating that Edwards and Church were considered good men the enquiry concluded that "Private Duckworth, who was employed on the books on account of his writing well, was not a man of good character."[6] Although the enquiry gives no reason for this, it is interesting to note that Duckworth was one of the men who had benefited from a false date of engagement with two years and seven months more service to his credit than was correct. Yet one cannot help but wonder if the only reason much of the blame stuck to Duckworth was because he was a private and thus could not pass the buck further down the line.

The other officer to be criticised, and who was perhaps one of the main culprits when it came to creative accounting, was Quartermaster William Mansfield. Of Mansfield, the enquiry concluded that although he had given many years of good service to the regiment, "It is however clear that he procured false bills and signed certificates in the pay lists which he must have been well aware were

5   NAM: 8303–105, Gough Papers, 'Court of Enquiry', 26 October 1829.
6   NAM: 8303–105, Gough Papers, 'Court of Enquiry', 26 October 1829.

not founded on fact."[7] Indeed there does seem to be a certain 'creativity' to Mansfield's approach to his work that no doubt came from the time spent during the war and overseas when such methods were ignored. There is a quite damning letter amongst Gough's papers where Mansfield suggests such 'creative accounting'. He recommends moving payment of the "varnishing of fire-locks [muskets]" from one year to another in the accounts. A postscript to this letter suggests that Mansfield, and possibly even Gough, were party to the practice of falsifying discharge lists. The problem we have when making such judgements is that this letter is the only one surviving of what is clearly continued correspondence. It could possibly be taken out of context, as one does not know what went before. There is however a troubling phrase, used by Mansfield, when alluding to the moving of payment between the years in the accounting process, when he states that this will be possible, "if the return you [Gough] have has not been seen by any one." Although far from conclusive this does suggest a level of duplicity and secrecy, at least on Mansfield's part. We do not know what reply Gough gave to this letter.[8]

Exactly what part Gough played in the events is difficult to say. Whilst somewhat critical of him, the Court of Enquiry did not conclude that there had been any deliberate wrong doing on his part. The closest he came to indulging in the irregularities himself was in the case of Private James Lowe. Major Craster, whose judgment might not have been the best, called Private Lowe a man of "infamous character." There does appear to be some truth to this judgement as Lowe had been sentenced to 500 lashes and then to be drummed out of the regiment. However Gough, in what appears to be an act of compassion, gave him a blank discharge rather than a dishonourable one.[9]

We do not know all the details of the case but Gough had clearly exceeded his authority, albeit with perhaps the best of motives hoping that a blank rather than dishonourable discharge might give Lowe a second chance, and enable him to keep the pension for his 18 years' service. This would be consistent with Gough's behaviour to his men and was not the first or the last time that his care for the men under his command led him to flout regulations. In the case of Lowe, Gough had received a rebuke from the Adjutant General and had been forced to issue a dishonourable discharge. However this was a fairly minor matter and, as a one off, had not caused any great concern. It was the wider issue of incorrect dates of enlistment and false bills done over a long period of time that was considered the real problem by the Court of Enquiry.

There were far greater concerns than one act of possibly misguided kindness. In short Gough's biggest sin in the eyes of the Court of Enquiry had been to sign incorrect documents. It was generally considered that his fault had been to place trust in officers who were not deserving of such confidence. In Gough's defence it has to be stated, as indeed the Court of Enquiry did, that the corruption and forgeries had been going on for many years before Gough joined the regiment and indeed continued after he gave up command. However the Court of Enquiry did not absolve him of blame in this regard:

> The returns annexed to the report of the Court of Enquiry details the particulars of the above cases and contains the strongest proof that a corrupt system in the forgery of service has extensively prevailed for a long period of years in the 22nd Regiment which can only be imputed to the gross and culpable neglect of those whose duty it was to inspect and preserve the Regimental records ... this Regiment exhibits an unusual and flagrant instance of the

---

7   NAM: 8303–105, Gough Papers, 'Court of Enquiry', 26 October 1829.
8   NAM: 8303–105, Gough Papers, William Mansfield to Gough, 25 December 1825.
9   NAM: 8303–105, Gough Papers, 'Court of Enquiry', 26 October 1829.

injury resulting to the public service by the disgraceful laxity with which the Regimental records have been kept.[10]

In a sense Gough was the ultimate authority in this regard. Regimental records were not commonly seen outside the Regiment at this stage and so he was the highest ranking officer responsible. To an extent the enquiry concluded that the 'buck' ultimately had to stop with him. In their summing up they said as much:

> The Court of Enquiry has not pointed out the name of any individual officer to whose neglect of duty these irregularities appear to be wholly or impart attributable, but, however painful it is the duty of the General Commanding in Chief to state that Lieutenant-Colonel Sir Hugh Gough has signed the major part of the erroneous discharges. He commanded the regiment from 1819 to 1826 and must be called upon for explanation which he has not yet had the opportunity of giving.[11]

The cost for the 'errors' was large, amounting to £1,125 (over £55,000 in modern money).[12] Although in the great scheme of things this might not appear to be a huge amount it is important to remember that the total amount would have continued to grow if the irregularities in the pension entitlements of former soldiers had not been discovered. Indeed, the Court of Enquiry calculated that the annual cost to the public purse just of the incorrect payment of pensions was £265 a year (over £13,000 in modern money). It is also important to point out that this was only what the Court of Enquiry was able to prove. There was a great deal that the court suspected as regards further fraudulent behaviour. The Court of Enquiry held Gough responsible for much of this, given that it was ultimately his signature which had allowed such expenditure. The Enquiry concluded that:

> [T]he amount should be required to be refunded to the public account, and that Sir Hugh Gough should be called upon for repayment unless he can justify the expenditure, and that he should also be called upon to explain why he issued orders at variance with His Majesty's Regulations and signed certificates in the paylists, which are proved not to be founded on facts.[13]

In short Gough was blamed for allowing the practice to take place rather than actually being accused of taking part in the fraudulent behaviour. Ultimately Gough deserves criticism for the fact that he signed fraudulent documents. Gough himself felt that this was a little harsh. He put forward the case that many of the alterations, and much of the corruption, had commenced before his tenure of command. He also considered that, given this, it would have been difficult for him to have uncovered such errors without a thorough investigation. In fairness it must be stated that it had taken a formal Court of Enquiry to uncover the full extent. If Gough had ever had any suspicions he had either not been confident enough, or had not had enough time, to take any action.

There were a number of people who defended Gough at this time. Sir Henry Hardinge, a name we will hear more of later in our narrative, was one such man. In 1830 Hardinge, who was then serving as Secretary of State at War in the Government of the Duke of Wellington, wrote to Fitzroy Somerset in defence of Gough declaring his, "conviction of the perfect integrity of purpose

10   NAM: 8303–105, Gough Papers, 'Court of Enquiry', 26 October 1829.
11   NAM: 8303–105, Gough Papers, 'Court of Enquiry', 26 October 1829.
12   NAM: 8303–105, Gough Papers, Sir Henry Hardinge to Lord Hill, 17 June 1830. This is where the figure of £1,250 comes from.
13   NAM: 8303–105, Gough Papers, 'Court of Enquiry', 26 October 1829.

of an officer of such high character."[14] In short Hardinge was stating his belief that anything Gough had done had been an error of judgement rather than deliberate deception. In a letter to Lord Hill, Hardinge placed most of the blame on the adjutant, Captain Edwards, stating that, "I must necessarily conclude, that the principal share of blame for neglect of duty, and want of command vigilance in allowing these irregularities in the orderly room is principally to that officer."[15] Hardinge gave mitigation pointing out that the alterations and forgeries had taken place before Gough had taken command and, "they were so carefully executed as to have escaped ordinary observation."[16] The response would be that Gough might have had due cause to be suspicious and might therefore have been wise to give the books more than "ordinary observation." As mentioned previously, he was obviously aware that Mansfield at least had a rather 'unusual' accounting system. Here however we have the problem that Gough was busy elsewhere. As we have seen, Gough was an extremely active officer whilst in Ireland. He therefore understandably left such work to others. Indeed in an age where far too many senior officers did not have the talent, understanding, or indeed faith to delegate to their subordinates, Gough's approach is, in theory, refreshing.

Gough's fault was to delegate to people who were dishonest, and perhaps his failure to pick up on the fact that there was something amiss is his greatest error in this instance. It also points to something that will occur again later in his career, in that he was not a particularly good judge when it came to his choice of staff. Admittedly in the case of the 22nd he inherited such officers; however he might have chosen to appoint more suitable candidates. However there is an interesting comment from Blakeney, the President of the Court of Enquiry, which suggests that it might not only have been Gough's judgement that was in error. In a letter to Fitzroy Somerset, Blakeney states that:

> The Quarter Master [Mansfield] has been upwards of thirty years in the 22nd Regiment nearly twenty of which I have known him, and always considered him to be particularly honest and correct, and I am confident that Colonel Sir Hugh Gough entertains the same opinion of him as also does Major General Dalrymple who formerly commanded the 22nd Regiment.[17]

If therefore Mansfield was, as the enquiry presided over by Blakeney concluded, guilty of corruption, it was not only Gough whose judgement of the man had been in error. Although it is a little harsh given the circumstances, Gough does deserve some criticism for not spotting that there was something wrong. He should have been in a better position to detect this than Blakeney. However one must also lay some blame at the door of Dalrymple, which surprisingly the enquiry failed to do.

Hardinge took a similar view to Blakeney, and made it quite clear that he believed there was no question of Gough having been party to the irregularities. As Hardinge summed up, in a letter to Fitzroy Somerset:

> Sir Hugh Gough candidly admits his error, and takes on himself the whole responsibility. I should wish to treat his case with every possible moderation, but I feel I cannot, in justice to other officers who have already been made to refund money so misapplied, in cases infinitely less irregular that Sir Hugh Gough's, and establish a precedent in favour of an officer of his

14   NAM: 8303–105, Gough Papers, Hardinge to Somerset, 17 June 1830. In July 1830 Hardinge would be appointed as Chief Secretary for Ireland, so this letter of June 1830 must be one of the last he wrote as Secretary at War. He only held the post in Ireland until November of the same year.
15   NAM: 8303–105, Gough Papers, Sir Henry Hardinge to Lord Hill, 17 June 1830.
16   NAM: 8303–105, Gough Papers, Sir Henry Hardinge to Lord Hill, 17 June 1830.
17   NAM: 8303–105, Sir Edward Blakeney to Fitzroy Somerset, undated but likely written towards the end of the proceedings Court of Enquiry.

rank, by relieving him of the same obligation which has been enforced against other officers of refunding a portion of the cost to the public.[18]

This suggests that Hardinge was prepared to accept the mitigating elements of Gough defence.

He was not alone as the President of the Court of Enquiry, Blakeney, also remarked in a letter written whilst the enquiry was on going that: "I am sure that any enquiry into the conduct of Colonel Sir Hugh Gough, as commanding officer of the 22nd Regiment must rebound in every instance to his credit."[19] Given that Lord Hill, the commander-in-chief, also wrote of his belief that Gough's motivates had been pure, one does wonder where the criticism of the Court of Enquiry actually came from. The simple answer would appear to be Fitzroy Somerset, and that it was at his urging that the Enquiry did not hesitate in allotting some of the blame to Gough. Why is unclear. It may simply be that Somerset felt that Gough, as the senior officer with direct responsibility, had to take his share of the responsibility for what went on. This would be entirely understandable.

The final outcome was that Gough was ordered to repay the amount of £53–14–00, as this was calculated to be the amount accountable for the duration of his command.[20] Given that the total amount which the public were said to have been defrauded of amounted to £1,125, this was a relatively small amount. It also backs up Gough's claim that the irregularities had been going on for many years before and after his tenure of command. What damage this affair did to his reputation is difficult to assess, largely because it was so little known. The Army was obviously keen to keep any example of waste or corruption quiet at a time of cuts to the military budget. Those who have looked at the career of Hugh Gough previously have also failed to make mention. It is in many ways a minor part of his career. Even the extensive biography produced by Sir Robert Rait makes no mention of this Court of Enquiry. Rait skips over Gough's command of the 22nd in a few pages. The large majority of Rait's biography is concerned with India. Cynically, it could be suggested that as his biography is intended primarily as a defence of Gough, the inclusion of such an event might have hurt this intention.

Yet it would be wrong not to acknowledge that it happened, and it did perhaps leave a black mark against Gough's name. It could also be used to question further his administrative abilities and his judgement. To the latter it should be remarked that he was far from the only one, as the irregularities had been going on before he joined the regiment and after he left it. As to his administrative abilities, it is difficult to know exactly what this tells us. It is clear that he had no great interest in such work. He was a 'fighting' soldier rather than a 'writing' soldier. Yet his earlier career shows us that he obviously had ability in this regard. During his time in command of the 87th, things had run relatively smoothly under very difficult circumstances. He had clearly kept a careful eye on things but had largely left the matters to those directly responsible for such matters within the battalion. During the 22nd's time in Ireland, Gough had clearly been occupied elsewhere and had left such matters to others within the regiment, such as the adjutant, quartermaster, and second-in-command. The problem was that, unbeknown to Gough, he did not trust the right people. It is difficult to know exactly what he could have done differently, as it appears the deception was so well carried out. Indeed it took almost 20 years before the authorities found out. Gough had to carry some of the blame because he was the senior officer who signed off on the reports and accounts, yet even the authorities seemed to appreciate that Gough had no blame attached to him other than this.

---

18   NAM: 8303–105, Sir Henry Hardinge to Fitzroy Somerset, 17 June 1830.
19   NAM: 8303–105, Sir Edward Blakeney to Fitzroy Somerset. This letter is undated but obviously written during the proceeding of the Court of Enquiry.
20   NAM: 8303–105, Fitzroy Somerset to Gough, 14 August 1830.

23

In the Wilderness

One cannot help but wonder if the aforementioned Court of Enquiry had any part to play in the fact that for the next 11 years Gough remained on the half-pay list. It does seem strange that one of the most experienced regimental commanders in the army remained unemployed for so long. It is quite possible that the enquiry had no bearing on this whatsoever and that his unemployment had more to do with the lack of a suitable vacancy. Certainly, things were complicated when in July 1830 he was promoted major general. Gough's reputation was that of a fighting commander but as a junior major general he would be at the mercy of the policy of filling vacancies by seniority. He would also be hampered by the perception of him as wartime commander, as indeed this was where his experience lay. This might have had a greater impact on his long absence from active employment, than the verdict of the Court of Enquiry in to the 22nd Regiment.

At only 46 it must have been frustrating to be out of an appointment. He was, as Robert Rait recorded, "in the very prime of life".[1] During this period away from the Army he spent the majority of his time on his estate at Rathronan near Clonmel in County Tipperary. This he had purchased in 1826 with a lease for the remainder of his life and that of his son. Indeed his family had played a key role in him not going with the 22nd to the West Indies, as he knew from experience the risk it would put his health in. Should he die he would leave his family in a difficult state financially. Given such conditions he had no intention of taking his family with him, particularly given the fragile health of his wife for much of this period. Also, having already lost one son he would not have risked the life of his remaining son at such a young age. At the same time, to leave them at home whilst he went overseas alone was not something he contemplated.

His new estate also needed considerable work and his first few years there were busy as he tried to put the estate in good order. Along with the estate came certain responsibilities to the local community and he once again served as a magistrate. One story remains of his time as a magistrate and it bears repeating. He and his fellow magistrates were called to consider the case of a local farmer who had been robbed by a gang, referred to in the story as 'moonlighters', and was now applying for compensation. The major area of debate was around the fact that the farmer had surrendered his gun without firing. This had divided the magistrates with some arguing that he should have fired the shot, some even suggesting the fact that he had not was tantamount to collusion, and others pointing out that had he fired both he had his family would likely have been killed.

It was common on such occasions for Gough to remain quiet, and it is a mark of his character that he only spoke when he felt obliged to. There is also a suggestion that as a relative newcomer to the district he felt slightly uncomfortable in opposing the more experienced magistrates and gentry. However on this occasion he felt compelled to speak and his words speak to the character of the man:

---

1   Rait, *Gough*, Vol. I, p. 143.

I beg pardon for interfering on an occasion like the present, when the regularly resident gentry are so much better able to form a correct judgement than I should be. But if I may presume to give an opinion, I would say that, if I were in that farmer's situation I would have done just what he did; and been, moreover, very much obliged to the midnight gentlemen for letting me off so easily, when such dreadful consequences might have resulted from refusing to comply with their demand. Nor do I think that the man who thus made discretion the better part of valour, would be one whit less brave than the bravest amongst us, on a proper occasion, when his courage could be turned to good account.[2]

Exactly how aware he was of the impact of his words is something we will never know. However Gough must have realised that once he had declared that he would have done the same any suggestion of cowardice on the part of the farmer would evaporate. Equally these were clearly the words of a family man who could appreciate the dilemma the farmer was in. Had it been only their own safety both the farmer and Gough in similar circumstances might have acted in the same way and defended themselves and their property. Gough was able not only to understand the farmer's motivation but willing to publicly defend it. This is yet another glimpse of that more thoughtful and caring side that was occasionally seen during his life.

Whilst he no doubt enjoyed the time with his wife and young family he was anxious to return to his profession. At the commencement of this period of inactivity his family consisted of his eldest daughter Letitia who was 17, his only surviving son, George, who was 10, his second daughter Gertrude who was eight, Jane who was seven, and Frances the youngest who was only a year old. Indeed he was at that period in life when his family was changing as children arrived and elder members of the family passed away. In 1822 he had lost his brother Major William Gough who was drowned when the troop ship he was on board sank. In 1829 his mother had died, and in 1833 his sister Jane, the widow of Lieutenant Colonel Lloyd, died. Then in March 1836 his father died at the age of 85, whilst on a visit to Hugh and his family at their house in Rathronan. The same year a happier event saw the marriage of his eldest daughter Letitia to Mr Edward Supple. The following year his next eldest daughter Gertrude was married to Archibald Arbuthnot, the son of the late Sir William Arbuthnot, 1st Baronet, and erstwhile Lord Provost and Lord Lieutenant of Edinburgh. His son would marry in October 1840 to Sarah Palliser. The marriage was brief as she died the following August, and in 1846 he married Jane Arbuthnot. Hugh Gough's third daughter Jane, called by her family by her middle name of Mona, married in 1840 to Lieutenant Colonel Gregory Haines, the son of a Peninsular War veteran, and brother to the future Field Marshal Sir Frederick Haines. The youngest daughter Frances married in September 1844 to the then Major, later Field Marshal, Sir Patrick Grant. Grant was a widower with two sons. He would have a further four sons and a daughter with Frances.

How active Gough was in the upbringing of his children is unclear however he would have been close at hand to witness some happy moments with his growing family. Given his kindly spirit he no doubt cherished these moments and this experience. At the same time however he would have been anxious to return to duty. To the civilian there is often a misconception of this desire for appointments as the manifestation of a desire for social advancement, power, or simple bloodlust. However it is often little more than a desire to advance in one's chosen profession, something that most people can relate to. As a lawyer may desire to be called to the bar there is a similar desire of a soldier to be called to the front. Whilst this might be an over simplification there is a parallel to be drawn. However with the soldier, particularly in Gough's era, there is also the calling of duty and social responsibility. Gough was born to a military tradition. It is helpful to remember that by 1826

---

2   Rait, *Gough*, Vol. I, p. 149.

he had already worn the King's uniform for over 33 years. Indeed with the exception of his wife and children, the Army really was his life. His father, his siblings, and even his mother and her family, were all in some way connected to Army life.

Gough had hoped that his promotion to major general was a signal that he was in line for some appointment or other. However nothing came. There was little to excite him during this period, even his appointment as Knight Commander of the Order of the Bath in 1831 was merely the fulfilling of a promised advancement in the Order. For service in the Peninsula, Gough had been recommended for KCB by Sir Thomas Picton. At the time he was made a Companion of the Bath, as the Order was in the process of being remodelled. There had been a 'promise' that upon his attaining general rank he would be favourable considered for advancement to Knight Commander of the Order of the Bath.

In one sense it appears that Gough became used to the disappointment of him being given no further employment. However there is no doubt that he was hurt by the events concerning the 87th. In August 1834, Sir John Doyle died and the appointment of colonel of the 87th Regiment fell vacant. Gough understandably felt that he had the best claim to be his successor. Given his achievements with the regiment in the Peninsula there was perhaps no better claimant to the command. However the Army did not work that way and instead the colonelcy was awarded to Major General Sir Thomas Reynell. Reynell had no experience with the 87th, but was undoubtedly an experienced officer having seen considerable service in the West Indies, Flanders, India, and Spain, as well as having the distinction of having served at Waterloo. Most recently he had served in India in the Army of the Bengal Presidency and commanded the 1st Infantry Division. In 1829 he had succeeded his brother as the sixth Reynell Baronet. After that he held no further active appointments other than the colonelcy of the 87th from 1834 to 1841 and then of his old regiment, the 71st, from 1841 to 1848.

The failure to achieve the colonelcy of the 87th was a bitter blow for Gough. Indeed it would have appeared to be the end of his military career. If he were not considered the right man for the colonelcy of the 87th, whose second battalion he had led so gallantly and indeed made his reputation commanding, what future was there for him in the Army? If not that appointment, which he seemed such a logical choice for, what appointment would there be for him? In these circumstances and with these questions going through his mind it is easy to understand why he seriously considered retiring fully from the Army, as Rait suggests was the case.[3] The fact that he chose to remain was perhaps due to two reasons. Firstly, if he was to leave the Army what would he do? A career in politics, or business seemed unlikely, and he was not a large enough landowner to survive on that alone for the remainder of his life. Secondly, there was still the glimmer of hope that he would gain useful employment in the Army at some point in the future.

In 1837 his inactivity came to an end. Somewhat to his own surprise, Gough was offered the command of the Mysore Division of the Madras Army in India. Gough accepted the offer. With what enthusiasm he undertook this is unknown. He was no doubt happy for employment, but India was not his first choice. It meant uprooting his family, and on the face of it there would have appeared little chance of any action. India was relatively quiet in the 1830s. More importantly, the area that the Madras Army was responsible for had little chance of action, and it was rare for troops to serve outside their Presidency. Thus it was not an overly attractive appointment. In one sense, many of the reasons he used for not following the 22nd to the West Indies in 1826 applied to taking up a command in India in 1837. Whether or not it was due to an anxiousness to get her husband's

---

3   Cunliffe, *Royal Irish Fusiliers*, p. 190 & Rait, *Gough*, Vol. I, pp. 143–145.

career back on track or not, it is clear that this time Lady Gough was keen to accompany him. Thus in the autumn of 1837 the Gough family sailed for India.[4]

On the way to India the ship called in at Mauritius. At that time six companies of the 87th Foot were based on Mauritius as its garrison. Gough received a warm and indeed joyous reception from the officers and men of the 87th. The enthusiasm with which they greeted him was no doubt partly influenced by the boredom of life on Mauritius and the excitement at Gough's presence helped provide a momentary lift from this tedious duty. As a historian of the 87th Foot recorded, this points to:

> what might be called the collective memory of the regiment, for not many of those who cheered him could have served under Gough. They knew of him because he had done so much to build up the regimental tradition; in this sense, no one who has served a regiment well, if it be a good one, is ever forgotten by it.[5]

A fellow traveller recorded that Gough

> received a most wonderful ovation from the officers and men of his old regiment, the fighting 87th. During the time the ship lay at the Mauritius, they were in a state of wild excitement. The whole regiment followed him down to the boat, waded into the water, and would even have followed it swimming if they had not been sternly ordered back. The headlands were lined with them, still cheering, and the last we saw of Mauritius was a bonfire with a number of their figures around it.[6]

Given the disappointment of three years previous when he had been ignored for the colonelcy of the regiment, it was no doubt comforting to Gough to know that the officers and men of the battalion had far from forgotten him. This sense of collective memory or history of the regiment, is what is really meant when the oft-used phrase *esprit de corps* is used in connection with the British regimental system. It seems appropriate that the last contact Gough should have before embarking on his new appointment, and a new period of his career, was a poignant reminder of the past and the events that had made his name and ultimately brought him to this point.

---

4   There is some question over exactly which ship they sailed on. Robert Rait refers to the ship as the *Minerva Castle*. However the present author has been unable to find a ship of that name
5   Cunliffe, *Royal Irish Fusiliers*, p. 190.
6   Cunliffe, *Royal Irish Fusiliers*, p. 190.

Part 4

India and China

24

Command in Madras

In October 1837 Hugh Gough landed at Madras, setting foot in India for the first time. At that stage he could not have known that he was embarking on one of the most active periods of his career. This was the start of a period of considerable active service and command experience. It is unlikely that he expected such as he arrived in India. Indeed, one gets the impression that he almost viewed it as one final piece of service before retirement. After so long out of an appointment there was no doubt a sense of relief, but also some trepidation. This was of course new ground for Gough. Although still technically an officer of the British Army, in India he would be in the service of the Honourable East India Company (HEIC), more commonly simply referred to as the East India Company (EIC).[1] Until 1858, British interests and territory in India would be governed by the East India Company in the name of the Crown. There is not time here to go into a detailed account of the way in which this worked, or to look at the relationship between the Crown authorities in Britain and those of the East India Company in Asia. Sufficient to say this was a duality of control. The home government could make its feelings known, but the men on the ground, although approved by the British government, were the men of the Company. The Company was controlled by the Court of Directors in London, but increasingly they came under the influence of the government. In short it would be wrong to believe that the East India Company independently ruled British India, but equally it would be incorrect to believe that the British Government had direct control.

Although there is not space, nor indeed the need, for a detailed account of the history and organisation of the East India Company, further information in this regard will be helpful in setting the scene and providing understanding of the situation into which Gough now entered.[2] The British Empire was one founded upon trade. The expansion and development of the 'Empire' particularly in its early days, had more to do with merchants than politicians, soldiers, sailors, or missionaries. Whilst all played their part, it was the merchant and mercantile requirements that drove the process. Although there had been limited contact with India beforehand, the starting date of 31 December 1600 is often used when chronicling British ventures in India. This is because on this date Queen Elizabeth I granted a Royal Charter incorporating "The Governor and Company of Merchants of London trading into the East Indies". This East India Company, as it became known,

---

1   For the majority of this work the term EIC will be used for the sake of simplicity.
2   There are numerous books on the history of the East India Company. So many in fact that it is difficult to recommend further reading due to this fact. However Philip Lawson's *The East India Company: A History 1600–1857* (London: Longman, 1993), is a good scholarly introduction to the subject, if perhaps somewhat dated. John Keay's *The Honourable Company: A History of the English East India Company* (London: Harper Collins, 1991), is perhaps an easier read more in the style of a popular history. A good modern economically focused history is to be found in Nick Robins, *The Corporation that Changed the World: How the East India Company shaped the modern multinational* (London: Pluto Press, 2012).

had started off under the leadership of Sir Thomas Smith, an experienced merchant, with 125 shareholders and starting capital of between £68–72,000, roughly £7,000,000 in modern money.[3]

Although the subcontinent was always part of the commercial drive of the Company, in the early days it tried to focus more on the islands in the East Indies, the majority of which are to be found in modern day Indonesia. However competition from the Dutch turned the British company more towards the subcontinent. In 1605 the EIC had started trading at Surat, on the west coast of India. This had many advantages. Firstly it was convenient for trade with Persia, where an overland trade route had already been developed by the Muscovy Company. Secondly, Europeans, in this case the Portuguese were already trading from Surat, although this did ultimately lead to clashes with them, it meant that the British were trading in an area already used to Europeans. Thirdly, Surat was also convenient for diplomatic links to the Mughal Empire at Agra.

The main staple of the EIC in the early days was the trade in pepper. A lack of interest in English goods, such as woollen and iron products, in India meant that trading took place in silver bullion, which at the time was the closest thing there was to an international currency. Although initially there was a great concern about the effect of so much bullion leaving the country, the fears proved unfounded. The pepper was traded in Europe for silver bullion, and it was calculated that they paid four or five times what it had cost to buy in India. After English naval victories over the Portuguese in 1613 and 1615, British supremacy in Surat was assured, and an imperial *firman* (decree) from the Mughal court allowed the establishment of a British trading post, or factory, on Indian soil. Surat was just the beginning. In 1640 Fort St George was established at Madras, and in 1651 Bombay was received from the Portuguese as part of the wedding settlement of Charles II. As this was a crown 'property', and not part of the EIC until 1668 this marked the first deployment of English/British troops as opposed to those of the EIC, when in 1665 about 100 soldiers landed at Bombay.[4] The need to defend the new possessions, from local rulers and European rivals, meant that the EIC was allowed to enrol its own military forces. Although 'private armies' had been unpopular with monarchs and governments in the past it was the lesser of two evils. The alternative would have required the deployment of large-scale 'crown' forces to defend English interest in the area. Thus between 1663–64 the first Company soldiers were enrolled for the defence of Bombay, which became the principle British post from 1687.

Domestically it was not plain sailing for the EIC. There were the obviously problems created by the political turmoil in England during the mid 17th century. Yet the bases in India kept going even when the Company at home was struggling. There was also competition from other English traders. However by 1709 the EIC's monopoly had been secured from other English completion by the merger with the English India Company. There was now a renewed prosperity as the Company entered the 18th century. Trade began to grow from the three main bases: Bombay (having replaced Surat as the trading centre on the west coast), Madras, and Calcutta in the Bay of Bengal (where EIC trading had been established in 1690). In time the three trading posts would form the three presidencies into which EIC control in India was developed: namely Bombay, Madras, and Bengal. During this period the commercial impact of the EIC grew, particularly in Calcutta where the local stability aided trade. The EIC was now very much a commercial force, accounting for roughly 20 percent of the imports to England during the early 18th century. Indeed taxes paid by the Company, not to mention a loan of £3 million to the British government, were an important, and increasingly vital, part of national revenue.

---

3   Whilst this might sound a lot, but when the Dutch launched their own East India Company (VOC) two years later, they did so with £500,000 worth of capital (roughly £50,000,000). See Lloyd, T.O., *The British Empire 1558–1983* (Oxford: Oxford University Press, 1984), pp. 12–14.

4   The sending of the first formal British regiment to India would not occur until 1754 when the 39th (Dorsetshire) Regiment of Foot would land in India.

In terms of European competition, the British found that as Dutch and Portuguese influence declined, it was the 'old enemy' France that provided the main rival. This broke into open hostilities between the EIC and their French equivalent when the two nations were at war, such as the War of Austrian Succession and the Seven Years War.[5] The fighting in India during the latter conflict saw the cementing of British power and influence over that of France. This was particularly due to the victories over the French and her native allies by Sir Robert Clive at Plassey on the 23rd June 1757 and by Sir Eyre Coote at Wanderwash (Wandiwash) 22 January 1760. As a result of the conflicts the EIC's military forces grew in size and, whilst continuing to require the support of Crown forces, became a military power in its own right.

By the late 18th century Britain, through the auspices of the EIC, had become the predominant European power in India. The rise of Britain to this dominant position had coincided with the decline of the Mughal Empire. This provide the opportunity for the EIC to expand its trade, power and influence, but also brought it to increasing conflict with Indian states as the 18th century wore on. Wars were fought against the state of Mysore, the Mahratta Confederacy, and numerous other minor states. The conflicts developed out of the growing influence of the EIC and its desire to interfere in the local politics of the areas in which it was based, largely to defend trade interests or expand operations. The EIC armies consequently grew in size.

It is important to understand that there were three armies in India, divided upon the lines of the Presidencies mentioned earlier; Bengal, Madras and Bombay. There were also three different 'type' of soldier in 'British' uniform in India. There were the Crown forces, those of the British Army (often called 'King's Regiments' or after 1837 'Queen's Regiments'). There were also the 'european' troops of the Company armies. The majority were from the British Isles, and in the early days a number were former English/British Army soldiers who were offered incentives to stay in India. As with the British Army of this period there was a disproportionately high number of Irishmen making up the EIC's 'european' regiments. By the end of the 18th century one third of the 'European' army of the Company was Irish. The 'European' regiments were habitually under-strength and recruiting in this regard was as much of a perennial problem for the EIC as it was for the British Army. Finally there were the 'native' soldiers of the Company armies. The native troops were an important part of the army, and provided a large part of the numerical strength of forces in India.[6] Their quality, and indeed the amount of confidence and trust that was placed in them, varied over the years. Yet without them the Company, and indeed British, rule in India would not have been possible. The EIC military presence grew dramatically to the point where, by 1809, it numbered 132,469 (in addition there were 19,843 British Army troops in India at the same time). The majority of the native troops were infantry, and like their British counterparts they were a volunteer rather than a conscripted army. Unlike their British counterparts recruitment was not the 'last resort' option. Indeed military service was popular and seen as an honourable profession. It was often a family business with fathers, sons, brothers and cousins carrying on a long military tradition. Regular pay, accommodation, allowances for active service, and a pension were far more attractive to the India recruit than the British one. The majority of recruits came from the countryside, which it was argued produced a physically and morally stronger recruit. The majority of recruits were also from higher castes; indeed the lower castes were denied entry into the infantry

---

5   The conflict in India during the War of Austrian Succession is often referred to as the First Carnatic War (1746–48). The Second Carnatic War (1749–54) was when the two nations were technically at peace and was therefore largely fought through support for local rulers. The Third Carnatic War (1756–1763) refers to the India theatre of the Seven Years War.

6   For more information on the Company Army in general and the native troops specifically, see Kaushik Roy's *War, Culture and Society in Early Modern South Asia 1740–1849* (Abingdon: Routledge, 2011) & *Military Manpower, Armies and Warfare in South Asia* (London: Taylor & Francis, 2013).

of the Bengal Army.[7] Whilst largely equipped, drilled, and trained in European manner, or at least that of their British Army counterparts, it would be wrong to see the EIC's army as purely a European import imposed upon Indian soldiers. As Kaushik Roy points out:

> The Raj's military machine represented a complex amalgam of both western trends and indigenous aspects. This was because the Raj's military machine had to utilize the financial, animal and human resources of the subcontinent. For instance, the irregular cavalry, the recruit boys scheme, the invalid establishment comprising of ex-soldiers turned farmers, and care for the sepoys and sowars' religious, cultural and linguistic sensibilities on the part of the British officers, were unique to India. Even recruitment policy was somewhat guided by the preferences of the high castes.[8]

The EIC became not only a financial and military power, but the expansion of the Company from its original trading posts had also turned it into a territorial power. It was at that stage that the British Government sought to exercise some sort of control, through Parliament, upon the EIC. In 1773 the governor of Bengal had been raised by the Government to the rank of Governor General, and whilst he would continue to be appointed by the EIC through the ruling Court of Directors, his appointment was now subject to Crown approval. In 1784 a board of control had been established in London by Parliament to supervise military, political and financial matters conducted by the EIC. The President of the Board of Control was the forerunner of the Secretary of State for India. In 1813 this power of supervision was expanded to include commercial transactions also. Thus as the 19th century developed, the EIC was increasingly controlled by the Crown.

Little of this would have been familiar to Gough, as he had no previously experience of India or the Company. One wonders how much Gough knew about the workings of India. The answer is probably very little about the political workings, but he may have been better aware of the military affairs of the EIC. Either way it is perhaps slightly surprising that he should get such an appointment. However there was always a demand for officers of general rank in India. On the one hand it was a popular appointment: costs were much lower than in the British Isles and one could live in luxury with numerous servants at a fraction of the cost. There was in theory more chance of active service, and therefore opportunity for career advancement, in India than elsewhere, although at the time of Gough's arrival this did not look likely in his case. On the other hand, service in India had its drawbacks. You were far from British society and it was possible to become quite isolated in this regard. The climate was not always conducive to good health and a long stay in India, particularly during this era, could reduce your life expectancy by a good number of years.

At this stage of Gough's career the advantages outweighed the risks. To say he was desperate would be an exaggeration, and perhaps a misinterpretation, of his situation. However, if he wanted to remain in the Army this was perhaps his last chance. He was at a crossroads. Given the length of time between his last employment and the offer of a command in India, it was unlikely that another offer would come along any time soon. Thus if he wanted to remain in the Army he really had little option but to take the offer of a division in the Madras Army. To refuse it would be tantamount to accepting the end of his military career, and this was something Gough was not prepared for at this time. Thus in October 1837, a month shy of his 58th birthday, Gough and his family landed in Madras at the commencement of a new chapter in his life. From Madras he made the journey in land to his new headquarters at Bangalore.

---

7   For more information on the social composition of the native army see Roy, *War, Culture and Society*, pp. 49–58.
8   Roy, *War, Culture and Society*, p. 69.

We know little of the years spent in command of the Mysore Division. Little record survives of what impact he was able to have. It should not be forgotten that this was the largest command he had held in his career to that point, and it would be interesting to know how easily he took to this new responsibility. Indeed we know little of his life between that point and November 1840, due to a lack of papers for this era. To the biographer it is one of those annoying gaps that leave a lot of unanswered questions. It would in particular help to place his future command progress in context if we knew how easily he took to the command of a larger formation. The fact that no criticism of this period in command of the Mysore division is to be found might lead one to believe that he was successful in the appointment and experienced no great problems in making the 'step-up'. There were many who in the aftermath of the Sikh Wars were all too critical of him, so if there had been any problem with his command of the Mysore Division then surely this would have come out. On the other side of the argument, it could be stated that, at this level and under these circumstances, the command of the division was not very different from the command of a regiment. The lack of activity, and a more established administrative organisation, meant that any shortcomings in the command were only likely to be visible during active service.

It was in November 1840 that Lord Auckland the Governor General of India, and the first of the four to hold that position during Gough's time in India, approached Gough with regards to China. By this stage the conflict had already started and some 4,000 troops had been despatched. Already the campaign had lost momentum and most the troops were stuck in various garrisons, largely through lack of an overall strategy. This proved fatal, quite literally for many, as disease and a climate not conducive to good health conspired to reduce the ranks of the British. It is clear that the British authorities wanted someone more active, and by his reputation Gough fitted the bill.

It is easy to be critical of the initial commanders and accuse them of only 'playing at war', as one historian put it.[9] However this was more to do with the political side rather than the military. The military could not plan for campaigns without knowing what their aim was. The political situation was such that no one knew exactly what they were trying to achieve. One feels sympathy for Charles Elliot, the civilian representative in China. His instructions from London, and even India, could take such a long time to reach him that by the time they did they had been overtaken by events. Also when instructions from London came they were often vague. It was no wonder that more and more responsibility devolved upon the Governor General in India. He was at least within reasonable communication distance from China. More importantly he had assets, both naval and military, that were far closer to the scene. In one sense it was inevitable that the main direction of the war would devolve upon India.

It was now the responsibility of the Governor General to provide extra troops for China, and also to provide a commander. When Lord Auckland approached Gough, offering the command of the expedition in China, it was clear that Auckland was displeased with the progress and performance of the expedition to date. Indeed one can see Gough being positioned as the new broom to sweep away the inactivity. To that end Gough had the foresight to take with him a rudimentary staff. That Auckland was aware of Gough's active command style might suggest that he was not only familiar with his past career in the Peninsular War and in Ireland. Auckland must have at the very least heard reports of his command of the Mysore Division, if not witnessed it himself. Whilst we do not know that these reports were positive, it is unlikely that had they been negative Auckland would have approached Gough with a view to his commanding in China.[10]

---

9   Holt, Edgar, *The Opium Wars in China* (London: Putnam and Company, Ltd, 1964). 'Playing at War' is the title of chapter 8 of this book.
10   Rait, *Gough*, Vol. I, pp. 160–161.

That Gough accepted this offer was not surprising. For any officer the chance to command in conflict is a strong desire, particularly in this era. Careers could be made, as could fortunes, by a successful campaign. After years of inactivity, when he believed his military career was over, Gough was delighted to have the chance to command such an expedition. His delight at the appointment is illustrated that after accepting the command he immediately set off for China. His alacrity pleased Lord Auckland who felt that if he showed the same active approach in China then his decision would have been vindicated.[11]

---

11   Rait, *Gough*, Vol. I, p. 167.

25

The First Anglo-China War

The First Anglo-China War 1839–1842 is one of the many conflicts of the age of imperialism that remain controversial to this day. Much of this is to do with the alternative name for this conflict: the Opium War. However the opium trade was only part of a far more complex and wide ranging set of causes that led to war between Britain and China. Indeed it was more than simply a conflict about trade. It was also a clash of cultures and empires. The opium trade might well have been the trigger, but conflict would have arisen regardless of that trade in the fullness of time. Whilst the concern of this book is the life and career of Hugh Gough, it will be helpful to the reader to understand something of the background to the conflict in which Hugh Gough would find himself thrust. Whilst the following chapters will look at Gough's actions during the war itself, this chapter, by way of setting the scene, provides a brief overview of the background and causes of the war that commenced in 1839.

There have been numerous books written about the conflict between Britain and China.[1] Many veer to one extreme or the other. Although largely forgotten in modern Britain the war still looms large in the conscience of the Chinese nation, where it is still seem as the first move in what would be perceived as a century of Western imperialism designed to humiliate and control China. For Britain the conflict was largely about commercial interests, but there was clearly also a clash of cultures, with each side believing in their own cultural superiority. However the spark that caused the tensions to spill into open warfare was clearly the opium trade.

Opium has a long history in China, and it is important to note that opium use in that country predates Britain's arrival on the scene. Reading many histories of the conflict, one would be forgiven for thinking that opium was a British invention. In fact, exactly how opium was introduced to China, or, more to the point, who by, is something of a mystery. We do know that the first reference to it being used in China dates back to the early 8th century AD. At that time it was largely used as a medicine for pain relief, but also numerous other ailments and maladies. However it soon started to be used for what today we would call recreational purposes. There was a theory that it

---

1   Whilst sources are numerous there are two in particular that are recommended reading for anyone wishing to better understand the conflict, its causes, and its consequences. Edgar Holt's *The Opium Wars in China* (London: Putnam & Co Ltd, 1964) remains a thoroughly readable account. It is perhaps a little dated, but as a basic introduction to conflict it is still extremely useful. Of the modern works by far the best is Julia Lovell's *The Opium War: Drugs, Dreams, and the making of China* (London: Picador, 2011). This is an excellent book written by someone who understands not only Chinese history but its people, culture, and language. Whilst not defending the actions of the British, it highlights some of inconsistencies and hypocrisy in the Chinese approach. It takes advantage of many Chinese documents. For additional reading see Jack Beeching *The Chinese Opium Wars* (London: Hutchinson & Co, 1975) for a good political account of the war. John Selby *The Paper Dragon: An Account of the China Wars* (London: Arthur Baker Ltd, 1968) is like Holt a somewhat dated but informative account. Professor Harry G. Gelber *Opium, Soldiers, and Evangelists: Britain's 1840–42 War with China* (New York: Palgrave Macmillan, 2004) is a very interesting if academically-orientated book.

helped control male ejaculation and became popular amongst the elite as a sexual aid. Julia Lovell states that its use, or overuse, by the Ming Emperors might explain why 11 of the 16 failed to live past their 40th birthday.[2] There developed a belief that it was the panacea for all ills. The drug had been mixed with food or drink up until the late 16th century, when tobacco arrived in China. The two were soon mixed, and the Portuguese started to import opium syrup that made this easier to achieve. This dilution of opium made the product cheaper and more accessible. As a consequence pure opium, being more expensive, became highly sought after as a status symbol. This increase in the status of pure opium, added to the other properties of the drug, made it a greatly sought after commodity.

In the late 1700s the British, through the East India Company, started to enter the picture. At first they were extremely welcome, as they could supply the drug in large quantity and of high quality. In fact this would be the defence that the British merchants would put forward; that they were satisfying demand rather than creating it. Although a rather hollow, not to mention morally ambiguous, response it did have a ring of truth. Indeed one of the inconsistencies of this period is that even the Emperor Daoguang was himself a recreational user of opium to the extent that he wrote a poem documenting the experience.[3] However within 20 years of his becoming Emperor he would launch a campaign to eradicate it from China. It was even rumoured that he had his own son executed for taking opium. The evils of opium were such that the Chinese ultimately banned the product. The lack of understanding and communication between the two sides was illustrated by the fact that the Chinese were astonished to find that opium was legal in Britain. Some Chinese diplomats thought they were not only asking the British to respect Chinese laws but also their own. In fact, the first controls upon opium in Britain only came in 1868 with the Pharmacy Act, which regulated the sale to registered pharmacists and chemists. Stricter controls did not really come about until the Dangerous Drugs Act of 1920.

The banning of opium may seem a logical step to the modern reader. However in the 19th century opium was not understood as a drug. Many felt it to be a beneficial and useful substance, and the chemistry of the drug was not accurately known. The detrimental effect that it had on Chinese society was obvious. However the reason for the crackdown on opium usage was not simply moral. Nor was it due entirely to the social impact that the drug was having upon China. There was behind all the rhetoric a strong economic argument. Whilst there had been attempts in the past to combat the smoking of opium, the real impetus came from the fact that the opium trade had in a short period of time severely damaged the Chinese economy. Indeed it is important to recognise that the main target was the opium trade – and, after the trade was made illegal, opium smuggling – rather than opium smoking. The latter carried on regardless, to the extent that in the coming conflict it was common for the British to face Chinese soldiers under the influence of the drug. Indeed in the aftermath of the Battle of Amoy Gough's men made a collection of a great many opium pipes.[4]

The opium trade, and the knock-on effect it had upon the silver trade, were extremely serious for the Chinese economy. Indeed the impact on the silver trade was extreme, and the Chinese government found itself running out of silver. Silver was the currency of the country, used to pay for imports, and government spending. Initially there was a trade imbalance in the opposite

---

2   Lovell, *The Opium War*, pp. 21–22.
3   Lovell, *The Opium War*, pp. 22–23 & 24. The Emperor Daoguang was born in September 1782. He reigned from October 1820 until his death in February 1850.
4   National Library of Ireland (NLI): MS 638 'Gough China War Despatches', 5 September 1851. The despatches are handwritten, but although similar it does not appear to be Gough's handwriting, but is presumably that of a staff officer, possibly his son George. The capture of opium pipes is also recorded in Beeching, *The Chinese Opium Wars*, p. 135. This refers to the capture of Amoy, but gives no source for the report.

direction as the British paid for everything in silver, which they themselves had originally imported to Britain.[5]

Originally this affected Britain's balance of payments and trade with China: to meet the demand for tea at home required the purchase of a large quantity of silver to pay for this. The sale of opium, produced widely in Bengal and some of the princely states of India, to China helped Britain to balance its trade and then start to make considerable profits, such was the demand for 'British' opium. The need for China to import silver to an even greater extent, added to the increase in the size of opium imports, had a severe effect on China's balance of payments. Whereas between 1800 and 1810, around $26 million entered the country, between 1828–1836 over $38 million left the country. In this period not only did the balance of payments enter the red, but it is estimated that the wealth of the country dropped by 20 percent.[6]

The opium trade became the popular scapegoat for this economic downturn and many in China did, and indeed still do, see it as part of a western plot to undermine China and weaken it in prelude to invasion. As a result a moral crusade against opium was started. The easy target for this was perceived to be the foreign traders. This ignored the fact that there was a great deal of domestic production of opium, and also allowed a rather insular society to play on its fear of foreigners. Indeed the way in which China viewed itself, and indeed the rest of the world, was a fundamental problem for any interaction with other nations. Yet there was a much wider problem than opium and its trading.

There is an oft quoted speech that John Quincy Adams made in 1841, once war had started. Adams was a previous Secretary of State, and the 6th President, of the United States, and at that time Chairman of the House of Representatives Committee on Foreign Affairs. He denied that Opium was the cause of the war:

> It is a general but I believe altogether mistaken opinion that the quarrel is merely for certain chests of opium imported by British merchants into China, and seized by the Chinese Government for having been imported contrary to the law. This is a mere incident to the dispute; no more the cause of the war than the throwing overboard of tea in Boston harbour was the cause of the North American Revolution … The cause of the war is the kowtow – the arrogant and insupportable pretentions of China that she will hold commercial intercourse with the rest of mankind not upon terms of equal reciprocity, but upon the insulting and degrading forms of the relation between lord and vassal.[7]

Adams was not a man with any great love for the British. His comments were extremely controversial and drew much criticism in the United States. Indeed the United States had a rather ambiguous relationship with China during this period. They were themselves engaged in trade with China, and suffered the same ignominy and humiliation from the Chinese as cultural inferiors. Although unknown to most Americans both at the time and to this day, US merchants were also involved in the opium trade and it has been calculated that a tenth of China's imports of opium were coming from US merchants. American opium came from the Ottoman Empire, and was slightly cheaper

5   Holt, *The Opium Wars*, pp. 64–65.
6   Figures vary widely, with some Chinese sources claiming almost 50 percent of the country's wealth being wiped out. The figure of 20 percent seems to be closest to the real figure. Lovell, *The Opium Wars*, pp. 36–37. The original research was done in the US so the prices are in dollars. Converting to sterling is not easy to do accurately. Converting $26 million into a modern valuation in sterling comes to around £3.5 billion. Similarly the $38 million mentioned above converts to roughly £6.4 billion in modern money.
7   Inglis, Bryan, *The Opium War* (London, Hodder & Stoughton 1976), p. 176.

than that sold by British merchants, albeit of inferior quality. Once a ban on opium was in place in China, US merchants also assisted their British counterparts in smuggling. It was therefore pragmatic for the United States to be in support of the actions of the British, if it opened China up to further western trade; at the same time, they did not wish to be politically linked to British actions.

Yet Adams also made an important point in his speech about the Chinese view of the world. To the Chinese, the rest of the world were 'barbarians'. There was a fundamental belief in the moral and cultural superiority of the Chinese. Here was the obvious problem when dealing with the British, who had similar ideas about their own position in the world in the early 19th century. Each side felt the other was inferior, and each side felt the other were 'barbarians'. Under such circumstances it was all but impossible to hold trade negotiations on equal terms. Indeed the arrogance of both sides had been demonstrated during the earlier trade mission of George Macartney, 1st Earl Macartney, in 1792–3. Much has been made of the fact that Macartney refused to kowtow, that is to bow in a prostrate manner with the head upon the floor. Macartney did refuse to do this, but the greater problem was his failure to acknowledge the supremacy of China and accept the Chinese way of thinking that Britain was merely a client state of China. The latter sounds bizarre, but this was the policy under which China undertook foreign diplomacy during this era. All the states on earth were vassals of the divine Emperor.[8]

The British for their part attempted to demonstrate their superiority through presenting examples of their technological advancements. This included Macartney attempting to impress the Chinese by the demonstration of matches! The arrogance, bordering on imbecility, of Lord Macartney in trying to impress the Chinese with something they had originally invented back in the 10th century is almost beyond belief. Indeed of all the gifts presented to the Chinese intended to impress, it was only the pottery of Josiah Wedgewood that caused any interest. It points to the difference between the two cultures, that what impressed the Chinese eye was not a military, technological or scientific piece of equipment but what might be called a cultural achievement in the form of pottery. As the Emperor said in his official reply:

> Our ways have no resemblance to yours, and even were your envoy competent to acquire some rudiments of them, he could not transplant them to your barbarous land … Strange and costly objects do not interest me. As your Ambassador can see for himself, we possess all things. I set no value on objects strange or ingenious, and have no use for your country's manufacturers.[9]

For their part the Chinese seem to have been somewhat amused by the whole enterprise. The response however to the trade delegation was negative, and the official letter to King George III was of a style that he had surely never received before.

> You, O King, from afar have yearned after the blessings of our civilization and in your eagerness to come into touch with our converting influence have sent an Embassy across the sea bearing a memorial [memorandum]. I have already taken note of your respectful spirit of submission, have treated your mission with extreme favour and loaded it with gifts, besides issuing a mandate to you, O King, and honouring you at the bestowal of valuable presents. Thus, has my indulgence been manifested.

The start of the letter was to set the tone for its remainder. To the Chinese this was meant to be kind and conciliatory, forgiving the British their indiscretions with paternalistic kindness. Yet to

---

8   Lovell, *The Opium War*, pp. 87–89.
9   Beeching, *The Chinese Opium Wars*, p. 16–18.

the British, so sure of their own cultural, technological, and military superiority it would have been the proverbial red rag to a bull. The letter went on to dismiss the British:

> Hitherto, all European nations, including your own country's barbarian merchants, have carried on their trade with our Celestial Empire at Canton. Such has been the procedure for many years, although our Celestial Empire possesses all things in prolific abundance and lacks no product within its own borders. There was therefore no need to import the manufactures of outside barbarians in exchange for our own produce. But as the tea, silk and porcelain which the Celestial Empire produces, are absolute necessities to European nations and to yourselves, we have permitted, as a signal mark of favour, that foreign *hongs* [merchants] should be established at Canton, so that your wants might be supplied and your country thus participate in our beneficence. But your Ambassador has now put forward new requests which completely fail to recognize the Throne's principle to "treat strangers from afar with indulgence," and to exercise a pacifying control over barbarian tribes, the world over. Moreover, our dynasty, swaying the myriad races of the globe, extends the same benevolence towards all. Your England is not the only nation trading at Canton. If other nations, following your bad example, wrongfully importune my ear with further impossible requests, how will it be possible for me to treat them with easy indulgence? Nevertheless, I do not forget the lonely remoteness of your island, cut off from the world by intervening wastes of sea, nor do I overlook your excusable ignorance of the usages of our Celestial Empire. I have consequently commanded my Ministers to enlighten your Ambassador on the subject, and have ordered the departure of the mission.[10]

Although the Emperor and his officials thought that Britain was a remote island, they seemed to ignore the fact that there was a large military presence in India. Indeed when war came between the British Empire and China, it was troops and ships of the East India Company that provided the bulk of expeditionary force. Indeed, up until 1833 all British trade with China had been done through the East India Company which held the monopoly on this. The Chinese stance also ignored the fact that at this stage Britain had mastery of seas and whilst the journey from Britain to China could not be called easy, it was perfectly within the grasp of the world's largest navy, both militarily and commercially. Whilst the letter, and Chinese attitudes in general, may seem amusing rather than insulting to the modern reader, their impact upon certain British officials should not be underestimated. However the idea that there was a conspiracy to teach China a lesson in the realities of the world is to overestimate the importance of China to British politicians during this period. Whilst the men on the ground in China might have felt that way there were few in Britain who shared the view or were even aware of what was happening in China. The British government, and the East India Company, faced far more pressing concerns both domestically and internationally. Indeed if China was ever debated at Cabinet level, it was usually well down the agenda and so late on in the meeting that little time was spent upon it. Internationally, Syria, Mexico, South America, and Afghanistan were far more pressing concerns. Domestically, in both Britain and India, by the 1830s the governments faced increasing civil unrest.[11]

In 1833 the Company's monopoly on trade in China came to an end. At the same time another trade mission was despatched to China in an attempt to expand British trade. This time William

---

10   Whilst exerts of this letter appear in numerous books covering the period, a translated version can be found on line on the website of the University of California. <http://www.history.ucsb.edu/faculty/marcuse/classes/2c/texts/1792QianlongLetterGeorgeIII.htm>.

11   Lovell, *The Opium War*, p. 100–103.

Napier, 9th Lord Napier, a retired Royal Navy officer, was placed in charge of the mission.[12] Despite Napier having no knowledge of China himself, the British had at least made sure that he had a staff of experienced 'China hands', including John Francis Davis – the son of HEIC Director Samuel Davis and later the second Governor of Hong Kong – who had spent time in China where he had worked as both an interpreter and translator. However, Napier's trade mission, based in Macau, fared no better than Macartney's. There was the same level of misunderstanding, arrogance and failure to understand the Chinese mentality, despite him having a better prepared and experienced staff than the previous attempt. Napier's success is well illustrated by the name said to have been given to him by the Chinese Governor Lu Kun. Not knowing how to translate Napier into Chinese he instead used characters which when translated into English stood for 'laboriously vile'.

Napier faced the same Chinese superiority complex, failing to recognise even his existence, let alone accept a letter from him. Napier quickly turned in favour of a military showdown with China. To assert British authority Napier despatched his two frigates HMS *Andromache* and *Imogene*, upriver from Macau towards Whampoa anchorage midway between Macau and Canton (Guangzhou) in early September 1834. On the passage the two frigates were fired upon by the Chinese batteries in the forts along the river. Although the fire did little damage, the act of firing upon the British flag was in itself a cause for war. The fact that no such conflict came in 1834, and that the events of September did not of themselves lead to further military clashes, does therefore somewhat undermine the Chinese argument that this was all part of a plot to undermine China. The events of September could easily have been the spark for a conflict. Certainly there were those in China who wished it. However the whole episode was anti climactic, 'Napier's Fizzle' as one American merchant called it at the time.[13]

There had been little support for military action from the home government, and when during 1834 the government had fallen, this view point continued under the new administration. Lord Palmerston had not been interested in Chinese affairs, but his successor as Foreign Secretary, the Duke of Wellington, was adamant that there should not be any military action. Writing to Napier, he reminded him of his responsibilities and that he was to act in accordance with Chinese customs and practices. The latter was a difficult thing to ask and one wonders if Wellington really understood what this entailed. However Wellington reminded Napier that:

> It is not by force and violence that His Majesty [William IV] intends to establish a commercial intercourse between his subjects and China, but by other conciliatory measures so strongly inculcated in all the instructions you have received.[14]

Although the letter had been addressed to Napier it never reached him, as in October 1834 Napier had died of fever in Macau. The fact that writing in February 1835 Wellington was still unaware of this illustrates some of the problems faced in this area. Whilst it is easy to blame the men on the spot for taking matters into their own hands at times, and acting against the wishes of the government, the delay in communications made this inevitable. It was impossible for the representatives in China to carry out the wishes of the government, when there was a delay of four months. Let us not forget that between the action involving the two frigates and Wellington's letter had been a period of almost five months, which had included a change of government.

---

12   William Napier should not be confused with his near contemporary the historian William Napier. They were related and part of the wider Napier clan.
13   Holt, *The Opium Wars in China*, p. 56. The American merchant was W.C. Hunter.
14   Holt, *The Opium Wars in China*, p. 58.

26

Early Engagements of the First Anglo-China War

After Napier's death things settled down again, and there were no further military confrontations. There was clearly no appetite in London for war with China, and the Chinese believed that they had dealt with the 'barbarian' problem. John Francis Davis had replaced Napier and had followed the old Company policy of avoiding unnecessary clashes with the Chinese authorities. Although Davis's attitude, and that of his successor Sir George Best Robinson, was approved of by the home government it proved unpopular with the merchants. It is easy to look at such merchants and say they were simply motivated by profit: there is some truth to this but it must be remembered that it was they who suffered the indignity of the behaviour of the Chinese on a daily basis. Most of them were also disillusioned because after the ending of the Company's monopoly they had believed that they would benefit from free trade with China.

That this had not occurred was largely due to the Chinese, but some of the merchants seemed to lay the blame at the door of the British government and its officials for not forcing the issue and defending the rights of their citizens to trade and conduct business where they wished. The main problem with this was that the primary article of trade had become opium. Once China banned the opium trade, to defend the merchants was to defend the illegal trade. This was an ambiguous position for the government: whilst supporting the principle of free trade with China they could not support the trading of an illegal product. At the same time the merchants could honestly say that they were not doing anything that was illegal under British law. Were they to be forced to adhere to the laws of a 'barbarian' society? The latter was a question that certainly embarrassed the British government.[1]

After opium had been declared illegal the trade largely continued, as Chinese officials and merchants were prepared to turn a blind eye. That was until the arrival of the Lin Zexu as Imperial Commissioner. Commissioner Lin, as he is generally known in British translations, was certainly one of the more capable Chinese officials during this era. Whilst he had a more realistic view of the British, he still failed to grasp many of the key concerns and more importantly that the British had the military capability to do great harm. The modern Chinese interpretation is to view him as a good and honest man who stood up to imperialism and he has developed into a national hero in modern day China.[2] What Lin was able to do in a very short space of time was to severely reduce Chinese cooperation with the smuggling of opium. This included the punishment of merchants,

---

1   Lovell, *The Opium War*, pp. 62–64.
2   Lin Zexu has become not only a hero in China but somewhat strangely a global symbol against drug trafficking. Whilst this is a naïve interpretation of his role, and somewhat rectified by Julia Lovell's previously mentioned work on the Opium Wars, it has become the popular interpretation. So much so that the International Day against Drug Abuse and Illicit Trafficking is celebrated on 26 June, the day Lin destroyed a large amount of British opium. Lin Zexu is commemorated by a Memorial Hall in Fuzhou, the town of his birth, by a statue in New York City, and most unusually an asteroid belt discovered by Chinese astronomers that has been named in his honour.

coastguard officials, and various others who at the very least had turned a blind eye to smuggling if not actively participated themselves. At first there was little to worry the British merchants, but after having dealt with Chinese involvement Lin turned his attention towards the British.

The British had themselves had a change of leadership, both in China and at home. In April 1835 Lord Melbourne had returned as Prime Minister and had reappointed Lord Palmerston as Foreign Secretary. In early June Lord Palmerston despatched letters to Macau dismissing Robinson and appointing Captain Charles Elliot, RN, as the new British representative. It was not until 14 December 1835 that the letters reached their destination. Elliot had decided that to be effective in his negotiations with the Chinese he needed to be in Canton rather than Macau. In asking for a passport for Canton he rather naively marked his letter 'Pin' which translated to the Chinese as petition. This, the Chinese took as proof that the new representative accepted the inferiority of his position and recognised Britain as a client state of the Celestial Emperor. In a bizarre way it seemed to work. Lin responded positively saying that he would ask for Imperial approval for Elliot to go to Canton. At the same time the perceived tone of the letter was not lost on Lin, who told the local merchants that 'the phraseology and subject-matter of the barbarian's address are reverential and submissive'.[3] To have such a misunderstanding from such a minor and inappropriate use of a Chinese character demonstrates the difficulty of such diplomacy. Elliot's use of the word 'Pin' was not popular with his superiors, and Palmerston told him that he should never use such a character again on any such document. However the damage had been done and there was no hope that the Chinese would treat the British as anything other than inferiors. The use of the term had gained Elliot access to Canton, yet in reality this did little good and the situation did not change.

By this stage Palmerston was becoming impatient and was starting to lean towards the gunboat diplomacy that he would become renowned for. Through his urging, the Admiralty despatched Rear Admiral Sir Frederick Maitland to China. Maitland commanded the East Indies Station and it was felt that he should now be required to keep part of his squadron in Chinese waters wherever possible. By this time the Chinese were cracking down on opium smugglers but were being careful only to target Chinese nationals. This meant that the owners of the opium and the vessels supplying the trade were not being attacked. In late 1838 the Chinese authorities attempted to make their objections clear to the foreign merchants without directly moving against them. A Chinese opium smuggler, sentenced to death, was to be publicly executed by strangulation outside the factories of the foreign merchants in Canton. Indeed the point for the execution was close to the American Consul. When the apparatus for the execution was put up by the Chinese, British and American merchants came out and removed it. This intervention by the foreign merchants incensed the local population and a crowd of around 6,000 Chinese gathered outside the factories. Stones were thrown, and threats were made. Chinese troops arrived and the mob was dispersed, but the foreign merchants had to an extent been put in their place.

A similar incident in 1839 was more dangerous when the crew of a British ship in Canton joined in the destruction of the execution site. A similar response from the local population ensued against the foreign merchants, and again it was the arrival of Chinese soldiers that saved the situation. One wonders exactly what the Chinese authorities, or more precisely Commissioner Lin, were doing at this stage. It may be that he was subtly attempting to show the foreign merchants that their safety and security depended upon the Chinese authorities and their soldiers. If so it was lost on the foreign merchants, and the British authorities at home. In March 1839, Commissioner Lin turned his attention squarely against the foreign merchants. Lin's first move was to remind the Chinese hong merchants that keeping the foreigners in line was their responsibility. He also made it clear to the foreign merchants that in return for continuing to trade tea, and also rhubarb, with foreign

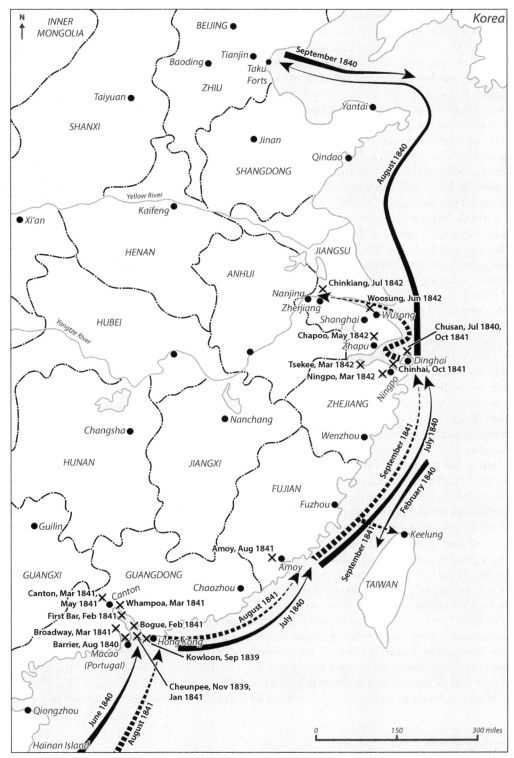

Map 7 The First Anglo-China War.

merchants the Chinese insisted on an end to the opium trade. The rhubarb story is an interesting aside and it has been suggested that Commissioner Lin believed that if he were to withhold the sale of rhubarb the foreigners would die of constipation! It might not be true and whilst it might sound bizarre there was much attached to this era that was.

Lin's proposals were not in and of themselves an unfair request. The problem was the manner in which it was done, for it was worded as a demand. The Chinese had demeaned themselves by agreeing to trade with foreign merchants, and in return for graciously allowing them to buy tea, and Rrhubarb, from them they expected them to stop trading opium. Like so much during this period it was the translation and interpretation from Chinese to English that caused so many problems. What followed is generally called the 'siege of the factories'. Lin demanded that all opium then held in the factories or the ships in the harbour must be handed over and that no further trade would be allowed. Until this happened all interaction and trade with the merchants was stopped. All Chinese labour was removed, soldiers surrounded them on land, and a fleet of war junks blockaded the harbour. Whilst the siege was not particularly unpleasant it was the final straw for Elliot. He was by this stage a tired and depressed individual. He was fed up and felt abandoned by the home authorities and had a particular animosity towards Palmerston. Thus, three days into the 'siege' Elliot gave in to the Chinese. As Julia Lovell has pointed out, this had two far reaching effects. Firstly by agreeing to give up the opium Elliot had lost the confidence of the merchants. Secondly, and even more significantly, he had stated that the crown would be responsible for reimbursement of the confiscated property. As Lovell states, "In two brisk moves, Elliot turned a private economic quarrel into a matter of state: a negotiation between the Queen of England and the Chinese Emperor."[4] Whatever Elliot's intention, he had given a victory to Commissioner Lin. By acting in a forthright manner Lin felt he taught the barbarians a lesson. The easy surrender convinced Lin and many others that their opinions of the barbarians were correct.

Lin made the most of his victory, and at Humen in May 1839 he publicly destroyed the 20,000 chests of opium. Lin now followed up with the second part of his agreement which was that the British would sign a declaration, or more accurately a bond, stating that they would no longer participate in the opium trade. On receipt of this bond some accounts say that Elliot tore it up. What was quite clear was that he could not sign such an agreement. He attempted to bluff Lin by stating that if signing of this bond was insisted upon then he and the foreign merchants would have no choice but to leave. Lin found no threat in such a statement, and his response was simply to make it clear that if they left they would not be allowed to return.[5] Elliot had badly misjudged the situation and on 23 May he ordered all British merchants and ships out of Canton: the Americans decided to stay. The British community now became a floating one. They anchored off Hong Kong in a move that would echo Britain's future in China. Hong Kong, with its natural harbour was a sensible place to anchor. It was also close to Macau and the foreign traders.

In July there was another incident when a group of British and American sailors went ashore on the Kowloon side of Hong Kong. After a period of heavy drinking, they assaulted a number of Chinese and in the brawl that followed one local was killed. Elliot acted quickly to hush up the incident and tried to pay off the deceased's family. To an extent he succeeded and the family signed a declaration stating that the death was an accident. However Commissioner Lin took advantage of the opportunity to further enforce his authority over the foreign merchants. He demanded of Elliot that the murderers be handed over to him for trial. Elliot could not hand over the individual, and even had he wanted to it is doubtful that he could have enforced the decision. What he did by way of response was to order a trial on board a British ship. He was technically within his rights

---

4   Lovell, *The Opium War*, p. 66.
5   Lovell, *The Opium War*, p. 71.

to do this, and it was the only way he could see out of the situation. There were precedents where Europeans had been handed over to the Chinese authorities in the past and the penalties had been death, and the idea developed that Chinese justice demand a life for a life: as in fact did British justice in this era.

Elliot reported that it was impossible to discover who had actually committed the offence and thus nothing could be done. Lin responded on 15 August 1839 by ordering that all supplies be cut off from the British, whether in Macau or on board their ships. Lin's response was also motivated by the fact that his success at destroying the British opium had not, as he believed it would, ended the trade and indeed it seemed to be growing despite the restrictions placed upon the British. The Portuguese authorities in Macau were ordered to expel all British merchants and civilians. By 26 August, all British civilians and merchants were anchored off Hong Kong in a variety of ships. Food supplies soon became a problem.

On 31 August HMS *Volage*, a 28-gun frigate commanded by Captain H. Smith, RN, arrived off Hong Kong. A few days later it was joined by the 20-gun frigate HMS *Hyacinth*. Elliot now had something with which to back up his defiant words. Escorted by the two ships, he sailed into Kowloon on 4 September 1839, where he managed to arrange for the delivery of food to the ships in the harbour. This was in clear defiance of Lin's instructions. As such some of the war-junks, somewhere between 20 or 30 in number, attempted to stop Elliot on the return journey and Elliot opened fire. This, although a minor skirmish, is often used as the starting point of the First Anglo-China War. Indeed they were the first shots fired in anger. In reality all that happened was an exchange of gunfire which caused a few minor casualties on the British ships and forced some of the Chinese ships to run aground. What the exchange did do was point to the great superiority of British ships. These were of course a second and third class frigate, yet they had easily outclassed a numerically superior force. The Chinese reports that reached the Emperor told a different story. In what would become part of a familiar pattern, the events were exaggerated to portray Chinese forces in the best possible light. The Emperor was thus informed that a two-masted British ship was sunk, that the British had suffered upwards of 50 casualties, and that the Chinese ships had suffered no losses and had won a victory against superior forces.[6]

The actions of that day had brought short term relief by the opening up of regular supplies to the fleet. However in the long term the situation was intolerable. The British community in China could not be seaborne indefinitely. War to resolve the issue seemed inevitable. That was not simply the British position; Commissioner Lin was thinking along similar lines. The latter was confident in the superiority of Chinese arms and had a very low opinion of the ability of Europeans to fight. Even in Britain such a course of actions was starting to be accepted. In late September the Cabinet decided that a military expedition was necessary. It is important to note that this was before they had heard that the first shots of the war had been fired. There was at first reluctance to do anything, as both domestic and other international events seemed more pressing, but the need to act became increasingly apparent. Palmerston believed that the despatch of a naval squadron was all that was required, whilst others in the Cabinet, including Lord Melbourne, doubted that it would be so easily achieved.[7] Indeed that was the question, what was the war aim? To restore pride? To gain compensation? To open up China to commerce on equal terms? If so how was this to be achieved? Few, if any, of these questions seemed to have been answered before the decision to act was made.

A more pressing question for some was who would fund the expedition. The East India Company was concerned that it would be asked to cover the cost as well as provide the bulk of the military forces necessary. They were relieved when the British government declared that they would pay

6   Holt, *The Opium Wars in China*, pp. 89–90.
7   Lovell, *The Opium War*, p. 101.

for the campaign. After that there was more enthusiasm in India than there had been hitherto. This was important, as the burden of finding troops for the expedition would fall on India. Lord Auckland started to put together a force, calling in the 18th Foot from Ceylon, the 26th from Calcutta, and the 49th from Madras.

In the months that followed, Commissioner Lin continued to try and resolve the barbarian situation. It was at around this time that he wrote to Queen Victoria asking her to intervene and stop the opium trading of her subjects. The letter was however rather naïve and divorced from reality. It has been argued that Lin had been heartened by reading an English book, translated into Chinese especially for him, entitled *The Iniquities of the Opium Trade with China*: this was written by the Reverend Algernon Sydney Thelwall, an evangelical Church of England clergyman who was hardly typical of British opinion. This had convinced Lin that not only was British law on his side, but also the British people and political elite. It was a naïve interpretation, but an understandable one. It did rather illustrate an ignorance of both British opinion and British interests. The latter, particularly in financial terms, was likely to have more impact on governmental decision-making than a few angry clergymen expressing their opinions in print.

In January 1840 Commissioner Lin seems to have had a slightly different change of opinion, deciding firmly that the British could not be trusted and should therefore not be allowed access to the Chinese Empire. An edict was issued that theoretically ended trade between Britain and China completely and permanently. All ports were to be closed not only to British merchants but even to British goods being sold by third parties. This was a slight miscalculation on the part of Lin, and allowed the British to continue with the argument that the disagreement was about wider trade issues than purely opium. By banning all British trade Lin had supported this view. It also ignored the practicalities of the situation, and the British ships anchored off Hong Kong continued to trade and find numerous ways around this edict. This also included the continued smuggling of opium. In Britain orders had been issued that the military force was to be gathered at Singapore by the end of April 1840 in preparation for transportation to China should military action be required. On 7 April 1840, a debate on China commenced in the House of Commons. This would have far reaching consequences. The debate started when the Conservative opposition moved a resolution condemning the handling of events in China by the present Whig administration. The resolution had been moved by Sir James Graham who, when previously First Lord of the Admiralty, had been against military action in China. The Whig government took the same line that Palmerston had taken in his official correspondence with the Chinese Emperor. This was that British citizens had been treated with violence, their property had been confiscated, and that the actions of the Chinese government were an insult to Britain. It was therefore urged that in defence of British citizens, property and honour that action against the Chinese, military if necessary, was required.[8]

The Conservative opposition took a very different line, arguing that there was no justification for war, and placed considerable blame for the situation on the government for not having dealt with the opium trade more effectively. Graham's opening remarks were answered eloquently by the great Victorian historian Sir Thomas Babington Macaulay, who at the time was Secretary at War in the Whig Government. However Macauley's eloquence for the Whigs was answered later in the debate by the passionate nature of W.E. Gladstone's response for the Conservatives.[9] Gladstone concentrated almost entirely upon the role that opium had played in leading to what he called this

8   Holt, *The Opium Wars in China*, pp. 97–100.
9   Although renowned as one of the great Liberal Party Prime Ministers, it is often overlooked that Gladstone began his political career as a Conservative. He had already held junior ministerial appointments in Sir Robert Peel's previous Conservative Government. He would later serve as President of the Board of Trade and Secretary of State for War and the Colonies in future Conservative government's before joining Sir Robert Peel in his split from the Conservative party.

most 'infamous and atrocious' war. He later stated in the debate that, "A war more unjust in its origins, a war more calculated to cover this country with permanent disgrace, I do not know and I have not read of."[10]

In summing up for the Government, Palmerston condemned the opium trade but tried to point out that there was far more at stake here than the opposition seemed to appreciate. It was for national honour and the protection of citizens and property of that nation that the insults and injuries performed by the Chinese Empire upon the British Empire needed to be answered. It was an eloquent if not entirely convincing response, but it had the desired effect. The Whig government sat with a majority of 14. In the vote that followed, the opposition amendment was defeated by a margin of nine votes. The consequences were, however, far greater than this would at first suggest. During the debate the subject had shifted to being about whether or not Britain could go to war rather than simply a condemnation of the Government's actions. Palmerston now felt he had the approval of the House of Commons for war with China.

On 30 May 1840, the British force at Singapore sailed for China. The army side of the expedition was to be commanded by Colonel George Burrell, of the 18th Foot. He had the local rank of brigadier but would soon find himself appointed major general. In military terms the contest would be one sided. The British had superiority in all arms. British ships were from a different century, and the use of steamers illustrated the technical edge they had. However it was not simply these ultra-modern vessels that were superior to the Chinese. Even elderly frigates were more than a match for the strongest Chinese war junk. The latter were brightly painted and adorned with such fearsome animals as tigers, but were in reality not even as powerful as a sloop-of-war. They carried a crew of about 50 and their guns, on average 10 in number, were of limited value. They were designed largely as costal patrol vessels and had limited capacity away from the calm inshore waters. To use modern military language, this was a conflict between a blue-water navy and a brown-water navy. Yet even that does not adequately describe the discrepancy in naval power. This was the world's largest and most modern navy against a fleet that was over 200 years behind in terms of naval technology.

Chinese war junks were intended as a support to coastal forts, which were considered by the Chinese to be the main line of defence. Such forts were in theory very strong with thick walls, impressive height, and as many as 60 guns. However there were many weaknesses. They had no roofs, and high-angled shellfire could be pitched over walls with relative ease and cause enormous damage. Whilst they gave reasonable protection from assault from the sea, there was little protection from land based attack. Indeed they had been designed largely to protect against pirate raids and were thus not concerned about amphibious assaults. There were also other practical problems. The guns were not maintained, and the forts were generally in a state of disrepair after years of neglect. There had also been a failure to construct them along scientific lines so as to make the most of each fort in support of the others. For example often the guns of one fort were not able to support those of another due to the position and angle at which they had been built.

Chinese artillery in general flattered to deceive during the conflict. The Chinese possessed a great many guns, but the quality varied dramatically. There was a story of a captured Chinese gun foundry in which was found a not unimpressive attempt to copy a British naval gun that had been captured from a shipwreck.[11] Generally, though, Chinese cannon tended to be rather elderly, and little care was taken to protect them from the elements. They were generally guns of position, fixed to a point and never moved. They therefore had no mobility, but also very little manoeuvrability.

---

10   Lovell, *The Opium War*, p. 107.
11   NLI: MS 638, 'Return of Ordnance Captured at Chusan, 1st October 1841' & NLI: MS 638, Gough to Lord Auckland, 18 October 1841. The latter specifically mentions the copying of guns found on the shipwrecked British vessel *Kite*. Gough called it 'an excellent imitation', although these were likely the words of Captain Herbert of HMS *Blenheim* who actually discovered the gun.

They were unable to swivel, not placed on rails, and could for the large part only fire straight ahead. The quality of the gunners also left much to be desired. Most had limited knowledge of their guns, and showed little determination in manning and defence of them. Perhaps most surprisingly was the poor quality of Chinese gunpowder. Given the lack of industrial process it was, like so much of Chinese military equipment, from a bygone age.

Whilst the majority of British infantry still carried the flintlock musket, some had started to carry the new percussion cap, or lock, musket that was more efficient and effective. The Chinese invariably lacked firearms and there was still a great reliance on swords, spears and bows. This often included the use of a shield made of rattan, which whilst effective against the normal enemies of the Chinese Empire, gave no protection against a musket ball. The exact number of Chinese soldiers who carried firearms is difficult to ascertain. It may be that as few as one in 10 had a firearm of some description. The majority were of a type that had long since disappeared from European service, the matchlock. In this type of weapon slow-burning matchcord was used to ignite the powder in the firing pan and create the explosion in the barrel that propelled the shot. Early types of this weapon had been seen since the middle of the 15th century in Europe, but by the early 18th century the weapon had largely disappeared from European armies. It is likely that such weapons were indeed developed from Chinese inventions: however whereas the European powers had sought to improve the weaponry, the Chinese had not. It was an inefficient and slow weapon, even when compared to the flintlock never mind the percussion cap.

The discipline, training and drill of the Chinese was woefully inadequate for a conflict against the British. The military elites, such as the Manchus and Mongolians, had rather taken their position for granted, becoming a sort of military/social elite rather than a professional force. Training was limited, and as China's financial position had deteriorated the military had suffered the brunt of the cuts. Pay had not improved but prices had risen dramatically. As a consequence, wide-scale corruption was commonplace. The financial limitations had also had their effect on training. Practice with ammunition had largely been stopped because of a want of ammunition and powder. Theoretically the Chinese Empire had the largest army in the world, approximately some 800,000 strong. Yet the majority of such soldiers were spread out to protect the vast Chinese Empire. As a result the Chinese were rarely able to have a force of more than 50,000 in the region of operations. Even then, a portion of such troops were needed for garrison duties. Troops were moved from neighbouring regions to support operations, yet their progress was so slow. Even for some of the closest troops to arrive at the front lines would take upwards of 40 days. By comparison, the British could transport troops from India in about the same amount of time. The slow movement of Chinese troops held back their ability to ever coordinate an effective counter-attack.

British military supremacy was therefore assured, although perhaps not fully appreciated until later in the war. One can see from Gough's despatches that he is genuinely surprised at the lack of fight shown by the Chinese. As a consequence he often starts to wonder whether or not he has missed something. It is almost as if at times he believes it is too easy, and this leads him to think that he must be missing something. Yet Gough had not yet arrived on the scene. There was general disquiet, in both India and Britain, as to the conduct of Charles Elliot and the way in which matters were being dealt with. As a consequence, there was a change in the political and naval command. rear admiral George Elliot, at that time commander-in-chief of the Cape Squadron, was to travel to China to assume the dual role of commander of the naval forces and senior plenipotentiary. He was the cousin of Charles Elliot and it was no doubt hoped by Palmerston that his supersession by his cousin would soften the blow. However his journey was delayed and he did not arrive off the China coast until the end of June 1840.

George Elliot was under instructions from Palmerston to deliver a letter to the minister of the Emperor of China, and then meet to discuss the signing of a treaty with the Chinese, a draft of which had been sent to him. In the meantime, to attract the attention of the Chinese Empire, he was to blockade Canton until such time as a treaty could be agreed upon. Of the tasks he had been given, blockading Canton was by far and away the easiest. Elliot would have great difficulty in getting the Chinese to accept his letter let alone sit around the table and negotiate.[12] On 4 July 1840 the British fleet sailed into the harbour of Chusan. Both Chusan and Tinghai fell easily, indeed they were hardly defended and there was no battle as such. Whilst the occupation was easy the holding of the towns was made all the harder by some serious blunders during the occupation. The sites chosen for the British troops to camp in could hardly have been worse. No reference had been made to the medical officers. The tents were pitched in low lying paddy fields surrounded by stagnant water. The soldiers were to suffer in extreme heat, surrounded by flies of all sort and subject to all manner of diseases and maladies. The biggest enemy to the British in that first year was disease.

The Elliots then continued their advance, mainly using a naval force. With 10 warships they sailed up the Pei Ho (or Hai) River towards the Taku Forts. On the way, George Elliot despatched two ships to blockade Ningpo and two to blockade the mouth of the Yangtze River, and with his remaining six he reached the Taku Forts by 15 August. Here he finally managed to find a Chinese official who would accept the letter and arrange for it to be passed on to Peking. It is not necessary to go into detail of the negotiations of the next month. Little was achieved and the Elliots became alive to the fact that the Chinese were just stalling for time. In a sense this worked, due to the poor planning of the British military. By September 1840 British forces in China, particularly Chusan, had been decimated by disease. Solar apoplexy, diarrhoea, dysentery, malaria, and physical exhaustion had severely affected a garrison of nearly 3,000 men. At least 450 had died from the various diseases by the end of September.[13]

In the words of Major Armine Mountain, a name we shall hear more of later, 'We have been playing at war instead of waging it'.[14] This neatly sums up the state of affairs. The Elliots had been reluctant to commit fully to war. They clung to the hope that the Army of Demonstration, as they referred to it, would be sufficient to induce the Chinese to accede to their demands. At times they had been given hope in this direction, but it had come to naught. In late November George Elliot suddenly resigned due to ill health and Charles Elliot became the sole plenipotentiary. Yet he would not last long, and would have been removed sooner had it not been for the delay in communication. His problem was that he was unable to bring a satisfactory conclusion to the confrontation with China. He displayed a great reluctance to really press a military campaign and this was ultimately his downfall.

The military solution was the only one that would bring the Chinese to accept British terms. Whilst it is easy to see British military action as an attempt to cut the Chinese down to size, there is also a practicality to this. In the same way that the Chinese would not trade on equal terms, they would not negotiate on equal terms. The British actions were seen as 'banditry', and not without some justification. The Chinese could not see any difference between the British who attacked their sea borders and the 'barbarians' who attacked the land frontiers of the Empire. It was therefore unlikely under these circumstances that an acceptable agreement could be reached. To create this new attitude new leaders were required. Gough was to be one of them.

---

12   Lovell, *The Opium War*, p. 116 & Holt, *The Opium Wars in China*, p. 107.
13   Holt, *The Opium Wars in China*, pp. 111–112.
14   Mountain, Mrs Armine (editor), *The Memoirs and Letters of the late Colonel Armine S.H. Mountain* (London: Longman, Brown, Green, Longmans & Roberts, 1858), p. 167.

27

Gough's Arrival in China

When Gough arrived on the scene, it is abundantly clear that he saw his main aim as being to humble the Chinese military. By doing this the British would then be in a position to dictate terms, whatever the politicians might decide these should be. Gough's reputation as an active commander, and his considerable experience in the greatest campaign in British history within living memory, made him an obvious candidate for the job. He was also convenient, both geographically and in terms of employment. His absence from the command of a division in India would not be missed in the short term. George Burrell, who Gough superseded, had been in command simply because he was the senior British officer of the regiments sent to China. There was no thought given to the command structure and he had no staff. This goes to further illustrate the rather ad hoc and limited nature of the early deployment of troops. Even by the standards of the British Army during the Victorian era, this was a very amateur arrangement. Once again this is largely due to the fact that there was no direction from the politicians as to what the military were to achieve.

Although in this respect Burrell does deserve defending, he does appear to have been a some-what rigid and 'by the book' officer. Despite temperatures of up to 38–40 degrees Celsius, Burrell insisted upon his troops wearing their regulation serge coates fully buttoned up, even when engaged in manual labour. Unsurprisingly this added to the suffering and casualties. At best he seems to have been indifferent to his men's suffering, cancelling his visit to the hospital to see them despite the fact that the naval commander and the civilian representative had paid a similar visit, and refusing to listen to the surgeons' requests for a ship to be provided for the wounded to give them a 'change of air' and hopefully a slightly less oppressive temperature. However the death toll was not simply down to the questionable actions of any single officer, and Burrell failed to alleviate the suffering rather than being the cause of it.[1]

By the end of September 1840 there had been 450 casualties as a result of disease. This was exac-erbated by the poor quality of the food supplied, particularly when the food came from India. The 26th Foot (Cameronians) were renowned for their arrangements, which in India, had seen them have the lowest rate of sickness and death in the subcontinent. The extreme nature of the condi-tions in China is demonstrated by the statistics attached to this regiment, considered to be one of the healthiest in the army. When they arrived in China in 1840 they boasted 28 officers and 902 men. By the end of that year they had only one officer and 110 men fit for duty. Of the rest, the majority were in hospital but 240 had already died through sickness and disease. Part of the reason why the 26th suffered such high casualties is said to have been down to the fact that they relied wholly on food supplies from India, whereas the 18th Foot had been transported by ships originally sent from England and thus carrying food supplies from there. The food from India is said to have been poorly packed. Biscuits were placed in insanitary boxes or bags. Much of the cured meat was

---

1   Holt, *The Opium Wars in China*, p. 111. Barthorp, Michael, *The British Army on Campaign 1816–1853*, (London: Osprey Publishing, 1987) p. 45.

so poorly done than it did not last the voyage from India to China before it went bad. The 18th also benefitted because, with Burrell elevated to command the whole force, there was a more relaxed approach: their officers allowed them to unbutton their coatees and carry their stocks under their shoulder straps.[2]

A large part of the problem was down to the fact that a force had been despatched without any clear aim or objective. As a consequence they had been held in 'reserve' in unhealthy garrisons and in severe climatic conditions which was an act of extreme folly. Of the two alternatives, namely camping in fields or being kept aboard the ships at sea, neither was conducive to good health. The former, due to the damp conditions was even worse for the health of the men than the cramped garrisons, whereas the latter was impractical as many of the ships that had initially transported the troops had either left the scene or were full of civilians who had been evacuated from the mainland. As the century wore on the British Army became aware of the need to get troops in and out of such unhealthy areas as quickly as possible. Largely this was due to such experiences as China in the 1840s.

Despite sailing in December 1840, it was not until 2 March 1841 that Gough arrived in China. By this stage much had changed. The Chinese were now looking to negotiate, and Commissioner Lin was replaced by Qishan (Chi-shan): whilst Lin's reputation in China remains high, Qishan is remembered as 'Shameless capitulationist-robber Qishan'.[3] The Chinese Emperor had been influenced in his decision to replace Lin by the official letter from Lord Palmerston. The Emperor's selective reading of the letter had convinced him that the main source of grievance was the attitude and actions of Lin rather than wider issues of trade and prestige. However this willingness to negotiate was not an acceptance of defeat or surrender; rather, it was a continuance of a diplomatic tradition going back to the Han dynasty. This policy, known as the 'loose rein', was an attempt at controlling the 'barbarians' by kindness rather than military force.[4] Whilst not an acceptance of inferiority it was, perhaps, an acceptance of the practicalities of the situation. A long war against the British would be costly and not what the failing Chinese economy needed. To think of it as appeasement would be to misinterpret the Chinese mind. However to an extent this was the way the British interpreted it.

Whilst Elliot was happy to negotiate, he was in his own mind convinced that the military action up to this point had been the reason for the Chinese negotiations. He therefore felt it prudent to threaten Canton and used this as an 'aid' in his negotiations, threatening that if an agreement was not reached that he would launch the attack. Orders were issued in London for Elliot to occupy Chusan and blockade Canton, but whether Elliot actually received these orders before his decisions were made is unlikely. On 7 January 1841, he made good on the threat. Twelve ships commanded by Commodore James Bremer sailed along the Pearl River delta towards the Bocca Tigris and the island of Chuenpee (Chuanbi). This was the gateway towards Canton, and was a clear indication that the British could move and take the city if they wished. A force of around 1,500 soldiers, British and Indian, Royal Marines, sailors, and three artillery pieces were landed to attack the fortress. Over 2,000 Chinese commanded the fortress with numerous, though hopelessly outclassed, artillery pieces. The land based British guns and those of the British ships had silenced the enemy guns within an hour. Operations had begun at 0800 and by 1000 the upper fort had been captured, and the Royal Marines were about to storm the lower fort. The British had triumphed with ease and the loss of just 38 men. The Chinese had not only lost two important forts, but over 190 guns, and maybe as many as 600 dead. The Chinese reports would claim the British

---

2   Barthorp, *The British Army on Campaign 1816–1853*, p. 45.
3   Lovell, *The Opium War*, p. 120.
4   Lovell, *The Opium War*, pp. 121–124.

victory was due to treachery from within the Chinese camp, and that the secrets of the forts and the waterways had been sold to the British.

This act of force encouraged the diplomatic process and the Chinese agreed to the Convention of Chuenpee on 20 January 1841. This act of diplomacy however satisfied neither side. Elliot felt he had achieved a good deal for Britain and believed that he had satisfied the instructions about any such deal with China that he had received from Lord Palmerston. These had included return of the captured opium or financial recompense for such, an indemnity for the indignities suffered during the siege of the factories, guarantees on future trades on equal terms, payment of outstanding debts by Chinese merchant and payment for the cost of the British expedition. Finally Elliot was charged with securing an 'island' along the Chinese coast which could be used as a base for trade. The Convention of Chuenpee secured most of this. It secured trade on equal terms, the reopening of trade at Canton, the ceding of Hong Kong to the British, and an indemnity of six million dollars.

Both Elliot and Qishan thought they had done a good deal and were pleased at the results. It was not long before they realised that their political masters did not share their enthusiasm. The Emperor rejected the Convention immediately upon hearing of it. He was particularly angered that the island of Hong Kong had been ceded and that trade, which Lin had in theory ended forever, was restored. Qishan was dismissed and stripped of his rank. Taken to Peking in chains, his property was confiscated and he was sentenced to death, although it was never carried out. A story exists that Qishan attempted to avoid his fate by trying to bribe Elliot to return Hong Kong. The offer was said to include considerable artwork and curios and a beautiful Chinese mistress. As was so often the case with Chinese officials, Qishan's disgrace was only temporary and in 1842 he was appointed Imperial Commissioner to Tibet. In 1854 he died whilst leading an Imperial army against the Taiping rebels. The Emperor's mood was illustrated by the fact that he now appointed three new generals to command in the area around Canton, with the aim of driving the British out of China.

Elliot's problems started when the Convention document was sent via India. Lord Auckland added his opinion before forwarding the documents to London, making it clear that he thought the terms "fall very far short of the expectations with which this powerful expedition was fitted out."[5] He felt the evacuation of Chusan was a mistake, that the agreement to continue to pay Imperial charges and duties on business done in Hong Kong was unacceptable, and that the financial indemnity was not only too small but too lenient as it would be paid in the amount of 1,000,000 Chinese dollars a year. His views were shared in London. Whilst Elliot felt he had obtained a good deal, the British Government dissented from the Convention. The problem was that Elliot had 'negotiated', in all good faith, and thus had inevitably compromised to agree a settlement. Elliot no doubt felt this was what was needed, whereas the British and Indian governments wanted him to dictate terms without compromise.

Inevitably, hostilities broke out again on the in February when British warships sailing up river to Canton were fired upon. Commodore Bremer dispatched five ships and a force of about 1,500 mixed troops to attack the forts at Anunghoy on the route to Canton. On 26 February the forts were taken. When Gough arrived on 2 March 1841 he found that a three-day truce was in effect, whilst negotiations took place with General Yang Fang, the only one of the three generals appointed by the Emperor to have reached the area. Upon his arrival Gough immediately planned for further operations. Appreciating that the nature of the area in which they were operating was a largely naval scene he placed his forces at the disposal of the naval commanders. This act of cooperation should not be underestimated. All too often, pride got in the way of cooperation between naval and military commanders during this era. Gough arrived and immediately summed up the situation,

---

5   Holt, *The Opium Wars in China*, p. 120.

knowing that any advance needed to be amphibious in nature and that therefore it was better that such operations be organised by naval officers. That is not to say that Gough took a back seat, as he provided all the assistance he could in making the naval commanders aware of what his force could achieve.

Gough also consolidated his forces. On his arrival the senior officer in the area around Canton was Major Alexander Peat who commanded a small attachment under the naval commanders.[6] It was under Gough's orders that the force in Chusan under Major General Burrell were brought up to join him outside Canton. Gough how had his entire military force before Canton. This act, in and of itself, means little but it does highlight the fact that there was now an element of organisation, order, and indeed purpose to military operations. Gough's character was such that he was not going to sit around and wait. By placing his forces at the disposal of the naval commanders he was also urging them to take action. They now had the resources to seriously threaten Canton.

On 6 March, troops under Gough's command occupied one of the forts overlooking Canton itself. The city was now under direct threat. On the 18th, British troops took possession of the foreign quarter or factory area of Canton. The British factories that had once been besieged and then evacuated now had the Union Flag hoisted above them. This was not only an event of great symbolic importance, it also had a profound effect on the Chinese commander Yang Fang. The latter, although under Imperial instruction not to, felt obliged to return to the negotiating table. With such a clear threat to Canton he accepted a ceasefire and agreed that trade should be reopened. This allowed the British to replenish their stocks of food and supplies, without having to resort to plundering, which Gough had made it quite clear in the short space of time since his arrival, would not be tolerated.

At this stage the British position was, on the face of it, a strong one. Trade had been restored at Canton, and a British base at Hong Kong had been established, although at this time as little more than a giant storehouse for British goods. However beneath the surface was the belief that this was only an interlude, an event which was welcomed by both sides. The Chinese continued to prepare, and it was clear that the lesson of their military inferiority had not yet been appreciated. They proceeded to build a large military camp outside Canton, as troops were finally arriving in large numbers after long journeys from other parts of the Chinese Empire. During this period of armistice and trade Gough had much to occupy him. One of his first duties upon arriving had been to ask for fresh troops. Before he left India, Lord Auckland had urged him not to make this request, largely because Auckland had little to spare. Gough appeared to have agreed to this before his departure, and it was surely with some surprise, if not to say annoyance, that Auckland received Gough's request.[7] However it was for 'fresh' rather than 'extra' soldiers that Gough was asking. The battalions that had been in China for some time were tired and had been greatly reduced by death and disease. Gough's argument was that due to this he could not place in the field the number of troops that was presumed to be his total strength. In short, the number of troops Auckland had told Gough he would have under his command when he agreed to make no further request for troops were not available. Eventually the 55th Foot were sent, along with some Madras Native Infantry, to reinforce Gough's command.[8]

Early on in his time in China, Gough had to preside over a court of enquiry. Sadly he makes little comment in his surviving papers on this point. It would be interesting from his point of view

---

6   Although his name appears in the Army List and India List as Alexander Cumine Peat, his name occasionally appears in histories of the period as Peath. Peat was an officer of the Bombay Engineers who spent most of his career as a staff officer.

7   Rait, *Gough*, Vol. I, pp. 160–161.

8   The views were expressed in a letter to Archibald Arbuthnot, a Director of the East India Company, dated the 24 April 1841. This letter was reproduced in Rait, *Gough*, Vol. I, pp. 169–172.

to know how he felt in regards to this process given his own experience of such an enquiry from the other side. The subject was a difficult one, as the court was asked to report on the prevalence of sickness and disease amongst the troops. Whilst an unpleasant task it was no doubt helpful to the new commander to hear in detail the failings and faults of the previous campaigning. There was a great deal of concern over the high levels of disease and death, from a practical point of view if not necessarily a humanitarian one. The majority of the British troops had come from India where the number of European troops was always a concern. The fear persisted that Europeans were needed to give backbone to the native units. To lose such a large number of troops through disease caused practical concerns for the authorities in India and at home. The fact that the high rates of ill health also included a battalion with a high reputation for fitness and low sickness rates, the 26th, drew further attention to the matter.[9]

The court of enquiry laid the majority of the blame upon the conditions and climate, adding that they had the misfortune to be in China in a particularly bad year in this regard. There was also criticism of the fact that there had been too few camp followers to support the troops. As a consequence the soldiers had to undertake extra work in exhausting conditions. At the same time, the rather unintelligent actions of men like Burrell had not helped. Having to do manual work alongside their military duties in conditions 38–40 degrees Celsius was bad enough without having to keep their coatees on and fully buttoned up. Gough concluded that the proper thing to have done would have been to re-embark the troops. However he conceded that this was difficult as the soldiers had no authority over the naval forces and there were insufficient available ships for the majority of the time.[10] Gough did suggest that a system of rotating troops between the ships and the garrisons could have been used. However this was reliant on the naval commanders not the military. It would also have required a level of administration and organisation which was lacking in the existing arrangements. We see in the report of this court of enquiry further evidence as to why Gough had from his arrival tried to build up relations with the naval commanders and had taken the practical step of placing his forces at the disposal of the navy. He was not abrogating his responsibility, nor was he showing a lack of pride or confidence in his men: it was purely a case of practicality. Up to that point the combat had largely been naval in nature, and if Gough were to get his men involved in the war and take the fight to the enemy, as he had clearly been instructed to do, he would have to rely on naval support.

Gough's instructions had initially revolved around strikes against shipping and coastal areas. Lord Auckland felt that this was all that could be achieved for now, as he was particularly concerned about the drain upon the resources of India, both in terms of shipping and soldiers, which the conflict was having.[11] Gough, however, had resolved from the start that any action needed to go further than this. Not only was this contrary to his instructions it was also at odds with the opinion of Elliot, who was technically his superior. Gough was of the belief that such costal attacks were merely a preliminary and that more drastic movements in land had to be undertaken to convince the Chinese that the British were in earnest. Threatening the coastline and trade was one thing, but to really get the attention of the Chinese more drastic action was necessary. Gough's plan was to attack and occupy the city of Canton, not as an end but rather as a means to then pushing on towards Amoy to destroy Chinese shipping, and from there to Shanghai and up the Yangtze river.

---

9   Whilst suffering the aforementioned high rates of sickness whilst in China, it is said that the 26th Foot received a request from the commander-in-chief, India's office asking for details of the arrangements within that regiment that had led them to have such a good record of health. The request must have seemed in rather macabre humour to a regiment slowly dying in Chinese garrisons. Holt, *The Opium Wars in China*, p. 112.

10   Rait, *Gough*, Vol. I, p. 163.

11   Rait, *Gough*, Vol. I, pp. 164–165.

This would be a serious threat to the Chinese, not only cutting off their trade but with an inland movement threatening the Chinese Empire in a more serious way. It was here that the shallow draft of many British ships, and in particular the impressive iron steamer *Nemesis*,[12] was of great value. Although still using naval assets as the means of transportation, it allowed the British to take the fight into the heart of the empire and to threaten more than just the coastal towns and cities.

Whilst planning for this campaign, Gough also had something of a professional problem during this period. On 19 January 1841 the commander-in-chief of the Madras Army, Gough's old Peninsular War colleague, Sir Samuel Whittingham died unexpectedly. Correspondence of the time makes it clear that the position had been all but promised to Gough, and it was presumed that when Whittingham had served his term Gough would have succeeded to the command. However at the present moment that was impractical. It seems that there was the hope that the appointment of a successor could be delayed, and indeed it was not until September 1842 that a new commander-in-chief of the Madras Army was appointed. It is clear that Lord Auckland felt bad about the position Gough had been placed in.

> I fear I shall have done you a bad turn, by naming you to this appointment, for the sudden death of Sir Samford Whittinghame [sic] might otherwise have given you for a time an advantageous position at Madras, and if the anticipations of Captain Elliot should be true, there will be no demand for active service in China. It will be for you, with reference to a judgement formed on the spot, on experience and events, to decide on your future course, I must bear a grateful remembrance of the readiness with which you complied with my wishes, and shall much regret it if such alacrity should turn to your disadvantage. At the same time, I conceive that for the arrangement which may be necessary either for future service or for the settlement and protection of the island of Hong-Kong, your presence in the Canton River may be of much importance and benefit.[13]

Indeed the position was somewhat disappointing for Gough. He wanted the command of the Madras Army, and one wonders whether or not he had been convinced to take up the command of a division within it on the hint that he would one day assume overall command of the army. If this were the case, it had never been anticipated that it would be vacant so soon. Furthermore, despite what Elliot thought, Gough was certain that further military action in China would be necessary.

---

12   *Nemesis* was an Iron paddle frigate built and launched in 1839 in just three months. She used a mixture of steam and sail. Nemesis was built for the HEIC, but was for many years not on their official list. She mounted two pivoted 32 pdrs, four 6pdrs, and a rocket launcher.
13   Rait, *Gough*, Vol. I, pp. 166–167. Auckland misspells Whittingham's surname and uses the name by which he was known to his friends, 'Samford'. This was a combination of his two given names Samuel and Ford.

28

Battle for Canton

In April Elliot had felt confident enough about the situation to remove the guard of Royal Marines that had been defending the factories since trade had been reopened. However by the end of May 1841 Elliot had advised all Europeans to leave the factories. By sunset on 21 May the British flag had been lowered and all whites had left the factories except for two Americans. Elliot's decision had been well timed as that same evening of the 21st the Chinese opened fire on the factories. At the same time they attacked both the ships in the harbour from land and by the use of fire-ships. However this was all without success. The hopeless inferiority of the Chinese in naval terms was illustrated in the following days when over 70 Chinese war junks were destroyed for little damage to the British ships.

In response to the attack on the factories Gough now reiterated his call to attack Canton, which Elliot now backed. Gough had previously planned for action further along the coast at Amoy. However on 18 May Gough had written to Lord Auckland making him aware of the

> temporary abandonment of the movement on Amoy, in order to resume active operations against Canton, consequent upon the constant arrival and concentration of a large force from the enemy's provinces, and other demonstrations indicative of an interruption to our friendly intercourse with the provisional Government.[1]

With Commodore Bremer absent in India, Gough consulted with the temporary naval commander Captain Sir Humphrey Fleming Senhouse on how best to attack the city. Gough managed to collect around 3,500 troops for the attack, of which about 2,500 were soldiers the remainder being made up of Royal Marines and sailors. The Chinese troops inside Canton were said to number around 45,000, added to this were over a million inhabitants of the city and Gough had to take into account whether any of the latter would act as auxiliaries. On the face of it, looking purely at the numbers, it was an almost impossible task for the 3,500 men, even with naval gunfire support. However such was the military superiority of British arms that the attack was feasible, and indeed likely to succeed if conducted properly.[2]

By 18 May, Senhouse had prepared the naval task force to sail, and Gough later paid tribute to his considerable exertions in this undertaking. However due to variable winds the fleet did not sail until the morning of the 19th. Although HMS *Blenheim*, the flagship, and many of the men-of-war arrived off Canton on 21 May it was not until the 23rd that all the ships of the fleet arrived. On that day Gough went ashore to inspect the preparations of the city and plan his attack. He was also

---

1   NLI: MS 638, Gough to Lord Auckland, 3 June 1841. This mentions the previous correspondence of 18 May 1841.
2   NLI: MS 638, Gough to Lord Auckland, 3 June 1841. See also Lovell, *The Opium War*, pp. 153–154.

assisted by the reconnaissance by Commander Edward Belcher of the bomb-vessel HMS *Sulphur*.[3] It was almost exclusively Gough's own reconnaissance and that of Commander Belcher that informed his plan of attack. This was important in terms of the position for the landing: Belcher determining it was a feasible position to land the men, equipment, and stores, and Gough determining that it was a good position to gather in preparation for an attack on the enemy. Intelligence in general was hard to come by as it had been some time since any European had been allowed inside Canton, and intelligence from the Chinese had to be taken with a pinch of salt. The Chinese had a habit of telling the British what they wanted to hear, as they were anxious for the 20 dollars that Elliot had offered for intelligence. In recent months thousands of extra Chinese soldiers had arrived, and it was to be presumed that at the same time as reinforcements arrived, preparations for the defence of the city had also been undertaken.[4]

Gough and Senhouse held a meeting with Elliot on 23 May. It is clear that both military commanders wished to commence operations the following day. Gough also remarked that, given that 24 May was also Queen Victoria's birthday, it would be an auspicious day to commence the attack on so valuable target as Canton. Elliot still wished to negotiate, and firmly believed that he could obtain favourable terms without the need to assault Canton. It may be that he feared the outcome of such an assault both materially and politically. Casualties could be high, and once such an attack had been made, and Canton taken, the British were firmly committed to continuing further military operations. Up to that point their attacks had been a mild irritation to the Chinese Empire. However the seizure by force of an important trading city as Canton would inevitably lead to a response.

Gough had decided that his main force would attack from their position north west of the city, whilst the Right Column of 15 officers and 294 men, mostly of the 26th Foot, along with artillery consisting of one 6pdr, and one 5½ inch mortar, and one officer and 20 sappers, were to take possession of the factories. This column was commanded by Major Thomas Pratt of the 26th Foot.[5] The aim of this was not only to secure British property before the attack, but also to divert the attention of the Chinese from the main attack. The men of the 26th Foot, supported by naval gunfire, also succeed in capturing one of the island forts known as Dutch Folly. The remainder of the force, under Gough's direct command, was split into four brigades. The 4th Brigade consisted of 28 officers and 273 men of the 49th Foot commanded by Major Thomas Stephens, 11 officers and 219 men of the 37th Madras Native Infantry commanded by Captain Daniel Duff, and one company, of 1 officer and 114 men, of Bengal Volunteers under Captain G. A. Mee. The 3rd Brigade consisted of the artillery and 141 sappers and miners, under the overall commanded of Captain John Knowles of the Royal Artillery. The force was largely made up of artillery from the Madras Army, although there was a detachment of the Royal Artillery. Between them they had

---

3   HMS *Sulphur* was a Hecla Class Bomb vessel, mounting one 13 inch and one 10 inch Mortar, along with ten 24 pdrs, and two 6 pdr carronades. Due to the fact that they were heavily built and sturdy ships all eight of the class were converted, or altered during building, to survey ships in the years after the Napoleonic Wars. As such they played a considerable role in Arctic and Antarctic exploration. Indeed Captain, later Admiral Sir, Edward Belcher would become well known for his surveying efforts around the world, although his final mission to rescue the expedition of Rear Admiral Sir John Franklin saw him forced to abandon his ships that were trapped by ice. Court-martialled, standard practice for losing a ship, he was exonerated.
4   NLI: MS 638, Gough to Lord Auckland, 3 June 1841.
5   Major, later General Sir, Thomas Simson Pratt is perhaps better remembered for his service during the Maori or New Zealand Wars. He commanded British and colonial forces during the Taranaki campaign in New Zealand, where his lacklustre support for the war brought him into conflict with the governor and his over-cautious approach when dealing with Maori defences led to him being ridiculed by the settler community.

four 12 pdr howitzers, four 9 pdr field guns, two 6 pdr field guns, three 5½ inch mortars, and 152 32 pdr rockets. The 2nd Brigade was designated the Naval Brigade and commanded by Captain Thomas Bourchier of HMS *Blonde*, being made up of sailors from the ships of the fleet formed into the 1st Naval Battalion of 11 officers and 172 men commanded by Captain Thomas Maitland from HMS *Wellesley*, and the 2nd Naval Battalion of 16 officers and 231 men commanded by Captain C. A. Barlow from HMS *Nimrod*. The 1st Brigade was on the extreme right of the deployment commanded by Major General Burrell. It consisted of 25 officers and 494 men of the 18th Foot commanded by Lieutenant Colonel Henry Adams and 9 officers and 372 men of the Royal Marines commanded by Captain Samuel Ellis.[6]

Operations began at 1400 on 24 May. Whilst the main force landed, the right column commenced their capture of the factories and the fort known as Dutch Folly. This was achieved by 1700. The landing of the main body, the left column, took a little longer. The majority of troops were towed in boats by the steamer *Nemesis*, whose shallow draft of barely six foot made it possible to take the boats almost to the shore. It took some time for the troops to be landed. The 49th Foot were deliberately landed first so that they could provide a guard for the rest of the landing. Perhaps somewhat injudiciously Gough went ashore with them; although it was a risk he was at least able to continue his reconnaissance and was on hand in the event of an attack. Gough moved forward with the 49th to make sure the area was clear of the enemy. After establishing pickets they fell back on the village of Tsingpu (although in his report Gough called it Tsinghae). In the days of limited communication between ships and shore it was probably a calculated risk for Gough to go ashore with the first landing. He also had full confidence in the naval commanders to successfully complete the landing. That the naval commanders were competent was just as well given that the landing of the artillery continued during the night. Landing artillery at the best of times was fraught with danger, but to do it at night was an added risk. Although the naval crews deserve credit for achieving this successfully, Gough also remarked on the "zealous efforts of the artillery."[7] The landing of the remaining infantry followed during the night and early hours of the morning.

On the morning of 25 May, Gough ordered the advance. His reconnaissance had shown him that to the north of the town were four strong forts. In order to take the town they would have to be captured, as otherwise their guns would attack any force advancing on the city walls. It would also be dangerous to leave such strong positions in the hands of the enemy when advancing forward. Although the forts were physically strong, the guns were outdated and poorly manned. Also the position of the forts was such that Gough's artillery could fire on them from raised positions around them. The forts were about three and a half miles from where the troops had landed. Moving through undulating ground, paddy fields, and hollows meant that the movement took some time. Almost inevitably the infantry arrived before the artillery. Although this meant the British came under fire before their artillery was in a position to fire back, fortunately there was plenty of cover for Gough to protect his men.

When finally the artillery and rockets were able to open fire at around 0800, they quickly silenced the enemy guns, once again demonstrating the superiority of British artillery. Although the British troops were considerably outnumbered there was no hesitation in going on the attack. This was not simply the natural response of Gough, but was a vote of confidence in his soldiers. Nor was it only due to technological advantages. Gough also placed great faith in the discipline of British troops. For a man who had witnessed the triumph of British infantry over the hitherto-invincible French infantry during the Napoleonic wars, this was an understandable conclusion. Whilst it also says

---

6   For full details of the force listed above see NLI: MS 638, Gough to Lord Auckland, 3 June 1841. Over three pages Gough sets out the full deployment of his force.

7   NLI: MS 638, Gough to Lord Auckland, 3 June 1841.

something of the perceived strength and discipline of the Chinese troops, it should be pointed out the Gough had expected a far more determined resistance than he encountered. After the battle Gough wrote to Lord Auckland regarding the soldiers under his command, stating of their discipline and confidence that, "no disparity of number could dishearten, and no difficult could check." He went further and stated that, "They nobly realised, by their steadiness under fire, their disciplined advance and their animated rush, my warmest anticipations."[8]

After the artillery had silenced the Chinese guns Gough drew his men up for the attack.

> I now made the dispositions for attack in echelon columns from the left, and directed the 49th Regt to carry a hill on the left of the nearest eastern fort , supported by the 37th Madras Native Infantry and Bengal Volunteers under Lt Col Morris of the 49th Regt. The 18th Royal Irish supported by the Royal Marines under Major General Burrell, I directed to carry a hill to their front which was strongly occupied and flanked the approach to the fort just mentioned. This movement was to cut off the communication between the two eastern forts, and cover the advance of the 49th in their attack and storm of the nearest. Major General Burrell had directions to push on and take the principal square fort, when the 49th made their rush. Simultaneously with these attacks, the brigade of seamen was to carry the two western forts, covered by a concentrated fire from the whole of the guns and rockets.[9]

During the advance it became clear to Gough that a large party of Chinese had left the city ramparts and were moving towards the two western forts, against which the brigade of sailors was advancing. To support the sailors, Gough detached the Royal Marines under Captain Ellis.

Gough spoke of the discipline with which his forces advanced. He gave particular credit to the sailors and native troops, in whom he had clearly not had the same confidence prior to the battle as he had the British soldiers. Speaking of the native troops he gave them what to his mind would have been the highest praise he could muster; that they had performed to same standard as their British counterparts. The advance of the sailors he called, 'a noble rush' and commented that despite being under heavy fire they never wavered.[10] Although a great many of the sailors may have had some experience of being under fire, it would have been in the somewhat different surroundings of a naval battle. However their advance during this battle was greatly to their credit. Although Gough had chosen the slightly weaker target for their advance, he must have had confidence that they could carry the day.

The two forts were captured with little loss of life. As Gough reported, "in little more than half an hour after the order to advance was given the British troops looked down on Canton, within 100 paces of its walls." For the first time Gough was able to see the Chinese camp to the north east of the city which he described 'as being of considerable extent'. Gough's keen eye spotted that behind the camp lay paddy fields which would block the retreat of the Chinese in the event of a defeat, and he therefore started to plan for an attack which would potentially drive the Chinese into this land and thus precipitate a rout. The Chinese continued sporadic attacks in an attempt to drive and remove the British from their positions. They had little success, but Gough found that any attempt to follow the retreating Chinese exposed his troops to heavy fire from the city walls, that were in part still held by the Chinese.[11]

---

8   NLI: MS 638, Gough to Lord Auckland, 3 June 1841.
9   NLI: MS 638, Gough to Lord Auckland, 3 June 1841.
10 NLI: MS 638, Gough to Lord Auckland, 3 June 1841.
11 NLI: MS 638, Gough to Lord Auckland, 3 June 1841.

For now, Gough was largely prepared to sit and wait, as it was still early in the day, around 1000. The exception to this was that a party of Chinese had occupied a small village to his rear. Although exact details are not available, it would appear that this was a party of Chinese who had been dislodged from the hill earlier in the day and being unable, or unwilling, to return to the city had found refuge in the nearby village. Although they did not pose a major threat to him, Gough could not take the risk of leaving them in possession of the village and despatched the 49th Foot to take the village. This was done with ease.

By 1400, Gough believed that the Chinese were planning a concerted counter-attack, with General Yang in command. To counter this Gough prepared an attack on the aforementioned camp to the north east. There was a narrow causeway which was the only approach to the camp. Any movement along here would be exposed to fire from the city walls, and could not be done in secret. It was estimated that there were around 4,000 Chinese troops currently in the camp. At around 1500, Gough despatched the 18th Royal Irish and one company of Royal Marines to reinforce the 49th Foot. In effect Gough was combining the pick of his troops to attack the camp. Major General Burrell commanded the attack. Gough seems to have made good use of Burrell, and on such an occasion the latter's by-the-book attitude helped to maintain discipline under fire. The Chinese were routed, the camp burnt to the ground and destroyed, and several Chinese powder magazines were destroyed.

The attack was a complete success. The Chinese artillery fire from the walls of Canton had not proved as effective as was feared, or indeed as perhaps it should have been. This was partly down to the quality of guns, and the way in which they were handled, but also spoke of the effect that British artillery was having upon Canton. From their newly acquired positions British artillery, particularly the mortars, were firing directly into the city. Chinese accounts record that the British guns never fell silent and that parts of the city were set on fire. The constant barrage had also destroyed Chinese discipline, which had not been strong to begin with. Soldiers ran wild and looting was prevalent, whilst the civilian population packed up what they could in the hope of leaving the city before the British attacked.

By the time the attack on the Chinese encampment had succeeded the day was starting to fade. Gough admitted later that he had been tempted to rally his troops for an attack on the city in the late afternoon. However he wisely decided against it, as there were many factors against such an idea. His men had been on the go since the early morning and were tired from the exertions of the day, and from illness.[12] The weather had been an unpleasant mixture of heat and thunderstorms. May was the start of the 'hot' season in Canton, and in normal circumstances the heat could be oppressive. However when one takes into account that the men were engaged in strenuous labour and fighting in full uniform, the effects on their health can be imagined.[13] Gough's artillery was also causing havoc throughout the city and it was wise to continue this, as the number of guns being brought forward increased through the night. Waiting until the morrow also gave him the chance to bring up extra supplies, equipment, food and ammunition. Whilst one can understand Gough's desire to keep up the momentum his force had created, his decision to wait until the 26th was a wise one in military terms.

The troops spent an unpleasant night in bad weather conditions and without proper shelter, although some units did improvise some kind of bivouacs. However the morning of 26 May was

---

12   Lovell, *The Opium War*, p. 153, suggests that diarrhoea and sickness had spread through the British ranks. Gough makes no mention of this in his correspondence with Lord Auckland.

13   Lovell, *The Opium War*, p. 156. Lovell recounts the story of a British major who collapsed and died of heatstroke during this period. Although she does not name the officer it is possible that she means Major Belcher, the Quarter Master General, who collapsed and 'died within minutes', according to Gough, on 30 May. Gough recalls the incident regarding Major Belcher in his report to Lord Auckland.

one of great anticipation. The great city of Canton, the source of all European trade with China, was set to fall to the British. However it was a city that the Chinese had always been reluctant to allow westerners to actually enter, other than the factory area. This had always been a source of annoyance and grievance, and on that morning it appeared that it would fall to the British force that lay just outside its walls. The morning also brought the sight of thousands of Chinese streaming out of the north of the city, in anticipation of the British attack.

In the morning flags of truce could be seen flying from the city walls. Gough sent Mr Robert Thom, an employee of the trading house of Jardine-Matheson who was acting as an interpreter, to ascertain what was going on. "A Mandarin stated that they wished for peace. I had it explained that as General commanding the British I would treat with none but the General Commanding the Chinese troops." Whilst this was a necessary piece of protocol, it also ensured that Gough would be talking to the man most likely to be able to carry through on any promises that were made. Gough took the opportunity for a little politics and made it known:

> that we came before Canton much against the wishes of the British nation, but that repeated insults and breaches of faith had compelled us to make the present movement, and that I would cease from hostilities for two hours to enable their General to meet me and Sir Le Fleming Senhouse who kindly accompanied me throughout the whole operation.[14]

Despite Gough repeating the message several times his Chinese counterpart did not appear. As a consequence, at 1600 Gough hauled down his white flag. The Chinese did not follow suit and Gough took advantage of the fact that the Chinese did not fire to move his guns closer to the city and bring up further ammunition and supplies ready for an attack. Due to the Chinese negotiations he had lost a day but it did not appear to be of any great consequence. During the night Gough continued his preparations and formations were decided upon and orders issue for the attack on the 27th.

The right column consisting of the Royal Marines was to attack the north gate, blow it, and enter the city. Also on the right, the brigade of sailors was directed to attack a low part of the city wall near the North gate that seemed to be defended by only a few guns. The 18th Foot were ordered to attack near what Gough described as a 'five storied pagoda'.[15] Although the walls at this point were very high, the position was flanked by only one gun. On the left of this position, the 49th were to launch their attack. In theory this was the strongest point of the wall. However in practice the defenders had a choice as to whether to use their guns or their musketry, and the close positioning of the two types of firearms would create so much smoke as to make it difficult to view the advancing enemy. The ground ahead of all the advancing troops would be shelled before the advance took place as Gough feared that the Chinese might have mined the approaches to the city walls.

At daylight on 27 May, Gough was still surprised to see the flags of truce flying from the city walls. At 0615 the flags were still flying. As Gough reported, "I was on the point of sending the interpreter to explain that I could not respect such a display after my flag had been taken down and should at once assume hostilities." It was at this point that matters were taken out of Gough's hands.

> At this moment, an officer of the Royal Navy, who had been travelling all night, having [lost] his way, handed me the accompanying letter from Her Majesty's Plenipotentiary. Whatever

---

14   NLI: MS 638, Gough to Lord Auckland, 3 June 1841.
15   NLI: MS 638, Gough to Lord Auckland, 3 June 1841.

might be my sentiments, my duty was to acquiesce. The attack which was to have commenced in forty-five minutes (0700hrs) was countermanded, and the feelings of the Chinese were spared.[16]

The officer had in fact been despatched by Elliot the night before, at around 2200. However he had lost his way in the dark and had decided to sleep in a rice field before continuing his journey at first light. Gough was not happy. There were strategic, logistical, and welfare concerns to the cancelling of the attack. However it is clear that Gough also felt that he had personally been 'betrayed' by Elliot. The fact that Elliot had decided the day before to negotiate was contrary to the instructions Gough had given to the Chinese as senior military commander. In a land where 'face' was every-thing, Gough had clearly lost face by the actions of Elliot. A more tactful man then Elliot might have visited Gough in person to discuss the matter. That Elliot had the authority to take such action was never debated by Gough, it was merely the way in which he did it that rankled. Elliot's letter informed Gough of the negotiations taking place, giving some details of what this entailed, and concluded that, "For the purpose of completing this arrangement, I have to request that you will be pleased to suspend hostilities."[17] Canton was at their mercy, and although the British would have suffered some casualties in an assault their technological superiority, not to mention their greater discipline, would have meant that Canton would have fallen to their attack.

At 1000 General Yang finally put in an appearance and as Gough described it, "a long and unin-teresting parley ensued, in which I explained that Her Majesty's Plenipotentiary having resumed negotiations with the local authorities, I should await a further communication from him." At noon Captain Elliot arrived in camp and no doubt received a somewhat frosty reception. Gough simply recorded that upon his arrival, "all further active operations ceased."[18] Elliot negotiated a treaty, historically known as the Ransom of Canton, in which the Chinese agreed to pay an indemnity, or ransom, of 6,000,000 dollars; that compensation would be paid for the damage to the factories; and that the Generals and the governor leave the city along with all non-Cantonese troops. Having learnt a little from his previous treaty Elliot declared that the British would not withdraw until the money had been paid. The agreement included a clause by which if the 'ransom' had not been paid within seven days it would increase to seven million dollars, if not paid within 14 days eight million dollars, and if not within 20 days nine million dollars. Presumably if not paid after that point hostilities would recommence, although the treaty never made that clear. This is why the event is often called the Ransom of Canton: Gough disliked the name, feeling it gave the expedi-tion a somewhat buccaneering feel. It made it seem that money rather than honour was the main concern of the British. An argument for this can certainly be made, but this was not the spirit in which Gough was fighting the campaign.

The Ransom also necessitated the army remaining around Canton. Whilst sensible from that point of view, it created problems for Gough. Indeed Gough was not happy about the whole situ-ation. Not only did he feel a touch of betrayal in Elliot's actions, he felt that the terms negotiated were too lenient.[19] Also they did not end the conflict, but merely declared a ceasefire that surely could not last long. To a man who had been sent to China under instructions to take the war to the enemy, this appeared to be just the sort of games that had undermined previously military efforts.

16   NLI: 638, Gough to Lord Auckland, 3 June 1841.
17   NLI: 638, Elliot to Gough and Senhouse, 26 May 1841. A copy of the letter is included along with despatches held in the National Library of Ireland. Elliot's letter was marked '10 pm'.
18   NLI: 638, Gough to Lord Auckland, 3 June 1841.
19   Both Gough and Senhouse signed a formal complaint to Elliot over his actions. Elliot 'politely' ignored it. See Rait, Gough, Vol. I, p. 191.

Gough did not think highly of Elliot, and it was around this time that he remarked that he was 'as whimsical as a shuttlecock'. He wrote to Elliot in strong terms that:

> You have placed us in a most critical situation. My men of all arms are dreadfully harassed, my communications with the rear constantly threatened and escorts attacked. My men must suffer dreadfully from the necessity of continued watchfulness; for however you may put confidence in the Chinese I do not, nor should be justified in relaxing in the least.[20]

Gough was not alone in his point of view and his naval counterpart Senhouse, upon reading the contents of the treaty declared, "I protest against the terms of the treaty *in toto* [completely]". Although Elliot did not hear of his dismissal until July 1841, due to disquiet at the terms of the Treaty of Chuenpee rather than his actions at Canton, he was surely aware that he was in a dangerous position and that his time might soon be up. It is likely that the Ransom of Canton was an attempt to go out on better terms.

Gough's relationship with Elliot perhaps deserves further comment. There is no doubt that Gough was critical of Elliot's actions. His decision to negotiate with the Chinese was, as we shall see, to leave Gough's army in a false position. In his despatches Gough does not hold back on his opinions of Elliot and is understandably critical of him. This hardly places Gough in a unique position; there were a great many others more critical than Gough of Elliot's actions. Yet Gough's criticism has been misinterpreted on occasion by historians. References to Gough's "grievous mortification and disappointment" at not being allowed to attack Canton are often misinterpreted. It was not that he desired to "rape and pillage" Canton, as one historian has noted.[21] Yet, having attacked so far, to take Canton was necessary. Gough seems to have grasped the political reality of the situation more readily than Elliot. Canton in and of itself was not sufficient to grab the attention of the Chinese Emperor and his officials. Gough would later continue a policy of taking the war closer to the Imperial court as the only way of bringing the reality of the situation home to them. Had Canton been taken it would clearly have placed the British in a stronger position to negotiate with the Chinese. It would also have placed them inside the city, rather than in a dangerous position outside it which, under the terms of the Treaty of Canton, they needed to maintain until the ransom was paid in full.

Gough's criticism of Elliot suffers from the fact that it is made by a soldier. As such Gough's attitude is automatically taken to be one in favour of death and destruction, or 'rape and pillage', which as we have already shown was not part of Gough's character. We shall see later in the China campaign that Gough actually stood up to oppose political demands to 'sack' Chinese cities. A more thoughtful man than he was given credit for, Gough could see that taking Canton was a necessary evil on the road to bring the war with China to an end. As it was, Canton and many other towns and cities would have to be taken before the war was ended. Elliot and Gough had not seen eye to eye on the prosecution of the war, but there were few of his contemporaries who agreed with Elliot's handling of the conflict.

Over the next few days Gough watched the majority of Chinese troops depart. Gough was a little annoyed that they were allowed to leave with their arms and baggage, and it may well be that the fact that they did not leave with their banners, or colours, was due to Gough insistence on the matter. To Gough's mind it looked too much like the Chinese were leaving with honour intact.

---

20   Rait, *Gough*, Vol. I, p. 193.
21   See Hoe, Susanna and Roebuck, Derek, *The Taking of Hong Kong* (London: Curzon Press, 1999), p. 192. This is also repeated in Lovell, *The Opium War*, p. 171 who places emphasis on Gough's supposed desire to "rape and pillage Canton."

Whilst the treaty was respected by the Chinese authorities, it was not by the Chinese people. Gough alluded to the fact that his communications were threatened, and the chaos of the action before Canton had induced many Chinese towards banditry. Far worse than this was a popular movement amongst Chinese peasants designed to remove the 'invader' from their land. Indeed this was in many ways a far greater threat than the regular Chinese troops. The latter were professionals, many close to being classed as mercenaries. Their desire to fight the British was never as strong as that of the ordinary citizens who were fighting to protect their homes their families and their way of life. Consequently there was a determination and tenacity to the peasant organisation that there had not been to the regular Chinese soldiers. This peasant movement almost gave the Chinese nation a major victory over the British, and it is that to which we now turn our attention.

29

After Canton and the Sanyuanli Incident

Matters came to a head on 30 May, as Gough recalled:

> About twelve [...], I perceived numbers of men, apparently irregulars, and armed for the most part with long spears, shield and swords, collecting upon the heights, three or four miles to my rear. As they continued rapidly to increase, detaching bodies to their front, I directed General Burrell to take charge of our position, and hold every man ready in case of a sortie or other act of treachery, under cover of a flag of truce, should be intended.[1]

The last point illustrates that the situation placed Gough in a difficult position. Technically a flag of truce was still in force, yet the forces threatening him were not military but largely civilian in composition. At the same time as holding Burrell ready Gough detached a wing of the force which consisting of the 26th Foot, now having re-joined the main force, three companies of the 49th Foot, the 37th Madras Native Infantry, with the company of Bengal Volunteers and the Royal Marines as a reserve. Gough took personal command of this detached wing. The reserve was designed to protect his flanks, as Gough was unsure of what lay before him. He feared that many more 'peasant troops' might well appear on the scene.

As Gough advanced with this part of the army, some 4,000 to 5,000 men appeared before him.[2] Gough ordered both the 26th Foot and the 37th Madras Native Infantry to advance and drive the 'peasants' from a theoretically-strong position they had taken on an embankment. This they did with ease before destroying, on Gough's orders, a village which had been turned into a military post. Despite the weaponry that this new enemy had been using Gough was somewhat surprised to find a powder magazine in the village and immediately ordered it to be blown up.[3] This is an interesting discovery which suggests possible collusion with the regular troops or Chinese authorities, or at the very least points to the ambitions of this 'peasant' army to obtain and operate firearms or artillery. It perhaps helps to illustrate that this was the start of a more concerted effort by the local population against the British rather than an isolated response to the defeat at Canton and the subsequent treaty. However the fact that these were not trained soldiers was illustrated by the fact that at the first volley fired by the British troops the large majority ran away.

The climatic conditions were now taking their toll on the British force. As midday approached the heat became almost unbearable, or as Gough recalled "the sun was hardly supportable." Major Belcher collapsed from the heat and died and Captain George Gough, Hugh's son and aide, had to

---

1   NLI: MS 638, Gough to Lord Auckland, 3 June 1841.
2   It is interesting to note that Gough calculated the lower figure of 4,000. Many other sources name the higher figure of 5,000.
3   NLI: MS 638, Gough to Lord Auckland, 3 June 1841.

be ordered back to camp when, "he became alarmingly unwell."[4] Having succeeded in driving the enemy away from a position that threatened him directly, Gough recalled the troops and took care to have the 49th Foot, the Royal Marines and the Bengal Volunteers so positioned as to cover the withdrawal in the event of the Chinese returning to the field. Although this points to the careful nature with which Gough approached matters, there was soon to be an incident that illustrated the weaknesses in the staff system.

About two hours after the withdrawal a greater body of Chinese, around 7,000 to 8,000 strong, began to appear again. By this stage the rockets of the Royal Artillery under Captain Knowles had started to arrive and Gough decided to make use of them. In the normal course of events, the main use of the rocket was against irregulars such as this who would be easily frightened by the noise and unpredictability of the weapon. Perhaps in China, the land of the rocket, this was too much to hope for. However Gough's decision to bring them along was logical, if only because they were the easiest part of his artillery to transport and could easily be moved should he need to withdraw quickly. When they fired, despite their accuracy, they did not disperse the Chinese who continued to advance. In a clear comment of the quality of the Chinese regular soldiers he had faced up to this point, Gough remarked that the attack "bespoke more determination than I had previously witnessed."[5]

A thunderstorm looked likely to break and Gough was anxious to disperse the Chinese before the rain began. Gough ordered the 26th to meet the advance on the left and then clear the hills to the front of him of the enemy. At the same time, the 37th Madras Native Infantry supported by the Bengal Volunteers were ordered to attack to the front, in the direction of where the village had been. Both movements were successful and the enemy started to disperse. Exactly what happened next is debated. Gough reported that the 37th Madras Native Infantry continued its advance further than he had intended and he ordered the Bengal Volunteers up to support them. At the same time he urged the Madras Regiment to detach a company, under Lieutenant Hadfield, to open up communications with the 26th Foot on his left.

At this point, with the thunderstorm starting to break and the light beginning to fail, Gough understandably considered that it would be injudicious to follow the retreating enemy. He there-fore ordered all of the advanced units to fall back. The rain was now starting to fall. This in itself started to undermine the technological superiority of the British. The majority of soldiers still had the flintlock musket, which was difficult, bordering on impossible, to use in wet conditions due to the need to keep the powder dry so as to create the spark which ignited the musket. Only some units had the modern percussion lock design which, using fulminate of mercury held in a cap on the musket lock to ignite the weapon, was not susceptible to wet weather. This slackening of fire due to the wet weather emboldened the Chinese, who started to return to the field and harassed the withdrawing British. As a consequence of the weather most of the fighting at this point turned to hand-to-hand. Record exists of the 26th Foot leading bayonet charges to clear the enemy when they got too close. Remarkably only one British soldier was killed. The withdrawal had been orderly until it was discovered that a company of the 37th Madras Native Infantry, the one that had been tasked to link up with the 26th Foot, was unaccounted for. The error seems to have arisen due to the assumption that they had joined with the 26th Foot, and thus orders were not issued for the single company of the 37th.[6] Although this might appear a rather foolish error, given the circumstances it is understandable, and it is unclear exactly how that single company got so detached that it was neither within sight of its own regiment or the 26th Foot. There is also further mitigation for the

---

4   NLI: MS 638, Gough to Lord Auckland, 3 June 1841.
5   NLI: MS 638, Gough to Lord Auckland, 3 June 1841.
6   NLI: MS 638, Gough to Lord Auckland, 3 June 1841.

staff as, according to Gough, Captain Duff of the 37th Madras Native Infantry had informed him that his detached company was with the 26th. It thus was a shock to all concerned to find that they were not and had been left behind. As Gough recorded, he "was exceedingly annoyed on the force concentrating to find that the detached company, under Lt Hadfield, had never joined the 26th."[7]

The single company of the Madras Native Infantry had found itself cut off and surrounded. They had done the only thing they could do and formed square. At first they tried to withdraw: however, once surrounded they held their position and fought off the attack using bayonets and the occasional shot fired from a musket that they were able to clean and dry. This became increasingly difficult as the rain had soaked the field so much that the majority of the soldiers were up to their waists in water.

Gough had despatched the Royal Marines to find the company and rescue them, the Marines being armed with percussion lock weapons would not be affected by the rain. Probably in a desire to make a point, and hold the man Gough held responsible accountable for his actions, Captain Daniel Duff, the commander of the 37th Madras Native Infantry was despatched with the Royal Marines. It is very clear from Gough's account that he held Duff responsible for not knowing or making sure where his company was before withdrawing, rather than seeing it as a failure of staff work. Without knowing Duff's side of the story it is difficult to argue with Gough's assessment.

Around dusk the relief party found Lieutenant Hadfield and his men. By this stage they were surrounded by several thousand Chinese. Remarkably they had only lost one man killed and had 15 wounded, including Ensign Berkley whom Gough praised for continuing to do his duty despite his severe wound. The Royal Marines fired a single volley on arriving on the scene, and this was all that was required to make the Chinese leave the field. A possibly fatal situation had been saved by the Royal Marines and their percussion cap weapons, but also by the prompt action of Gough on discovering that a company was unaccounted for. By 2100 all British units had safely been brought into their makeshift camp.

In the morning, upwards of 25,000 peasants were witnessed gathering in the vicinity. They had come from over 80 villages in the surrounding area, and this helps to illustrate the popular nature of the uprising. Rather than attempt to deal with them Gough decided to pass the burden back to the Chinese authorities. Indeed his message was simple. In effect: they are your people, deal with them. Gough made it clear to the authorities in Canton that if he were threatened in any way similar to that of the previous day he would, "at once haul down the white flag and resume hostilities." Gough was not only concerned about the peasant army that was now visible on the surrounding hills. Under the treaty arranged by Elliot 7,500 Chinese Tartar troops had been allowed to leave the city with their weapons. Despite instructions to the contrary Gough was aware that they were still in the general vicinity. Gough was anxious regarding this and recalled that, "I felt some doubt whether treachery was not contemplated." He therefore felt that whilst lining his troops to face the threat from the peasants he had to keep sufficient troops in reserve should the Chinese regulars decide to join the fight.[8] This was partly the reason why Gough insisted that the Chinese take care of the issue. It was certainly a breach of the truce, and Gough would have had no hesitation in attacking Canton. The Chinese authorities also believed that Gough would be as good as his word, and in the afternoon Canton's prefect Yu Baochun was given safe passage to go and talk to the peasant army, accompanied by Captain Moore, of the 34th Bengal Native Infantry, who was acting as Deputy Judge Advocate General. Yu persuaded them that peace had been signed and that they must disperse.

---

7   NLI: MS 638, Gough to Lord Auckland, 3 June 1841.
8   NLI: MS 638, Gough to Lord Auckland, 3 June 1841.

Now convinced that the Chinese authorities were not contemplating treachery, Gough turned his entire force to meet the peasant army should it not heed the words of the prefect. Indeed the prefect convinced Gough that this had been a spontaneous uprising with no influence from the Chinese authorities, and that they were as concerned about it as the British. What for the British had been a series of minor skirmishes was, and indeed is, an occasion of great note for the Chinese. The British do not even have a name for the events of 29–31 May 1841, but for the Chinese it is known as the Sanyuanli Incident or 'Sanyuanli People's Anti-British Struggle'. Sanyuanli is the name of the village that had been converted to a military post and was burnt down by the British. The status of the movement grew under Marxist rule as a demonstration of 'people power', taking on legendary status in China. Consequently perspective has been lost. Lurid stories of hundreds of British soldiers killed, begging for mercy and howling have ensued, which do not stand up to closer scrutiny. There were in fact only four British soldiers killed during the whole of this episode, and little more than 20 injured. Chinese accounts have dramatically increased this number to 300 dead and over 750 total casualties.[9] There is no reason to believe that the British deliberately tried to hide casualty returns – indeed, in such a small force it would be impossible to do so – and the simple fact that British accounts hardly mention the incident or deign to give it a name illustrates the unimportance attached to it rather than a cover-up.

The exact cause of the uprising is unclear. There have been suggestions of rape, and certainly at least one Chinese woman was raped by a British soldier. There was also some looting. It is possible that one of these incidents was the spark for the uprising. However for the most part it appears that the British soldiers behaved themselves by the standards of the time and did far less damage than the Chinese troops had to the local population. According to Gough's despatch there were only two occasions of drunken soldiers being reported, and this despite the easy access to alcohol in the area. There is also a suggestion that the rising had more to do with a disappointment at Imperial officials and their lack of fight. The very nature of the uprising makes one think that it was a case of, 'if the army cannot drive the British out of China, we will'.[10]

At the end of the week 5,000,000 dollars' worth of the ransom had been paid. As Elliot was, "perfectly satisfied with the security for the payment of the remaining million for the ransom of Canton", Gough was ordered to withdraw his troops.[11] Such was the bizarre relationship that had developed with the local authorities that they even provided Gough with 800 coolies to pull his guns, including the 42 captured guns, to the boats. It had been a difficult time for all concerned, one of great danger, trial and exhaustion. Yet throughout this, Gough had been at the forefront of the action. This had endeared him to his men and gained him much credit. As one historian put it:

> Whenever there was fighting he was constantly among them, and he took no notice when shots from Chinese matchlocks passed over his head or cannon-balls dropped in a paddy-field a few yards from where he was standing. The idea of taking cover never seems to have occurred to

---

9   Lovell, *The Opium War*, pp. 157–162, describes the Sanyuanli Incident and gives an insight into how it has been represented, or perhaps misrepresented, in modern Chinese society. It is difficult to ascertain exact British numbers of wounded in battle as opposed to those suffering from heat exhaustion and disease. Chinese figures are so fanciful that they even include the death of Commodore Gordon Bremer who although in China for much of this period had returned to India at the time of the battle to bring back reinforcements. He did not return to China until late July 1841. Bremer died in February 1850, killed not by the Chinese but by diabetes.
10   Lovell, *The Opium War*, pp. 158–159.
11   NLI: MS 638, Gough to Lord Auckland, 3 June 1841.

him. It was a general officer's duty to set an example of bravery to his men, and Gough did so by standing erect and fearless in the face of Chinese fire.[12]

This view is also supported by the words of Armine Mountain in his memoirs.

> Sir Hugh was always on the alert, always on foot, day and night, never thought of himself in anything; and during the approach to, and halt in front of, the heights, though he was careful to post the men under cover, he was always exposed, eagerly reconnoitring the ground, for which he has a capital eye. The matchlock balls whizzed over and around him, cannon balls ploughed up the paddy fields within a few paces of him; he never seemed to notice them in the least and never once deviated from his erect posture.[13]

In the age in which we are discussing, such acts of bravery and courage by a general were as important as tactics, or orders. Discipline was enhanced by confidence in the man in charge, and such acts of bravery and courage were one way in which to achieve this. This literally was leading by example.

After eight days before Canton, Gough's army left the vicinity and were transported to Hong Kong. Exact figures for casualties on both sides during the eight days of operation are difficult to ascertain. Gough's own belief was that the Chinese had lost over 500 Tartar troops killed and 1,500 wounded, this being based on a conversation with the prefect of Canton. The problem was that the Chinese officials were desperately trying to reinterpret events for the Emperor in a way that would hopefully allow them to keep their lives. Thus defeats were often portrayed as victories, and when defeat had to be confessed it was due to the work of Chinese 'traitors'. Consequently British casualties were dramatically exaggerated, to the point that if anyone had ever bothered to calculate the figures the entire British force was reported as having been wiped out during the events. In fact the British had a total loss of one officer and 12 men killed in battle, along with nine officers and 78 men wounded. There were of course many who suffered from illness, largely due to the weather. The real consequence of this was not felt until they returned to Hong Kong where the effects of the recent operation took their toll on many. This included the naval commander Captain Senhouse, who died on 13 June 1841.

The embarkation of the troops, supplies and artillery went smoothly. In his despatch Gough paid credit to all the brigade commanders and to the officers of the Royal Navy. He had been well served by the officers under his command. It is tempting to say that they covered up for any shortcomings Gough himself had, however this might be a little unfair as there is very little to criticise Gough for in his conduct of this operation. Indeed he had shown both political and military nous, tactical discipline, and good control of his troops. The incident with the detached company of the 37th Madras Native Infantry had been an isolated incident and one for which Gough shares little blame. If he was guilty of anything, it was trusting the word of Captain Duff and his staff. However it would be unfair to expect a general to check such a relatively minor detail. Indeed, that was why he had aides and staff officers. He gave particular thanks to his deputy adjutant general Lieutenant Colonel Armine Mountain and to Major F. S. Hawkins his commissary general. Mountain would later serve under Gough during the Second Sikh War. Mountain was only a major at this stage and whether or not he actually held local rank of lieutenant colonel or this was a mistake by Gough is unclear.

Gough understandably felt pride in what he had been able to achieve during this period, and in the conduct of the army under his command. It had of course been a very difficult operation. This

---

12   Holt, *The Opium Wars in China*, p. 130.
13   Mountain, *Memoirs of Colonel Mountain*, p. 185.

is perhaps best illustrated in his own words, in a letter to his wife written on 6 June 1841, shortly after the events we have just examined.

> I shall be accused of making too much of the affair, but those who really know the situation under which I have been placed will do justice to the devotedness of my gallant little band. It must be remembered I had to land in a country totally unknown, never before trodden by European foot, unconscious of what difficulties I might have to encounter, or the numbers I had to oppose. These were enough to make caution necessary. Look to facts – the difficulties of the country as to advance of troops, in any other than that of file, the impossibility of a rapid move of artillery, an enemy 45,000 strong (or thirty men to one) of regulars, to oppose, besides a militia of equal amount, the former posted on fortified heights, impregnable to any but European soldiers, with a Town in their rear containing upwards of one million of inhabitants, who considered you as barbarians, strongly fortified, its walls being, at the point of attack, from 28 to 35 feet. These were obstacles which may not be well understood at home. These obstacles were to be and were, overcome by about 1,500 bayonets, unsupported and without the power of support – I might say of retreat, as the only two ships, the *Sulphur* and the *Nemesis*, were both aground the first day. I mention not this to enhance this business, but I merely mention facts to prove that I am not, nor have I been, too lavish of praise. This and this alone I care for; personally, I am indifferent, but I own I shall be jealous of the lowering the exertions and the devotedness of my noble band … Let your anticipations join with mine in thankfulness, in deep unaltered gratitude to that Being who in my old age enables me to serve my country.[14]

Gough's pride in, and devotion to, those under his command is another reason why he was so highly thought of by his soldiers, particularly the rank and file. In an age when the common soldier rarely received much thanks, Gough's attitude and actions were all the more appreciated.

---

14   The letter is reproduced in Rait, *Gough*, Vol. I, pp. 198–199. The letter to his wife, now feared lost, is dated 6 June 1841.

30

Changes in China Command and Strategy

The period after the ransom of Canton was one of recovery and preparation for future operations. Gough was slightly hampered by the fact that the conditions in Hong Kong did not help the recovery of his men from their recent exertions: during June he had over 1,000 men in the hospitals at any one time suffering from a mixture of heat exhaustion, fever and a particularly severe outbreak of dysentery. In late July things were made worse by a typhoon which destroyed the hospital and many of the new buildings being built in Hong Kong. It also wrecked several ships in the harbour.

For Gough personally there were two pieces of relatively happy news. The first was contained in a letter from Lord Auckland dated 18 June 1841 which contained the news that Gough was to be appointed Commander-in-Chief of the Madras Army on his return from China, for as Auckland stated, "I trust that you will not repine at being asked to continue in the conduct of your present most important command."[1] The positives to this were that as the position was normally filled by a lieutenant general it was likely that a promotion to that rank was on the cards. Indeed after Gough's services in China one would have been surprised not to have found that promotion. There was also the fact that despite being 61 years of age, he was a relatively junior officer for this appointment. It was normally reserved for a lieutenant general of long service. All this suggests that his success in China was being appreciated. He was fortunate to have the opportunity to command in combat, as any success in such operations was usually a short cut to promotion. In this regard he was fortunate that he had been given a mandate to take the war to the enemy. Although Gough was undoubtedly pleased at the appointment there was not the unconfined joy that one might expect. The Madras Army was unlikely to see much future action after China. The appointment also meant that he would be spending another five years in India. This was not exactly a thrilling prospect for Gough himself, but was of particular concern given the fragile health of Lady Gough.

Whilst the appointment to command the Madras Army was tinged with a little concern, he had no such problems with the second piece of news he received at this time. In June 1841 he discovered that he had been appointed colonel of the 87th Foot. To be appointed to the colonelcy of the unit that was so close to his heart was a great prize for him both as a soldier and a man. After the disappointment of having been overlooked for the appointment on the death of Sir John Doyle, there was no doubt added satisfaction that he was colonel of the 87th. In a letter to Sir Jasper Nicholls, Commander-in-Chief, India, he recorded:

> My appointment to the 87th comes much more home to my feelings as a soldier and a man. Such unsolicited acknowledgements of Lord Hill's [C-in-C of the Army] sentiments as to my

---

1   Rait, *Gough*, Vol. I, p. 200.

exertions at the head of that dear old corps in by-gone days, makes me feel proud of my profession and of its head.[2]

The acknowledgements of Lord Hill were pleasing to Gough. However they show something of the fact that he was still best remembered for his commander of the 2nd Battalion of the 87th during the Peninsular Campaign. With his success in China that was starting to change.

This was also a period of change in the command of the British forces in China. Although Elliot had been relieved of his appointment some months previous it was not until 9 August that his successor arrived in China. Indeed it was the Convention of Chuenpee rather than the Ransom of Canton that sealed Elliot's fate. It had been met with disbelief in England, and whilst Elliot thought he had secured a good deal for Britain the Foreign Secretary Lord Palmerston, and indeed Queen Victoria, felt otherwise. In an oft quoted letter to her uncle King Leopold of the Belgians, Her Majesty stated that, "The Chinese business vexes us much, and Palmerston is deeply mortified at it. All we wanted might have been got, if it had not been for the unaccountably strange conduct of Charles Elliot [...] who completely disobeyed his instructions and tried to get the lowest term he could."[3]

Although Elliot had not actually deviated too far from Palmerston's original instructions, it had been sufficient to ensure his removal. His actions had met with disapproval, but even Lord Auckland, not one of his admirers and a man who was deeply critical of his actions, was content that Elliot had acted "as he thought for the best."[4] He had acted honourably, but not with sufficient vigour or tenacity, and his replacement by a more dynamic man was inevitable. However due to the lengthy nature of communication and transportation to China it was only now that the change took place. On 24 August 1841, Elliot his wife and his family sailed for England. In the aftermath of Elliot's removal it was rumoured amongst the Chinese that he had been beheaded on his return to England for his failure. Although this was untrue, he did perhaps meet with the diplomatic corps equivalent and was posted a year later to be *charge d'affaires* to the Republic of Texas.

Elliot's successor as Her Majesty's Plenipotentiary was Sir Henry Pottinger. Like Gough he was from an Anglo-Irish family. A former HEIC employee, he had also served as an officer in several campaigns in India reaching the rank of colonel. Pottinger was a man more to the liking of Gough. He was a first-rate administrator and acted both firmly and decisively. To a soldier such as Gough such honest and open hard work, combined with a determination and drive similar to his own, was an attractive combination. There was another change in the commander structure with Rear Admiral Sir William Parker, an extremely experienced and battle hardened naval commander, replacing the late Senhouse in command of the fleet. Unlike his predecessors, and because of his experience and seniority, Parker was not directly under the command of Pottinger but directly responsible to the Admiralty. Indeed Parker had been given instructions to consult and cooperate with both the Indian authorities and Pottinger rather than be under their direct command. It was also made clear to Parker by Lord Auckland that whilst he was to be in charge of all matters whilst afloat that, "in the government of all that concerns the troops, and their employment on shore, the military officer in command [Gough] will be paramount."[5] This clearly set-out demarcation

---

2   NAM: 6210–168, 'Sir Jasper Nichols Papers', Gough to Nichols, 1841. The letter is undated. See also, Cunliffe, *Royal Irish Fusiliers*, p. 190.

3   Holt, *The Opium Wars in China*, p. 121. The criticism of Elliot was not confined to Royalty. Around this time *The Times* stated that Elliot was 'unfit to manage a respectable applestall'.

4   Holt, *The Opium Wars in China*, p. 131. This is a quotation from a letter by Lord Auckland to Commodore Bremer.

5   Phillimore, Augustus, *The life of Admiral of the Fleet Sir William Parker*, (London: Harrison, 1879), Vol. II, pp. 443–444.

helped to make a clear system of operation and chain of command, something which, whilst not entirely lacking up to this point, had not been so clearly defined. This in turn led to an alteration in which operations were planned and carried out. Unlike his predecessor, Pottinger was in effect the chairman of a three man committee including Gough and Parker. Pottinger would explain what was desired from a political point of view and would then leave the two commanders to determine the military and naval measures necessary to carry them out.

It was Gough's view that further action was needed, as it was only this that would force the hand of the Chinese. As he told Lord Auckland:

> While going forward our power is felt and respected. The moment we pause the Chinese false representations and ingenuity come into play. I have before stated to your Lordship, and I beg to repeat the opinion, that the Chinese individually are by no means despicable, and that their militia, as I witnessed on the 30th and 31st May, showed as much boldness as any irregular troops I have ever seen. In short, my Lord, the longer we continue the war, the more formidable the Chinese will become. It is for this reason that I regret our present inaction.[6]

Such comments spoke not only of the practicality of the situation that faced the British, but also highlighted the problem with operations up to that point. There had been little active fighting and what there had been was well spaced out. There had been no continued campaign against Chinese targets to truly place pressure on the Imperial authorities. As a consequence, the Chinese dealt with such matters as a series of incidents rather than a continued campaign. Gough's appreciation that sustained operations were the only way to win the conflict with the Chinese are more than simply a manifestation of his nature and desire to press home the attack. They speak to a greater awareness of the problems facing the British and the solution needed. This is a good understanding of the strategic understanding that Gough demonstrated.

However, others did not see it that way. In writing to Lord Auckland Gough was trying to convince him that land forces would be vital to future operations. The authorities both at home and in India were largely of the opinion that future operations should be largely naval in nature: a blockade to trade and the destruction of Chinese shipping. In short, they proposed what would today be termed economic sanctions against China as a means to getting what they wanted. History shows that such sanctions rarely work: in this instance, whilst they could damage China they were unlikely to obtain for the British what they wanted. Eventually the realisation came upon the authorities that the Army would be needed to bring the campaign to a successful conclusion.

Gough however did have problems in regards to placing an effective force in the field. Sickness and disease had taken its toll on his command, and there was also a severe lack of commissariat and medical supplies for any future operation as everything that was available was being used in Hong Kong. The 55th (Westmorland) Foot were sent to Gough as reinforcements. They left India on 23 May and arrived in Hong Kong in early August 1841 – exact dates vary as the entire regiment did not arrive in one transport. One of the ships, the *Nerbudda,* was wrecked on its journey. The story is a rather unpleasant one: there was only one boat on the ship and this was taken by the officers and men, who left the 240 Indian bearers and deck hands to their fate. Many were drowned and those who survived were taken prisoner by the Chinese. Only two survived as many were either tortured to death, starved to death, or simply beheaded by their Chinese captors.

Just before leaving India, the 55th had exchanged their flintlock muskets for the new percussion lock musket. It is interesting to note that this is before the incident with the 37th Madras Native Infantry took place and it shows a desire to send troops out well equipped, perhaps also giving one

---

6   Rait, *Gough*, Vol. I, p. 204, quoting a letter by Gough to Lord Auckland dated 1 July 1841.

the sense that the conflict was starting to be taken seriously. To make best use of such weapons Gough had created a company of 'rifles' as he called them, although perhaps a better term would be skirmishers. They were then formed into a company designed to go ahead in front of the army and act as skirmishers or light infantry. They were all equipped with either the percussion musket or a rifle. Although Gough reports that he 'created' this unit, he did have the basis of a rifle company. In 1830 the Madras Rifle Corps had been dispersed amongst the Madras Native Infantry Battalions so that each battalion had a rifle company. However the fact that this company stood at over 100 men, particularly after losses that must have been experienced in conflict or through sickness and disease, indicates there must have been some argumentation from other units. It is quite possible that this was that rare thing, a mixture of European and native soldiers. Few details remain of this unit and we do not know whether they used the standard Baker rifle or the new Brunswick rifle. The Brunswick was a percussion lock rifle that never really lived up to expectation. It had only started to be issued to specialist units in 1840. The Baker rifle, although tried and tested, was slow to load and somewhat dated.

The realisation that a more aggressive attitude was needed was demonstrated by Pottinger's attitude, as he was no longer prepared to deal simply with local officials on a town-by-town basis as Elliot had. He now determined only to deal with representatives of the Imperial court and to this end he needed to get their attention. This would require a movement further north. He was therefore happy to accept the ideas of both his naval and military commander for such a movement. Accordingly, it was set that Saturday 21 August 1841 would see the commencement of an expedition against Amoy, nowadays known as Xiamen. The attack was designed to bring the war nearer to Peking, as part of a movement along the coast. Indeed this is important to understand, as the attack on Amoy was not an end in itself but the commencement of a much wider operation against the Chinese. The war was now turning serious.

31

Amoy

Although the expedition to Amoy set off on 21 August, due to unfavourable winds it was not until the 23rd that the fleet was really able to leave the sea around Hong Kong. As a consequence it was not until the evening of 25 August that the fleet arrived off the coast of Amoy. A few shots were fired by Chinese batteries upon their arrival but they were of no consequence. The following morning Gough along with Pottinger and Parker met aboard the HEIC paddle steamer *Phlegethon*. From her, they reconnoitred the enemy's defences with a plan to commence operations later that day. Amazingly as the *Phlegethon* steamed up and down the coast examining their defences the Chinese did not fire a single shot in her direction.

The British had demanded the surrender of both the town and the forts. The defences of Amoy were strong, containing many newly constructed forts, over 400 guns, the majority of them new, and over 15,000 soldiers. As Gough recalled, "Every island, every projecting headland, from whence guns could bear upon the harbour, was occupied and strongly armed."[1] Any assault was also restricted by the natural defences of the sea, hills, or paddy fields, which would hamper any attacker. For almost a mile outside the town extended a stone wall with slate roofs and batteries of artillery placed along it. The Chinese had also covered the roofs with clods of earth to absorb any artillery fire. The natural rocky terrain acted as its own defence along with smaller defensive embrasures positioned at intervals. This was the problem that faced the army once ashore. However getting ashore would also be difficult. The channel between the island of Amoy and the island of Gulangyu was only 600 yards wide, and the latter island was strongly fortified with guns in stone batteries.

Given the two strong enemy positions it was decided that a simultaneous attack would be required. Thus an order of battle was decided which would see the two largest line-of-battle ships of the fleet, the 74-gunners *Wellesley* and *Blenheim*, with the two steamers, concentrate their fire on Amoy. Some smaller ships were detailed to protect the landing just outside the city walls by the bulk of Gough's troops. At the same time the two 44-gun heavy frigates, *Blonde* and *Druid*, and the 18-gun sloop *Modeste* would attack the defences upon the island of Gulangyu and cover the landing of a company of artillery, three companies of the 26th Foot, and 170 Royal Marines in a small bay on the east of the island and to the left of the island's defences.[2]

At about 1330, the attacks commenced. Although there were slight problems with the landing of the troops, the operation proceeded well. However even the heavy guns of the larger ships had little effect upon the strong stone defences of the Chinese. Fortunately there appears to have been a lack of skilled gunners amongst the Chinese defenders and the guns did not cause any real damage to the fleet. Nor did they prevent the landing, and by 1500 the majority of British soldiers were ashore

---

1   NLI: MS 638, Gough to Lord Auckland, 5 September, 1841.
2   NLI: MS 638, Gough to Lord Auckland, 5 September 1841. This contains a full description of preparations and deployment for the assault.

and before the strong defences of Amoy. However the strongest defences in the world are of little use unless they are well defended, and the Chinese made little attempt to defend the works outside the city. Whilst the British guns may have had little effect on the enemy's fortifications, they were able to offer such fire so as to protect the landing. It is difficult to say how much the lack of success of Chinese artillery was down to their lack of ability and trained gunners and how much to the ability of British naval artillery to make them keep their heads down and thus render it difficult for them to fire on the British landing. The 18th Foot took the wall without any difficulty, and the 49th Foot took the other more isolated defences with no major casualties. Thus the entire sea defences of Amoy had been taken with little resistance. On the island of Gulangyu the fighting was a little harder but the 26th and the Royal Marines succeeded in climbing the defences and overcoming the defenders. This was achieved by 1530hrs.

By the end of the day the island of Gulangyu had fallen and Gough had taken the heights surrounding the town of Amoy. A day which had potentially been full of difficulty had passed off relatively easily. The main reason for this was, as Gough recorded, the inability and unwillingness of the Chinese to stand firm.[3] A spirited defence might have inflicted many casualties on the British and checked their advance. Yet the Chinese contented themselves with firing off their guns until the British closed upon them, at which point they withdrew. Indeed there is one story from that day of a Chinese fort being taken by a lone British officer, outnumbered 40 or 50 to one. Entering the fort he fired off his two pistols, this was sufficient to cause the Chinese defenders to retreat.[4]

Through the night Gough continued to bring up his supplies and the remainder of the troops. Indeed the weather had been so 'boisterous', to use Gough's own words, so as to delay the landing of the 55th Foot until after dark. This was not without risk and indeed the most significant casualties of the day were from a boat that overturned and drowned five of its occupants. Gough undertook a reconnaissance of the remaining city defences in the early evening. From his despatch it appears that he felt that the Chinese had pulled back their troops to defend the city, and he expected a significant resistance to be put up when he attacked the following day. One gets the sense that Gough was wondering if there was something he was missing. Why had the Chinese so easily abandoned their new forts and defensive walls? Was it some trick to lure him on to the defences of the city? Throughout the early evening and early morning of the following day he intently studied the city, looking for something he had missed. In the morning to the surprise of all, the Chinese had abandoned the walls.

Still a little uncertain of the actions of the Chinese, Gough ordered the 18th Foot to advance, supported by the 49th and with the 55th as a reserve. It does seem unusual, given that they were his freshest troops and least affected by disease and the months of campaigning, that Gough chose to use the 55th only as a reserve. Possibly it was because they were in such a relatively good condition that Gough wanted them in reserve in case he needed fresh troops. It is perhaps an indication to another of Gough's character and command traits, that he did not yet feel confident about them. That is not to say that he necessarily distrusted them, but the 18th and 49th had both proved themselves under his command up to this point. Gough therefore, and understandably, had confidence in their ability. It appears that often Gough needed time to appreciate a unit before giving them his full confidence. For a man who believed in the power of the infantry attack this is again understandable. Such an attack required discipline, determination, and steadfastness. Gough needed to have confidence that a unit had these qualities. Where some commanders would be able to make instant decisions in this regard, either rightly or wrongly, Gough took a little longer to get used to

3   NLI: MS 638, Gough to Lord Auckland, 5 September 1841.
4   Lovell, *The Opium War*, p. 183.

a unit and to see how they operated. Much of his correspondence during this period, talks of the character of his officers and men, and it is clear that he was assessing their ability.

The 18th Foot took the walls with ease, using ladders they had taken from the defences captured the previous day. Without any fighting they were then able to open the east gate and this allowed the rest of the force to enter the town. There was still a sense of disbelief, and Gough, with perhaps untypical caution, occupied the defences in anticipation of attack. It might be given his experiences at Canton that he perhaps feared a peasant uprising more than the Imperial troops. Gough placed his artillery in a 'commanding position' overlooking the town, where he could have fired into it with devastating effect had he needed to. However there was no threat. The city had descended into looting; the worst being carried out by the Chinese troops who had been tasked to defend the city. Yan Botao, the governor of the region, who had done so much good in building and preparing the new defences found the situation too much to take. He is said to have burst into tears and run away leaving the city to its fate.[5]

In the two days of fighting, British casualties had been two killed and 15 wounded. There had been some hard fighting on the 26th but the 27th had been no contest at all. No accurate figures exist for the Chinese casualties. Gough could only record that his belief was that they had been 'severe'. Once again Gough paid particular tribute to the work of his staff, Lieutenant Colonel Mountain, Captain Gough, Major Hawkins, Dr French, and Lieutenant Gabbett. It is also important to recall how grateful Gough was to the support he had been given by Rear Admiral Parker, and in terms of the landing, also the support of Captain Henry Wells Giffard of the sloop HMS *Cruizer*.[6]

The general disorder and looting in Amoy posed a problem for Gough. Before the attack he had issued strict instructions to his officers and men that there was to be no looting. However with a city in chaos, and large-scale looting already taking place, it was asking a lot for his men to resist the temptation. On occasions Gough had to order his troops to fire on 'mobs' that were near to British positions. However unlike Canton they were not there to attack the British; they were more inclined towards looting. On the whole Gough felt his men had behaved well, particularly given the temptations in front of them. This included vast quantities of rice liquor.[7] Gough had however already issued in general orders a stern warning with regards to looting. He made it clear to his officers that they were not to allow soldiers to become stragglers in the hope of breaking away from the unit and engaging in looting. To the camp followers he made it clear that any of them caught looting would be immediately executed. To the soldiers he made no such direct threat, surely hoping that the previous advice to officers would reduce the opportunity for looting. He did however issue in general orders a very clear statement that such behaviour would not be tolerated.

> Sir Hugh Gough will only observe that, as Amoy is a principal commercial town, where there was once a British factory, it is an object of great national importance that no act should occur, that would preclude future friendly intercourse. The Government and the Military must be overcome, and public property of every description secured, under instructions that will be

---

5   NLI: MS 638, Gough to Lord Auckland, 5 September 1841. Lovell, *The Opium War*, pp. 183–184.
6   NLI: MS 638, Gough to Lord Auckland, 5 September 1841. Captain Henry Wells Giffard, RN was the son of Admiral John Giffard. Henry Giffard was one of the few men in the Royal Navy at the time of the China War who had a 'steam certificate' i.e. he could command a steam vessel. During the Crimean War he commanded HMS *Tiger*, a paddle steamer, during the bombardment of Odessa in 1854. In May of that year she ran aground in thick fog during the bombardment. Under heavy fire from the Russians the ship was forced to surrender and the crew were taken prisoner. Captain Giffard was severely wounded, losing his left leg. His wounds later became gangrenous and he died on 1 June 1854.
7   NLI: MS 638, Gough to Lord Auckland, 5 September 1841.

issued; but private property must be held inviolable; the laws of God and man prohibit private plunder; and the individual appropriation of the goods of others, which in England would be called robbery, deserves no better name in China.[8]

No doubt his orders were somewhat influenced by Pottinger, although there is no evidence that there was ever any instruction in this regard from him to Gough. What it illustrates is that Gough had obviously understood and appreciated the thoughts of Pottinger. It shows a more harmonious relationship between Gough and Pottinger than that with his predecessor as Her Majesty's Plenipotentiary.

Gough's orders to his officers and his warning to his men certainly had an impact. In a situation that could have descended, quite easily, into large-scale British looting, the attitude and instructions of Gough played an important part in preventing this. He later informed Lord Auckland that:

> I am most happy to be enabled to state that the conduct of the troops has been exemplary; some instances of misconduct have no doubt occurred; but when it is considered that they were in the midst of temptation, many of the houses being open with valuable property strewn about, and many shops in every street deserted, [...] it is a matter of great satisfaction that these instances were so few.[9]

Such was the plundering of the locals and Chinese troops, that Gough felt it unsafe to let any of his troops, or to venture himself, into 'the interior of the island'. Gough had considered marching through the island as an attempt to quell the looting and rioting but as he later confessed to Lord Auckland, he feared that "our marching through the island might rather have frightened away the peaceable householders, and led to further plundering by the mob, than have been of any advantage."

Gough showed concern for not only the local population and merchants, but also for the wider rule of law. Although this might seem unusual given that the conflict has often been viewed as one where the British were actually subverting the rule of law, in regards to the opium trade, we have already seen that this view is perhaps a somewhat limited one that does not appreciate the full picture. To Gough, however, the moral ambiguity of the war would not have been a consideration. The decision to go to war was politics, and not his province. However for the local population of the country Gough was capable of great sympathy. Perhaps this had something to do with his own experience in Ireland, or even in Spain, where he had seen how war could affect innocent civilians who simply had the misfortune to live in the vicinity of the area of conflict. His despatch to Lord Auckland gave a glimpse of this concern when speaking of his wish to help the islanders.

> I did all in my power to prevail upon the respectable merchants and householders, who had so much at stake, to aid me in protecting property, which they readily promised but their apprehension of appearing to be on friendly terms with us was so great, that I could obtain no effectual assistance from them, and was unable even to get a Chinese to remain with the guards at the gates, and point out the real owners of households.[10]

---

8   Rait, *Gough*, Vol. I, p. 215. This is a copy of the original order to the army composed by Gough.
9   NLI: MS 638, Gough to Lord Auckland, 5 September 1841.
10   NLI: MS 638, Gough to Lord Auckland, 5 September 1841.

Whilst this was an 'official' record of events around him, he wrote a more personal account to Lady Gough on 4 September. In this one senses once again his more sensitive side and his appreciation of the horror of war.

> The sight about me now is heart-rending. Every house broken open and plundered, in most instances by the Chinese robbers, of whom there are 20,000 now in the Town, ready to sack it the moment we leave. I have had many conferences with the respectable Chinese merchants, urging them to aid me, for it is ten to one when I send out parties to protect property, I may be preventing them from taking away their own. The moment a house is broken open, what between Chinese, soldiers or followers, every article is destroyed. The wanton waste of valuable property is heart-rending, and has quite sickened me of war. [...] For the first two days, the [Chinese] soldiers were well in hand, but when they found we were to give up the place, and saw the crowds of miscreants ready to plunder every house the moment we turned our backs, it has been most difficult to restrain them.[11]

This illustrates the difficult position Gough was in. Indeed it was a no-win situation. If he remained in the town he would have to take action against Chinese civilians, if only in the name of restoring law and order. Also, the longer he remained the greater the chance of a similar peasant uprising to that in Canton. If he withdrew completely from the town he was leaving the law-abiding citizens to their fate. Given his previous comments it was no doubt with a heavy heart that he had to leave Amoy.

The looting and general disorder was part of the reason why they chose not to stay at Amoy for long. However the more important factor was that Amoy had only been a stepping stone as the British moved along the coast. Indeed the British force remained only long enough to destroy the defences of the town so as to make sure that there was not a strong strategic post behind them before advancing onwards. The need to advance was clear, as at first the capture of Amoy had little impact on the Chinese authorities, and in particular the Imperial court. Indeed the usual series of distortions and lies were placed before the court by Chinese officials. They claimed to have sunk one of the British steamers and six other ships of war. The story continued that they would have destroyed the entire fleet but for a sudden change of wind which blew the smoke of the burning British Ships into the Chinese sailor's path so that they could not see to fire.[12] It was even recorded that Amoy had not fallen to the British at all but to 'Chinese Traitors', who had then allowed the British to occupy the city. The British decision to withdraw was also distorted to have been a rout in which over 1,600 British troops had been killed, and a further 18 British ships destroyed along with the capture of seven British 'chiefs'. Whilst such amusing distortions are interesting to read, it further illustrates the deluded nature of the Chinese authorities, and in particular the Imperial court. It also vindicates Gough's previous comments to Lord Auckland that the only thing that would make the Chinese take notice and meet British demands, was to press forward and attack. It was only when the Chinese began to realise that the attack on Amoy had just been the opening salvo in a new campaign that it was looked at more closely.

Somewhat ironically, the next target was Tinghai (Dinghai) on the island of Chusan (Zhoushan), which the British had captured and held the previous year. The decision to abandon Chusan, in return for Hong Kong, had deeply harmed the reputation of the previous Plenipotentiary Elliot. Although Chusan had little commercial value, it was an important symbol given Britain's previous experience. It was also a strong defensive and strategic position from where it could have been

---

11   Rait, *Gough*, Vol. I, pp. 216–217. Rait reproduces part of a letter to Lady Gough, but gives no date for it.
12   Gelber, *Opium, Soldiers, and Evangelists*, p. 128

possible to threaten the movement of the fleet further up the coast. Since the initial occupation, the Chinese had built new defences: it was clear from the outset that not only was Chusan well defended, but that unlike Amoy the Chinese intended to put up real resistance. The original intention had been to attack Chinhai (Zhenhai) further along the coast. In due course this would be captured, but the decision to take Chusan first was due to the practicalities of the situation. Gough records that 'contrary winds and the lateness of the season' led Rear Admiral Parker to propose that Chusan be attacked first. Gough agreed with this decision.[13]

The British fleet sailed from Amoy on 5 September, save for the ships *Druid*, *Pylades*, and *Algerine* which were left with a small detachment to defend the island of Gulangyu. Bad weather not only delayed the movement but obliged the force to scatter to ride out the storm. It was not until 25 September 1841 that the fleet finally regathered in the anchorage off Silver Island, halfway between Chusan and Chinhai. It was at this point that Rear Admiral Parker recommended to Pottinger and Gough that to attack the former might be easier than the latter. Parker was concerned about the weather and in particular concerned about the fleet reaching Chusan. Gough concurred with this decision, and indeed had another reason for wanting to attack Chusan without delay.

In Chusan there was a new Imperial Commissioner, a tough Mongol General whom the Chinese called Yuqian. He had determined to treat the barbarian British with the methods they merited: namely barbarism. He was convinced that if the Chinese put up a fight rather than run away, that the British would not be able to stand against them. He arrived in Chusan in February, three days before the British abandoned the island. Yuqian used this to convince the Chinese that the British were scared of him. Whether he truly believed that, or was simply using it as a means to motivate citizens and soldiers alike, is unclear. However he determined to show the British that he was a ruthless general and not to be taken lightly. His first act was to dig up all the British who had been buried in Chusan, many who had died from disease and sickness, and have their bodies mutilated and then thrown in the sea. In March an unfortunate ship's captain named Stead, who had landed on Chusan unaware that the British had abandoned it, was captured. He was publicly sliced to death. In May 1841 another unfortunate captain and an Indian sailor, who were most likely opium smugglers, were captured. The captain was flayed alive and then sliced to death. The Indian was beheaded and then his head was flayed and displayed to the masses. One could perhaps draw an interesting conclusion from the difference in the treatment of the British and Indian sailors. The harsher treatment to the British captain was clearly not just one motivated by rank but one of nationality. To make an example of the British man was to warn any future expedition of what they might expect should they be captured.[14] At the same time as delivering such warnings by acts of such severity, Yuqian was also preparing the defences around Chusan. Although on the face of it the defences were extremely strong he did perhaps underestimate his enemy when he concluded that if the British attacked he would be able to exterminate their entire expedition. This overconfidence would prove fatal, as so convinced was he in the strength of his defences and the difficulty of the hilly terrain that he posted the majority of his troops to the south of the island. Furthermore, whilst on the face of it the defences were strong they had been unscientifically constructed and did not make the best use of their strength.

Whilst waiting for the remainder of the fleet to arrive, the three British leaders, Pottinger, Parker and Gough, had undertaken a reconnaissance of Chusan in the paddle steamer *Phlegethon*. The reconnaissance showed that the Chinese had learnt from the previous occupation of the island. The inner harbour, where the British had landed previously, had been reinforced with a number of batteries. Due to the fact that the tides made it difficult for the major ships of the fleet to bring their

---

13   NLI: MS 638, Gough to Lord Auckland, 3 October 1841.
14   Lovell, *The Opium War*, p. 186.

guns to bear on these new defences, it made landing there all but impossible. New defences had also been constructed on the hills around the island. However one important factor that Gough observed was that many of the new defences, whilst generally finished from a structural point of view, had not yet had guns placed in them. Thus an attack on Chusan now would be easier than if they had sailed along the coast to take Chinhai first.

Gough formed the opinion that the best place to land in light of this was to the west of the city in the area known as Tinghai (Dinghai), where the forts were nearly completed but lacking in guns. "This reconnaissance confirmed me in the opinion which I had previously formed, from the reports of officers acquainted with the ground, that this (Tinghai) would be the most eligible point of attack." The belief that the harbour previously used was not an option for a landing was confirmed by the fire from the batteries upon the *Phlegethon* as she made her reconnaissance. It will be recalled that at Amoy no such fire took place as the reconnaissance was made. Gough recalled that the fire demonstrated to him that, "the sea line of battery was efficiently armed."[15] Perhaps more importantly, the Chinese had crews who knew how to operate their guns. The attack on the island of Chusan promised to be a more testing occasion for Gough and his force than either Canton or Amoy had.

On 29 and 30 of September Gough had landed a party of Madras and Royal Artillery, alongside some engineers, on Trumball Island to establish a position where they could fire upon Pagoda Hill, a position which the Chinese had heavily fortified. The Royal Artillery had one 8 inch howitzer and a party of two officers and 31 men. The Madras Artillery had two 24 pdrs and a party of one officer and 12 men. This force was completed by one officer and 20 engineers. This was done as the prelude to a general attack on 1 October.[16] The remainder of Gough's force was split into two columns, although in his despatch Gough referred to them as divisions. The left column, or First Division, consisted of the 55th Foot, 25 officers and 720 men commanded by Major David Fawcett, the 18th Foot, consisting of 14 officers and 286 men commanded by Lieutenant Colonel Henry Adams, the specially formed rifle company mentioned previously, consisting of 4 officers and 110 men, and 8 officers and 204 men of the Madras Artillery manning four mountain howitzers and two mortars. Finally, 6 officers and 117 engineers were attached to this force. The column was under the command of Lieutenant Colonel Peter Craigie. The right column was commanded by Lieutenant Colonel Edmund Morris and consisted of 34 officers and 435 men of the 49th Regiment of Foot commanded by Major Thomas Stephens, 7 officers and 201 men of the Royal Marines commanded by Major Samuel Ellis, and 15 officers and 250 sailors, also under the command of Major Ellis. They were supported by 2 officers and 50 men of the Madras Artillery operating two 2 pdrs, and two officers and 50 engineers.

The first division were placed in boats towed by the steamers, with this flotilla being under the overall command of Captain Giffard RN. Their landing was made all the more difficult by the extremely strong tides, and the fact that the landing was successful despite the obstacles was a feat that Gough credited to the skill of Captain Giffard. Certainly the role of the naval officers in the conflict is one that deserves the greatest credit and which Gough readily and frequently admitted.

Once the landing had taken place the men found themselves under heavy fire from the heights around the beaches from a mixture of cannon, muskets and Gingalls – the latter being a type of heavy musket often mounted on a swivel. Gough sent forward orders that they were to press on as quickly as possible. In short, like any amphibious landing, the key was to get off the beaches as soon as was practical. To this end he ordered the three companies of the 55th who had been the

---

15   NLI: MS 638, Gough to Lord Auckland, 3 October 1841.
16   NLI: MS 638, Gough to Lord Auckland, 3 October 1841. This includes a full description of the preparations and deployment for the attack.

first to land to press onwards and attack the heights. This included the two flank companies: the light company and the grenadier company. At the same time he ordered the other units to press on in support once they had landed and they formed a reserve for the advance of the three companies of the 55th.

Despite a difficult attack, and a defence by the Chinese that was far more disciplined and intense than anything the British had come across up to that point, the heights were captured. As Gough recorded:

> This duty was gallantly performed under the directions of Lieutenant-Colonel Craigie, commanding the column, and Major Fawcett, in the temporary command of the regiment, and notwithstanding the steepness and ruggedness of the ascent, and a heavy and well sustained fire from an infinitely superior force, this gallant corps carried the whole extent of the ridge of the hills terminating in a fortified camp, and drove everything before them.[17]

This attack could be used to prove several points. Firstly, that even when the Chinese stood and fought they were still no match for the British infantry. Secondly, that even the toughest obstacles appeared to be surmountable to a disciplined and well-led attack by British infantry. If Gough held an unshakable believe that British soldiers could overcome any obstacle in a frontal charge then it was battles such as this, and his experience in the Peninsular War, that confirmed such a point of view. It also interesting to read that he referred to the 55th as a 'gallant corps', the same phrase he had used to describe his own beloved 87th in the Peninsular. The use of this term should not be taken too lightly and clearly points to the great respect he had now developed for the 55th Foot.

However this was more than just a simple frontal attack. At the same time as the 55th made their assault, the 18th Foot had outflanked the enemy line on the right and captured a bridge which gave them access to the whole line of the Chinese sea defences. An amusing anecdote exists regarding this bridge, which was too narrow for the bass drum of the regimental band to cross, so that it had to be taken across by boat. The Chinese upon observing this immediately opened fire on the drum presuming it to be some new sort of weapon!

Another important factor of this battle was that Gough had the good sense to alter his plan during the engagement to match the changing circumstances. Rather than pressing on against the sea defences with his whole right column as he had originally planned, this turning movement by the 18th Foot allowed him to send that unit, along with artillery support, to attack the line of the sea defences. As Gough remarked:

> This was executed with equal gallantry by Lieutenant-Colonel Adams in the face of a very large force, which contested the whole line with more than ordinary spirit, apparently led by one of the principal Mandarins, who, with several of inferior rank, was killed on the spot, when the Chinese fled, and the 18th pushed on and occupied the top house hill, which the well-directed fire of the guns on Trumball Island, under the able Lieutenant Spencer, of the Royal Artillery, and the detached squadron under Captain Bourchier, had compelled the enemy to evacuate.[18]

Although a minor change in the great scheme of things, it is important to note that not only did Gough have the confidence to make such an alteration, but that he also had confidence in his staff to carry it out during the middle of a battle.

---

17   NLI: MS 638, Gough to Lord Auckland, 3 October 1841.
18   NLI: MS 638, Gough to Lord Auckland, 3 October 1841.

At the same time as the 18th attacked, Gough had moved the three companies of the 55th to watch the west gate of the city to prevent any support being sent. Whereas the 18th had been a reserve to support the attack of the 55th earlier in the day the position was now changed. In this sense this was a good use of his limited resources. With Gough in personal command, he moved with his staff and the remainder of the 55th to take the heights overlooking the town of Tinghai to the northwest. At some point Gough was hit in the shoulder whilst undertaking a reconnaissance with Major Mountain, who had previous knowledge of the ground over which they now operated. The wound was not serious enough to delay him or prevent him from moving forward with his men. He covered this advance by the use of his recently formed rifle company. The value in creating this unit was borne out by this battle where it gave greater protection to advancing infantry. Once the column were on the heights the light guns of the Madras Artillery were moved to join them, and brought their fire to bear on the city walls itself.

At this stage in the operation the Chinese were in retreat and were in the course of falling back on the city. Some of the guns on the city walls along with the occasional matchlock musket were being fired. Sensing an opportunity Gough ordered the 55th, less the three detached companies, to advance upon the city walls supported by the Madras Engineers carrying scaling ladders. Once again he made good use of his newly formed rifle company to cover their advance. At the same time the rifle company was also cutting off the enemy's retreat to the north. Whilst the sappers with Captain Pears leading the way were first to climb the walls Gough reported that, "I had soon the satisfaction of seeing the colours of the 55th Regiment waving on the wall of Tinghai while those of the Royal Irish [18th Foot] were planted on the top-house Hill above the suburb."[19] By continuing the momentum that his advance had built up, Gough was able to take the walls far easier than he had expected.

The right column consisting of the 49th Foot, the Royal Marines, and the battalion of sailors, was not landed in time to take part in the attack on the sea defences, and once again the strong tides were responsible for this. In one sense this was helpful to Gough, as now fresh troops were appearing on the battle field as the enemy retreated. By the end of the day the city had fallen. What had at times seen some difficult fighting had in affect been a relatively easy day. It had not been the intention to take the city of Tinghai on 1 October. Instead the idea had been to secure the landing and the outer defences, and then attack on 2 October. That fact that Gough was able to seize the initiative, deviate from his plan of campaign, and take advantage of the circumstances is greatly to his credit. Whilst it is easy to criticise the defence put up by the Chinese it should never be considered that this was an easy operation.

On 2 October Gough moved to secure the rest of the island, and to either capture, kill, or force to withdraw from the island the remaining Chinese soldiers. To this end he sent out various raiding parties. To the west he despatched Lieutenant Colonel Adams with the 18th Foot and the rifle company to secure that side of the island. They were in turn supported by two frigates sent by Rear Admiral Parker to provide artillery support if necessary. Gough also despatched 300 men under Major Blyth of the 49th Foot to the east where they were also supported by two warships, and to the north three companies of the 55th Foot under Captain Campbell. In short order they secured the island. The campaign had been a great success. Despite difficult obstacles and a more determined level of resistance than had been experienced up to that point, British casualties had been relatively light. Gough recorded one officer, two sergeants and 25 men wounded, with 19 of those men coming from the 55th Foot. Surprisingly, given the level of resistance, only one officer, an Ensign of the 55th Foot, and one soldier of the Madras Engineers were killed.[20]

19   NLI: MS 638, Gough to Lord Auckland, 3 October 1841.
20   NLI: MS 638, Return of Officers and Men killed and wounded at the capture of Chusan, 3 October 1841.

32

Pressing Onwards: Chinhai and Ningpo

One gets a sense that there was a great desire on the part of the committee of three who were directing British strategy, to keep the momentum going that had been gathered in the previous operations. This was combined with a desire to press on before the winter came, and to that end to secure a position in which the British could winter safely. As a consequence operations progressed swiftly. By 3 October the island of Chusan had been cleared of the Chinese. So swift was the movement forward that by 8 October the British force was ready to continue its movement. On the same day they undertook a reconnaissance of Chinhai (Zhenhai) further along the coast. The intention was now to move on both Chinhai and Ningpo (Ningbo), important commercial towns and a movement nearer to the imperial court.

Chinhai is situated on the left bank of the River Yong (sometimes referred to as the Ningpo River). Once again the city and its fortification appeared on the face of it to be strong, and at Chinhai the Chinese would once again put up a more determined fight. This had much to do with the presence of the aforementioned Mongol General Yuqian. Having managed to escape from Chusan he returned to his headquarters. This happened to be in Chinhai, which Gough referred to as 'the giant military depot of this province'.[1] Yuqian had made the by-now-usual excuses for his previous defeat, by claiming a reduced number of his own soldiery and adding a zero to the number of British troops. However once again the Emperor was informed that misfortune and Chinese treachery had been the main reason for British success.[2] This time Yuqian relied upon the natural defences of the city of Chinhai rather than building elaborate defences as he had attempted at Chusan. On either bank lay a large fort with reasonably modern artillery. The main approach to the city was also well known for the muddy nature of the river. Any boat entering this area, even the shallow draft steamers, would be talking a huge risk and should they run aground they would be at the mercy of the guns of the two forts and the city itself. Reports suggest that some of Yuqian's senior commanders were not as confident as he. Indeed some were said to have suggested a return to the 'loose-rein' approach of previous years. In short they suggested negotiating their way out of the present situation. Yuqian's response was to say that this time there would be no retreat; if Chinhai fell Yuqian would fall with it. Once again Yuqian was to be guilty of overestimating the strength of his defences, and underestimating the power of British naval gunfire.

Perhaps there was also a somewhat complacent approach on the part of the Chinese. When, on 8 and 9 October, Gough and Parker undertook reconnaissance of the area in one of the steamers, they were not fired upon at any point. This allowed Gough and Parker to carefully plan their attack with a reasonable expectation of the difficulties and obstacles such a landing would encounter. Gough reported of Chinhai that, 'The walls are nearly three miles in circumference, and their sea face runs for about a mile along a massive stone embankment, that extends for three or four miles

---

1   NLI: MS 638, Gough to Lord Auckland, 18 October 1841.
2   Lovell, *The Opium War*, pp. 190–191. See also Rait, *Gough*, Vol. I, p. 217.

further, up the coast'.[3] Gough went into further detail on the defences of the city, but it is sufficient to say that they were formidable. The majority of Chinese troops appeared to be stationed on
the right bank of the river on a series of hills with strong artillery batteries. In short the defences
appeared strong and any landing would be a formidable undertaking. Gough later informed Lord
Auckland that:

> It appeared to me advisable, in which Sir William Parker concurred, that we should make a
> conjoint attack on both banks of the river, first drawing the attention of the enemy to the right
> bank, and the dispositions were accordingly made for attacking with three columns, while the
> two line of battle ships, with the "Blonde" and "Modeste" were to cannonade the joss house
> hill and the sea line of the city defences; the smaller vessels and the steamers to cover the
> landing and to support when practicable the advancing columns by their fire.[4]

Whether or not this plan of attack was advisable, it was in reality the only real option open to him.
Although it is not necessary to detail the alternative landing sites, it is sufficient to say that they
presented more daunting prospects such as gorges, swamps, and jagged rocks. In reality the decision was in this case probably more that of Rear Admiral Parker than that of Gough. In short the
decision rested upon where it was possible for the navy to act at their most effective. The chosen
landing site enabled full use of naval gunfire. Once again it is worth noting the key role that the
navy played in the operation. The ships, both in terms of guns and men, supported Gough's small
force. They were also the key to his movement, both logistically and strategically. Indeed Gough
was the first to give praise to the naval support he received. All his despatches to Lord Auckland
give full praise to the naval officers and men.

At day break on 10 October the attack commenced. The attacking force was split into three
columns, but unlike previous campaigns there was no attempt to land more than one column at a
time. This was partly due to the difficult nature of the landing. However it was also linked to the
fact that Gough's force was now reduced in numbers. Such was the reduction that it would have
been difficult to land two forces at the same time and be confident that they had sufficient strength
to defend themselves until reinforced. For the attack on Chinhai, Gough could call on a little over
2,000 men, 508 of whom were Royal Marines and sailors. Sickness had taken its toll on his force
as had the need to leave garrisons at previously captured areas. The reduction in number is seen
particularly when looking at the British Army battalions. For instance the 18th Foot went into
battle with only 12 officers and 280 men, and even the newest arrivals, the 55th Foot, only placed a
force of 18 officers and 417 men in the field. There was therefore a need to concentrate his strongest
and most reliable units together. Particular as only one column, the left column commanded by
Lieutenant Colonel Craigie with Gough in attendance, was to land initially.[5] This disposition made
the left column the main striking force. On paper it was certainly the strongest, combining both
the 18th and 55th Foot alongside the rifle company Gough had created, which now comprised 4
officers and 110 men. This was supported by over 120 artillerymen with four mountain howitzers
and two mortars, and 104 engineers. The total of this initial landing force was 45 officers and 1,025
men. In addition to this number were 112 'Dooley Bearers and natives to carry shot'.[6]

3   NLI: MS 638, Gough to Lord Auckland, 18 October 1841.
4   NLI: MS 638, Gough to Lord Auckland, 18 October 1841.
5   NLI: MS 638, Gough to Lord Auckland, 18 October 1841. This includes a full list of the disposition and
    deployment of the force which Gough commanded.
6   A Dooley, more often spelt dhoolie or doolie, was an Indian style palanquin normally used to carry the
    wounded. In short they were stretcher bearers, pressed into service as ammunition carriers.

Once again, we see an example of Gough's personal bravery in accompanying what was likely to be a difficult landing. Whether or not this was the role of the commander-in-chief of land forces is another matter. It could be argued that he would have been better served observing the landing from a ship of war and directing reinforcements or naval gunfire to support the landings. In his defence on these charges, it can be argued that he had full confidence in his naval counterparts to do what was necessary and appropriate. Also, if he went with the landing he was on hand should any emergency arise and could direct operations if necessary. One cannot help but feel that Gough's motivation was his desire to get to the front, however even if that was his main motivation it does not necessarily mean that his decision was incorrect.

Exactly what happened during the landing is unclear, as the expected opposition did not arise. Gough does make the comment that when the column advanced it had to do so over several steep hills, so it is possible that these hills, along with the confusion caused by the naval bombardment, masked the British landing. Gough later reported that:

> At eight o'clock the steamers having run in close to the shore, the troops were promptly landed without any opposition under the judicious superintendence of Captain Giffard ably aided by Lieutenant Somerville of the Royal Navy, at a rocky point, having the low flat (of land) and the canal already mentioned to their right.[7]

We do know that the naval artillery had overwhelmed the Chinese defences. The British ships overpowered and outranged the Chinese artillery. Thus the British ships could take position out of range of the Chinese guns and obliterate their defences. Seeing that there was no resistance, Gough ordered the landing of the centre column about a mile to the right of his position, and on the opposite side of the canal. The centre column, commanded by Lieutenant Colonel Morris, consisted of the 49th Foot, reduced to 23 officers and 346 men, supported by one officer and 40 men of the Madras Sappers, one officer and 50 men of the Madras Artillery and four men of the Royal Artillery operating two 12 pdr howitzers and two 9 pdr field guns. In total the column consisted of 25 officers and 440 men. This was the weakest column. From his account it appears that Gough was concerned that the Chinese were preparing to attack the centre column as it landed. Whether there was intelligence to support this or it was simply Gough's explanation for why the Chinese had not attacked the left column, is unclear. Perhaps this supports the notion that he would have been better remaining at sea where he could have better observed events. However he was now able to advance quickly upon the enemy, who appeared to be in some confusion due to the severity of the naval bombardment.[8]

The left column, accompanied by Gough, climbed the several steep hills to their front, still without opposition. When on the crest of one Gough was able to see the picture more clearly. Ahead of him were two bridges over the canal. Realising that it was important to secure them, Gough detached the rifle company to protect the bridge directly in front of him by occupying several houses on the bank. Gough held the 18th Foot in reserve to support the rifle company if necessary whilst despatching Lieutenant Colonel Craigie, still nominally in command of the column, to secure the second bridge with the 55th Foot and the engineers. However once they had secured the bridge Craigie was ordered to press on and take the hills beyond the bridge, thus turning the right flank of the enemy, and threatening to cut off their retreat back to the city of Chinhai. By the time this was achieved the centre column had climbed the hills in front of it and threatened a frontal attack on the Chinese position.

7   NLI: MS 638 Gough to Lord Auckland, 18 October 1841.
8   NLI: MS 638 Gough to Lord Auckland, 18 October 1841.

Having captured the bridge, Gough now moved to cross it covered by the rifle company. The bridge had been partly blocked and although some of the obstacles had been removed men could only cross in single file. It is unclear as to whether the bridge had been blocked deliberately by the Chinese or from debris from the British artillery bombardment. Moving the 18th down to cover the bridge, Gough ordered the rifle company to cross and take up defensives positions on the other side of the canal. A large body of Chinese soldiers appeared during this movement on a hill only 150 yards away from the bridge. Bizarrely they did not fire a single shot and Gough even records that they, 'cheered our advance'.[9] Once the rifle company was in position Gough ordered across the 18th Foot. By the time this had been achieved Gough received information that the 55th and the engineers had crossed the second bridge and reached their position on the right of the Chinese line. With the news that the 55th were in place, Gough ordered the centre column to advance. The nature of the ground made the advance of the guns difficult, however the Madras Artillery were able to bring forward their rockets and open fired on the enemy.

With the support of rocket fire a complex movement from three directions now took place upon the Chinese position. The 49th attacked from the front, but this was largely a feint to cover the advance of the 55th from the second bridge and the 18th Foot and the rifle company from the first bridge. As Gough later recalled, "I have seldom witnessed a more animated combined attack: the Chinese cheering until we got close to them, now poured in a very heavy but ill-directed fire, and displayed in various instances acts of individual bravery that merited a better fate- but nothing could withstand the steady but rapid advance of the gallant little force that assailed them."[10] In a short period of time the colours of the 49th were visible from the highest of the hills. The 18th, who had charged through a deep gorge to the left of the Chinese position, now broke into the central encampment of the Chinese force. What remained of the Chinese troops had been driven from the force down towards the river and in some cases literarily into the river as they tried to escape. Their retreat had been cut off by the movement of the 55th and many Chinese drowned whilst attempting to escape across the river to the city. Others sought safety on a number of large rocks in the middle of the stream. They were persuaded to surrender and were carried to safety by the very boats the British had used to land earlier in the day.

Whilst the centre and left columns had driven the enemy from the heights and secured the route into the city the right column had been landed a little further along the coast on a narrow spur of land at around 1100. Given that this was largely a naval force consisting of the Royal Marines and the battalion of sailors, Gough had placed the force under the overall control of Captain Herbert of HMS *Blenheim*. Supported by naval gunfire they had landed and taken a hill, the fort originally sited upon which had largely been destroyed by the aforementioned naval bombardment. Gough allowed Captain Herbert to decide, based on his success, how far he was to push on with his advance. Due to the fact that the naval bombardment had been so devastating, and that the two other columns under Gough's command had engaged and defeated the majority of the Chinese soldiers, there was little to stop the advance of the Royal Marines and sailors. Due to their success they pressed on to the city. As Gough recalled:

> Captain Herbert, with his usual sound judgement, instantly determined upon taking advantage of the general panic, quickly followed up the retreating enemy, and cleared the city ramparts in his front by a sharp fire of musketry. At this moment a tremendous explosion took place in a battery below the hill, by which the Chinese suffered severely, and a drummer of the marines received so severe a wound that he soon after died. The Column escaladed [the city wall] at the

---

9   NLI: MS 638, Gough to Lord Auckland, 18 October 1841.
10   NLI: MS 638, Gough to Lord Auckland, 18 October 1841.

South Eastern angle, where the city wall is about twenty feet high, the enemy flying before it, as it rapidly pushed along the ramparts, and escaping through the western gates.[11]

Further reading indicates that Gough was not the only senior commander who delighted in leading from the front. According to Gough, Rear Admiral Parker accompanied the force that attacked the city and was said to be one of the first to set foot on the walls of the city.[12] One wonders in this case who exactly commanded the fleet at sea, given that Herbert was the next senior officer and he was also on shore. Pottinger held a civilian rather than a military appointment. In short there was little for the ships to do other than to keep firing and each ship's captain had sufficient skill to do that. There were risks to the scheme; particularly had they needed to withdraw in a hurry, but given the opposition that was never really likely. Indeed it was the sort of campaign where pluck and courage were the key. Both Gough and Parker displayed these qualities in their personal conduct and willingness to share in the danger and lead from the front.

The city was taken with ease. Gough recorded his success in triumphalist tones and can perhaps be forgiven for a slight error when he claimed that the enemy had been strengthening Chinhai for a year at great expense. In reality, whilst the defences had been strengthened the sort of time, money, and effort had not been spent on them as had been on Chuan. Gough also overestimated the Chinese force he had faced, although he admitted that "I have not been able to ascertain the exact strength of the Chinese." He went on to say that he believed them to be around 8,000 strong, whereas most modern scholars estimate the Chinese strength to have been at most 5,000. Gough based his estimation on the number of weapons found and by calculating the number of men needed to garrison the city and the forts.[13] However this should not detract from the scale of the defeat that the Chinese suffered. They had been in a strong position and had squandered their opportunities. They had suffered over 1,500 soldiers killed, with at least the same number wounded or captured, out of a force of around 5,000. However, as Yuiqan had been using Chinhai as his headquarters, the Chinese had built a gunfoundary and a large arsenal in the city and their loss was a great blow. As mentioned previously, Gough recalled that in the arsenal was found one of the guns from the wrecked ship *Kite* alongside what Gough called 'an excellent imitation', illustrating that the Chinese were attempting to learn from their 'barbarian' adversary. Yuqian had attempted to stay true to this promise that if the city fell he would fall with it and had attempted suicide by drowning himself. However his retinue managed to resuscitate him and transport him away from the city. As they left the city he achieved his desired end by taking poison which, somewhat ironically, was believed to be an overdose of opium.[14] Whilst the defeat had been humiliating for the Chinese it had been a great triumph for the British, and one can forgive Gough having a somewhat arrogant tone in his dispatch to Lord Auckland. The British had lost at most 16 soldiers killed. Gough recorded only three killed at the time of his dispatch, however there were also 16 wounded recorded of whom 10 were said to be severely wounded and may subsequently have died of their wounds.

The British advance continued its momentum and no sooner had Chinahi fallen than preparations were being made to press on towards Ningpo. Two days after the battle for Chinhai, Rear Admiral Parker sailed in the *Nemesis* to determine whether the river was practicable in the advance towards Ningpo. He reached a boat bridge on the outskirts of Ningpo before returning and at no point was he fired upon. Although they did not know it at the time, resistance to the British

11   NLI: MS 638, Gough to Lord Auckland, 18 October 1841.
12   NLI: MS 638, Gough to Lord Auckland, 18 October 1841.
13   NLI: MS 638, Gough to Lord Auckland, 18 October 1841.
14   Lovell, *The Opium War*, p. 190.

advance had evaporated. With the death of Yuiqan there was no order or leadership. On 13 October the steamers and other shallow draft craft set sail for Ningpo. Gough left a sizeable garrison behind including the 55th save the light company, 100 Royal Marines, and a detachment of artillery and sappers. Although it would appear a strange decision to split his already weakened force there were several reasons for it. Firstly little resistance was expected at Ningpo. Secondly Chinhai was in danger of falling into chaos following its capture and looting was widespread. Thirdly there was a limit to how many troops could be carried up the river at any one time. It is interesting to note again that Gough clearly saw the 55th's light company, skirmishers, as being useful to the type of warfare he was fighting.[15]

For further operations Gough therefore retained a total of around 750 men not counting artillery and sappers. They sailed at 0800 on the morning of 13 October and by 1500 they reached Ningpo. There was no enemy to greet them, although the bridges into the city were thronged with curios Chinese onlookers. The town fell without resistance and Gough attempted to return the city to normal life, ordering that all shops be opened as usual and promising their safety. The dispatch to Lord Auckland demonstrates not only Gough's delight in what had been achieved, his thankfulness that casualties amongst the civilian population were relatively light, the good order and conduct of his men, but also a rather patriotic sense of pride, speaking of 'the true British feeling which exists in this little force'.[16] Gough again took the opportunity to mention in dispatches the excellent work of Major Mountain as Adjutant General, and Captain Gough, his son, as Quartermaster General. They had clearly done good work, although they were greatly assisted by the navy in their ability to transport and supply the force. It is interesting to note that Gough sent the dispatches of all the action that year up to the fall of Ningpo to Lord Auckland via Lieutenant Gabbett of the Madras Artillery along with his personal recommendation of the officer. Gabbett's name appears nowhere in the dispatches other than the mention of him being sent with them. Normally such an honour was reserved for an officer who had distinguished himself in the field as a special mark of honour. It is strange that an artillery officer from the Madras Army, rather than a line officer from the British Army, was so chosen. There may have been a desire to reward one of 'his' soldiers, with Gough being c-in-c of the Madras Army, but we do not know.

Gough settled down to garrison Ningpo and stationed his troops so as to not only defend against Chinese insurrection but to be able to defend the Chinese citizens against looting and robber bands who now roamed the country. To that end he also created a police force made up of local Chinese largely aimed at defending local property: the idea was to raise 5,000 Chinese police/militia to maintain law and order.[17] One imagines that Gough felt similarly about the maintenance of civil law and order and the defence of property and livelihood as he had when garrisoned in Ireland. He also showed sensitivity to Chinese culture when placing troops in a temple. Strategic necessity forced him into using the temple as a base for the 18th Foot, however he issued strict instructions that the building was not to be damaged, defaced or defiled in any other way.

There is a suggesting that Gough's attitude in regards to protecting Chinese property and sensibilities was somewhat at odds with others in the force, not least of all Pottinger himself who had told the Foreign Secretary that he had been "looking forward with considerable satisfaction to

15 NLI: MS 638, Gough to Lord Auckland, 18 October 1841.
16 NLI: MS 638, Gough to Lord Auckland, 18 October 1841.
17 NAM: 8303–105, Gough Papers, Gutzlaff to Gough, 21 Jan 1842. Charles Frederick August Gutzlaff deserves further comment. Gutzlaff was a Prussian missionary. Well versed in several Chinese dialects he was an invaluable aide to Gough during the campaign acting not only as interpreter but also as an unofficial intelligence chief. Gutzlaff Street in Hong Kong is named in his honour.

plundering Ningpo."[18] It does appear the Rear Admiral Parker supported Gough in his decisions. It was also supported by Lord Aberdeen, now Foreign Secretary and generally opposed to action in China but forced to support it, who had been disturbed by Pottinger's allusion to 'plundering'.

That Gough took a very different view to Pottinger is illustrated by the following passage written in November 1841:

> My great object is prospective, and, though a poor man, I would much prefer leaving a conviction of the minds of the [Chinese] people that we are not only a brave, but a just, a liberal, and a humane nation, than realising a large proportion of prize money. My views on this head are not in accordance with those of either Sir Henry Pottinger or the Admiral. They say their instructions are to press the Government through the medium of the people, so as to make the war unpopular. Now this might apply to France, where the people's voice must have a strong influence on the acts of the Government, but in China it is chimerical. The Government care not for the people, and I verily believe the most annoying thing you could do is to prove to the people by our moderation and our justice that our characters were foully belied. The great object of the present expedition is to prove this, and to obtain, from such knowledge, future commercial intercourse; and that can alone be obtained by mutual confidence.[19]

Again we see not only benevolence to Gough's character but also a thoughtful aspect. No doubt the situation in his own country of Ireland influenced his thinking. The modern reader might interpret Gough's policy as an attempt to win over 'hearts and minds'. Whatever his motivation it appears a genuine and quite sensible approach, albeit again perhaps more to the modern reader than to his contemporaries. Although Gough was often criticised, and with some justification, for his lack of political sense we see here a clear demonstration that he understood the politics of the situation in China better than many of his contemporaries. It demonstrates to us that Gough was a far more intelligent man than might readily be believed.

There was also the question of the paying of an indemnity, rather than the city being plundered. Gough opposed this, with similar reasoning for objecting to plundering. However this time Gough was outvoted. Later both Lord Auckland and his successor Lord Ellenborough sided with Gough. Sir Robert Rait, in his biography of Gough, put this incident forward as an example of Gough's 'political wisdom'.[20] This might be to take things too far and give credit for something that was borne more of practical, strategic and paternalistic concerns rather than any great political vision or nous, but it clearly points to a greater intelligence than is readily believed of him. Gough was not a politician and he found it difficult to play the game of politics. Indeed the somewhat duplicitous nature of the profession ran contrary to his nature. He was also governed too much by his passions to play the game of politics effectively. However whatever his motivation he appears to have been on the right track as captured Imperial correspondence later confirmed. A letter from the Imperial Court stated that:

---

18   Holt, *The Opium Wars in China*, p. 139 & Beeching, *The Chinese Opium Wars*, pp. 139–140. This refers to the communication with the Foreign Secretary. Pottinger believed he was writing to Lord Palmerston, but by the time the letter arrived there had been a change of government and the Tories were now in office and Lord Aberdeen was Foreign Secretary. Phillimore, *The Life of Sir William Parker* Vol. II, p. 460. The latter states that the comments also appeared in a memorandum addressed to Parker and Gough. In this account Pottinger states that 'After the manner in which the city has come into our hands' he felt it would be 'impolitic' to plunder the place.

19   Rait, *Gough*, Vol. I, pp. 235–236.

20   Rait, *Gough*, Vol. I, p. 239.

The mass of the people remain neutral, for these rebellious barbarians (the British) issue edict after edict to tranquilize them. They do not oppress the villages, and we have therefore lost our hold upon the fears and hopes of their inhabitants. [...] Consider, moreover, the numerous city guards the barbarians have established, and how cunningly they proceed to manage matters, in order to keep the people in their interests.[21]

---

21   Rait, Gough, Vol. I, p. 246.

33

Wintering in Ningpo

The capture of Ningpo seemed to get the attention of the Emperor. His initial response was to set a series of punishments for Yuiqan. However upon learning of his death at Chinhai, if not necessarily the method, he was given substantial honours and the equivalent of a state funeral. Instead his second in command, and ironically the man who had put up the most resistance at Chinhai, Yu Buyun, was executed. The Emperor looked around for a new commander and decided to appoint his nephew Yijing.[1] He had achieved success fighting rebels, but only as a junior officer and had no experience of higher command. Indeed at that point he was the Imperial Director of Gardens and Hunting Parks: a great contrast with his predecessor. Unsurprisingly Yijing wondered whether fighting was the best course of action in regards to dealing with the British, and favoured negotiations. However it was made clear by his uncle that he was desired to fight. Making Suzhou (Soochow) his headquarters, he attempted to establish a force of 12,000 regulars and 33,000 militia. He also took the strange step of placing a suggestion box at the gates to the city and inviting suggestions on how to defeat the British. He received over 400 suggestions none of which seemed practical.[2] Indeed, Yijing seemed both unwilling and incapable of going to war. His juniors took the opportunity of his lack of interest to make themselves wealthy off the funds being provided for the prosecution of the war.

Whilst the new Chinese commander was taking suggestions on how to fight the war, the British had chosen to winter in Ningpo. This was not without opposition from Gough, who felt that other captured cities, particularly Chinhai, were better suited as a winter garrison. Gough was worried that his force was spread too thinly amongst the captured towns. He had advocated abandoning Ningpo, but had been understandably overruled by Pottinger and Parker. Although to give up an important city captured with such ease, particularly when there was a likelihood of having to recapture in the face of resistance, would seem a great folly, one can understand Gough's concerns if not necessarily agree with them. Gough was not alone in this view, and indeed upon hearing of the thinly spread nature of British troops, Lord Auckland expressed similar concerns to those made by Gough. However once Lord Auckland was aware of the matter the decision had already been made.

Cholera broke out in both Chinhai and Ningpo in the immediate aftermath of their capture. In Ningpo no soldiers died of the disease, although many had suffered from it. However in Chinhai 10 Royal Marines died of the disease. Gough attributed the success in fighting the disease to, "the unremitting attention and judicious arrangements of Dr French, the superintending surgeon."[3] As

---

1 Exactly what relation Yijing, or in some accounts I-ching, was to the Emperor is debated. Julia Lovell states he is the Emperor's nephew, whereas Edgar Holt refers to him as a cousin. It is likely that the former is correct. Lovell, *The Opium War*, p. 192. Holt, *The Opium Wars*, p. 140.
2 Lovell, *The Opium War*, p. 194 & Holt, *The Opium Wars in China*, p. 140.
3 NLI: MS 638, Gough to Lord Auckland, 18 October 1841.

it turned out Ningpo was a good winter quarter for the army, which was kept supplied by the ships sailing up the river from Chinhai. From various accounts it appears that officers enjoyed hunting local pheasants, ducks, snipe, woodcocks, wild pigeons, and anything else unfortunate enough to show its face, whilst the men engaged in snowball fights, and enjoyed the fresh local bread and vegetables. To that end Gough had made an allowance of 8d a day per man for such food.[4] Little was to happen during the winter of 1841 and 1842. In late December Gough led a column of men to Yuyow and Tzkee to disperse the 'enemy' and relieve pressure on Ningpo. Neither was a particularly serious operation, and both are normally left out of accounts of the conflict. They are mentioned here to illustrate the point that although the winter prevented major operations, Gough was not inactive. However there was not much he could do in way of preparations for the campaign season of 1842.

It was during this stage that a curious letter came into his possession. Unsurprisingly the letter was intended to persuade Gough to quit China, but the tone demonstrated the usual distance from reality of official Chinese communications. After a long preamble regarding how the world was created and how China had become supreme ruler of the world, it urged him in curious language to leave. It seemed to be offering him a way out from what the writer obviously saw as his 'error' and allowing him to leave with face, excusing his ignorance of how the world worked.

> You have now all of a sudden sneaked into the eastern part of Chekeang, and without obeying the ancient laws, taken forcible possession of a frontier country. The reason of this is that you did not know, that the Celestial dynasty, with the aid of worthies and sages, has successfully over several centuries ruled over all who are in the central country and foreign parts.[5]

Although a letter full of fanciful ideas, one suspects that whoever composed it had a better understanding of the real world than the tone suggests. Not only did they give him a chance to leave without losing face, for he had simply made a mistake and in their 'benevolence' the Imperial Court would overlook this, they offered more practical inducements. They promised him that, "rich rewards will be showered upon you, you will become an object of the highest favour, and your name become illustrious." There were even promises that his descendants, after appropriate training, would be allowed to attend the Imperial College. Although the latter probably held little significance to Gough it was an extraordinary honour in the eyes of the Chinese. The offer went further and even seemed to ask Gough to change sides.

> You of course are the best judge of the present state of affairs, and will look forward to the education of your children. You, like a clever bird, will choose the proper tree to perch there, and as a shrewd servant select your master and serve him.[6]

This extraordinary offer demonstrates the lack of understanding of their adversary on the part of the Chinese. The idea that Gough would change sides and become a 'servant' of the Chinese Emperor is ridiculous. It does perhaps illustrate once again that the Chinese saw no difference between the British and any other 'barbarian' enemy they had faced. In effect they were trying what had worked

---

4   Lovell, *The Opium War*, p. 198, Beeching, *The Chinese Opium Wars*, p. 141, & Holt, *The Opium Wars in China*, p. 140.
5   Rait, *Gough*, Vol. I, pp. 242–245. It addresses him as 'The English Minister Gough'. It is interesting to note that the Chinese obviously see him as an official rather than a soldier or are perhaps unable to make a distinction between the two.
6   Rait, *Gough*, Vol. I, p. 245.

elsewhere in the empire and on their borders. Gough's reaction to this letter is not recorded, but it is hard to think that it was anything other than amusement.

Throughout the winter Gough had attempted to keep the garrison on its toes, fearing a possible attack. This was not so much based on intelligence of Chinese activities as a fear that his troops were spread out too thinly particularly between Chinhai and Ningpo. The Chinese for their part were indeed planning large-scale operations. Yijing could not be faulted for his ambition. His plan to raise over 40,000 troops had failed, yet he still went ahead with the same plans. He proposed to attack Ningpo, Chinhai and Chusan simultaneously. However this had been based on manpower figures that he was unavailable to make a reality. The plan had been for a force of 36,000 to attack Ningpo, 15,000 Chinhai, and for 10,000 to cross the sea to Chusan. The latter was particularly ambitious given the dominance of British naval power. However, had he developed the manpower he had hoped for he might have been successful to an extent as the overstretched British would have found it much harder to defend all three cities simultaneously. Exact figures for the Chinese are uncertain however the number were not what had originally been planned for. It is said that at most Yijing had 10,000 men with which to attack Ningpo and Chinhai, whilst the fleet that sailed for Chusan had no more than 3,000–4,000 men. The plan was further hampered by its timing. Had it been launched earlier the deep snow might have worked to the advantage of the Chinese, however by 9 March when the attacks commenced, heavy rain had reduced the snow to slush and turned the roads to mud. Despite these setbacks the Chinese still launched their attack as originally planned.[7]

Yijing would have been better served by throwing his entire force at Ningpo, and it is quite possible that he might have been successful. Gough's concerns about the difficulty of defending Ningpo were to be realised during the attack. The Chinese however made two notable errors just prior to the attack. Firstly the early deployment of fire ships to attack the fleet just off the city alerted the British to attack and thus the garrison had stood to before the Chinese launched their operation. The Chinese also carried lanterns when they attacked which gave the British excellent targets at which to shoot. Simultaneous attacks were launched against the southern and western gates. At the former a detachment of 140 men of the 49th Foot faced an attack by around 3,000 Chinese soldiers. The fighting was hard, often hand-to-hand, but the timely arrival of the remainder of the 49th saved the situation. At the southern gate in particular the Chinese were said to have enjoyed the support of a 'fifth column' from within the town that supported the attack. Whether or not this is true is unclear but it does appear that at the very least someone from within the town opened the gate for the Chinese attackers.[8] At the western gate the 18th Foot found themselves in a similar position, and facing a similar number of Chinese. The defensive position was, however, harder to maintain and the fighting soon became a brawl of hand-to-hand fighting, with the British soldiers even breaking up walls to throw stones at the enemy. If anyone had ever doubted that the Chinese could fight here was an example of their ability. Eventually the Chinese were beaten back by the deployment of a howitzer which halted their advance.

The attack on Ningpo was repulsed but the fighting had been hard and bloody. Indeed many officers, who had seen harrowing scenes in the Peninsular War, declared that this was the worst they had seen since Badajoz. The narrow streets of the city had meant that the gunners had an easy and mass target to aim for. The severity of the clash is partly demonstrated by the fact that few Chinese wounded remained; they had either been killed outright or were able to escape.

The attack on Chinhai was similar in nature but was not as well led or supported from within the town. The story exists that the garrison was alerted to the imminent attack by a small boy who passed a note to British soldiers. Exactly who had sent him and where the note had come from

7   Lovell, *The Opium War*, pp. 202–203.
8   Lovell, *The Opium War*, p. 203 & Holt, *The Opium Wars in China*, pp. 141–142.

remains a mystery.[9] However it gave the British chance to prepare. With Chinhai being easier to defend, and the Chinese attack lacking direction or determination, it was easily repulsed. The attack on Chusan never took place at all and the fleet carrying the landing force simply sailed up and down the coast. The intention was that the three attacks would take place simultaneously, but due to the tide being against them the fleet did not sail until after the attacks against the other two cities had failed. The fleet set sail unsure of their intentions, with low morale, and with crew and soldiers drawn largely from landlocked provinces who suffered terribly from seasickness.

There had been a chance of success for the Chinese. They had conceived a good plan. Had the manpower numbers been up to what Yijing had desired, and had a three pronged attack been launched simultaneously, there was a real chance that they might have overwhelmed the thinly spread out British force. Gough's fears about his force being overstretched were genuine, but one can understand the desire of Pottinger and Parker to hang on to Ningpo once it was captured. It also illustrates that whilst the British enjoyed superiority over the Chinese, they were not invulnerable. Importantly, they had survived the most concerted attack the Chinese were able to make. Gough immediately urged that, having repulsed the enemy action, it was time for the British to renew their attack. By doing this Gough hoped to exploit the Chinese disorder after the failed attacks.

9   Lovell, *The Opium War*, p. 204.

34

Continuing the Advance

Gough had not been at Ningpo when the attack of 9 March took place. He had deliberately wintered in Ningpo so as to be on hand should any attack be made. However Parker had largely remained aboard his flag ship, and Pottinger at Chusan. On the day the attack took place Gough was in Chusan along with Rear Admiral Parker visiting Pottinger to discuss future operations. There is a suggestion that the Chinese had spotted Gough's departure and had taken it to be the first step in an evacuation. It is possible that this influenced their decision to attack when they did.[1] In turn the simultaneous attacks upon the British held towns determined Gough upon action against the Chinese in the vicinity.

The winter had necessitated a halt in the momentum of the British advance. However with the Chinese renewing the war Gough realised that there was a need to restore the momentum to the British campaign. Gough returned as soon as he could and by 13 March he was leading his men out to meet the enemy. "I deemed it right promptly to follow up these successful repulses, taking the attacking columns in detail, and understanding that General Yu-poo-yun was advancing from Funghwa with from 6 to 7,000 men, I moved out to meet him on the 13th."[2] The Chinese had around 8,000 men positioned about 18 miles from Ningpo at what had been their base just prior to the attack. Many of the soldiers were the elite of the army, Qing warriors dressed in the purple and black of the Imperial Guard, who Yijing had held back as a sort of personal bodyguard rather than commit to the attack. Gough took with him a force of around 600 men composed of the 18th and 49th Foot, some Madras Artillery with two guns, and 50 engineers. Added to this was a force of three companies of the 26th Foot, the rifle company, and some Royal Marines and sailors who were on board the steamers that accompanied his force. The steamers *Queen*, *Nemesis* and *Phlegethon* were able to guard his flank as he marched and provide artillery support if needed. In total, Gough had around 1,000 men under his command.

By the 14th Gough had reached the village where the Chinese had last been spotted. His lack of information meant that he had missed the Chinese by less than a day. Gough, now joined by Rear Admiral Parker who accompanied him throughout the action, decided to move upon Tskee. On 15 March they arrived to find the 8,000 Chinese had taken position on the hills above the town. Gough himself was unsure of the exact number and in his dispatch calculated between 7,000 and 10,000. The figure of 8,000 was his best guess. At 1200 Gough commenced his attack. The town itself was barely defended. Although Gough noticed guns had been placed on the walls and in the gateways, they had so little effect when they fired that Gough became convinced that the Chinese had never intended to seriously defend the town. This gave him a moment's anxiety, feeling that he was being led into a trap. However he decided that either way it was important to take the city

---

1   Rait, *Gough*, Vol. I, pp. 248–249.
2   NLI: MS 638, Gough to Lord Auckland, 19 March 1842.

without further delay.[3] Gough ordered the Royal Marines and sailors to scale the walls and then work their way along to the north gate. This was part of a three pronged movement that also saw the 49th move along a shallow canal under the city walls towards the south gate. Having blown the gate they were to join the naval contingent on the walls and make their way to the north gate. The 18th Foot marched around the outside of the city walls and drove off a portion of the enemy from a hill on the north west of the city. They were then to move around to the north gate and if not already taken, to engage the enemy in support of the naval force and the 49th. The 26th Foot were kept in reserve and to protect the movement of the guns.

The aim was to take the city by this movement and then for the whole force to join up again at the north gate. Gough stated later that he decided upon taking the city before dealing with the main force on the hill so as to prevent them from having a place to retreat to. It would also have been dangerous to have had a portion of the enemy behind him no matter how slight and how ineffective their guns were. The Royal Marines and sailors scaled the walls unopposed. The 18th dispersed the enemy and then rapidly moved on the north gate. Gough himself accompanied the 49th Foot as they moved along the canal, because the bridge had been destroyed and Gough, conscious of the need for a quick movement, decided that there was insufficient time to rebuild it. Gough was able to coordinate this movement with that of the naval detachment on the ramparts thus each covered the other's advance.

The force secured the town and then gathered by the north gate. The town was surrounded by hills and at the north gate the spur of one of the hills met the city wall. To the north west of this position were slightly higher hills where the camps of the Chinese were based and where they now made their stand. However the Chinese had not occupied the highest point of the range of hills. Gough quickly seized upon this error: "I at once perceived that the [Chinese] position was faulty, as the hills on our right commanded their left, while their left commanded their right, and I made my dispositions accordingly."[4] Once again he organised a simultaneous attack. The 18th and the rifle company were ordered to move along a ravine and occupy the high position on the enemy's left, and thus turning the enemy's flank. The naval detachment was ordered to occupy two large buildings in front of the right encampment of the Chinese. This was to be secured prior to them advancing on the Chinese position. At the same time, Gough accompanied the 49th in a frontal attack on the other encampment. As Gough later recalled, "My great object being to make a simultaneous attack with the three columns pushing the 18th down in rear, while the naval brigade should cut off all communication with the city."[5] The speed with which this, and the previous movement, had been achieved had been so rapid as to prevent the guns coming into action in time. As it happened only one gun managed to be moved into position in time to take part in the engagement.

The plan was ambitious, and the synchronising of the movement of three columns problematic. As it was, the 18th Foot and the rifle company took longer climbing the narrow ravine than Gough had anticipated. The steepness of their ascent was also a reason for delay. Gough realised that, despite the fact that they had not reached their position, if he were to delay much longer it could have consequences for the rest of his troops as the Royal Marines and sailors were already coming under fire:

> Finding that the naval brigade might probably suffer more by the delay than in an immediate attack, and that the enemy appeared to gain confidence by this delay, I ordered the advance to

---

3   NLI: MS 638, Gough to Lord Auckland, 19 March 1842.
4   NLI: MS 638, Gough to Lord Auckland, 19 March 1842.
5   NLI: MS 638, Gough to Lord Auckland, 19 March 1842.

be sounded, when the 49th with their accustomed spirit, pushed up the hill, overcoming all opposition, and crowning its height within a few minutes, driving everything before them.[6]

Once on the height, Gough observed that the naval brigade had also come into action and attacked the other encampment with similar success. It is interesting to note that whilst Gough accompanied the 49th in their advance, Rear Admiral Parker personally led the naval brigade in their attack. As the naval brigade battled to the top of the hill Gough observed that coming up the other side of the hill was what he described as 'a large body of Chinese'. The naval brigade was unaware of their presence and Gough feared for them as they were still engaged in battle and likely to have another sizeable force of the enemy engage them at the same time.

Gough ordered his nephew, Major John Bloomfield Gough, to lead forward the grenadier company of the 49th Foot to support the naval brigade. However, they were to be positioned in such a way as to not only bring fire support but also to cut off the retreat of this large body of Chinese. As a consequence, "The carnage at the foot of this hill was extraordinarily great. The 49th in rear and the naval brigade in front almost annihilated this body."[7] At the same time the remainder of the 49th pursued the retreating enemy. Having arrived too late to take part in the initial battle, the 18th and the rifle company, operating under their own initiative, had descended the far side of the hill and blocked the retreat of the enemy. Gough ordered the 26th Foot, least one company left behind to protect the guns, to join in the pursuit. The rout was completed by 2000, and Gough's men returned to the Chinese encampment where they found much baggage and many luxuries. The following day, 16 March, Gough set fire to the encampments along with several houses that had been used by the Chinese as arsenals.

Exact figures for the number of Chinese dead have never been clear. The minimum appears to have been 1,000, although it is quite possibly far greater. Gough called them the elite of the Imperial Army. Although they wore the imperial uniform they were perhaps not the elite. However they were certainly a cut above the troops they had faced up to this point, as shown by their willingness to die rather than surrender. Although many offers were made, few prisoners were taken and by the end of the battle the British troops had rather morbid target practice at the fleeing Chinese. There is certainly controversy to this, as many of the Chinese were not only retreating but had thrown their weapons away. The British were therefore shooting unarmed and fleeing men. Whilst distasteful this was after all one of the practicalities of war, and as a British soldier is said to have stated, "If we don't kill them now sir, they will fight us again, and we shall never finish the war."[8] This was a simplistic and rather brutal assessment, but one that was not too far from the truth.

The Chinese put up greater resistance than usual, yet the British had only lost three dead and 22 wounded. Yijing for his part had retreated from Ningpo, already planning his excuses for the Emperor. They were the usual mix of fanciful nonsense, although they had a touch of flair that some of his predecessors lacked. One of the most amusing comments, amongst the usual expression of how wonderfully they had fought, was to report the death of the 'Barbarian Chief Palmerston'! Lord Palmerston, roughly 5,800 miles away in the safety of England, was said to have been amongst the 500 British soldiers the Chinese had killed.[9] This was out of a supposed British force of over 17,000 who had been defeated by the Chinese, only for the latter to be betrayed by Chinese saboteurs who had burnt their camps during the battle and had necessitated their withdrawal. However, even this description was surpassed by that of the expedition to Chusan, which

6   NLI: MS 638, Gough to Lord Auckland, 19 March 1842.
7   NLI: MS 638, Gough to Lord Auckland, 19 March 1842.
8   Lovell, *The Opium Wars*, p. 206.
9   Lovell, *The Opium War*, pp. 206–207.

it will be recalled never landed or even engaged the British. Yijing only now reported this to the Emperor and claimed a great victory in which one British man-of-war and 21 smaller ships had been destroyed by fire rafts. Feeling that this was insufficient, later reports claimed five men-of-war and over 600 British sailors killed. It is said that the account was so improbable that even some of Yijing's officials refused to endorse his account.

Despite Chinese attempts to cover it up, the engagements of this period had been a disaster for the Chinese and a great triumph for Gough and the British. In the aftermath Gough made one notable error. In an act to appease the local population of the town he had ordered the grain stores opened. This resulted in them being emptied and him having to rely on supplies coming up before he could continue his march. It was therefore not until 1200 on 16 March that he was able to continue his movement. His target this time was the Changki Pass where he believed the enemy had taken up position. The prospect of having to force this was not one he relished, as he considered it to be a formidable position that was almost insurmountable. However once again through reconnaissance and the local knowledge of Lieutenant Colonel Mountain, he determined that the position could be turned on the left where the hills were slightly easier to ascend. At 1500 he ordered the 18th Foot to ascend the hills on the left whilst Gough moved with the 26th, 49th, the Royal Marines and sailors to a wooded spur to the front of what was presumed to be the Chinese position. However, once the 18th were in position Gough became aware that the Chinese had abandoned their position: if, indeed, they were ever there. After three hours in the pass, and no sign of the enemy, Gough decided to return to Tskee which they reached at around 2100.[10]

Although a severe blow had been dealt to the enemy, if Gough had moved sooner he might have been able to inflict another heavy loss on the retreating enemy. This was largely due to his error over the grain stores in Tskee. However, given the formidable position that Gough believed the Chinese to have held it is perhaps just as well for Gough that the Chinese withdrew before he could reach them. Any significant loss of life to the British force would raise questions over continued operations, and indeed there were more important objective left ahead. The action of this period had been in response to a Chinese attack. With the winter passing the British were preparing to move on against other Chinese towns to bring the war to the very heart of the Chinese Empire.

10   NLI: MS 638, Gough to Lord Auckland, 19 March 1842.

35

Advance along the Yangtze River

In his dispatch, Gough wrote with pride of the behaviour of his troops in hostile territory where no houses had been ransacked, no private property looted, and no civilians killed. On 17 March he returned with the entire force to Ningpo. Two companies of the 26th were sent to Chinhai under Captain Henry Strange to reopen communications between that place and Ningpo, which had been severed during the attack. This was also intended to deal with any straggling Chinese soldiers who might be in the countryside between the two places.[1]

After the previous Chinese attack, Ningpo was never quite the same for the British. Whether as part of the attack or just the understandable reaction of the inhabitants of the city after seeing the Chinese force heavily defeated, there was a hardening of attitude towards the British. Acts of sabotage, and indeed the abduction and murder of British soldiers, became common. Over 40 men were believed to have been abducted in this manner during the period after the attack and before the main force departed the city. This 'fifth column' in Ningpo had a detrimental effect upon the local police force Gough had organised to patrol the city, to the extent that it collapsed and looting became commonplace. It was during this time that Gough made a remark that is often used in books detailing this conflict. In looking at the poor state of Ningpo after the attack and the collapse of the local police force and of law and order he wrote in a letter home that, "When I look at this place, I am sick of war."[2] However this was not the condemnation of British actions that it is often portrayed as. It was a soldier's weariness with war, and not a comment on the specific conflict in which he was presently engaged. No doubt it brought back to Gough painful memories of the Peninsular Campaign and the hard fighting he had seen there. Again it is a demonstration of the more thoughtful side of his nature.

In the months that followed, there was a continual debate between the three British leaders, and the government in India, as to where future operations should take place. Gough had often expressed the opinion that an attack up the Yangtze River would be the most effective and would include taking Shanghai, Nantong, Chenkiang and Nanking. Lord Auckland, the Governor General of India, proposed a movement along the Pei Ho River (also known as the Hai) towards Peking for the campaigning season of 1842. Whilst to move against the capital made sense from a political point of view, from a military perspective it created many difficulties in terms of military preparations, the length of time such an operation would take, and the likelihood of extremely strong resistance. Gough however felt compelled to go along with this course of action, presuming that this was the will of the Home Government expressed through the Governor General. However such a movement would require a greatly reinforced army to attempt it. Gough proposed that whilst waiting for reinforcements, which were on their way, he should begin operations along the Yangtze River so not as to waste any of the campaigning season.

---

1   NLI: MS 638, Gough to Lord Auckland, 19 March 1842.
2   Rait, *Gough*, Vol. I, p. 261.

The situation changed with the arrival of Lord Ellenborough to replace Lord Auckland as Governor General. Ellenborough officially replaced Auckland as governor general on 28 February 1842, yet Auckland was still conducting official business with Gough until at least late March whilst he awaited the arrival of his successor. It became clear that the suggested line of attack put forward by Auckland had been a personal one and not the view of the home government. Indeed Gough's planned movement up the Yangtzee had the approval of the Duke of Wellington who felt that the operation would be easier and more effective in its financial impact upon the Chinese.[3]

The taking of the capital Peking could be a double edged sword that might only serve to stiffen the resolve of the Chinese and bring the Chinese people further into the conflict. However the situation was complicated again when Wellington changed his military advice after a conversation with Admiral Sir George Cockburn, First Naval Lord at the Admiralty.[4] Cockburn convinced Wellington of the importance of the anchorage at the mouth of the Pei Ho River. This was the advice that they gave to Lord Ellenborough. Fortunately what Ellenborough understood, but neither Wellington nor Cockburn grasped, was that a movement along Pei Ho would leave the land forces largely without naval support. There was even a question as to whether or not the shallow draft steamer *Nemesis* would be able to operate in such conditions, as it would be easy for the Chinese to cut the river banks, flood the plains below, and dramatically alter the water level. Ellenborough also pointed out the climatic conditions. Whilst the advance might be made in good order, after several months fighting and with wearied troops the movement back could have been disastrous for the health of the army. Ellenborough decided that it was best to leave such decisions to the discretion of the naval and military commanders. Rear Admiral Parker concurred with Gough's view and, thanks to the sensible approach of Lord Ellenborough, it was decided that operations would take place along the Yangtze River.[5]

With reinforcements not yet arrive, and with an ever-dwindling force of fit soldiers, Gough was compelled to abandon the towns in which the army had wintered save for Chinhai where a fort or 'joss house' overlooking the town was maintained as a defensive position. This in turn also protected the entrance to Ningpo by sea. On 7 May 1842 the British abandoned Ningpo, which the Chinese subsequently claimed as a victory.[6] It was not until the 13th that all the ships and men not only from Ningpo but also from Chinhai and Chusan had been gathered together. The entire fleet then moved along the coast towards Chapo (Zhapu). The aim was not only to take the town but to destroy a Chinese force of over 8,000 gathered there. The tides were extremely strong and many of the ships struggled to make the journey and did not arrive until 17 May. Gough and Parker had arrived the previous day and had undertaken a detailed reconnaissance of the area in preparation for the attack. Despite the detailed reconnaissance, they could not successfully ascertain the strength and defensives positions of the town itself without going ashore. However, they had been able to determine appropriate landing points from where they could advance on the town.

---

3   At this time the Duke of Wellington was not serving as Commander in Chief: between January 1828 and August 1842 this position was held by Lord Hill, before Wellington returned to the post. At the time in question he was part of the government of Sir Robert Peel acting as Minister without Portfolio and Leader of the House of Lords.

4   It is perhaps interesting to note that in July 1846 William Parker replaced Cockburn as First Naval Lord, albeit for only a week before ill health forced him to give up his political position. There is some suggestion that although announced he never actually accepted the appointment. One wonders at the real reason for his resignation as he was immediately returned to commanding the Mediterranean Fleet.

5   Law, Edward, 1st Earl of Ellenborough, *History of the Indian Administration of Lord Ellenborough, in his correspondence with the Duke of Wellington*, (London: R. Bentley & Son,1874), p. 296–298.

6   Lovell, *The Opium War*, p. 207. Lovell quotes the correspondence of the Chinese commander Yijing to the Emperor stating that he had, 'forced the British troops – terrified at the advance of the great Qing army – to retire'.

The heights outside the town appeared well defended with artillery batteries and around 1,000 to 2,000 men. By the time battle commenced, the majority of the 8,000 strong Chinese force lined the heights. However Gough was sure that once again he would be able to turn their position. Not only that, Gough was also convinced that if he moved rapidly enough he would be able to cut off their retreat and surround the men defending the heights outside the town. If not, he hoped to be able to follow the retreating enemy into the city and secure the gate and then move on with his entire force. The reconnaissance identified a bay four miles to the east of the town, which both Gough and Parker felt afforded the opportunity to land despite the disposition of the enemy as it was so easily covered by naval gunfire.[7]

At daylight on 18 May the troops started to land and by 08.00 the entire force was ashore. This was a feat that owed much to the experience of previous operation, so that the crews, particularly those of the three steamers, were adept at making such landings. Indeed this type of warfare was becoming so commonplace that the movement of the troops was an excellent example of a tactical operation of this nature. The left column commanded by Lieutenant Colonel James Schoedde, consisting of the 26th Foot, the 55th Foot and one officer and 55 sappers, turned the flank of the enemy on the heights and cut of the route back to the town, whilst Gough and the right column commanded by Lieutenant Colonel E. Morris, consisting of the 18th Foot, the 49th Foot, and one officer and 25 sappers, attacked the heights from the front. Consequently the enemy was attacked from two directions, whilst at the same time the movement of the infantry had been covered by naval gunfire.[8]

The bombardment undertaken by the fleet was a huge success and had done damage to the enemy before the British soldiers reached them. The right column swept the enemy from the heights with, as Gough called it, 'the usual spirit'. The Chinese broke, many throwing away their weapons and fleeing from the hill straight onto the waiting left column. One Chinese unit, actually believed to be Tartars, of around 300 men however could not escape. Gough later reported that they, 'took possession of a house and enclosure which they defended with wonderful obstinacy, and would not surrender until the house was in flames from our rockets and breached by powder bags'.[9] The defence made by the 300 men only delayed the British advance temporarily. Indeed whilst that had been ongoing Gough had order Lieutenant Colonel Duncan Montgomerie, commanding the centre column, consisting of the Royal Artillery, the Madras Artillery, two officers and 74 sappers, and the rifle company, to move with both the left column and the centre column towards the town. Using the rifle company Gough then occupied a house near the city wall. From here they could provide fire support for movements against the city wall, which were undertaken by the 55th Foot and the sappers. They took the city walls, entering initially through a canal that ran into the town, and Gough then moved on with the rest of his force to secure all the gates into the town.

Seeing the enemy fleeing from the town, Gough ordered the 55th, the furthest forward unit, to pursue them and attempt to bring them to battle. He would in the meantime secure the city and move on to support the 55th as quickly as he could. Gough also feared that many of the Chinese soldiers were actually still in the city but were difficult to identify, noting that 'It is so easy for a

---

7   NLI: MS 638, Gough to Lord Stanley, 20 May 1842. Lord Stanley, later the 14th Earl of Derby, was at the time serving as Secretary of State for the Colonies. He would later serve as Prime Minister on three separate, but relatively brief, occasions.

8   NLI: MS 638, Gough to Lord Stanley, 20 May 1842. This includes a full list of the deployment of the British force.

9   NLI: MS 638, Gough to Lord Stanley, 20 May 1842. The 'house' as Gough calls it is recorded by Julia Lovell as actually being the Temple of Heavenly Respect. Lovell, *The Opium War*, p. 212.

Chinaman to divest himself of the appearance of a soldier, that I have no doubt that many escaped by throwing off the outward uniform by which alone they are distinguishable from the peasantry'.[10]

Once in the town, he realised that the Chinese had never really intended to defend it in any real way. The walls of the town did not lend themselves to this and the gun emplacements were limited and few in number. Indeed the city itself was divided by an internal wall which complicated any defence. The main defence had therefore been made on the heights outside the city. This defence appears to have been undone by the fact that the British landed in a position that the Chinese had thought impossible to land due to the strong tides and currents. Indeed , such a landing would have been impossible for the Chinese but because of the steamers of the British fleet it was practicable. As a consequence Gough was able to turn the enemy position with relative ease. Due to their having been trapped on the hill Chinese losses were high. Gough recorded some 1,500 Chinese casualties, but this was likely a conservative estimate and the real number might have been as many as double that number. The British had lost nine dead and 55 wounded. This figure would have been smaller if it had not been for an unfortunate piece of regimental rivalry. It is recorded that the initial attempt to dislodge the 300 who had taken up position in the house was undertaken by a small detachment of the 18th Foot. Having failed in the initial attempt they decided to wait for the rest of their battalion and the 49th Foot. The Colonel of the 49th is said to have made a disparaging remark about the 18th Foot, probably including the fact that they were an Irish regiment. This was overheard by Lieutenant Colonel Tomlinson of the 18th who in a fit of pique ordered his battalion to attack despite the urgings of his junior officers.[11] The 18th Foot suffered particularly, losing Tomlinson, a sergeant and three rank and file all killed. As they had taken the lead in the attack on top of the heights they had also more than their fair share of wounded including two officers, a sergeant, and a drummer and 27 rank and file wounded. Gough lamented the loss of Tomlinson, an experienced commander, but also the temporary loss of the severely wounded Lieutenant Colonel Mountain, who Gough hoped would be able to return to duty before long. Mountain was an excellent administrative officer who freed him from such responsibilities and his loss was greatly felt by Gough.

Gough had never intended to occupy the town for long, as it was merely a stepping stone of his advance along the Yangtze. When the British force re-entered the town after the battle they were faced with a horrific sight. It will be recalled that the force of 300 on the heights that caused them such trouble was thought to be comprised of Tartars. Whether or not this was the case we do not know for sure, yet their defiant actions makes one believe they were. In the town there certainly were Tartars who showed a similar defiance of the enemy. The devoted Tartars had refused to surrender. At the end only 50 were captured, and many of them later tried to commit suicide.[12] This example was repeated inside Chapo. Many Tartars remained inside the city and rather than face the ignominy of capture they committed suicide. However before doing so they attempted to kill both their women and children. Indeed, Sir Robert Rait in his biography of Gough declares that the Tartars had 'destroyed' their wives and children, and that is perhaps a fitting if slightly disturbing word for the events that had taken place. It was clear from the scenes that greeted the British that many of them had attempted to resist. The Chinese on the other hand had no such scruples about surrender, and indeed there appears to have been a change of attitude. The resistance that had been visible in Ningpo in the winter was not seen here. One cannot help but wonder if the gruesome scenes of the Tartars killing themselves and their women in the aftermath of defeat gave them a new perspective and made them less alarmed of the British and perhaps more concerned

---

10   NLI: MS 638, Gough to Lord Stanley, 20 May 1842.
11   Holt, *The Opium Wars in China*, p. 143.
12   Lovell, *The Opium Wars*, p. 212.

about their own leadership. Gough also demonstrated great kindness in releasing the Chinese prisoners taken that day. Later correspondence from the Chinese side shows that this act would be remembered when later in the war British prisoners were released in return for the act of kindness shown at Chapo.[13]

By 27 May the fleet was ready to sail again. Chapo was abandoned, having had its defences and arsenal destroyed. The fleet now sailed into the Yangtze River for the first time. In the day that followed there were various naval engagements which do not really concern our purpose as Gough was merely a spectator. On 13 June the felt reached Woosung (Wusong) about 14 miles from Shanghai, and on the following morning Rear Admiral Parker and Gough made a reconnaissance of the area but were largely disappointed. There did not appear to be any practicable landing point from which the army could turn the Chinese position. However they did obtain useful information as to the defences of the town. The only place to land was heavily defended: indeed the Chinese were fully aware that this was the only point at which the British were able to come ashore and had prepared accordingly. Parker and Gough decided that they would have to force a landing at this point. To enable them to achieve this it was decided that a large-scale bombardment by all the ships of the fleet would be necessary. To accomplish this many of the larger warships had to be towed into position.

At 0600 on the morning of 16 June, a large-scale bombardment of the Chinese defensive positions was begun. Whilst the Chinese batteries had been firing, even before the naval bombardment commenced, their guns did little damage. The naval bombardment soon silenced the Chinese and destroyed most of their defences. At the same time the ships transporting the landing force had started to move. Unfortunately they ran aground and as many of them were shallow draft steamers this goes to show the difficulty of the task and the need to know the correct route to the shore. It therefore fell to the naval brigade, a mixture of sailors and Royal Marines, to take the remaining defensive positions. It was not until 1200 that the Army managed to get ashore. By the time they reached the town they found that the Chinese had abandoned it. This again highlights the lack of fight put up by the Chinese. It probably also illustrates the awe with which the British were starting to be viewed. They had obliterated the defences with naval gunfire and landed at a place thought almost impossible. Given that one can hardly blame the poorly equipped, poorly trained and poorly disciplined Chinese for running away.

---

13   The National Archives (TNA): FO 682/1975/2, 7 July 1842. I am grateful to my friend Anna Coombs (or to use her Chinese name, Qing Wang) for the translation of this and other letters written in Chinese found in the National Archives.

36

Advance on Shanghai

With the capture of Woosung the way was open to attack Shanghai. Shanghai was an important city not only for goods coming in but more importantly for internal trade within the Chinese Empire. The loss of Shanghai would be a major blow to the economy of China plus the prestige of the Imperial Court. An attack was planned for 19 June. Gough split his force into three columns as usual. However in a change to his normal practice he ordered one column, under the command of Lieutenant Colonel Montgomerie, to make its way the 15 miles to Shanghai by land whilst the other two columns moved by sea.

The exact reason for this is unclear. It may have been that Gough thought it best to attack from two different directions at once. However it is possible that after the events at Woosung Gough, or possibly even Parker, were a little nervous about their ability to transport the army purely by water. They were now in waters that were largely unknown to them. The local knowledge that had been so valuable in previous assaults was lacking in regards to this area. Tides, currents, depths and obstructions in the water were largely unknown, other than that which they had ascertained in the brief time they had been there. As at Woosung, and indeed throughout the campaign, the naval bombardment was invaluable. The majority of Chinese guns in range of the landing sites had been put out of action before the landing was undertaken. Montgomerie's column arrived on the scene first and found that the city itself had been abandoned by its soldiers and richer inhabitants the previous night.

Shanghai had fallen largely without a fight. The attitude of the Chinese also appeared to be changing. Whereas in the past they had feared the arrival of the British they were now starting to appreciate that they meant no great harm to the wider population. It was never expressed quite so bluntly, but the British argument was with the regime not the Chinese people. Indeed the Chinese merchants were now appreciating that they could make money out of the British. Stockpiles of vegetables and meat had been prepared for trading with the British once the city had fallen. Gough attempted to use the locals to police their own city, with a varying degree of success. This was largely due to his desire to move on with operations and to leave the city as soon as possible.[1]

The campaigning seasons was going by fast and Gough wanted to continue the momentum of their advance. He was still 170 miles from the objective of the campaign for that year, namely Nanking. Gough was also starting to receive reinforcements, in particular detachments of the Madras Army, which he welcomed as experience had shown him that the Sepoy dealt better with the climatic conditions than the Europeans. However he was also delighted at arrival of another British regiment the 98th Foot.[2] The reinforcements were under the overall command of Major General Lord Saltoun, an experienced commander who had served at Waterloo, and at the head of

---

1   Rait, *Gough*, Vol. I, p. 268. See also Phillimore, *The Life of Admiral Sir William Parker* Vol. II, p. 490.
2   Then known only by number; later the Prince of Wales's Regiment (1873) and later still the North Staffordshire Regiment (1881)

the 98th was the future Field Marshal Colin Campbell. Another officer to arrive at this time was Captain James Hope Grant, later General Sir James, an officer of the 9th Lancers who was acting as Saltoun's brigade major.[3] There is an amusing story that bears repeating that says that Hope Grant owed his appointment as Brigade Major to his ability to play the violoncello. Lord Saltoun was a keen violinist and liked to have men of his staff who could accompany him.

The arrival of reinforcements, and the quite considerable preparations that the fleet required to sail further up the Yangtze, meant that it was not until the evening of 6 July that they finally set sail. On the evening of 16 July, Gough and Parker undertook a reconnaissance of Chinkiang or Chinkiagfoo (modern day Zhenjiang). Once again the reconnaissance was a rather bizarre affair, with no attempt made by the Chinese to prevent it. Indeed, many of the locals came to the river banks to marvel at the steamer in which the reconnaissance was being conducted. Delays with the movement of the fleet up the river meant that it was not until the 20th that the fleet assembled off Chinkiang.

Gough now had an army of about 9,000, including the sailors and Royal Marines. He divided his force into three columns as per usual. This time he had three major generals commanding the brigades: Schoedde, Bartley and Lord Saltoun.[4] The 1st Brigade, commanded by Saltoun, consisted of the 26th Foot, the 98th Foot, nine companies of the Bengal Volunteers, and the flank companies of the 41st Madras Native Infantry. The 2nd Brigade, under Schoedde, was made up of the 55th Foot, the 2nd and 6th Madras Native Infantry, and the rifle company. The 3rd Brigade, under Bartley, consisted of the 18th Foot, the 49th Foot, and the 14th Madras Native Infantry. The artillery and engineers were maintained separately under the command of Lieutenant Colonel Montgomerie.[5]

The attack was arranged for the morning of 21 July. By around 0700 most of the force had been landed. However one of the consequences of the extra numbers for this campaign was a delay in the navy's ability to land the force. Gough and Parker had perhaps been over-ambitious in attempting to land all of the troops. Indeed the limits upon shipping meant that some units did not get ashore until the fighting was almost over. The approach to Chinkiang was a difficult one for an assaulting force. The Imperial Canal and the Yangtze itself formed a kind of moat around the majority of the city. To the north and east of the city were a range of heights topped by a fort, or joss house, which made an approach difficult. After landing Gough had planned that the three columns would attack independently. The 2nd Brigade was first into action attacking the heights to the north whilst the 1st brigade protected the landing of the 3rd Brigade. After all the troops and artillery had been landed they moved upon the encampments outside the city. The Bengal Volunteers were engaged to turn the enemy's right flank. They did this unseen and as a consequence were the first to attack the encampments. They were soon supported by the rest of the 1st Brigade and the enemy was soon despatched. By this stage the 3rd Brigade and the artillery had been drawn up facing the city walls, and Gough had decided to force an entry to the city via the west gate. The 3rd Brigade was joined by the 26th Foot detached from Lord Saltoun's command for the attack on the west gate. Sappers blew the gate and started to enter the city but found another gate blocking their entry to the city. At the same time the 2nd Brigade had attacked the city from the other side.

Having cleared the heights to the north, Gough had given Schoedde discretion to attack the city where he felt best. Gough had recommended the north east gate, but had realised that a better opportunity might present itself. The handing of such discretionary power to a brigade commander

3   Hope Grant would lead the British contingent of the Second Opium or China War.
4   Schoedde is attributed the rank of major general. This may be a mistake as he was not officially promoted to full major general until June 1854: however it is possible that he held acting or local rank; his substantive rank at the time was lieutenant colonel.
5   Rait, *Gough*, Vol. I, p. 272. This includes an order of battle for the assault.

was acceptable so long as he exercised good judgement. In this case Schoedde appears to have done so. He had decided that a better course of action was to escalade the north wall and force his way across the western ramparts to join up with 3rd Brigade at the western gate. It is to the credit of the staff that he had been provided with scaling ladders and engineers so as to cover both possibilities.

Gough had accompanied the 3rd Brigade's attack on the west gate. Once this part of the city had been cleared, Gough ordered a temporary halt. The heat of the day was causing serious fatigue upon his men, and indeed there were some fatalities as a consequence. Gough felt he would be unable to take the whole of the city before nightfall. He determined however to clear the ramparts and secure all the gates. If the exits to the city were under his control he could safely wait until morning before finishing the capture of the city. The clearing of the rampart and the enclosures of the city was however a difficult task that needed to be accomplished before nightfall.

Once again they came up against the determined resistance of the Tartars. At one point on the western outwork of the defences a party of Tartars were trapped and fought to the death, those who were not shot being burnt alive in the defences. On the walls themselves some 1,000 to 1,500 Tartars stubbornly resisted the British attack. It even appears that at some point the British advance was, in an event almost unparalleled in the war, pushed back. Whether one interprets this as the British advance being stopped or that Gough ordered a respite to allow the men to recover is debatable. One thing is certain and that is that the heat of the day was certainly taking its toll on the British and would account for a good number of their casualties. Whatever the reason for the respite the Tartars knew they had no chance of escape and in the intervening period the majority chose to end their lives, and, as witnessed previously, also that of their women and children. The sights before the British were horrendous and Gough echoed his previous words when he wrote of the sight that, "I am sick at heart of war and its fearful consequences."[6]

British casualties were high by the standards of the campaign. Figures vary slightly but between 34 and 39 officers and men were killed and between 110 and 130 wounded. One has to consider that for the difficulty of the task and the severity of the opposition put up by the Tartars, these were relatively 'good' casualty returns. One also has to remember that about 17 of the deaths were as a consequence of heat exhaustion or sunstroke rather than enemy action. Exact returns for the number of wounded suffering in such a way are unknown.[7] The battle had however been a difficult one. Many of the problems and loss sustained during the attack came about by the late arrival of the 3rd Brigade. This led to a rather ad hoc attack being made, rather than the detailed plan Gough had envisaged. It would be unfair to heap too much criticism on the naval forces for their late arrival. The navy had performed wonders throughout the campaign in moving the army and its supplies and equipment and supporting it with naval gunfire. Yet the failure to land all the troops together did disrupt Gough's plan, as did the fact that the Chinese within the city put up such strong resistance. Had the large Chinese force outside the city decided to intervene rather than running away at the first sign of battle, even greater losses could have been sustained. Although it was a constant problem, the heat played a particular part on this occasion in restricting the actions of the British. Temperatures of considerably over 90 degrees Fahrenheit were experienced.

Exactly what happened in the city after this is a point of some conjecture. Due to the severe heat and the toll the battle had taken upon his force, Gough felt unable to deploy his forces against the robbers who took to plundering the city. The vast majority of these were Chinese; however it appears that there were some incidents involving British soldiers. There was no doubt some looting and rape committed by British soldiers, as reported by the Chinese. However it is less likely that

---

6   Rait, *Gough*, Vol. I, p. 275.
7   The figure of 17 comes from Hall, W. H. & Bernard, W. D., *Narrative of the voyages and services of the Nemesis* (London: Henry Colburn, 1845), p. 429.

the Chinese account that the British were drugging the locals with a 'potion' that turned them into 'black' soldiers has much truth to it![8] The large number of dead bodies and the high temperature in the city led to an increase in disease and in particular a severe outbreak of cholera. This necessitated Gough moving the troops out of the city itself and he established a camp on the heights outside Chinkiang. This had the unfortunate effect of adding to the lack of law and order in the city and left a situation that was little short of anarchy.

This would turn out to be the last military action of the campaign. In taking such an advanced position along the Yangtze the British had really brought the war to the Emperor. Major trading cities had fallen to the British and the naval forces were now blockading the Imperial or Grand Canal which had a real impact on the Imperial Court. By 29 July Gough had his force ready to continue the advance on Nanking. The intention was now to sail straight to Nanking. Poor winds delayed the fleet and it was not until 9 August that the British arrived outside Nanking.

Nanking was an important city not only due to its size and importance as a centre of trade but also the significance of the city as a former capital of the Chinese Empire. Fearful of similar resistance and scenes that were likely to follow such a defence, the political decision was taken to offer to spare the city in return for its surrender and a ransom. However this was rejected. Gough therefore started to plan for operations against the city. The walls of Nanking were 35 miles in length, although arrangements had been made to defend inner walls that made the circumference only 20 miles. This made it difficult to defend, as did the fact that there were many heights that over looked the city, and Gough selected those to the east as a placement for his artillery, where they could have fired into the city.[9] Gough had decided that by threatening the city at three distant points he could prevent the Chinese from collecting a considerable force at any one point to resist attack. At the same time the naval forces would bombard the north east of the city. Gough would feint an attack against three gates whilst launching his main attack at the central gate on the eastern side where his artillery could effectively support his attack. However they were not required. The author Demetrius Charles Boulger wrote of the plan of attack that, "Although they exhibit the tactical skill of the commander, and no officer was more skilful than Sir Hugh Gough in drawing up a plan of action, their interest and importance have long departed."[10] Throughout the campaign Gough's planning had been thorough and thoughtful. He used all elements of his force effectively. However it would be wrong not to reiterate the great assistance he was given by the naval force.

It had been likely for some time that a peaceful settlement to the conflict was becoming likely. The reality of the war was now being realised by the Chinese authorities. In June correspondence with the Imperial Court had given Pottinger the opportunity to state the terms of the British Government. Even as the force was leaving Chinkiang, reports were coming through that imperial commissioners had arrived at Nanking with the authority to negotiate a peace. By 12 August Gough was ready to strike at Nanking but diplomacy was starting to overtake events and he stayed his hand. However, Pottinger had wisely left the option of an attack open and in an attempt to prevent Chinese delaying tactics had announced that the attack would be launched on the 15th unless an agreement had been reached by that point. Even then the Chinese left it until the last minute not sending notice until midnight on 14 August.

The British had been sensible in setting deadlines and in keeping their forces ready for war. Both Parker and Gough were ready to renew hostilities at a moment's notice. This was sensible as the Chinese had not entirely abandoned their military options. Even as the imperial representative Zhang Xi negotiated, he was preparing for further military action. He planned to use a large fleet

8   Lovell, *The Opium War*, p. 221.
9   Rait, *Gough*, Vol. I, pp. 278–279.
10   Boulger, Demetrius Charles, *History of China* Vol. II (London: W. H. Allen & Co, 1882), p. 132.

of fire ships to destroy the British fleet and leave the army cut off and marooned, whence he thought they would be easier to despatch. There was some justification in the theory although he seems to have been ignorant of the fact that the same strategy had been tried several times before and had always failed. The majority of British ships were too manoeuvrable and their gunfire too accurate to be troubled by slow-moving fire ships. However whilst the Chinese played at brinkmanship they were unwilling to provoke further action by the British. The consequences of the failure of such an attack could be dire, and it was therefore not attempted.

The Chinese Emperor, who had never truly understood what was going on or what the British wanted, had reached the end of his endurance in July 1842.[11] The reports of the large death toll at Chinkiang, and a rather desperate plea from the governor of Nanking for assistance seemed to have been the final straw. His officials thus received a communication on 1 August that they were to settle matters with the British. In short they were given a free hand to end the conflict on whatever terms they could get. What followed has become known as the Treaty of Nanking. Officially called the *Treaty of Peace, Friendship and Commerce between Her Majesty the Queen of Great Britain and Ireland and the Emperor of China*, it was the first of the so-called unequal treaties 'forced' upon China by the west over the next century. The treaty was indeed unequal but was in a sense only a reflection of the inequality of the military campaign. Nanking would have fallen to the British, and with their reinforcements Gough and Parker would have ultimately taken Peking had it been necessary. The campaign had been so one-sided that it was hardly surprising that so was the peace. That said, in one sense the treaty actually set the British and Chinese on equal footing. No longer were the Chinese to officially cling to the deluded notion of the British as an inferior subject nation. The basic principles of the Treaty of Nanking were the cession of Hong Kong to the British, the opening up of five ports, known as the Treaty Ports, to western trade, namely Canton, Amoy, Foochow, Ningpo and Shanghai, the payment of 21,000,000 dollars, and the abolition of the Hong trading monopoly. Although certain issues, such as the opium trade, were left unsettled it was enough to avoid further hostilities at that time. On 29 August 1842 the Treaty of Nanking was signed by Pottinger and the Imperial representatives on board HMS *Cornwallis*.[12]

The British had in short got all they wanted from the war. It has to be clearly understood that from a military point of view there was little contest. The superiority of British weapons and technology, in particular superior artillery, shipping, and as the war wore on the percussion lock musket, meant that it was extremely one sided. British casualties reflect that, as so do Chinese casualties. In that sense it is easy to belittle Gough's achievements in China. However technological superiority has never been a guarantee of success in war as history demonstrates time and time again, and one should not believe that it was an easy campaign. The lack of detailed knowledge of China, the climatic conditions, disease, logistical problems, and the sheer size of China, made it a daunting campaign. Gough deserves credit for the way in which he handled the army. He showed skill in his handling of the battles. His use of flanking movements and his ability to turn the enemy's flank was well used. He also made good use of skirmishers and artillery. He took good care of his men's health as much as he could, relying on the competent surgeon Dr French and following his

11   Lovell, *The Opium War*, pp. 223–224. Lovell shows that as late as May 1842 the Emperor was still asking such basic questions of his officials, such as where is England? Why are there 'Indians' in their Army? Are they really ruled by a twenty-two year old woman [Queen Victoria]?

12   HMS *Cornwallis* was a 74 gun third-rate ship of the line that had been launched in Bombay in 1813. In 1855 she was converted to screw propulsion and reduced to 60 guns. She saw action in the Crimea under the command of George Wellesley the nephew of the Duke of Wellington. *Cornwallis* was renamed *Wildfire* in 1916 and became a base and depot ship at Sheerness. She served in total for some 144 years finally being broken up in 1957.

instructions where ever possible.[13] Indeed, like so many of Britain's wars of Empire, the real opponent was as much the geography and climatic conditions.

At the same time, Gough had been greatly helped by the relationship he enjoyed with both Parker and Pottinger. Parker's warships were an excellent support to Gough during the landings and in terms of naval gunfire. It is obvious from Gough's writing of the time that he greatly and genuinely appreciated Parker's assistance. A friendship developed between the two men at the time. Despite only sporadic contact in the following year Parker would publicly speak in defence of Gough when the latter was criticised for his handling of the Sikh Wars. Parker also wrote a personal letter of congratulations to Gough on the ending of the Second Sikh War, which Gough greatly appreciated. As for Pottinger, his greatest attribute was his ability to trust both his naval and military commanders to do their job. The interference that Gough had experienced when Elliot had been plenipotentiary was gone. Pottinger dealt with the political side and the wider aims of the campaign.

Gough had shown many great qualities during this period. However on a man of 62 years of age, the campaign had taken its toll. Remarkably, given the unhealthy conditions and oppressive heat, Gough suffered no major illness. Perhaps it was more on the emotional side that it affected him, as evidenced by his comments on his being sick of war. Indeed it appeared to him that this was his last campaign. Yet it was to be far from that, and the demands of the future years would test him to breaking point. There was to be no easy retirement after China.

---

13   NLI: MS 638, Gough to Lord Stanley, 20 May 1842.

Part 5

Commander-in-Chief and Gwalior Campaign

37

After China

Almost as soon as the war was over Gough started to receive praise and rewards for the role he had played in the conflict. It is worth reiterating the words of the Duke of Wellington which paid tribute to Gough's work, emphasising the difficulty of the task:

> There can be no doubt that the operations of this war were exceedingly difficult. Little was known of China except its enormous population, its great extent, and its immense resources; we knew nothing of the social life of that country; we knew nothing more of its communications than a scanty acquaintance with its rivers and canals; and whether their roads ran along rivers, or in any other way, nobody in this country could give any information, nor could any be acquired.[1]

Wellington continued that there was, "no individual, however sanguine, who could have expected such success as has been produced by the cordial co-operation of the admiral commanding the fleet and the general commanding the army." In a private letter dated 5 January 1843, but received by Gough in late March, Wellington added that, "I cannot omit to congratulate you upon the complete success of the service in which you have been lately employed, so much to your own Honour and the publick [*sic*] benefit."[2] It was not surprising therefore that Gough, who had already been awarded a GCB after the assault on Canton, was further honoured by being made a baronet and receiving the thanks of both Parliament and the Honourable East India Company.

Gough remained in China for a few months after the ending of hostilities overseeing the implementation of the terms of the Treaty of Nanking. This included organising several garrisons that were to be maintained in China until the indemnity had been paid in full. Gough left Nanking in late September 1842 and after visiting the various garrisons it was not until late November 1842 that he reached Hong Kong. He had planned to return to India in early December 1842; however, the outbreak of violence in Canton meant that he felt unable to leave. Indeed in an interesting incident he decided to journey to Canton to assess the situation for himself in the steamer *Proserpine*. Despite Gough's conviction that the violence was the work of individuals rather than the inspiration of the Chinese government, the merchants at Canton were extremely concerned. To provide

---

1   *Hansard*, House of Lords Debate, 14 February 1843 Vol. 66, cc525–45. A somewhat unusual scene seems to have taken place during the Duke of Wellington's speech. Initially he named the Admiral in command as H. Senhouse. Whilst Senhouse had commanded in the early stages it was Admiral Parker who had commanded for the majority of the operations. This appears to have been pointed out to Wellington during his speech. Presumably a colleague handed him a note. It was therefore only towards the end of the speech that thanks was given to Admiral Parker. This story is mentioned as it will seem familiar later in our narrative when the Duke omits the name of Gough in his vote of thanks for the First Sikh War.

2   Rait, *Gough*, Vol. I, p. 293. Rait includes a copy of the letter from Wellington to Gough dated 5 January 1843.

for their protection, and if necessary a means of escape, Gough arranged for the *Proserpine* to remain at Canton. He did this despite the fact that this required him to return to Hong Kong on a cramped schooner. He could not stand up in the cabin, which he had to share with nine other passengers, and the voyage took him two days. This act illustrates much about Gough's lack of pretension and the way in which he did his duty without thought to his own personal discomfort. Although in the great scheme of things this was a minor incident it is by such actions that the true character of a man is shown.[3]

On 20 December 1842 Gough left China, handing over command of the military force to Lord Saltoun. He returned via Singapore and landed in Calcutta in early January. Whilst on the face of it he had been treated well by his nation there were a couple of points that would cause him a little bitterness. The first of these concerned the payment or *batta* he was to receive for active service. In 1845 Gough wrote a rather bitter letter to the Honourable East India Company complaining about his treatment. His point was this: at Canton he had received 47,200 rupees, the appropriate amount for a major general. Rear Admiral Parker, who held what amounted to the equivalent rank in the Royal Navy, received the same. At Nanking Gough received the same amount but the now Vice Admiral William Parker received 62,796 rupees. As Gough now held the equivalent rank in the army, lieutenant general, he felt he deserved the same amount. In this view he was supported by Parker, who indeed had brought this discrepancy to Gough's attention. Eventually he received the same amount. Parker had a similar complaint regarding the awards given out for China. In reply he was told that Gough had received his GCB for service at Canton, before Parker arrived on the scene. Parker had to complain to get his pension for China raised to £2000 a year, the same as Gough. This was actually a little unfair as Gough had been there far longer. This matter was also raised by the Earl of Haddington, First Lord of the Admiralty at the time, in the House of Lords during the debate on the vote of thanks for the campaign in China.

Gough claimed in his letter that his main motivation for seeking redress was due to circumstances as much as 'equality'. Whether one believes that or not is a matter for debate. However Gough stated that:

> I have a great disinclination to come forward as an applicant in pecuniary concerns, except forced to it in justice to myself as in the case of my having been detained in India nearly six months by the late Governor-General, without drawing pay or allowance whatever.[4]

The claim that it was only due to circumstances that he was making this claim does have some justification. He was not a particularly wealthy man and the fact that he had been stuck in India without employment was the other great cause for concern and of some initial bitterness.

Having missed out on the appointment as commander-in-chief of the Madras Army in January 1841, Gough had expected that he was now the obvious choice for the appointment. Indeed he seems to have been promised as much by the Governor General. Despite Whittingham having died in January 1841 it was not until late 1842 that a replacement was appointed. It almost appears as if the posting had been held open for Gough's return. Contrary to some accounts, Gough was never officially appointed commander-in-chief of the Madras Army. However Gough presumed it would be him, and it did seem a fitting reward for his services in China. However politics intervened. It had been considered for some time that it was desirable for the offices of Governor General of

3   Mountain, *Memoirs of Colonel Mountain*, p. 204.
4   NAM: 8303–105, Gough to Phillip Melvill, 5 June 1845. Phillip Melvill was from 1837–1858 the military secretary to the East India Company. He was the father of Lieutenant Teignmouth Melvill, who was awarded the Victoria Cross posthumously for his attempts to save the Queen's colours in the aftermath of the Battle of Isandhlwana on the 22 January 1879.

Madras and commander-in-chief of the Madras Army to be combined. With the appointment of George Hay, 8th Marquess of Tweeddale, as governor general it was considered an opportune moment to put this theory into practice. Although Hay could point to a distinguished war record during the Napoleonic Wars, it must be remembered that this was around 30 years ago. Indeed Hay had no experience of war since July 1814 when he had been captured at the Battle of Chippawa.

The argument could be made that an army would be better off in the hands of a commander who had more recent experience of war: in other words, Gough. Despite the weakness of the opposition he had faced, Gough had handled the army well had embraced new elements of strategy and weaponry and had developed good experience in amphibious and expeditionary warfare. If indeed the Madras Army, being the least active of the three presidency armies domestically, were to be used as a sort of imperial reserve for British interests in the east, then there was a strong argument for Gough's appointment as commander-in-chief of the Madras Army based on his recent experience. However the politicians in London were concerned with the lack of discipline and poor organisation of the Madras Army. It was argued that to effectively combat this political authority was needed. The argument was therefore made that the need was for a good political and administrative man rather than an experienced fighting general.[5]

Whatever logic there was to the appointment of Tweeddale, it did have the look of being somewhat ungrateful to Gough: indeed a slap in the face. Had he not been in China he would have been appointed commander-in-chief in January 1841 when Whittingham died. Indeed he was informed that on his return the position was his, and this was why no successor to Whittingham had immediately been appointed. Lord Auckland's communication with Gough makes this very clear. The sense that he had missed out because he had been undertaking important work for the Crown on active service meant that it looked as if Gough's career had suffered by doing his duty and doing it well. Had he not been successful in China no one would have been unduly concerned at his missing out on the appointment. It was indeed because he had done well, because he had been successful, that it was felt that he should be rewarded for his triumph not penalised.

Gough officially took a somewhat sanguine attitude, at least initially. Still physically and emotionally tired from the China expedition this is understandable. Perhaps his expressions of being 'sick of war' and its consequences should also be viewed in this light. Indeed it is only when the government's indecision about what to do with him began to drag on that he started to get concerned. The main reason for this was financial. Without any active employment his meagre personal finances were being drained by having to maintain both his wife and family in India without allowances or accommodation. It appears from his correspondence that he would have been happy to return home. In response to a letter from Lord Hill, commander-in-chief of the army, Gough replied that:

> However mortifying it may be to me to find myself deprived of the appointment to which I had been so graciously nominated, I beg to assure your Lordship that I bow, without repining, to any measure that may be considered beneficial to the interests of my country. To serve that country in the higher walks of a profession which I entered as a child, I came to India, and especially to China, and I trust your Lordship will believe that, while my Sovereign considered my services useful, they were, as they shall ever be, freely and, I hope, energetically rendered. [...] That I feel rather disappointed, I cannot deny; but I am not the less grateful to my Sovereign for her gracious kindness towards me; or the less sincerely and warmly thankful to your Lordship for the renewed proof of kind consideration which your letter conveys.[6]

---

5   Rait, *Gough*, Vol. I pp. 286–287.
6   Rait, *Gough*, Vol. I pp. 287–288. Rait includes a copy of the letter between Gough and Lord Hill dated 15 September 1842.

The letter is intriguing. Whilst publicly saying that he accepts the decision, because of course he can do nothing else, there is an element of trying to gain sympathy. Perhaps a hope that some other appointment will be found for him, either military or civilian to make up for his 'disappointment' and that he will be seen as a loyal servant of the crown placing the interests of his country before his own. It would be interesting to know who actually read the letter. It was dated 15 September 1842 and, unbeknown to Gough, Lord Hill had stood down as commander-in-chief in August 1842 due to ill health. Indeed it is probable that by the time the letter reached London Hill was dead, dying as he had on 10 December 1842. If it was indeed Wellington, returning as commander-in-chief, who read the letter then this might explain why in later years Wellington would constantly appeal to Gough's spirit of doing what was in the best interests of his country; however that is to get slightly ahead of ourselves in the narrative of Gough's life.

Gough visited Lord Ellenborough on 7 February 1843 with the hope that he might obtain some appointment or other, but with no specific expectations. It was therefore a genuine surprise when on that day Ellenborough informed him that it was planned that in the autumn he would replace Sir Jasper Nicholls as commander-in-chief of the Army of the Bengal Presidency. Being the senior of the three armies this conferred with it the title of Commander-in-Chief, India. No official announcement was made for some time. However the decision must have been planned for a little while before Ellenborough informed Gough, as the aforementioned letter from Wellington dated 5 January, which Gough did not receive until late March, made mention of the offer stating:

> It has given me great pleasure to have had it in my power to suggest, and that the Government should have so readily attended to my suggestion, that you should be appointed Commander-in-Chief in India. This is one of the highest, if not the highest situation which an officer in Her Majesty's service can hold, and I do not doubt that you will equally as heretofore in other situations perform its duties with honour to your own character, and to the publick [sic] advantage. You may rely upon my affording you every assistance in my power.[7]

Wellington rather suggests in the letter that it was his idea, but it is likely that the idea originated with Ellenborough, who in turn asked Wellington's opinion. It was thereafter the newly reappointed commander-in-chief of the British Army who formally suggested it to the Government. Wellington was obviously open to the idea and supportive of it, but it would be wrong to believe that he was the originator of the idea of appointing Gough as Commander-in-Chief India.

There is a sense in which politicians, both at home and in India, felt almost compelled to find an appointment for Gough so as to publicly acknowledge and reward his success in China. In many ways the appointment as commander-in-chief in India was the most powerful in British arms, even more so than commander-in-chief of the British Army. The latter was largely a political appointment, and mainly an administrative one. Whilst there was an element of this with the appointment in India, there was much more of a practical hands-on control of the British and Company forces in India and the expectation that the commander-in-chief in India would lead the army in the field.

One could perhaps argue that Gough was not suited to such a higher command appointment, being perhaps better suited as a corps or divisional commander, and we shall return to this matter later on. This is not to be unduly critical of Gough as the story of the British Army is one of a constant problem to find higher command leaders, throughout the 19th and early 20th centuries. There are but a few figures during this era that showed such ability. The fact that expeditions during the 19th century rarely rose above the size of a division, and often fell short of that, did not help matters. In terms of higher command leadership, that is commanding an army or multiple corps

7   Rait, *Gough*, Vol. I p. 293.

in a prolonged campaign, there were only a handful of officers in British service at that time that had the ability.

Although the appointment was a great honour, and Gough appreciated it as such, it may be that Gough did not relish the idea of taking on such an appointment. It meant staying in India and the oppressive climate would do little to aid the health of either his wife or himself. However, at least Gough now knew that his future was secure. He also anticipated being in the north of India more often and therefore in a slightly less oppressive climate not only for himself, but particularly for his wife given that the heat in Madras and Calcutta had not helped her frail health. In some senses Gough would have been happy to leave India. Indeed plans had been made in this direction until the private meeting with Ellenborough. The heat, his wife's poor health, his advancing age, the recent exertions in the field, all meant that India was not quite the attractive prospect to Gough as it might be to other men. Had his financial future been secured he would happily have returned to Ireland and largely retired from public life. One also feels, reading between the lines, that he felt his victories in China were a fitting end to his military career. He was by now 63 and the years of active service were starting to catch up with him. Let us not forget that he had in his life been severely wounded several times, and this had naturally affected his general health. At the same time it was a great honour to receive the appointment.

It appears that there was something else behind Lord Ellenborough's motives in wanting to keep Gough close at hand. The former was concerned about the state of affairs in China, where things had not settle down and the possibility of further military action appeared, at least to Ellenborough, as a very real possibility. Before the appointment as commander-in-chief he had written to Gough:

> I should with much regret see your Excellency leave India for England at a period when your services may still be required in China, where the knowledge of your presence would be worth Battalions in the pacific settlement of all unadjusted questions; and I should hope that your Excellency would find it convenient to remain at Bangalore, or at some place where the Government can easily communicate with you. If there should arise in China a state of affairs indicating a probable renewal of hostilities, or the expediency of making a demonstration of Force, your Excellency has full authority at once to return and to resume your command.[8]

There is a sense that in light of this letter from Ellenborough, Gough felt honour bound to remain in India for the foreseeable future. Thus when he complains about the financial repercussions of having to remain in India, out of employment and without pay or allowances, we see that Gough was in this position because of the urging of the Governor General. This perhaps casts a different light on his requests over pecuniary matters.

At this time there is certainly a strong relationship between Gough and Ellenborough. The latter clearly respected the judgement of the former. It is telling that Ellenborough was so inclined to keep Gough around. Later comments Ellenborough would make about Gough should be seen in this context, and it is very clear that Gough's decision to remain in India was largely influenced by Ellenborough, even before the private notification of his appointment as commander-in-chief.

Indeed the two men seemed to have been of the same opinion on most matters. On the deployment of troops in China after the Treaty of Nanking, Ellenborough agreed almost in its entirety with Gough's dispositions. The only difference was that Ellenborough recommended the deployment of a battalion to be stationed in Singapore to provide a reserve for the forces in China, and in particular Hong Kong. It is slightly unusual that it was the politician who suggested this rather expensive, and some might claim, unnecessary, expenditure. Despite this difference of opinion it

---

8   Rait, *Gough*, p. 292.

is clear that there was at this stage great respect and a good working relationship between the two men.[9]

Although Gough had complained of this period without employment, there had been much in the way of entertainment and adulation for his victory in China for him to enjoy. There were many dinners, functions, and balls given in his honour. He was for a time the guest of choice for the elite of India. Gough certainly enjoyed this, but after a while he found it tiring. He was particularly delighted that whenever the toasts were given at events during this period his own name was second only to Her Majesty. However being on show in this way did not help him to recover from the exertions of China. Nor did the fact that whilst his wife remained in Bangalore, he was in Calcutta. This caused him anxiety as to her state of health.

In March he travelled to Madras, where he stayed with his second daughter Gertrude Sophia Gough and her husband Archibald Arbuthnot, a junior partner in the merchant bank Arbuthnot Latham. This opportunity to meet with his daughter and grandchildren was a pleasant occasion for Gough. By this stage his daughter had three children and was pregnant with a fourth. They would ultimately have six children, five sons and a daughter. Since her marriage in December 1838, Gough had seen little of her and it is thought likely that this was his first meeting with his grandchildren. Having arrived on 6 March his visit was relatively brief as by 18 March he had reached Banaglore and enjoyed a reunion with his wife. About a week later, the hard work and travel finally took its toll on Gough who succumbed to 'Chinese fever'. Given the severe conditions in China, given the amount of travel and subsequent engagements Gough had endured since his return, and given his age, it is not surprising that this finally came upon him. In fact if anything it is surprising he did not succumb sooner. A change of air was prescribed and Gough moved on to Mekara in the Coorg (Kodagu) district of southern India. Gough was still here in May 1843 when official confirmation of his appointment as commander-in-chief was received. Although keen to get on with the business of his new appointment recurrent attacks of fever meant that he had to remain where he was until late summer of 1843.

---

9   NAM: 8303–105, Gough Papers, Ellenborough to Gough, 14 October 1842.

38

Commander-in-Chief, India

Although it is not necessary to detail the history of British India it is important to remind the reader that India was still nominally governed through the Honourable East India Company. Over time the power of the Company had been diminished and greater control exercised by the British Government. By the time of Gough's appointment India was still officially governed by the East India Company through its Court of Directors. Since the East India Company Act of 1784, also called Pitt's India Act, a body often simply referred to as the Board of Control was established, consisting of the Chancellor of the Exchequer and four privy councillors nominated by the crown, and a President. The President of the Board of Control was the forerunner to the Secretary of State for India. The Board of control officially acted through the Court of Directors. However this was often only honoured technically, whereas in practice the Board dealt with the governor general who was also governor general of Bengal, which, as we have seen, was the senior of the three presidencies. This was similar to Gough own position where he was head of the Bengal Army, but as such Her Majesty's Commander-in-Chief in the East Indies.

Since the 1833 Government of India Act, the commercial nature of the Company had been lost and it was largely concerned with the government of its territory. Appointments were still within the patronage of the Court of Directors; however the control of the British Government was such that appointments to the great offices of India required the consent of the Crown through the government of the day. It appears that in Gough's case the nomination saw the agreement of the home government, the commander-in-chief of the British Army, and the governor general in India. However such harmony over appointments was rare. Gough also had, and retained, a good relationship with the Court of Directors who held a high opinion of his abilities.

Gough entered the post at a difficult time for British India. The East India Company was in decline and there was a somewhat uneasy and ambiguous governance of India during this period. This was just one of any number of problems for the British in India. Britain's hold of India did not appear as secure as it now appears looking back with the benefit of hindsight. The prestige of the British in India had been reduced by the First Anglo-Afghan War. The shadow of this military reverse would be cast over Gough's period in command. The British response to this was to look to firmly secured Britain's hold on India. The conquest and annexation of the Sindh in February 1843, by forces under the command of Major General Sir Charles Napier was part of this. There remained two main threats to British power in India. The first was the Mahratta state at Gwalior. Although the once powerful Mahrattas had lost much of their land and power since the three Anglo-Mahratta wars of the late 18th and early 19th centuries, the geographical position of this Kingdom was such that it remained a threat. The second, and far more potent threat, lay further north in the Sikh state.

Gough also faced internal problems with the Indian Army. Much of his early correspondence as commander-in-chief deals with 'mutinies' or at the very least insubordination within the native army. A detailed examination of the causes of such incidents is beyond the scope of this work but they were many and varied. Again, the shadow of defeat in Afghanistan can be seen at work. There have been suggestions that there was already a rise of nationalism amongst native troops. This is perhaps an attempt to make the evidence fit the theory, and takes advantage of the fact that 14 years later there was a major sepoy mutiny. This is also to misunderstand the role of nationalism within the Mutiny of 1857, but again this debate is beyond the scope of this work. During this era such incidents of 'mutiny' and insubordination had more to do with a lack of respect, and often of interest, from British officers towards native troops. Many of the incidents could have been avoided if the British officers had better understood their men. It is interesting that in his private correspondence Gough does not hold back in criticising British officers in their handling of native troops. Often it appears that prompt action by a regimental officer might have avoided the need for Gough's involvement.[1]

There were also genuine concerns about pay and allowances that were badly handled at a political level. A system of payment for active service, or service outside the normal geographical area of the army, was paid. This, like most allowances, was generally referred to as *batta*. The *batta*, loosely translated from Hindustani as 'donation', was a payment over and above regular pay. Often soldiers relied on this to care for their families in their absence. Some would even take out loans or receive credit based on the promise of *batta*. If therefore the *batta* was suddenly withdrawn it created real problems for the native soldier and his family. In China there had been a reluctance to pay *batta* to native soldiers serving under Gough's command. However this issue was largely solved without incident. Gough had personally championed the cause of his men, and this no doubt assisted in the granting of the extra payment.[2] What caused greater problems was the sudden removal of the *batta* from soldiers serving in the Scinde. Traditionally any service there would justify a payment as it was service outside the usual area of the army. However once the Scinde had been conquered by Napier and annexed to British India, the payment was abruptly removed. For the Indian soldiers, many of whom had already made financial decisions based on the promise of this payment, this was of real concern.[3] It is easy to see from their point of view why they were so disconcerted. Little had changed other than a political decision that now included the Scinde in British possessions. However the conditions of service, the expenses, and the distance from their homes had not altered. Gough attempted to deal with the series of mutinies throughout this period with a mixture of firmness and clemency. He was willing when he felt it necessary to pass sentence of death or to disband a battalion if he felt it necessary. At the same time he was also prepared to commute death sentences and give battalions another chance.[4]

The problem was that by the time such matters found their way to the desk of the Commander-in-Chief a great deal of harm had already been done. Again we come back to this point of officers not understanding their men, and not acting promptly enough. This perhaps points to a wider

---

1   This is a running theme but see specifically NAM: 8303–105, Gough Papers, Gough to Ellenborough 22 February 1844. This concerns the 7th Light Cavalry and Gough criticises the handling of the situation by the commanding officer Major Benjamin Phillips.

2   NAM: 8303–105, Gough Papers, Ellenborough to Gough, 14 October 1842. Ellenborough refers to previous communication from Gough regarding this matter.

3   NAM: 8303–105, Gough Papers, Gough to Ellenborough, 17 July 1844. Gough admits in this that whilst he shares the concerns of the native soldiery and beliefs the financial hardship this will create is very real, 'nothing however can justify or ever extenuate this glaring breach of discipline'.

4   Pollock, John, *Way to Glory: The Life of Havelock of Lucknow* (London: John Murry, 1957) pp. 103–104. Gough and Havelock, who was serving on the commander-in-chief's staff at the time, had a brief falling out over the matter. Gough asked Havelock his advice. Havelock believed that an example had to be made and Gough accordingly passed sentence of death on 39 mutineers. Gough later commuted the sentence of all but six.

problem in the falling off in quality of the Company forces. For a commander-in-chief this should have been more alarming than it appears Gough considered it to be. In the years that lay ahead the poor leadership at battalion and company level would be a constant problem for the Commander-in-Chief as he now entered into a period where he would be leading the army in war.

The First Anglo-Afghan War had also highlighted many problems with the organisation and supply of troops. It had made it clear that the British were not invincible, a point of view which up until then had been held by many British and natives alike. It was for Gough a difficult time to be commander-in-chief as the British now appeared vulnerable. It was not surprising that in such circumstances he made mistakes, and that there were errors of judgement. He was most certainly not alone in that regard. There is some mitigation for Gough. Although Gough would appear by this stage to be an experienced commander, the size of the task now facing him was beyond anything else he had previously encountered. This was a failing of the British system and British experience. From never having commanded more than 9,000 men he was now ultimately responsible for over 200,000 troops spread over a vast area. It is easy to say that this was beyond his ability, but that could be said for the vast majority of officers of the crown.

Such was the nature of the British Army, and for that matter East India Company Army. Few officers had experience of higher command or the organisation and administration of large numbers of troops. It was not something that the British Army planned for. In the era after the Napoleonic wars and until the early 20th century, British military thoughts generally revolved around expeditions and campaigns that were rarely larger than 20,000 men. In such a situation the management of a large military machine was rarely thought about. Even in India where such a force existed, there were problems. Although Gough was nominally commander-in-chief, he did not have the freedom of command that the title might suggest. Firstly, governor generals were increasingly keen to interfere in matters concerning the army. Secondly, his authority over the Madras and Bombay army was not absolute, and any wider-scale reform of them was going to be difficult. Thus the magnitude of the task that faced Gough should not be forgotten.

Gough had previous experience of administration on a smaller scale. He also had experience of leading men in battle. The latter was more important for a commander-in-chief in India of this period than the former. Gough was perhaps seen by Ellenborough and others as a safe pair of hands. Although that would seem a strange comment based upon the future opinions of many in power in India and at home, based upon the correspondence of the time it does appear to be the view that was taken. Wellington raised no concerns at this stage about Gough's ability or his suitability for the post. Ellenborough seems, based on his correspondence, to have been keen to secure the service of Gough. If people subsequently changed their mind about Gough it is important to remember that they once held the opposing point of view and had indeed engineered his being in so high a position of command. The demands that would be placed upon the commander-in-chief and the army in the years ahead would have been too much for most men.

Gough might not have been the ideal commander-in-chief, either from an administrative or field command point of view. However one area of his command that should not be underestimated is the understanding he developed of both India and the Indian people, in particular its soldiers. Throughout his career, Gough always seemed to be able to understand his men. In India he had to deal with many difficulties, including the numerous acts of disobedience and 'mutinies'. Gough's understanding of India and the military and political situation there is best illustrated by his comments before a House of Commons select committee in 1853. Gough offered the rather prophetic words that:

India is a very peculiar country; you do not know the hour when some outbreak may take place: and we all know that the people of India have their heads up like leeches looking for anything that may occur.[5]

Less than four years later Gough's words took on their prophetic nature when the Indian Mutiny broke out to the surprise of many. Whilst it cannot be said that Gough predicted the Mutiny, his comments do show that during his time in India, contrary to what some historians would say, he had come to understand its people and society, if only from a military perspective. For a man who had no knowledge of India before his arrival in October 1837 it is clear that he had learnt something from his time. It is also interesting that a man who, as we shall see, one Governor General said had no understanding of the political situation in India, seemed to better understand the potentiality of mutiny than many seasoned 'professional' politicians. It perhaps helps to illustrate once again that whatever faults Gough might have had as a senior commander, he had a good understanding of men.

---

5   *British Parliamentary Papers: Indian Territories*, Vol. 13, 116.

39

Gwalior Campaign

The first major military duty of Gough's time in command was the Gwalior Campaign of December 1843. In short, the Gwalior State was what remained of the once powerful Mahratta Empire. The three Anglo-Mahratta Wars of the late 18th and early 19th centuries had destroyed much of Mahratta power. What remained was a shadow of its former glory but Gwalior's location near the Punjab and Scinde meant that it was still a threat to British interests. If war came in the Punjab, as was looking increasingly likely, the British did not want to have a major enemy behind them as they advanced. Although the military might of the empire was gone, Gwalior still maintained an army of 15,000 cavalry, 20,000 infantry and 250 guns. Although largely still a native force, there had been a degree of training and drill undertaken by European mercenaries. The Maharaja Doulut Rao Scindia, who had opposed the British in the Second and Third Anglo-Mahratta Wars, died in 1827 without a clear heir. The succession of the state had been left by Rao Scindia for the British to decide. A distance relative, Jankoji Rao Scindia, was raised to the throne. When he died in February 1843 another distant relative Jayajirao (Jayaji) Scindia became Maharaja. However the power remained with the previous Maharaja's uncle Mama Sahib. Such was the concern of the British that Lord Ellenborough himself journeyed to Agra to keep a close watch on events.

At first it appeared that matters had been settled to the satisfaction of the British. However, in the May of 1843 things changed and a faction opposed to Mama Sahib, led by the late Maharaja's wife and a minister known as Dada Khasjee seized power. Ellenborough at first did nothing other than advising Mama Sahib to leave Gwalior and promised him protection. Later the British minister to Gwalior also felt it appropriate to leave. This in and of itself was not a great concern, and was little more than a momentary set back to British interests. More problematic was the appointment to the ruling council of men who had previously been removed from that body for their anti-British behaviour. To Ellenborough this was a clear signal that the Gwalior was now hostile towards the British. As war in the Punjab seemed to be an increasing possibility Ellenborough ordered that a 12,000 man army of observation be posted at Agra. This was initially as a precaution but soon it became clear that military action was planned.

It should be remembered that at this time Gough had only just received official confirmation of his appointment as commander-in-chief and had not really taken over command in any serious way. Indeed Gough did not reach Calcutta, and thus officially take up his appointment, until August 1843. On his arrival he found a letter waiting for him from Ellenborough.

> I am delighted to hear that you have arrived. We want you very much. You can have but little rest in Calcutta, for the state of affairs at Gwalior makes it necessary that your own Camp should be formed at Cawnpore on the 15th of October, and a large Camp of Exercise and Observation in the vicinity of Agra by the 1st November.[1]

---

1   NAM: 8303–105, Gough Papers, Ellenborough to Gough, 8 August 1843.

It was a difficult task to hit the ground running as commander-in-chief and take the army straight into the field with the possibility of action. To have arrived in August and to be expected to have an army of observation ready for action by the beginning of November was a difficult task. Even if one accepts that all the administration had already been put in place, it was asking a lot of Gough to command such an unknown force. It should also be remembered that he had only arrived back in India in January 1843. Now in the August of the same year he was being asked to prepare for another campaign, after several years of hard and exhausting campaigning in China.

Gough had no experience as a commander-in-chief, and indeed his command in China had for the majority of the time concerned a force of around 3,000. He now had a force four times that size to command against the Mahrattas. He also had no experience of the Bengal Army who would make up the bulk of this force. Even his experience of the Madras Army was limited. This should be remembered when considering his subsequent actions. He had been placed in a difficult position with little time for planning or consideration. At the same time, just as the situation in Gwalior had become serious, British attention was diverted to the far greater concern over events in the Sikh Empire where the murder of Maharaja Sher Singh at Lahore in September 1843 had raised tensions. To this end, a second army of observation was raised, after Gough's prompting, to watch over events in the Sikh Empire under the command of Sir Robert Dick. It was hoped, and indeed planned, that Gough should relieve Sir Robert once the situation in Gwalior had been resolved. After barely a month officially in the position of commander-in-chief, Gough faced the possibility of simultaneous conflict on two fronts. He was certainly being thrown in at the deep end.

The rushed nature of the deployment to Gwalior caused problems. The logistical situation of moving an army in India was difficult and is best described by Colonel Harry Smith, later Lieutenant General Sir Harry:

> To assemble an army in India requires much arrangement and consideration. There are various points at which the maintenance of an armed force is indispensable; the extent of country in our occupation entails in all concentrations particularly long and tedious marches; lastly, the season of the year must be rigidly attended to, for such is the fickleness of disease and its awful ravages, that it would need an excess of folly to leave it out of account.[2]

In short, at the best of times such an operation was difficult, but with a commander-in-chief newly appointed and newly arrived on the scene this was exacerbated. The obvious answer was that the staff should make the preparations. However there was a serious deficiency in staff arrangements in this era and often the staff of an army were little more than the private staff of the general in command. Given the financial position in India it was also difficult to obtain permission from civilian authorities to make such preparation in anticipation of events.

Gough intended to gather an army of 20,000 for proposed operations against the Gwalior State. Somewhat controversially he decided to divide his force. The main force under his command would move from Agra, whilst a slightly smaller force commanded by Major General Sir John Grey would move from Bundelkhand. Harry Smith was amongst the critics of this decision, and in light of what we have just read with regards to the difficult logistical nature of deploying and operating a force in India there is certainly some justification to his criticism. Smith also feared that whilst the main body would be sufficient to handle a confrontation with the entire army of the enemy, some 25,000 strong, Grey's command could be in peril if confronted by that force. As Smith points out, this had been considered by Gough who felt it was an acceptable risk. Smith's point in a sense was

2   Smith, Sir Harry & Moore Smith, G. C. (ed) *The Autobiography of Lieutenant-General Sir Harry Smith* (London: John Murray, 1902), Vol. II, p. 124.

that this was not what he would have done, but that did not in itself mean that it was the wrong decision. Whilst critical, Smith did not imply that Gough acted in folly. In short Gough had taken a command decision which in his view gave him the best chance of success, and Smith made it clear that he accepted it as such.[3]

Gough did later concede that he felt he had been slightly mislead by the intelligence he had received. Smith's experience and understanding of the Gwalior Army gave him an advantage, emphasising the problems that Gough suffered from being so newly on the scene. He relied on intelligence, from political officers or agents, which led him to believe that he would face little opposition. He later conceded that, "The Politicals entirely deceived me. I thought I should have a mob without leaders, with the heads at variance. I found a well-disciplined, well-organized army, well led and truly gallant."[4] Perhaps Gough was also still in 'China mode', believing that the enemy would be unable to show much resistance, and it may be that a level of complacency had developed because of his recent experiences in that part of the world. That would be understandable. There was also some justification in Gough again attempting to turn the position of the enemy. Indeed his dividing of the army caused the Mahrattas to do the same. Thus rather than attempting to overwhelm one force before moving to meet the other they attempted to deal with both British columns at the same time.

Gough's plans were fully sanctioned by the Governor General who commented that "We entirely approve of the detailed arrangements your Excellency has communicated to us."[5] In a letter to the Duke of Wellington, Gough outlined his plans and went into more detail as to reasons for his planned deployment.

> Your Grace will not, I trust, consider that I have decided on an injudicious movement by advancing from such opposite points, and leaving to an enemy the option of attacking either Wing, when no support could be afforded it by the other. But I feel perfectly confident that either Wing would be amply sufficient not only to repel, but to overthrow the whole Mahratta force in the field, while, by such a movement, the attacking force would be cut off from the Capital and stronghold of Gwalior, together with what the Mahratta's place so much reliance on, their immoveable park of 300 Guns, by a rapid march of the other Wing. On the other hand, I shall place their Army between two powerful bodies capable of taking in reverse, or of turning the flank of, any position they may take up. It will also enable me, in a great measure, to prevent what I have so long apprehended, the dispersion of their force into bodies of armed men, who would assuredly become bands of Robbers, and make incursions into our territories.[6]

When read in this light, Gough's plans make perfect sense on paper. His belief that either wing of his army would be able to defeat the entire force of the enemy makes sense only if they were able to choose their own positon from which to give battle. Given a reasonable defensive position Gough is probably correct in this assumption. Indeed Smith agreed that this was probably the case, but felt it was a risk. Gough also points out the risks that the Mahrattas would be taking in attempting to deal with one force whilst leaving the other to move unopposed, and the Mahrattas' decision also to divide their force is proof of this. It is also interesting to note that Gough made it clear that he wished to defeat the army in a pitched battle, rather than risk a prolonged guerrilla campaign. As an experienced Peninsular War veteran Gough, would have known well the power of a guerrilla

3   Smith, *Lieutenant-General Sir Harry Smith*, pp. 125–126.
4   NAM: 8303–105, Gough to George Gough, 20 January 1844.
5   NAM: 8303–105, Ellenborough to Gough, 14 October 1843.
6   Rait, *Gough*, Vol. I, p. 312.

force and the difficult in attempting to confront and control such an insurgency. No doubt this passage also met with the approval of the Governor General. Like all politicians, he wished for a short, sharp, relatively inexpensive, and victorious campaign.

By October Gough's plans were in full swing. However there were many problems. There were political considerations, largely beyond his control. There were also many logistical and topographical issues. The latter were probably the hardest for Gough as he was unfamiliar with the terrain and the country in particular, having in reality spent little time in India in general never mind that region. In his defence it does need to be stated that he did ask for investigations to be undertaken and attempted to fill the gaps in his knowledge. There is perhaps a case to be made that he was let down by those who undertook the investigations. In their defence it can be argued that they simply did not have the time or resources to carry them out in the detail that was required. For example Gough had ordered an investigation into the depth of rivers, and decided that he would have to take with him material to build at least one boat bridge. Had his intelligence of the area been better he would have been better aware of the areas where he could cross without a bridge. This would have saved him from the burden of taking with him the means of building a boat bridge, which placed a considerable burden upon his logistical organisation.[7]

The main aim of the expedition was the fort of Gwalior which stood upon an isolated rock 65 miles from Agra. The fort was accessible from certain directions. Comparison has been made with the situation of Edinburgh Castle.[8] The fort at Gwalior had been captured by the British twice during the Anglo-Mahratta Wars, the last time being in 1803. Sadly no attempt seems to have been made by Gough or his staff to examine previous history in this regard. In early December the Right Wing of the army which Gough was to command started to assemble at Agra. At the same time the left wing under Grey started to gather with one division at Jhansi and one at Koonch (Konch). On 11 December 1843, Lord Ellenborough arrived at Agra, officially in the hope of finding peace but in reality to be on hand for the coming campaign. Ellenborough was claiming Britain's right to become involved in the political situation in Gwalior under the Treaty of Surji-Anjangaon that had concluded the Second Anglo-Mahratta War in 1803.[9] This gave the British the right to intervene to help the Maharaja maintain law and order. This clause had largely been forgotten by both sides, but gave Ellenborough the justification needed to intervene. Indeed, when the British entered Gwalior a proclamation was issued on 14 December stating that the British had entered, 'not as an enemy but as a friend of the Maharajah whose person and whose rights the British Government is bound by treaty to protect'.[10] It was also believed by the government of India that many Mahratta chiefs would side with the British. In reality only a little over 1,400 Mahrattas joined with the British.

Such was the confidence of the British force that the wives of senior officers were allowed to accompany the army. This was not uncommon in warfare of the age, and any number of civilians could be found travelling with an army. In this instance the ladies present included Lady Gough and her daughter Frances, Juana Smith (the famous Lady Smith) who was used to accompanying her husband on campaign, Mrs. Curtis the wife of the commissary general, and several other ladies. Indeed the whole impression given by official documents is that it would be a walkover. No real resistance was expected. In that sense one can understand why Gough later felt he had been deceived, as events were to prove that the Mahrattas still had the ability and willingness to fight.

---

7   Rait, *Gough*, Vol. I, pp. 315–316.
8   Rait, *Gough*, Vol. I, p. 314.
9   In Rait's biography of Gough he refers to this as the Treaty of Burhampur, as many older works do. He also gives the date as 1804, but as the treaty was signed on 30 December 1803 this is perhaps understandable.
10   NAM: 8303–105, Gough Papers, Proclamation on entering Gwalior.

Yet despite the fact that little resistance was expected it would be wrong to believe that little preparation or detailed planning was undertaken by the British. As the Deputy Adjutant General Major Patrick Grant, a future field marshal and knight, recorded, "It may be a mere military promenade, but our progress will be attended with every precaution and vigilance necessary in marching through an enemy's country, and that will give it some degree of interest".[11] As has already been mentioned, even the movement of such a sizeable force in India was a considerable logistical undertaking, and could therefore not be taken lightly. Yet one feels that Grant's statement suggests more than this. He was counselling caution.

---

11   Rait, *Gough*, Vol. I, p. 320. Rait is quoting from a letter written by Patrick Grant to his mother and dated 18 December 1843.

40

The Battle of Maharajpore

War was now imminent and Ellenborough had decided upon this as a necessary cause of action. The campaign was expected to be short-lived. This would prove to be the case, but it was not to be as straightforward a case as many thought. The Mahrattas were to show that whilst they were a shadow of their former glory, they could still fight. Before moving on to look at the main battle of the campaign, it will be helpful to consider briefly the army that Gough commanded and the movement it made that would take it into its first battle.[1] Gough had a considerable force under his command and it will be helpful just to outline its composition and movement. The right wing under Gough's command, consisting of 12,000 men and around 40 guns, most of them light, was to cross the Chambal River at Dhaulpur moving from the north. The movement of its right column started on 22 December and by the 25th the entire right wing had crossed and gathered just outside Hingonah. The left wing commanded by Major General Sir John Grey, consisting of 4,000 men, was moving from the south crossed the Jumna (Yamuna) River on 24 December at Calpee (Kalpi). The intention was that both columns would meet at the city of Gwalior.

Gough had made a reconnaissance with his staff 20 miles forward of his camp, but had seen no sign of the enemy. This added to the belief of his staff and the Governor General that there would be no resistance worth the name. However Gough had been told on 25 December that a large body of the enemy with strong artillery was moving towards him. Although he did not know it, this was a force of 3,000 cavalry, 14,000 infantry and around 100 guns. The right wing under Gough's command consisted of a right column of mounted men and horse artillery under the command of Major General Joseph Thackwell. This included Lieutenant Colonel Charles Cureton's Cavalry Brigade – the 16th (The Queen's) Lancers, the Governor General's Bodyguard, the 1st Bengal Light Cavalry, and the 4th Irregular Cavalry – supported by two troops of horse artillery under Brigadier G. E. Gowan. The centre column commanded by Major General Thomas Valiant consisted of the 40th (2nd Somersetshire) Foot, and the 2nd and 16th Bengal Native Infantry. This column, made up of a single brigade, was largely considered a reserve. The left column was the largest and consisted of two infantry divisions, a brigade of cavalry, horse field artillery. The 2nd Division of Infantry, under Major General James Dennis consisted of the 14th and 31st Bengal Native Infantry, and 43rd Bengal Native Light Infantry. This Division was supported by a battery of light field artillery. The 3rd Division of infantry, under Major General John Littler consisted of 39th (Dorsetshire) Foot and 56th Bengal Native Infantry, supported by a battery of light field

---

1   A good history of the Gwalior Campaign is still lacking. Many of the general histories of Victorian campaign do make some mention. See, Featherstone, Donald, *Colonial Small Wars, 1837–1901*, (Newton Abbott: David & Charles, 1973), pp. 48–52. Haythornthwaite, Phillip, *The Colonial Wars Source Book* (London: Arms & Armour Press, 1995), pp. 88–89. Farwell, Byron, *Queen Victoria's Little Wars* (London: Allen Lane, 1973) pp. 32–36.

artillery. The Brigade of Cavalry, commanded by Brigadier Scott, consisted of the 4th and 10th Bengal Light Cavalry, supported by Captain Grant's troop of horse artillery.[2]

Gough's previous reconnaissance had convinced him that the army would have to move in three separate columns due to the terrain ahead. Given the power of the two flanking columns, the risk of splitting his force was minimised. Each part had artillery and cavalry attached to it and should be able to meet any initial attack made. Although the centre column was just a single brigade of infantry its position meant that any attack upon this column would be enveloped by the two wings of the army. Gough attached an officer of the Quartermaster General's department to each column to lead the way, as they had all been present on Gough's previous reconnaissance.

On the morning of 29 December 1843 the army split into three columns and started to move. Gough sent the left column forward a few hours before the rest of the army began their march. This was not only because they had the most difficult route, over what Sir Harry Smith called 'Pigmy Mountains', but also so that they could act as an advanced guard. With the largest force of cavalry this made perfect sense.[3] The precise time at which the army arrived at their destination, just outside a village known as Maharajpore, is unclear. However having set off at dawn the men had not breakfasted and so Gough ordered the army to rest and eat what food they had. Exactly what happened next is unclear and has been debated by historians. Gough clearly knew that the village was defended by the Mahrattas, as the previous day the Quartermaster General Major General Churchill had been fired upon from the village whilst undertaking reconnaissance. It likely that Gough expected the Mahrattas to hold the village and that he would have to attack it later in the day. In this light his decision to allow his men to rest and eat is understandable. Even when the Mahratta guns opened fire, there was no panic as most of the men were still out of range. Indeed the story is told that so unconcerned were the 39th Foot by the cannonade that they piled their arms and had breakfast whilst it continued.[4]

What certainly did surprise Gough was that the Mahrattas had moved part of their army forward and away from the defensive position of the village itself. However this was not necessarily a bad thing, as Gough appreciated commenting that, "I was surprised, and most agreeably surprised, to see that they had pushed forward, into a plain open for all arms, so large a body of their force." However, despite the fact that Sir Robert Rait makes a strong defence of Gough's handling of the battle which now ensued, it is clear that Gough made several mistakes. Whilst Rait raised some legitimate points regarding Gough's handling of the battle, and the point that Gough was not surprised by the enemy in the conventional sense of that term, it is difficult to argue that Gough was not forced to rush his plans. He might not have been taken by surprise in the sense that he knew where the enemy were, but he certainly had not planned to act as quickly as he did.[5]

Gough moved his artillery forward in an attempt to silence the enemy guns. However this was a forlorn hope as the Mahratta guns greatly outranged and overpowered the smaller British guns, with inevitable heavy loss amongst British gunners. This raises an important issue in regard to Gough's handling of his guns. Whilst it is incorrect to say that he did not appreciate them, it appears to be true that he did not understand them. In China, for example, the control and direction of his guns had largely been taken out of his control. The naval artillery was the responsibility

2   Cardew, Lieutenant F. G., *A Sketch of the Services of the Bengal Native Army to the Year 1895* (Calcutta: Office of the Superintendent of the Government of India, 1903). This includes a description of the entire order of battle. A similar description appears in Rait, *Gough*, Vol. I, p. 323. As is so often the case in British colonial campaigns, the use of terms such as division and brigade seem somewhat unusual. The 'divisions' only consisted of a single brigade at most.
3   Moore Smith, *Sir Harry Smith*, p. 132.
4   Rait, *Gough*, p. 324.
5   Rait, *Gough*, pp. 324–326.

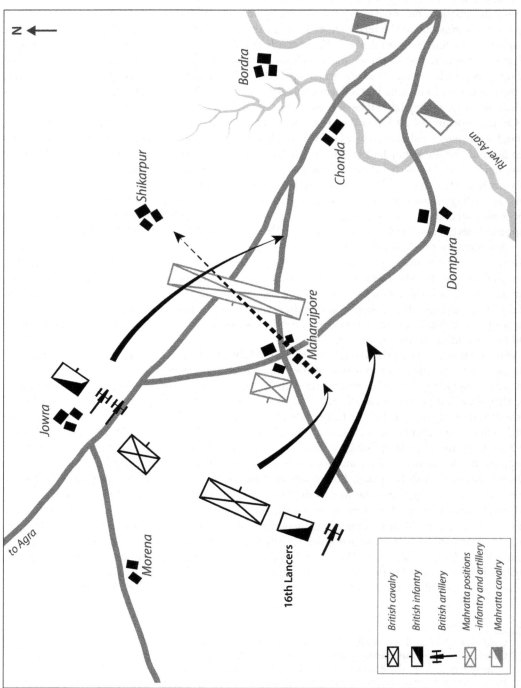

Map 8 The Battle of Maharajpore.

of Rear Admiral Parker, and Gough had left the able Lieutenant Colonel Montgomerie to his own devices when it came to his land based artillery. Brigadier Gowan commanded the largest contingent of artillery at Maharajpore, and whilst he was no doubt a good gunner he perhaps did not have, or had indeed been used to, such freedom to use his own initiative. Gough also seemed to take the rather common view of generals of the age that the role of the guns was to silence the enemy's guns and then prepare the way for an infantry assault. Therefore if Gough's guns could not silence those of the Mahrattas', what use was there in an artillery duel? The range of the Mahratta guns proved a great problem, and because British artillery had been unable to silence them, the army would have to advance for almost a mile under heavy fire. There was some success in silencing enemy guns, but this was largely against smaller calibre pieces on the flanks of the enemy position. This had been achieved by exploiting the mobility of British guns, the majority of them being horse artillery, against the Mahratta guns that were largely fixed in defensive positions. Yet against the larger calibre guns in the centre of the enemy line there was little the British artillery could do.

The basic problem was there were too few guns and what they had were not heavy enough to match the Mahrattas'. Amongst the Mahratta ordnance captured after the battle were 18 pdrs, 12 pdr howitzers, and other 12 pdr guns. To this the British could answer with only 6 and 9 pdr horse artillery. The British had heavier guns but Gough had been dissuaded from taking them by Lord Ellenborough, who for reasons that were largely political and economic urged that the 'siege train' should remain at Agra and only go forward if a siege was necessary.[6] Gough had acquiesced and not taken the only guns capable of matching the Mahratta's heavy artillery. To call this an error is to have the benefit of hindsight. It must be remembered that Gough hoped to move swiftly and engage the enemy in the open. Moving swiftly with such heavy guns would not have been possible. Gough did consult with Colonel Tennant, the officer responsible for the siege train, as to the possibility of it accompanying him.[7] Gough came away from this meeting convinced that to take it with him would slow him down and prove very difficult to transport. It was said that to make them capable of transport it would, after arrival at any point, require 24 hours to get them ready for battle.

The Spectator criticised Gough for, "his great rashness in sending back the heavy guns and mortars, and taking only pop-guns to the field."[8] This comment was made without any discussion as to Gough's reasons for so doing or the political pressure that was placed on him to leave such guns at Agra. Gough did attempt to bring some 8 inch howitzers with him. They arrived during the battle but did not take part. Here we see an example of the lack of initiative within, and poor command structure of, the army. Arriving on the battlefield they had no instructions to open fire and so remained silent throughout the battle. Gough angrily wrote to his son regarding this matter after the battle deploring the lack of initiative and saying, "as if I had sent them three staff messages to come up and be fired at!"[9] Whilst to Gough it seemed logical that if he sent for the guns he wanted them to take part in the battle, this was perhaps a rather simplistic approach. One can understand that the officer commanding the guns had no orders to fire, knew not what targets to aim at, and having come into the field during the battle did not perhaps have the benefit of knowing the course of the engagement. The argument can also be made that it was better that they held their fire rather than fire at the wrong targets and possibly hit their own side. One gets

6   Ellenborough, *India Administration of Lord Ellenborough*, pp. 410–411. Ellenborough tells Wellington that he has 'requested' that Gough leave the siege train at Agra. Gough, in his natural manner, would have taken this as an order.
7   Rait, *Gough*, p. 333.
8   Rait, *Gough*, p. 333. In reality he had not 'sent them back', they had never accompanied him in the first place.
9   NAM: 8303–105, Gough Papers, Gough to George Gough, 31 December 1844.

the sense that Gough did not know of their arrival until after the battle, which begs the questions as to whether the officer commanding the guns notified anyone as to his arrival or whether or not it was spotted by anyone on the staff. Perhaps a commander who paid more attention to detail, or who was possessed of a staff that did, would have detailed an officer to meet the 8 inch howitzers, bring them onto the field of battle and give them their targets.

Lack of artillery support aside, Gough had perhaps been in error to have stopped where he did, however it was the first appropriate point where his three columns could meet together. Knowing that the village of Maharajpore was defended, Gough had obviously planned to attack it given his campaign plan of bringing the enemy to battle. To wait was dangerous, not least of all because some of his men were coming under fire from the enemy. To withdraw would be difficult and could become chaotic. If Gough had learnt nothing else from General Graham at Barrosa it was surely the danger of retreating in the face of the enemy, something which had led the latter to attack a numerically superior force as the lesser evil. Also, to withdraw in the face of the enemy would have shattered morale and would have sent out the signal that the British were frightened of the Mahrattas. Finally, to attack the enemy quickly and decisively had been considered the key in India since the French Captain Louis Paradis had attacked a numerically superior force at the Battle of St Thome in 1746. As that great chronicler of the British Army, Sir John Fortescue remarked, "The memory of Paradis should be honoured in England since he taught us the secret of the conquest of India."[10] A cautious commander might have chosen to withdraw his men as best he could from out of the range of the enemy's guns. However Gough was not a cautious man and the cannonade from the enemy was to him a challenge that must be met.

Gough ordered an advance. His intention was to use the 3rd Division under Littler's command to make the frontal assault whilst supported by 2nd Division under Dennis, whilst the centre column commanded by Valiant would attempt to work around behind the enemy, take the nearby village of Shikarpur, and then attack Maharajpore from the rear. The cavalry under Major General Thackwell was ordered to be on hand to support either attack as it developed. Whilst the plan was sound in theory there were several points that it raised. In some sense it seemed overly complicated and the movement of the centre column behind the Mahrattas was a difficult manoeuvre to make under enemy fire. It also relied heavily on Thackwell being able to ascertain correctly the course of the battle and not commit his cavalry too soon. Whilst Thackwell was an excellent and highly efficient commander he was perhaps not best suited to make such a judgement, due to the fact that he could not see the whole battle. Nor was he kept fully informed of the course of the battle by Gough's staff. In the normal course of events the cavalry would have been directed when to attack by a staff officer of the commander-in-chief. Again this is perhaps an example of Gough's desire to delegate a great deal of responsibility, leaving senior commanders to use their own initiative. In some sense this was refreshing and sensible. Yet at same time it meant that decisive commands from the top were lacking when they were most needed. It required a delicate balance between decisive command and delegation that Gough seems to have misjudged on a number of occasions.

The movement of the divisions across the killing ground of almost a mile inevitably took its toll on the infantry. Given that there was often the need to climb in and out of ravines, the fact that some order and cohesion was lost is not surprising. Indeed given the difficulty of their task it was surprising that the infantry reached the enemy in such good order as it did. Gough had been anxious for the movement to be swift so as to reduce the time spent under fire. In one particular instance he was aided by the then-Major Henry Havelock, later Major General Sir Henry, who was officially acting as an interpreter but had in reality became another ADC on his staff. Gough, concerned at the slow movement of his infantry, commented of a particular native infantry regiment, the

---

10   Fortescue, Sir John, *History of the British Army*, (London: Macmillan & Co, 1899) Vol. II, p. 184.

56th, part of Littler's 3rd Division. Given that they were there to support the British 39th Foot his anxiety at their slow movement was understandable. According to Havelock, Gough exclaimed, "Will no one get that sepoy regiment on?" which Havelock took as an instruction. Riding over to them, Havelock, using his local knowledge, addressed then in Hindustani and called them by their native name of 'Lamboorun-ke-Pultan' and encouraged them on leading from the front and waving his hat in encouragement. As Havelock led the way the sepoys followed enthusiastically.[11]

Around 60 yards short of the enemy position, the battalions halted to re-form into line and prepare to fire. This inevitably halted the momentum of the advance but also presented an excellent target for the Mahratta gunners. The Mahratta artillery kept firing with everything they had, including old iron and horse shoes once the cannon balls had run out. As the infantry charged, the Mahratta's were driven from their guns. It was now the Mahratta infantry largely armed with elderly muskets and swords came forward to engage the British. The fighting was hard, considerably harder than had been expected, as the disciplined Mahratta's held firm against a strong British attack. Much of the fighting fell upon the 39th Foot, which had got slightly ahead of the rest of the army. As the other battalions came up so the enemy was driven back. Indeed the 56th Native Infantry with Havelock in the lead joined the 39th as the first to break through the Mahratta lines and take the guns. Valiant's men had taken the village of Shikarpur with ease before moving on to attack Maharajpore. At the latter they attacked and became engaged in a fierce and confused melee: so much so that by the time the action was finished Valiant's brigade was now on the left and Littler's command on the right, the opposite of their starting positions.

Despite this initial success, and the capture of the village, this was only the first defensive position that needed to be taken before victory was assured. About 1,200 yards behind Maharajpore lay a strong defensive position with 12 guns. No sooner had Gough's force moved out of the village than they came under a heavy fire. It had been felt that it would be difficult to re-form the formations successfully within the confines of the village and that this could be done once they left the village. However, this could certainly have been handled better and the men came under a heavy fire as they attempted to reform just outside the village. The advance was now even more difficult than before. The guns were firing at a shorter range and worked smoothly and efficiently, and the terrain that the British had to cross was even more difficult than before. The lead battalions suffered large casualties but the discipline and resolve of the units meant that they reached the enemy positions and drove them away in close quarters battle where bayonets were predominate and muskets were used as clubs.

The main thrust of the attack was once again led by Littler's division. Gough did have slightly fresher troops available; however they were not European. He only had two British regiments available, the 39th and 40th Foot, both of which had already been heavily involved. Gough was reluctant to commit an attack without one of the two British regiments leading the way, thus the 39th ended up bearing the brunt of both attacks. Like most British commanders of this period Gough held the belief that the sepoy would only follow the British soldier into battle, rather than lead the attack himself. It is quite likely that the slow advance of the 56th earlier that day and the need for Havelock to encourage their advance had enhanced this belief. This feeling that he could not rely on non-European troops to lead an attack, only to support it, would prove problematic both now and in the future. One does wonder whether in Gough's case there was slightly more to this. In China he had not held the same reticence and used his sepoys to full advantage, particularly the rifle company of the Madras Native Infantry. In may be that it was now that they were facing fellow Indians that Gough was hesitant. Havelock certainly encouraged the 56th earlier that day by reminding them that their fellow Indians were watching and would hold a low opinion of them.

---

11   Pollock, *Havelock*, p. 102.

This suggests that there was a certain belief on the part of the staff that there might be problems with such native loyalties.

Throughout this period, the difficult nature of the ground had meant that it had proved impossible for the cavalry to support the infantry in the way that Gough had planned. However, with the support of the horse artillery, they had been able to disperse the Mahratta cavalry and were on hand later in the battle as Gough attempted to prevent the enemy from retreating. Unfortunately once again the terrain meant that the cavalry was unable to achieve this. The cavalry had also become badly out of position due to movements in anticipation of supporting the infantry that did not come to fruition.

There was one last defensive position once the village of Shikarpur had also fallen to Valiant's command as described previously. This was in effect the Mahratta final stand, made in a small defensive position containing three guns. This was cleared by the grenadier company of the 39th Foot. This ended Mahratta resistance and the defeat might have been even more decisive had the cavalry not been out of position. There is a suggestion that Gough had ordered the cavalry to stay closer to Valiant's command. Had they done this they would have been able to prevent the retreat or at the very least turn it into a complete rout inflicting many more casualties on the enemy. In Rait's biography of Gough the reason for this failure is put down to a mistake by a staff officer, although he provides no further details.[12] Despite this, Maharajpore was a crushing defeat for the Mahrattas. Perhaps Gough had not had the best control of the army and there is a sense that he was slightly rushed into battle and forced into action that inevitably resulted in high casualties. The idea that, "Gough displayed no Generalship whatsoever and gave but one order 'On and at them'" is unfair and indeed inaccurate.[13] Orders were rushed, but they were not non-existent. Whilst the casualty returns were high it was hardly surprising given the nature of the battle. Gough was forced into attacking well prepared defences. Even if one does not believe that he had to give battle, it must be remembered that Gough, Ellenborough and the Indian Government, wanted him to do just that and bring the war to a successful conclusion.

A year after the battle, and having received some criticism from politicians, an angry Gough remarked in a letter to his son that:

> What Lord Ellenborough and the non-military set by whom he was surrounded wanted to have seen, was a Field-day—guns and cavalry, with a host of skirmishers to have galloped about, to be well peppered by the Mahratta guns, and then to have fallen back behind the infantry; all this time enabling the enemy to bring up his support from Chonda, only a mile and a half distant, and giving confidence to the foe. This might have been all very pretty if both parties were to fire blank cartridge, but would have been murderous in the face of such an artillery. I took the shorter way of at once subdividing their force, and if the cavalry had acted according to my order, not a man from Maharajpore would ever have got to Gwalior; as it was, within half an hour their retreat was completely intercepted by Valiant's Brigade.[14]

This letter shows Gough's thinking and his motivation for his actions. In short, he took a command decision quickly and under fire from the enemy to act and act decisively, in accordance with the instructions from the Governor General and the accepted tactics of fighting in India by going on the offensive. That mistakes were made, and that perhaps better tactics could have been employed,

---

12   Rait, *Gough*, p. 235.
13   Featherstone, *Colonial Small Wars*, p. 50.
14   NAM: 8303–105, Gough Papers, Gough to George Gough 31 December 1844.

is not disputed. However his actions were not incompetent, or unnecessarily reckless by the standards of the time or the tactics of warfare in India.

Gough's force lost 6 officers and approximately 100 men killed. As for the wounded they numbered 34 officers and 650 men. Littler, Valiant and Wright, three senior commanders, had all been wounded. Two senior officers, Major General Horace Chatham Churchill and Lieutenant Colonel Thomas Sanders, were killed. Although in public Gough praised Churchill, in a private letter to his son written after the battle he expressed his disappointment at his work as quartermaster general, stating that "poor Churchill did practically nothing." [15] Unsurprisingly the British regiments bore the brunt of the casualties. The 39th Foot lost 30 officers and men killed and 196 wounded. The 40th Foot lost 24 officers and men killed and 160 wounded.[16] The 40th lost their commanding officer, Major James Stopford, and his successor Captain Fitzherbert Coddington, both wounded. In the battle itself Gough had lost 106 men killed, which was not an excessive figure. What made it look worse was the high number of wounded. Thus overall casualties, that is killed and wounded, amounted to 790. Occasionally one will find historians who are confused by this number and state that the number killed is 800. This is not the case and is a misreading, and rounding up, of the figures for killed and wounded.[17]

Given the need to attack strong defensive positions such numbers, particularly in terms of wounded, were likely. It must be added that some of the killed and wounded had even occurred after the battle itself, due to the explosion of mines and ammunition. Indeed the ladies, who had already had an eventful day, had to abandon their 'tea tent' sharply in the aftermath of the battle when a nearby mine exploded. The ladies had been mounted on elephants during the battle and had attracted the fire of the enemy. When later in the day a magazine exploded the elephants were frightened and ran away carrying the ladies with them. Their anxiety was added to by the fact that having been taken from the field they were unsure of the events of the battle until Major Patrick Grant brought them news of the victory. It appears that the ladies were removed from the tea tent by soldiers who had just discovered the mine. The ladies who were present at the battle were presented with special medals by Lord Ellenborough.

Whilst there is no attempt to belittle the number of casualties, or to deny that they were higher than people had come to expect from a campaign in India, they were not excessive or proof of incompetence. It was however proof that Maharajpore was a fierce battle against a stronger-than-expected enemy who occupied a strong defensive position and had superiority in artillery. It is also worth remembering that whilst the casualties for the Mahrattas are not accurately recorded it is believed that they exceeded 3,000, the majority of whom were killed, and was quite conceivably over 4,000.[18]

---

15 NAM: 8303–105, Gough Papers, Gough to George Gough. Undated but given its content likely May or June 1844.

16 As with all casualty returns there are discrepancies between killed and wounded, as inevitably some of those initially listed as wounded died subsequently.

17 Knight, Ian *Go to Your God Like a Soldier; The British Soldier Fighting for Empire, 1837–1902* (London: Greenhill Books, 1996), p. 45, states that Gough lost over 800 men killed. This is completely wrong as even total casualties, wounded and dead, were less than 800. This is perhaps the prime example of the misunderstanding mentioned above. Featherstone, *Colonial Small Wars*, p. 50, is partly guilty of this and the misleading nature of the previous sentence makes his remark regarding total casualties seems as if 800 were killed.

18 Featherstone, *Colonial Small Wars*, p. 52. Even the deeply critical Featherstone admits to 3,000 Mahratta casualties. The battle and its results are not to dissimilar to the Battle of Assaye on 23 September 1803. This was an early victory for the future Duke of Wellington and a battle he would later describe as his finest achievement on the battlefield.

On the same day as Maharajpore Major General Grey also fought a decisive battle at Punniar. This battle is often used to criticise Maharajpore by comparison. Grey had advanced from Bundelcund and had reached Punniar on 28 December 1843. This was about 12 miles away from Gwalior itself. At Punniar the Mahrattas had made a parallel movement to Grey's force as he manoeuvred his way towards Gwalior. Without warning the Mahrattas opened fire upon Grey's baggage train. Grey managed to defend from attack by the deployment of his cavalry and horse artillery. By 1500 on the afternoon of 29 December the Mahrattas had taken up a strong position on a hill at a place called Mangore. This threatened the British position and Grey determined to take the hill and destroy the enemy force. Grey sent the 3rd Foot and some engineers to attack the front. At the same time he sent the 39th Native Infantry to turn the left flank and kept a strong reserve of the 50th Foot and the 38th and 50th Native Infantry. The 3rd made a determined attack under heavy fire and drove the Mahrattas back to where the 39th Native Infantry had occupied a hill after turning the enemy's left, and were able to delivered a series of extremely effective volleys upon the retreating Mahrattas. At that point Grey decided to commit his reserves and they made a devastating attack on the enemy's right and completed the rout. Grey lost 35 killed and 182 wounded. Again, figures for the Mahrattas are not easily available but total casualties were around 1,000.

It is easy to paint the picture of Punniar being a more successful action than Maharajpore, and to an extent it was. Grey was certainly able to better plan and organise his attack than Gough was. Perhaps this once again is a matter of numbers. It was certainly easier for Grey to have a more direct control over a force of 4,000 men than it was for Gough with over 12,000. This takes us back to the point about higher command leadership in the British Army. On the face of it Grey certainly seems to have had an easier task. The enemy force was smaller, in a weaker defensive position than at Maharajpore, and without such decisive superiority in artillery. Both men had attempted to outflank the enemy, with Grey having greater success in this regards. Gough's biggest problem was that he had the battle somewhat hurriedly forced upon him. The other major problem he faced was having to advance almost a mile under enemy gunfire. It also appears that Gough faced the cream of the Mahratta army. This is understandable from the Mahratta point of view as Gough's force was the largest and clearly the greatest threat, and it is therefore understandable that they sent their best units to oppose him. It is clear that at Maharajpore the Mahrattas put up a more stubborn resistance than at Punniar. It is also worth pointing out that for the campaign Gough had only four available European regiments. The idea that European soldiers were needed to give backbone to the native infantry has already been covered above and is one we shall return to later. Although Gough faced the more difficult task and was likely to engage the larger part of the enemy army, he had decided to divide his European regiments evenly between the two wings.

In the aftermath of the campaign Gough received a personal letter from the Duke of Wellington. It read, "I sincerely congratulate you on the Battle of Maharajpore. I have perused the details thereof with the greatest satisfaction; they are highly creditable to the officers and troops engaged as well as to yourself."[19] However Lord Ellenborough was quite critical of Gough in the aftermath of the battle. There is clearly a personal angle to this in the sense that Ellenborough, who accompanied Gough's command, was annoyed and felt personally slighted that Gough had not kept him fully informed of his plan throughout the battle. This was particularly difficult as the actions of the Mahrattas forced Gough into a number of last minute changes.[20] To have the Governor General looking over his shoulder during battle, figuratively if not literally, was a difficult position for Gough to be placed in. It was also one he was not used to as in China Pottinger, and even to an extent Elliot before him, had kept a discreet distance and left Gough to fight the battle his way.

---

19   Rait, *Gough*, pp. 332–333.
20   Ellenborough, *India Administration of Lord Ellenborough*, p. 435.

There is also a sense that Ellenborough's views on the battle were tainted by the fact that he himself came under fire. Ellenborough's movement, from a position which Gough had determined would be safe for him to watch the battle, was on the initiative of an unnamed staff officer. The Mahratta gunners did not know who he was but had grasped that he was a figure of some importance and commenced to fire on his position. As a non-military man Ellenborough understandably found this unnerving. At the same time however he seems to have failed to grasp the fact that such things happened in war. Ellenborough, who had been so keen on Gough's appointed and had written that 'We want you very much', now started to change his mind.[21] He had now had the opportunity of witnessing Gough in battle and given the course of Maharajpore one can understand his change of heart. However Ellenborough had watched the battle from a somewhat obscured position. It is important to understand the position Ellenborough was in. The relationship between him and Gough had soured a little during the campaign, the saga over the siege train being only one example.

Perhaps his criticism of Gough was also an attempt to defend himself. Ellenborough had received much criticism from home over his actions whilst Governor General. Partly this was due to Afghanistan. Although the war had been commenced by his predecessor Lord Auckland, Ellenborough's concluding of the conflict was met with much hostility and indeed for a time there was even talk of his being impeached. Although this passed, the annexation of the Sindh created new problems for him. To many in Britain the annexation seemed unjust and more to the point unjustifiable. He had also fallen out with the HEIC directors.[22]

Shortly before Ellenborough was recalled, he wrote to the Duke of Wellington that Gough, "despite his many excellent qualities, had not the grasp of mind and prudence essential to conduct great military operations." This in and of itself was not too serious a criticism, and one must appreciate the aforementioned personal considerations that Ellenborough had. However it perhaps takes us back to Sir Hew Strachan's point that Gough was a Blucher who never found his Gneisenau. The talents he had were fine if the skills he lacked were present in the character of another; for example a chief of staff.

Gough also ran afoul of the Indian press. They were a difficult audience for a military commander to please and even generals such as Roberts, Charles and Robert Napier, and the Duke of Wellington himself, were strongly criticised for their military actions. Charles Napier even went so far as to say, "There is no falsehood that the Indian Press – with one or two exceptions – does not proclaim against me! One mass of spite, jealousy, malice, hatred, fury, is poured out upon me and all I do."[23] So Gough was far from being alone in receiving such criticism. The aftermath of the Gwalior campaign was the start of a rather acrimonious association with the Indian press that would dog the remainder of his time in the subcontinent. Relations with the press need to be nurtured over time. Gough was however either unwilling or unable to play the political game with them and was at times openly hostile in response. Relations started to sour when it was claimed that one of Gough's staff officers, Colonel Garden, had deliberately mislead both Gough and the correspondent of the *Delhi Gazette* as to where the battle would be fought. The suggestion being that Gough thought he was fighting the battle of Chonda rather than Maharajpore. Gough categorically denied this and went so far as to lead an enquiry into the source of this report. A problem with such a situation as the relationship with the press in India was that any officer with an axe to grind could pass on such stories. It turned out that a disgruntled officer of the Horse Artillery was the source of the story,

21   Rait, *Gough*, p. 309.
22   For an impression of the contemporary condemnation of Lord Ellenborough see Anonymous, *India and Lord Ellenborough*, (London: W. H. Dalton, 1844).
23   Napier, William, *General Sir Charles Napier and the Directors of the East India Company* (London: C. Westerton, 1857), p. 5.

and although Gough could not dismiss him he had him transferred to a less glamorous appointment in the Field Artillery.[24] However this was the start of a war between Gough and the press in India. Gough had not handled the issue with any tact, nor did he see any reason to so do. Gough dismissed the press to the point that he did not even read the Indian press. He was quoted as saying, "I can afford abuse but I cannot afford to pay for it."[25] This somewhat sanguine attitude towards the media was common of his era but the power of the press was starting to rise.

The battles of Maharajpore and Punniar had effectively ended the war. On 31 December 1843 negotiations began, although it was not until 13 January 1844 that the treaty was actually signed. Although the independence of Gwalior continued the Gwalior army was to be converted into a British unit of 10,000 men maintained at the expense of the Gwalior state. As a historical note it is interesting to point out that this new 'British' Gwalior contingent was to play a considerable part in the mutiny of 1857. Indeed one of the most celebrated leaders of the mutiny, Tantia Topi, had been part of the Gwalior force. The fort of Gwalior, which dominated the town, was transferred to British control. The war had been incredibly short. It had lasted less than three weeks. Indeed with the first battles fought on 29 December 1843 and negotiations opening on the 31st, one can argue that the campaign only lasted for three days.

Whatever criticism there might justifiably be of Gough's command and control during this campaign, it is clear that he had by his actions done a great service to British India. The defeat of the Mahrattas removed a dangerous threat. As events would prove, it was just as well that the British did not have to face the possibility of an alliance between the Mahrattas and the Sikhs. Such an alignment, although unlikely, could have proved fatal to British ambitions in India. In that sense Gough had done good service to his country. Whilst the total casualties were high, the total number of killed standing at around 150 for the expedition, for what had been achieved this cannot be considered an excessive number. Against an army with considerable artillery, such casualties were inevitable and this should have been understood.

24   Rait, *Gough*, pp. 338–340.
25   Rait, *Gough*, p. 340.

41

India Between Campaigns

_____

The business in Gwalior was over by the end of January 1844, although a detachment remained until March at the Maharaja's request. Although Gough would be called to the field again in December 1845, for the time in between he had to deal with a myriad of issues surrounding the Indian Army. It is not necessary to go into details but the HEIC and the possessions in India were short of money. Such was the expense of running the country that economies were sought to improve the financial position. As is so often the case, the military were an easy target for such cuts. A strange paradox now emerges where politicians in India, not least of all Lord Ellenborough, were calling for reductions in the size of the army, whilst continually warning of the threats posed by the Sikh Empire and further north in Afghanistan, along with the usual domestic concerns of law and order.

The Indian army stood at over 240,000 men. This should be placed in context and it must be remembered that they held guard over a territory which at that stage was of around 1,100,000 square miles and a population of over 100,000,000. This is without considering the possibility of action against unfriendly forces, and the need to gather an army for service in the field. As Gough found out on three separate occasions, the army in India was so thinly spread that it was never an easy task to find sufficient troops for such operations. At the same time, it needs to be said that despite the size of the Company army there was still a strong reliance on British Army battalions to form the backbone of military power in India. Given this it is perhaps understandable that politicians thought there could be some reduction in the native army. Whilst the politicians were seeking cuts, Gough was attempting to improve the state of the Indian Army. To an extent this was based upon his experiences of the army in China, but particularly on the Gwalior campaign. Given what we have seen in the previous chapter, it will hardly be surprising to learn that one of his major concerns was the state of the artillery, which he thought was under strength. His desire was to improve not only its size, both in numbers and calibre of guns, but also its mobility. This was always going to be a difficult task in an atmosphere of economic retrenchment.[1]

The fact that, during the Sikh Wars, British artillery failed to have superiority in number, calibre or quality until the last battle of the Second Sikh War is testament to the validity of Gough's argument. Nevertheless, he failed to persuade the civilian authorities that this was necessary or convince them to release the necessary money. It cannot be said that he did not try or that he did not recognise the problem and attempt to amend it in the years after the Gwalior campaign. Whatever he might have said publicly about artillery, it is clear from this that privately he appreciated its value.

Gough also desired to have a greater proportion of 'european' regiments, be they the Company's own 'European' units or British battalions, to native ones. Again we can see the influence of

---

1   Rait, _Gough_, Vol. I, pp. 342–357. Rait dedicates an entire chapter to what he calls 'The Army Policy of Sir Hugh Gough'. Specifically on improvements to artillery, see NAM: 8303–105, Gough Papers, Gough to Ellenborough, 5 March 1844.

Gwalior in his thinking. In that campaign, he had been forced to rely heavily upon British regiments. Although he makes no direct reference to it, Gough might have been considering what he would require for possible military action with the Sikhs. At the same time Gough was concerned about the quality of native units. Interestingly he laid the majority of the blame for this with their European officers. Indeed the poor quality of officers for native regiments would ultimately have a role to play in the major mutiny of 1857. The problem was that command of a native regiment was near the bottom of the pecking order for British officers. Any officer who demonstrated any particular skill or knowledge, or who was well connected, needed to spend little time with his battalion before being employed as a political officers on the frontier, in a civil service appointment, or in a staff appointment. As a consequence, Gough believed the native regiments were left with officers who showed little skill and little imagination, or very young officers new to India and new to command in general.[2]

It was partly the drive for economy that exacerbated some of the problems with regards to the native units, and created events that required Gough's attention during early 1844. The main problem was to do with 'mutiny' within the native army. The main source of the problems was once again the withdrawal of the *batta* for soldiers serving in newly conquered lands. In short, Scinde was no longer classed as a foreign territory and therefore the batta for such service was not to be forthcoming. In the subsequent wrangling over this matter the government would seek to lay the blame at the feet of the pay department of the army. Their argument was that there had never been an official order from the government to the effect of striking off the batta. This was an action that Gough would later describe as, 'unworthy of a government'. Although correct, in the sense that no order had been given, the fact remained that the Scinde was no longer foreign territory and therefore the batta should cease. One can imagine that had it not been stopped immediately there would have been an outcry against the army for 'waste' and 'inefficiency' by the government of India. Within the letter of the law the pay department had acted correctly, and if the government had planned to make an exception for the newly conquered territories then notification of this should have been given to the commander-in-chief for him to pass on to subordinate departments. No such orders were ever received by Gough. Indeed there appears to have been no consideration given to this matter by the government before the outbreak of 'mutiny', whereas Gough had been aware of this potential problem since the very early days of his appointment as commander-in-chief.

As has been previously mentioned many soldiers relied on the batta to support their families whilst they were away. As a result, certain units refused to move when ordered because of the effect it would have on their families. It is interesting from a historical perspective to note that one of the units involved in such a 'mutiny' was the 34th Bengal Native Infantry: it was in this regiment that the Mangal Pandey incident took place in April 1857, widely considered to be one of the first moves of the Mutiny of 1857.[3] In January 1844, the 34th had refused to march due to the withdrawal of batta. Whilst Gough had some sympathy for the sepoys' point of view, he wrote to Lord Ellenborough that, "nothing however can justify or ever extenuate this glaring breach of discipline and the most stringent measures must be taken with the 34th."[4] The problem was to find an appropriate compromise. There were those who argued that it would be best to disband the regiment.

---

2   NAM: 8303–105, Gough Papers, Gough to Ellenborough, 27 Feb 1844.
3   Mangal Pandey was a soldier in the 34th who with a loaded rifle threatened to attack the first European he saw. Attempts were made to arrest him, in which he was assisted by other sepoys. It was a guard of Sikhs who ultimately arrested him with the support of Major General John Bennet Hearsey. Eventually Pandey attempted to kill himself, and despite shooting himself and point blank range he did not die. On 8th April 1857 he was hanged for mutiny. The exact nature of events and the incident in general has been debated over the years.
4   NAM: 8303–105, Gough Papers, Gough to Ellenborough, 17 February 1844.

Gough argued that this would turn trained men into enemies of the British, and who could tell to whom they would offer their services? It would also be unsettling for the army as a whole. Although against the idea of disbandment, he did not rule it out. To Lord Ellenborough he wrote that, "The supremacy of order must be upheld, whatever the consequences even that of placing in our enemy's rank, whole regiments."[5] With the benefit of hindsight, and bearing in mind events 12 years later, one can argue that Gough might have done a service to the Indian Army had he disbanded the regiment at this time. Yet his point about releasing trained men to join a potential enemy was well made. In the end other means of punishing the regiment were perhaps the best course.

1844 also saw a similar incident of 'mutiny' in the 64th Bengal Native Infantry. The 64th had a good reputation and had played an important role in Afghanistan. When ordered to Scinde they requested the same batta as they had received when in Afghanistan. To the soldiers, and indeed many of their officers, this did not seem an unreasonable request. At first it was simply a reluctance to move without a promise of batta rather than an outright refusal, and the situation seems to have been resolved by some experienced staff officers who convinced the native officers that if they moved the men they would do their best to gain the allowance they requested. Gough even wrote a letter promising minor allowances and concessions and that they would not be in the Scinde for more than a year.[6]

With this, the situation could have been resolved had it not been for the subsequent actions of their colonel, an officer called Moseley. Moseley used Gough's letter to bribe his men to move. This was never the intention, as Gough had written it partly as a reward for the tactful way the men of the 64th had dealt with the matter. They had not openly refused to move, but had expressed their concerns. Moseley also lied to his men telling them that they would receive the full batta they had received in Afghanistan. This exacerbated the matter when on pay day the extra money was not forthcoming. The lies of one officer reflected badly on all Europeans and one can understand the reluctance of the men of the 64th to believe in the concessions that had genuinely been offered. Brigadier George Hunter attempted to persuade them to continue their journey, even promising to pay the money out of his own pocket. There was a standoff for 24 hours. Hunter sent their own officers away and eventually managed to persuade the men to move. On hearing the details Gough's decision was to initially pass sentence of death on 39 men of the 64th. This decision had been reached with the advice of Henry Havelock. Whilst Havelock could also appreciate the concerns of the 'mutineers' he stated that, 'exemplary punishment should always be inflicted without hesitation on mutinous troops – whether British or Indian'. Charles Napier, the conqueror of the Scinde, supported this view. As for Colonel Moseley, he was justly cashiered, with Gough particularly annoyed at the misuse of his letter.[7]

Despite having ordered the execution of 39 men, Gough later backtracked and remitted the sentence for all but six; those considered the main instigators of the 'mutiny'. It is easy to think of this as an example of Gough's kindly nature, similar to that which had led him to act injudiciously during his command of the 22nd Regiment. It is quite possible that there was a more practical reason behind the decision. The actions in the 64th were minor, and exacerbated by poor leadership, however in other units the situation was more serious. The 34th had openly refused to move and there was a level of defiance absent from the actions of the 64th. In short, the situation threatened to spiral out of control. Disturbing reports were reaching Gough of further mutinies. The 7th Light Cavalry had mutinied in an event which Gough felt was more serious than that in

5   NAM: 8303–105, Gough Papers, Gough to Ellenborough, 18 February 1844.
6   Mason, Phillip, *A Matter of Honour: an Account of the Indian Army its Officers and Men* (London: Macmillan Publishers Ltd, 1986) p. 227
7   Pollock, *Way to Glory*, p. 103 & Farwell, *Eminent Victorian Soldiers*, pp. 37–38.

the 34th as the 7th Light Cavalry had not only refused to march to Scinde but had used, "deceitful language towards the government."[8] At the same time, there were reports that the 4th and 69th Bengal Native Infantry were on the verge of 'mutiny'. The 69th did indeed partly mutiny. The regiment was split, Gough reporting to Lord Ellenborough that, "a portion of the 69th Reg. were ready to obey, consisting of 8 Subedar, 8 Jemadar, 52 Havildar, 16 Brahmin and 340 sepoys, indeed the whole of number 4 & 5 companies, but that the remainder refused to embark in the boats."[9] Gough regretted the actions of the remainder, amounting to 169 men, and now felt he had no choice but to act against them:

> I have directed them to be disarmed, and Lt Col Buck has my directions to select the most prominent for trial. The remainder I shall discharge. I have no doubt but that ere two days elapse the 4th will equally succumb. I will own this has been a great relief to my mind, as I am almost confident that if any general manifestation were made I could not depend upon the 60th which Regiment is not trustworthy.[10]

Despite the tone of Gough's letter it was apparent that the situation was not resolved, and would not be as the batta was not going to be paid. The situation still had the potential to turn ugly and Gough was keen to find a solution.

However the most disturbing news to reach Gough was that the discontent had spread to a British regiment. The 31st (Huntingdonshire) Foot were said to be in agreement with the mutineers. Gough informed Lord Ellenborough that, "private reports go so far as to say that the 31st Queens have declared they will not act against men contending only for their rights."[11] What effect this had on the ever nervous Ellenborough is not recorded. Although Gough was concerned, it was more to do with the fact that this was being reported rather than his believing in its validity. He feared that the rumour that British soldiers were in sympathy with their Indian counterparts might embolden the latter with the belief that they would not act against them.

Gough did not believe that the report on the 31st's behaviour could be entirely accurate, for as he later told Lord Ellenborough, "the first principle instilled into a British soldier is obedience to command – afterwards to appeal."[12] Gough later wrote to Lord Ellenborough that:

> As to the report relative to the 31st having said, they would not act against men only claiming their rights – I do not believe it – a drunken scoundrel may have made use of such an expression, but I would have no hesitation in going out with them to act against the native corps- much as I should regret the two services in collision.[13]

Indeed it was not just the native troops that Gough was aware of. All this was taking place under the watchful eye of the Sikhs. In communication with Lord Ellenborough, Gough alludes to intelligence which concludes that the movement of Sikh troops towards the border is in response to

---

8   NAM: 8303–105, Gough Papers, Gough to Ellenborough, 22 February 1844.
9   NAM: 8303–105, Gough Papers, Gough to Lord Ellenborough, 29 February 1844. The ranks of subedar and jemadar were native officers, equating to captain and lieutenant respectively; havildars were native NCOs.
10   NAM: 8303–105, Gough Papers, Gough to Lord Ellenborough, 25 March 1844.
11   NAM: 8303–105, Gough Papers, Gough to Lord Ellenborough, 26 February 1844.
12   NAM: 8303–105, Gough Papers, Gough to Lord Ellenborough, 26 February 1844.
13   NAM: 8303–105, Gough Papers, Gough to Lord Ellenborough, 27 February 1844.

reports of 'mutiny' in the British forces. There was also a suggestion that they were trying to entice sepoys to join them.[14] In a letter to his son Gough later remarked of the sepoys that:

> [T]hey look upon us as their conquerors, and only serve us from interested motives; whilst we pay them better than our neighbours and treat them justly, they will serve us. But if we, as we did in Scinde, strike off a great part of their allowance, when at the very moment the Sikh army in their immediate neighbourhood was receiving 12 Rupees, while ours only had, at the most, eight and a half, it was not to be wondered at that the sepoys hesitated.[15]

The significance of the 'mutinies' during this period should not be underestimated. With a large and fearsome army on the borders anticipating and prepared to seize any opportunity to exploit the situation, it was one full of danger. Gough feared for the possible consequences of any action he might take. "I cannot conceal from myself that the government are in a most unpleasant dilemma. To give in would be a most fearful blow to discipline, to attempt to force corps to act, will eventually lead to further acts of disobedience and consequent punishment of whole corps."[16]

Whilst Gough might have demonstrated leniency towards some of the mutineers, his reaction to events is surprisingly active. He ordered Sir Robert Dick, commanding the division in question, to disarm – and in the case of the 7th Light Cavalry dismount – any unit that threatened mutiny. At the same time Gough ordered the 16th Lancers and 40th Foot to be ready to move to support Dick's command at short notice. He even considered travelling to the scene himself. His active hands-on approach to command is illustrated by the comments in a letter to Lord Ellenborough that, "Could I speak the language I would at once go up."[17] That said, he did move himself on a strategically timed tour of inspection which meant he would be reasonably close at hand should events threaten to spiral out of control.

Had Gough not handled the situation as well as he did there could have been dire consequences for British India. Indeed it is possible that a mutiny along the lines of 1857 might have occurred far sooner. In balance it should be added that perhaps all Gough had done was to delay matters for a future time rather than deal with any of the long term concerns; then again, some of the concerns in overall treatment and the perception of the Europeans were beyond Gough's ability to alter. He had demonstrated a good mix of firmness and restraint that had helped to prevent matters from getting out of control. In following such a middle ground, Gough was open to criticism from two directions. There were those who urged a firmer line, such as Havelock who in particular disagreed with Gough's commuting of death sentences. On the other hand Gough had not resolved any of the concerns of the native soldiers to any real extent. Again this was perhaps beyond his power. It was perhaps Gough's concern for the ordinary soldier, which was manifested throughout his career, which was his greatest strength at this time.

Eventually matters calmed down and a solution was found. Thus what had threatened to turn into a large-scale mutiny within the Company's native forces remained a relatively minor event that has largely been forgotten. Of the units that mutinied only the ringleaders were dealt with,

---

14 Such attempts were common throughout this period, even during the two Sikh Wars. In reality it appears that they had limited success. For example in September 1845, in the build up to the First Sikh War, a Sikh vakil (emissary) tried to tempt sepoys in the garrison at Ferozepur to desert to the Sikh cause. Despite his efforts only 30 sepoys, out of a garrison of 10,000, deserted. This was in reality little more than the regular rate of desertion. See British Library: Add MSS 40, 127, 391: George Broadfoot Papers, correspondence between George Broadfoot and Captain Peter Nicholson, 1845.
15 NAM: 8303–105, Gough Papers, Gough to George Gough, 30 June 1844.
16 NAM: 8303–105, Gough Papers, Gough to Lord Ellenborough, 26 February 1844.
17 NAM: 8303–105, Gough Papers, Gough to Lord Ellenborough, 26 February 1844.

the large majority being executed. The exception to this was the 34th regiment. Such was the level of disobedience that despite Gough's reluctance he found it necessary to disband the regiment in March 1844: reconstituted in 1846, the 34th Bengal Native Infantry would be disbanded again in 1857 after the Mangal Pandey incident. Although there is no account of what happened to the men it was clearly a necessary evil. Gough had hoped that it might be possible simply to transfer the men to other units. On reflection he decided that this might only serve to spread discontent to previously unaffected units. Indeed the example of disbanding the regiment was such that Gough believed it deterred further mutinies. In a letter to his son Gough claimed that, "I strongly remonstrated against the striking off the allowances, before the disaffection took place; when it did, I gave it as my opinion, no concession should be made by the Govt, until obedience was manifested."[18] In this he believed that the government had acted against his advice on each occasion. They had allowed, if not directly ordered, the allowances to be withdrawn, and had then been prepared to make concession to the 'mutineers' before order had been restored. Whilst Gough was displeased with the actions of the government in India he was pleased that on both points, and throughout his handling of events, he had received the full confidence and support of the HEIC Court of Directors.

There was also an unfortunate situation with regards to Sir Robert Dick, in overall command of the troops on the frontier that had mutinied. Gough had been critical of him writing to Lord Ellenborough on the 26 February 1844 that, "If Sir Robert Dick had acted with discretion he might, and in my opinion he would have succeeded [in supressing the 'mutiny']. He has however allowed the malcontents to appear in such strength as to render coercion of very doubtful effect."[19] Gough was also slightly concerned that Dick seemed to take the rumours that the 31st Foot would refuse to move against the 'mutineers' as fact. Unfortunately the mention of such opinions to Lord Ellenborough hardened the latter against Sir Robert Dick. Ellenborough removed Dick from his command, using a seldom-used privilege of the governor general. Gough felt this was too severe for the offence. Given the language of his letter to Lord Ellenborough this is somewhat surprising. However when Dick was removed from his command by Lord Ellenborough Gough complained strongly about it. This might have been the fact that Gough perceived this as an undermining of his authority. Ellenborough was in no doubt that, as he wrote to the Duke of Wellington, that Dick had to go: "really the errors of Sir R. Dick were so serious that we all felt we could not venture to leave him where he was."[20] Dick, feeling slighted by his removal, immediately sent in his resignation to the Horse Guards. This was refused, and by the time the decision reached India Lord Ellenborough had been replaced as governor general by Sir Henry Hardinge. Hardinge agreed with Gough's opinion that his removal had been too harsh a punishment and Dick was appointed to command the Cawnpore Division. Gough had perhaps acted injudiciously in so openly criticising a subordinate commander and one can forgive Ellenborough for acting in the way he did under the circumstances.

The solution to the problems with the Bengal Army had been to make Scinde part of the responsibility of the Bombay Army. Thus the problems in the Bengal Army were eased. At the same time the problems over the payment of batta were limited within the Bombay Army. It appears that the idea originated with Gough, and it was certainly he who first mentioned it to Lord Ellenborough. Whether or not the idea was mentioned to Gough by someone on his staff or in some private correspondence we have no record. Gough wrote that:

---

18   NAM: 8303–105, Gough Papers, Gough to George Gough, 30 June 1844.
19   NAM: 8303–105, Gough Papers, Gough to Lord Ellenborough 26 February 1844.
20   Ellenborough, Lord & Colchester, Lord (editor)*History of the India Administration of Lord Ellenborough in his correspondence with the Duke of Wellington*, (London: Richard Bentley and Son, 1874) p. 434.

I find I have not mentioned the only alternative I now see, to which I recommended in my public letter, namely ordering the Bombay troops to occupy the Scinde. [...] I sensibly feel this is degrading to the Bengal Army, but it would be far more degrading to recommend to the government concessions to a mutinous army. By no other name can it be called. Deeply humiliating as is this alternative, still, situated as our corps are, on the borders of an unfriendly nation [the Sikh Empire], with its mutinous army exercising almost unbounded sway-I really see no other measure that can be adopted to meet the present exigency.[21]

The problems of discipline had come at an unfortunate time. Gough was very well aware of the possibility of having to fight a campaign against the Sikhs. He was extremely concerned about military preparations near the border and the arrangements for such a campaign. One notable example was the magazine at Delhi. Along with the magazines at Cawnpore and Agra, it was key to the security of India. In regards to Delhi Gough concluded, "That it could not be worse placed is quite evident, that it cannot be made secure on its present site is equally evident, except at an enormous outlay."[22] The Duke of Wellington had indeed argued for some time that the magazine should be better placed so as, "to render it impregnable as a citadel."[23] However to do so was a difficult, and more importantly expensive, task, that would temporarily at least render the magazine useless during any operations against the Sikhs. Gough did however make it clear that he felt the threat to the magazine at Delhi came not from the Sikhs, who would be cut off from their retreat if such an attack was made, but from internal revolt. The Mutiny of 1857 would prove his judgement to be correct.

The recall of Ellenborough momentarily delayed any movement on this topic. Gough did press the matter with Ellenborough's successor Henry Hardinge. In September 1844 Gough wrote to Hardinge about the seriousness of this situation as he saw it.

The insecurity of the Delhi magazine, situated within the city, three miles from the military cantonment, and defended only by a plain brick wall of no strength has been long noticed, and measures have from time to time been under consideration for rendering it secure against any assault which the population, under any cause of excitement, might be induced to make upon it. All the measures yet proposed to attain this desirable end would, however, be attended with such an enormous expense that no steps have yet been taken to carry any of them into effect.[24]

Gough continued by recommending that the magazine be moved to Meerut or Ambala (Umbala) where he planned to gather a large military force to meet the Sikhs if necessary. He initially favoured Meerut. However as Gough became better acquainted with the position around Meerut he decided that Umbala would be a better solution and recommended this accordingly. This was still before the First Sikh War, and he recommended Ambala for its ability to quickly support the exposed towns of Ferozepore and Ludhiana, which he believed to be vulnerable should any Sikh attack take place. At the time there is no recorded response from Hardinge. However in the aftermath of the First Sikh War Hardinge took up the matter and concurred with the view Gough had expressed with regards to the magazine at Delhi which Hardinge said was in an "Objectionable position [...] and ought to be gradually abolished."[25]

---

21   NAM: 8303–105, Gough Papers, Gough to Lord Ellenborough, 27 February 1844.
22   NAM: 8303–105, Gough Papers, Gough to Lord Ellenborough, 22 February 1844.
23   Rait, *Gough*, Vol. I, p. 344.
24   Rait, *Gough*, Vol. I, pp. 346–347.
25   Rait, *Gough*, Vol. I, pp. 347–348.

The problem was that after the First Sikh War Hardinge did not see the sense in repositioning the magazine at Ambala. He believed that the defeat of the Sikh Army in the first war had altered the position to the extent that Ferozepore and Ludhiana were no longer at risk. Indeed they were to be used to support Lahore, which under the treaty that ended the First Sikh War was to be occupied for seven years. Although the Second Sikh War proved that this was a false assumption, at the conclusion of that and the annexation of the Sikh Empire, similar arguments could, and indeed were, made.

Despite the point being raised with three separate governor generals, Ellenborough, Hardinge and Dalhousie, and all three seeing that the position in Delhi was not only impractical but highly dangerous, no action was ever taken. The main reason was cost, although it would be unfair to not to mention that the two Sikh Wars contributed to no action being taken. After each conflict there was a period of retrenchment due to the cost of the war. Once the Sikhs had been defeated there appeared to be no great urgency. It was only when the mutiny broke out in 1857 that the failure to support Gough's decision as to the movement of the magazine to Ambala proved costly from a strategic point of view and from an economic one required greater expense in fighting the mutineers. As Sir Robert Rait commented:

> Soldiers who fought in India in those troublous (sic) times [the 1857 Mutiny] will bear ample evidence to the effect which the removal of the magazine to Umballa [Ambala] would, in all probability, have produced upon the history of the Mutiny. It would not have prevented the seizure of Delhi, but it would have made the success of the rebels less important and the subsequent siege much less costly. Nearly fourteen years had elapsed since Lord Gough had asked Lord Ellenborough to sanction that removal, and nine since he had suggested it to Lord Dalhousie. On the Commander-in-Chief who was in office from 1843 to 1849 no responsibility can be said to rest, if the Commander-in-Chief who was in office in 1857 found his task unnecessarily dangerous and perplexing.[26]

Whether the above statement is entirely accurate, and the removal of the magazine would have altered the course of the mutiny, is open to debate. However the account of Gough's efforts to move the magazine is mentioned to give evidence to the fact that Gough was active in his role as commander-in-chief. It helps to show that he was alert to the dangers, and attempted to introduce necessary reforms. That he was not able to achieve this was due to the same problem that has afflicted generations of army commanders, namely that strategic planning and logistics were subject to economic pressures. It is very difficult to see Gough's failure to get action out of three different governor generals as anything else. This is particularly apparent when one considers that they accepted his basic argument about the unsuitable nature of the Magazine at Delhi.

Although the arrival of a new governor general brought no joy for Gough on the movement of the magazine, it did bring much needed changes in the treatment of the troops. Hardinge, an experienced soldier, could as a new governor general make concessions in this regard that Ellenborough could not. The latter would have looked weak whereas the former looked like an active new appointee anxious to deal with the situation. A revised set of Articles of War for the army were introduced which saw an increase in sepoy pay, a return of privileges and certain allowances made for service away from their families. At the same time the ease with which 'mutiny' had so easily been contemplated and enacted required an answer. It was in this light that flogging was reintroduced in the Company Army. Gough supported this move and whilst the use of 'the lash' had never been something he was afraid of using, he had also acted with a sensibility around it. He used in primarily as a deterrent, but in his time commanding the 87th he had not been afraid to use it when required for the good of the discipline of the battalion as a whole.[27]

Yet despite the reintroduction of flogging, the reforms that Gough and Hardinge put in place were by in large to the benefit of the native soldier. Gough had wanted to go even further and in some regards urged equal treatment between European and native soldiers. This was particularly true in the case of kit. For example, Gough wrote to Hardinge that, "I do not see upon what just grounds one [the European] should have a greatcoat given him free of expense, whilst the other [native soldier], with infinitely smaller pay, should be forced to pay for it."[28] Gough's desire to see a fairer treatment of European and native soldiers was not only paternalistic but also practical. British India needed its native soldiers and a disaffected army was a great danger, as events of 1857 were to prove.

Although he and Gough were able to introduce such measures, Hardinge does seem to have been somewhat disaffected by the state of the army and his level of influence over it. On 18 March he wrote to Walter James, his stepson, "With the army I can do very little. The force cannot be reduced whilst affairs are in their present condition in the Punjaub [sic.] & the com. in ch. [Gough] who is 1,000 miles off, renders any communication on reforms & alterations a very uphill task."[29] Yet despite this they were able to institute some reforms and one wonders what lies behind Hardinge's comments. It is interesting to compare it with Gough's comments in a letter to Hardinge the tone of which makes clear that Gough believed they had the potential to make an important impact on the army. In April, almost a month after Hardinge's comments, Gough wrote to Hardinge congratulating him on "such just and enlarged views on our Military Policy, views that, when carried into effect, will rest on the popularity of the military profession, banish every embryo seed of discontent, and make the Indian Army as loyal as they have ever proved themselves brave."[30]

Gough's opinions in this regard were wildly optimistic and perhaps illustrate a character flaw in his understanding of wider issues with native soldiers. It was a flaw of his paternalistic view of soldiers, and belief that they would appreciate such reforms for what they are: in his eyes an act of paternalistic kindness. However to many a soldier such reforms in pay and conditions were seen as either restoration of conditions or no more than they deserved. Thus Gough was in this sense over-optimistic and Hardinge had a more practical view and realised that greater reform was required.

Perhaps this affair is also an early indication of Hardinge's desire to take a very active role in the command of the army. As an experienced soldier and military administrator, this would be entirely understandable. It may be that his aim was to help rather than supersede the authority of Gough as commander-in-chief. It is also relevant that he remarked on the distance between himself as governor general based in Calcutta and Gough in command of the army based near the northern border with the Sikhs. It is difficult to know what to make of this comment. Perhaps it was an indication that Hardinge desired to have the commander-in-chief closer at hand and therefore more easily under his influence. In a time when communication and transportation in India was still quite limited one can see the sense of such a point of view. However at the same time if anyone was to move during this period, given the present emergency, it should surely be the governor general not the commander-in-chief. Given that, by the time of this letter, matters in the Punjab seemed to indicate that military action would shortly occur it would have been foolish, and left Gough open

27 Singh, *The Letters of Viscount Hardinge*, p. 113. This is a copy of a letter to Hardinge's stepson Walter. This includes details of the new order and the reactions to it. Hardinge is clear that Gough supports the idea.
28 NAM: 8303–105, Gough Papers, Gough to Hardinge, 14 April 1845.
29 Singh, Bawa Satinder (editor) *The Letters of the First Viscount Hardinge of Lahore to Lady Hardinge and Sir Walter and Lady James, 1844–1847* (London: Office of the Royal Historical Society, University College London, 1986), p. 55.
30 NAM: 8303–105, Gough Papers, Gough to Hardinge, 14 April 1845.

to justifiable criticism, if he had been over 1,000 miles away from the front at a time when he was expected to lead the army in a campaign.

Perhaps this is an example of an officer, Hardinge, coming to India and not appreciating the difference in duties between commander-in-chief of the British Army and the Indian commander-in-chief in India. If so he was not the first and certainly not the last to fail to appreciate the difference. In Britain such an officer was an administrator leading the army from the War Office. In India a commander-in-chief had such responsibilities but also a duty to command the army in the field and to be a fighting commander. Here we see an early indication of the tension that existed between governor general and commander-in-chief, based upon the nature of their positions and upon aspects of control rather than any personal tension. It should also be noted that both men were under pressure with the impending conflict in the Punjab utmost in their minds.

The Sikh problem was one which Gough was aware of. The last major threat to British India would have to be dealt with at some point. In this sense, the fact that the reforms had at least for the time being halted the threat of 'mutiny' and obtained in the short term the loyalty of the native army was an important factor. Indeed during the years leading up to the First Sikh War it was a strong possibility that the Sikhs would attack before the British were prepared, and thus the loyalty of the army was vital. As early as March 1844 Gough was making preparations for the coming conflict, on paper at least.[31] It needs to be remembered that at this point Gough had been active as commander-in-chief for barely seven months, much of which had been taken up with operations in Gwalior and the consequences thereof. This point really does need to be emphasised as does the point that he was still relatively new to India. Although officially appointed to India 1837, he had spent considerable time outside of the country serving in China. Even on his return he spent almost a year without an appointment and little practical experience of command in India.

The coming conflict with the Sikhs would test Gough's ability, and highlight his character flaws and weaknesses. Yet the magnitude of the challenge that Gough and British India were about to face can all too easily be forgotten. The Sikhs were not only the last independent state to threaten them, they were perhaps the strongest threat that British India had ever faced. Before turning to examine the course of the conflicts with the Sikh State it is therefore first helpful to understand something of the Sikhs, both as a race, a religion, and a nation.

---

31 NAM: 8303–105, Gough Papers, Gough to Ellenborough, 5 March 1844. Gough discusses some of the preparations in this letter but also alludes to previous discussions of this nature.

Colonel George Gough, the father of Hugh Gough. (Private collection)

Hugh Gough's mother Letitia Gough, née Bunbury. (Private collection)

Gough's brother William, the third son of George and Letitia Gough. William was a major in the 6th Foot and served extensively in the Peninsular War. He was drowned off Kinsale in 1822 when returning from Canada with his regiment. (Private collection)

Sir James Henry Craig. Commander of the expedition to Cape Colony in which the young Gough got his first taste of action.

Arthur Wellesley, 1st Duke of Wellington, was the dominant force in the British army for the first half of the 19th century. His relationship with Gough was often strained.

General Sir Thomas Graham, 1st Baron Lynedoch. An underrated general whose victory at Barrosa deserves greater praise than it receives.

General Graham directing his troops at the Battle of Barrosa.

The Battle of Barrosa, 5 March 1811.

Siege of Tarifa. The painting depicts the French attack on 31 December 1811.

This image is very hard to date. Although Gough looks quite old, the absence of the whiskers that were a constant feature of his old age makes one wonder. There is a similar engraving from 1842 on which the painting might have been based. It might be that the painting is set a little later, and there is a suggestion that Gough's uniform is that of a Colonel of the Horse Guards and thus after 1855. (Private collection)

The Daoguang Emperor was a curious individual. The version of events his 'courtiers' reported to him often meant that he was a deluded individual.

Nemesis in battle against Chinese warships on 7 January 1841.

Negotiations on board HMS *Wellesley* on 4 July 1840, the day before the capture of Chusan.

The destruction of Opium being overseen by Commissioner Lin in 1839.

On the right of the painting the steam powered iron warship *Nemesis* can be seen.

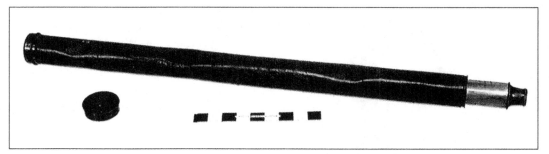

Made by John Gilbert of Tower Hill, London circa 1840, this telescope accompanied Gough to India, and was presumably used during his campaigns both there and in China. (National Army Museum, NAM 1966-05-14)

British troops being unloaded before the advance on Canton 24 May 1841.

The British bombardment of Canton from the surrounding heights, 29 May 1841.

Brigadier General Armine Mountain.
His support for Gough during the
First Anglo-China War was greatly
appreciated by the former.

Sir William
Parker developed
a good working
relationship with
Gough, providing
great logistical and
firepower support
for the campaign on
land.

A Chinese scroll recording the *Nemesis* and another British ship.

Sir Henry Pottinger, who managed to work well with Gough and Parker, and was reluctant to overrule them.

Boats loaded with soldiers being towed by a steamer ready for the attack on Amoy, August 1841.

The 18th Foot (Royal Irish) in action at Amoy on 26 August 1841.

The fleet preparing for the assault on Chinhai.

The Battle of Chinhai, 10 October 1841.

The 18th and 49th Foot attacking a 'joss house' at Chapo, 18 May 1842.

Commissioner Lin Zexu. Although an extremely accomplished and remarkable individual, the modern day hero worship of the man is somewhat unseemly.

Troops being landed in preparation for the assault on the west gate of Chinkiang.

The aftermath of the battle of Chinkiang, where the Tartar soldiers chose to end their own lives and those of their families, rather than be captured.

A portrait of Gough in military uniform, surprising for the fact that his trademark whiskers are missing. Circa 1842. (Private collection)

John Cam Hobhouse, 1st Baron Broughton. Served twice as President of the Board of Control from April 1835 to August 1841 and then from July 1846 to February 1852.

Sir Robert Peel. Twice Prime Minister, from December 1834 to April 1835 and from August 1841 to June 1846, and one of the leading British politicians of the 19th century.

Edward Law, 1st Earl of Ellenborough, was Governor-General of India from 1842-1844.

The Battle of Maharajpore. Battle scene depicting the death of Major General Sir Charles Horace Churchill.

Henry Hardinge. An excellent soldier who, often inadvertently, caused Gough many problems.

Gough, circa 1845.
(Private collection)

Ranjit Singh's reform of the Sikh military produced a formidable fighting force.

The exact nature of Lal Singh's actions and motivations during the First Anglo-Sikh war will probably never be known.

Hugh Gough in Staff
uniform circa 1845.
(Private collection)

The Battle of Mudki.

A scene from the Battle of Ferozeshah.

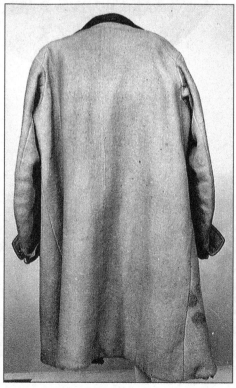

One of Gough's non-uniform 'White Fighting Coats', believed to have been worn during the First-Anglo Sikh War, and possibly the Second Anglo-Sikh War. Although now faded and stained, this was indeed once white in colour. (National Army Museum, NAM 1960-03-155).

Frederick Haines was a
loyal supporter of Gough.
Haines would himself
become Commander-in-
Chief in India.

Tej Singh, a Sikh Army commander
who has been dogged by reports of
collusion with the British during the
First Anglo-Sikh War.

Herbert Edwardes was in
many ways a talented and
impressive individual. He
played a vital role in The
Second Anglo-Sikh war.

Chatar Singh was the father of Sher Singh and an important player in the Second Anglo-Sikh War.

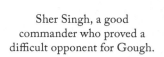

Sher Singh, a good commander who proved a difficult opponent for Gough.

James Andrew Broun-Ramsay, 1st Marquess of Dalhousie. A remarkable man, but ever the politician.

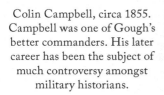

Colin Campbell, circa 1855. Campbell was one of Gough's better commanders. His later career has been the subject of much controversy amongst military historians.

Brigadier General Charles Robert Cureton was a remarkable man and one of Gough's finest commanders. His death at Ramnagar was a great blow to the army.

Acting Brigadier John Pennycuick deserves some of the blame for the losses at Chillianwala, but died a 'noble' death leading forward the men of his own regiment the 24th Foot.

A plaque to the memory of Brigadier Pennycuick and his son, who died by his side at Chillianwala.

The Battle of Chillianwala.

Monument to the Battle of Chillianwala.

The Battle of Gujrat.

Walter Raleigh Gilbert.
Despite the reservations
of others, Gough held
Gilbert in high regard.

Gough in triumphant mode at the end of the Second Anglo-Sikh War, painted c 1850 by an unknown artist. A copy of this portrait hangs today in the entrance hall of the Radisson Blu St Helens hotel that was once Hugh Gough's home. (National Army Museum, NAM 1999-02-24-1).

Awarded to staff and field officers largely, although not exclusively, for service in the Peninsular War. Gough received clasps for Vittoria, Nivelle, Barrosa and Talavera. (National Army Museum, NAM 1966-10-27)

Sometimes incorrectly called the Mahrajpoor Star, but was awarded to those who also fought at Punniar. The only difference is the inscription on the silver disk in the middle of the medal which has the name of either of the battles. (National Army Museum, NAM 1966-10-27)

The medal for the First China War, although obviously it was just called the China War Medal at the time. Originally the medal was to have been issued only by the EIC to its officers and men. However it was issued by the British Government on the orders of Queen Victoria to all ranks of the army and navy. No clasp was ever issued for the First China War, so it is unclear why one appears to be missing. (National Army Museum, NAM 1966-10-27)

The Sutlej Medal was issued for the First Anglo-Sikh War. The first battle a soldier participated in was engraved on the reverse, hence no clasp for Mudki. Somewhat surprisingly, given that he was not there, Gough is awarded a bar for Aliwal. The National Army Museum assured the author this was the medal awarded to Hugh Gough. (National Army Museum, NAM 1966-10-27)

The Punjab Medal was issued for the Second Anglo-Sikh War. In a first for a British campaign medal it was issued to those troops who had been present in the Punjab but not taken part in any fighting. In this case it was obviously issued without claps. (National Army Museum, NAM 1966-10-27)

The Knight's Cross of the Royal and Distinguished Order of Charles III of Spain. Awarded to Hugh Gough for service in the Peninsular. (National Army Museum, NAM 1966-10-27)

'Miniature Medals' of the Army Gold Cross and the Knight's Cross.
(National Army Museum, NAM 1966-10-27)

The gold leaf in the centre of the broach is said to be taken from the eagle that was captured at Barossa by the 87th Foot under Gough's command. (National Army Museum, NAM 1966-10-27)

This portrait of Hugh Gough's wife, Frances, shows her at around 56 years of age, painted c.1844 by an unknown artist. She is wearing the Mahrajpore Star, which she was awarded for coming under enemy fire whilst accompanying the army during the Gwalior Campaign. (National Army Museum, NAM 1997-08-20-1).

Portrait of Hugh Gough by Sir
Francis Grant, PRA. Although it
depicts Gough commanding during
the Second Anglo-Sikh War, Gough
actually sat for the portrait in 1852.

Miniature, watercolour on ivory, of Gough
by unknown artist. Although listed as
circa 1850 this does not look like the face
of a seventy year old man, and might
perhaps be earlier than that. (National
Army Museum, NAM 1979-09-23).

An 1850 daguerreotype of Hugh Gough, illustrating that he was still a physically impressive looking man at the age of seventy. (Private collection)

Hugh Gough in civilian clothing wearing his Army Gold Cross. (Private collection)

Whilst the modern addition to the property either side can clearly be seen, the main house is much as it would have been in Gough's day. The author was informed by the management that it was apparently the first property in Ireland to have a preservation order placed on both the exterior and interior. (Courtesy of Radisson Blu Group)

The front of St Helen's, now a hotel in the Radisson Blu chain, once owned by Hugh Gough. Taken by the author on his 2013 visit to Ireland.

Lough Cutra Castle, County Galway, purchased by Hugh Gough in 1854. He seldom visited it and his son George seems to have had more to do with than he ever did.

The Coat of Arms of Viscount Gough of Goojerat and of Limerick. (Private collection)

This image appeared in the *Illustrated London* News on 6 March 1880. It gives some sense of the significance that was placed on the unveiling of the statue.

The statue of Lord Gough by John Henry Foley as it stands today in the grounds of Chillingham Castle, Northumberland.

Part 6

First Anglo-Sikh War

The Sikhs

The Sikhs are an extraordinary people. Although that great chronicle of life in British India, Rudyard Kipling, is rather out of fashion nowadays his comment in one of his short stories that, "There is no land like the Punjab. There are no people like the Sikhs", still rings true.[1] The Sikh Empire was by far and away the strongest force the British had to face during the conquest of British India. Sikh culture and religion, which are difficult to separate, had created a powerful force, ideologically, administratively and ultimately militarily. Surrounded on all sides by potential enemies, a strength and unity had developed. It was not perfect, and disagreements and personal agendas remained, but on the whole a powerful force emerged over the centuries leading up to the two Anglo-Sikh Wars. Sikh power often fluctuated, but they remained a potent enemy for anyone. Often it needed a powerful leader, either under the Gurus or a military leader like Ranjit Singh, to unite the Sikhs. Although a detailed account of the Sikh nation and its military is beyond the scope of this work, it will prove useful to provide some background. So doing will see the power of the Sikh Empire placed in an appropriate context and emphasise the difficulty of the task that Gough faced.[2]

To most historians, the strength of the Sikh Empire was its military prowess and warrior culture. However this is to miss the much wider strength of the Sikhs and ultimately the Sikh Empire, in terms of administration, culture and religion. They were in many regards an oppressed people who had sought military strength to defend themselves and maintain their culture and way of life. They were not originally a nation or even a people in the defined sense. Sikhism started in the Punjab as a religious movement. Indeed the name Sikh is simply translated as 'disciple' or 'learner'. The origins of the Sikhs date back to Guru Nanak (1469–1538). It is perhaps not surprising that the area for this new interpretation of faith was in the region where Hinduism met Islam. The basic tenant of the teaching was that both Hinduism and Islam were 'confused' on their teachings of a divine creator

---

1   Kipling, Rudyard, *Rudyard Kipling's Collected Short Stories*, Vol. IV (London: The Folio Society, 2005), p. 49. This is taken from the short story *A Sahibs' War*, first published in Kipling's *Traffics and Discoveries* (London: Macmillan & Co, 1904).

2   There are many books dealing with the strength of the Sikhs as a military force, indeed too many to mention. A very interesting modern account is Amandeep Singh Madra & Parmjit Singh, *Warrior Saints: Four Centuries of Sikh Military History*, Vol. I (London; Kashi House, 2013). Also Patwant Singh & Jyoti Rai, *Empire of the Sikhs: The Life and Times of Mahraja Ranjit Singh* (London: Peter Owen Publishers, 2008), is an interesting and useful account of the rise of the Sikh people under their most effective leader. For the purely military side Ian Heath, *The Sikh Army 1799–1849* (Oxford: Osprey Publishing, 2005) and Bajwa, Fauja Singh, *Military System of the Sikhs during the period 1799–1849* (Delhi: Motilal Banarasidas, 1964), are a very helpful starting point. To understand the Anglo-Sikh relationship throughout the years of Empire see Phillip Mason, *A Matter of Honour: An Account of the Indian Army its Officers and Men* (London: Macmillan Publishers Ltd, 1986). Also both George Bruce, *Six Battles for India* (Calcutta: Rupa & Co, 1969) & H. C. B. Cook, *The Sikh Wars 1845–6 & 1848–9* (London: Leo Cooper, 1975) each give a chapter to explaining briefly the history and nature of the Sikhs.

and that to separate the spiritual and the secular was wrong. Nanak taught that the two were in effect the same, and encouraged the principles of truthfulness, equality, fidelity, meditation, self-control and purity. To this, over time, were also attached ideas of fighting against tyranny which in turn promoted a peculiar kind of militarism. From this developed over the centuries the Five Ks. This was introduced by the 10th Guru Gobind Singh (1666–1708) who did much to formalise and develop the faith and culture of the Sikhs. The Five Ks are to be adhered to by all 'baptised' Sikhs as means of identification and to remind the individual of their duty and responsibilities. It was also Gobind Singh who introduced the name Singh, 'Lion', to be used by male initiates and Kaur, 'Princess', by female initiates.

The five articles of faith are the *Kesh*: the uncut hair tied and wrapped under a Sikh turban sometimes referred to as a *Dastar*. *Kangha*: a wooden comb, usually worn under the turban, which symbolises discipline and cleanliness. *Katchera*: cotton undergarments that also had a military value in that they were looser fitting and enabled greater movement on the battlefield. They were tied with a draw string. The idea of the garment was to encourage self-control, and it is said that the idea of the drawstring was that untying it gave the individual time to think about their actions. *Kara*: an iron or, more commonly, steel bracelet which acts as a symbol of restrain and reminds the wearer of the omnipresence of God. *Kirpan*: a sword which symbolises dignity and the struggle against tyranny and oppression. This varies in size, and in modern times is often more like a dagger. However historical accounts show that in the past Sikhs were heavily armed with many weapons adorning their turbans and attire.[3] It is easy to regard the aforementioned as symbols of a religion. That would be slightly to misunderstand their significance. Rather than symbols they are reminders to a Sikh of his responsibilities, of the decisions he has made, and path he has chosen. In that sense they are far more powerful than mere symbols. Such a constant reminder of the path they had chosen was particularly significant to the Sikhs when surrounded by Hindus, Muslims, and later Christians, and their religious and cultural ways. This in turn also led to a militaristic spirit, more in terms of a defence of culture and religious freedom than aggression or territorial aggrandise-ment. This was defined by Guru Gobind Singh as 'Dharam Yudh' or a war of righteousness. Guru Gobind Singh also wrote *Dasam Granth* which was the military scripture of the Sikhs. Again, this was more in the terms of defence of the Sikh people, but it would be wrong to think that territorial aggrandisement was completely absent.

The Khalsa, translated as the 'pure', were those who followed the Five Ks. This was also the name of the Sikh Army that would emerge and be a key force in the forming of the Sikh Empire. Over the years, Sikh teaching was resented by Muslims and Hindus. The former were the greater problem for the time being as the dominant religion of the Mughal Empire. The Mughals were largely suspicious of the Sikhs and their hostility saw several Gurus allegedly murdered on the orders of various Mughal emperors. Indeed it is said that the Guru Gobind Singh was presented with the severed head of his father by the Mughal emperor. This understandably gave him a strong desire to free the Sikhs of Mughal influence. Although prepared to use military force, his was a more tactful way.

An interesting figure in the Sikh military struggle during this period is Banda Singh Bahadur. Born Lachman Dev, he was a convert to Sikhism after a meeting with Guru Gobind Singh. His new beliefs led him into battle against the Mughal Empire. In 1709 he captured the Mughal city of Samana, in a large-scale slaughter that saw perhaps as many as 10,000 dead Mughals. This was an important conquest as it was a major source of minted coins for the Empire. Although he led an army of Sikhs, he was often supported by Hindus who feared the Mughals more than the Sikhs at this stage. The following year he took Sirhind and became its ruler. Although a strong ruler he did

---

3   I am grateful to the Leicester-based Sikh scholar Gurinder Singh Mann for pointing this out to me.

at the same time practice the principles of his faith and gave the land over to the peasant farmers to operate giving them a level of dignity and self-reliance. Later in that year, when Banda Singh was away from the city it was attacked an overrun by the advanced guard of the Mughal Army. Banda Singh managed to recapture the city but the arrival of further Mughal troops, around 60,000 of them, led to another siege. Although Banda Singh managed to escape it was the start of a difficult period for the Sikhs, but one which served to galvanise the Sikh population to action. Although there were considerable Sikh victories during this period, they were largely of a hit and run nature, and Banda Singh had been forced to retreat into the foothills of the Himalayas. In December 1715 Banda Singh was captured after having been starved into submission. There was mass slaughter of the Sikhs. Banda Singh was captured and taken to Delhi where it is said after three months of torture he was finally executed in a gruesome manner.[4]

Until the mid 18th century the Sikhs were largely under the power of the Mughal Empire. When the Persians invaded in 1738 the Mughals had been unable to resist them. Delhi had fallen and although ultimately the Persians would withdraw the decline of the Mughal Empire had begun. The Persians carried off much of the wealth of the Empire. Included amongst this treasure was a very famous diamond. On seeing it Nadir Shah of Persia exclaimed 'Koh-i-Noor', which translated means 'Mountain of Light'. The diamond, which we will read more of later on, has been known as the Koh-i-Noor ever since.

There followed a series of Afghan invasions between 1747 and 1769, which the Mughals had difficulty in combatting. In was into this void that the Sikhs and the Khalsa moved. As the people most at threat from such an invasion, it was a natural act of self-preservation. However it was more than that. It was the emergence of the Sikhs as a power. It was the demonstration not only of military might and professionalism but of unity. Even then the Sikhs were not able to break entirely from outside control. As the Mughal Empire declined, the Hindu Mahratta Empire was beginning to grow. The Afghans were also a powerful force. Often the Sikhs resorted to hit and run operations again, known as 'Dhai Phat' or two and half strikes, which brought them wealth, weapons, horses, and much needed supplies.

Although the Sikhs had developed a strong military and a good reputation they remained a loose association of Misls or confederacies under the *Buddha Dal* (older guard) and *Taruna Dal* (younger guard). The period from 1748 to 1799 is that of the Sikh Confederacy. During this period the 12 Sikh Misls, sovereign states, joined together in a confederation largely based on self-defence. They held bi-annual meetings. Each Sikh community was largely drawn upon feudal lines with its own chief. At the same time there was a degree of democracy. As the Swiss adventurer Antoine Polier wrote it was an 'aristocratic republic'.[5] Under Jassa Singh Ahluwalia, leader of the *Buddha Dal*, the Khalsa grew in strength, but although a force to be reckoned with in the Punjab it could still not contest with the Mughals, Mahrattas, or the main Afghan army. The problem was that there was still too much independence of spirit and it was only when danger threatened that the Misls would even consider banding together to support each other. For the majority of the time they might even be fighting each other for influence and territory. During the period of the Sikh Confederacy territorial gains were made at times, however there was an inability for the most part to maintain them. What was required was a strong leader to unite the Sikhs and bring the people together. For this the delicate balance of strength, tact, ruthlessness, diplomacy and cunning was required. Ultimately the Sikhs found this in Ranjit Singh, who would become known as the 'Lion of the Punjab'. Born in 1780, by 1799 he had already captured Lahore and taken a large step in uniting

---

4   <http://sikhcybermuseum.com/history/sikhmassacredehli1716.htm>.
5   Singh, Khushwant, *A History of the Sikhs: 1469–1838* (London: Oxford University Press, 2004), Vol. I, p. 165.

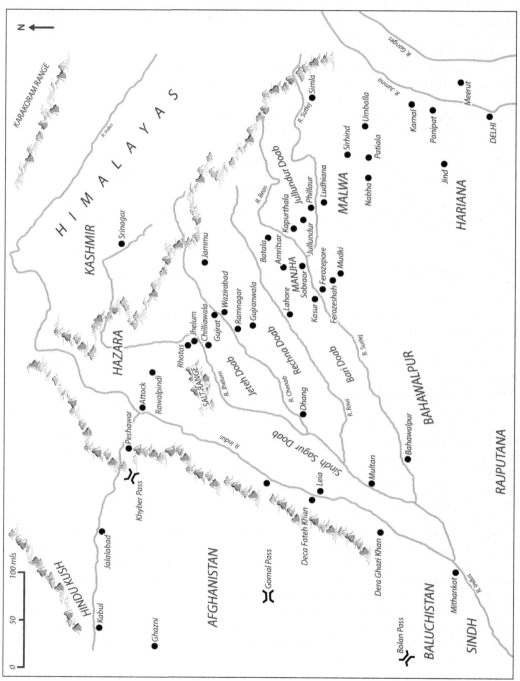

Map 9 The Sikh State.

the Sikhs. There was now a change from hit and run raids, and a loose confederation to a strong army and a central authority.

When in 1796 the Afghans under Zaman Shah Durrani had invaded the Punjab, those Sikhs not under Ranjit Singh's direct control fled to the hills in anticipation of using hit and run raids upon the Afghans until they withdrew, something they had done many times before. However Ranjit Singh had decided by 1798 that the time was right to stand and fight. He held the numerically superior Afghans at bay until a rebellion in Kabul and a Persian invasion of Afghanistan forced Zaman Shah Durrani to return. After this Ranjit Singh moved in to fill the void and after a brief siege took the important city of Lahore in July 1799. It was an important moment in the development of Sikh power. In April 1801 Ranjit Singh declared himself Maharajah of the Punjab, after taking Amritsar.

Ranjit Singh was said to be an unimpressive man to look at. Due to a childhood incident he had only one eye. He could neither read nor write but was an intelligent man who had an inquiring mind. He was also shrewd. Despite his religious upbringing he had a great love of wine, women, and song. His sexual appetites might have been exaggerated in the aftermath of his death. However the view that he drank heavily and to excess seems to be accurate. A story exists that suggests his favourite drink was one made of orange spirit, crushed emeralds, and brandy. It was said that it was best to drink it down quickly, avoiding contact with the lips which it was said it had a habit to burn if it touched!

Ranjit Singh was quite prepared to use 'outsiders' if they gave him something he needed. For example his foreign minister Azizuddin was a Muslim, his Prime Minister Dhyan Singh was a Hindu, and his finance minister Dina Nath was a Brahmin. In no area was this use of outsiders greater than in the training of his army in European tactics. Ranjit Singh had witnessed both the Mahratta and British armies at close quarters when the Second Anglo-Mahratta War spread into the Punjab. It is said that Ranjit Singh, accompanied by a small bodyguard, disguised himself to move amongst the two armies. What he witnessed there and in observing the two forces in battle was the need for his own forces to adopt European training and tactics. The Mahratta's had already adopted this to an extent, but it was British forces, both European and sepoy, that he wished to emulate.[6] The other factor was the might of the Akali Nihangs who were the religious military order of Guru Gobind Singh. They were the 'Knight errants' who would lay down their lives for the Khalsa Commonwealth. However their tactics were not to the liking of Maharaja Ranjit Singh, perhaps because they bordered on the 'fanatical' rather than the professional, and were seen by some as being antiquated. Adopting European ideals allowed Ranjit Singh to move past this.

There was at this time a slight incident with the British. It stemmed largely from the definition of the border between British influence and the Sikh Empire as it was now becoming. In September 1808 negotiations began between Ranjit Singh and the British representative Charles Metcalfe, a 23-year-old political officer who had been attached to General Lake's force during the Mahratta conflict and would later become governor general of India. The tact and cunning of Ranjit Singh is illustrated by one incident during the negotiations when Metcalfe alluded to an area that was not entirely under Sikh influence but being claimed by them. Metcalfe awoke the next morning to find Ranjit Singh and a large part of his army gone. On their return Ranjit Singh had captured Faridkot, Maler Kotla, Patiala, Ambala, and Shahabad, settling the question as to whether or not he controlled the area!

In December 1808 the negotiations resumed. The British were concerned with keeping areas south of the Sutlej River, including Sikh communities, out of Ranjit Singh's hands as a buffer between British possessions and the Sikh Empire. A British base at Ludhiana near the border

6   Bruce, *Six Battles for India*, pp. 34–35.

was to be established and a force under Major General David Ochterlony was despatched to the region.[7] Ranjit Singh was continually asked to move his troops back beyond the Sutlej. Only when Ochterlony's force was in striking distance was the threat of military force used. Ranjit Singh refused to comply and readied his army to meet any coming threat. There was reluctance on the part of the British to use force. This was not so much to do with the strong impression made by the Sikh Army but more to do with a feeling that this was unnecessary and indeed wrong. Lieutenant General George Hewett, the commander-in-chief in India, wrote that the idea of invading Sikh territory made him feel, "considerable embarrassment and uneasiness."[8]

What happened next is open to debate, however one of the more reliable accounts tells the story as follows. Metcalfe and his troops were stationed at Amritsar, the Sikh holy place and the site of the Harmandir Sahib or 'Golden Temple'. The British sepoys were parading to celebrate the Muslim festival of Muharram. Given the sensitivity of Sikhs towards Muslim practices and the fact that they had suffered at their hands for some many years, it is not surprising that the local Sikhs were deeply upset at this. A force of several thousand Sikhs, with drums beating and flags flying, moved forward to attack the sepoys for this affront, which was even more shocking for happening so near to such a holy site. The Sikhs who attacked were largely the Akali Nihangs, often called simply the Akali in contemporary sources, under their leader Akali Phula Singh. It was such men who had been at the heart of the hit and run raids performed over the previous years. There were little over 200 British sepoys at Amritsar. However, in keeping with the prescribed tactic of the age for meeting native forces in India, they advanced to attack the Sikhs. The sepoys launched a determined and disciplined attack and repelled the Sikhs. Ranjit Singh arrived on the scene in an attempt to prevent bloodshed but was only in time to witness the Nihang driven off at bayonet point.[9]

The reason such a story has been included in our narrative is for the consequences it had upon Ranjit Singh and as a consequence upon the Sikhs. Metcalfe, having now demonstrated British power, was able to obtain the deal he wished and Ranjit Singh removed his forces from the area that had been in question and returned all the towns he had captured during the 'negotiations' save for Faridkot. The fact that such a move was a humiliation for Ranjit Singh is illustrated by the rise in dissent amongst Sikh chiefs after this event. However it taught Ranjit Singh an important lesson. He had already seen the necessity to reform his army and the tactical superiority of European tactics and drill convinced him that this was the way to go. One can imagine the impact on him that seeing some of his finest and most devout warriors driven off by an enemy outnumbered 10 to one had. Yet his practical nature and pragmatism prevented him from panicking, merely alerting him to his need to improve his own forces.

One particularly point he learnt was in regards to the need to move away from an over-reliance upon cavalry. To this end he wanted to adopt European infantry tactics, weapons, training and drill. His plan was to go even further than the Mahrattas had gone, the latter having adopted elements of such warfare as they thought best. By instead creating in effect European troops in terms of drill, weapons and uniform, and combining them with the characteristics of discipline, determination and tenacity that the Sikh religion imbued, Ranjit Singh would create a unique and extremely powerful army. The growth in infantry was dramatic. For example in 1809 he had barely 1,500 infantry in disparate and relatively unorganised units. By 1821 he had 10,000 infantry divided amongst 14 battalions of around eight to 10 companies. This was his regular army, and

7   It is interesting to note that although Ochterlony was a British general he was born in Boston, Massachusetts in 1758, thus before the American Revolution.

8   Bruce, George, *Six Battles for India: The Anglo-Sikh Wars; 1845–6, 1848–9* (Calcutta: Rupa & Co, 1969), p. 43.

9   Bruce, *Six Battles for India*, pp. 43–44.

was designed to be a field army. For the time being, irregular infantry were being used to maintain garrisons. At the same time Ranjit Singh developed a fascination with artillery. He established his own foundries and works in Lahore in 1807 and would copy designs and innovations from European weapons. Many of the guns were of poor quality to begin with as designers and manufactures developed their skills. The major problem was to create the quality and sustainability of the barrels. Ranjit Singh was also not averse to 'acquiring' guns wherever he could. It is said that if he heard of a town or fort that had an interesting gun he would venture there with his army and either take the gun by force or demand the weapon as his price for sparing the town from attack. It was not just the guns themselves but limbers, carriages and means of transportation that he started to develop.

To train such an army he needed soldiers skilled in European tactics.[10] With the ending of the Napoleonic Wars there were a considerable number of experienced soldiers looking for gainful employment. This was particularly so of the defeated French Army, where many of Napoleon's officers were either not wanted or not welcome anymore. There were four men who were largely, although not exclusively, responsible for the development of the Sikh Army during this period.[11] They had also been in the service of Napoleon, and whilst Jean-Francois Allard and Claude Auguste Court were French born, both Jean Baptise Ventura and Paolo Di Avitabile were of Italian birth. They had all been carefully interviewed and judged by Ranjit Singh before their employment, and he was convinced he had the best men for the job. Such men were needed not only to drill and train units but also to train Sikh leaders who could ultimately replace them. Ventura, who had been a colonel in Napoleon's army, seems to have had overall responsibility for training the army, and was indeed overall commander of the Fauj-i-Khas. The latter freely translates as 'model corps', and was an elite part of the Sikh Army, consisting of four infantry battalions, two regiments of cavalry and two troops of artillery. It was in that sense a 'model' for what Ranjit Singh wanted the rest of the army to be.

Avitabile had partial responsibility for the artillery alongside Court: the former responsible for the gun foundries and arsenal, and the latter for the training of the artillery and organising them along European lines. Avitabile also assisted with the training of the infantry. The infantry were equipped with European muskets, some French, some British or East India Company patterns. There were even some Baker Rifles issued to the elite Sikh units. Uniforms were largely of European design, including some idiosyncratic touches For instance the Fauj-i-Khas standard included the Napoleonic Imperial Eagle with the letter 'N' displayed. As the drill book for the Sikh Army was a translation of that used by Napoleon's army this was not entirely inappropriate. Uniforms and equipment were largely based on British models and in a similar vein drums were copied straight from British designs, including such battle honours as 'Peninsular' or 'Waterloo'. Neither this nor the Napoleonic Eagle can have had little significance for the Sikh, who, it is suggested, viewed them as having some mystical significance.[12]

Allard had responsibility for the cavalry. As many of the local chiefs were protective of their own mounted men it was a much smaller force that Allard had responsibility for. It has also been suggested that Ranjit Singh failed to appreciate the importance of 'regular', and in particular, heavy

---

10   A good account of the development of the army can be found in Roy, Kaushik, *War, Culture and Society*, pp. 140–150.
11   Whilst the 'French' officers were the most important 'mercenary' officers they were not the only ones. A number of British and Irish soldiers, some deserters from the EIC army and other merely adventurers, served in the Sikh Army. There are also records of American, Polish, Russian, Spanish and Prussian officers serving in the Sikh Army.
12   Haythornthwaite, *The Colonial War Source Book*, pp. 95–96.

cavalry on the battlefield.[13] Allard raised and trained two dragoons regiments and one of lancers, after the French fashion, to be a force of regular cavalry. The quality of this cavalry is demonstrated by an interesting story that comes from 1823. With the British blocking Ranjit Singh's expansion south he turned north for further territorial gains. As the British largely wanted peace at this stage, having more significant enemies to deal with, it was understandable that Ranjit Singh would turn against his more natural enemy, the Afghans. As has been previously mentioned, the majority of the cavalry remained irregular. When crossing the Indus River into Afghan territory, the irregulars charged into the crossing in total disorder and as a consequence around 500 of them were said to have been swept away by the current. The regular cavalry, under Allard's watchful eye, success-fully crossed, clearly obeying orders and only moving on the word of command, without a single man lost. This event is said to have impressed Ranjit Singh and was to him a clear justification of the reforms and the officers he had selected to introduce them. However he retained a love for his traditional Ghorcharas. These were Ranjit Singh's personal cavalry and although better trained and more disciplined than other irregulars were still trained and equipped in the traditional manner. He was certainly not alone in his desire to cling to his traditional cavalry, something which seems to be a continual theme in armies throughout the world. Thus it was only the three regiments raised by Allard, around 3,000 men, that ever matched the infantry or artillery in terms of quality or training. After Allard died in 1839 the quality and discipline even of this small force fell away dramatically.[14]

An argument could be made that this disparity in terms of training led to mixed opinions amongst the British as to the quality of the Sikh forces. For instance Captain Osborne, the governor general Lord Auckland's military secretary, had a low opinion of the army due to having seen largely irregular cavalry forces. As a consequence he did not have the strongest of opinions of the army as a whole, whereas Lieutenant Barr, who had witnessed the forces of the Fauj-i-Khas, presented a very different view.[15] At the same time there were clearly those on the British side who believed that despite training, weapons, and tactics developed from European ideals there was still an innate inferiority in the Sikh Army. Such views clearly had racial undertones and a belief in the superiority of the European races. However as we shall see Gough did not share this opinion and was under no illusion as to the strength of the Sikh Army and the difficulty of the task he faced. Whilst many excuses can be offered for Gough's performance in the subsequent Sikh Wars, underestimation of the enemy is not necessarily one.

What Gough was guilty of if anything was perhaps an overestimation of his own strength, which is a very different thing entirely. Indeed this belief in the superiority of the British soldier is not the same as a belief in the poor quality of the Sikh. An example of this can be seen by the rather strange actions of the aforementioned Captain Osborne. He was with Ranjit Singh when they witnessed the training and manoeuvres of the Sikh army. Osborne pointed out that the Sikh skirmishers were firing volleys under orders. Osborne explained to Ranjit Singh that this defeated the object of skirmishing. He explained that each man should pick out his target and fire at will without orders. Ranjit Singh is said to have taken the advice on board and had the training and tactics changed accordingly. Thanks to Osborne's comment the Sikhs started to develop the skill of skirmishing. It was not only the skirmishing problem that Osborne pointed out to Ranjit Singh. He also made comments on the use of cavalry to protect the flanks and suggested ways in which this could be better used.[16]

---

13   Bajwa, Fauja Singh, *Military System of the Sikhs during the period 1799–1849* (Delhi: Motilal Banarasidas, 1964), p. 351.
14   Roy, Kaushik, *War, Culture and Society*, pp. 141–142.
15   Roy, Kaushik, *War, Culture and Society*, pp. 141 & 144, Bruce, *Six Battles for India*, pp. 48–49.
16   Bruce, *Six Battles for India*, pp. 52–53.

It does seem bizarre that a British officer would be giving tips on tactics and deployment to the ruler of the state who was clearly a potential enemy. The reason was partly arrogance, partly belief in innate British superiority, but much more a belief that without greater European leadership the Sikhs would never be able to mould their soldiers into a disciplined force on the same level as the British. As Osborne commented on seeing the Sikh Infantry:

> Their movements are very steady, but much too slow, and a European light infantry regiment would find little difficulty in working around them. This might be easily remedied by having a higher proportion of active European officers, but nothing can be worse than the system now in vogue. The commanding officer beats and abuses the major, the major the captains, the captains the subalterns, and so on till there is nothing left for the privates to beat but the drummer boys, who catch it accordingly.[17]

Although this might be a rather unfair view, and not too greatly dissimilar to the situation in the British or Company forces, it does raise some points regarding the perceived discipline of the Sikh Army. It was from this sort of thinking that an opinion developed that despite training, despite tactics, and weaponry, the one thing that the Sikhs would never master was the level of discipline that the British had.

To an extent this is supported by the experience of the army in action. In fighting in the north the Sikh Army would start in good discipline and order, as they did on the parade ground. However when the battle began it proved difficult to maintain this discipline and order, particularly when advancing. Often the infantry attack descended into a rush, and would be all too often diverted by the desire for looting. Whilst the British and Company soldiers were certainly not above a bit of looting, they did tend to be kept in order and good discipline until the battle was over. The British, in this case largely due to Osborne's testimony, took this to be due to the inferiority of non-Europeans. However if one looks a little further it is easy to argue that what we are really seeing is a lack of experience and more importantly an attempt to overcome years of tradition. This view is described by George Bruce's comment that, "Though continually drilled, the Sikhs could not entirely subdue a fiery individualism that found outlet in the tumultuous uncontrolled charge, any more than they could forget their age old urge for battlefield looting."[18] This however is due to the traditional way of fighting and could be changed, rather than an innate inferiority.

Yet it was clear that if officers like Osborne were assisting the Sikh Army it was because they believed that they could never match the discipline of British troops. Ranjit Singh is alleged to have said that, "The system of the British is so good that even if the enemy threw gold coins in the course of their fight, the soldiers would not even look at them."[19] Although an exaggeration, and a theory which was thankfully never put to the test, it does suggest this concept of discipline being the main British advantage. If one accepts this, then it does perhaps place a slightly different slant on Gough's subsequent tactics. Although clearly not the only general to believe in the supreme and superior discipline of his troops he could speak to having witnessed such discipline and order in dramatic effect during the Peninsular War, and at no battle greater than that of Barrosa where he was so heavily and personally involved.

Ranjit Singh had developed a formidable force, regardless of its drawbacks. The new regular army of the Sikhs was organised into what have been called 'mini-divisions', but would perhaps be better described as 'mini-corps' as they were a combination of four infantry battalions, a regiment

---

17 Bruce, *Six Battles for India*, p. 50.
18 Bruce, *Six Battles for India*, p. 51
19 Bruce, *Six Battles for India*, p. 51.

of cavalry, and two batteries of artillery. Needless to say that like all military forces this was the established and theoretical size. Sometimes there would only be three battalions of infantry, or perhaps not a full regiment of cavalry or perhaps only one battery of artillery. The artillery tended for the most part to be horse artillery. The battalions of infantry were about 800 strong and divided into eight companies. In line with their French training such companies were called *pelotons*, with two *pelotons* forming a *region*, and two *regions* a *demi-bataillon*, and two *demi-bataillons* a *bataillon* or battalion.[20]

Although deployed along French lines the battalions certainly looked British. They wore red/scarlet jackets for winter and white for summer, which were a direct copy of those worn by the British and Company soldiers. They even copied the use of different coloured collar facings for each regiment. Blue trousers with a red stripe were worn. Turbans were worn coloured white or blue and were generally after the Sikh pattern. Yet not all soldiers in the regular army were Sikhs. Indeed there was initially a great reluctance on the part of Sikhs to join the infantry. This was largely due to their historical tradition of fighting on horseback which had led to the development of contempt for fighting on foot. By the mid 1840s 52 of the 62 infantry battalions were Sikhs, the others made up of Muslims and Hindus. There were even some Gurkha battalions, although these were often said to be Kashmiris rather than Nepalese. Such Gurkha battalions wore the uniforms of British riflemen, green, with red facings and black headgear, yet there is little evidence to suggest that they were designated as riflemen or especially equipped with Baker rifles.

The cavalry also wore red tunics and blue trousers, although often wearing a red turban. They were split into troops in the same manner as European cavalry regiments. Indeed their equipment was similar. The majority were armed with sabre and carbine, although Sikh sabres or talwars were considered greatly superior to that used by the British army during this period. They were both heavier and sharper, and there was indeed a great deal of envy of Sikh talwars during the two Anglo-Sikh Wars. The main reason for having a sharper edge was a difference in drill. The British cavalryman was taught to attack with the point, whereas the Sikh cavalry would use the blade in a slashing motion. Indeed so effective were the blades that body parts of enemy soldiers were easily removed during battle.

However the greatest success of the reforms and re-equipment along European lines was the development of one of the finest artillery formations in the world. Like their infantry and cavalry comrades their uniform was based upon that of the British, wearing as they did black or dark blue tunics with red facings and yellow lace. It was even said that some wore a black bearskin with red cord for their headdress. The artillery itself was a powerful collection of guns and this alone meant that the Sikhs should never be thought of as a 'native' army. It was indeed a European artillery formation, and one which a good number of European countries would have been envious of. Indeed a strong argument could be made to the extent that it was a more powerful force than that possessed by the British. The basic formation for such artillery was the battery, in this case made up of eight to 10 guns. In keeping with European style there were numerous types of artillery. The light batteries, often called *Aspi*, contained 4 pdr or 6 pdr guns. At the outbreak of the First Sikh War they possessed 32 batteries so armed. Although not horse artillery in the accepted sense they were pulled by horses. There were also much heavier batteries often pulled by bullock or on some occasions elephants. Some of the batteries possessed heavy guns with anything from 18 pdrs up to 42 pdrs, and many points in between. At the outbreak of the First Sikh War it estimated that the Sikhs possessed 381 field artillery pieces and 104 howitzers amongst the heavier guns. At the other

---

20   For a description of the Sikh army, uniform, formations, and equipment see Ian Heath's book *The Sikh Army 1799–1849.*

end of the scale were *Zamburaks*, light swivel guns, often mounted on animals, the favourite being camels, and able to deploy rapidly around the battlefield.

Another important factor to remember in regards to Sikh Artillery was that they produced their own equipment. On other occasions during the 19th century the British came up again relatively modern artillery that was equivalent if not superior to their own. However they were guns that had been purchased largely from outside the country and there was little hope of obtaining replacements, spares, or ammunition from such foreign sources when at war with a British Empire that controlled the sea lanes. This was not the case with the Sikhs who not only built their own guns, but also produced their own ammunition and fuses. The foundries in Lahore were becoming increasingly skilled at such production. They could equip and maintain their artillery by themselves and this gave them a huge advantage. Indeed Sikh ammunition was in theory superior to that used by the British Army or the Company forces. The Sikhs used what was called 'prepared ammunition': that is that the projectile and propellant were in one. This gave them a great superiority in terms of rapidity of firing over the British, who still had projectile and propellant separate. The only problem in terms of ammunition was in regards to its supply given the many varied calibres of guns and lack of standardisation. Whilst this must have complicated the supply system it does not seem to have had any serious effect on the use of artillery by the Sikh Army.

Indeed Ranjit Singh had developed the Sikhs to the point where they were self-sufficient as regards the production of weapons and munitions.[21] Raw materials such as saltpetre sulphur and flints were provided from within Sikh territory, and iron was imported from the region north of Peshawar. Ranjit Singh had established cannon foundries, gunpowder magazines, musket factories and all manner of equipment factories at both Lahore and Amritsar. From here he was able to equip, and just as importantly maintain, sufficient material for his army. This gave him great power and meant that he was not dependent upon imports that the British could potentially have prevented from entering his territory. Nor should it be though that the skill and expertise for such arrangements existed solely with his European experts. Lehna Singh Majithia played an important role in developing the gun foundries at Lahore and Amritsar. Many of the guns designed and cast by him would be used in the coming conflicts with the British.

This new Sikh Army proved almost unstoppable in its northwards advance. The Punjab was largely under Sikh control. In 1818 the Sikhs took Multan, and the city of Peshawar was captured in the same year and continued to pay tribute until being formally annexed in 1834. The Sikh Army was making this possible. The combination of the regular army, the Fauj-i-Ain, in particular its artillery, alongside the irregulars proved more than a match for all they faced. Ranjit Singh was still desirous of peaceful co-existence with British India despite his new found military might. Yet this state of affairs ended with his death in 1839. It is slightly unusually to think of Ranjit Singh as both a calming influence and a great advocate of peace. However he certainly played an important role in the maintenance of such peace. The attitude of both sides changed with his death. Each believed now that a conflict was inevitable. The Sikhs were confident in the power of their new army. They felt threatened by the continual territorial expansion of the British and felt that this made conflict inevitable. At the same time they were starting to doubt the strength of the British Army in the light of the First Anglo-Afghan War, and there is no doubt that the conflict had a profound effect on the perception of British power. Some historians go so far as to suggest that had it not been for the turmoil in the Sikh Empire due to the death of Ranjit Singh in 1839, an attack would surely have been made on British territory at this time. Perhaps this is to go too far, however it is clear that the Sikhs saw the time as being right to secure their independence for years to come. On the British side the forward school still dominated Indian policy despite the departure of Lord Ellenborough.

---

21   Roy, Kaushik, *War, Culture and Society*, p. 143.

Exactly what Hardinge, his successor, believed in connection with the need to deal with the Sikh threat is difficult to ascertain, and to some extent beyond the scope of our concern. Hardinge seems to have favoured military action, but only to subdue rather than conqueror. He hoped that a Sikh state, with nominal British control and influence, would secure the north of the country without the need for annexation. However there are holes in Hardinge's thoughts on this subject, and a detailed examination of this is not necessary for our aim.

However it was clear that war was coming. With the death of such a powerful and established leader as Ranjit Singh it was not surprising that a power vacuum was left after his death. There was no leader with the power to maintain the unity created, control the disparate factions, and most importantly wield the power of the Khalsa. Ranjit Singh was succeeded by his son Kharak Singh. Kharak was proclaimed king on his father's death in June 1839 and installed as Maharaja in September 1839. Little is known of Kharak and he has in the past been dismissed as an 'imbecile'.[22] Whether this is true or he was simply not up to the unenviable task of following in his father's footsteps is unclear. However by October he had been removed from the throne and imprisoned and by November he was murdered by poison. He was in turn replaced by his son Nau Nihal Singh, who himself met with an 'accident' when it is said that masonry fell on him as he was passing by. It all seemed rather convenient to have happened just by chance. Nau Nihal's wife was pregnant at the time with the future heir to the throne, and whilst awaiting the child's birth Maharani Chand Kaur, the widow of Kharak and mother of Nau Nihal, acted as regent. When the child was still-born the Maharani stood down as regent and Sher Singh was recognised as Mahraja of the Sikh Empire. The Maharani Chand Kaur was assassinated in June 1842. Despite standing down she was still considered a threat, and her servants were paid to kill her. Sher Singh is widely considered to have been a naïve and even uninterested ruler who allowed others to control the country. However he himself was murdered and the throne passed to Duleep Singh. Duleep was the youngest son of Ranjit Singh and given the recent course of events he entered the scene at a very dangerous time. As Duleep was only five years old, his mother the Maharani Jind Kaur acted as regent. His half-brother was seeking to replace him, the Sikh chiefs were seeking greater freedom, a clash with the British seemed inevitable, and the power of the Khalsa seemed to be uncontrollable.

In such circumstances the move towards war seemed inexorable. Whilst the expansion of British India and British Imperialism were certainly part of the outbreak of war it would be wrong to assign it a prominent place. One can make an argument to say that even if there had never been a movement northwards of behalf of the British, and even if the forward school had not played a dominant part in British policy in India, a clash with the Sikhs was inevitable. Indeed at the outbreak of war came at a most inauspicious time for the British. The misadventure in Afghanistan and the mutinies in the native army meant that British prestige was a little fragile. The economic position had certainly not improved due to both reasons. The Afghan expedition had been expensive, and added to an already difficult financial situation. In turn the number of mutinies had meant that cuts to a usually easy target for economy, the military, were complicated and to cut the size of the army or reduce the British Army contribution would be fraught with danger. Such moves had the potential to be political suicide should there be an outbreak of war or further mutiny. Also, with the Sutlej providing a natural frontier for British India there was also a reluctance to expand further for fear of the consequences to the exchequer of a permanent military commitment north of the Sutlej and the construction of encampments, fortresses, magazines, and means of transport and communication. Whilst there were certainly those military and political figures within Britain and British India who looked towards expansion in the north they were a minority, albeit a quite

---

22   Cook, *The Sikh Wars*, p. 19 & Sidhu, Amarpal, *The First Anglo-Sikh War* (Stroud: Amberley Publishing, 2010) pp. 23–24.

powerful and influential one. Indeed the point has been made that the spirit of expansionism was more readily alive within the Sikh camp than the British one. This was partly due to the fact that they had effectively gained all they could by moving northwards, without becoming engaged in a prolonged campaign in Afghanistan and the recent British campaign illustrated the dangerous nature of such a campaign.

The call for war on the Sikh side was also a manifestation of the frustration of some Sikhs, particularly within the Khalsa, at Ranjit Singh's policy of détente and rapprochement. With the turmoil of royal and political affairs in the Sikh Empire the power and influence of the army grew. The army's power had become a threat to the political stability of the government. Whoever was in power held on to it so long as the Khalsa were on side. This has even led to suggestions that there were those in the Sikh ranks who secretly hoped that the British would destroy the power of the Khalsa. To an extent they could point to the recent conflict with the Gwalior state as an example of this. The former Maharaja had been placed back on his throne once the Mahratta army had been destroyed. Whether or not such conspiracies on the Sikh side are valid or not is beyond our concern. Regardless, the Sikhs were a powerful force, and Gough was now to embark upon the most trying and difficult period of his military career. He would face a strong enemy that had been taught, trained, equipped and drilled along European lines. It is now to the course and actions of what would become known as the First Anglo-Sikh War, and in particular Gough's part in it, that we now turn our attention.

43

Outbreak of the First Anglo-Sikh War

In the previous chapter we looked at the moves towards war. The aim of this chapter is to provide a little background to the problems facing Gough in the build up to war. In a sense there was an inevitability that the two strongest powers on the subcontinent would eventually clash. Suspicion existed upon each side and this did not ease matters. By late 1845 war seemed inevitable. The immediate concerns of the British had been the chaos in the Sikh Empire since the death of Ranjit Singh and the almost tyrannical power that the Khalsa seemed to wield. To British eyes the events of December 1844, when the Vizier Hira Singh and his finance minister Pandit Julla had been murdered by the Army, enforced this belief. Various intelligence reports of this time suggest that even in early 1844 the Sikh Army was inclined to invade British territory, with the specific aim of annexing the buffer area between the two nations.

British attempts to interfere in Sikh governance were viewed with suspicion and many Sikhs believed that the British were eyeing the Punjab as their next conquest. This belief grew after the annexation of Scinde. There was now a 'game' of escalation. To guard against the power of the Sikh Army, a British division was moved to reinforce the border. This in turn led to the Sikhs moving their army nearer the border, which in turn saw the British despatch further troops. Eventually such action was bound to lead to direct confrontation unless one side backed down, which neither was likely to do. It was the Sikhs who made the first move and crossed the Sutlej River and thus violated the treaty with the British.

When the Sikh Army crossed the Sutlej, on 11 and 12 December 1845, and thus made the first move in the conflict, Gough had mixed feelings. In so doing they had taken matters out of his hands. He had been anxious about being forced into making the first move. This was largely due to the fact that he had not been able to complete his preparations due to political considerations and judgements outside his control. There was also a little hesitancy and trepidation in having to face the Sikhs. Publicly he had no doubt that British arms would overcome. However he most certainly did not share in the belief that the Sikhs would prove no harder to defeat than any other foe the Britain had encountered in India.[1] He knew that he now faced a difficult task. Not only was he confronted by a skilled, well trained and armed enemy, but he also had to face them on their terms. They had crossed the Sutlej; they were setting the direction and pace of the conflict. They were not going to wait for the British to make the first move, to allow them to take the offensive, as Gough had experienced when fighting the Mahrattas and the Chinese.

It would be wrong to say that the apprehension about the actions of the Sikhs had only been on the military side. Lord Ellenborough, although now gone from India, had expressed his concerns at a forthcoming campaign against the Sikhs. This is perhaps surprising coming from one of the

---

1 NAM: 8303–105, Gough Papers Gough to Hardinge, 26 August, 1844. This letter, written considerably before the war, demonstrates clearly that whilst Gough respected the Sikh Army, and in particular its artillery, he believed his forces to be superior.

forward school. His main concern was the preparedness of the army to face the Sikhs. In February 1844 he had written of the coming 'contest' with the Sikhs that, "I must frankly confess, that when I look at the whole condition of our Army I had rather, if the contest cannot be further postponed, that it were at least postponed to November 1845."[2] He got his wish, plus an extra month, but of course this mattered not to Ellenborough now he had been replaced. It is interesting not only to hear the words from a former civil head of India, but also to read further of his diagnosis as to the main deficiency of the British forces. In short, it was the quality of Sikh artillery and the weakness of British artillery that was the main problem Ellenborough identified. In light of the subsequent campaign it could be argued that he was entirely justified in his views.

Ellenborough made his opinions on the matter known to the Duke of Wellington. Of this we have clear record, and although we do not have any account of him mentioning this to Gough it would be hard to imagine that it were not a topic of conversation at some stage.[3] If such conversations had taken place it would be intriguing to know what response his views received from Gough. Did he agree? Was he already aware of the problem? Did he try to rectify it? Given Gough's reputation, one could argue that he cared little for this deficiency, believing that cold steel won battles. However as we have already seen during his time in China he made great use of his artillery and in light of this experience would surely appreciated the concerns expressed. On the other side, one wonders what Wellington thought of this matter when Ellenborough brought it to his attention. Although only having limited control over such matters there does not seem to have been any great effort made by the commander-in-chief at Horse Guards to strengthen British artillery in India. It is also interesting to note the language Ellenborough used. He was not simply concerned about the numbers or calibre and range of artillery. To Wellington he wrote that, "it is very necessary that every possible measure should be previously taken to make our artillery most efficient."[4] It is that last word that is key; efficient. In the use of that word we see an appreciation of the quality of Sikh artillery, and perhaps even their whole army. The coming conflict would not just be about numbers, or weapons, but about efficiency, and in using such language Ellenborough made it clear that he appreciated that the Sikh Army would be a strong opponent, and a cut above what the British had been used to fighting in India.

The strange thing about this incident is that it was with Ellenborough, not Gough, that the ability to resolve this situation lay. The financial control that would be needed to improve the state of the artillery was in his hands. Given Gough's use of artillery in China, and his annoyance that the heavy guns of the siege train were not available for the campaign in Gwalior, it is likely that Ellenborough would have been supported in any move by his commander-in-chief. A combination of governor general and commander-in-chief should have been able to make good the necessary deficiencies in the artillery. The problem was that Ellenborough was on borrowed time in India. Afghanistan presented an excuse to recall him. However it was much more than just that. As George Bruce puts it:

> Ellenborough was still anxious about the army, but the East India Company directors in London had become far more anxious about him – about the aggressive trend of his policy, in face of the need for peace which they had urged upon him; about the arrogant tone of his letters, and about his open favouritism of the army at the expenses of civilians.[5]

2   Bruce, *Six Battles for India*, p. 81.
3   Ellenborough, *India Administration of Lord Ellenborough*, pp. 424–425.
4   Ellenborough, *India Administration of Lord Ellenborough*, pp. 420–421.
5   Bruce, *Six Battles for India*, pp. 82–83.

It is important to point out this very different approach between Ellenborough and Hardinge. Hardinge, understandably given the circumstances of his appointment, was more inclined to follow the instructions of the Court of Directors. He attempted to follow their policy of peace and, as we have already seen, was inclined towards military reductions but did not feel able to undertake them due to the threat from the Sikhs. We see the beginning of a strange policy whereby there was a desire to avoid war, but also an appreciation that war was likely.

Whilst Hardinge, and even Gough, might have been anxious to avoid war, there were many who were not so inclined. An important figure in this regard is Major George Broadfoot (1807–1845). As an officer in the Company Army he had played a vital part in the defence of Jalalabad during the First Anglo-Afghan War when he had convinced his superiors not to abandon Jalalabad. He then served as Ellenborough's aide-de-camp for a period, before service in Burma. It was Hardinge who appointed him as political agent for the Punjab and the North West Frontier. This was a rather foolish appointment for as one historian put it Broadfoot was "a very dangerous man indeed in this very sensitive situation. Paranoically liable to see grave insults to the British Government where none was intended he was also arrogant, pompous and bellicose."[6] Hardly the appropriate man if peace was the desired objective. One gets the impression that Broadfoot lived off his reputation gained at Jalalabad, where being 'arrogant, pompous and bellicose' had been to his advantage under those circumstances. Most of his reports include lurid accounts of affairs at the Sikh court, often depicting the supposed drunkenness and debauchery of that place. A regular target in this regard was the 'notorious immorality', as Broadfoot put it, of the Maharani Jind Kaur, using such examples to justify a call for the imposition of 'Christian Government' upon the Sikhs. He was liable to use the slightest excuse for sabre rattling, as illustrated by his demand to the Sikh Empire about the whereabouts of a young officer of the East India Company who had disappeared in Sikh territory. It subsequently turned out that the reason for his disappearance was due to the officer being drunk and losing track of the day. On another occasion Broadfoot turned back Sikh 'police' sent by the government in Lahore to administer the lands in Malwa that had been claimed by the late Ranjit Singh. Although he would later gain the support of Lord Ellenborough for refusing to recognise such claims he had taken the decision not to allow passage of the official party on his own initiative.[7]

Whilst Broadfoot does deserve credit for the creation of supply dumps at 20 mile intervals along the frontier these were not sufficient to allow for a large army to move. However one can say that at least they created a basis upon which further supply needs could be built. Yet whilst he did good work like this he did not really hold with the new policy of Hardinge to avoid war if at all possible. Broadfoot could be viewed as a warmonger but it is more likely that his experiences in the area had convinced him that war between the British and the Sikhs was inevitable. Yet it also appears clear that he did not fully appreciate the might of the Sikh Army. With men like Broadfoot carrying on direct correspondence with the Sikh state it was hardly surprising that war broke out. Broadfoot was also a strong critic of Gough. His comments criticised Gough both for doing too little to prepare for war and making Broadfoot's positon difficult by provocative acts. The latter accusation was reserved for when Gough attempted to reinforce the army at Ferozepore as a precaution.

Gough was in a difficult position as he tried to balance the need to be prepared for any possible action by the Sikhs with a desire not to provoke them. His preparations were certainly hampered by political interference.[8] With the support of Lord Ellenborough he had done what he could to strength the frontier, but once again a major problem with this was the difficulty of communication.

---

6   Bruce, *Six Battles for India*, p. 85.
7   Bruce, *Six Battles for India*, pp. 85–86 & Sidhu, *First Anglo-Sikh War*, p. 27.
8   Rait, *Gough*, Vol. I, pp. 382–384.

Several examples of this are seen in Gough's correspondence of the time. On one occasion Gough remarked that, "There is great neglect somewhere in the transportation of letters". This was after he received on 5 March 1844 a collection of letters dated from 26 February to 4 March. When correspondence was likely to turn up in 'bundles' like this it added to the problems.[9]

There were four key stations on the frontier with the Sikhs: at Ferozepore and Ludhiana, both theoretically in Sikh territory under a British guarantee of protection, and at Umballa and Meerut. Ferozepore was about 80 miles from Ludhiana, and Umballa was about another 80 miles on from that. The final station at Meerut was 130 miles from Umballa. This illustrates the great distance of the frontier and the fact that it was extremely difficult for each point to support the other in anything but general terms during an attack. A generation on, with the development of the rail network, it would still have been a difficult task, but when reliant on dirt roads and animal transport it was especially so. The most obvious point for a Sikh attack, due to it being a direct route from Lahore and one of the best points at which to cross the Sutlej, was Ferozepore. To avoid alarming the Sikhs by ordering extra troops to the frontier, a degree of subterfuge was used by Ellenborough and Gough. Troop formations had already been ordered to Scinde and as this was public knowledge it would not alarm the Sikhs. However orders were drafted to change their destination to the frontier and this force was then split amongst the garrisons to strengthen them.

The events in the Gwalior State allowed Gough to go further. Mention has already been made of the fact that as an army was prepared to take the field against the Mahrattas, another force was prepared to watch the frontier with the Sikhs. In such circumstances the movement of large numbers of troops towards the border with the Sikhs would not look overly provocative. This was the second army of observation under the command of Sir Robert Dick that totalled around 16,500 men of all arms. As a consequence, the garrisons at Ferozepore and Ludhiana were increased to around 3,500 men. Each garrison had one British regiment supported by native units. Between the two garrisons Gough planned to deploy a brigade of light cavalry about 3,000 strong under Brigadier General Cureton. Their job was to keep open communication between the two garrisons. They were also there to act as support for either garrison should they come under attack. Gough also prepared a force of two European regiments, the 29th (Worcestershire) Regiment of Foot and the 1st Bengal European Regiment, slightly understrength and numbering around 1,500 men in total. They were placed in the hills at Kasauli and Subathu to be ready to move to support either garrison should they be required. At Umballa a force of 6,000 was placed, including a regiment of European cavalry and two European battalions of infantry.[10]

The problem was that political considerations meant that the numbers of troops mentioned above were never fully dispersed. With the situation in Gwalior quickly resolved, the justification for large-scale movement of troops disappeared. This meant that the cavalry brigade was never deployed, and the major force at Umballa was understrength and particularly lacking in mounted men. In short, what had been accomplished was to provide infantry on the border who could resist any initial attack. However for the ability to then cross into Sikh territory and destroy the Sikh Army, preparations were needed that Gough found it very difficult to get official approval for, such as the building of new grain stores, increased barracks, and more general logistical preparations. Gough was aware that far greater preparations were needed. This was particularly true of the commissariat; that is to say the support or logistical services. It is clear from Gough's correspondence that he understood the importance of this and was doing his best not only to urge it upon the

---

9   NAM: 8303–105, Gough Papers, Gough to Lord Ellenborough, 5 March 1844.
10 The term European is used as they included non-British Army units that were made up of Europeans rather than natives. In other words these were the 'white' troops of the EIC's army.

civilian authorities but to undertake what measures he could through his own authority. In March 1844 he wrote to Lord Ellenborough:

> Our commissariat is another subject of deep importance and interest. The first great point is the power to cross the Sutlej as well as the other rivers in the heart of the country. The want of these ample means may either paralyse our operation or give us a decided advantage.[11]

At the same time Gough made such preparations as he could for the coming campaign, including the purchase of an extra 1,000 horses 'for all purposes' at a cost of £1,084. Perhaps the failure to undertake all necessary preparations were not so much Gough's put those of his staff. An example of this frustration is seen in his correspondence with Ellenborough in regards to the provision and preparation for the movement of artillery through difficult country. Gough's frustration with his staff can be viewed through a rather pointed remark of his movement of artillery in China when he says that he had in this capacity Armine Mountain, "an officer who did not understand what the word difficult meant." This clearly shows a great deal of frustration with his staff arrangements and a clear wish that he had people of similar quality to his staff in China.[12]

We have already seen that Gough was full of praise for his staff arrangements in China. There, to an extent, he had been able to appoint his own staff, because it was an ad hoc staff raised for a specific campaign. Upon becoming commander-in-chief he inherited a staff and staff arrangements that were not what he was used to or what he required. Whilst over time he might have been able to change this it is worth remembering the relatively short period of time he had occupied the position as commander-in-chief. By the time he made the above comments he had been in the appointment officially for only seven months. Yet as we know he had spent a great deal of time engaged with the Gwalior campaign. Indeed even by the time the First Sikh War broke out he had occupied the appointment for less than 18 months. One can clearly make too much of this, and certainly not all the faults were those of the staff. Had there been a strong staff in place when Gough arrived, this might have helped him settle in better, and get off on the right foot. It does perhaps lead further towards the conclusion that a man such as Gough was dependent upon a strong staff. Whilst ultimately Gough as commander-in-chief was responsible for the actions of his staff, it would be wrong not to acknowledge the difficulties such staffing arrangements caused him. For a man such as Gough the need for an effective and efficient staff to support him, and make good his own deficiencies, was very great.

Some of Gough's preparations did not always meet with the approval of his political masters. Gough was convinced that Ferozepore was the key to British preparations.[13] This was based largely upon his assessment that it was the obvious and easiest point at which the Sikh Army would attempt to cross the Sutlej. This opinion was reinforced when in December 1844 Gough and his staff made a detailed and careful study in person of the frontier, with particular emphasis on Ferozepore. During this journey along the frontier the importance was so clear in Gough's mind that he wrote immediately to Hardinge emphasising the importance of Ferozepore. "Ferozepore, is within an hour's march of a river the whole navigation of which is in their [the Sikhs'] hands, and that river is within 24 hours' march of their capital."[14] This demonstrates that Gough not only appreciated Ferozepore as a defensive position, as the most likely point of any Sikh attack, but also its importance and location for any attack by the British upon Sikh territory.

---

11   NAM: 8303–105, Gough Papers, Gough to Lord Ellenborough, 5 March 1844.
12   NAM: 8303–105, Gough Papers, Gough to Lord Ellenborough, 5 March 1844.
13   NAM: 8303–105, Gough Papers, Gough to George Gough, 5 November 1845 & 27 November 1845.
14   NAM: 8303–105, Gough papers, Gough to Hardinge, 7 December 1844.

He was therefore keen to strengthen Ferozepore, but in this desire he had previously been opposed by Ellenborough in 1842. Prior to Gough's appointment as commander-in-chief, construction of improved barracks and defences at Ferozepore had been halted on Ellenborough's orders in 1842. Ellenborough commented that he felt Ferozepore was 'a position in the air'. Whilst it has been suggested that this comment suggests that he felt it had little importance, it could be argued that he had other concerns. It may be that he felt a strong defensive position would not be necessary given the intention of pressing on into Sikh territory.[15] However although Gough clearly felt that Ferozepore was where the Sikhs would make there crossing, and therefore perhaps the point of the first action, he also saw it as a main base and depot from which to launch his attack. Whilst it was the easiest point for the Sikhs to cross it was also the easiest point from which Gough could cross the Sutlej and attack the Sikhs.

Although Ellenborough had been a slight brake on Gough's ability to make correct preparations for the coming conflict, the situation if anything, became worse under Hardinge. The latter was genuinely convinced that war could, and indeed should, be avoided. At the same time he was under pressure to provide a more considered approach to affairs in India in succession to the forward school advocated by Lord Ellenborough. Whilst under orders from the home government to avoid war with the Sikhs if at all possible, Hardinge's role is slightly ambiguous. On the one hand he felt that the need for military action was receding. In an early letter to Gough he pointed out that, "When Lord Ellenborough left Calcutta the probability of offensive operations in the Punjab had almost subsided into a conviction that the case of necessity compelling us to interfere by arms would not arise."[16] This was an overoptimistic assessment of the situation. Indeed the statement almost suggests that the reason why conflict with the Sikhs was near at hand was due to the actions of Ellenborough and the forward school. Whilst there might be some justification for believing this there is a much wider sense in which a clash between the British and the Sikhs was inevitable as they were the two strongest powers on the subcontinent. The worst that can be said of Ellenborough's policies was that they helped to bring the situation with the Sikhs to a head sooner rather than later.

At the same time, and indeed in the same letter to Gough, Hardinge conceded that the situation was still dangerous. As a practical soldier and administrator Hardinge told Gough that the situation was such that, "It is therefore not advisable, however strong the conviction that the case of necessity will never arise, to relax in any of our military preparations."[17] This met with the approval of Gough. He too was anxious to avoid conflict, believing that it would be a severe test of the native forces under his command. We now move on to look at the forces – British and native – that would fight the coming campaign in a little more detail.

15   Rait, *Gough*, Vol. I, pp. 366–368.
16   Rait, *Gough*, Vol. I, pp. 368–369.
17   Rait, *Gough*, Vol. I, pp. 368–369.

44

British Military Power in India and Outbreak of War

The aim of this chapter is to allow us an opportunity to look briefly at the army Gough was to lead in the field, in the same way that we have looked at the Sikh Army. The majority of the troops Gough commanded came from the Bengal Army. Although the largest, it was in some ways the weakest of the three East India Company armies. Whilst the previous chapter illustrated the challenges posed by the enemy Gough faced, this chapter aims to identify and introduce many of the challenges he faced on his own side. Many of the points raised in this chapter will be looked at again in further detail.

One of the first letters to arrive on Hardinge's desk when he took up his appointment as Governor General was from Gough urging greater preparations on the border with the Sikhs. It is interesting to note that in this Gough highlights that one of the reasons for the growth in hostility towards the British from the Sikhs is, in his opinion, due to the debacle in Afghanistan which Gough clearly believed has done much to damage the reputation not only of the British Army but of the British as a race in the eyes of the Sikhs. The somewhat anxious tone of this letter was due to the fact that Gough felt that he had lost much vital time in preparations due to the change in governor general. Gough informed Hardinge that he had told Lord Ellenborough that to undertake a successful campaign against the Sikhs he would require an army of at least 40,000 men.[1]

One of the more interesting remarks in this letter is in regards to artillery. Gough's plans called for ten troops of horse artillery, ten batteries of field artillery and what he refers to as seven 'reserve companies of foot artillery'.[2] At the same time he urges that the Horse Artillery should be 'up-gunned' from 6 pdrs to 9 pdrs and that the field artillery should similarly be up graded to 12 pdrs. Some batteries of field artillery in India were already standardised upon the 12 pdr: what Gough was calling for was for all batteries to use that pattern. This he was not able to do to the extent that he had hoped before the outbreak of hostilities. Indeed only one horse artillery battery had been equipped with 9 pdrs by that time. Another interesting move was his attempt to have them once more pulled by horses. Although they maintained the name 'horse', the vast majority of artillery in India depended upon a mixture of horses and bullocks. Gough complained that this not only made them slower but also reduced their mobility on the battle field. With horse drawn artillery he could move them across the battle field with relative ease to support any units that needed it, as he had in China with his mule and pony-drawn artillery. At the same time with horse he would be able to despatch them with the cavalry to support that arm, which he could not expect bullock-drawn artillery to achieve. At the same time, Gough called for the creation of what he called a 'Mountain Train' of artillery, presumably mountain guns that could be carried into the

---

1   NAM: 8303–105, Gough Papers, Gough to Hardinge, 26 August 1844. Although Hardinge was appointed governor-general in May 1844 it was not until late July 1844 that he took up his duties.
2   It will be noted that horse artillery operated in units called 'troops', denoting their links to the cavalry. Field/ foot artillery operated in batteries. In each instance they consisted of between four to five guns.

282

most difficult places. The latter clearly speaks of his experience in China where he had artillery carried on ponies, and he had already told Ellenborough that, "my little pony battery in China was a powerful auxiliary."[3]

All of this shows that whilst Gough felt he was no expert on artillery, once remarking to Ellenborough that when it came to artillery he was "not a competent judge", he clearly appreciated, or had been made aware of, the importance of artillery and in particular the strength of Sikh guns.[4] In a letter to Hardinge he wrote that, "The Sikh Artillery are good ; they are bringing into the field a much larger force than we are, even as aggressors; if on the defensive, they will treble ours, with much heavier metal. Our advantage will, and ever must be manoeuvre, and the irresistible rush of British Soldiers."[5] Such a view helps us to better understand the decisions Gough would make in the coming war. A reliance, possibly overreliance, on the power of British Infantry did not just come from the experience of over 45 years of fighting Dutch, Spanish, French and Chinese where he had seen its strength proved time and again often against overwhelming odds, but also from the practicality of the moment. He knew that he would be unlikely to win any large-scale artillery duel with the Sikhs. However we see from his correspondence that he did not simply accept this as fact without trying to change the picture. Instead he he asked for heavier guns, and for a high proportion of horse and mountain artillery, thus helping with the principle of manoeuvrability by which he hoped to negate the superiority of Sikh guns.

Gough also emphasised the point that he was criticising the guns of the artillery not the men, stating, "Our six pounders are pop-guns, very well and effective against Infantry, but unequal to cope with the heavy Metal of the Native States, when outnumbered as we shall be".[6] Here perhaps we see illustrated the purpose of artillery used by the British in India up to this point. Whilst it clearly had a role in silencing enemy guns its main use was as a system of force multiplication. With the British continually outnumbered, the use of artillery against enemy infantry was important. As a consequence this was how guns had been developed, being lighter, more manoeuvrable, and largely firing case shot. To Hardinge, Gough also wrote that, "I do not mean by any means to throw a slur on our Artillery; I know them to be almost invariably the elite of the Bengal Army, and that they will ever nobly do their duty; but if we have to go into the Punjab, we may look forward to being opposed by from 250 to 300 Guns in position, many of them of large Calibre."[7] This debate over artillery is one that has not been appreciated when considering Gough's performance in the Sikh Wars. It is important to note the fact that Gough not only appreciated this problem but was also attempting to resolve it in the build up to the declaration of war. That his solution was to rely on cold steel will always be controversial, but if one appreciates the problems of the artillery debate, then it becomes understandable.

Whilst Gough made it clear that 40,000 men was the force he felt he would need to advance into Sikh territory, including in his plan at least 10 European infantry battalions, 28 native infantry battalions and two battalions of rifles, he did also propose a much smaller force that could act purely on the defensive. The reason he proposed this was that he was mindful of the political consideration that might make the deployment of a large force appear an overtly hostile act. He felt that a smaller defensive force should include five troops of horse artillery, two field batteries, five European infantry battalions and five native infantry battalions, along with cavalry, sappers and engineers. This he felt would be sufficient to repel any Sikh incursion into British territory. Gough had long desired the deployment of the siege train, the heavy guns possessed by the British, from

---

3   NAM: 8303–105, Gough Papers, Gough to Lord Ellenborough, 5 March 1844.
4   NAM: 8303–105, Gough Papers, Gough to Lord Ellenborough, 5 March 1844.
5   NAM: 8303–105, Gough Papers, Gough to Hardinge, 26 August 1844.
6   NAM: 8303–105, Gough Papers, Gough to Hardinge, 26 August 1844.
7   NAM: 8303–105, Gough Papers, Gough to Hardinge, 26 August 1844.

Delhi to either Ferozepore or Umballa. This was rejected for understandable political reasons, given that it could not be construed as anything other than a hostile act. There would also have been logistical problems about their accommodation at either Ferozepore or Umballa, and it is difficult to believe that they could have been stationed at either point without considerable, and costly, improvement to the buildings. Obviously any further building work near the border would arouse Sikh suspicions. Whilst cavalry, infantry, and some artillery, could be explained away as a defensive precaution, it was quite difficult to do that with the siege train. Hardinge's fear that the Sikhs would perceive this as a hostile act is quite understandable.

It was not just how such troop movements would be viewed by the Sikhs that was in Hardinge's mind. He was also concerned as to how the actions might be perceived by a home government that had encouraged him to avoid war if at all possible. Such troop movements near the border could be interpreted as a breach of these instructions should they provoke war with the Sikhs. Gough on the other hand was not concerned with such matters, or at least not to the extent that Hardinge was. Gough was concerned with having to fight a difficult campaign and to that end he had many tactical considerations in his mind that were more important to him than how troop movements could be interpreted.

The importance of British or European infantry lay at the heart of Gough's military thinking. When the time came there was a deliberate attempt to create wherever possible brigades that consisted of one European and two native battalions. At times, the lack of European infantry meant that brigades sometimes consisted purely of native infantry. In a letter to Hardinge he expressed the view that "Cavalry and Artillery are excellent arms in aid, but it is Infantry alone that can in India decide the fate of every battle."[8] As Gough's previous biographer Sir Robert Rait eloquently puts it these were words that "form either the vindication or the condemnation of his whole military policy."[9] Further analysis of Gough's tactical awareness and strategic thinking will be undertaken later on, and it is perhaps sufficient to point out at this stage that the majority of general officers in the British army at this time would have whole heartedly agreed with Gough. The British approach throughout the late 18th and the large part of the 19th centuries was that artillery was there to silence the enemy's guns and if possible soften up the enemy infantry. Cavalry was there to perform reconnaissance, to prevent the enemy from outflanking you, to deal with the enemy cavalry, and to follow up any infantry attack and drive the enemy from the field with a series of cavalry charges that would complete the rout of the enemy force. Both arms were there to support the ultimate aim of the battle which was the charge of the infantry against the enemy infantry. Numerous contemporaries of Gough would have supported this view. Specifically to India, this was supported by the notable Indian official and soldier Sir Henry Lawrence. Lawrence wrote that "Our infantry must ever be our mainstay; if it is indifferent, the utmost efficiency in other branches will little avail."[10] We have already explored the fact that to a large extent Gough's artillery was inferior to that of the Sikhs. So perhaps the point is not really Gough's overreliance upon infantry but how he used his infantry, and that is a subject we will return to later in our narrative.

As we are discussing the tactical use of the three arms, now is an opportune moment to briefly look at the equipment and organisation of the three arms. The infantry of the time, both British and EIC, wore similar uniforms. Indeed, as we have already seen, so did the Sikhs, meaning that the battlefield had a somewhat uniform look to it. Muskets were not necessarily so uniform, although it is common to see the term 'Brown Bess' used to describe all such weapons. The major change was that by the time of the First Sikh War the majority of troops were armed with the

---

8   NAM: 8303–105, Gough Papers, Gough to Hardinge, 26 August 1844.
9   Rait, *Gough*, Vol. I, p. 374.
10   Rait, *Gough*, Vol. I, p. 374.

percussion lock musket as opposed to the older flintlock. As already mention in looking at events in China, the percussion lock was a far more reliable weapon. Of this there were several types. There were conversions to percussion lock of the flintlock Indian Pattern musket which had been the standard weapon of the Company forces and also extensively adopted by the British Army. There was also a Pattern 1839 British Army version that had been in use. The strength of this weapon was first seen in China by the Royal Marines under Gough's command at the Battle of Canton, where they had been able to fire in wet conditions. This was essentially the old 'Brown Bess' design with a new percussion lock. This had been superseded by the 1842 Pattern. This model also introduced a new bayonet design. This was the traditional socket design but with an added spring catch. It had been found through experience in India that the previous bayonet design could be pulled off easily by an enemy during battle.

Some units had special rifle companies equipped with the percussion lock Brunswick rifle, designed to replace the better known Baker rifle. The Baker was a very popular and effective weapon during the Napoleonic Wars. The only drawback was that it was slow to load and really needed a great deal of training to be used effectively. It was also now quite dated and a newer design was desired, and was found in the Brunswick. The Brunswick was an excellent weapon in theory, however in practice it proved very difficult to load, as the ammunition barley fitted the barrel thus with a dirty barrel loading was almost impossible. It was also under-powered and this led to a lack of rotation on the bullet and meant that over 400 yards it had very limited effect. As well as regimental rifle companies, at the start of the war there were two Gurkha battalions acting as rifle units, which tended to have a mixture of the two types of rifle.

The primary weapon of the cavalry was either the sword or the lance. The effect of French lancers during the Napoleonic Wars had deeply impressed the British and something of a fad for lancer regiments was seen throughout the 19th century. This was despite the fact that they proved to be a relatively limited weapon, rather cumbersome, and of little strategic value. The standard lance was 9ft long, made of ash and having a steel point and shoe. British swords of this period have a poor reputation; however this might have more to do with their negative comparison to the excellent swords wielded by the Sikhs. Neither the Light Cavalry sword nor the Heavy Cavalry sword was very impressive. Each had a single edge so could only be used on one side. There was also a difference in tactical use with the British preferring to attack with the point whereas the Sikhs used the blade in a slashing motion and therefore kept a much sharper weapon. Cavalry were also equipped with firearms, pistols and carbines, but were reluctant not only to use them but even to train with them.

Infantry weapons, and artillery for that matter, did not change dramatically from that of the Napoleonic era until the introduction of rifling and then later on breech loading. It was only then that the weapons became very effective. The standard infantryman of this era had a largely inaccurate weapon, which struggled to fire with any sort of accuracy over 300 yards, and was indeed only truly effective firing in massed volleys. The decision to largely retain the tactics of the Napoleonic era was not simply due to the forces of conservatism, although these were prevalent enough in the British Army. Until the advent of a rifled weapon as the main firearm, and the added advantage of a quicker firing breech loader, volley fire would remain the most useful manifestation of infantry firepower. Added to this was a belief in a well-tried system that had proved its worth against Napoleon. It is therefore unsurprising that a largely unimaginative commander such as Gough stuck to the principles of the Napoleonic Era.

Gough's main concerns were not so much tactical as strategic: that is his ability to move and manoeuvre his army. Whilst Hardinge appreciated Gough's military and strategic concerns, and indeed agreed with him in theory, there were political considerations that affected strategy. Gough urged that to accommodate these new troop deployments that the construction of new barracks, particularly at Ferozepore, be restarted and completed with alacrity. It will be recalled that similar construction projects had been halted on Lord Ellenborough's orders. In August 1844 Gough had written to Hardinge that "the brigade at that important frontier post [Ferozepore] is insufficient without a[nother] Regiment of Europeans."[11] Gough also identified many other problems with Ferozepore. There was only temporary stabling for the troop of horse artillery stationed there, the magazine was only a temporary building and not very strong, and Gough also felt the commissariat buildings were too close to the magazine. The latter point is interesting as it clearly illustrates that there were other important problems with Ferozepore beyond a lack of barracks for European troops. The magazine was not as Gough put it, 'bomb proof'. Indeed it appears to have been an ordinary stone building used for the purpose. Also, its close proximity to the commissariat buildings was dangerous as in the event of it blowing up it had the potential to take the majority of the commissariat with it. So although Gough viewed Ferozepore as an important place in terms of its geographical position he also considered it, "essentially faulty, it having no support, and there being at present no positon of strength to which the garrison could retire." In short Gough was trying to point out the strategic importance of Ferozepore whilst making clear that in its present state it was not fit for purpose.[12]

Whilst Hardinge shared Gough's view, and appreciated them from a military point of view, he felt, from the political standpoint, that to construct new barracks so close to the Sikh border would be viewed as a hostile act. In Hardinge's mind the enemy was not so much the Sikh Empire but the Sikh army, which he continually referred to as the Khalsa. Hardinge had even talked about the possibility of the British becoming involved to support the Sikh Maharaja against his own army, such was the power of the Khalsa particularly when there was weak civilian government. The concern over how construction work on barracks would be perceived was sensible; why else would you construct new barracks if you did not mean to man them? The question was now whether the Sikhs would respond to this.

It was for this reason that Hardinge refused to sanction the building of extra facilities at Ferozepore. As he communicated to Gough, "It is with regret I abstain from completing the barracks for an Infantry Regiment at Ferozepore, but I am so firmly resolved to give the Lahore Government no cause for questioning our good faith, or by a hostile attitude to justify their alarm, that I prefer for a time to suffer the inconvenience."[13] It could be argued that the problem was more than an 'inconvenience' as Hardinge put it, but that is to use the benefit of hindsight knowing as we do that war occurred. Had the 'inconvenience' been overcome and proper facilities built, the British would have been in a far stronger position when the Sikhs crossed the Sutlej. Again this depends on the belief that war was inevitable at some stage. Whilst this would have been an understandable standpoint Hardinge continued to hope, almost against hope, that war could be avoided.[14]

Although Hardinge's decision was regrettable it was understandable. However that did not lessen Gough's frustration. Hardinge did suggest that construction might be possible in late November when troops were moving up country to replace battalions already in service, yet this was to prove too late. The problem with not constructing such new barracks was that it was not possible to house more than one European infantry regiment at Ferozepore or Ludhiana, due to them not being up to the standard for European troops. This meant that at the outbreak of the war the garrisons at Ferozepore and Ludhiana consisted of one European and seven and five native infantry regiments respectively. For Gough this had wider implications. Gough had a firm believe that he needed a minimum of five European battalions to defend from a Sikh attack. Without the new construction

11   Rait, *Gough*, Vol. I, p. 372.
12   Rait, *Gough*, Vol. I, p. 376.
13   NAM: 8303–105, Gough Papers, Hardinge to Gough, 8 September 1844.
14   Rait, *Gough*, Vol. I, p. 373.

this meant that this would not be possible. He calculated that the earliest juncture at which he would be able to deploy five battalions was four days after news of an initial attack. This could prove costly if the Sikhs were to follow up their crossing of the Sutlej with a determined advance. Again he pressed the transfer of the magazine at Delhi, now suggesting that a move to Umballa would greatly strength his ability to gather large numbers of troops rapidly upon the border.

Even up until the 11th hour, Gough continued to be restricted in his deployment of troops. In late November Broadfoot reported that there were large-scale movements of the Sikh Army towards the Sutlej River. Broadfoot wrote to Gough that the Sikhs planned to cross the Sutlej with 40,000–60,000 men. Gough, whilst perhaps having his doubts about Broadfoot's objectivity in this matter, could not afford to ignore such intelligence. He ordered the garrison at Meerut to be prepared to move forward, whilst at the same time despatching the 9th Lancers to monitor Sikh movements, and ordering forward the 8th and 4th Irregular Cavalry and the Sirmoor Rifle Battalion. However both decisions were overturned by Hardinge who was still attempting to follow his orders from London to do nothing that might precipitate war. It was also made to look as if Gough was overreacting. In point of fact his orders look more like very basic preparations. Gough was not helped by the fact that a few days later he received a conflicting report from Broadfoot, who now believed that a Sikh advance was unlikely. This conflicting information perhaps shows us not only Broadfoot's slightly doubtful judgement, but also the great difficult in discovering exactly what was going on. Whilst Gough accepted Broadfoot's view, he urged that the precautions he had made by moving extra troops to the border be maintained. Given that there was clearly doubt as to what Sikh intentions were, this did seem a logical precaution. Hardinge, however, maintained the view that to move any further troops to the border could only serve to antagonise the Sikhs and could possibly precipitate the very thing it was designed to guard against.

On 26 November Gough and Hardinge met in person at Karnal. Gough was so anxious for a face-to-face meeting that he rode 50 miles to Karnal and then back all in the same day. A round journey of 100 miles would have been a tiring exercise for any man but especially so for a man who had just turned 66.[15] Hardinge tried to convince Gough that his decision to countermand the latter's orders was the sensible course of action, and that further deployment to the border was not necessary at this time. Hardinge left the meeting believing that he had convinced Gough that the movements were not necessary. Gough's first biographer, Sir Robert Rait, takes a slightly different view and believes that Gough was not convinced, but merely appreciated that any further protest was pointless. He believed that as his orders had already been countermanded on the 24th it would only serve to 'poison' relations between him and the Governor General if he continued to protest the decision.[16] Rait also records that when some months later an attack was made by the *Quarterly Review* upon Hardinge for not having taken sufficient preparation for war, Gough, rather than point to this debacle, chose to defend Hardinge and shared with him the responsibility making no mention of the fact that his orders for precautions had been countermanded.[17] This not only points to the honour of the man but also suggests that he might have been more inclined to Hardinge's position than would be believed at first glance. Perhaps Hardinge had, as he believed, convinced Gough at their meeting after all.

Gough appears to have shared Hardinge's desire to avert war with the Sikhs and was therefore prepared to acquiesce to Hardinge's position if this aim might be achieved. This failure by Gough, when criticism came on the lack of preparations, to defend himself and make it publicly known

---

15 NAM: 8303–105, Gough Papers, Gough to George Gough, 2 December 1845.It is interesting to note that in a letter complaining about the age of all around him Hardinge stated in March 1845 that Gough was 68. At the time of writing he was only 65 and would not turn 66 until 3 November 1845.

16 Rait, *Gough*, Vol. I, pp. 384–385.

17 Rait, *Gough*, Vol. I, p. 384.

that he had urged reinforcements was indicative of his sense of honour. However it caused Gough pain when he learnt that Hardinge had not followed suit, and in his correspondence with the Prime Minister Robert Peel had blamed Gough for failure to take necessary precautions.

It would be wrong to believe that there were not tensions between the two men at this time. That Gough acquiesced to the Governor General's point of view was largely down to Gough's understanding of the relationship between commander-in-chief and governor general. However it is clear that Gough was concerned about the situation. In a letter to his son, written on 2 December 1845, Gough recalled the events and spoke of his relationship with Hardinge. A large portion of this letter is reproduced here:

> I like him much, and he appeared ready to place every confidence in me. But he is very anxious not to fall into the error of Lord Ellenborough, of making war without ample cause for doing so. This may be all right politically, but it hampers me, so as to give perfect security to all points. He asked me if I intended to fight the whole Sikh army with the force I had here. I said decidedly I would, were they to cross and threaten seriously Ferozepore or Ludhiana. He said I would be greatly abused in England for fighting with so few men, when I had so many at my command. I pointed out that it was the Government that should get the blame, not me. If they gave me cover, I saw the expediency of the measure, but without cover I could do nothing. He has provided temporary cover for 5,000 additional natives, but it is Europeans I want to the front. So if I am forced to fight with inadequate means, and thereby lose some men, the onus must not be attached to me.[18]

This letter is interesting for many reasons. It illustrates that the tension was real between Hardinge and Gough, but that they enjoyed generally good relations, at least on a personal level. It also demonstrates very clearly the age old clash between was is politically expedient and what is necessary from a military point of view.

However, the letter also demonstrates the rather bullish nature of Gough. Perhaps it would be better to think of his reaction as that of a soldier whose belief it was to engage the enemy whenever possible. Given the likelihood of a Sikh invasion Gough was in a difficult position. If he stood and fought he would be criticised for fighting with so few men, but if he withdrew and waited for reinforcements he would be criticised for abandoning important strategic positions and retreating in the face of a native enemy. It was an unenviable position.

Again on 2 December Gough urged the movement of reinforcements with renewed reports of the movement of the Sikh Army. This time there had even been an appeal by Major General Sir John Littler, who commanded the troops at Ferozepore, for reinforcements. Yet Hardinge continued to hope for peace and despite receiving the letter on the 3rd it was not until the 5th that he agreed to the deployment. However this order did not reach the troops until 7 December. It is difficult to criticise Hardinge too much. His difficult position, the incomplete nature of the intelligence he was receiving, and his distance from the scene of events, all hindered his decision making process. Sensibly he decided to move nearer to the scene of events and by 8 December had reached Ludhiana, with Gough now at Umballa.[19]

Although they were still 80 miles away from each other, this was the nearest in terms of communication that Gough and Hardinge had been for some time. On that same day Hardinge, now better acquainted with the situation, acceded to Gough request to move the 80th Foot forward to reinforce him at Umballa. By the 10th, Gough received orders to move the army forward. Yet it was

18   NAM: 8303–105, Gough Papers, Gough to George Gough, 2 December 1845.
19   Rait, *Gough*, Vol. I, pp. 388–389.

only about to set off on its march when on 12 December 1845 the Sikh army crossed the Sutlej, and despite all Hardinge's best efforts war was now unavoidable. For Gough's part he was annoyed that he had not been able to take the preparations he had wished. In a letter to his son on 13 December 1845 he wrote that "I got the consent of the Governor-General too late, as the Sikh Army were between me and it [Ferozepore] before they [the reinforcements] had even moved." Thus Gough started a war against a formidable opponent on the back foot due to political concerns that had been beyond his control.[20]

---

20   NAM: 8303–105, Gough Papers, Gough to George Gough, 13 December 1845.

45

Early Stages of the Conflict

The day after the Sikh Army crossed the Sutlej River, Hardinge, who had done so much to try and avoid conflict, formally declared war on the Sikh Empire. His honourable attempts to avoid war and thereby follow the instructions given to him by the home government cannot really be criticised. In short, he was doing what he had been sent to India for. However they did have an unfortunate knock-on effect for the preparations for war and the course of the conflict. It meant that his commander-in-chief was immediately on the back foot. It was not simply the orders for troop movements that had been cancelled but also the movement of supplies and the requisitioning or purchase of extra waggon, oxen, mules and camels needed for transport.

Gough was primarily concerned with supporting the frontier garrisons that were dangerously isolated. Gough had long wanted to build proper forts along the border but Hardinge had not permitted this: partly due to cost but also his fear of antagonising the Sikhs. On 2 December 1845, Gough again lamented this failure to build proper buildings to garrison soldiers along the border. In a letter to his son he remarked that "the Governor General is indisposed to the expense of building barrack accommodation [along the frontier]. I hope we shall not live to regret it."[1] Hardinge, perhaps slightly concerned at how his decisions had hampered preparations, became very active. He moved from Umballa to Ludhiana, which despite his bodyguard of cavalry was a risky enterprise. On 12 December, the day the Sikhs crossed the river, he ordered Gough to 'meet the emergency'. With Gough preparing forces to move against the main Sikh Army, Hardinge attempted to deal with the problem of defence on the frontier.[2]

Historians have all too often seen the work of Hardinge and Gough at this time as being contrary to each other and in conflict. There has almost been a suggestion of one-upmanship regarding what they attempted to do. This has not been helped by biographers, such as Hardinge's son and Robert Rait, who in their attempts to vindicate the actions of their subject have sought to do so at the expense of the other. Although it is true that in April 1845 Hardinge had written to his stepson, Sir Walter James MP, that "I don't think much of Gough's abilities", this is perhaps taken somewhat out of context.[3] It has been used to condemn Gough's military capabilities, but if one reads the whole letter it is clear that he is not specifically referring to his leadership or command in terms of leading an army in the field. Hardinge is writing from a political point of view, as he is also discussing the Court of Directors and others in the government of India. Gough's name is simply mentioned as one of the advisers to the Governor General. If Hardinge had his doubts, it was in terms of Gough abilities in administration and wider political terms. It is worth remembering that Hardinge had been involved in the fallout of the court of enquiry into the financial goings on in the 22nd Foot during Gough's time in command. Although Hardinge had defended Gough against

---

1   NAM: 8303–105, Gough Papers, Gough to George Gough, 2 December 1845.
2   Rait, *Gough*, Vol. I, p. 389.
3   Singh, *Letters of Viscount Hardinge*, pp. 74–75.

any suggestion of collusion in the irregularities, it is understandable that he had his doubts about Gough's administrative abilities, and perhaps his judgement in such matters, as a consequence of this. The memory of this must have coloured Hardinge's opinion of Gough even before the two met in India

It should also be recalled that Hardinge's letter was written in March 1845 and that Hardinge had only arrived in India at the end of July 1844. At the beginning of 1845 Hardinge confessed that correspondence with the Commander-in-Chief had been difficult up to that point. Even in July 1845 Hardinge was writing to his wife that, "Sir H Gough is somewhat jealous of his authority, but when we get together I hope we shall go on smoothly."[4] The first part of the sentence is interesting and is perhaps evidence that Hardinge has already allowed his interest and experience in military affairs to push the boundaries of his authority as governor general. From Gough's point of view it is understandable that he was 'jealous' about his authority, as any criticism of the decision making process in regards to the army would naturally rebound upon Gough as commander-in-chief more than on Hardinge as governor general. Thus it is understandable that if Gough was to be criticised he wanted it to be for his actions and not those forced upon him by the governor general, or anyone else for that matter.

It is quite conceivable that the views that inspired Hardinge's comments made in general about the lack of support he had around him in India made in March 1845 in a private letter to a family member were subject to change. Indeed in a letter to his wife written in early December 1845, just a week before the war would begin, Hardinge stated, "He [Gough] is a fine soldier-like looking man, Lady Gough sensible and clever, & I think we shall always get on well as long as we are together."[5] This quite different appraisal of Gough, although speaking more of his personality than ability, perhaps shows us that not only were Hardinge's comments of the previous March taken somewhat out of context but that as he had gotten to know Gough better he had improved his opinion of him.

There is of course another way of looking at the actions of the Governor General during this period. From Hardinge's point of view he was trying to make himself useful, and in some ways trying to buy time for Gough whilst he gathered his forces together. He was of course an experienced staff officer. It is perhaps in this light that Hardinge's decision to take charge of affairs at Ludhiana should be viewed. It was a somewhat unconventional situation. It was unusual for the governor general to give orders directly to a garrison commander, as he did to Brigadier Wheeler at Ludhiana. Yet it must be remembered that Hardinge was an experienced British Army officer, still technically on the Army List with the rank of lieutenant general. As we have already seen, delays in communication were a problem. It was therefore understandable that rather than making a recommendation through proper channels via the commander-in-chief, which could have taken several days even for the letter to arrive, he decided to act on his own authority. It is easy to see tension between Hardinge and Gough where perhaps, at this stage at least, there was no more than would be expected. One historian has commented that at this time, "Conflict and mistrust existed and would grow between the ambitious Sir Henry Hardinge and the mercurial Commander-in-Chief, Sir Hugh Gough."[6] This does not take into account the difficult situation they were in, or the great problem of delay. If either man had waited to hear back from the other before acting the British response would have been crippled. At the very best such communication would take a day, often more.

Hardinge decided to move the majority of the garrison at Ludhiana forward to Bussean where there was a large grain store which he felt it important to secure. The decision is understandable

4   Singh, *Letters of Viscount Hardinge*, p. 93.
5   Singh, *Letters of Viscount Hardinge*, p. 131.
6   George Bruce *Six Battles for India*, p. 107.

and one wonders what Gough's plans were in this regard. There is no evidence to show that Gough made any plans to defend Bussean. It is quite likely, given the great difficulties he had in securing the necessary troop numbers to maintain the four main garrisons on the border, that he considered Bussean as indefensible. Hardinge made what turned out to be a good decision, although it was risky and had the potential to go horribly wrong. If the Sikhs had decided to move in his direction there was little he could have done with around 4,000 men against the main Sikh army. However if he could not secure the grain store he would at least have been in a position to destroy it and thus deny it to the enemy.

It is interesting to recall the comments Hardinge had made to Gough about advancing to meet the enemy with such a small number of men, and the negative way in which this could be viewed in Britain. In effect this was the chance that Hardinge was now taking. Had he been defeated not only might the grain supply at Bussean have been lost, but with it an important force designed to protect the frontier until the main army could arrive. In such circumstances Ludhiana would have become untenable and Umballa would have been at great risk. There was not, contrary to some reports, advice from Gough against such a move. Indeed Gough had written to Hardinge that he believed Ludhiana would be indefensible against Sikh heavy guns, and he therefore understood the movement. However it is clearly not what Gough would have done, although in this instance, as is often the case in war, it was success that justified the risk. Hardinge secured an important source of supply for the army. Gough's main concern appears to have been for the safety of the Governor General. It was quite possible that he could be captured, or even killed, if the Sikhs fell upon his force. As Gough later wrote to Hardinge, "I really do not like your position. It would be a fearful thing to have a Governor-General bagged."[7]

Gough was starting to gather the army at Umballa. Gough's correspondence makes it clear that he had been at Umballa for some time, and was certainly there when war broke out. In the criticism of Gough, and Hardinge for that matter, that followed the conflict there were suggestions that Gough had been at Simla when war broke out. This suggestion, made initially by Colonel George Malleson, was intended to demonstrate that Gough had been negligent in his preparations and far from the scene of action. This was not the case. From Umballa, his intention was to move towards Ferozepore. His major problem was a lack of animals readily available for transport duties. As they were coming from all over Bengal, many of these followed on later. There seems to have been a lack of camels for some reason, which Gough had planned to use as a major source of transportation. As a consequence Gough had to use many bullock-carts, known as hackberries, as a substitute. In this instance it is hard not to blame Hardinge for his refusal to allow the purchase and movement to the frontier of large numbers of animals before the conflict.

For the time being, the garrison at Ferozepore under Littler's command had been ordered to hold their position. Littler's force of a little over 7,000 men still only contained one European regiment of infantry. Although there had been a few desertions amongst the native troops, the large majority had stood firm and Littler was confident in his ability to hold Ferozepore. Yet at the same time there was naturally a state of anxiety and as a precaution he had been keeping his men fully dressed and armed at all times and ready at a moment's notice. Ferozepore had no strong defensive positions and Littler had ordered that his men dig trenches, but these were at best ad hoc and their use if the Sikhs decided to attack was debatable. Contrary to his orders, and somewhat daringly, Littler decided that his best option was to move forward. Whilst on the face of this might seem an odd decision, as he took with him less than 7, 000 men, leaving one native regiment to defend the cantonment and another to defend the town, there was some sense to it. He was not in a strong defensive position at Ferozepore whereas in the open he might be able to take up a strong position.

7   NAM: 8303–105, Gough Papers, Gough to Hardinge, 12 December 1845.

He had both artillery – and in particular horse artillery – and cavalry to support his infantry. There was also the continued tactical belief that the way to deal with native armies was to attack. Over three days, 15–17 December, elements of the Sikh Army approached Littler's force but whenever he moved to attack the Sikhs they withdrew.

The true course of events in the Sikh Empire at this stage may never be known and is largely beyond the scope of this work, but there were some curious occurrences at this time. Although Gough seems to have been largely unaware of them until later, there was communication between one of Broadfoot's officers, Captain Peter Nicholson, and the Sikh Prime Minister Lal Singh.[8] It is said that during this correspondence Lal Singh expressed his friendship for the British and asked what he should do. If this was true it is a remarkable event. We have already looked at how those in power in the Sikh Empire were scared of the Khalsa and may secretly have hoped that the British would destroy it for them. This seems to support that view. Nicholson for his part wrote back that Lal Singh should divide his force, leaving one part under the commander-in-chief Tej Singh to threaten, but not attack, Ferozepore, whilst he himself led the other half towards the Governor General. This suggests that Hardinge was aware of this correspondence, but it does appear that Gough was not. Nor does Littler seem to have been aware, or he would surely not have left Ferozepore to seek out the enemy. However it does explain why the Sikhs withdrew from his advance, and why they did not attempt to overwhelm the strategically important position at Ferozepore. The exact nature of this conspiracy, if conspiracy it was, will likely never be known. It is therefore difficult to say exactly how much Hardinge knew.[9]

From a military point of view there was logic for the Sikhs in not attacking Ferozepore. It has already been stated that it was not a position which was easily defended, and had the Sikhs taken it this would have presented a problem to them as much as it did to the British. The large army, commanded by Gough, on its way towards them was surely the primary concern for the Sikh commanders. Ferozepore could be dealt with at a later stage. In this sense it could actually be suggested that Nicholson had given Lal Singh very sound advice. Whilst Nicholson clearly under-rated the Sikh Army and overestimated the strength of the British force moving up to meet it, for the Sikhs to attack the main British force was sound strategy. The British had the potential to get stronger whilst the Sikhs were already at their strongest. Had events gone the other way we might be talking of Nicholson as a possible collaborator rather than Lal Singh. This is why it is difficult to fully understand exactly what went on at this period within the Sikh military hierarchy. There was clearly a lack of enthusiasm for the fight on their part, although this does not seem to have been matched by the Khalsa itself.

In the meantime, the few units Gough had readied to support Ferozepore in an emergency were ordered forward, with Gough still believing that this was the most likely place for a Sikh attack. This again supports the view that Gough was not aware of the correspondence between the Sikhs, Nicholson, and – possibly – Hardinge. The 29th Foot and the 1st Bengal European Regiment, which had been stationed in the hills at Kasauli and Subathu respectively, were ordered to march to Ferozepore. However it proved difficult for them to get through and the majority ended up joining Gough's main force. Having received from Hardinge permission to start moving the army on 10 December, by the following day Gough's cavalry had started for Ferozepore and the following day his infantry began their march. It is important to note that Gough started to move troops forward not only before the Sikhs crossed the Sutlej but also before war had been declared. Gough waited

---

8   Some references erroneously say that this correspondence was with John Nicholson, later known as the 'Hero of Delhi'. John Nicholson was at this time serving on the staff of Gough. Cook, *The Sikh Wars*, p. 42 has this error.

9   Sidhu, *The First Anglo-Sikh War*, pp. 36–39. Sidhu quotes from the diary kept by Peter Nicholson.

until all his troops had started before leaving Umballa, anxious that he should see them all march off before he departed. By the evening of the 12th he had reached Rajputa, the following day Sirhind and the day after that Isru. From here he wrote to Charles Napier asking him to gather all possible troops from the Scinde and to move to support the main army. This last act was not that of a man who was underestimating the enemy. He already had a large army with him, yet still he called for reinforcements of both men and supplies. Whatever else Gough may have got wrong he had not underestimated the difficulty of the task before him. In public he appeared bullish and confident of victory, as was expected of him as commander-in-chief. Yet it is clear from his private actions that he knew that he had a tough fight ahead of him.

Gough also wrote to his son, explaining the problems he faced and once again lamenting the delay caused by political concerns. "We delayed too long moving, and the troops I put in motion being in part countermanded has crippled us." Perhaps this was a slight exaggeration but it was clear that the Governor General's decision to countermand Gough's orders had been an unfortunate delay.

According to Gough, Hardinge now regretted having countermanded his orders. "The G.-G., is now with me, he has placed all at my disposal, and now sees that it would have been better had my proposals been carried before into effect."[10] The likelihood is that Hardinge did not actually regret the decision, having taken it with the hope of avoiding conflict, but could now see with the benefit of hindsight that it would have been better if the troops had been moved forward earlier. Gough clearly saw it as a personal vindication and in a personal letter he is always only too pleased to point out when he was right and others were wrong.

There are those who have suggested that Hardinge had failed diplomatically during the build up to war, that he had left too much authority in the hands of the bellicose Broadfoot. For example it was the latter who formally severed diplomatic relations with the Sikhs, not the Governor General. This was true but Hardinge had at least attempted to move himself nearer to the scene. Yet he had failed to take a hands on approach to the diplomacy, which, as governor general was really what was required of him.[11] This failure of Hardinge to engage in diplomatic overtures, has led one historian to comment that:

> He had no conception of the statesmanship that the great post of Governor-General called for. He was afflicted with a sort of mental paralysis – he had been too long a soldier in uniform. In face of instructions not to go to war his sole act was the blind military one of refusing to reinforce troops on the frontier, to avoid alarming the Sikhs, when they had already been frightened out of their wits.[12]

However in this instance, in regards to the deployment of reinforcements along the frontier, Hardinge acted honourably, if perhaps misguidedly, whilst trying to adhere to the orders he had received to avoid conflict.

In the same letter to his son quoted previously Gough spoke of his army and his plans.

> My fellows are in great spirits. I move to-morrow [16 December] thirty miles. I shall push on so close that, if they attack me, Littler will fall on their rear; if they attack him, I shall be in the midst of them. I shall not precipitate an action if they do not, but wait for my force moving up

---

10   NAM: 8303–105, Gough Papers, Gough to George Gough, 15 December 1845.
11   See, Sidhu, *First Anglo-Sikh War*, pp. 26–29 & Bruce, *Six Battles for India*, pp. 85–90
12   Bruce, *Six Battles for India*, p. 101.

within one day's march of me, under Major-General Gilbert. This, by one day's delay, would give me 10,000 fighting men, whilst Littler has at Ferozepore 7,360 fighting men.[13]

It is interesting to note the tone of this letter, and the fact that he emphasised that he did not intend to 'precipitate an action'. This was perhaps partly due to the fact that Gough's plans and his army were still coming together. It may also be taken as indicating a desire for the enemy to attack him. If so this might be as a consequence of the actions of the Gwalior campaign, and to a lesser extent China. In both campaign Gough was largely on the offensive, and whilst this was considered to be the standard tactic in India for dealing with native armies, it was perhaps not the correct tactic for dealing with the Sikhs. It might be taking it too far to infer this from Gough's comment, but it does appear to at least indicate a reluctance to attack the Sikhs in open battle. Also, if he could trap the Sikhs between himself and Littler's force, he would then be in a strong position to coordinate an attack from two directions and perhaps inflict a severe reverse on the Sikh Army.

There is a very interesting account of the army gathered to meet the Sikh invasion that is found in the letters of William Hodson, at this stage a young officer in the 2nd Bengal European Regiment and later better known as a light cavalry commander of the unit that bore his name. It is included here as it gives a good description of the force which Gough would command during the campaign against the Sikhs. Hodson recorded that,

> I never saw so splendid a sight: 12,000 of the finest troops were drawn up in one line, and as I rode slowly along the front, I had an excellent opportunity of examining the varied materials of an Indian Army. First were the English Horse Artillery, then the dashing dragoons of the 3rd Queen's, most splendidly mounted and appointed, then came the stern determined looking British footmen side by side with their tall and swarthy brethren from the Ganges and Juma – the Hindoo, the Mussulman, and the white man, all obeying the same word and acknowledging the same common tie. Next to these a large brigade of guns, with a mixture of all colours and creeds. Then more regiments of foot, the whole closed up by regiments of native cavalry; the quiet looking and English dressed Hindoo troopers strangely contrasted with the wild irregulars in fanciful un-uniformity of their native costume, yet these last are the men I fancy for service. Altogether it was a most interesting sight, either to the historian or soldier, especially as one remembered that these were no men of parade, but assembled here to pour across the Sutlej at a word.[14]

By 16 December, the force from Ludhiana and the advanced units of Gough's army, mainly the cavalry, joined at Wadni. Even at this early stage of the conflict the army was suffering from ill effects of moving through northern India. The heat, particularly in the middle of the day, took its toll upon the soldiers, which was not helped by a general shortage of water. The lack of anything resembling a proper road made marching hard. Gough was pushing them, and himself for that matter, hard to reach the enemy as soon as possible. This is where the failure of Hardinge to allow for fuller preparation started to take effect. The forced march was also because Gough feared not only for the safety of his troops in the border garrisons, particularly Ferozepore, but also the safety of the Governor General who were in amongst them. This in itself had a knock-on effect as having moved his infantry forward as quickly as he could they had outstripped the movement of their own supplies and equipment, which moved slowly in a huge convoy of various types of pack animal. Thus, at the end of a long days march, with little water, the soldiers would settle down often

---

13   NAM: 8303–105, Gough Papers, Gough to George Gough, 15 December 1845.
14   Trotter, L. J., *The Life of Hodson of Hodson's Horse* (London: J. M. Dent & Sons, 1912), p. 19.

without food and without anything by means of support other than what they had been able to carry themselves. This often meant they did not even have their greatcoats to ward against the cold nights. All this was the real impact of not having been allowed to prepare the way for the advance of this army and reinforce stations along the border, not only with extra troops, but extra supplies.

As a consequence of this, Gough felt compelled to give his men a rest day at Wadni. Although this decision could be questioned, there is sense behind it. The march had been very hard and to throw such troops against the enemy would be a risk. It could have been done, but Gough had made such good progress that he felt to rest his men was now an option. If there was to be any major trouble he did now have the vast majority of his cavalry present and rested, having arrived the day before the infantry, and could deploy them if necessary.

After a day of rest Gough pushed on his army and they covered 21 miles in that day which took them to a place called Mudki where there was a fort. The fort was initially reported to be in the hands of the Sikhs but in actuality had only been occupied by a unit of Sikh irregular cavalry which withdrew as Gough's army advanced. Unsure of what lay before him, Gough had ordered the army to advance upon Mudki in line of battle, a sensible precaution, but after a long march not conducive to the condition of his men. The army was moving towards what would be the first major battle of the war.

46

The Battle of Mudki

Gough now faced a problem. The presence of enemy cavalry told him that he was nearing the main Sikh Army. Their departure from the battlefield in such a hurry was an indication that they had in effect been a scouting party. Gough now faced a position in which the enemy would know where his force was but he did not enjoy the same luxury. With daylight fading he understandably took the decision to make camp at Mudki. It gave him a reasonably strong position. It also allowed his men to rest and just as importantly for baggage and straggling units to reach him. The latter point is particularly relevant as it helps us to understand the difficult nature of the march. Often even battalions were unable to march as one unit, due to the poor nature of roads and the difficult nature of terrain. Thus when the army reached Mudki many battalions had perhaps only half their men with them. In what is perhaps an extreme example it is said that when they reached Mudki the colonel of the 31st Foot had only 50 men present with him.[1] Having endured a long day's march and with only three hours of daylight left, Gough probably made a wise decision. Nevertheless, he can be criticised for not pressing his cavalry forward, firstly to harry the enemy but also in the hopes of finding the location of the main enemy force. He sent out only minor patrols when perhaps a reconnaissance in force was called for. As it turned out, the Sikh force was only some two or three miles from him, and a deployment of his cavalry would quickly have discovered this. Indeed, had Gough deployed his cavalry forward earlier the Sikhs may have decided to withdraw and he would have saved his exhausted men from the prospect of battle.

An unusual conversation is recorded taking place in the village of Mudki as the British force continued to arrive. Hardinge had now arrived, but was still unsure as to the action required. He expressed doubt to his staff as to how British actions would be viewed at home. Still concerned at his failure to fulfil his instructions from the government and avoid a war, he seems to have had doubts about pressing on. In some senses what he was saying was an expression of him 'thinking out loud' rather than an expression of intent. He wondered whether there was justification for war, this despite him having signed a declaration of war five days previous. The Sikhs, after all, had only entered the disputed territory south of the Sutlej under British protection, rather than actually enter British territory itself. Given the fact that Ferozepore had not been attacked, and it was clear that relations with Lal Singh were still cordial, Hardinge was concerned over the justification for his action. This does seem quite bizarre in the face of the enemy and one wonders what Hardinge proposed to do if he decided that there was not a justification for war. The idea that he was perhaps rather naively thinking out aloud is supported by a letter written to his wife on 20 December 1845, in which he recalled that "There never was a juster quarrel or more unprovoked aggression. War has been forced upon us, & we must now do our duty".[2]

---

1   Cook, *The Sikh Wars*, p. 44.
2   Singh, *The Letters of Viscount Hardinge*, p. 132.

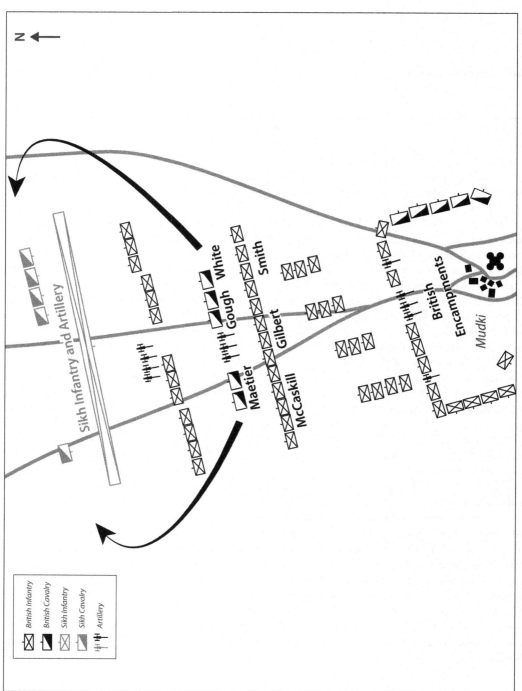

Map 10 The Battle of Mudki.

We will never know exactly what size the Sikh force ahead of Gough was. Estimates vary widely, and here the lack of information from the political agents who were acting as intelligence officers, based on the premise that they knew the country and the language, were at fault. Criticism has been made of Gough for exaggerating the numbers he faced at Mudki. However if one reads his reports it can be seen that they clearly state that the numbers quoted, 15,000 infantry, 20,000 cavalry, and 40 guns, are what was reported to him from the political officers. Gough never wrote that this was what he faced; only that it was what was reported to him. If one reads further on in the report it is clear that he was fully aware that he never had to face that number of men. That the intelligence officers and scouts wildly exaggerated is without doubt. More accurate estimates for Sikh strength at Mudki are 2,000 to 4,000 infantry, 10, 000 cavalry and about 22 guns. As previously mentioned, Sikh intentions at this point are difficult to ascertain due to the allegations of duplicity on the part of the high command of the army. However it does appear that the intention of the force heading towards Gough at Mudki was to delay his advance. This would seem logical given the high proportion of cavalry.[3]

Gough's force consisted of around 10,000 men. Given the number of stragglers and the long line of march it is unclear exactly how many were present. It is also extremely unlikely that all of the slow moving artillery had arrived by the commencement of the battle. The army was just starting to rest when news of the Sikh advance came. There are at least three different accounts of how the Sikh force was spotted. One has Captain Frederick Haines discovering the advanced guard. Haines, who would end his career a field marshal and a knight, was an officer on Gough's staff and is said to have been despatched by Gough to find the enemy. There are also two different accounts given of it being Broadfoot who discovered the enemy force, whilst others that Christie's Horse, who had been scouting ahead, had discovered them.[4] It is possible that Broadfoot's information was a confirmation to Gough of the message sent back by Haines. It is also possible that Broadfoot was delayed in telling Gough as he decided to inform Hardinge first of all. As a political officer he was technically responsible to Hardinge, but as a serving officer of the army he was under Gough's command, and common sense would suggest that the commander-in-chief should have been the first to be informed. Haines' message is said to have been sent at 1500hrs and as he was only a short distance from camp it is likely that Gough received this inside half an hour. Robert Napier, at that time a young Bengal Engineers officer attached to Gough's staff but later to be known as Field Marshal Lord Napier of Magdala, recalled that Broadfoot informed Gough of the approaching Sikhs at 1530hrs. Robert Napier had presented himself to Major General Gilbert, to whose division he nominally belonged but had not travelled with them due to other duties. Upon presenting himself he was informed by one of the Gilbert's officers that, "this was not the time when engineers were wanted." Napier therefore decided to present himself to the commander-in-chief to see if he could be any use. His offer of service was warmly welcomed by Major Grant, the Deputy Adjutant-General, and thus Napier became attached to the staff of the commander-in-chief.[5]

---

3   Unknown, *The War in India: The Despatches of Viscount Hardinge, Lord Gough & Sir Harry Smith* (London; John Ollivier and Ackermann & Co, 1846), pp. 40–49. This is a copy of Gough's despatch to Hardinge dated 19 December 1845.

4   Christie's Horse were by this stage technically the 9th Bengal Irregular Cavalry. It had originally been raised by John Christie, a captain in the 3rd Bengal Light Cavalry for service under Shah Shuja of Afghanistan.

5   Napier, Robert, *Personal Narrative written shortly after the Actions of Moodkee and Feroze-shuhur by Captain R. Napier, Bengal Engineers*, (Hertford: Printed for private information only, 1873), p. 4. This extremely interesting but seldom used account of the First Anglo-Sikh War can be found in the British Library. Sidhu, *The First Anglo-Sikh War*, pp. 45–46, discusses the various theories as to who spotted the Sikhs first, and see also Bruce, *Six Battles for India*, pp. 108–109. The latter gives credit to Broadfoot for discovering the enemy were advancing, but gives Haines the credit for identifying where the enemy was

Regardless of how the news came to Gough, it presented him with a difficult problem. A Sikh force, of he knew not exactly what size, was bearing down upon him. From what reports he had, it appeared they intended to attack. His men were tired after a long day of marching and there were barely two hours of daylight left. As a consequence Gough's decision to take the offensive seems odd. However, if he were to wait until the following day, that would create several problems. Firstly the Sikhs might get behind him and harry not only the straggling units making their way into camp but perhaps more importantly his supply lines. Given that the Sikh force had a large contingent of cavalry this was a distinct possibility. Secondly, his camp could be threatened during the night and the Sikhs would be quite capable of launching cavalry raids during the night which would have a detrimental effect not only on the amount of rest his men would get during the night but also on their morale. Indeed Robert Napier recorded that Broadfoot had warned Gough that the Sikhs planned a night attack. If this is accurate this would also have influenced Gough's decision to take the offensive.[6] Thirdly if this was just the Sikh advanced guard, even if 30,000 strong, it was still possibly only a portion of the army and he waited till the morrow he would potentially face a far greater enemy.

Gough decided, despite being fully aware of the risks, to take the offensive and to attack the force coming towards him. This decision has been understandably criticised, not least of all by Harry Smith and Hardinge at a later date. A strong argument can be made that Gough should have held his position. After all, his army was in a weakened state not only through a gruelling day's march but also as there were still elements of missing. For instance, one of his infantry divisions was lacking its European battalion and was thus comprised entirely of native infantry. Gough held what was theoretically quite a strong defensive position, and the Sikhs would have to cover considerable open ground to attack him. Not only was the light against him, but his army was not as well organised as he would have liked. His brigade and divisional formations had only really existed on paper up to this point. As the army had not been fully formed before war was declared, much of this was still ad hoc and the system of command was tenuous to say the least. Higher command functions would be largely irrelevant and he would be reliant on his battalion and regimental commanders to a far greater degree than would have ordinarily been the case. He had some experienced cavalry and infantry, both European and native, but completely untested brigade and divisional arrangements.

However Gough's decision to attack did have its merits. Firstly, as has already been mentioned, it was the convention of the time that to defeat native armies the offensive should be taken. Secondly, Gough naturally had a desire to send a clear message to the Sikhs. As this was the first engagement of the war a decisive British victory might shorten the conflict. At the same time a failure to attack might be seen as a sign of weakness and have a positive effect on Sikh morale whilst having a negative effect on that of Gough's own army, particularly the native contingent. Gough was mindful that despite his high opinion of the Sikh Army he did not want to do anything that might give the impression that he was either afraid of them or doubtful of his own men. Thirdly, whilst in theory he held a strong defensive position there had been no preparation for its defence. Indeed the call to arms necessitated by the news of the Sikh advance had been so hurried that many of the men formed line in shirt sleeves and officers attended the field with drawn swords without having time to put on their sword belts, let alone have time to prepare any defences. This in turn presented a problem, given that Sikh artillery outranged Gough's own. Had he stood to wait the attack, the Sikh advance could have been partly covered by their artillery without Gough being able to return fire. Again, this would have had a detrimental effect on morale. History indicates shows that the

---

and where they were moving. Frederick Haines is sometimes erroneously referred to as Gough's son-in-law. In fact it was Haines's elder brother Gregory who had married Jane Gough.

6   Napier, *Personal Narrative*, p. 4.

morale of soldiers advancing and sustaining casualties does not fall as quickly as the morale of soldiers awaiting an attack who are coming under fire and sustaining casualties without being able to fight back.

There is a good argument to be made for each course of action: either holding their position or advancing to the attack. The latter was certainly the bolder approach, and given Gough's temperament and his previous experience in the Peninsular and in China it is not surprisingly that he decided upon the attack. Had he stayed on the defensive he would probably have sustained fewer casualties, but he could not have known that at the time. As the desire was to deliver a decisive defeat to the enemy attack was obviously the best option. Yet whilst the decision to attack can be defended, it is harder to defend the way in which this was carried out, particularly in regards to the way in which the infantry advanced. Gough's plan started off well. He deployed his artillery forward, which not only bought his infantry some more time to prepare but also partly covered the advance of his cavalry. The artillery duel went slightly better for the British than should have been the case, considering that they were both outgunned and outranged. As Gough had stated before the war, he was relying on the one advantage his artillery had: manoeuvre. On his right the horse artillery and two field batteries were faring well, but the rest of his artillery was failing to make an impact and suffering from the return fire of the Sikhs. At best such a duel was a stalemate.

Gough's cavalry, deployed on either flank, fared much better. On the right of his line Gough had ordered the cavalry to threaten the Sikh left and attempt to outflank them if possible. This was undertaken by his nephew Brigadier John Bloomfield Gough, commanding the 2nd Cavalry Brigade, consisting of the 5th Bengal Light Cavalry, the Governor General's bodyguard and a portion of the 4th Bengal Light Cavalry (Lancers), and Brigadier Michael White commanding the British 3rd Light Dragoons. Their movement was successful and they managed to get behind the Sikh line on their left and sweep around the back onto the Sikh infantry and artillery. The latter was silenced and the Sikh cavalry on that flank withdrew under the onslaught. On the British left a similar, although not as successful, flanking movement was undertaken by Brigadier Mactier commanding the remainder of the 4th Bengal Light Cavalry and the 9th Irregular Cavalry.

It could be argued that at this point Gough was in full control of the battle. He had silenced the majority of his enemy's guns and his cavalry were causing havoc behind the Sikh lines. His horse artillery had pressed forward, as had one or two field batteries. Now might have been the time to recommence the bombardment. With the enemy horse withdrawing and much of their artillery silenced, Gough's batteries could have inflicted real damage on the enemy's infantry, his remaining artillery and retreating cavalry. In short, the action of his cavalry had levelled the playing-field, and Gough's artillery could have proved decisive. He could then have used his infantry to finish off the enemy position, before allowing his cavalry to attack the retreating enemy. Brigadier George Brooke, commanding the artillery, did attempt to recommence the artillery bombardment at this juncture with limited success. However with the advance of British infantry he decided to halt the bombardment. Had Gough ordered him to, he would gladly have continued the bombardment, but he received no such order.

The question is whether Gough should have delayed the infantry attack to allow his artillery to cause further damage to the Sikh line before he committed the infantry. Gough's decision to instead press on with an infantry attack is a debatable one, bringing about several possible problems. Firstly, the enemy guns had not been completely put out of action: it was merely that many of the gunners were either dead or had sought refuge with the infantry. To reopen an artillery bombardment would require the movement of Gough's cavalry away from their threatening position, to avoid firing on his own men. Secondly, a major problem in this regard was the exercise of control on a mid 19th century battlefield. The only way for him to have delivered messages to the units concerned was via a member of his staff riding over with the order. The Sikhs had positioned marksmen around the battlefield, many of them sitting in the occasional trees that spotted the area.

Such a horseman was an obvious target to such men. At Mudki, three staff officers were killed and three wounded whilst undertaking such tasks. Apart from such casualties, Robert Napier had his horse shot from under him whilst on such a mission to deliver a message, although Napier escaped serious injury. It was really this problem of communication and coordination on the battlefield that would have hampered any plan for attempting to finish off the enemy with an artillery bombardment. Given the somewhat chaotic nature of the battle, Gough might have been rather limited in the information he received during the battle. Yet had he given the order for the artillery to recommence their bombardment he may have gained a less costly victory.

However it is unlikely that such a consideration was given much time by Gough. His desire was to finish off the enemy at bayonet point as he had when fighting the French and the Chinese. However his deployment of the infantry was poor. Rather than have a shortened line, Gough positioned all his infantry in one long line. This had two important consequences. Firstly it left him without any reserve of infantry to call upon to exploit any weakness his line of infantry might create. In the context of the battle of Mudki, this was perhaps not a bad thing. Indeed it could be argued that his aim was to get all his infantry engaged as soon as possible. Secondly, however, the positioning of his army on the battlefield was such that not all his infantry could appear in a straight line. On his left there were great problems with organising the infantry due to the nature of the terrain and the position chosen for the camp. The battlefield was not an ideal one. Sandy hills obscured some of the terrain, whilst there were dense thorn bushes and jungle, with 'dwarf' trees in which enemy marksmen took up position.

When the infantry lined up they were facing at right angles across the battlefield to where the British troops were lining up on the right. A more tactically astute commander may have attempted to exploit this by advancing his right whilst initially refusing his left, thus advancing in a crescent moon shape that threatened to envelop the outnumbered enemy infantry. However, without knowing many details about the battlefield which are now lost to us, such as the exact enemy position and the intricate nature of terrain, it is difficult to say whether this could have worked. As always, it is perhaps best that Gough stuck to what he knew, as he had neither the capacity nor the staff around him to be able to adopt radical changes from his plan of action. Indeed an example of the rather rudimentary state of his staff work is illustrated by the account left to us by Robert Napier. Gough was concerned about his position on the left and was aware that the line needed to be straightened. He therefore wanted to urge the infantry on the left forward into open ground where they could take up a position facing the enemy. Gough is said to have called out in this regard, "Someone desire them to take more ground." Napier took this as an order to urge on the infantry on the left flank and immediately rode over with the message. His horse was shot from under him, and he barely made it back to the safety of the British lines before some Sikh cavalry descended. This again illustrates the confused nature of the battlefield because although much of the enemy cavalry had been driven off, pockets of enemy horse remained on the battlefield and had to be considered a danger. By the time Napier reached the left he found that Major Grant, the Deputy Adjutant General, had also been sent to the left to try and restore order.[7]

By the time the infantry reached the Sikh position night was already falling. However, committed to the battle as he was, Gough could do little but press on. The failing light, the undulating nature of the terrain, the disjoined nature of the British line, and the dust thrown up by the movement of so many men and horses, not to mention the smoke of weapons, had created made it an even more confused place than the average battlefield. Gough later wrote to his son about the battle and said that the conditions made it, "hard to distinguish friend from foe, which may account for our fearful

---

7   Napier, *Personal Narrative*, pp. 4–5.

butchers bill."[8] It is interesting to note that, in private at least, Gough accepted that the casualties were high and lamented the fact. It is easy to view Gough as someone who simply accepted high casualties and did not give them a second thought. This would be wrong. He was certainly under no illusions as to the fact that casualties would occur, but this was the nature of war in this era. However it is clear that he had great regrets over such numbers. The cynic would say this was because it reflected poorly on him as a commander, whereas the defender of Gough would point out the great concern he had for his men.

The Sikh infantry, however few in numbers they were, put up a fearsome display. So much so that Sir Harry Smith, a man who had seen much fighting on several continents and who commanded the 1st Division at Mudki, described what faced his division as 'an overwhelming force of Sikh infantry'. That the Sikhs acted with bravery should hardly be surprising, but there does seem to have been something more than the bravery and courage normally associated with the Sikh. Some have referred to the Sikh behaviour as 'fanatical', and authors writing in the late 19th and early 20th centuries would often compare them to the Dervishes of the Sudan. Fanatical is perhaps the wrong word, but there is a sense in which the Battle of Mudki demonstrated that there would be a level of courage and bravery exhibited by the Sikhs in this war that was beyond that normally associated with them. Perhaps this was recognition, consciously or not, that this was a fight for the very future of the Sikh way of life. There was certainly a grim determination on the part of the Sikh infantry.

The last two hours of the battle were extremely confused. As the Sikhs withdrew, they would occasional stand and fight, sometimes even launching into a charge on the British infantry. As Gough's own account states that,

[T]heir whole force was driven from position after position with great slaughter, and the loss of seventeen pieces of artillery, some of them of heavy calibre; our infantry using that never failing weapon, the bayonet, whenever they stood. Night only saved them from worse disaster, for this stout conflict was maintained during an hour and a half of dim starlight, amidst a cloud of dust from the sandy plain, which yet more obscured every object.[9]

The numerical superiority of British infantry eventually told. Given the difficulties it faced, it is not surprising that the great burden of the fighting fell upon Smith's 1st Division on the right. Smith lost five officers and 73 men killed and 20 officers and 319 men wounded. This was out of a total of 215 killed and 657 wounded for the army as a whole. These figures do tell us something about the nature of the battle. The cavalry losses were unsurprisingly high given the extremely active role they had played in the battle. The Cavalry Division lost 81 killed and 87 wounded, along with 164 horses killed and 63 wounded. The high number of horses killed and wounded shows that the Sikhs were shooting at the horses rather than the man. This loss of horses would have an effect as the war went on. Despite Gough having ordered the purchase of extra horses before the war began, after the first two battles of the campaign a number of cavalrymen were reduced to fighting on foot.

The losses in the artillery not only illustrate the part they played in the battle but also the skill and ability of their opponents. The artillery division, as Gough referred to it in his despatch, lost two officers and 25 men killed, and five officers and 44 men wounded. Added to this were 45 horses killed and 25 horses wounded. Brigadier Brooke deserved, and received from Gough, great credit for his activities during the battle. He had made good use of his artillery and their manoeuvrability.

8   NAM: 8303–105, Gough Papers, Gough to George Gough, 25 December 1845. In this Gough gives an account of both Mudki and Ferozeshah to his son.
9   Unknown, *The War in India, Despatches*, p. 44.

It is also interesting to note the high number of officers who fell.[10] Major Generals Sir Robert Sale and Sir John McCaskill, respectively Quartermaster-General and commander of the 3rd Division, were killed. So too was Brigadier Samuel Bolton, one of Smith's brigade commanders, although he was listed as severely wounded in the initial casualty returns. The list of wounded senior officers was even longer, including Brigadiers W. Mactier and H. M. Wheeler, and Lieutenant Colonels T. Bunbury, and J. Byrne. It is also interesting to note that a great number of the killed and wounded officers were on the various staff appointments. As well as the officers already named, two officers were killed and two wounded on Gough's personal staff. One officer was killed and one wounded on Hardinge's staff. The ADC of Brigadier Gough of the cavalry division was severely wounded. Smith's staff had two killed and three wounded and his first brigade also had their surgeon severely wounded. The 2nd Division had one staff officer severely wounded, and the 3rd its commander killed. Added to this, Major General Sir James Lumley, the Adjutant General, was so ill that he was unable to take part in the battle. This is why so much responsibility devolved upon his deputy, Major Patrick Grant.

These heavy staff losses help to emphasise the confused nature of the battlefield, the use of Sikh concealed marksmen, and the closeness of the staff to the action. It must also be said that there was a rather adventurous spirit in many of the staff officers that took them into places where perhaps they should not be. For example Sir Robert Sale, a hero of the Afghan campaign, rode with Sir Harry Smith at the head of the 1st Division. Although an act of great bravery it was perhaps not the appropriate place for the quartermaster general of the army to be. However it could be argued that they were simply following the example set by the commander-in-chief, who had been right in the thick of the action and had attracted much enemy fire. It also points to the standards of the age and the need for such officers to not only lead by example but to encourage their men forward. Gough, Smith, Sale, and many other officers managed to lift the flagging spirits of the men by personal encouragement through a tiring and difficult battle.

---

10   This was a continual theme throughout the wars with the Sikhs. Sikh soldiers, and in particular their gunners, had been trained in the art of firing at officers and the command element of an enemy formation. This deliberate tactic became apparent early in the First Sikh War. See BL IOR: Thomas Pierce Papers, Mss Eur A106, 5.

47

The Aftermath of the Battle of Mudki

Although the high number of casualties was a concern, there were other worrying things to come out of the battle. Firstly Gough's army had failed to finish off the enemy. Although exact numbers for Sikh casualties have never been determined it is likely that they lost slightly more than the British. An officer who toured the field after the battle estimated 300 Sikh dead, however such figures never account for those who managed to leave the field of battle to die elsewhere. Regardless of the exact figure, it was hardly a crushing victory. However it was a victory nonetheless and with the capture of 17 of the 22 Sikh guns that took part in the battle there was a certain justification in being satisfied with the result. A second problem, and one which does not seem to have been fully explored, was the actions of the British native units. Accounts exist that they deliberately held back from attacking the Sikhs. Hardinge's son Arthur recalled witnessing many native units deliberately firing into the ground rather than at the enemy. Their courage was put to the test when advancing on the Sikh positions, and many wavered and some even ran away. The prompt action of Gough, who at one point rode over personally to rally the troops, and Harry Smith who grabbed one of the colours of the 50th Foot and waved it to rally the men, proved a temporary solution.[1]

A detailed account of the actions of the native troops is beyond the scope of this work, but a brief comment is relevant to help us understand the problems Gough faced. The burden of the battle had fallen, somewhat unsurprisingly, upon the European units. The casualty figures bear this out: if one looks at Smith's division, the infantry formation most heavily engaged, he had six battalions under his command. Two were Europeans and in this case both were British Army regiments, the 31st and 50th Foot, and the other four were native infantry. Total casualties for the four native infantry battalions were 136 men, whereas the 31st had 175 casualties and the 50th 125. The 47th Native Infantry's casualties were only 10 percent of that suffered by the European battalion, the 31st Foot, with which they were brigaded.[2] It is also clear that a number of British casualties were caused by friendly fire from the native infantry. It is possible to see treachery in this fact and see it as a forerunner to the Mutiny in a little over 10 years' time. However it appears to be more to do with the poor quality and discipline of the native infantry and the generally confused nature of the battle. However the battle made it clear that generally the native infantry could not match the Sikhs. Their role would be to support attacks led by European troops. If in future Gough relied more heavily upon his European troops this is hardly surprising.

---

1 Bruce, *Six Battles for India*, p. 116 & Cook, *The Sikh Wars*, p. 50. See also Crawford, E. R., 'The Sikh Wars, 1845–1849' in Bond, Brian (ed.), *Victorian Military Campaigns* (London: Hutchinson & Co, Ltd, 1967), p. 41. Crawford's opinion is based upon his reading of the Rev. J. Coley's *Journal of the Sutlej Campaign 1845–6* (London: Smith, Elder, 1856). Coley, with a charitable nature that one might expect of someone in his profession, credits that the actions of the sepoys might have been by accident or in light of some confusion. Whilst possible it seems there were more 'sinister' motives at work.
2 Cook, *The Sikh Wars*, p. 48.

The battle was disappointing for the British not only from the point of view of casualties, but also because it was not the decisive and overwhelming victory that had been aimed at. As Gough said in his despatch, "Night only saved them from worse disaster."[3] The fall of night had further obscured what was already a confused battlefield. In the dark and in a very fluid battlefield, potentially fatal mistakes were made. One example involves Gough's cousin, Lieutenant Colonel Thomas Bunbury commander of the 80th Foot. Bunbury had been wounded in the battle but remained in command until he believed the battle was over. He then handed over to his second in command and rode off alone to get his wound treated. Going back towards his own lines he suddenly found himself in the middle of a Sikh unit. Each was equally surprised to see the other, and in the confusion Bunbury managed to escape.[4] Although not specifically stated it is likely the Sikhs he met were horsemen. Isolated pockets of Sikh cavalry were to be found all over the battlefield in the confusion, so much so that at several points advancing British infantry took the precaution of forming square in response to sightings of such groups. It was this general confusion created by the battlefield that had assisted the Sikhs in their withdrawal. Sir Harry Smith, reviewing the battlefield the following day, believed that the Sikh infantry had been able to retreat through the British lines given the confusion and disjointed nature of the British attack that had been created by a number of factors.

The battle has been called one of, "the most untidy actions the British Army in India had ever fought."[5] It is hard to disagree with this statement. In the aftermath everyone had their opinion as to why this was. Hardinge came up with an interesting and not entirely inaccurate point of view. In a letter to Lord Ripon he stated:

> The troops having been collected from various points, and constantly engaged in marching, had only been brigaded on paper. […] The troops therefore were not in that state of organization and formation so essential to discipline and field movements. The brigadiers and their staff were unknown to the men, and the men to the brigadiers, while at Mudki the confusion of the attack, combined with the facts above noticed, had created a feeling that the army was not well in hand.[6]

The above comments have often been seen as a criticism of Gough. If one did not know the full story it would be possible to view them in that light. However, as we have already seen, the reason the troops were collected at various points and that brigade formations existed only on paper was not of Gough's doing. Gough had urged for greater concentration near the border. It was Hardinge who had countermanded orders and prevented Gough from creating such formations near the frontier. Here we see an early example of the fact that whilst Hardinge was reporting his version of events to those in power back home, Gough was not.

Also, in the time since the Sikhs had crossed the Sutlej, Gough had barely had a moment's rest as he had attempted to create an army out of the various individual units, and all this whilst on the march and aware that a confrontation with the enemy was only a matter of days away. For Hardinge to have meant the above as a criticism of Gough would have been foolish, given Gough's ability to respond and show clearly that it was the continual countermanding of his orders that had left the army in such a poor state of preparation. It is only when looking back with the knowledge of what Hardinge would say later in regards to Gough, that some have come to view this as criticism.

---

3   Unknown, *The War in India, Despatches*, p. 44, quoting Gough's despatch dated 19 December 1845, pp. 40–49.
4   Cook, *The Sikh Wars*, pp. 49–50.
5   Cook, *The Sikh Wars*, p. 49.
6   Hardinge, Charles, *Rulers of India: Viscount Hardinge*, (Oxford: Clarendon Press, 1891), p. 86.

Gough remained on the field of battle until 0200 the following day. He was anxious about the whereabouts of the remainder of the Sikh army and was extremely anxious that his men should be properly taken care of. There was no central field hospital, which complicated matters. Gough's order for the formation and movement of a field hospital to the frontier, issued in early December was one of the orders countermanded by Hardinge. As a consequence, the field hospital had not been formed until the outbreak of hostilities and was making its way slowly to the frontier. Thus the regimental surgeons and the occasional private doctor who accompanied the force were stretched to the limit. The fort at Mudki had been converted into a makeshift reception area for the wounded, but it was far from being a field hospital of the type that even a generation later would have been a common sight. This also meant that there was no transportation to medical treatment. Robert Napier leaves us a record that many of the officers loaned their horses so that the wounded could be taken from the field. This had the consequence that Napier's, and no doubt other officers', horses were unable to move the following day due to overwork and a lack of food. As a consequence Napier spent the following day attempting to perform his duties as a staff officer on foot. Eventually the vast majority of the wounded were collected from the battlefield. It is typical of the man that it was only when he was convinced that the latter had been dealt with that Gough chose to rest.

Gough managed to get four hours rest, although whether or not he slept is something we may never know. Although not a man given to deep introspection, one wonders what thoughts crossed his mind in those early hours of 19 December. There would certainly have been a sense of disappointment that he had not overwhelmed the enemy, as this had been a key factor in his mind when deciding to attack. He had hoped that in the first engagement of the campaign he would have been able to inflict a heavy defeat on the enemy that might not only have sapped the morale of the Sikhs but also their willingness to fight. Whilst the latter was probably a forlorn hope, the effect that a crushing defeat of the enemy would have had on his own men was another consideration. He was also anxious about the wounded, the lack of facilities for their care and the consequences this would have for the effectiveness of his army. At the same time he was concerned as to the whereabouts of the main force of the enemy. In an ideal situation Gough would have liked to follow up his success by continuing his movement at first light. However the practicalities of the situation prevented this. An already tired and tested army had just undertaken a demanding late afternoon and evenings work. The rest of the night had seen exhausted men barely able to rest as Gough felt it appropriate to keep most his men at the alert for fear of the arrival of the rest of the enemy.

Gough's decision to attack at Mudki is one that, with the benefit of hindsight, can be criticised. However, given the facts as they presented themselves before the battle, his decision is defendable if perhaps questionable. Hypothetical questions as regards to what would have happened had he remained on the defensive are hard to gauge. He may have avoided battle altogether on that day; the Sikhs preferring to wait until their entire army arrived. This would have only delayed the problem, and confronted with an overwhelming force a day or two later Gough would have then been forced to decide whether to defend his position at Mudki, advance against far greater numbers or withdrawal altogether. The first would have put him at the mercy of heavy Sikh guns and would have stretched the courage on his infantry on the defence against far greater numbers; this could have been a particular problem in the case of the native infantry. The second could only have resulted in casualties higher than those sustained at Mudki. Against a larger force it was also doubtful as to whether his cavalry and artillery would have been as effective in weakening the enemy position as they had been at Mudki. The third option, of withdrawing, would have been disastrous for the morale of his army although it would have allowed Gough time to bring up his entire force and properly organise it. However any criticism Gough received for fighting a questionable action at Mudki would have been far greater had he withdrawn.

Whatever point of view one takes upon the matter of the decision to fight, the way in which the battle was fought was less than satisfactory. To describe the battle as 'untidy' is perhaps to be kind.

It was disorganised, disjointed, and disappointing. Again we see that whilst Gough's plans and intentions were sensible and correct, the way in which they were put into practice was not. It is a fair criticism of Gough to say that he often found it difficult to put theory into practice. Again his staff has to take some of the blame, as he could not be expected to do this alone. Yet at the same time one wonders how able Gough was to make them fully aware of his plans and intentions so that they could act accordingly. Whilst Gough had a degree of disappointment over the battle of Mudki it would be wrong to suggest that he was overly disappointed or felt that he had in any way failed. It was a victory, albeit a costly one, and the Sikhs had been defeated. Gough's only major regret was that it had not been the overwhelming and crushing defeat he had desired.

Gough decided that the day following the battle, 19 December, needed to be a day of rest for the army and an opportunity not only to bring on the remainder of his troops but also whatever reinforcements and supplies were possible. Gough was no doubt anxious to press on, and whilst the state of his army was partly the reason, he was also concerned about leaving the large number of wounded behind. The evening of the 19th brought the welcomed arrival of two extra European regiments, the 29th Foot and the 1st Bengal European Regiment. Although the European battalions were particularly important there was also the welcome arrival of the 11th and 41st Bengal Native Infantry and two 8 inch howitzers. However, Gough knew these were the last reinforcements he was likely to get for some time. Whilst his force would be swelled as it joined with other units in the area, most notably Littler's command, there were to be no fresh troops.

The evening of the 19th also brought a remarkable event which has been well documented elsewhere. Whilst it is not the intention to go into great detail and discussion of the matter here it is impossible for any biography of Gough to ignore the discussions between Gough and Hardinge on that evening. It will be recalled that Hardinge was, as well as governor general, a serving officer in the British Army. Although equal in rank to Gough, both being lieutenant generals, he was lower than him on the list of officers and thus Gough had seniority. Also, Gough held the local rank of general, and had done since March 1843, so there was no doubt in purely military terms as to who was senior. This created a problem as Hardinge was present with the army throughout the campaign. Hardinge had, as we have already seen, countermanded Gough's orders before the campaign began. On the morning of the 19th, he did so again. This time it was more serious as it took place in the field.

Early on 19 December, the reluctant Sikh commander Lal Singh was 'forced' by his disgruntled commanders to send reinforcements to Mudki. Exactly what size of force he sent is unknown but it was the arrival of this force near Mudki that caused the order for British troops to prepare for battle to be given. Reports of Sikh cavalry had forced the army to stand-to ready to engage, before the Sikhs withdrew upon ascertaining that there were no troops remaining in the area for them to support. Gough believed this was the entire Sikh Army coming to attack him, which is understandable. Hardinge however seems to have known better, but not passed on any specific information to Gough. It may be that Hardinge was aware, through the communications the political officers were having with the Sikh leadership, that it was not their intention to attack, and it may be this that accounts for the following unusual encounter. As Robert Napier recalled shortly after the war:

> Then ensued a scene which I hope never again to witness. Orders were given by the Commander-in-Chief –counter orders by the Governor-General. Troops were told to go to their lines to cook, then to stand fast, then to cook, until the (men), wearied, said they preferred to remain where they were![7]

---

7   Napier, *Personal Narrative*, p. 6.

The ambiguous nature and blurred lines of control between the governor general and Commander-in-Chief confused matters. It will be remembered from previous discussions on Gough's return from China that he missed out on an appointment because there was a desire to combine the civil and military roles in one person.

Hardinge now approached Gough with a somewhat unusual offer and said that he would act as his second in command. The idea that Hardinge could have exercised his right as governor general to take overall command is a somewhat troubling concept. It would have created a very dangerous precedent. Not only would it have dramatically weakened the role of the commander-in-chief but it was not always guaranteed to be as opportune as the case between Hardinge and Gough appeared to be. For example, Hardinge's successor as governor general, Lord Dalhousie, had no military experience. It was fine if the positions of governor general and commander-in-chief were to be combined, but even this had a danger of over centralisation and placing too much of a burden on one man's shoulders. It placed Gough in a difficult position and he had little choice but to accept such an offer. In a letter to Hardinge he replied:

> On this evening [19 December] in addition to the valuable counsel with which you had in every emergency before favoured me, you were pleased yet further to strengthen my hands by kindly offering your services as second in command of my army. I need hardly say with how much pleasure the offer was accepted.[8]

In private it is likely that he was less than thrilled by this. However it can be argued that as Hardinge had decided to take the field he might as well do this in his proper place as a soldier. It did however make for a rather unusual situation which almost inevitable led to further controversy.

With new units and a day of rest behind them, Gough planned to move his troops to engage the main Sikh army. Mudki had been indecisive and costly and Gough was anxious to fight another battle and hopefully inflict a major reverse on the Sikhs that could mark the beginning of the end of the conflict. However what would follow was a far bloodier battle even than Mudki. It would also see Gough's worse fears about the role Hardinge would play become reality.

---

8 Rait, *Gough*, Vol. II p. 9.

48

Divided Command and the Movements Towards Ferozeshah

Although on 19 and 20 December there had been rumours of a Sikh attack on the British position at Mudki this had never materialised. The Sikhs had instead taken up a strong defensive position around the village of Ferozeshah. Understandably they had decided to hold this position and await a British attack. Gough, for his part, had decided to attack on the 21st. To this end, on 20 December orders were sent to Sir John Littler to leave a small force to protect Ferozepore and then bring the vast majority of his 7,000 men to join the main army under Gough's command. However there is much more to this story than the basic facts suggest.

The new command arrangement between Gough and Hardinge was already starting to creak. Hardinge had been in personal correspondence with Littler on the evening of the 19th and had informed him of the battle at Mudki and urged him to march at once to join Gough at Sultan-Khanwalla about ten miles from Ferozepore. The problem was that Hardinge had failed to pass on this information to Gough, who had no plans to move until the 21st. This had the potential for disaster for Littler's division. As it happened Ferozepore was threatened by the Sikhs on the 20th and as a consequence Littler did not march off until the morning of the 21st. At the earliest he would not reach Gough until 1000.[1] This was a problem for Gough as he intended to attack early in the morning of the 21st. On the evening of the 20th Gough summoned his divisional and brigade commanders to a briefing where he outlined the intelligence he had of the Sikh position, its strength, number of men, and number of guns, and his intentions for the following day. Apart from the usual scouting reports Gough had a useful source regarding the Sikh strength. Captain George Bidulph of the 3rd Irregular Cavalry had arrived at Mudki before the rest of the army and had been attempting to ride through to join Littler's force, when he was taken prisoner by the Sikh advanced guard of the force that would fight at Mudki. He was returned to the main Sikh camp at Ferozeshah and treated with great respect. After having spent the evening of the 18th and the 19th in the camp he was released and returned to the British lines. Some have interpreted this as a gesture of good faith by Lal Singh, whereas others see it as a deliberate act of treachery on his part. It does appear that Bidulph had seen much of the Sikh camp and was able to provide Gough with much intelligence regarding their strength and disposition.

Bizarrely, although invited, Hardinge declined to attend the conference that Gough had called. As governor general there was no requirement for him to be there, although one would have thought curiosity about the proposed events for the following day might have compelled him to attend. However as a lieutenant general and nominally second in command of the entire army it is almost unbelievable that he decided not to attend in person but instead sent his military secretary Colonel Robert Blucher Wood. This was strange behaviour and has led some to believe that it was a deliberate affront to Gough, and indeed even a challenge to his authority. This is perhaps going too far. However it is odd to think why he chose not to attend and what he was doing whilst the briefing

---

1 Rait, *Gough*, Vol. II, pp. 10–11. As we shall see, Littler was delayed and thus did not arrive until midday.

was underway. With the fact that he was corresponding privately with one of Gough's subordinate commanders', Littler, without communicating this to the commander-in-chief, Hardinge was very close to either exceeding his authority as governor general or insubordination as second in command. This highlights the dilemma that Gough faced as due to Hardinge's actions he did not know who he was dealing with; a civilian representative or a subordinate soldier.[2]

One might interpret Hardinge's failure to attend the briefing both as an indictment of his willingness to be a subordinate and of Gough's strategic ability. Cynically it could be argued that there was no need for Hardinge to attend as Gough's tactics could be guessed at given his lack of original tactical thinking. Why he did not decide to attend in person is not really clear, but it certainly would not have helped the increasingly ambiguous relationship he had with Gough. It also had an unfortunate consequence. Whether Wood forgot to mention it, or Hardinge chose to ignore it, the fact that Gough had declared at the briefing that he intended to launch an attack early on the morning of the 21st was not part of Hardinge's plan and would lead to a further clash the following day.

On the morning of 21 December the army awoke at 0200 and by 0400 was ready to move, in line with Gough's plan outlined the previous evening. The light was still dim as they commenced their march and Gough had order the army to move in extended line of columns: in other words in battle order as a precaution against surprise attack from out of the dim early morning light. Once in the light of day it was easier to see what lay ahead, and Gough ordered the army to move back in more general columns which eased the march. By 1000 the army was in sight of the Sikh positions around Ferozeshah.

Gough had decided to attack as soon as possible. The Sikh position was strong and given his experience at Mudki he wanted as much daylight as possible in which to attack. The large bulk of the Sikh force at Ferozeshah had been there since they crossed the Sutlej at the commencement of the war. They had thus been able to prepare strong defences in a quadrilateral shape around the village. The defences held a resemblance to a rectangle, but the sides were not quite straight. There were trenches and ditches, earthworks of varying heights, and around the defensive line the land had been cleared of trees, bushes and so forth to create a 300 yard killing ground. This area had also been mined in various places. Even if Gough had possessed heavy artillery with which to soften up the enemy defences, the prospect of taking such a position was an unenviable one. Yet without heavy artillery and against a well disciplined and resolute army the task was almost suicidal.

Gough had been advised that the northern stretch of the camp was largely undefended. This advice had come from Broadfoot and might explain why it was less than welcome to the Commander-in-Chief. Harry Smith for his part had urged that an attack on the eastern side of the Sikh position would cut off their retreat and could lead to a complete rout of the enemy. The problem with this latter plan was that it would also require a movement upon the battlefield. This was also risky as this proposed attack not only cut off the Sikh line of retreat but also prevented the British from withdrawing in the direction of British territory. Any reverse or circumstances that required withdraw would mean that their only fall back would be Ferozepore. Smith also seems to have been unaware of the possible approach of Tej Singh's Sikh army, which had been threatening Ferozepore but was now moving to support the main Sikh force at Ferozeshah. If the British attacked from the western side of the Sikh camp they would have their back to this force when if it arrived on the battlefield.

Gough had undertaken his own reconnaissance and decided to attack the south-eastern part of defences. Given that this was possibly the strongest part of the Sikh defensive position, the decision is obviously open to question. However to attack the northern position would have required the vast majority of the army to undertake a flanking movement of great difficulty, and, as we shall see,

2   Bruce, *Six Battles for India*, pp. 123–124.

movement on this battlefield was confused at the best of times. It was very likely that any movement would be time consuming and it would almost certainly be detected long before Gough's troops closed on the enemy position giving the Sikhs plenty of time to reinforce the northern position. The southern positon favoured by Gough was nearer and could be attacked more quickly. Given that his artillery was weaker than that of the Sikhs, both in terms of numbers and calibre, he was unlikely to win any artillery duel. Thus the shorter the distance his infantry had to cover, and the less time that they were therefore vulnerable to fire from the Sikh artillery, the better. He also felt that he would be able to attack this in force rather than splitting his limited number of European troops to undertake a flanking movement whilst covering the southern position.

Under Gough's plan of attack, when Littler's force – now designated as the 4th Division – arrived on the field it would become a reserve, and be able to support the attack where necessary. It was also likely that Littler's movement would be able to threaten the rear of the Sikh position. The arrival of 7,000 extra troops on the battlefield to attack an already engaged enemy would be a potentially battle-winning moment. This was indeed the best use of Littler's force and did not require waiting for them to arrive and get into position before commencing the battle. As Gough was anxious to make the most of the daylight hours, this was sensible. The time factor involved in any flanking movement was also uttermost in Gough's mind. Not only did he want to be able to take advantage of as many hours of daylight as he could, but he was aware Tej Singh's detachment was likely moving to join the force at Ferozeshah. This was the contingent that had been sent to watch Ferozepore, but not attack it. The Sikh soldiers in this force had become disgruntled at not being allowed to attack. When it became clear that the force they were meant to be watching, Littler's division, were marching to join the main British force, there would have been mutiny if Tej Singh had not moved to join the main army at Ferozeshah. This force however was always going to arrive on the battlefield later than Littler's division, and indeed perhaps too late to take any part in the battle.

By about 1030 Gough was ready to attack. It was now that one of the most controversial actions of the entire war took place. Gough was anxious to attack as soon as possible, whereas Hardinge wanted to wait until Littler's reinforcements arrived. Both positions had their merits. Gough was anxious about the need to have enough daylight, the arrival of Sikh reinforcements and the negative affect on morale that a prolonged delay might have. Hardinge was anxious to have every soldier possible to face the Sikhs, not only because of the strength of their position but because his opinion of the Sikh Army had dramatically increased after the events at Mudki. However Littler had not been able to set off until 0800 and would not join up with the main army before midday at the earliest. Gough had already decided that with or without Littler he had to fight Lal Singh's force as quickly as possible before Tej Singh's reinforcements had chance to join him.

At 1100 the army was about to attack and as Robert Rait wrote, "the army occupied such a position that the words, 'Right wheel into line', would have brought on an action."[3] Yet before giving this order Gough had ridden up to Hardinge and greeted him with the oft quoted words "I promise you a splendid victory." It is unlikely that Gough was seeking approval for the attack but merely greeting Hardinge. Hardinge of course had other ideas. Here we have the consequence of his failure to attend the briefing the previous night. Had Hardinge been present he could have taken the Commander-in-Chief to one side after the briefing and made his concerns known. Instead a situation now transpired where, with an army straining at the leash to engage the enemy and all lined up for battle, a most unusual conversation now took place between the Commander-in-Chief and the man who was both governor general and his second in command.[4]

3   Rait, *Gough*, Vol. II, p. 14.
4   Rait, *Gough*, Vol. II, pp. 14–15.

Exactly what took place has always been slightly debatable. Hardinge's son would later claim that Gough's proposal to attack was a shock and that, "it was with no small surprise that the Governor-General found himself confronted with such extraordinary proposals."[5] This seems hard to credit, even if Wood had failed to pass on Gough intentions. Was Hardinge so detached from events that he was not even aware that for the last few hours the army had been lining up for battle? If so, it hardly speaks well of his offer to act as second in command. As Rait also wrote, "It was certainly with no less surprise that the Commander-in-Chief discovered that the Governor General desired him to spend the precious hours of daylight in waiting for General Littler's arrival."[6] With what was no doubt going to be a heated discussion brewing, Hardinge decided quite properly that it would be better it took take place in private. He led Gough over to a small grove of trees where they could discuss the matter. They were accompanied by a few staff officers, including Frederick Haines, on Gough's staff, and the future 2nd Viscount Hardinge. Haines, who records that his back was used as a makeshift map table for Hardinge and Gough, provided a personal account of the meeting to Rait in preparation for his biography of Lord Gough.

It is said that Gough stated his case vigorously for an immediate attack. He pointed to the need to usefully employ every hour of daylight, of the fact that not only were British reinforcements on their way but also Sikh reinforcements and that his desire was to have largely resolved the battle before either should arrive on the scene. According to the account left by his son, Hardinge was actually in favour of the battle starting later in the day. Exactly why he does not say, but it does appear once again that Hardinge was in possession of intelligence from those officers in communication with the Sikh leadership that Gough was not made aware of.[7] Not only did Hardinge not want to attack, he wished the army, now lined up for battle, to march to meet Littler's force as it moved from Ferozepore. At this remark Gough was close to losing his temper, and believed that Hardinge did not fully understand the implications of such a movement. To move towards Littler would leave Mudki isolated and open to attack. Gough understanding the potential consequences of such a move is said to have remarked, "What! Abandon my communications with India, and my wounded at Moodke!"[8] When placed in those terms it did seem a strange request from the Governor General. Such a movement was open to great criticism. Firstly there was the humanitarian aspect. The large number of wounded remained at Mudki with only a small guard of native infantry for protection. Had they so desired, the Sikhs could have seen off the guard and slaughtered all at Mudki. Again, perhaps Hardinge knew that the Sikh commanders would not allow such actions to take place. Gough certainly did not know this and his concern in this regard was genuine. The second point was that he would be allowing the enemy to get between him and the route back to India. Normally such a movement would be avoided at all costs and the fact that Hardinge would propose it shows the unusual nature of the conflict.

Gough continued to express his desire to attack immediately. It appears he was starting to lose his temper and some accounts say that he reminded Hardinge who was commander-in-chief.[9] It is at this point that it is said that Hardinge remarked, "Then Sir Hugh, I must exercise my civil powers as Governor-General and forbid the attack until Littler's force has come."[10] Gough's thoughts at this behaviour can be guessed at. However no records exist of an angry response, an

5   Hardinge, *Viscount Hardinge*, p. 91.
6   Rait, *Gough*, Vol. II, p. 14.
7   Hardinge, *Viscount Hardinge*, pp. 90–91 & Rait, Robert, *The Life of Field Marshal Sir Frederick Paul Haines*, (London: Constable & Co, 1911), pp. 29–31.
8   Rait, *Gough*, Vol. II, pp. 15–16. Although Rait gives no credit for it, it is to be considered likely that this came directly from his interview with Haines.
9   Bruce, *Six Battles for India*, p. 127.
10   Hardinge, *Viscount Hardinge*, p. 90.

action which would have been understandable under the circumstances. Gough would have been forgiven for thinking he was fighting two enemies; the one in front and the one behind. Hardinge, however honourable or well-intentioned his actions might have been, had continually made the difficult task that Gough faced even harder. He had blocked troop movements before the war, along with any serious preparations. On the eve of war itself he had countermanded the orders of his commander-in-chief. He had carried on private communications with senior officers in the army and through political officers with the Sikh commanders, all without communicating said correspondence to the commander-in-chief. He had placed Gough in a difficult position with his strange offer to serve 'under' him. Now to top it all he had countermanded his orders in the face of the enemy and with the army lined up for battle. This would have been to a different man than Gough a final 'slap in the face' which he could not tolerate. Many other officers would have resigned on the spot. Historians have been divided in their opinion of this event. Rait generously remarks that, "the second in command could not divest himself of his supreme powers, or his supreme responsibility."[11] Although there is no doubt some truth to this, one only has to look at the political fallout from Ferozeshah where the blame is laid squarely on the shoulders of the commander-in-chief, which makes one questions who truly had supreme responsibility. As commander-in-chief Gough was ultimately responsible for the control of the army and would be held accountable.

Gough however accepted that he had no choice, and really had no option. The only other possibilities were either to openly defy the Governor General or resign. Each course of action would have had serious repercussions. To defy the supreme civilian authority would have set a dangerous precedent which politicians at home would not allow; namely that military commanders could defy civilian authority in the name of military expediency. This of course was far different from a commander in the field who was unable to communicate with civilian authority and had thus exercised his own discretion. Here the civilian authority was right alongside him and had given him direct instructions. To resign in the face of the enemy, no matter what provocation and justification he could point to, would have been career suicide and would have left his reputation in tatters. Even to have simply handed over the army to Hardinge and become his second in command would have been questionable. In any case, it is doubtful that such ideas every crossed Gough's mind. As he rode away fuming he simply accepted the situation, and somewhat reluctantly issued orders for the entire army to march in the direction of Ferozepore until they got sight of Littler's force. Further evidence of Hardinge's collusion with the Sikh commanders is seen in the fact that whilst undertaking a withdrawal near to the enemy no attempt was made to attack the British force. Despite protestations from his soldiers Lal Singh would not allow an attack on the exposed flank of the British force as it marched away. Some accounts say that it was at that point that his subordinates started to plot his removal, if necessary by resorting to murder.[12]

Gough's frustration no doubt grew as the day wore on. It was not until 1230 that Littler's force was spotted and Gough halted the army to await their arrival. Littler himself arrived at 1300, however it was not until 1330 that his entire force of two cavalry regiments, six infantry battalions and 21 guns arrived in the British camp.[13] By this stage the British force was over a mile and a half from the Sikh entrenched position. Gough now had a force of around 18,000 men which he had to lead back to the Sikh position and then draw up into formation to attack. There was now a confused situation as the army took far longer than was necessary to form up. There was

---

11   Rait, *Gough*, Vol. II, p. 16.
12   Sidhu, *The First Anglo-Sikh War*, p. 63.
13   There are many differing times recorded not only for the initial conjunction of the two armies but the time by which all of Littler's command had entered the field. Sir Harry Smith claims that the conjunction took place at 1000hrs, but this is clearly a mistake. The times given here seem to be the most generally agreed.

certainly some faulty staff work and orders do not seem to have been clearly sent out to brigade and divisional commanders. As Sir Harry Smith recalled, "The army was one unwieldy battalion under a commanding officer who had not been granted the power of ubiquity."[14] Although Gough does deserve criticism for a failure to communicate and slowness in deploying the army there is a degree of mitigation. In regards to the staff work it will be recalled that in the morning the army had deployed with few problems in about an hour, before being 'forced' to march off. It will also be remembered that by this stage the main army had already been on the move for the best part of nine hours.

Littler's additional men, were slightly fresher and had only been on the move for about four and half hours by the time they reached the army. It took time for them to reach their position on Gough's left. Indeed the taking up of a new position for the entire army certainly confused matters but not to the extent that competent staff officers should not have been able to deal with. The problem was that whilst complaints existed that the brigade and divisional staffs were somewhat ad hoc and had existed on paper rather than in practice, the same could be said of Gough's staff. It was also a difficult manoeuvre on the battlefield as Littler's division and the rest of the army were moving in different directions as they formed line. As a result, it was not until 1600 that Gough finally had the army in position. It could cynically be argued that the delay was a display of petulance by Gough at not having got his own way earlier in the morning. Indeed he was urged to attack as soon as possible after the conjunction of the two forces. Yet Gough insisted on waiting until every man was in place before launching his attack. Although this seems a sensible precaution, it could be argued that he could at least have commenced the artillery duel. This might have provided some cover whilst his army formed up, however it could equally have drawn the fire of the enemy artillery upon his infantry. The decision to wait until all his men were in position was in many ways sensible.

Nevertheless, it is quite unusual that in the build up to the same battle Gough was to be criticised first for being too enthusiastic and impetuous and later for displaying lethargy and a lack of drive. Norman Dixon through his important work *The Psychology of Military Incompetence* does suggest that these two characteristics can go hand in hand as an example of incompetence of command.[15] However in this case it would appear that this is not the case. Gough's plans of earlier in the day were not particularly impetuous. For example, he was not contemplating fighting the battle without Littler, merely commencing it without him. When Littler entered the field, presumably during the battle, he would have in effect turned the flank of an already engaged enemy. It could be argued that this was a better use of Littler's command than that envisaged by Hardinge. Even if this had not necessarily been Gough's intention it would have been the likely consequence of his original plan.

---

14   Smith, *Sir Harry Smith*, p. 151.
15   Dixon, Norman, *On the Psychology of Military Incompetence*, (London: Jonathan Cape, 1976).

49

The Battle of Ferozeshah: The First Day

Gough's frustration that the battle started six hours later than he had anticipated can be imagined. With the benefit of hindsight one could argue that he might have been better to make camp for the night and wait the following morning before making his attack. However, this would obviously have meant an increased likelihood that Tej Singh would arrive with reinforcements. It will also be recalled that he was now in a difficult position in that he was not directly linked to Mudki and the lines back to India.

Although Gough's decision to start the battle so late in the day can be questioned, his reasons for so doing were understandable. Henry Havelock best summed up the position that Gough faced:

> It was one of those cases in which it would have been better to have attacked at midnight, rather than not to have anticipated the junction of the two armies. The object was to defeat the one before the other should come to its aid. No sacrifice is too great to complete such a manoeuvre. Every risk must be run, and every fatigue endured to attain such an object in war. The entrenched camp was attacked and carried. The resistance was indeed terrific, and the loss on our side tremendous. But—this is war.[1]

Gough's troops were disposed as follows. Brigadier White commanded the 3rd Light Dragoons and 4th Bengal Light Cavalry, with a troop of horse artillery, on the right of the British line. They were next to Major General Gilbert's 2nd Division consisting of Brigadier Taylor's 3rd Brigade of the 29th Foot, the 80th Foot and the 41st Native Infantry, and Brigadier Mclaren's 4th Brigade consisting of the 1st Bengal European Regiment and the 16th and 45th Native Infantry. In between Gilbert's and Wallace's divisions were a battery of 8 inch howitzers and two batteries of 9pdrs. Brigadier Wallace, who had assumed command of the 3rd Division with the death of Major General McCaskill at Mudki, had a small/weaker division consisting of the 9th Foot and the 2nd, 26th and 73rd Native Infantry. Next came what was in theory the strongest part of the line consisting of Littler's 4th Division and considerable cavalry support. This was despite the presence of only one European infantry battalion. Littler's command was made up of Brigadier Reid's 7th Brigade, consisting of the 62nd Foot and the 12th and 14th Native Infantry, and Brigadier Ashburnham's 8th Brigade, consisting of the 33rd, 46th and 54th Native Infantry. He was supported by two batteries of 9 pdrs and two troops of horse artillery. He was also supported by Brigadier Gough's brigade of cavalry consisting of the Governor General's Bodyguard and the 5th Bengal Light Cavalry. To the left of Littler the British line of battle was completed by Brigadier Harriot's brigade of cavalry consisting of the 8th Bengal Light Cavalry and the 3rd Irregular Cavalry.

Smith's division was held in reserve, although its two brigades were actually split and were about a mile apart from one another, either side of Wallace's third division. Smith's division consisted of

---

1   Cooper, Leonard, *Havelock*, (London: The Bodley Head, 1957), p. 68.

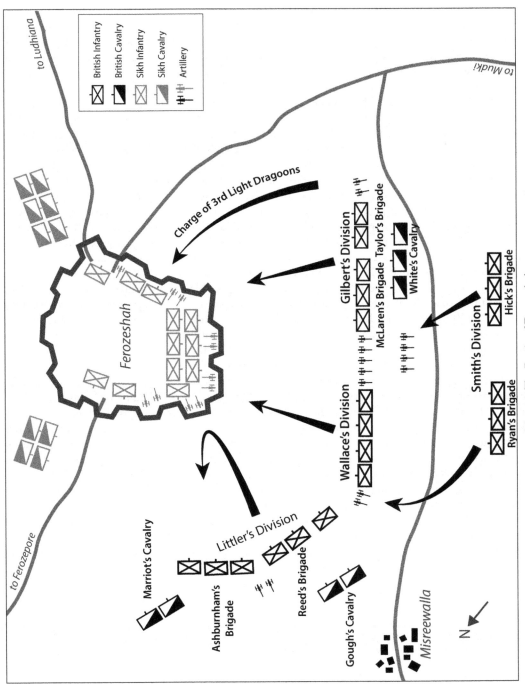

Map 11 The Battle of Ferozeshah.

the 1st Brigade commanded by Brigadier Hicks consisting of the 31st Foot and the 24th and 47th Native Infantry, and Brigadier Ryan's 2nd Brigade of the 50th Foot and the 42nd and 48th Native Infantry. Possibly Smith's men might have been better employed in attempting the flanking movement that Gough had rejected earlier in the day. Perhaps a more flexible commander, or a more imaginative one, would have seen this as an opportunity to now undertake the desirable strategic movement that earlier in the day he had rejected for sound reasons. With the extra troops Littler brought, it was now easier for Gough to spare a force for a flank attack. Yet he chose to stick to his original plan, even though the position from which he was to attack had altered.

As so often in the war, Sikh numbers are not known. Indeed figures vary widely from barely outnumbering the British at around 19,000 men to vastly outnumbering them at around 35,000. A good estimate seems to be around 25,000 men, and of this force around 17,000 were infantry who manned the defences of the position around Ferozeshah.[2] Whilst the extent of their numerical advantage is open to debate, one undoubted area of Sikh superiority was in artillery. The Sikhs had around 103 guns at Ferozeshah compared to the 69 that the British brought to the field. Yet this tells only part of the story of their superiority. Not only were Sikh guns more numerous but in general they were of far heavier calibre. Many of the guns were 24, 32 and 36 pdrs and it was even said that there were some 62 pdr guns amongst the Sikh artillery at Ferozeshah. This compared to the average British gun being a 6 pdr. Indeed the only British guns that had any real effect were the 8 inch howitzers, but they were too few in number to make any significant impact.[3]

The nature of the battlefield and the nature of the advance meant that the manoeuvrability of the artillery used to such good effect at Mudki was not possible at Ferozeshah. Indeed, the lack of impact of British artillery in general is attested to by the fact that no damage was found to have been sustained by the Sikh guns. The Sikh gunners were also using the old tactic of targeting officers and colour parties of British formations, hoping that without leaders the formations would fail to effectively press home the attack.[4] At the same time, the Sikh gunners appeared to be of better quality managing three rounds a minute compared to the one that British guns averaged. Such was the ferocity of the Sikh bombardment and its effectiveness in the artillery duel that Brigadier Brooke, commanding the artillery, warned Gough that his gunners risked being 'blown out of the field'.[5] Littler's artillery was faring slightly better. The two troops of horse artillery under Colonel Edward Huthwaite were well handled. They would unlimber their guns, fire a few rounds, limber up the guns and then move to another position, unlimber and fire a few more rounds, continuing this process as Littler's infantry advanced. In this way they were able to provide something of a cover for his advance in a way that the guns under Brooke's direct command could not.

Yet even this local advantage was limited, and once again the lack of British heavy guns, and the superiority of Sikh gunners, was telling. The Sikhs were firing quicker and with greater accuracy than their British counterparts. Indeed one account from a British officer suggests that the Sikh victory in the artillery duel was overwhelming:

2   Sidhu, *The First Anglo-Sikh War*, pp. 66–67. Sidhu discusses the varying figures and decides, quite sensibly that the figure of 25,000 is the most likely. However the usually reliable Roy, Kaushik, *War Culture and Society*, pp. 153–154, goes with a much higher figure of 12,000 irregular cavalry, 30,000 infantry and 98 guns.
3   Sidhu, *The First Anglo-Sikh War*, pp. 66–67.
4   There are numerous accounts of Sikh artillery targeting officers throughout the two wars. For Ferozeshah in particular see British Library, India Office Record and Private Papers, Mss Eur A106, 5, private papers of Major General Thomas Pierce.
5   Rait, *Gough*, Vol. II, p. 18.

We had not a gun left, or if they were, the ammunition was all expended; but most of them were smashed; and dead horses and broken limbers were lying about, having been completely outmatched by the heavier artillery of the Sikhs.[6]

Although this account is perhaps not indicative of all British artillery, as no one officer was likely to have seen all the artillery in action due to the large nature of the battlefield, it does raise some interesting points. It does show us that serious damage was being done to British guns. It also shows that having the guns in fixed position was a rather wasteful exercise, and the adoption of tactics similar to that used by the guns accompanying Littler would have served better. In fairness it must be added that, from the position he was placed in, Brooke was unable to do this. His artillery might have been better served attached directly to a brigade or placed on the flank of the British line. The quoted account also highlights the supply problem. The lack of supplies had been a problem at Mudki a few days earlier. Some supplies had come in since then, but it once again demonstrates the folly, from a military point of view, of countermanding the orders for preparation that Gough had put in place. With two major engagements taking place so close together this placed a strain on a supply system already experiencing difficulties.

We have already seen that the orders given to the various commanders were criticised for their lack of detail. Exactly what orders were given to Littler has never been entirely clear. It appears that Gough had a relatively brief conversation with him when he arrived on the field, but that little information other than the fact that he was required to attack the south western part of the Sikh defences was imparted. For reasons that have never been explained, Littler launched a premature attack on the Sikh lines. This was in fact premature in two regards. Firstly it was before all his troops were ready to attack and secondly it was before the other two first-line divisions had started to move. Indeed Gough was still struggling with the artillery duel when reports came in of Littler's men having started the attack. In a sensible precaution, Gough had ordered his men to lay down so as to make less obvious targets for the Sikh gunners. Gough is recorded as saying that "Littler will be in the trenches unsupported", with an emphasis that barely disguised not only his concern but his annoyance.[7] Littler's 7th Brigade, commanded by Brigadier Reed with the 62nd Foot taking the lead, had advanced beyond the 8th Brigade under Ashburnham. Suggestions, perhaps more appropriately referred to as allegations, have been made over the years that this was due to the fact that the latter's command was made up entirely of native infantry. For understandable reasons there does appear to have been a lack of drive in the native brigade and one gets the sense that the two native battalions in Reed's brigade were almost pulled along by the British battalion.

It has also been suggested that the reason for the premature attack was the jungle between where the British had lined up and the Sikh positions.[8] If the jungle had confused the movement of Littler's division it had at least covered them from the fire of the Sikh artillery, but when they came out of the jungle into the 300 yard killing ground that the Sikhs had cleared they were met with a heavy bombardment of both canister and grape shot. It has been calculated that the vast majority of the 62nd Foot's casualties were sustained at this time. Their total casualties for the battle were five officers and 97 men killed and 11 officers and 186 men wounded. That the majority are believed to have fallen during the opening minutes of the cannonade is testament to the quality and skill of the Sikh artillery and gunners. Although no doubt partly due to the fact that majority led from the front, there was a particular targeting of officers by the Sikhs: at least four officers were killed whilst carrying the regimental colours during the advance on the Sikh position. Of the 62nd 24 officers,

6   Sidhu, *The First Anglo-Sikh War*, p. 69, quoting Colonel James Robertson of the 31st Foot.
7   Rait, *Gough*, Vol. II, p. 18.
8   Cook, *The Sikh Wars*, p. 57.

17 were either killed or wounded. With such a large number of officers down, some companies were now being commanded by sergeants.

The ferocity of the fire upon the 62nd had understandably caused them to quicken their advance. As a consequence the regiment found itself alone in the trenches outside the Sikh position. An element of the 12th Native Infantry seems to have kept up with them, but it appears that the 14th Native Infantry deliberately held back their advance. A few men seem to have reached the Sikh lines, based on the number of sword wounds inflicted, but the vast majority of those who made it that far could make it no further. For around five minutes the battalion stayed in position and exchanged fire with the enemy, but the position was hopeless and Brigadier Reed ordered a retreat which was conducted in good order. Reed unfortunately used the term 'panic' to describe the withdrawal of the 62nd but later withdrew the remark, however it was one of a number of slurs against different regiments that would come in the recriminations of what was a difficult and testing battle.

The sight of the repulsed attack, and in particular of a European battalion being seen off, was the cause of much delight and great shouts from the Sikhs could be heard as the remainder of the British force marched on the Sikh position. The withdrawal of Reed's brigade slightly confused and affected the momentum of Wallace's division. The 62nd had withdrawn completely, and, given the casualties they suffered – particularly to their leadership – this is understandable. The 9th Foot now led a renewed attack. Least it should be thought that the courage of the native infantry has been unduly criticised, it must be pointed out that the 9th's attack was ably supported by the 26th Native Infantry. Whilst the majority of Littler's division had hung back and not become engaged, there were two notable exceptions to this. The 33rd Native Infantry, of Ashburnham's brigade, seem to have become seriously engaged in the attack and whilst the 14th Native Infantry had largely been ineffective until now, the adjutant Lieutenant Paton had led a party of men and the Colours in support of the attack now launched by the 9th Foot.

The withdrawal of the majority of Littler's division from the field presented a problem. Now the left flank of Gough's army was exposed. A more immediate concern were the guns of the artillery, which were now undefended and in danger of being cut off. At the same time the cavalry on that flank were now without infantry support. The role of Littler's command will be assessed later, but in short it had caused nothing but problems and the divisions commanded of Wallace and Gilbert would now have to bear the brunt of the battle. Gough might have been well served at this point to have moved Smith's division, still in reserve, to support the left flank but he did not order any such movement. Given the angle of the advance, the 29th Foot, on the extreme right of the British line, were furthest forward and drew the majority of the enemy fire. The advance was difficult as the jungle, although not particularly thick, did tend to obscure what lay ahead. The infantry were therefore marching into the unknown, which neither aided the speed of the advance nor the confidence of the men.

When they emerged into the killing ground that the Sikhs had cleared, they were met with a fierce cannonade. Accounts of its ferocity exist written by officers who were present. What makes their testimony even more compelling is that many of them were Peninsular War veterans. One such veteran, Major George Congreave commanding the 29th Foot, managed to steady his battalion when it appeared to be on the verge of breaking. The 80th Foot had now caught up to the 29th and the two British battalions now launched their attack against the Sikh line, pausing to fire a volley before attacking the Sikh guns. By all accounts the Sikh gunners defended their guns to the last man with admirable determination. However once through the Sikh gun line the 29th and 80th were met by Sikh infantry, many of them the elite of the Sikh troops raised under European officers. Their fire was accurate and effective. However they were too close to their gun line and the British battalions quickly closed on them and drove them away at bayonet point. Lieutenant Colonel Thomas Bunbury of the 80th recalled at this point the attack halted, and rather than continue their advance the soldiers of the two British battalions spent time examining the guns.

Given their unusual calibre and their excellent manufacturing they caused great interest.[9] At the same time elements of the native infantry, notably the 47th, now entered the Sikh camp and began large-scale looting, to the point that the 47th ceased to be a cohesive fighting unit. The aforementioned should not be viewed as being suggestive of an unwillingness of European soldiers to loot. Indeed, given the opportunity, they were masters at the art. What it does illustrate is the greater control and discipline which was maintained of British Army units in particularly and the rather lax discipline of the Company Army in general.

A counter-attack was now mounted on the 29th and 80th, many of the Sikh troops employed being Akalis (or Nihang) who wore chain mail and attacked with ferocity mostly using swords. These were ideal soldiers, shock troops, to try and force the British to withdraw. A brutal clash of sword and bayonet ensued. After a dramatic fight the counter-attack was repulsed. This fight not only illustrates why Gough had so much confidence in the power of British infantry and the bayonet, but also now much easier it was in warfare of this age to be on the defensive rather than the offensive.

Elsewhere on the battlefield the 3rd Light Dragoons had once again undertaken a highly successful cavalry charge when attacking Sikh artillery on the right of the British line. The artillery there had the ability to fire into the flank of the 29th and 80th Foot, and the 3rd Light Dragoons had been desired to clear them away. The 3rd then attacked the infantry that lay behind the guns and drove them away, being then able to sweep through the Sikh camp. Their loss was heavy but it had a dramatic effect of Sikh morale on that side of the battlefield and hindered their ability to launch a counter-attack.

Mclaran's brigade, part of Gilbert's division, had success in breaking through the Sikh line. The main assault fell upon the 1st European Regiment. The two native infantry battalions of this brigade provided varying degrees of support. The 16th Native Infantry followed the 1st closely and provided useful support. The 45th Native Infantry, however, held back. Indeed their firing was so wild that it is thought they caused more casualties to the 1st and 16th than they did the Sikhs. This brigade did not face such stiff opposition as their comrades on the right, and once through the enemy lines were able to left wheel and join the attack made by the 9th Foot. The 1st European Regiment would suffer their worst casualties when passing by a Sikh magazine that suddenly exploded. Indeed there would be a number of such explosions. Many were magazines, but a number were mines. The advance towards the village itself was slightly delayed by this explosion.

Further resistance was met by the majority of the army as they moved through the Sikhs defences towards the village itself. Smith's division had come into the fray late in the battle. On seeing Littler's attack fail, Hardinge ordered Smith to bring up his division, although this seems to have been intended more to support Wallace than fill the gap left by Littler. Smith could not actually bring forward his whole division, split as they were, but advanced with the brigade that he was with.[10] Hardinge did not consult the commander-in-chief before giving this order. Presumably now acting once again as second in command, this was an understandable instruction. A certain degree of latitude to a senior commander in the field should be allowed. However given what went before Gough would have been forgiven for thinking that Hardinge was again overstepping the mark and interfering where it was not needed. Smith's division took time to form, and it will be recalled that the two brigades had been separated by some distance before the battle began. Smith's attack on the left was delayed further for unknown reasons: Smith himself would claim that it was due to stragglers from the 9th Foot who blocked their way, but this seems doubtful. The 50th Foot performed well in driving off one of the elite Sikh regiments, clearing not only the entrenchments

9   Cook, *The Sikh Wars*, p. 60.
10   Bruce, *Six Battles for India*, pp. 132–133.

but the oncoming infantry at bayonet point. The 50th then pressed on into the village itself where in the narrow streets the Sikhs put up a determined resistance before being cleared. The 50th also proved their worth when the native infantry battalions broke and ran during a Sikh counter-attack, the situation being saved by the steadiness of the British battalion. Smith secured the village and lined his men up in battle order – in this case something rather like a semi-circle – to await a possible counterattack.

As night fell the British appeared to have won the battle, but the situation was confused to say the least. Isolated Sikh units remained and would launch counter-attacks. British battalions were scattered and many were disjointed, such had been the confused nature of the battlefield that day. Throughout the former Sikh encampment, fires burned and periodic explosions occurred either from mines or ammunition magazines. Yet the British held the camp and had captured many guns. Casualties had been heavy. Yet when one considers the strength of the Sikh position, both in terms of men, guns and entrenchments, this was inevitable.

The battle speaks to the power and discipline of the infantry, particularly the units belonging to the British Army, and to the units of British cavalry. The Sikhs held a strong position, and this was no typical 'native' army. They were a disciplined and well-trained force with equipment that was the equal, and in the case of the guns the superior, of their British counterparts. So, heavy losses were inevitable. Indeed when looking at events with the benefit of hindsight and detachment from the ideals of the era, it is somewhat surprising that the position was taken at all. Rait argues that "had there been another hour of daylight, success would have been complete."[11] This is perhaps wishful thinking, and obviously alludes to the controversy over the delay in commencing the attack due to the interference of Hardinge. We can never know for sure, but it does appear likely that had the attack been started at around midday as Gough wished he would have been able to follow up his attack on the camp by driving the Sikhs from the field.

During the battle on the 21st, Gough had continued to move around the battlefield urging on his men. The considerable risk he took, particularly given his conspicuous appearance with his white fighting coat on, is shown by the number of staff officers who rode with him who were either killed or wounded. Five officers on the personal staff are listed amongst the killed and wounded. Two further officers, Saunders Abbott and Robert Napier were both wounded but neither is recorded as such in Gough's returns for the battle.[12] Whilst this approach to his role as commander-in-chief might appear somewhat anachronistic to the modern reader, it was not unusual for the time. It did draw the fire of the enemy, and whilst they continually missed Gough, his unfortunate staff officers often had to pay the price.

Gough's biggest problem on the night of the 21st was lack of supplies, and in particular a great shortage of ammunition. Events had moved so fast that what supplies there were had quickly dwindled and further supplies were still making their way up to Mudki. The confused nature of the battlefield was such that Gough was unable to ascertain exactly what was going on. Understandably, but regrettably as it turned out, Gough chose to move the army 300 yards away from the Sikh entrenchment where they could camp for the night. The Sikh camp contained a large number of dead bodies and considerable risk of disease. There were also the continuing explosions and the fear that the camp had been extensively mined. The night was to prove a most unpleasant one for the British. There was virtually no water, few food supplies, and no chance of either a hot meal or a warming fire, so close were they to the enemy. It was recorded as a bitterly cold night, even bringing

---

11   Rait, *Gough*, Vol. II, p. 25.
12   Napier, *Personal Narrative*, p. 8. Napier records the wounds to both Abbot and himself, yet neither appear in Gough's official despatch which includes the killed and wounded officers. The despatch can be found in *The War in India*, pp. 57–60.

with it a ground frost. Not only were the men unable to light fires, the majority had stored their greatcoats before battle and thus spent the cold night laying on the ground with only their uniform for warmth. Gough had decided that rather than try and reform the army in the darkness he was best to wait until morning, when he hoped the picture would become clearer. One might question the decision but given the problems in organising the army earlier in the day, when people could see what they were doing, Gough can be forgiven for not attempting such an enterprise in the dark.

The decision to withdraw 300 yards presented a problem for Smith's division. Gough was unaware of exactly where he was and indeed the entire army was in great confusion. Given that Smith's orders had come from Hardinge rather than Gough, and that the former had not bothered to inform the latter of this fact, this is an entirely understandable if deplorable chain of events. Smith, still in the village itself, had formed his men into two squares, one made up of the 50th Foot and the other made up of a collection of other units that had partly made it to the village. Smith was in a difficult position. He did not know where the rest of the army was. Although the Sikhs made no major attack upon his positon there was a degree of harassing fire directed against him. Realising his position was precarious, at 0300 he decided to withdraw from his positon in an attempt to find the rest of the army.[13] The word eerie has been used to describe the setting Smith's men were in, and it seems as good a word as any. The darkness was broken by the burning magazines, tents, and so forth. This in itself would be slightly disconcerting, but added to this were the noises of the wounded and the dying, the shots of Sikh sharpshooters, and now as they made their retreat the bodies of the fallen of earlier in the day. Reports say that many of the troops were jumpy, and that it not surprising. Given Smith's experience, perhaps Gough's decision not to attempt such a movement in the dark unless absolutely necessary was sensible.

Smith retreated along almost the exact same route he had advanced earlier in the day and ultimately found his way to where Littler's division had camped at Misreewala. Despite being urged by his fellow divisional commander to fall back on Ferozepore, Smith determined that he must remain in the field as he correctly surmised that battle would be renewed the following day. It is just as well that Smith reached Littler during the night as it appears that at first light Littler intended to fall back upon Ferozepore and would thus have robbed Gough of an important part of his force. From Smith's account it appears that Littler was in somewhat of a state and had convinced himself that all the attacks had been repulsed. Reading between the lines of Smith's account one almost gets the impression that Littler believed that a major defeat had been suffered and that he commanded the only British force left. Smith reassured Littler that battle would be re-joined the following day and convinced him to stay. This goes to further illustrate the disjointed nature of the army after the battle and the lack of communication and coordination.[14]

During the night another example of the staff problems within the army was to take place. Captain James Rutherford Lumley Jnr was acting Assistant Adjutant General. It will be recalled that the Adjutant General, his father Major General James Rutherford Lumley Snr, had been too ill to take part in the battle at Mudki. The latter's deputy, Major Patrick Grant, had been wounded at Mudki and was unable to take part in the battle. Thus the role of adjutant general, in effect the chief of staff, fell upon a captain. Lumley Jnr appears to have had a good reputation up to this point, and although there was the suggestion that nepotism had played a considerable part in his appointment, in truth that could be said throughout the army. Lumley's previous record points to a stable if unspectacular officer. However his stability deserted him during the days of the battle of Ferozeshah and he issued some unusual orders. Whether it was the heat – some say he had 'a touch of the sun' – nervous exhaustion, or a vision of impending doom, has been debated. It may

13   Smith, *Sir Harry Smith*, pp. 157–159.
14   Smith, *Sir Harry Smith*, pp. 159–161.

simply have been that such great responsibility at such a time of emergency proved too much for him. Lumley on his own initiative started to issue orders that would have dramatic consequences.[15]

Smith, who was unsure of the whereabouts of Gough, let alone his intentions, was at first delighted to see Lumley. This soon altered when Lumley issued extraordinary orders. The incident is perhaps best retold in the Smith's own words:

> He (Lumley) said, "Sir Harry Smith, you are the very man I am looking for. As senior officer of the Adjutant-General's department, I order you to collect every soldier and march to Ferozepore". I said, "Do you come direct from the Commander-in-Chief, with such an order? If you do, I can find him, for, by God, I'll take no such order from any man on earth but from his own mouth. Where is he?". "I don't know, but these in my official (position) are the orders". "Damn the orders, if not the Commander-in-Chief's. I'll give my own orders, and take none of that retrograde sort from any Staff officer on earth. But why to Ferozepore? What's the matter?". "Oh, the army has been beaten, but we can buy the Sikh soldiers". "What !" says I, "have we taken no guns?" "Oh yes", he says, "fifty or sixty". "Thank you", I said; "I see my way, and want no orders". Turning round to my A.G., Captain Lugard, I said, "Now get hold of every officer and make him fall in his men".[16]

Although this story has a ring of truth about it given events we shall discuss a little later on regarding Lumley, Smith should always be taken with a 'pinch of salt'. He is a 'dramatic' teller of events. He also wrote his account many years after the events in question. Even allowing for Smith's over-dramatic style, this was a remarkable and extraordinary incident. It is bizarre enough to believe that any captain, no matter what position he held, thought he could order around such an experienced officer; and a major general no less. The actions seem to be a panic reaction to the events of the day. Fortunately Smith knew better than to obey them. Unfortunately not all were as confident of their position to obey what on the face of it appeared to be an official order. For example the commanding officer of the 8th Light Cavalry simply obeyed the order when Lumley approached him and rode his regiment off towards Ferozepore.

As for Smith, he was fortunate that just after the incident with Lumley, Captain Christie arrived with a detachment of irregular horse and said he knew where Gough was. Thus Smith marched with his entire force, with Christie leading the way, to join up with Gough. Smith recorded that, "The Commander-in-Chief was as delighted to hear of me and my troops as I was to find His Excellency." It quickly became clear to Smith that the orders he had received from Lumley had certainly not originated with Gough. Indeed Gough's first action was to move Smith into place for the attack he envisaged in the morning. Smith was slightly shocked to find that the intended target was the very spot he had evacuated earlier in the night, and he clearly felt aggrieved that he had not known of the Commander-in-Chief's intentions before he decided to move.[17]

This lack of communication was always a problem on the battlefields of this era, and particularly so at night. Perhaps Gough could have done more to better ascertain exactly where his army was. The only way to have done this would have been to send mounted men across the field to bring in all

15   Bruce, *Six Battles for India*, p. 150, calls Lumley "half-crazed". Cook, *The Sikh Wars*, p. 66, calls him "Insane". Sidhu, *The First Anglo-Sikh War*, p. 89, is somewhat more charitable and declares that he had 'temporary insanity' quite possibly due to the heat. Lumley later resigned and was given a medical discharge after a court martial had found that he had been in an unsound state of mind when he issued the order. Br Lib IOR/Z/E/4/19/G434, is the letter of resignation submitted by Captain J. R. Lumley to the Commander-in-Chief and Gough's response.
16   Smith, *Sir Harry Smith*, pp. 159–160.
17   Smith, *Sir Harry Smith*, pp. 160–162.

straggling units to his location. Over a large battlefield this would have been a major undertaking. It would also have been a dangerous operation given the parties of Sikhs that were still around the battlefield, the number of unexploded mines, and the dark of night made the possibility of 'friendly fire' incidents increasingly likely.

Smith would later change his tune in regards to the evening. He would later claim that the moonlight was such as to make it 'as bright as day'. This was in attempt to substantiate his view that Gough should have been able to support Smith in Ferozeshah itself and that there was no need to withdraw. No other account by anyone there at the time makes mention of the bright moon. Indeed many accounts record the problems that the dark created. At the time Smith made no mention of such an occurrence in his report of the battle. Sir Robert Rait went further in his efforts to show that Smith's claims as regards the moonlight were false by enlisting the help of Professor Herbert Hall Turner, Savilian Professor of Astronomy at the University of Oxford. Turner demonstrated that amongst other things the moon was in its last quarter and would not have had the effect that Smith alluded to.[18]

Smith was no doubt trying to criticise Gough for not supporting him at Ferozeshah. Smith had also become bitter when many of the details of his report were not expressed in the despatches of Gough. Very little reference to the fine actions of Smith on that day made it into Gough's despatch. Despatches are always a contentious issue, and the commander-in-chief cannot include everything that happened in the day and whatever is left out is bound to offend someone. In this case Gough's reason for leaving out much of what Smith wrote might be quite simply, in that he wished to avoid reporting Smith's criticism of others. Smith's report was extremely critical of many of his own officers and men, of the staff officers he met in the day, and of many of the other senior commanders, in particular Littler, and in more general terms of the way in which the battle was fought.[19]

Whilst Smith may well have been correct in much of what he said, that was not material for the despatches. It is interesting to note that in his report Smith called Ferozeshah, "the most glorious battle ever fought in the East, adding additional lustre to H.M. and the Honourable Company's arms, and to the already acquired glory of the Commander-in-Chief." In his autobiography many years later he said that the battle was poorly conceived and poorly carried out. Obviously opinions do change over time and circumstances allow one to speak many years hence in a way that was not possible at the time. However it does illustrate that Smith is an authority who should be taken with a 'pinch of salt'.[20]

During what was a difficult night, Gough welcomed the arrival of Smith and his men. He would need every man he could to retake the defences in the morning. For much of the night the men tried to get the best sleep they could. At one point in the early hours of the morning Gough was forced to undertake an action against the Sikhs. Many of them had returned to their guns and their defences once the British had withdrawn. One large calibre gun started to cause problems for the British, firing directly into where they had camped for the night. Although it is unlikely that the Sikhs knew exactly what they were doing, they were firing directly at the area of the camp where Gough, Hardinge and their respective staffs were. More than this, it was having a negative effect on the already low morale of the army. Thus, despite his reluctance to undertake any movement during the hours of darkness, Gough determined to silence this gun. He ordered the 80th Foot supported by the 1st European Regiment, to attack. They advanced to within 70 yards, firing a volley and then giving a loud cheer before charging the gun. The gun was taken and spiked, and there were no

18   Rait, *Gough*, Vol. II, pp. 23–24.
19   Rait, *Gough*, Vol. II, pp. 23–24.
20   Rait, *Gough*, Vol. II, p. 24 & Smith, *Sir Harry Smith*, pp. 152–153.

further problem of this nature through the remainder of the night. Indeed the exploits of the 80th Foot provided a much need boost to the flagging morale of the army.

Morale was a problem during that night, and Gough and Hardinge did all they could to lift the men's spirits by moving from unit to unit. Gough's distinctive appearance always raised a cheer from the men, even on a night such as this. Hardinge also helped to lift the men's morale. It is said he made sure that everyone saw the empty sleeve where his hand was missing. At other times he tried to disguise it, but on this particular night the loss he had suffered at the Battle of Ligny was used to illustrate that he was an experienced soldier who knew what he was talking about.[21]

Yet the men were cold, hungry, and thirsty. Many of them had been at arms for around 24 hours, which in and off itself would have been tiring. However when added to the morning march to Ferozeshah, the march to join Littler, the march back to Ferozeshah, and then the battle itself it is hardly surprising that the men were suffering from fatigue. This, and the hard fought nature of the battle, was bound to lower morale.

It is unsurprising that there were those who took advantage of the night to slip away. This was particularly the case with civilians, such as the native drivers of the artillery, but it was also true of the native infantry. No doubt there were many 'Europeans' who considered such a cause of action, but we know little of this. Indeed for many it would have been easy to do as there were many stragglers who had become disjointed from their regiment during the day. Anyone subsequently caught could make a strong case for having become 'lost' and unable to find the rest of their unit.

However it was not just the men who were suffering from low morale. During the night many officers are said to have approached Gough urging him to withdraw. Gough gave them short shrift, and dismissed them with a sense of anger. He later wrote to his son, "Were I to have taken the strenuous representations of officers, some of rank and in important situations, my honour and my army would have been lost".[22] To withdraw would mean the likely destruction of Mudki and the loss of all the wounded there. He would have been stuck at Ferozepore, as despite the supplies that were there, they were insufficient to meet the needs of such a large army. Also withdrawing the army was not the easy and risk free enterprise that those who championed it presumed it to be.

There were some officers who even claimed that they had been sent to Gough by the Governor General. In the same way that Lumley had presumed to talk for Gough, they now presumed to talk for Hardinge. Gough reply is recorded as being, "Well, I shall go to the Governor-General, but my determination is taken rather to leave my bones to bleach honourably at Ferozeshah than that they should rot dishonourably at Ferozepore".[23] As it turned out there was no question of the officers having been sent by Hardinge. Whatever reservation Hardinge might have had about the battle of the following day, he was as determined as Gough that there must be a battle.

Despite being in agreement over the need for action the following day they had differing views over the likelihood of its success. Gough wrote that, "I saw nothing to make me despond. We were well collected, and our Europeans all in good heart and in hand. I had not a doubt in my mind as to our success in the morning, when daylight showed me friend from foe". Gough did later experience a minor moment of doubt but as he wrote to his son, speaking of himself in the first person, "But it was only for a moment, and Hugh Gough was himself again". That he had this doubt is to his credit, as not to have experienced a moment's doubt under the circumstances would have seemed to indicate ignorance of the magnitude of the position he was in.[24]

21   Sidhu, *The First Anglo-Sikh War*, p. 75.
22   NAM: 8303–105, Gough Papers, Gough to George Gough, 16 January 1846.
23   NAM: 8303–105, Gough Papers, Gough to George Gough, 16 January 1846.
24   NAM: 8303–105, Gough Papers, Gough to George Gough, 16 January 1846.

Hardinge, whilst putting a brave face on in public, seems to have been more alive to the potential for disaster. As a precaution he sent away the Crown Prince of Prussia, who had been an observer with the army, much to the latter's chagrin. He also sent his sword, presented by Wellington and said to have been the sword Napoleon carried at Waterloo, away from the field of battle.[25] He also burnt his private papers, lest they should fall into enemy hands, and issued orders that in the event of a British defeat that his secretary Frederick Currie who was at Mudki should burn all the state papers there. This unfortunately led to a belief amongst those at Mudki that the British had been defeated on the 21st. Indeed Robert Cust, one of Broadfoot's political officers and therefore not enamoured of the Commander-in-Chief, wrote in his diary that Gough had been defeated on the 21st.[26] This was, as we have shown, not true but it was an understandable assumption for Cust, who was with the wounded at Mudki, to make on receiving such an unusual order. Somewhat controversially Hardinge, without informing Gough, ordered that should they be defeated the garrison at Mudki was to surrender in the hope that the wounded could be saved.

---

25 Although it is generally believed that Hardinge sent his sword away with his surgeon, some sources do say that he sent it away with his son Charles.
26 Robert Needham Cust was an intelligent and articulate officer who had been an assistant to Broadfoot as agent for the North-West Frontier. On Broadfoot's death he actually took over as chief agent. After leaving India in 1867 he became a noted writer and philosopher and something of an expert on Asiatic studies.

50

The Battle of Ferozeshah: The Second Day

There is a sense in which the darkness and the eerie feel of the battlefield led to a despondence amongst the army that started to recede as daylight came. Both Gough and Hardinge did all they could to help this gloom to lift as they rode up and down the line of battle. As Gough recalled, "The line halted as if on a day of manoeuvre, receiving its two leaders as they rode along its front, with a gratifying cheer, and displaying the captured standards of the Khalsa army."[1] The conditions of the night before, and the difficulties of the day, left men who were tired, hungry and thirsty, without much optimism and with decreased morale. It is easy for the historian to concentrate of the events of the evening and early morning, but it needs to be placed in context. When the morning came, it was with remarkable ease that Gough formed up his line and he had little difficulty in raising its morale and preparing it for the task that lay ahead.

In a strange way it probably helped that Gough had ordered an attack. To have had to stand and await an enemy attack would have added to the tension. In this, Gough was not only following the tactical imperative of warfare in India, but also addressing the practicalities of the situation. With a shortage of ammunition the main weapon of the day would have to be the bayonet. It was far easier to use this as a weapon of attack rather than defence. To have had to stand and await a Sikh attack without being able to fire in any great degree would have weakened the British morale and encouraged the Sikh attack. Thus, whilst it might seem unusual, given the circumstances, to go on the attack it was not without good reason.

The Sikhs had only partly reoccupied the entrenchment. Whilst many authors concentrate, understandably, on the difficulties experienced by the British after the first day of the battle, the problems were no less for the Sikhs. Their command structure, and indeed discipline in general, had broken down. There are reports of the Sikhs undertaking looting, with even the disciplined Akalis joining in. At the same time Lal Singh, who no doubt feared for his own life with an increasingly angry soldiery about him, had abandoned not only his men but his command and had left the field. This perhaps explains why there was no coordinated attempt to reoccupy the defences of the previous day. Whilst one can point to treachery and personal agendas being behind the difficulties the Sikhs suffered, it would be wrong to completely ignore the impact that the previous day had upon them.[2] That said, Amarpal Sidhu takes a slightly different view and claims that the Sikhs had "vast resources of food and munitions." Whilst this can be debated, he correctly makes the important point that the Sikhs controlled the wells that serviced the village. Sidhu certainly acknowledges the falling off in discipline amongst the Sikhs.[3]

Whilst much has been written about the British suffering, the Sikhs had lost even more men, and had been driven from what would have appeared to them to be very strong positions. Also, if

---

1   Unknown, *The War In India, Despatches*, p. 52.
2   Cook, *The Sikh Wars*, p. 64.
3   Sidhu, *The First Anglo-Sikh War*, pp. 77–79

Sikh 'treachery' and particularly that of Lal Singh had been so assured, why had Hardinge – who is supposed to have been aware of such correspondence – taken such precautions for the aftermath of a possible defeat the night before? It is a question we cannot really answer, but it is tempting to believe that some historians, and those present at the time, have subsequently used such reports to explain away events. To speak of 'treachery' on the enemy's side disguises the deficiencies of the British and Company armies as a whole. It also weakens the presumed strength of the Sikhs. Whilst they were no doubt great soldiers and determined fighters, this raises a question mark over their discipline, leadership and morality. In the aftermath of the war, and when Sikh soldiery were being harnessed for the empire it would have been attractive to show that they needed British leadership and discipline to reach their full potential. However, like so many things attached to the Sikh War, we can never know for sure exactly what was happening. Better Sikh leadership and a more cohesive command would no doubt have made it harder for the British on the morning of 22 December 1845. Yet to argue that under such circumstances Gough would not have been successful in retaking the Sikh camp is to underestimate both him and the British Army regiments upon whom would have devolved the main responsibility of capturing the position.

As it was the taking, or perhaps retaking, of the Sikh defensive position was achieved with little difficulty. Only a small number of Sikh guns were still manned, and it has been argued that the fire from the Sikh guns was largely ineffectual due to many of the trails of the guns having sunk into the earth due to the heavy firing of the previous day. The gunners manning them had either not realised or not had time to do anything about this. Whilst the British were particularly short of artillery ammunition, there was sufficient to engage the Sikh guns. Indeed spirits had been slightly lifted when in the early morning a small number of camels arrived carrying ammunition. Although it was not nearly enough for the army it did allow some men to receive a few extra rounds and did ensure at least that every European had a loaded musket. It was under the cover of the artillery duel that the British line advanced. Many of the Sikhs who had manned the line of defence understandably withdrew against overwhelming odds. Once again it was the Sikh gunners, defending their guns, who proved the sternest test.

It does appear that the morale of the Sikhs had been dealt a blow, not only by the previous day's fighting but by the problems with the command system and an overall lack of leadership. As a consequence the British now swept through the Sikh encampment with an ease that they had certainly not experienced the previous day. Having commenced the attack at just after 0700, by 1000 the camp had been cleared. There was no question of the British following after the retreating Sikhs, as neither supplies nor the condition of men and horses allowed for this. Such was the relief at this victory, and such was the hunger and thirst of the men, that the army disintegrated as it entered the camp. Each man went looking for what succour he could find. There was surprisingly little food in the camp, and as the Sikhs had no opportunity to withdraw such supplies after the battle it illustrates that the Sikhs were also suffering from a lack of supplies. As for water, the only well that was found had been polluted with dead bodies and the ropes of the well cut. The former did not bother men almost driven mad with thirst and the latter was solved by tying the ends of pairs of trousers and lowering them into the well on the end of a rope.[4]

Just at the moment of triumph there was a cloud on the horizon, both literally and figuratively. The large dust cloud heralded the arrival of Tej Singh and his army from Ferozepore. Exactly what size of force he had is unclear. It has been estimated that it may have been as high as 30,000 men. This included a large number of guns. With the already inferior British artillery reduced in number

---

4   Sidhu, *The First Anglo-Sikh War*, p. 80, recounts the story of the tied together trousers. Bruce, *Six Battles for India*, p. 146, states that the British found one bucket for use. Although the ropes had been cut they were able to tie together tent robes to enable the bucket to be lowed to the water.

and largely out of ammunition, there was nothing they could do to trouble such artillery as the enemy possessed. Indeed in all areas the Sikhs were superior in numbers. To a British force, now around 15,000 men at most, battle weary, hungry, 30 and thoroughly exhausted, the presence of such a large Sikh force presented a real danger. It came at a terrible time in terms of the morale of the men. After a night full of trepidation they had faced the morning and battle, and had won. With obvious feelings of relief they had sought to slake their thirst and resolve their hunger. The fact that just at the point of presumed victory and the hope of succour, a large force of the enemy came fresh to the field would have dealt a terrible blow to the confidence of any man. Indeed it was at this point that even the indomitable spirit of Gough fell for a moment. As he later wrote to his son:

> The only time I felt a doubt was towards the evening of the 22nd when the fresh enemy advanced, with heavy columns of Cavalry, Infantry and guns, when we had not a shot with our guns, and our Cavalry Horses were thoroughly done up. For a moment then I felt a regret (and I deeply deplore my want of confidence in Him who never failed me nor forsook me) as each passing shot left me on horseback. But it was only for a moment, and Hugh Gough was himself again.[5]

Perhaps Gough's recovery of spirits was not simply his faith in God, but also an acceptance that battle was unavoidable. To have attempted to leave the field would have been full of risk. His men were so exhausted that few of them would have been able to march at the speed necessary to withdraw. Also where could they withdraw to? Ferozepore would be difficult, as the Sikh cavalry had the ability to cut of this route. Back to Mudki would only delay a fight, perhaps allowing a few extra supplies to be brought up but with an army greatly reduced in terms of morale. In short, he had little choice but to stand and fight. By so doing he would be playing to the strength of the British soldier who has always tended to be better on the defensive than the offensive, and no doubt memories of the defence of Tarifa came back to him. The question would be for how much longer could the British battalions stand given the exertions and exhaustion of the last few days.

Goughs's exhausted men were formed up into a large defensive square around the village of Ferozeshah, using the previous defences of the Sikhs wherever they could. Gough ordered his artillery forward to try and slow the advance of the enemy. After only a few rounds were fired, each troop of artillery was badly hit by the Sikh return fire and eventually forced to withdraw back to the British square, with their ammunition all but exhausted. The Sikh artillery was now turned upon the British infantry. The British square was heavily shelled with large numbers killed and wounded. At the point where the Sikh cavalry was about to attack, a heroic and courageous charge against them was led by the 3rd Light Dragoons supported by two native cavalry regiments. It is recorded that several mounted officers, including Major General Gilbert commanding the second division, bravely, but perhaps rashly, joined the 3rd Light Dragoons in their assault. Although reduced in number due to their heroics both at Mudki and on the 21st at Ferozeshah, the 3rd Light Dragoons managed to turn around the advancing Sikh cavalry. Although there was a lack of leadership within the Sikh army at large, and the cavalry in particular, this action by the British cavalry ranks with any display of bravery and courage in the history of the Army. To say it appeared a suicidal assault would perhaps be hyperbole, but it does at least give us an idea of the nature of the charge they undertook.

Whilst this cleared the imminent threat, the Sikhs returned to bombarding the infantry square with their long range guns and there was little, if anything, that the British could do in response. In fact such was the severity of the fire, and the effect it was having on the steadfastness of the British infantry, that Gough undertook a remarkable act of personal courage. Wearing his distinctive

---

5   NAM: 8303–105, Gough Papers, Gough to George Gough, 16 January 1846.

white fighting coat and accompanied by one aide-de-camp, Gough rode out ahead of the infantry to draw the fire of the Sikh guns. One has to question the appropriateness, and the sanity, of the action, but it demonstrates not only the courage of Gough but the desperate nature of the situation. Gough recounted his drawing of the enemy's fire in a letter, stating that he "rushed forward with my gallant A.D.C., to draw a portion of the artillery fire on us from our hard pressed infantry. We, thank God, succeeded, and saved many unhurt, my gallant horse being a conspicuous mark – unheeding the thunder of shot (both round and grape) – ploughing up the earth around him."[6]

Although Gough drew great fire, remarkably he was not hit. The need for such an act, that is to relieve the pressure on the infantry, cannot be questioned, even if the propriety of the course of action the commander-in-chief took can. The infantry were hard-pressed, and already those who could were starting to leave the field. This was particularly true of the native forces. The infantry slipped away where they could, but it is recorded that one irregular native cavalry regiment when ordered forward did as it was told but quickly returned. Thus Gough's action gave a momentary relief by giving the Sikh gunners an alternative target. However it was just that: a momentary relief. The situation seemed hopeless as the Sikh infantry started to advance under the cover of their guns against a battered British infantry square made up of tired, thirsty, hungry, despairing men who were expecting to die within the next few moments.

It was at this point that a most remarkable event took place. Some historians have written that only a miracle could save the British from the position they were in.[7] If it was a miracle is was a miracle in error. Just at the time when every man was needed for a desperate defence, all the British artillery and cavalry started to leave the field of battle. Bizarrely this was done under orders which the men who obeyed them believed had come from Gough himself. However the orders had not come from Gough but from his 'deluded' acting adjutant general Captain Lumley, who almost beyond belief was still in possession of this important appointment despite the actions in regard to the orders issued to Harry Smith. Whether or not Gough was fully aware of exactly what had taken place between Lumley and Smith in the early hours of the morning is unclear. If he was it was clearly a gross error to have kept Lumley in his appointment.

Yet it was an error that with the 'luck of the Irish' would end up saving Gough and his army. Lumley had ordered all the guns to ride from the field, and to protect them he had ordered all the cavalry to accompany them. Once again, Lumley issued these orders in the name of the commander-in-chief, only this time the officers in question had neither the wisdom nor independence of mind to question the orders. One can indeed understand that they were relieved to be leaving the field. Lumley said that the intention was to move to Ferozepore to restock with ammunition. Given that the guns were now down to a few rounds per gun at most, one can understand how any officer used to obeying orders without question would have seen some kind of logic in what Lumley said. The problem was that this left the infantry completely without support. Although this account is largely accepted by historians some have questioned it: Amurpal Sidhu questions how significant the withdrawal was and states that only a few light guns left the field. He also doubts that any of the cavalry left the field.[8] Certainly, however, some troops began to depart.

The rest of the army watched amazed as the artillery and cavalry marched away. Both Gough and Hardinge sent riders after them to try and get them to return to the field, but it was to no avail. Yet at the very moment when defeat looked a distinct possibility the Sikh army started to withdraw.

6   NAM: 8303–105, Gough Papers, Gough to George Gough, 25 December 1845. His 'gallant' aide was Charles Sackville-West, later a major general and the 6th Earl De La Warr. Sackville-West died in 1873 by drowning in the River Cam (or more accurately one of its tributaries the River Granta), in what is believed to have been an act of suicide.
7   Bruce, *Six Battles for India*, p. 149.
8   Sidhu, *The First Anglo-Sikh War*, p. 83.

Exactly why has never been understood. Some have pointed to this being another act of treachery by the commanders of the Sikh army and in particular Tej Singh. Whilst there might be some truth in this, as Tej Singh was a reluctant participant in the war at best, it is not an entirely satisfactory explanation. The explanation that Tej Singh, and other Sikh commanders, gave to explain away this extraordinary decision is that they feared a flanking movement, possibly supported by fresh troops. One can understand that the sudden and inexplicable movement of most the guns and cavalry away from the main field of battle would unnerve an enemy commander. At the very least one would expect him to wonder if he had missed something. It was quite possible, and indeed plausible, that Tej Singh felt that this was an attempt to outflank him. He might even have thought that they were trying to block his retreat.

Tej Singh must have known that the British infantry in front of him had been shaken but did he know the extent to which they had been damaged by the events of the last two days. If Tej Singh saw a mass of red-coated infantry ahead of him and feared the possibility of artillery and cavalry at his rear then the decision to withdraw has a degree of plausibility about it. He may even have believed that there was another infantry force on its way to the field, and that the artillery and cavalry were moving to support this. This is not as far-fetched as it sounds as the exact numbers of the garrison at Ferozepore cannot have been accurately known. Whilst Littler had marched off to support Gough with the majority of the garrison, Tej Singh might have suspected that there were further infantry reinforcements marching from Ferozpore and that the artillery and cavalry were marching to join them. The likelihood is that it was a mixture of both 'treachery', or perhaps more appropriately a lack of enthusiasm, and uncertainly as to what the movement of British cavalry and artillery indicated, that led to Tej Singh decision to withdraw. Whatever the cause, the decision was welcomed by the British. Pursuit of the retreating enemy was not even considered. Partly this was due to the fact that the army was so exhausted and worn down by the action, but also because the main arm of pursuit was the cavalry, which was now heading towards Ferozepore.

The main problem that now faced Gough was not pursuit of the enemy but care for his wounded. He put as many men as possible to the task of bringing in the wounded that were scattered over the battlefield. Care for them was difficult. There were few supplies, other than those found in the Sikh camp, and much of the transport had left the field. The lack of a field hospital, the movement of which had been ordered by Gough but countermanded by Hardinge, increased the suffering. The burden of the task again fell upon the already overworked regimental surgeons.

That Ferozeshah was a British victory, albeit it a costly one, cannot be doubted. Yet it was clearly a very narrow victory that it could be argued owed more to luck than judgement. The disappointment lay in the fact that, just as at Mudki, it had not been a crushing victory. The Sikh army, although battered and bruised, had not been annihilated and remained a force to be reckoned with. The greatest consequence of the casualties suffered by the British was that the majority were again Europeans and the small number of European units had again borne the brunt of the battle and suffered accordingly. This meant that whilst Gough still had a large army, his most important units were reduced in number and could not go on suffering such casualties for much longer. Gough had suffered a total of 694 officers and men killed and 1,721 wounded. Of this number 37 British officers and 17 native officers had been killed. Of the men 462 were Europeans and 178 were natives. This illustrates the important part that British troops had played and that the burden of the battle had fallen upon them. The figures for wounded also serve to illustrate this point. There were 78 British officers and 18 native officers wounded, and 1,054 British and 571 native men wounded. This put total casualties at 2,415.[9]

---

9   Unknown, *The War In India, Despatches*, pp. 56–60. This includes Gough's full and detailed casualty returns for the battle.

As at Mudki, Sikh casualties are not known. An estimate of 3,000 is often made, and this does seem reasonable. Some accounts put the figure lower but often this is based on an account of officers who based their figure on the number of casualties they saw around them. Given the large size of the battlefield this does not always produce an accurate figure. Robert Rait puts forward a figure of 5,000 Sikh casualties but this does seem a little high. In short, we can never know for sure. The Sikhs had sustained heavy loss not only in terms of men but also supplies and guns. They were however in a better position to replace the losses.[10]

Gough's conduct of the battle will always be questioned, and rightly so. It was not his finest hour. However he had been placed in a very difficult position from the outset. The need to fight so soon after the action of Mudki was partly a problem of his own making, and this placed an added burden upon his army. The actions of the Governor General, however honourable and well intentioned they might have been, certainly did not help matters. From the moment Hardinge offered to theoretically serve 'under' Gough, he created the potential for the incident that took place the morning of the 21st. By undermining Gough's authority by overruling his plan and exercising his authority as governor general, Hardinge placed Gough in a very difficult position. A lesser man than Gough might have simply renounced responsibility and turned over the command fully to Hardinge in an act of petulance. If that had happened one wonders how Gough would now be remembered given the inevitability of large casualties when attacking such a strong position as Ferozeshah without artillery superiority.

The issue of large-scale loss, both in terms of dead and wounded, is one that it is hard to escape. Casualties in such a battle are always inevitable, but when attacking such a strong position held by an enemy in many ways one's equal, and in some ways superior, the high number was to be expected. One could actually argue that under the circumstances 694 dead was not excessive. The problem was that it was unexpected. Up to that point India had been conquered with far fewer casualties, and there was a failure in Britain, particularly amongst the press to appreciate the quality of the enemy that was faced.

At this time, however, Gough did receive the support of one who knew much about war and India, and could perhaps appreciate the magnitude of the difficulties Gough faced better than many others: namely the Duke of Wellington. Wellington wrote to Gough that:

> I sincerely lament the loss, as all must, of the services of so many gallant officers and soldiers. But long experience has taught me that such operations could not be carried on, and such achievements performed, and such objects attained, as in these operations under my consideration without experiencing much loss, and that in point of fact the honour acquired by all is proportionate to the difficulties, risks and dangers met and overcome, by those who have attained such objects for their country. We may regret the loss and even lament the fall of individuals, but we never can the event itself.[11]

From the most experienced British soldier of the age, such words would have brought comfort to Gough. Wellington had already spoken of the underestimation of the 'Indian soldier' and no doubt recalled his own battles in the subcontinent. Gough had lost slightly under 15 percent of his army either killed or wounded. At Wellington's great battle Assaye, which made his name, his total

---

10   Sidhu, *The First Anglo-Sikh War*, p. 88, suggest that the figure of 3,000 is quite possible.
11   NAM: 8303–105, Gough Papers, Wellington to Gough 7 March 1846. For unexplained reasons a slightly different quote from Wellington is sometimes used. The one mentioned here is taken from the handwritten copy found in the Gough Papers at the NAM. It may be that the other quote is a copy of the original letter that was slightly altered. In either case, the overall message and intent of the letter remains the same.

casualties had accounted for 31 percent of his total force. When one recalls that the Sikhs were a warrior race, who had been trained by former officers of Napoleon's army, and were equipped and trained in the European style, perhaps it is equally fitting to compare the casualties with that great battle of Gough's earlier career: Barrosa. At Barrosa Graham's total casualties had accounted for just under 24 percent of his total force.[12]

The Battle of Ferozeshah had been a difficult one for Gough. He had faced problems that had proved difficult to surmount. The interference of Hardinge, and therefore the dilution of command, did not help an already difficult situation. Had Gough been allowed to stick to his original plan and not been overruled by Hardinge exercising his powers as governor general, the camp would have been in British hands far earlier in the day. The men would have been in far better physical condition and the extra hours of light would have allowed for better provisioning and the preparation of a better camp for that night.

Littler's force had really contributed little earlier in the day. Had they arrived early in the afternoon their presence as a reserve could have been invaluable to Gough. The direction in which they would have arrived on the field would also have blocked part of the Sikh retreat and therefore the combined cavalry of both Gough and Littler might well have inflicted a far greater loss of life upon the retreating Sikh army.

Also, if Tej Singh had then arrived the following day he would have found a fresh army ready to fight and fully occupying a strong position. Even Hardinge seemed to acknowledge the problem of the lack of daylight at the end of the battle. To Lord Ripon he wrote, "the want of daylight, while it rendered our decided success less secure, caused the enemy to abandon that portion of the position which had not been attacked, and was as detrimental to him as it was hazardous to us."[13] The first part of this statement seems to acknowledge that the lack of light, caused by Hardinge's intervention, had prevented a more secure victory. The second part seems to be an attempt to defend this, and ignore the consequences not only of later that night but the following day. However if Hardinge ever regretted his decision to intervene and overrule his commander-in-chief he never acknowledged it in public.

Yet sadly this is just conjecture and we can never know the course the battle, and indeed the war, would have taken if Gough's original plan had been enacted. What added salt to the wound was that the overruling of Gough by Hardinge was kept quiet for many years and few knew of the events of that day. As a consequence Gough was blamed for the delay by various sources. It was upon Gough that the criticism fell for attacking so late in the day, and he was accused of being reckless for so doing. It was not until the publication of the biography of Lord Hardinge written by his son, that the truth of events on that day became public knowledge. The problem was this was a little too late, as many had already pronounced their verdict upon Gough's actions.[14]

Gough was also let down by his staff arrangements. Some of this was out of his hands, due to the illness or wounds of important officers. Gough should perhaps have paid more attention to this. Indeed it must be question whether it was right that a captain of limited experience should by default have been acting as Adjutant General for the entire army. There were surely better suited men around him. Perhaps this would have been a better use of Hardinge's experience, and he would have been a useful chief of staff and adjutant general to Gough. Maybe Gough considered this, although there is no record of it, but decided that it was beneath an officer of Hardinge's rank.

---

12   Rait, *Gough*, Vol. II, pp. 74–75. Rait also uses for comparison the battle of Blenheim (23 percent casualties) and Talavera (25 percent casualties). The figure of 24 percent is a rounding up of the 23.8 percent that can be found in Haythornthwaite, Phillip, *The Peninsular War: The Complete Companion to the Iberian Campaigns 1807–14*, (London: Brassey's, 2004), p. 225

13   Rait, *Gough*, Vol. II, p. 32.

14   Rait, *Gough*, Vol. II, pp. 33–34.

Whilst historians have spent much time dwelling on the deficiencies of Gough and the British in general, not enough credit is given to the Sikhs. Despite their own problems, not least of all the lack of commitment of many of their higher command leaders, they had fought a determined action. Their success should not be seen simply in terms of British deficiencies or underachievement. Their performance was a credit to the officers who had trained them over many years and to the military reforms of Ranjit Singh. Robert Rait perhaps summed up best the battle of Ferozeshah when he wrote that, "Our death-roll was certainly heavy, but we had to face a brave enemy, and the accidents of warfare had been, on the whole, against us."[15]

The two battles of Mudki and Ferozeshah had been hard fought, costly, and largely indecisive in that a hammer blow was not delivered to the Sikhs that could end the war. In reality the strength of the Sikh army was such that one battle was never likely to have resolved the conflict. However what the two battles had achieved was the withdrawal of the Sikh army back across the Sutlej. In the sense that a renewed invasion of territory under British protection was unlikely, India had been saved.

---

15   Rait, Gough, Vol. II, p. 31.

51

A Lull in the Storm

After Ferozeshah the Sikhs withdrew across the Sutlej River. Gough was not entirely sure of what happened, nor was anyone else on the British side for that matter, and throughout 22 December the army remained at Ferozeshah half-expecting a renewed assault. There was certainly a lack of command and coordination at this time, and Hardinge continued to issue orders without consulting Gough. Much of what was ordered was sensible, and somewhat ironically, included orders that Gough had himself issued previously and which had been overruled by Hardinge. This included the movement of extra ammunition, heavy artillery, hospital equipment, and now most importantly, extra troops.

There was agreement between the two men that no major action could take place against the Sikhs until such reinforcements and supplies arrived. Hardinge accompanied Littler's division back to Ferozepore, whilst Gough remained camped about four miles from Ferozeshah. This was largely to allow for the placing of a camp away from the now insanitary conditions of Ferozeshah. The night of 22 December saw an event take place which with the benefit of hindsight is amusing but at the time had the potential for disaster. Robert Napier gives us an account of the evening, during which Gough and his staff toured the battlefield and then visited the troops. By the time this was completed darkness had fallen and Gough and his staff decided to spend the night on some full sacks they had found, which apparently made good beds. Their sleep might not have been quite so restful had they known what they were sleeping on. It was only in the light of the new day that they discovered they had spent the night on bags of gunpowder. The potential for disaster was all too obvious, and it is said that the fact that Gough disliked smoking saved them all from being blown sky high.[1]

On 23 December it was felt that there might be a need to retire from the field, and Gough received deputations from officers, including Napier, that they should stay if at all possible. Napier proposed clearing the camp at Ferozeshah and using it as a future base. To Napier, Gough replied in kindly and appreciative terms, saying that he had every intention of staying unless ordered to do otherwise by Hardinge.[2] Perhaps this illustrates something of the uneasiness that Gough still felt over the presence of Hardinge. Normally the governor general would not interfere with the decisions of the commander-in-chief in the field as to where to place the army. Yet Hardinge had already done it once, and Gough no doubt feared he might do it again. It is only natural to believe that Gough must have been concerned with his own position at this time, alongside that of his army.

As it was, Gough remained close to Ferozeshah until 27 December when he moved to Arufka. The Sikhs had crossed back over the Sutlej in some disarray and although they had lost numerous guns and most of their supplies they received supplies, extra guns and reinforcements from Lahore

---

1   Napier, *Personal Narrative*, p. 10.
2   Napier, *Personal Narrative*, p. 14.

far quicker than Gough could expect similar support. Once again Gough and Hardinge differed in their opinions. Hardinge believed, particularly in the light of recent events, that the British needed to wait until they were fully reinforced before attempting to cross and attack the Sikhs. It may also be the case that Hardinge hoped to receive a reply to his letter to London suggesting a change in command before it was necessary to attack again, but we will look at Hardinge's correspondence regarding Gough later on.[3] Gough for his part, unaware that any permanent changes to the command structure were being considered, was against waiting. Partly this was due to his nature. Never good at waiting, he wanted to get at the enemy. Perhaps he felt a little uneasy that he had been unable to decisively defeat the Sikhs and was anxious for another attempt. Although these personal considerations undoubtedly played a part in Gough's desire to attack the enemy, there was also a strong military argument. The Sikhs were starting to build strong defensive positions along the river. It was therefore wise to attempt an attack before these were ready. It was also true that if the Sikhs were able to place their heavy guns in strong positions not only would they make any attack a costly affair, they would also make British positions on their side of the river untenable.

Gough from his new position was able to keep a careful watch on all the crossings. However it was not possible, nor was it considered advantageous, to try and prevent any attempt by the Sikhs to cross back to the southern bank of the Sutlej. Indeed Gough and Hardinge were both agreed that it would be better should the Sikhs cross, as they could then be dealt with. In a sense this suited both their needs. For Gough it meant that although he was generally inactive he had something to occupy him, and for Hardinge it meant that his commander-in-chief was occupied whilst he awaited reinforcements.

The first considerable body of reinforcements arrived 6 January 1846. This consisted of the 9th and 16th Lancers, 3rd Bengal Light Cavalry, 4th Irregular Cavalry, the 10th Foot, three Native Infantry regiments, two batteries of artillery and a company of sappers. Gough had extended his line to cover all the crossing points, but after a personal reconnaissance he carried out on 28 December 1845, he established that the main Sikh position, where the majority of their troops were, was the crossing at Sobraon. On 13 January a short action took place at this point. Using light infantry and horse artillery he managed to drive the Sikhs from a small 'concavity' where a "considerable force of infantry had crossed over."[4] After driving the Sikhs away Gough considered permanently occupying the position and using it to destroy the boat bridge that the Sikhs had built earlier. However he decided that it was not that important, and given his limited number of troops, guns, and particularly ammunition that the holding of this position could not be justified. The Sikhs reoccupied the position but Gough was not concerned. As he wrote to the Duke of Wellington:

> I felt I could at any time dislodge him [the enemy] from this position and have been more than once inclined to effect it, but this could not be enacted without considerable loss of life, and as I have not, at present, the means of pushing on to Lahore, the 1st Division of the battering trains not having yet come up, I have contented myself with keeping him within the range of his guns.[5]

Thus the enemy now had an encampment, and started to throw up defences on the south side of the river. Gough does seem to have appreciated the situation at this time. Whilst there was a desire to be active, he appreciated that a full scale attack and advance was not yet possible. Waiting for reinforcements could be detrimental to the morale of his officers and men if he was completely inactive,

---

3   Singh, *The Letters of Viscount Hardinge*, pp. 138–140.
4   NAM: 8303–105, Gough papers, Gough to Wellington, 2 February 1846.
5   NAM: 8303–105, Gough papers, Gough to Wellington, 2 February 1846.

but there were practicalities to consider and Gough issued sensible orders. In the same letter to Wellington he added that, "I have given the strictest orders not to molest him [the enemy], with the hope of drawing him out, but in vain. I must therefore bide my time, which your Grace may be assured I shall not let slip."[6] Yet at the same time the need to keep busy, and not leave the Sikhs unhindered in their movements, called for some action. This was not only for the morale of Gough's army but by so doing he also helped to protect the northern territory of British India and the movement of troops through it. The great need for reinforcements had seen much of the north of India denuded of troops, particularly European ones. The Sikhs, fully aware of this, were tempted to raid into this territory. The tempting nature of this target was increased by the movement of a large British supply convoy, stretching over some 16 kilometres, containing over 4,000 wagons of various types, and protected by only 2,000 native soldiers. This slow moving convoy included the heavy guns of the siege train, 18 pdrs and 9 inch guns, without which an invasion of Sikh territory would be extremely difficult. With the military stretched thin in this district the Sikhs had the potential to deal a blow to the British and delay any attack on Sikh territory.

At the same time Gough was conscious of Sikh movements south of the Sutlej. This detachment of the Sikh Army was commanded by Ranjodh (or Runjoor) Singh. Little is known of him, but he appears to have been reasonable young – possibly mid thirties – and a competent, if not extraordinary, commander. There is also no doubt of his loyalty to the Sikh cause. He and a sizeable force of Sikhs crossed at Ludhiana. There was between 7,000–10,000 infantry, 2,000 irregular cavalry and 70 guns. Such a movement threatened several smaller garrisons, and in particular Ludhiana itself which both Hardinge and Gough agreed was difficult to defend. Only the small fort at Ludhiana was occupied, the village being left unguarded. Brigadier Godley held the fort with the 5th Native Cavalry, the 30th Native Infantry, two battalions of Ghurkhas, and four guns of the Horse Artillery. There was also a small force sent by the Raja of Patiala, who was anxious to show his friendship for the British: the exact number of soldiers sent by the Raja is unknown.

From Ludhiana the Sikhs were only 50 miles away from Bassian which held a large British depot, the key link in the chain of supply from British India to Gough's Army. With such an important target at risk, and with the obvious fear of what such raids could do to the loyalty of the locals, Gough decided that it was imperative to deal with this Sikh Army. To undertake the task he called on Major General Sir Harry Smith. Whatever Smith might have thought of Gough, and his opinion does seem to vary, Gough held Smith in high regard. He was certainly the outstanding division commander of the army. In reality he was the only officer to whom Gough could entrust a sizeable independent command. With news that the village of Ludhiana had been sacked and that the Sikhs were continuing their advance, Gough felt it necessary to detach an enlarged brigade under Smith to seek out the enemy and defeat them.

Initially Gough had asked Smith for a brigade to be detached from his force, and Smith had selected Hicks' Brigade. Gough seemed reluctant to ask Smith to command the force himself, although reading between the lines it was clear that this was what he wanted. Whether he thought such a force was inappropriate to be commanded by someone of Smith's seniority, or whether there was some other reason is unknown. Smith was keen to command and Gough was pleased when Smith said he would lead them himself.[7] For this task Smith was initially given a brigade of infantry consisting of the 31st Foot and the 24th and 47th Native Infantry, accompanied by the 3rd Light Cavalry and some irregular cavalry. Although in a biography of Gough the movements of Smith's force and the subsequent action at Bhudowal and Aliwal might seem somewhat peripheral they are important to our narrative. Firstly they show the way in which Gough supported his

6   NAM: 8303–105, Gough papers, Gough to Wellington, 2 February 1846.
7   Smith, *Sir Harry Smith*, pp. 165–166.

subordinate in these movements. Secondly they illustrate how a different commander to Gough faired against the Sikhs. Therefore it seems appropriate to take a few moments to consider Smith's movement and the subsequent actions.

52

The Battle of Aliwal

Sir Harry Smith's initial task when he set off in the early morning of the 17th January 1846 was to clear Fategarh and Dharmkote of the enemy. This was accomplished with ease: the former had already been abandoned, whilst the latter surrendered upon the advance of Smith's cavalry. Gough now urged Smith to move on to join with the garrison at Ludhiana and then move to attack Ranjodh Singh's force. Gough's main fear was for the siege train that would be transported through this area. Given that there were only 2,000 troops guarding the whole column, this was exposed to potential action if Ranjodh Singh's force was not dealt with. In this part of the country there was little concern at this stage about hostile 'locals'. The area was predominantly Muslim and as many had suffered under Sikh occupation in the past they were therefore more kindly disposed towards the British. As ever in India the old saying 'My enemy's enemy is my friend' rang true.

Given the importance to future operation that was attached to the safe arrival of the heavy guns Gough was anxious to secure their route. To this end, and to support Smith, Gough despatched the 16th Lancers, some extra irregular cavalry, and two batteries of horse artillery. Smith now had a force consisting of a brigade of cavalry, a brigade of infantry, and 18 guns. Gough also sent an extra British infantry battalion, the 53rd Foot, which would join Smith at Jugraon before he reached Ludhiana. The 53rd were also being used to escort a number of reinforcements for other European battalions and included amongst their number a party of dismounted men from the 3rd Light Dragoons. Amongst the dismounted men was the future diarist Sergeant John Pearman whose rather biased opinion would cloud historians' understanding of the Sikh Wars for many years after their edited publication by the Marquis of Anglesey. In fairness it must be added that Anglesey in his editorial notes did his best to act as a counterbalance to Pearman's class bias and dislike for the army in general. In the past Pearman had been extremely critical of Gough and was equally critical of Smith during the Aliwal campaign.[1]

Smith had also received a message from Brigadier Godby at Ludhiana asking him to move as quickly as possible to join with him. Smith used this to justify a quick and tiring march for his men. The commanding officer of the 53rd had wanted to rest not only his men but also his weary pack animals for at least 24 hours but Smith ordered him to march at once. Smith could justify this by Godby's letter but more likely was Smith's fear that the Sikhs would get away without him being able to bring them to battle. There was urgency about Smith's movement that was partly a quest for glory but also a practical desire to deliver a decisive defeat upon the enemy. Such a victory would improve morale, both British and native, as well as lowering Sikh morale and hopefully preventing any further incursions over the Sutlej. In this sense it would buy time for British reinforcements and for preparations to be made to cross the Sutlej in force and then press on towards Lahore.[2]

---

1   NAM: 8303–103, Gough Papers, Gough to Wellington, 2 February 1846. Anglesey, The Marquis of (ed.) *Sergeant Pearman's Memories* (London: Jonathan Cape, 1968).
2   Smith, *Sir Harry Smith*, pp. 172–178 & 187–188.

On 20 January Smith was joined at Jugraon by the reinforcements Gough had despatched. He now sent word to Godby to leave Ludhiana and join him at Bhudowal with as many men as he could. Smith left all of his heavy wheeled transport at Jugraon to speed his march, but as a consequence it left him desperately short of supplies. His men were also tired and weary. In an attempt to catch up with the enemy he had pushed them hard. Learning that the Sikhs were blocking his march, Smith decided to detour two miles south of Bhudowal, rather than confront them at this stage when the conditions and geography would have been in the enemy's favour and without Godby's extra men. However given that the Sikhs were moving along the main road rather than the largely sandy terrain that Smith's men had to cross, the Sikhs were able to manoeuvre ahead of him. The Sikh artillery opened fire, obviously hoping to provoke a response. However because the Sikhs showed no sign of advancing Smith continued his march, using his cavalry to cover his flank against a sudden rush and using his horse artillery in an attempt to reply to the Sikh guns. The infantry got through safely. However the baggage train was attacked by Sikh cavalry. Having left his wheeled transport behind, Smith was relying on pack animals, and the Sikh artillery fire had frightened the animals, particularly the camels, and had slowed the progress of the column.

A determined resistance was made by Quartermaster Cornes of the 53rd Foot with 30 men of his own regiment and a few men of the 16th Lancers and some native infantry. Under attack from around 1,000 Sikhs they gave a good account of themselves and were able to repel the attack. However they were unable to re-join the rest of the column and Cornes decided that their only course of action was to withdraw to Jugraon. A good deal of the baggage was looted and there has been some debate as to whether this was done by the Sikhs or locals after the engagement.[3] Many of the men made it back safely to Jugraon but the majority of the baggage was lost. The British had lost 69 killed and 68 wounded with around 70 being taken prisoner. Many of the dead were the sick and wounded who were being transported on Doolies. In the fighting the native bearers had understandably abandoned them to seek safety, and they were killed by the Sikhs, unable to escape. The Sikhs had no casualties. Smith had suffered a defeat, but so minor is it considered that it often fails to even appear in accounts of the First Sikh War. Sergeant Pearman was deeply critical of Smith in his memoirs. Pearman is also the source of a story that suggests that Smith had been led into a trap by his own local guides. Pearman goes further and states that shortly after the engagement Smith personally shot both guides.[4]

In his own account, Smith tried to pass some of the blame onto Godby stating that he "was astonished, I admit, at hearing nothing from Colonel Godby."[5] Smith presumed that Godby must have seen the movement of the Sikhs, and could not understand why he had not informed him. Yet this was unfair of Godby who had in fact done all he could reasonably be expected to do. Smith was looking for a scapegoat. Smith marched on towards Ludhiana and near the town met up with Godby who had heard the firing at Bhudowal and marched out in that direction. Although Smith's casualties were relatively light, he had inflicted no damage on the enemy and had lost the majority of his baggage. As a result his men were cold, tired, hungry, and exhausted as they rested that evening. It had not been an auspicious start to his independent command, but was not a disaster.

The one man Smith did not try to blame was Gough, whose actions he claimed had showed, "great foresight and judgement" by despatching reinforcements.[6] On the following day, 22 January,

---

3   Smith, *Sir Harry Smith*, p. 173. Smith was certainly of the view that the majority of the looting was undertaken by local villagers, stating of the baggage that 'little of it fell into the hands of the enemy's soldiers'. This view is contradicted by Sidhu, *First Anglo-Sikh War*, pp. 101–102. Sidhu gives evidence of a great deal of looting of the baggage being undertaken by Sikh cavalry.

4   Anglesey, *Sergeant Pearman's Memories*, p. 36.

5   Smith, *Sir Harry Smith*, p. 174.

6   Smith, *Sir Harry Smith*, p. 176.

Gough ordered Brigadier Wheeler, who commanded the other brigade in Smith's division, to march and join Smith. It is important to note that Gough must have ordered this before he had heard about the action at Bhudowal. Wheeler acted in a more cautious manner. He kept to the tracks and roads rather than attempting to move across country as Smith had done. Wheeler was anxious to save his men's energy, rather than being obsessed with speed as Smith had been. He was also careful to keep clear of any potential clash with the Sikhs and would march out of his way to avoid them.

As a consequence of this caution Wheeler's brigade did not reach Jugraon until 24 January. Here he met up with a regiment of native infantry and one of cavalry that Gough had ordered to support Smith. It is clear that Gough was attempting to despatch all possible aid to Smith. He was no doubt anxious to give Smith all the help he could in the hope that Smith would inflict a severe defeat on the Sikhs and thus relieve the pressure on Gough's position and improve the morale of his army but also that of local rulers and of the local populace who supported the British.

With Wheeler moving from one direction and Smith from the other, Ranjodh Singh feared an attack from two directions, and thus withdrew his troops back to the river at a place called Aliwal. Smith now had a force of around 12,000 men, and due to the reinforcements sent to him by Gough now felt confident to take the offensive. Leaving around 2,000 at Ludhiana as a garrison he marched out to attack the Sikhs. Just as important as the number of men was the fact that he had 28 field guns and two 8 inch howitzers, the latter giving him artillery that could match the Sikhs. Indeed the battle of Aliwal on 28 January was to be the first time the British and Sikhs had met on equal terms. Smith had sufficient cavalry, a little over 3,000 men, to be able to split them into two brigades. The whole of the cavalry was commanded by Brigadier General Cureton, one of the best cavalry commanders in the British Army who Gough had sent to aid Smith. Brigadier McDowell commanded the 16th Lancers, the 3rd Bengal Light Cavalry, and the 4th Irregular Cavalry in one brigade whilst the other brigade, commanded by Brigadier Stedman, consisted of the Governor General's Bodyguard, the 1st and 5th Bengal Light Cavalry and a detachment of Shekhawati Cavalry. Hicks' and Wheeler's brigades formed the bulk of the infantry, although Smith had replaced one of Wheeler's native infantry battalions with Sirmoor Gurkhas who had been stationed at Ludhiana. Brigadier Wilson commanded a makeshift brigade of infantry consisting of the 53rd Foot, 30th Native Infantry and the Shekhawati Battalion. Godby also commanded a similar formation containing the 47th Native Infantry and the Nasiri Gurkha battalion. There were 22 guns of the horse artillery, eight field guns and, importantly, the two 8 inch howitzers.

The number of men Ranjodh Singh had at his disposal is uncertain. Estimates vary from between 14,000 and 20,000 men. Whatever the exact number was, the majority of them were irregulars, and a great many would be classed as mercenaries. It has been suggested that only around 4,000 of Ranjodh Singh's army were regular soldiers. He had slightly over 70 guns, and again they varied dramatically in size and calibre. There was however no great battery of heavy guns as there had been at Mudki and Ferozeshah. Thus whilst the Sikhs had numerical superiority in artillery, in terms of calibre and weight of shot they were fairly equal.[7] Ranjodh Singh attempted to build rudimentary defences for his position but he had little time to affect anything other than very basic breastworks. Ranjodh's inexperience seems to have been demonstrated when on the morning of 28 January, as Smith started to advance, he commenced an advance of his own. It has been suggested that he hoped to out manoeuvre Smith and reach Jugraon. All this did was to tire and confuse his own men. His inexperience was also shown in the fact that he had placed himself with his back to the river. If he was beaten he had little hope of escape, and this might explain his desire to move

---

7   Sidhu, *The First Anglo-Sikh War*, p. 112, estimates the Sikh force as between 14,000–18,000 men and about 52 guns that could actually take part in the battle.

away from his position at Aliwal. However it does not explain his initial decision to take up this position in the first place.

The example of Ranjodh Singh helps to illustrate why one must be careful when ascribing 'treachery' to explain away the action of Sikh commanders. Had Tej Singh or Lal Singh placed the army in such a position and given such confused orders it would generally have been interpreted as an example of their 'treachery' and collusion with the British. Yet with Ranjodh Singh this was clearly not the case.[8] He had simply made some poor decisions. In war mistakes are made: indeed they are inevitable. Whilst there was clearly some reticence amongst the Sikh commanders to prosecute the war fully, not every mistake should be seen as an example of 'treachery' or collusion with the enemy.

As Smith made his advance he had no cover, but equally he had no obstruction. There was no thick jungle and the terrain was even and relatively easy to march across. Smith deployed his army well, using his cavalry not only to protect his flanks but to be in position to prevent any attempt by the Sikhs to break out. In short, the Sikhs were stuck if they were not victorious. They could not withdraw to their rear, and their enemy had placed his cavalry so as to prevent any attempt to move away in another direction. Smith's clear and concise orders brought the army to the field in near perfect order, although it must be added that there was nothing – topographical, geographical, political, or even in the actions of the enemy – to hinder his arrangements.

Smith had taken care of his guns, using the detachments of reinforcements for the 62nd and 80th that had arrived with the 53rd Foot to not only protect the guns but help manhandle them into position. Although slightly outnumbered in both the number of guns and average calibre of guns, Smith's artillery more than held its own. The 18 pdr field guns and the 8 inch howitzers gave the British something that could at least match the Sikh guns. There were other advantages in Smith's favour since, unlike at Ferozeshah, the Sikh artillery had poorly prepared positions from which to fire. It is also true that they were not handled by as experienced gunners as at Ferozeshah. Yet another factor in favour of the British was the fact that the enemy consisted of only a few regulars. The largely irregular nature of much of the soldiery meant that the British cannonade had a far greater detrimental effect on enemy morale than it had at Ferozeshah.

When Smith's infantry advanced, the first target was the village of Aliwal. Hicks' Brigade took this with relative ease, as the Dogra irregulars defending it seemed to have little desire to fight. With the support of Godby's brigade they pushed on and broke through the Sikh line. Wheeler's brigade joined the advance and after firing a volley they attacked the Sikh gun emplacements. Wheeler deployed his men with the 48th Bengal Native Infantry in the centre, against the convention that held that the European battalion should be in the centre. The 48th behaved excellently and fought determinedly. The reason for this was that Wheeler was a former officer of the 48th who understood not only the men but also the unit. It does perhaps add to the belief that the Sepoys would, and could, most certainly fight when they had confidence and respect in the officer commanding. By all accounts the Sikh infantry put up little fight against Wheeler's men. The same could not be said of the Sikh gunners who fought doggedly in defence of their guns.

The 53rd took the village of Bhundri and now threatened the route to the river. Between them and the river were the regular Sikh battalions that had been trained and organised in European tactics. Having been threatened by cavalry they had formed into square, as dictated by the tactics of the time, the sight of which caused the native light cavalry regiments to veer off. However a squadron of the 16th Lancers charged through a Sikh square, a feat that was followed by another

---

8   Sidhu, *The First Anglo-Sikh War*, p. 102. Sidhu shows that whilst some have tried to ascribe 'duplicity' to Ranjodh's actions, this tends to be the minority and much of this stems from an account by Captain Joseph D. Cunningham, a British engineer and political agent.

squadron. The rest of the Lancers attacked the remaining Sikh batteries. The Lancers' attacks on the Sikh squares was supported by the 30th Native Infantry and then by the 53rd Foot.[9]

With the defeat of the Sikh regular units, the battle was over and a pursuit followed. Cavalry from both flanks now fell upon the retreating Sikhs, who were routed. Fifty-four guns were taken by the British and another 11 were lost in the river as the Sikhs attempted to save them. Figures for the Sikh casualties vary wildly. Some sources of the time placed the figure as high as 3,000 whilst some more modern accounts of the battle are as low as 300.[10] Perhaps just an important was the fact that what remained of the army had fled as best they could, most abandoning their arms. In effect it became a mass of men rather than a cohesive army.

The British had suffered 151 killed, 413 wounded and 25 missing; of the 151 killed, 59 were from the 16th Lancers. It was a clear victory that did much to restore British morale and lift the spirits of an army deflated after the inconclusive victories of Mudki and Ferozeshah. Some modern research suggests that the total casualties for the British and the Sikhs were remarkably similar, and one could therefore interpret Aliwal as not being quite the overwhelming success it was portrayed as. However this would be to miss the point. Aliwal was an important and decisive victory not because of casualties inflicted but because the enemy broke and ran. The army that had faced Smith at Aliwal had evaporated after the battle and ceased to exist as a cohesive fighting formation.

The victory was welcomed by Gough. A staff officer who was present with Gough whilst the battle was being fought told the following story:

> We heard the cannonading which was, while it lasted, fearful. I asked him what he thought of it. "Think of it! Why, that 'tis the most glorious thing I ever heard. I know by the sound of the guns that Smith has carried the position and silenced their artillery".
>
> "I hope, sir", I said, "he has not found it too late, and retired to wait for our reinforcements". "Retire", he cried, "no! No British force would ever retire before such a cannonade as we have just heard". He spoke with such likely confidence that, although I had gone to him fully impressed with the conviction that Smith had failed, I left him perfectly assured that I was wrong, and that the victory had been ours. He sent Bagot and Becher to bring an express. When he heard the news he was nearly frantic with joy, but Bagot told me that ere the lapse of two minutes he saw the dear old man on his knees by his couch, offering up his thanks to that Power which alone gave the victory.[11]

This reaction was typical of Gough. His delight soon turned to thankfulness to his God for the victory. To describe Gough as a 'simplistic' man sounds like an insult. Yet there is no doubt that he was in many ways an uncomplicated man who knew what he believed in and believed what he

---

9 Cook, *The Sikh Wars*, p. 81, gives the traditional account of the squares being easily broken by the 16th Lancers. Crawford, 'The Sikh Wars, 1845–49', p. 46, indicates that whilst the squares were broken, the Sikhs inflicted heavy losses on the 16th Lancers. Sidhu, *The First Anglo-Sikh War*, p. 117. Based on his research Sidhu suggests the breaking of the square was not as easily achieved as some accounts make out. He points to evidence that suggest the Sikhs withstood four determined charges by the 16th Lancers, from different directions, plus stood up well to the artillery attack. He even suggests they retreated in square for some distance. Bruce, *Six Battles for India*, pp. 168–170, questions whether the Sikhs had been able to form 'proper' squares, which might help explain the unusual occurrence of a 'broken' square.

10 For many years the official British figure of 3,000 Sikh dead was taken without debate as an accurate figure. However more recent research has suggested that this might have been wildly inflated. Amarphal Sidhu, *The First Anglo-Sikh War*, pp. 118–119, suggests that Sikh casualties were, 'certainly no more than several hundred'.

11 Rait, *Gough*, Vol. II, pp. 47–48. Rait quotes the officer but does not name him. Of the officers Rait personally interviewed, the most likely candidate is the future Field Marshal Sir Frederick Haines.

knew. It is interesting to note Gough's interpretation of the events of the battle by the sound of the guns. Whether this was bravado or a real sense of how the battle was going is difficult to know. If one believes the latter it is another example of what Professor Richard Holmes called Gough's remarkable ability to judge the course of battle.[12] It perhaps also reminds us that Gough was an experienced soldier who had heard the cannon roar many times before, and perhaps was able to envisage a battle by the sounds of war. Even if it was only meant to be a display of self-confidence it was effective, as the testimony of the aforementioned officer affirms.

Gough deserved some credit for Smith's victory. Indeed this was the time at which he most acted as a traditional commander-in-chief, employing the delicate arts of delegation and support. Gough had sufficient confidence in Smith's ability to allow him freedom of movement. Indeed it was Gough who decided that he was the officer best suited for this independent command. Whilst there were few alternatives to Smith, Gough does deserve credit for appointing him. Gough had also supported Smith in his efforts. He had kept a close eye on events and when it appeared that the Sikhs had been reinforced, he sent extra troops, particular the remaining brigade of Smith's division and the two 8 inch howitzers. This had left Gough with only 10,000 men under his own personal command, against an unknown number of Sikhs across the river Sutlej. As Gough conceded in a letter to Wellington, "I did all I could, even to the appearance of running some risk, to enable Sir H. Smith to drive the enemy across the Sutlej at that point but I had the most perfect confidence in the troops with me." Although with a somewhat weakened force Gough held a strong defensive position and any movement of the Sikhs across the Sutlej could be harassed by cavalry and horse artillery. Although seen as a somewhat jealous man, Gough did not hesitate in giving praise to Smith. To Wellington he wrote that the victory, "has been most gallantly and successfully achieved by that very able officer, and I beg to bring to your grace's favourable consideration the officers of her Majesty's service brought to notice in the despatches of Sir Harry Smith."[13] Gough was grateful to Smith and did not miss an opportunity in the aftermath of the victory to say so. In one sense this could be interpreted as bringing credit to his own name by association, in that it was Gough who selected him for the task and enabled his victory. Yet there was clearly something more than this: In short what Gough was expressing was relief that the tide has been turned.

The modern reader will perhaps better appreciate the role Gough played than the Victorian reader did. At that time the battlefield role of the general, leading his troops directly, was the norm. Perhaps distant from the actual fighting but somewhere where he could see the battlefield and influence the fight if necessary. However we have no problem in appreciating that Gough, although not at Aliwal, had played a key role in the battle. As commander-in-chief he had despatched the force, selected its commander, briefed him on its objective, supported his march, reinforced him when necessary and as a consequence deserves a share in the spoils of victory. There were those at the time who could appreciate this. One such man was Major General Archibald Galloway, Deputy Chairman of the East India Company Court of Directors. In a private letter to Gough he commented upon hearing Wellington give a speech in praise of Gough, but remarked that Wellington had:

forgot, what I thought was the finest part of the campaign. Your great manoeuvre, your operations on the upper Sutlej by which you effected the destruction of that formidable division of the Sikhs by which your right was menaced. The time you choose for detaching Sir Harry Smith was just the right time. [...] Now the merit of all this was due to the Commander-in-Chief and the result was decisive. Nor does this detract one iota from the triumphant manner

12   Holmes, Richard, *Sahib: The British Soldier in India, 1750–1914* (London: Harper Collins, 2005), p. 15.
13   NAM: 8303–105, Gough Papers, Gough to Wellington, 2 February 1846.

in which the great movement was executed and which has most justly excited boundless praise on Sir Harry Smith.[14]

In a letter to his son shortly after Aliwal Gough remarked, "Thanks be to God, another glorious victory has been obtained and although not fought by me I take as much pride in it." He followed this by writing that, "I am in a position at any hour I please to take the initiative." Yet Gough was still reluctant to move too soon, and reading the remainder of the letter one gets the impression that Gough is concerned not only about the strength of his own army but the strength of Sikh artillery which is now firmly emplaced in strong positions.[15] However Gough's heavy artillery was now arriving, as were reinforcements of men, supplies and ammunition. An attempt to cross the river had to be made before too long. Gough seems to have been conflicted at this stage. In letters to Hardinge he urged attack as soon as possible, fearing that the Sikhs would only get stronger as they further entrenched themselves and prepared better defences. At the same time, particularly in his correspondence with his son, doubt was expressed. Gough clearly feared another bloody battle. Whether this was because of the political consequences, the fact that he was running out of Europeans – or as one Indian is said to have remarked they were running short of 'white cloth' – or simply his humanitarian concerns for the men he commanded, is difficult to ascertain. Yet this conflict between what he wrote in private communications and what he wrote to Hardinge in official correspondence is interesting to note and points to the conflicted nature of Gough's thoughts. In one sense it is analogous to having an unpleasant task to undertake: being torn between a desire to put off the inevitable or to get it over and done with.[16]

Gough decided to wait. Firstly for all of the siege train to reach his position and secondly for Smith's force to re-join him. The attack on Sobraon was likely to be decisive one way or another. If successful, a large Sikh army would be dispersed and whilst there was likely to be further fighting the British would be heading into the heart of Sikh territory and on the direct route to Lahore. If defeated then the war would surely have become a stalemate. It would have required fresh European troops and in that case and that would have tested the resolve of the British government to pursue the war. It would almost certainly have meant the supersession of Gough. So the fight at Sobraon would prove to be decisive not only for the course of the war but for the future of the commander-in-chief.

14   NAM: 8303–105, Gough Papers, Archibald Galloway to Gough, 7 April 1846. The present author has presumed that the date is the 7th of that month, but the number is not very clearly written on the original document.
15   NAM: 8303–105, Gough Papers, Gough to George Gough, 2 February 1846.
16   NAM: 8303–105, Gough Papers, Gough to George Gough, 2 February 1846 & 18 April 1846.

53

Political Decisions

Before moving on to look at the battle of Sobraon, it is important to take a moment to consider the political situation. The victory at Aliwal might have improved the situation from a military perspective, but the political picture was still confused. The disputed nature of command between Gough and Hardinge had not been resolved. It was certainly an unusual situation where the second-in-command of the army also held supreme political authority. The ability of the second in command of the army to use such authority to overrule his nominal superior in the field was unfortunate and unhelpful to the smooth running of the army and the conduct of an already difficult campaign. The situation that had developed before Ferozeshah had not been resolved. The battle itself had clearly shaken Hardinge. Indeed, in the days that followed Hardinge was considering Gough's position, unbeknown to Gough.

In a letter dated 30 December 1845 Hardinge wrote to the Prime Minister, Sir Robert Peel, what has been called, 'a strongly worded letter', about his concerns with regards to Gough.[1] In this letter, Hardinge suggested Gough be removed from overall command. This suggestion is not always placed in context. Gough knew nothing of this letter at the time. For his part Sir Robert Peel knew nothing of Hardinge's actions on 21 December when he had used his political authority to overruled Gough. Although it would be wrong to presume this was due to duplicity on Hardinge's part, it did mean that Peel's perception of events was not entirely accurate. Peel could only rely on the information provided by the press, which was already critical of Gough for delaying his attack at Ferozeshah, and when this distorted view of events was added to Hadringe's concerns the result was a rather different perception of events to the reality of the situation.[2]

Hardinge had not acted incorrectly in his correspondence. As governor general it was his right, indeed his duty, to acquaint the home government with anything that he felt was of such importance. Hardinge seemed to appreciate better than Gough that on the final day of the conflict at Ferozeshah it was not just the battle that hung in the balance but possibly the long-term future of British India. Whilst this might sound melodramatic, such a catastrophic defeat, coming so soon after the debacle in Afghanistan, could have proved fatal to the British military reputation. There was certainly a fear that such a defeat could lead to large-scale uprisings, and there were, as we have already seen, grave doubts about the loyalty of the native army. Whether Hardinge was making a grab for power is not really clear to see. Were these the genuine concerns of the senior political figure, or an attempt to gain full control not only of the political apparatus of India but also the military? There have been suggestions that Hardinge lusted not only after power but after glory. For a man who had largely been a staff officer throughout his career it is possible that he now saw the opportunity to go down in history as the conqueror of India. Such suggestions perhaps do Hardinge an injustice. However, it was not just Gough who Hardinge was criticising for a few days

1   Rait, *Gough*, Vol. II, p. 34
2   Rait, *Gough*, Vol. II, pp. 88–94. These pages included a reproduction of the letter Hardinge wrote to Peel

later he criticised his own council saying, "The Council are excellent men, but there is not one who is equal to any emergency."[3] A cynical reading of his correspondence could suggest that Hardinge was creating a situation and making the case for him being the only man who can resolve the present situation, with overall control of both the military and political means.

The contents of the letter to the Prime Minister is somewhat taken out of context. Hardinge wrote that:

> It is my duty to Her Majesty and to you as head of the Government, to state, most confidentially, that we have been in the greatest peril, and are likely hereafter to be in great peril, if these very extensive operations are to be conducted by the Commander-in-Chief. [...] I respect and esteem Sir H. Gough, but I cannot risk the safety of India by concealing my opinion from you.[4]

This has always been read in the vein of a condemnation of Gough's military ability, but that is not necessarily the way in which Hardinge meant it. If he meant it in a military sense then he was clearly duplicitous in his failure to explain the course of the battle, and in particular the role that he himself had played in it, to the Prime Minister. However, it could be argued that Hardinge was talking more about the political considerations of the campaign, hence his mention of the risk to India, rather than in purely military terms.

Hardinge clearly hoped to be offered the command as a compromise, but modesty forbade him from putting his own name forward. The name he did suggest, Charles Napier, was from a military point of view quite sound, and thus reflected well upon Hardinge's judgement, but from a political point of view the appointment of Napier was unlikely to be accepted due to his unpopularity with the government at home and in India and the HEIC Court of Directors. On the same day that he wrote to the Prime Minister, Hardinge also wrote to his stepson. Alluding to his relationship with Gough he wrote:

> My position has been most painful. My C.C is an honourable man, amiable, kind-hearted, and heroically brave. I had better not finish the character. The fault of any deficiency rests not with him. He does his best and never spares himself, but it is very critical work.[5]

This is perhaps slightly at odds with the perception of his comments in the letter to Peel. The line, "The fault of any deficiency rests not with him", is a curious phrase. On one hand it could be interpreted as recognition of the lack of support that Gough received from his staff: in a letter to Lord Ripon dated 27 December, Hardinge was particularly critical of Gough's staff calling them inefficient and asserting that they were of no assistance to Gough. Alternatively, however, it could also suggest that Hardinge was trying to excuse Gough by suggesting that a lack of intelligence was not his fault but rather the nature of the man. Neither is perhaps a fair reflection, and one is left wondering exactly what Hardinge was trying to achieve.[6]

There was much to criticise in the handling of the army, but there was also much mitigation, none of which Hardinge presented to the Prime Minister. In his letter to Peel, Hardinge went on to say that Gough, "has no capacity for administration. He is at the outposts wonderfully active; but the more important points, which he dislikes, of framing proper orders and looking to their

---

3   Rait, Gough, Vol. II, p. 34.
4   Rait, *Gough*, Vol. II, pp. 89–90.
5   Singh, *The Letters of Viscount Hardinge*, p. 136. This quotes from Hardinge's letter to his stepson Walter James dated 30 December 1845.
6   Singh, *The Letters of Viscount Hardinge*, p. 134.

execution, are very much neglected." Again this suggests that the staff system was poor as the commander-in-chief should not be expected to do such tasks single-handed.[7] Yet the criticism is unfair due to the fact that so many orders Gough gave before and during the campaign were countermanded by Hardinge. It could also be argued that Hardinge was presenting a case for Gough being a fine fighting commander leading the army in battle, but that he needed another in a position of authority to prepare the army, issue the orders, and deal with the administration and organisation. If one takes this view then Hardinge was not only making the case for himself having supreme command, but for maintaining Gough, albeit it as a subordinate command. It has also been said that Hardinge had a habit of portraying suggestions raised by Gough's in their correspondence as his own ideas. This gave the impression that Hardinge was supplying all the ideas. However Hardinge himself would later accuse Gough of the very same thing. In February 1846 he wrote to his stepson Walter that, "With regard to Gough, he consults me, adopts generally my suggestions, and with variations makes them his own."[8]

The fact that Hardinge was clearly playing a wider political game is also illustrated by the fact he seemingly contradicted himself in the same letter to Peel. Firstly he stated that 'our movements were so accurately combined with other posts on our line of operations that in our progress here we brought with us every available man' but then later he wrote that "the state of the army is loose, disorderly, and unsatisfactory."[9] It is hard to therefore understand exactly what complaint Hardinge had against Gough. Was it a lack of organisation and discipline, or was it a wider tactical one? It is interesting to note that in the majority of his correspondence of this time there was little criticism of Gough for his tactical approach and his methods of attack. Indeed, how could there be when Hardinge was claiming that they were his plans in the first place? What Hardinge did criticise was Gough ability to control the army and its administration, but he made no condemnation of his tactics or overreliance on the bayonet.

One does get the sense that Hardinge's correspondence of this time credits all the success of the campaign to his own ability and all the failures to his commander-in-chief. In reality, each shares the blame and each shares the credit. It would be wrong to claim that Hardinge was any less culpable than Gough for any failure in the campaign. Indeed, by exercising his powers as Governor General to overrule the commander-in-chief in the field, Hardinge had made it impossible for him to be absolved from blame. By interfering with Gough's plans he was tacitly taking on responsibility for the consequences. It could be suggested that this, rather than any attempt to maintain Gough's reputation, was the real reason why Hardinge 'forgot' to mention to the Prime Minister that he had overruled his commander-in-chief just prior to the Battle of Ferozeshah.

Much of Hardinge's correspondence relates to Gough's character. Although he never states it so bluntly, his theory was that Gough was brave and courageous, but lacking in intelligence. He also continually used the word 'jealous' when referring to Gough's guarding of his own authority. Given the number of times that he was overruled by Hardinge it is hardly surprising if Gough dug his heels in and did guard jealously what authority he had left. Hardinge never seemed to appreciate that whilst he might have been acting for what he considered the public good he had by his actions undermined and weakened his own commander-in-chief in the middle of a difficult campaign. Perhaps the repercussions of this on Gough's attitude towards the war and Hardinge in particular can never fully be understood. It would be almost inconceivable to think that the actions of Hardinge did not have a profound effect upon Gough's decision making in the future.

---

7   Rait, *Gough*, Vol. II, pp. 92–93.
8   Rait, *Gough*, Vol. II, p. 34, makes the claims regarding Hardinge passing off Gough's ideas and success as his own. Singh, *The Letters of Viscount Hardinge*, p. 146.
9   Rait, *Gough*, Vol. II, p. 35.

Hardinge wrote a similar letter to Lord Ripon, President of the Board of Control and responsible for overseeing the East India Company. This ran to 42 pages, far longer than standard reports of the day, and the length of the letter likely added to the seriousness with which it was received. The response to Hardinge's letters to Peel and to Ripon was to result in some extraordinary attempts to give Hardinge the authority he needed over Gough. In Britain, particularly during the Victorian Age, there was a great aversion to anything that seemed to smack of dictatorship. Yet quite extraordinarily this would have been the consequence of the alterations the Prime Minister, Lord Ripon, and the Duke of Wellington now proposed. Hardinge would effectively have been dictator of India, with full military and political control, because, as we have already seen, although he would be answerable to London, communication was such that they could have little control over his policy. Even as things already stood, the decisions of the governor general often presented London with a *fait accompli*. In February 1846, Lord Ripon wrote to Hardinge concerning future operation against the Sikhs and stated that, "The cabinet have decided that it is indispensably necessary that some means should be taken whereby the command of all operations in the field should be under you." Although this is seen as a condemnation of Gough's command ability, there were also more practical reasons for this change of command. As Ripon would go on to write:

> It has a very strange and somewhat unseemly appearance that the Governor-General should be acting as second in command to the commander-in-chief in the field; and as these Punjab affairs are and must necessarily be, so much mixed up with political matters, it is quite reasonable that the same head should direct both.[10]

Perhaps this concern over the political settlement was more than just an excuse. Hardinge would complain that he received no help in regards to the political settlement from anyone other than his private secretary Currie. Indeed he later described Gough in the context of the political settlement as, "a mere soldier [who] can give me no opinion". For Hardinge, the ability to coordinate the military and political angles of the campaign would be useful.[11]

In the same letter, Ripon suggested that there was precedence to such a combination:

> We think that the best mode in which this could be done is by giving you (as was done in the case of Lord Wellesley in 1800) the commission of 'Captain-General and Commander-in-Chief'. This would place you in the position in which we wish to see you upon public and obvious grounds, and the commission would be so worded as not in any degree to point to any distrust of Gough.[12]

One can read too much into such a statement, but one wonders what the phrase 'obvious grounds' actually means. It would be easy to presume that it alludes to the questions over Gough's ability to command, as mentioned in Hardinge's letter to the Prime Minister. However, it is not entirely clear. Certainly the fact that Lord Ripon states that they would not want to imply 'any distrust of Gough', clearly illustrates that there was at least the fear that this was how the new powers bestowed upon Hardinge could be perceived.

However Ripon wrote again to Hardinge in early March stating that the above suggestion had been ruled as inappropriate by the 'law officers'.[13] Indeed one wonders whether it was

10   Hardinge, *Viscount Hardinge*, pp. 104–105.
11   Singh, *The Letters of Viscount Hardinge*, p. 150.
12   Hardinge, *Viscount Hardinge*, p. 105.
13   Hardinge, *Viscount Hardinge*, p. 105.

simply a question of legality or the possibility of the precedent it might set. It is also unclear how making Hardinge captain general and commander-in-chief would have affected Gough. Surely there could not be two Commanders-in-Chief, so what was to become of him? If he were to be without an appointment it would be impossible for Ripon to pretend that there was not 'distrust' of Gough. Would Gough simply have remained commander-in-chief of the Bengal Army, but not be commander-in-chief in India? No details of what would have happened to Gough under Lord Ripon's scheme are known. If the government wanted to make it look as if there was no loss of confidence in Gough then there must have been some consideration given to what title Gough would continue to hold.

The task of approaching Gough on this matter fell to the Duke of Wellington. In some ways, as commander-in-chief of the British Army, it was understandable that he should deal with the matter. On the other hand it could be suggested that the politicians were passing the buck to Wellington. Also, receiving such a suggestion from the most distinguished British soldier of the age might induce Gough to accept the decision without argument. If the latter was the intention then it indicated that political London had certainly misread or failed to understand the character of Gough.

In early March 1846 Wellington wrote to Gough on this matter, not yet knowing that the war had already been successful concluded. Although Wellington tried to be diplomatic, the earlier part of his letter must surely have confused Gough and made him suspicious of his motives. Wellington started by lamenting the great loss of life suffered in the war to that point. The problem is that Wellington did not make it clear as to when he was speaking for himself and when he was expressing the views of the Government. So after lamenting the loss of life, but also saying that he believed it was inevitable, he turned to the delicate issue of overall command:

> Her Majesty and her servants are sensible that your former services have afforded every reason which should give confidence in your talents and your performance of ever duty with which you may be entrusted. But the law has certain powers to, and thrown responsibility upon another person filling another office: and they are anxious that he should have in his hands all the power and authority which can be conveyed to him, to enable him to provide for all the emergencies of the service as he may have reason to expect they will arise; and to resolve the public interest.[14]

After this rather curious, and hard to follow, preamble, Wellington finally got to the main topic of the correspondence with regards to the view of the division of command between Gough and Hardinge.

> Under these circumstances therefore they are anxious that Lt-Gen Sir H Hardinge should assume the direction of the movements and operations and the command of the army in the field on the north west frontier, and I have received H.M's Commands to transit to him a letter of service accordingly and a warrant to enable him to assemble Courts Martial for the trial of Officers and Soldiers.[15]

14 NAM: 8303–105, Gough Papers, Wellington to Gough, 7 March 1846. The date is interesting as in India two days later the Treaty of Lahore would be signed thus ending the war. This once again highlights the problems and length of time in communication between England and India.
15 NAM: 8303–105, Gough Papers, Wellington to Gough, 7 March 1846.

Although the last simply signified the responsibility that Hardinge would now have, it was poorly worded and must have confused Gough as to what was planned. Where there to be mass Court Martials for officers and men with regards to Ferozeshah? Although this was not planned, the rather clumsy wording used by Wellington did not help the situation. Indeed his whole approach was rather disjointed and confused. Wellington attempted to mollify Gough with such language as, 'respectful to you' and 'your great service'. Neither disguised the fact to Gough that he was being superseded by an officer of junior rank.

Wellington's rather rambling letter then exposed something of the dilemma the Government at home were in, suggesting that they clearly felt that it would be difficult, not to say embarrassing, to attempt to force this decision upon Gough:

> I feel the desire most strongly, and I am anxious not only to conciliate your mind to an arrange-ment considered here to be absolutely necessary in the existing crisis, but that you should manifest your desire to promote it.[16]

The motives of this rather unsuitable attempt to get Gough to personally advocate the desired course of action can be easily imagined. If Gough were to be seen to be advocating this course of action the Government would be able to answer any critics of the decision by presenting it in such a way as to make it seem as if Gough had asked for the above arrangement to be put in place.

Wellington concluded the letter with the most bizarre comment that, "I tell you fairly that if I was in your place and it suited Sir Henry Hardinge, I would change places with him, and act as Second-in-Command to him, as he did to you." This is an almost laughable comment. Even a cursory glance at the career of Wellington illustrates that he jealously guarded his authority far more than Gough could ever be accused of. The idea that Wellington would willingly act as anyone's junior is hard to believe. At the end of the letter Wellington stated again that he would himself do what he was asking of Gough if the roles were reversed, stating, "In the course of my military life, I have had occasion to adopt and have offered to adopt a course analogous to that which I have above recommended to you." The only time that Wellington might have possibly done this would have been in his younger days when he was junior in rank. That was very different to asking a lieutenant general with the local rank of full general, serving as commander-in-chief in India no less, to become the subordinate of a lieutenant general junior to him on the Army List. Wellington also presented Hardinge's decision to act under Gough as a 'benevolent' act rather than the product of the fact that Hardinge was simply his junior in military rank.[17]

By the time Gough came to respond to Wellington, which, with the delay in mail between England and India, did not occur until early May 1846, Gough was already a little aggrieved about the actions of Wellington. In mid April, reports from England of the reaction to the battles of Mudki and Ferozeshah reached India. Gough was disappointed at the press reaction, but given his fairly low opinion of the press this did not cause him great consternation. Yet what did upset him was the report of Wellington's speech in the House of Lords during the vote of thanks to the army. Gough's name was mentioned only once, and in the context it appeared that he only played a very junior role and he was never named as commander-in-chief. Wellington made continual references to the commander-in-chief but never stated that Gough held that position: at the same time he

16   NAM: 8303–105, Gough Papers, Wellington to Gough, 7 March 1846.
17   NAM: 8303–105, Gough Papers, Wellington to Gough, 7 March 1846.

continually mentioned others such as Hardinge and Sir Harry Smith by name. When reading the debate it would be easy to believe that Harry Smith or Henry Hardinge was commander-in-chief.[18]

It is almost unbelievable that in a vote of thanks to a victorious army that the name of the senior officer in command should not be mentioned. Wellington was by this stage an old man and reports abound of his failing memory and the rambling nature of his speeches during this period. Yet to suggest this was simply an accident, a moment of forgetfulness from an old man, would seem a little too convenient to believe. It could be suggested that by diverting the attention onto Hardinge the Government was preparing the way for the change to come. That said, it must be stated that if one reads the speech made in the House of Lords by the Duke of Wellington there are a number of times when he is speaking that he has to be corrected, particularly when it comes to dates, by his fellow Lords.

Gough was angry and hurt, not only by the attempts to remove him from command but by the inexplicable failure of Wellington to acknowledge him in the vote of thanks in the House of Lords. Perhaps Gough made too much of this, and it should be added that Lord Ripon mentioned Gough several times when initially proposing the vote of thanks. One gets the impression that Gough started to suspect a conspiracy against him. Hardinge and Wellington were very close, and Hardinge was an intimate friend of Robert Peel. In June Gough would write to his son that he feared his career was over and that he would not be given another command. Over three days he wrote letters to his son George that show us something of the bitterness and resentment he felt. In a similar vein of anger he wrote to the military secretary at East India House enclosing copies of the correspondence with the Duke of Wellington, including his own reply, and asking him to acquaint the Court of Directors with it.[19]

On 7 June Gough wrote, "Truth will out and justice must follow in spite of that old [unintelligible] the Duke and his followers. I feel quite satisfied that nothing will come of that villainous letter of his Graces", no doubt referring to the plans to make Hardinge senior to Gough. On 8 June, Gough wrote that, "I have no chance of such a command whilst the Duke is at the head of the Army!" On 9 June he added, "I am heartily disgruntled with the Duke's Speech. It is the first time I believe in English history when the senior military personage leaves out the name of the general who achieved victory in an expression of thanks." Later correspondence from September of 1846 makes it clear that he still felt resentment over his treatment and the actions of the Duke of Wellington, referring to the latter as being 'daft' and of having a personal grievance against him for, "If he did not he ought to have spoken favourably of my service", in his speak in the House of Lords.[20]

On 7 May, Gough wrote to Wellington in response to his initial letter. The anger and annoyance was barely contained.

> In the British Army there is not an officer with whom I would more cordially act, than with Lt-General Sir H. Hardinge, nor is there one to whom I would merge superior military rank and serve under, as second in command, more readily under any other circumstance. But, when I find Her Majesty's servants, in the very midst of a campaign where important military operations have been performed, and equally important ones anticipated, call upon me to resign my military command to a junior officer who had so nobly acted with me, throughout the whole

18   *Hansard*, House of Lords Debate, 2 April 1846, Vol. 85, cc412–435. This was part of a pattern, see also Hansard, House of Lords Debate, 2 March 1846, Vol. 84, cc354–379.

19   NAM: 8303–105, Gough Papers, Gough to George Gough, 8 June 1846 & Gough to Phillip Melville 6 May 1846.

20   NAM: 8303–105, Gough Papers, Gough to George Gough, 7 June 1846, Gough to George Gough, 8 June 1846, Gough to George Gough, 9 June 1846 & Gough to George Gough, 3 September 1846.

of these successful operations, I beg to say that I feel I should be justifying the withholding of all credit to myself, so unequivocally done by the head of the British Army in addressing the House of Lords on the vote of thanks to this army, were I to serve in the subordinate capacity to which it would appear by Your Grace's letter, it is proposed I should be reduced. I think it right, therefore, to apprize Your Grace that when the Official Communication from the Secret Committee of the Court of Directors, to which you allude, shall reach me, I shall consider it due to myself to resign the Command of the Army of India.[21]

An unkind reading of this letter would suggest than Gough was resigning in anger and throwing something of a 'tantrum'. Yet a kinder view would be to see it as calling the Government's bluff. They wanted him to advocate the change; they wanted him to quietly step aside and avoid an embarrassing and possible controversial course of action. Gough was clearly not prepared to do this. If they were to remove him from command it would mean his immediate resignation. Although Gough was not the sort to make public declarations, the Government were no doubt concerned about the possibility of him speaking out once freed from the constraints of command.

It is clear also from this letter than the failure of the Duke of Wellington to acknowledge him in his speech in the House of Lords has deeply upset Gough. One must remember that Gough knew nothing of Hardinge's letters home and their comments regarding him. Therefore Gough was not entirely sure why the Duke had acted the way he had. Gough believed that he had offended Wellington, and that the Duke's actions both in his speech and in his letter to Gough were because of this. He thought that the reason for this offence might have been the publication of Littler's despatch which had an unfortunate use of language in that it used the word panic when referring to the actions of the 62nd Foot during the battle. Wellington had taken great pains in his speech in the House of Lords to defend this regiment, and thus Gough could be forgiven for thinking that this might be the cause of bad relations between him and the Duke.[22]

The other possible reason he could see for why he might have offended Wellington was his granting of a commission to every sergeant major of a British regiment under his command. Given the large-scale loss of officers in the two battles such a move was essential and it will be recalled that some regiments were down to a handful of officers. Thus something needed to be done, but by his actions Gough had not only encroached upon the authority of Wellington but also Royal Prerogative. As it happened this only resulted in five NCOs being commissioned, but it was a controversial move none the less. Gough argued that he had no choice, as his deficiency in officers was such that something had to be done. Writing to his son Gough declared, "I did then what I should do again even with the bane of His Grace's displeasure." As Sir Robert Rait put it, "he declined to allow the proprieties to interfere with the actual military necessities in time of war."[23]

Yet due to his lack of familiarity with the correspondence Hardinge was having with those in London Gough's assumptions were wide of the mark. Yes, there had been annoyance with Littler's remarks, but it was accepted that Gough had no knowledge of this and no hand in their publication. There was also displeasure at him having exceeded his authority by awarding commissions to senior NCOs, but a tacit acceptance that he had little alternative given the heavy loss in officers the two battle had brought. As a consequence one sees at this stage a very conciliatory approach from Gough towards Hardinge, and a far kinder interpretation of the latter's actions than would come later on. In a letter to his son in May 1846 Gough wrote, "Remember, as Governor-General, he was not only head of the State, but head of the Army, and that it was an act deserving of all praise

21   NAM: 8303–105, Gough Papers, Gough to Wellington, 7 May 1846.
22   Rait, *Gough*, Vol. II, pp. 96–97.
23   NAM: 8303–105, Gough Papers, Gough to George Gough, 1 May 1848. Rait, *Gough* Vol. II, p. 97.

that he took a subordinate part, which showed confidence in the Head [i.e., Gough himself]." It is also interesting to note that Gough ended this correspondence with the words, "Lose no opportunity of lauding Sir Henry Hardinge; he merits it as a noble soldier, although he was not Commander-in-Chief."[24]

This is slightly at odds with the letters of Hardinge to his family in which he was critical of Gough, but urged them not to say anything in public that might suggest this. It might be too simplistic an interpretation, but there is certainly some credence to the idea that whilst Hardinge was playing politics, and not wishing to see his actions misinterpreted, Gough was simply acknowledging the bravery of a fellow soldier. Perhaps here is shown all that one needs to know about the two men. Gough was a simple soldier with either no ability or desire to play the game of politics, whereas, whilst Hardinge undoubtedly had great skill as a soldier, such had been his work since the end of the Napoleonic Wars that he was now more politician than soldier in his outlook and had after all come to India in a political capacity not a military one.[25]

Gough had communicated his intention to resign if the Letter of Service that Wellington had talked about arrived in India. This was largely kept secret. Gough sent a copy of his communication with Wellington, including his reply, to both Hardinge and the Secret Committee of the East India Company Court of Directors. Hardinge expressed his regret at Gough's decision writing that:

> The arrangements made by Her Majesty's Government for a Political Purpose had entirely gone by, when it came before me, and consequently it appeared to me that the most appropriate course to take for all parties was to consider the whole matter in abeyance until you or I should hear further from England. I should therefore have been gratified if you could have adopted this course, which would answer every purpose.[26]

The problem with this course of action was that it would have reflected badly on Gough. Had he resigned when the letter arrived it would certainly have looked like a decision taken in anger and petulance. Yet by giving the authorities notice of his intention he made it clear to them what the consequences would be of their actions. There was no way that his resignation could be then seen as unexpected.

In any case, the letter never arrived. The victories obtained at Aliwal and Sobraon effectively ended the war and therefore the need for such an immediate course of action disappeared. One cannot help but wonder why, if there were such obvious concerns about the Commander-in-Chief, that moves did not continue to replace him. Indeed in the aftermath of a victorious conflict it would be far easier to do. A command at home could no doubt have been found for him, to ease him into retirement. Gough could have been brought home as the hero with honours and rewards, and a solution to the problems of command in India could have thereby been arrived at. The fact that this did not follow through after the war tells us a number of things. There was perhaps a reluctance to undertake the action that the correspondence had proposed, which in turn points to an overreaction to events leading to the belief that such radical action was required.

It also shows us that victory brings its own justification. Had communication been quicker between London and India, there is little doubt that the removal of Gough would have been implemented before the end of the war. This problem with correspondence meant that it was often

24 NAM: 8303–105, Gough Papers, Gough to George Gough, 1 May 1848.
25 Singh, *The Letters of Viscount Hardinge*, pp. 134, 136, 138, 165. A letter to his stepson Walter dated 19 April 1846 is the most open in this regard, accusing people of making 'mischief' as regard the relationship between him and Gough and asking Walter to make sure that this is remedied.
26 NAM: 8303–105, Gough Papers, Hardinge to Gough, 6 May 1846.

many months before a reply to a letter was received. Let us not forget that Wellington's letter, dated 7 March 1846, finally arrived with Gough on 6 May. Not only had the battles of Aliwal and Sobraon been fought and won, effectively ending the war, it was nearly two months after the Treaty of Lahore had been signed, formally ending the war. It is therefore easy to understand why Gough was aggrieved at his removal, notwithstanding his belief that Wellington had attempted to write him out of the narrative of the campaign.

At the same time, it was not until early September that Gough received a reply from Wellington to what in effect had been his letter of resignation written in May. Wellington's response to Gough letter was dated 9 July 1846. The letter commenced, "I am concerned to observe that you imagined I had failed to express in the House of Lords my sense of your services upon the occasion of the motion for the thanks of the House to yourself and the Army under your Command."[27] Wellington tried to explain this by stating that he was only responding to the vote of thanks proposed by Lord Ripon. He also commented upon the fact that he felt he needed to defend the 62nd over Littler's remarks and stated that in this he, "succeeded entirely to my own satisfaction and that of the House and the publick [sic]." Wellington slightly contradicted himself in the same letter. To begin with he stated that he, "certainly did not omit to express to the House my sense of the service which had been performed particularly by yourself" but later in the same letter wrote that he, "certainly did not fulfil my own intentions, or perform my duty, as I ought, if I failed to state to the House my sense of the services performed by yourself." These two very similar sentences do not quite add up.[28] In fairness it should be pointed out that Lord Ripon only mentioned Gough by name four times, and on three occasions this is actually in summing up to what and to whom the vote of thanks should be proposed. Other than that he simply refers to the commander-in-chief. Yet he did at least mention Gough's by name at some point, unlike Wellington.

Wellington also touched upon the rather delicate subject of Hardinge superseding Gough which he had mentioned in his previous correspondence.

> In respect to an arrangement to which my letter of the 7th of March referred, the object of that letter was to render it palatable to you, and I took the liberty of suggesting to you a course which you should take, which I thought would rebound to your honour and credit, and I suggested that the course which I recommended was analogous to those which I had adopted upon more than one analogous occasion, and had been prepared to adopt upon many.[29]

It might be this rather unusual reply, and the previous contradictory statements, that led to Gough's comment to his son George, around this time, that he believed that Wellington had gone 'daft'. Later in the same letter the Duke of Wellington seemed to try and backtrack and state that he had been at odds with the policy of the Government.

> You have been long enough in command of Armies to be sensible that it happens to a Commander-in-Chief but too frequently, to find that the essential interests of the publick [sic] require that arrangements should be made not exactly consistent with his own views or his opinions of justice to the pretentions and claims of individuals—this is the view which must be taken of this transaction, and the part which I took in it.[30]

---

27   NAM: 8303–105, Gough Papers, Wellington to Gough, 4 July 1846.
28   NAM: 8303–105, Gough Papers, Wellington to Gough, 4 July 1846.
29   NAM: 8303–105, Gough Papers, Wellington to Gough, 4 July 1846.
30   NAM: 8303–105, Gough Papers, Wellington to Gough, 4 July 1846.

Although not entirely clear, it is probable that when referring to the commander-in-chief Wellington is speaking of himself as commander-in-chief of the British Army rather than Gough. If so, it appears that Wellington was trying to convince Gough that the contents of his last letter had not been his own thoughts or wishes but those of the Government which he was asked to transmit. In some ways this was correct as it is clear from Lord Ripon's correspondence with Hardinge that the Government felt it best that such news should be delivered to Gough by Wellington. It also meant that if there should be any controversy over the move it would look like a military decision rather than a matter of political interference.

When in September 1846 Gough was finally able to respond to this letter he struck a conciliatory tone thanking Wellington for his comments.

> Having been placed in the high position I now hold through your Grace's recommendation, I will confess I felt sensitively alive to everything connected with the creditable performance of the duties of Commander-in-Chief of the Army in India; added to which I was fully aware that your Grace's approval stamps the value of all Military achievements. I trust I may therefore stand excused for having been prepared to resign—valuable to me though it be—that to which I had succeeded through your Grace, when I supposed I no longer held that place in your estimation as a Soldier, which from your Grace's having previously recommended me, I was proud in the idea of possessing.[31]

It seems to have been something of a character trait of Gough's that he was quite easily mollified. He was capable of great anger and bitterness when he thought he had been wronged, yet it took very little to cause that to subside. Here the mere recognition of his service to the Crown was sufficient to cause this. Indeed, it should be pointed out that although he was aware that his service was to be recognised he was not yet aware that this would be in the form of a Viscountcy.

Although concerns about Gough's ability to command remained, they were perhaps seen as being less important. The majority of politicians believed that, with the defeat of the Sikhs, British India was now secured. Gough for his part had no doubt that there would be a need to fight the Sikhs again and that the settlement with the Sikhs had been neither one thing nor another: they did not become a true client state, nor were they annexed. However that is to get a little ahead of ourselves in the narrative of Hugh Gough and his life and career. Whilst we have taken time to look at the political fallout from the early battles of the First Sikh War, it is now time to return to our narrative and look at what was to be the final battle of that war. This was the action at Sobraon on 10 February 1846. Whilst much of the correspondence mentioned above took place after this battle, and therefore after the practical ending of the war, it has been felt appropriate to deal with it all in one place. Now, however, we return to our narrative of the conflict and to the events that followed the victory at Aliwal.

---

31   NAM: 8303–105, Gough Papers, Gough to Wellington, 1 September 1846.

54

Planning for the Battle of Sobraon

The Battle of Aliwal had clearly been a morale boast to the British, not least of all Gough. It also coincided with the strengthening of the British position with reinforcements and extra supplies. Perhaps most importantly was the arrival of the siege train with the heavy guns that in theory gave Gough something with which to match the Sikhs. The siege train brought with it five 18 pdrs and 14 9 inch howitzers. Alongside this heavy artillery were some of the existing 9 pdrs that had undergone a makeshift conversion to fire 12 pdr shot. Exactly how effective this alteration was is not entirely clear. These measures together at last gave Gough some artillery equivalent to that of the Sikhs. The Sikhs would continue to have the advantage in artillery, but it would not be undisputed as it had been up to this point.

The problem was that despite this improvement in the prospect and morale of the British, the Sikhs were still in a strong position. Although Aliwal had been a disappointment, the Sikhs knew that they still held a strong position at Sobraon, with strengthening defences and their artillery well emplaced and defended. There have been suggestions that the Sikh defences had been built unscientifically and that the sandy nature of the ground somewhat nullified the explosions made by Sikh artillery. Whilst no doubt true it does not detract from the difficulty of attacking any entrenched position particularly when at best there was parity of artillery rather than supremacy. Gough stated in correspondence with Hardinge that, "the enemy has placed himself in certainly a very strong, still, in a false position, with a river in his rear."[1] However any British attack would be met with a very strong response by the Sikhs. Whilst they were perhaps disheartened they were very far from defeated. A bloody conflict was inevitable if Gough were to take the position at Sobraon.

It appears that there were three different plans of attack considered by Gough and Hardinge at this stage. The first was to leave a holding force opposite Sobraon whilst a large force moved further down the river and attempted to cross elsewhere. From there an attack would be launched on Lahore. The hope was that by taking the enemy's capital the force at Sobraon would surrender without the need for a fight. This plan was never really taken seriously for a number of reasons. Firstly, it was an extremely risky proposition: Gough would have had to split his force in two, never advisable, particularly when in hostile territory. Secondly, there appeared to be no other crossing point that was suitable for a large number of men to move across, particularly with any great speed. Thirdly, it was doubtful that the taking of Lahore, without the defeat of a large Sikh army, would end the war. Finally, there was every chance that the Sikhs might launch another raid across the Sutlej. If they were to do that there would be little the British could do. In short there were simply

---

1   NAM: 8303–105, Gough Papers, Gough to Hardinge, 6 February 1846. See also in the same collection, Gough to Hardinge, 18 January 1846. In the latter Gough goes into great details about the position and his intentions and strategy for attacking it.

not enough men to protect the crossing at Sobraon, deal with any raiding force, and also send a large force across the river at another point.[2]

The second idea, and the one that Hardinge favoured, was to attempt a secret night river crossing with 12,000 men, using boats which had been sent to support any British attempt. It was certainly a bold plan, and credit must go to Hardinge for supporting such a brave course of action. The plan was that this force would launch a surprise attack and capture the key Sikh strategic point across the river. This would cut off the enemy and an attack could be launched from two directions.[3] Gough felt this plan was too complex and that there were too many things that could go wrong. In one sense the poor staff work of the army, for which Gough was only partially responsible, meant that the necessary preparation and orders for such an assault were perhaps beyond the commander-in-chief's staff. It does not appear to have been suggested, but one wonders if a possible way around this would have been to detach such a force under Sir Harry Smith, given his recent success with an independent command. This also had the advantage that if Gough were seen to be still with the force at Sobraon it would add to the chance of the surprise attack being successful, in that one would have expected any attack to have been made under the direction of the commander-in-chief himself.[4]

Gough, perhaps unsurprisingly, favoured the final option of a frontal assault. Indeed he considered this the only reliable form of attack under such circumstances. Whilst it is easy to see this as the product of an unimaginative mind, in one sense he was right. The two other schemes were risky, involved more that could go wrong, required dividing his limited force of Europeans, and created the possibility for the Sikhs to be able to defeat the British in detail. The war up to that point had demonstrated that the Sikhs were a match for the British, and thus Gough's numerical inferiority was more of a concern than was usual in the British experience of warfare in India. Gough also believed that, "we can make no move here that will not be known immediately to the enemy, giving him the opportunity of making a corresponding move."[5] In that sense, getting to grips with the enemy as soon as possible was necessary and thus the frontal assault the most suitable course.

Hardinge was prepared to countenance Gough's intention to attack providing that British artillery could effectively soften up the enemy defences before the advance. This had two drawbacks. Firstly, despite the arrival of the siege train, Gough's artillery was still inferior to that of the Sikhs. Furthermore, given that the Sikh guns were in strong defensive positions, even the heavy guns the British possessed might have little effect. The second drawback was that any bombardment would alert the Sikhs to British intentions. A bombardment would be taken as a clear signal that the British intended to attack. Gough consulted his artillery officers and engineers. Their response was perhaps overly optimistic, or at least represented an overestimation of their own strength. They expressed the opinion that one to two hours of firing by 30 howitzers and five 18 pdrs would be sufficient to reduce the enemy to a position where it was safe for the infantry to advance. However, they later altered their opinion, presumably on a closer examination of the enemy position, and concluded that it was not possible to reduce the Sikh defences to a position where it would be safe for the infantry to advance without coming under fire. The Sikh guns were protected by strong earthworks, in front of which lay deep ditches. Their guns were well positioned and were placed so as to allow additional guns on the other side of the river to support their fire and protect their position.

2   NAM: 8303–105, Gough Papers, Gough to Hardinge, 18 January 1846.
3   Rait, *Gough*, Vol. II pp. 51–52.
4   NAM: 8303–105, Gough Papers, Gough, to Hardinge, 6 February 1846. Rait, *Gough*, Vol. II pp. 52–54.
5   NAM: 8303–105, Gough Papers, Gough, to Hardinge, 6 February 1846.

Gough accepted this new advice from his artillery and engineers officers. Hardinge however sought alternative advice and asked Major Lawrence, the political agent, and Major Abbott, an officer of engineers, to consider the matter. They concluded that an attack was possible if the artillery could soften up the Sikh defences first, despite the artillery officers voicing their concerns as to whether this was possible. On condition that the defences were softened up by artillery bombardment, Hardinge decided to accept Gough scheme and abandoned his own preferred scheme. Whether Hardinge had started to doubt the likelihood of his scheme being successful or not is not clear. What is perhaps more likely is that given the objections, transmitted to Hardinge on paper by Gough, he felt that to go against the advice of his own military commander in a risky enterprise might be unwise.[6]

Had Hardinge forced his plan on Gough, given his objections, any negative consequences would inevitable fall upon Hardinge more than Gough. Thus to Gough Hardinge issued the following instructions:

> Upon the fullest consideration of this question, if the artillery can be brought into play, I recommend you to attack. If it cannot, and you anticipate a heavy loss, I would recommend you not to undertake it. I have great confidence in the opinion of Major Abbott on these professional points, relating to the destruction of defences.[7]

Gough how decided upon making the frontal attack, after what he hoped would be an effective artillery bombardment. The Army was in a relatively good condition. Morale had improved, as had the organisational side of affairs, although this was slightly tainted by the need to place a lot of new or inexperienced officers in appointments due to the high number of casualties amongst the officer corps in the war thus far.

Gough, as he often did, undertook a personal reconnaissance before the battle. Once again he placed himself in danger, as British patrols and working parties were regularly fired upon by the Sikhs. The only exception to this seems to have been to British officers who went pig-sticking, who for some unexplained reason were not fired upon despite being in range of the Sikh guns. An amusing story recounts part of Gough's attempted reconnaissance. In the area where the 80th Foot were stationed was a tower from which one could obtain a great view of the battlefield and in particular the Sikh positions. The problem was that it was an easy target for the Sikh guns, which also caused casualties for the 80th. Lieutenant Colonel Thomas Bunbury had therefore posted guards on the tower to prevent anyone from going up there. It appears that when attempting to ascend the tower to view the battlefield, Gough was not only challenged by the sentry but told he could not go up there. We are told that in good humour Gough replied, "Sure my good man, aren't I the Commander-in-Chief, and can't I do what I like?"[8]

The Sikh position on the south bank of the river was curved, and therefore it was not possible to attempt any flanking attack. A frontal assault would be just that; an attack at the very front of the Sikh line. With Sikh positions on the opposite bank supporting those south of the Sutlej, there was a considerable killing ground before reaching the enemy position. There had been skirmishing along the respective positions of the British and Sikh lines on and off for about a month. On 7 February Gough ordered that this should stop and that no British personnel were to advance forward of the British lines. This was partly to reduce the possibility of spies entering the camp but

6   NAM: 8303–105, Gough Papers, Hardinge to Gough, 7 February 1846.
7   NAM: 8303–105, Gough Papers, Hardinge to Gough, 7 February 1846.
8   Cook, *The Sikh Wars*, p. 86.

also to prevent British soldiers being taken prisoner. In short, it was an attempt to conceal his plans from the enemy.

However the lack of British movement forward was actually a sign to the Sikhs that something was afoot and that a British attack was being planned. Although Gough's order for no forward movement was a sensible precaution it did perhaps lack any flair. It might be a little harsh to criticise Gough in this regard, but perhaps a more imaginative commander might have attempted some sort of diversion or used the continued skirmishing as a form of deception. However it is unlikely that such measures would have been successful. The Sikhs were well aware that the British intended to attack, and had probably realised, as had Gough, that there was little alternative to a frontal attack.

The Battle of Sobraon

On the evening of 9 February 1846, orders were issued for the forthcoming attack. Exact numbers for the Sikhs at Sobraon vary wildly, as per usual. British accounts of the time estimated the Sikhs on the encampment on the south bank at around 35,000. However one eyewitness, engineering officer Captain Joseph D. Cunningham, estimated the Sikh at fewer than 20,000. Gough's official estimate was 42,626 however this included the Sikhs north of the river. South of the river they had 67 guns of varying calibre. Yet the majority of their guns were north of the river and, of these, the majority were able to support the defences on the south side of the river. It was therefore a formidable and strongly defended position that the British had to attack. It was almost inevitable that it would be another bloody battle.[1]

Gough's army stood at around 20,000 men and 108 guns. The right of the army was commanded by Smith and consisted of his own 1st Division. This comprised the 1st Brigade, commanded by Brigadier Penny, consisting of the 31st Foot, 47th Native Infantry and Nasiri Battalion of Gurkhas, and the 2nd Brigade, under Brigadier Hicks, consisting of the 50th Foot and the 42nd Native Infantry. In the centre of the British order of battle was Gilbert's 2nd Division comprised of the 3rd Brigade, under Brigadier Taylor, made up of the 29th Foot and the 41st and 68th Native Infantry, and the 4th Brigade, under Brigadier McLaren, of the 1st Bengal Europeans, 16th Native Infantry, and the Sirmoor Battalion of Gurkhas. Smith was supported by Campbell's cavalry brigade consisting of the 9th Lancers, the 2nd Bengal Irregular Cavalry and two troops of horse artillery.

On the left of the British line was Dick's 3rd Division, which was made up of the three brigades which were be used for the main assault. The plan was that one brigade would act as a reserve to exploit any breach made in the enemy lines. This role was assigned to the 5th Brigade under Brigadier Ashburnham, which to this end had two European battalions, the 9th and 67th Foot, along with the 26th Native Infantry. Also in the division were the 6th Brigade under Brigadier Wilkinson consisting of the 80th Foot and the 33rd Native Infantry, and the 7th Brigade under Brigadier Stacey consisting of the 10th and 53rd Foot and the 43rd and 59th Native Infantry. To strengthen Dick's Division further a brigade of cavalry, consisting of the 3rd Light Dragoons, 4th and 5th Bengal Light Cavalry and 9th Irregular Cavalry, commanded by Brigadier Scott, was attached to him. There were also three reserve battalions of native infantry, the 4th, 5th and 73rd, and a battery of heavy guns accompanying Dick's division. In addition similar batteries of heavy guns were placed between Dick and Gilbert's divisions and between Gilbert and Smith's division.

The overall commander of the cavalry was Sir Joseph Thackwell. The remainder of the cavalry, that not supporting Dick and Smith's divisions, was commanded by Brigadier Cureton. Cureton was directed to make a diversionary feint on the right flank beyond Smith's division at the crossing of the river near the small island of Harike. For this task Cureton had the 16th Lancers and the

---

1   Sidhu, *The First Anglo-Sikh War*, p. 152. Unknown, *The War in India, Despatches*, p. 116, gives the figure of 30,000, and on p. 129 quotes a Sikh source that states there were 37,000 men.

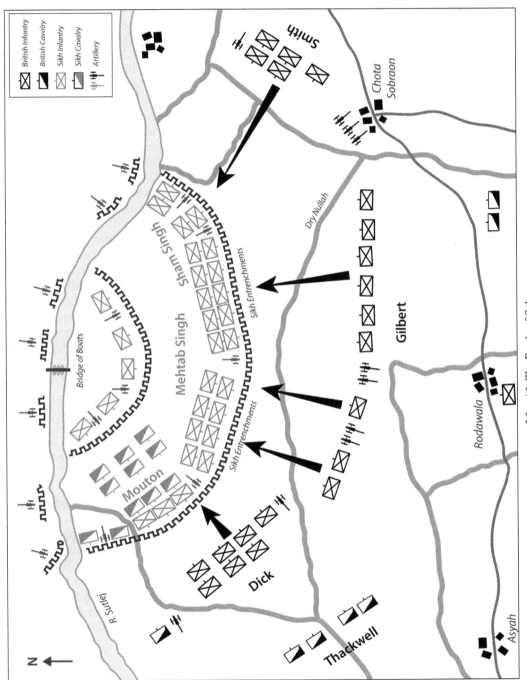

Map 12 The Battle of Sobraon.

3rd Bengal Light Cavalry, and 4th Bengal Irregular Cavalry. At another ford at Attaree to his left, between Sobraon and Ferozepore, Gough placed a force under Sir John Grey consisting of the 8th Bengal Irregular Cavalry and three regiments of native infantry. It appears that neither attempt at subterfuge worked. The Sikhs either understood the difficulty of attempting to cross in force elsewhere and thus identified the manoeuvre was a feint, or were convinced of Gough's tactical abilities to the extent that they knew his intention was the frontal assault.

By 0200 the British troops were prepared for battle. Due to a slight mist that hung over the battlefield, the attack was delayed until 0630. The battle commenced with an artillery barrage. Despite Gough's best attempts, and the almost silent movement of the British into position, the Sikhs were not taken by surprise. The Sikh guns replied with amazing alacrity, and it has been suggested that they returned fire before the British guns fired a second salvo. The artillery battle carried on for two to three hours. Little damage was done to either side. The Sikh entrenchments protected them from the worst of the British fire, although it was found after the battle that Gough's gunners had scored some direct hits on Sikh trenches and killed 30–40 men. Unusually, there was some success against the Sikh guns on the northern bank of the river, where the guns were not as well entrenched and two cannon were destroyed. As for the Sikh fire, it forced the British horse artillery, which had pushed forward, to withdraw but that was the limit of its success. Dick's forces, who were in direct line of fire, were largely defended by their presence in a *nullah*, a dry river bed, that acted as protection from Sikh artillery, the majority of it passing over their heads. After two or three hours the duel came to an end due to the fact that the British guns were running out of ammunition. Harry Smith later wrote that this was due to the fact that Gough's orders for extra ammunition to be brought forward had not been fulfilled. Whether this is entirely accurate is not clear, as Smith might have been alluding to Hardinge's previous overruling of Gough ammunition requests. However, Hardinge had reissued the order and the extra ammunition should have arrived by that time. It might also be the case that for some reason the ammunition did not reach the guns, as the battle field was somewhat extensive.[2]

Hardinge for his part, had already complained in the aftermath of Aliwal, when Gough urged immediate action at Sobraon, that Gough was:

> scarcely willing to understand that amn [ammunition] is necessary for artry [artillery]. We have to replace every shot we fire from Delhi 260 miles off; the enemy can replace his in 24 hours. In this army, rapidly brought together and living almost in an enemy's country from hand to mouth, I have to attend to all these details.[3]

This is perhaps a little rich coming from the man who had initially countermanded Gough's preparations, including extra artillery ammunition and dispatch of the siege train. One wonders whether Hardinge really did have to 'attend to all these details', or whether this was a consequence of his continual interference with the command of the army, both before and during the campaign.

On hearing that the ammunition was running out Gough is recorded as saying, "Thank God, then I'll be at them with the bayonet!"[4] This is often used as evidence for the argument that Gough neither understood nor appreciated the value of artillery but, as we have already seen from his time in China, this was clearly not the case. However, it is true to say that he believed firmly that no battle could be won by the use of artillery alone. In his view it was at best an arm used to soften up

---

2   Smith, *Sir Harry Smith*, pp. 191–192.
3   Singh, *The Letters of Viscount Hardinge*, p. 144.
4   Rait, *Gough*, Vol. II pp. 57–58. The quote originated from *The Times* of the 27 December 1886, the source being an anonymous 'Field Officer'.

the enemy prior to an infantry assault. This was not in any way to belittle the artillery. As he wrote in his despatch of the battle:

> notwithstanding the formidable calibre of our iron guns, mortars, and howitzers, and the admirable way in which they were served, and aided by a rocket battery, it would have been visionary to expect that they could, within any limited time, silence the fire of seventy pieces behind well-constructed batteries of earth, plank, and fascines, or dislodge troops, covered either by redoubts or epaulments, or within a treble line of trenches".[5]

Gough's words perhaps help us to better understand him. It is not a distain for artillery he was portraying, but more a belief in its limitations.

The news that the artillery ammunition was running out was delivered to Gough in some panic. Indeed it was a situation that could have proved distressing. Gough delivered his response in his usual powerful voice so that as many as possible could hear. Such confident words coming from the commander-in-chief would allay the fears of many. Gough gave the appearance of not being concerned for the benefit of the morale of his men. As Rait recorded, "now men felt that, artillery or no artillery, "old Gough" would pull them through." Through Gough's response to the news we see part of the reason why his men loved him. He displayed confidence in public. When doubts came upon him, as they do on all men, they were confined to the privacy of his tent. When he left his tent his expression was resolute and he stood tall and strong and looked as if nothing could trouble him.[6] Perhaps sometimes this outward display of confidence had detrimental effects. Perhaps his confidence was sometimes interpreted as a belief that victory would be easy. Whilst Gough had confidence in his European troops to take on all comers he was not, as we have already shown, under any allusions as to the strength of the Sikh army and the quality of their fighting men. It may also be the case that, to the staff officers around him, Gough's confidence gave them the impression that all was in hand. This may partly explain the poor quality of staff work at this time, as they felt Gough had everything under control and did not therefore undertake their work as seriously as they should. Perhaps this is to stretch a point too far, yet it is clear that whilst Gough's displays of confidence clearly had benefits there were also possibly negative consequences.

The artillery had not been as effective as was hoped in softening up the Sikh positions. Whilst the quality and handling of British guns was not as high as their Sikh counterparts, this was only a small part of why the artillery duel was not effective. As Gough had commented, it was never likely to have the effect that others such as Hardinge hoped it would against such strong positions. Exactly what occurred next has been debated for many years. Gough was preparing for the attack when Colonel Benson, an officer on Hardinge's staff, rode up to him. He claimed to come from the Governor-General and stated that if Gough "did not feel confident of success and without much loss, to withdraw the troops and work up to the enemy's entrenchments by regular approaches."[7] At such a suggestion Gough was close to losing his temper, not only because once again it looked like there would be political interference, but because the battle had already commenced. To withdraw now, after an artillery battle had taken place, could only be interpreted as a retreat before the enemy. The affect upon the morale of both British and native troops, and for that matter the Sikhs, can be imagined. It would also have left any retreat at the mercy of Sikh cavalry, and it is unlikely that withdrawal could have been affected without loss. Also the supposed idea of attacking by regular approaches for not possible without artillery protection, which would have necessitated

5   Unknown, *The War India, Despatches*, pp. 117–118.
6   Rait, *Gough*, Vol. II, p. 58.
7   Rait, *Gough*, Vol. II, p. 58.

waiting for the arrival of extra ammunition. Gough's reply was recorded as, "Loss there will be, of course. Look at those works bristling with guns, and defended as they will be; but, by God's blessing, I feel confident of success."[8]

The story did not end there, and it is recorded that Colonel Benson came with the same message three times. After the last time Gough's patience did wear out. He is said to have exclaimed, "What! Withdraw the troops after the action has commenced, and when I feel confident of success. Indeed I will not. Tell Sir Robert Dick to move on, in the name of God." The famous portrait of Hugh Gough, painted by Sir Francis Grant, in his white fighting coat pointing out across the battlefield is said to be at the moment the order "Tell Sir Robert Dick to move on, in the name of God" was given. Sir Francis Grant was the brother of the future General Sir James Hope Grant, who had served under Gough in China and was present for the Battle of Sobraon with the 9th Lancers. The popular account of the event comes to us from the pen of Patrick Grant, Gough's son-in-law and an officer on his staff throughout the campaign. Thus his impartiality can be questioned, but there seems to be widespread opinion that he gives an accurate portrait of events.[9]

Hardinge's son would later chronicle his father's life, and of this event was convinced that Grant was not only correct but that Benson must have misunderstood the orders given by his father. This is not too hard to believe. Firstly we have already seen that there was a tendency for staff officers during this campaign to rather freely interpret the orders of their superiors. Secondly the words that Benson is recorded as speaking to Gough are not too far removed from the instructions Hardinge had already given to Gough prior to the battle, namely, "Upon the fullest consideration of this question, if the artillery can be brought into play, I recommend you to attack. If it cannot, and you anticipate a heavy loss, I would recommend you not to undertake it." Benson seems to have rather freely interpreted Hardinge's instructions, and this was certainly the view of the younger Hardinge when several years later he wrote to Patrick Grant that, "All I can say is that Colonel Benson must have misinterpreted his orders, and as he is now no more, the matter cannot be further cleared up."[10] The idea that Benson had reinterpreted Hardinge's words appears to be true. Indeed Benson had previous form in this regard, having been one of the officers who visited Gough on that night at Ferozeshah purporting to come from the Governor General. The message that Hardinge is said to have asked Benson to convey was, "if Sir Hugh doubted the issue he might exercise his discretion, but if he only apprehended a severe loss, to go on."[11] This suggests that Hardinge expected there to be great loss, and if so it illustrates that he understood the inevitability of this when attacking such a strong defensive position. Read in this light, Hardinge was informing Gough that if he doubted that he would be victorious he was to exercise his discretion rather than to consider withdrawing if he expected heavy losses. Once again the problems of communication reared their ugly head.

Whilst Gough's natural instinct was in any case to attack the enemy with musket and bayonet, in reality he had little choice. To withdraw would be difficult, if not potentially disastrous, and the bait of the feint of two crossings elsewhere had not worked. With his guns running out of ammunition there was really little alternative. It was therefore at about 0900 that the infantry began to advance, with Dick's division leading the way. The reason for this division leading the advance was

---

8   Rait, *Gough*, Vol. II, p. 58.
9   *The Times*, 29 December 1886. In the same edition this point of view was supported by the then General John Bloomfield Gough. He stated that whilst he had been present and could vouch for the visits of Colonel Benson he could not vouch for the exact words because "I was not near enough to hear all that passed, but I believe Field Marshal Sir Patrick Grant's statement to be perfectly accurate."
10   This letter is quoted in Rait, *Gough*, Vol. II, p. 59. It was written on the same day as Grant's comments appeared in *The Times*.
11   *The Times*, 23 December 1886. It was this letter from the 2nd Viscount Hardinge that led to Grant and John Bloomfield Gough's response printed in the same paper on 29 December 1886.

that it had been discovered that the Sikh entrenchments opposite them did not quite stretch to the river bank, and there was therefore, in theory, an undefended stretch of land. In practice this was well covered by the Sikh guns, both in the entrenchment south of the river and those stationed on the north of the river.

As Sir Robert Dick's division advanced, Brigadier Stacey's brigade of four battalions took the lead. The plan was that this strong brigade, containing three European battalions, would make the initial breakthrough that could then be followed up by Brigadier Wilkinson's brigade of one European and two native battalions, and by the cavalry. That this was a prearranged plan put in place by Gough, who had reorganised the brigades especially, does show that he was learning and adapting, at least in part, from his experiences up to this point. It was also a realisation that it required European troops to create any breakthrough which could then be exploited by native troops. Also it demonstrated Gough's growing confidence in his cavalry. It should be recalled that Gough had little experience of commanding cavalry. In the Peninsular he had been an infantry commander; in Ireland he had cavalry under his command but this was an unconventional conflict; in China there had been little use of cavalry. Thus if Gough took some time to appreciate now best to use his cavalry then it is understandable due to his lack of experience in this regard. At Mudki and Ferozeshah his cavalry had proved their worth and had demonstrated what a powerful force they could be. Gough had become particularly enamoured of the 3rd Light Dragoons, which had more to do with their performance in the battle than the fact that it was the regiment of his nephew, John Bloomfield Gough.

Brigadier Stacey's advance was both steady and orderly as his brigade moved against the Sikh right. Stacey occasionally stopped a unit to allow other units to catch up so that the brigade continued to advance in good order. The advance was supported by a battery of horse artillery on the left, which unlimbered to fire at the enemy before reengaging the guns and moving forward to fire again. The effect of this fire upon the Sikh entrenchments was negligible, but at least it gave another target for the Sikh gunners to deal with apart from the advancing infantry. When the brigade was about 300 yards from the Sikh line they were threatened on their flank by a body of Sikh cavalry. The fire of the flank company of the 53rd Foot was sufficient to halt the Sikh advance, and the fire of the battery of horse artillery was sufficient to mean that the enemy cavalry left the field in disorder.

As they advanced, the 53rd Foot would also bear the brunt of artillery fire from Sikh artillery on the north bank and the battalion sustained casualties accordingly. Amongst the casualties were the staves of both the Queen's and Regimental Colours. This is hardly surprising as they provided such good targets for the Sikh gunners. Yet Sikh artillery was not sufficient to stop the advance, and although the 53rd had sustained casualties they were the first regiment to enter the Sikh trenches. Indeed the Sikh artillery was not its usual efficient self on the morning of 10 February. Much of the Sikh fire went over the heads of the advancing British troops. Exactly what caused this is unclear. It was likely a combination of factors, such as poor handling, less experienced gun crews, poor position and the terrain, but one should not rule out the fact that for the first time in the war the Sikhs had come under sustained artillery fire from heavy British guns. Whilst the British fire might not have silenced the Sikh artillery, it would be naïve to believe that it had not had some effect on its effectiveness and on the morale of the Sikh gunners.

Whilst the 53rd were breaking through on the British left, on Stacey's right the 10th Foot was suffering under Sikh artillery fire as they advanced. Yet it was not sufficient to stop them, and supported by Wilkinson's brigade and by three companies of the 80th Foot provided by the ever-watchful and efficient Colonel Bunbury, they managed to capture the artillery batteries. At this moment of triumph another battery opened fire and Sir Robert Dick was hit by grape shot as he urged his division onwards. This untimely loss of a commander who had led his troops well to this point was unfortunate. Dick was taken from the field but his wound would prove fatal and the veteran of the Peninsular War and Waterloo would die that evening. Command of the division now devolved upon Brigadier Stacey. Given that he was right in the thick of the action alongside his men, this had both a positive and negative influence on the battle.

Having broken through the first trench and silenced many of the Sikh guns the men of the 3rd Division were now faced with the Sikh infantry. The majority were lined up in front of the advancing British, however the Sikhs had developed a tactic of digging what were in reality large pits in which detachments of their infantry could hide until the enemy had passed by. They would then rush out and the enemy would be faced with a simultaneous attack from the front and the rear. The problem for the Sikhs at Sobraon was that the British were now wise to this tactic. Colonel Bunbury in particular had suffered with his regiment from this tactic in the past and at Sobraon he made sure that no chances were taken. As a consequence the tactic failed and after the battle these large pits were discovered with large numbers of Sikh dead inside them. Nevertheless, the Sikhs made a determined attack upon the British troops and for a time did retake some of the ground lost in the initial British assault.[12]

It was at this point that Gough took a questionable decision. He became concerned that the attack by the 3rd Division was becoming bogged down. He was also concerned by the Sikh counter-attack, and fearing they may be driven back from positions that had been won with such courage, he decided upon action. Up until now his two other divisions had been largely inactive, used more as a threat than in actual attack. Gough had ordered that both divisions deploy their skirmishers, in the hope that this would help to direct some of the attack from Dick's attack. When this had little effect Gough determined to use both divisions in the attack. The aim was to support the 3rd Division already engaged with the enemy, as Gough feared that as a large part of the Sikh army was now being directed towards them they might be overwhelmed and forced to abandon their gains. If this had happened all the exertions of Dick's troops would have been for nothing.

Thus, Gough's decision to deploy the other two divisions in the attack was understandable. The problem was that they faced very strong Sikh defences. The ditches in front of the Sikh position were steeper than those faced by the 3rd Division and just as well defended. The banks of the trenches were not only steep but very sandy in nature. Anyone who has tried to walk up a sandy dune at a beach will know that this is not an easy task, and here it was made far harder by Sikh artillery and musketry. As the men tried to climb the sand fell away from beneath their feet. Although they had scaling ladders, these were found to be too short. Gilbert's division had been covered from Sikh artillery fire by their presence in a large *nullah*. During the advance the line got somewhat out of order and the 29th Foot found itself ahead of the rest of Gilbert's battalions. Taking refuge in another *nullah*, only 70 yards from the Sikh lines, the division reorganised before making the final advance. When they went forward again, Gilbert's division was met by a storm of enemy fire that tore into the ranks of the British troops. Being unable to climb the aforementioned ditch in front of the Sikh guns, they fell back to the *nullah*. The commander of the 3rd Brigade, Brigadier Taylor, had been killed in the initial assault. It took two further assaults before Gilbert's division broke through. They finally got out of the trench by standing on the shoulders of their comrades before clambering up and over. Once men were on top of the Sikh entrenchments they could help their comrades up. However the assault had caused a fearful loss amongst the division.

For some reason Smith's division had not advanced at the same time as Gilbert's. Smith later recorded that he had been covering Gilbert's advance. However this had not been Gough's intention when the orders had been given, as he wanted to get as many men engaged as quickly as possible in an attempt to relieve the pressure on the 3rd Division and secure the advances it had made.[13] When it finally attacked, Smith's division had an even harder time of it. On their first attack they only got to within 30 yards of the Sikh position before being forced to fall back. Like Gilbert's division, it would take two more attempts before Smith was able to break through. Even once Smith's men were through the Sikh artillery lines, they were not safe from the gunners as they had failed to properly spike the Sikh guns or deal with the gunners in the way that Colonel Bunbury had. Thus once the attackers had passed through the lines the Sikhs came back, remanned their guns, and fired into the rear of Smith's division.

The casualties sustained by Smith's and Gilbert's divisions were unfortunate, and it can be debated as to whether or not Gough made best use of the two divisions. They attacked at a difficult point in the Sikh defences and suffered casualties accordingly. However despite the cost their attack did have the desired effect and the pressure on the 3rd Division was reduced as Sikh units that had made their way to the Sikh right to combat Dick's attack found themselves drawn back to their original positions to deal with threat posed by Gilbert and Smith's divisions.

As the British infantry pressed forward they created the opportunity for the British cavalry to launch an attack. Once again the 3rd Light Dragoons were at the fore as they pursued the withdrawing Sikhs. Some horse artillery also managed to make its way through the Sikh lines and was able to support the cavalry in an almost textbook combination of horse and horse artillery which broke the majority of the Sikhs' will to resist. It is recorded that some of the better trained Sikh infantry regiments attempted to conduct an orderly withdraw, but that was easier said than done. The Sikhs were now retreating on mass back towards the only bridge within their reach across the river. Now the problematic nature of maintaining a position on the enemy's side of the river came into play. The recent rain had swelled the Sutlej to an extent that it was impossible to ford at any point within their reach. Thus they were dependent upon the boat bridge. The mass of Sikh soldiery attempting to cross a small boat bridge was an easy target for the British. All arms were engaged upon the fight with the retreating Sikhs. Many of the native infantry regiments did much to restore confidence in them during this engagement. Many units fought with added vigour due to events earlier in the battle. When the British had attacked and withdrawn earlier on they had left many wounded behind, who had promptly been slaughtered by the Sikhs, mainly their ferocious gunners. This insured that there would now be no quarter given to the Sikhs: not that the latter would have expected any.

As so many Sikh soldiers attempted to cross the floating bridge at the same time the inevitable happened and part of the bridge broke away. Some accounts, particularly from the Sikh perspective, claim that the bridge had deliberately been sabotaged. The culprit it is claimed was Tej Singh, the Sikh commander, who had been one of the first to leave the field of battle. This is perhaps a stretch too far in the belief in the duplicity of the Sikh commanders. It is far more likely that a less-than-stable boat bridge simply succumbed under the weight of soldiers, horses and guns all trying to cross at the same time. Many were drowned as it broke away, and a great many more drowned as they attempted to swim across. This added to the high casualties they had already sustained during the battle.

As usual Sikh casualty figures cannot be known for certain, but it has been estimated that their losses were around 10,000. In the aftermath of the battle Gough would later revise this figure to between 13,000 and 14,000. This was based on the report of an unnamed officer but one that Gough called an 'undoubted authority'.[14] Either figure represented one of the most crushing defeats

---

13   Smith, *Sir Harry Smith*, pp. 192–193.
14   Unknown, *The War In India, Despatches*, p. 129. Sidhu, *The First Anglo-Sikh War*, p. 166. Sidhu usually errs on the side of caution when considering casualty figures, but even he estimates the Sikh losses were around 10,000.

in terms of enemy killed in the history of the British experience in India. Before the battle both Hardinge and Gough had issued instructions not to spare the Sikhs and the final stage of the battle descended into a massacre. Gough felt uncomfortable about this and later recorded that, "Policy prevented my publicly recording my sentiments of the splendid gallantry of the fallen foe – I could have wept to have witnessed the fearful slaughter of so devoted a body." This is yet another glimpse of the compassionate nature of the man, but also someone who truly understood and appreciated the suffering of war.[15]

At the same time Gough appreciated why the Sikhs were shown no mercy by British soldiers and why the slaughter was so great. Gough wrote that:

> Their awful slaughter, confusion, and dismay were such as would have excited compassion in the hearts of their generous conquerors, if the Khalsa troops had not, in the earlier part of the action, sullied their gallantry by slaughtering and barbarously mangling every wounded soldier whom, in the vicissitudes of attack, the fortune of war left at their mercy.[16]

However after the battle Gough showed the Sikhs the respect they had earned through their sacrifice. In an act of generosity which only the victor can normally demonstrate, he allowed the body of Sham Singh, the Sikh commander, to be retrieved.

> The body of Sham Singh was sought for in the captured camp by his followers; and respecting the gallantry with which he is reported to have devoted himself to death rather than accompany the army in its flight, I forbade his people being molested in their search, which was finally successful.[17]

This again demonstrates not only the respect Gough had for the Sikhs' part in the action but also for the personal courage shown by Sham Singh. This was the sort of conduct that Gough personally demonstrated and thus could admire in others.

Alongside the human casualties the Sikhs lost 67 guns and a large quantity of powder and ammunition. The fact that the battle descended into a rout did little for the morale of the Sikhs, nor did the early departure from the field of many of their leaders. Despite that, the soldiery had not surrendered without a severe fight, and it is remarkable when reading the account to hear how many of the Sikh regular units remained in formation until the bitter end. If ever an affirmation of the courage and discipline of the Sikhs was needed it was shown at this time.

The British casualties stood at 2,383, of which 320 were killed and 2,063 were recorded as either wounded or missing. Dick's division accounted for 85 of the killed, Gilbert's for 120, and Smith's for exactly 100. The artillery accounted for a further seven killed and the cavalry six. The remaining two killed were both on the staff. It is somewhat surprising, given the fact that they made the initial assault and had to contend with the large part of the Sikh army for a period of the battle, that the 3rd Division lost less than the other two. Yet given that both Gilbert's and Smith's divisions had to withdraw during their attacks, not once but twice, it is perhaps understandable. These high losses also point to the poor coordination between Smith and Gilbert. Had they attacked together, as

---

15   Rait, *Gough*, Vol. II, pp. 62–64. Peel, Sir Robert, *Speeches of Sir Robert Peel, delivered in the House of Commons*, Vol. IV, (London: George Routledge & Co, 1853) p. 159. The quote from Gough is actually taken from a speech in the House of Commons by Sir Robert Peel, the Prime Minister, from a letter written to him by Gough.

16   Unknown, *The War in India, Despatches*, pp. 119–120. This is taken from Gough's despatch of the battle of Sobraon dated 13 February 1846.

17   Unknown, *The War in India, Despatches*, pp. 129–130.

Gough's orders had intended, they might have overwhelmed the Sikh positions. Yet the problem remained that they attacked strong defences that could not be easily climbed, and for which they were not properly equipped. It says much of the courage and leadership of the officers and men who personally led the attack that they were able to overcome such fearsome obstacle and such a determined enemy.

Once again the Europeans formed the majority of the casualties. However, unlike previous battles, the discrepancy between Europeans and native losses was not as large. Of the 320 killed, 177 were Europeans and of the 2,063 wounded, 914 were Europeans. In a sense the larger number of native casualties was to be expected from the nature of the battle. The tactical idea was that the Europeans would create the breakthrough which could then be exploited by the support of the native infantry. In the battles up this point the severe losses suffered by the European regiments had weakened the morale of the native troops and having witnessed such losses they were understandably reticent about becoming engaged themselves. It was here at Sobraon, with European troops creating a breakthrough, that the native troops showed their courage and ability. Somehow, morale and discipline, that had seemed lacking in the native army, had been restored. Gough praised the native army in the aftermath of the battle with the following words found in a letter to Sir Robert Peel.

> Here let me observe one feature so highly honourable and creditable to the native army, that notwithstanding the numerous temptations held out to them by men of their own colour and religion –namely, greatly increased pay (from seven to twelve rupees a month), and immediate promotion, I had but three desertion from this large force, during the time we lay opposite to the Sikh army. [...] These are features which I well know you will highly appreciate, and which makes me justly proud of this noble army.[18]

Undoubtedly Gough could have coordinated the attack better, but to say so is perhaps a harsh criticism. The fact that it was not as well coordinated as would have been desirable was partly due to the need to relieve the pressure on the 3rd Division by committing Gilbert and Smith to the battle earlier than was planned. It was here that the ability of Gough and his staff to either anticipate the need for such a deployment, or better coordinate this event, can be criticised. However, to criticise him for using a frontal assault is somewhat unfair as he had little alternative. Indeed, he had attempted to attack the theoretically weakest point of the Sikh line and had his cavalry waiting to exploit any advantage that was made. The infantry attacking this sector had been especially reinforced with extra European troops, and was ably supported by horse artillery in their movement against the enemy position. Although relying on a frontal attack, Gough had a sound plan to commence the battle. The problem was that he was unable to influence events once the battle had commenced. It would be incorrect to characterise Gough's plan of attack as simply a frontal charge at strong enemy positions. He was attempting to exploit their weakest position and he was in effect attempting to turn the enemy position by this attack. On his left, the Sikh right, where Dick attacked, he was also coordinating infantry, cavalry and horse artillery into this strategy.

Given the nature of the task, the losses were neither unexpected nor excessive. However there has been some suggestion that the scale of the losses was due to Gough's error in allowing the Sikhs to build a camp south of the river. We have already seen part of the motivation for him not preventing the Sikhs from doing this. This would have required Gough to create his own entrenchment, which would have been in range of Sikh guns and would have taken a great deal of resources and manpower to maintain. In short had he done this it is unlikely that he would have been able to

18   Peel, *Speeches of Sir Robert Peel*, p. 159.

support Smith's operations around Aliwal to the extent that he did. Indeed he might have been so stretched as to be unable to spare Smith and his division at all.

There is another tactical reason for Gough allowing the Sikhs to form an entrenchment on the south side of the river. The argument goes that, wherever the British attacked the Sikhs, as they tried to cross the Sutlej they would come up against an entrenched position. It appears that Gough considered it favourable that this should happen on the south side of the river. The reason was simply, if he had to attack an entrenched position it was better that the enemy should be so placed as have the river behind. This way if the Sikhs were defeated the battle would quickly turn into a rout as such a large number of men tried to make their way over a narrow crossing. The Sikhs therefore made a tactical error by entrenching in a position with the river to their back. This was the key mistake they made at Aliwal and at Sobraon. Indeed, in his correspondence of the time Gough mentions his concern that the Sikhs, "would recross and place the Sutlej between us."[19] So what on the one hand could be interpreted as a poor command decision, letting the Sikhs entrench on the south side of the river, could on the other hand be interpreted as a shrewd move on the part of Gough that would ensure that, if the entrenchments were taken, there would be a crushing defeat inflicted upon the Sikhs.

Gough attempted to reduce British casualties by the use of his artillery. However this failed. The reason for this failure lies with Gough only in the sense that he should perhaps have waited a little longer before starting the attack, thus allowing more guns and ammunition to reach his position. However, Gough was anxious to take advantage of the victory at Aliwal and so was dammed either way. If he rushed in he would be accused of recklessness, but if he waited he would be accused of wasting Smith's victory and surrendering the initiative. Whether Gough could have made a better use of his resources is difficult to say. The simple fact remains that, costly as it was, he had won the battle, routed the Sikhs, driven them back towards Lahore, and dealt a major blow to their ability to continue the war.

---

19   Rait, *Gough*, Vol. II, p. 63.

Part 7

Second Anglo-Sikh War

56

An Interlude of Peace

In the aftermath of the Battle of Sobraon, the Sikh Empire sued for peace. It is interesting to note that it was only after Sobraon that the war came to Sikh territory for the first time. There was certainly a very real fear on the British side that the Sikhs would continue the war, and whilst their defeat seemed almost certain after the action at Sobraon it was likely that any continuance of the war would prove costly to the British. Thus it was with relief that both Hardinge and Gough received news of the Sikh offer of peace. The former was particularly pleased and it will be recalled that he had done much to try and avert war.

The campaign had been hard fought. Whilst, as we have seen, Gough had been severely criticised for the conduct of the war and specifically the high number of casualties, there had been much that could be said in mitigation. However once the war had been successfully concluded much of the bitterness towards Gough was forgotten. If anything, Gough held on to such feelings for longer than anyone else. The rewards that came his way for the work he had done helped to assuage such feelings, but there was a sense in which Gough continued to feel that he had been treated badly. Perhaps in some ways he had, but the concerns expressed by those in political authority both in India and at home were understandable if slightly ill-informed.

However with the war's end honours and recognition came quickly. Both Gough and Hardinge were raised to the peerage for their efforts. Gough became Baron Gough of Chinkiangfoo in China and of Maharajpore and the Sutlej in the East Indies. Gough had been anxious that the recognition of Maharajpore be included in the title, even going so far as to say "I would have much preferred declining the peerage, than that Maharajpore had been left out."[1] Perhaps this suggest that Gough felt that Maharajpore in and on itself could have earned him the reward of a peerage. The Court of Directors of the East India Company, who for the most part had not shared the general panic over Gough's performance during the conflict, conferred upon him the reward of a pension of £2,000 a year for life. This in turn produced a similar pension of £2,000 a year from the British Government, and one of £3,000 a year for Hardinge. The award of the pensions for Hardinge and Gough created much debate within the House of Commons. There was a degree of opposition to the awards, but it is widely considered that this was a political manoeuvre to embarrass the somewhat embattled Prime Minister Sir Robert Peel rather than any direct opposition to Hardinge or Gough.

Having been somewhat aggrieved at the comments in Parliament, or lack thereof, by the Duke of Wellington, Gough was delighted that on two separate occasions he now received a glowing tribute from the Prime Minister Sir Robert Peel. After congratulating Hardinge, in a speech in the House of Commons, Peel turned to Gough:

> The career of that other gallant officer whom Her Majesty has elevated to the British peerage has not been less distinguished. For fifty-two years has Lord Gough served in the British

---

1   Rait, *Gough*, Vol. II, p. 112.

army; and no one would have supposed from the vigour, the energy, and the heroism of his conduct, that fifty two years of active service could have passed over his head … I will not speak merely of his valour and his skill: these are admitted by all who are acquainted with the history of our Peninsular and Indian wars. But, I must take this opportunity of placing upon record an instance of his devotion to the service of his country, which he, probably, little thought would ever be mentioned within the walls of Parliament, but which I conceive to be at least as honourable to him as any services he has rendered in the field.[2]

The incident Peel would go on to talk of was with regard to the command in Madras after the China War, which Gough had willingly been prepared to give up. Peel again quoted directly from a letter from Gough stating that he would do what was in the best interest of the Crown. This probably helps explain further why, when it was attempted to appoint Hardinge to overall command during the First Sikh War, that they appealed to Gough that this was in the best interest of the state and the Crown. The public tribute from Peel was greatly appreciated by Gough. Whether Peel was playing politics, or this was a genuine tribute is unclear. It may be that Peel felt the need to praise Gough in case the details of the government's attempt to replace him with Hardinge became public. Either way, to Gough it appeared a welcome change of tone and he appears to have accepted it at face value.

Whether the rewards that came to Gough were intended as a salve to his wounded pride at the attempt to replace him, or recognition that the authorities at home had been hasty in their attempts in this direction is debatable. It is likely that none of the principle characters involved regretted their actions, whether it be Hardinge, Ripon, Wellington or Peel. All no doubt felt they had acted appropriately, and indeed prudently, in considering the new arrangement by which Hardinge would take overall military command. The concerns expressed were understandable, yet showed a lack of understanding not only of the general situation but the specifics of the task facing Gough. The task he faced was far from an easy one. At Mudki Gough had been in a difficult position and the tactical maxim of the era that one should attack native troops in India rather than sit on the defensive was followed. Perhaps this was unwise and most certainly the battle could have been better organised, but it is hard to think that any other British commander of the age would have done any differently. At Ferozeshah, political interference, indecision, and perhaps a little petulance on Gough's part meant that the battle was not successfully concluded until night fell. On the following day the British were certainly fortunate, but fortune has always been an important part of victory. The military maxim attributed to Napoleon when informed of an officers ability is recorded as, "Yes, but is he lucky." On that day at Ferozeshah Gough was most certainly lucky. His role in facilitating the victory at Aliwal has not been appreciated until now and the risk that he took in reinforcing Smith and dividing his force not fully understood. At Sobraon he organised a good plan of attack which almost worked. The casualties looked bad because he had to commit his two reserve divisions earlier than he had wished because of determined Sikh resistance on his left.

Regardless of the casualties, and it was in reality the high number of European casualties rather than total casualties that caused grave concern at home, Gough had successfully concluded the war in under three months. Indeed the serious fighting had lasted just under two months, with the whole course of the war running for just under three months, from 12 December 1845 to the concluding of the Treaty of Lahore on 9 March 1846.[3] Given the difficulty of the task, the quality

---

2   *Hansard*, House of Commons Debate, 4 May 1846, Vol. 86, cc9–35.
3   The 12 December, the day the Sikhs crossed the Sutlej is used as the start of the war. Sometimes the 13 December is taken as the official date as this is when the British responded to the Sikh 'invasion' with a declaration of war.

of the opposition, the lack of preparations beforehand, and the distances involved this was a very great triumph. To those who did not understand the situation the Sikhs appeared as just another native army. Yet this was like no other Indian army Britain had ever faced before. Even at the height of the clashes with the Mahratta Empire, the two armies had never been so evenly matched. The Sikhs were trained, drilled, organised and even armed in a manner that was equal and in some cases superior to that of the native troops under British command. Thus to have concluded the war in under three months and with only four major battles was a great achievement and should certainly have been a triumph for Gough rather than the somewhat pyrrhic victory it was portrayed as.

The role played by the senior Sikh military commanders in Gough's victory is difficult to ascertain. At best their prosecution of the war was half-hearted. At worst it was treacherous and intended to bring about the downfall not of the Sikh state but the uncontrollable Khalsa. There had certainly been correspondence with the British during the conflict, although it appears unlikely that Gough knew about much, if any, of the correspondence. To truly get at the heart of the motivation and conduct of the Sikh leadership is beyond the scope of this work, and also beyond the capabilities of the present author. With the passage of time it might now be impossible to ascertain what occurred during those months, but any attempt to do so would need to be undertaken from the Sikh perspective and largely through Sikh records and accounts.

Although there were certainly question marks over Gough's abilities, much of the problem came from the presence in the field of so distinguished a figure, and so well connected a man, as Hardinge. Hardinge was an insider, a man on first name terms with all the leading figures both military and civilian within the British Empire. Gough on the other hand was something of an outsider, not one of the smart set and certainly not well connected. Although to call him a humble Irish soldier might be a slight exaggeration, it was not too far from the way in which he was perceived by many in power. In fact, Hardinge was also from a relatively humble background being the son of a clergyman, the difference being that amongst his close personal friends were the Duke of Wellington and Sir Robert Peel. Hardinge had not only delayed Gough's preparations for war, albeit with honourable intentions, he had also forced him to adopt a plan at Ferozeshah that was not his own. He also prevented Gough from fighting the war the way he wished. Whilst this might have been wise, it was not conducive to the running of a smooth campaign. The difficulty this placed Gough under should not be forgotten.

Whilst Gough had his limits as a commander, in terms of his organisational and tactical ability, he was not incompetent, careless, or callous. He also had mixed luck during the campaign. He was undoubtedly lucky in that the Sikh higher command was half-hearted at best and at worst duplicitous. He was lucky that at Ferozeshah a blunder by a staff officer possibly saved his army. He was lucky that communication with London was not quicker as he would surely have been superseded by Hardinge. However he was unlucky that Hardinge, his military inferior but his political superior, chose to be present with the army. He was unlucky in that Hardinge made an offer to serve under him as second in command; an offer that, no matter how much he might have wanted to, he felt unable to refuse. He was unlucky that at a time when British politicians and the public had, in the words of the Duke of Wellington, forgotten that Indians could fight he had to face probably the greatest of the martial races of the subcontinent and a force that was European in all but ethnic heritage.

The Treaty of Lahore was not nearly as harsh as many might have expected. It has sometimes been suggested that Hardinge feared a renewed hostility and that the Sikhs would fall back on Lahore. The latter, if defended by the 20,000 Sikh soldiers in the area, could prove very difficult to take, particularly given the relative strengths of artillery. Yet in a private letter of the time written to his wife Hardinge stated clearly that, "We have given these Sikhs a great beating."[4] That does

---

4   Singh, *The Letters of Viscount Hardinge*, pp. 152–153.

not mean, in and of itself, that Hardinge did not fear the continuation of hostilities, but is does suggest that he was not overly anxious about the state of affairs. What the situation did prevent was annexation of the Sikh state, which would surely have been resisted strongly. However there was little appetite for this either from Hardinge or the authorities at home.

In late February Hardinge negotiated with the representatives of the Sikhs, and also met the eight-year-old Maharaja. The Sikhs lost territory and renounced claims to all territory south of the Sutlej. Although the treaty stated that "The British Government will not exercise any interference in the internal administration of the Lahore State", a British resident, Henry Lawrence, would henceforth be on hand to advise and assist both the regency council and the Maharaja. The Sikh Army was to be reduced and reorganised, and the heavy guns of the army were to be surrendered. In a further limit on the Khalsa, no European or American advisers were allowed to be employed. An indemnity by way of reparation for the cost of the war was to be paid to the British amounting to around £1,500,000.

It was hoped that the treaty would allow the two states to live in harmony and alliance. However, even whilst the ink was drying on the treaty many on both sides were either preparing for, or at least anticipating, a second conflict. The Treaty had brought the conflict to a temporary conclusion but had not resolved the issues that had led to war. The Sikhs still remained nominally independent. The Sikhs would seek to assert and increase this whilst the British wanted to control the state through influence rather than annexation. British troops stayed in Lahore until the end of the year whilst the terms were put into effect. Matters were sometimes tense but after a while settled down. In other parts of the former Sikh Empire there were sporadic outbreaks of violence but nothing that gave a sense of an impending revolt against British influence or of a renewal of conflict with the Sikh state.

With the pending departure of British troops, there were many within the Sikh regency council who feared the reemergence of the Khalsa as the dominant force. There was a unanimous request from the Sikh ruling council requesting the establishment of a British protectorate until the Maharaja came of age. This resulted in the Treaty of Bhyrowal signed in September 1846 which announced that the regency council would continue to rule but with some new members and most importantly under the control and guidance of the British resident. This now extended British influence allowing for the free movement and stationing of British troops in any part of the Sikh state, for which the Sikhs would contribute to the upkeep. There were now three British brigades permanently stationed within the Sikh state at Lahore, Jullundur and Ferozepore. Whilst in the short term this secured the continuance of a friendly regime it was storing up trouble and resentment for later on.

Despite concerns expressed during the war, and the rather tense relationship that seemed to develop, there was no further attempt after the First Sikh War to alter the leadership arrangements of the Army. Gough remained commander-in-chief, with Hardinge continuing as governor general. Whilst their relations remained friendly for the most part, there were the inevitable clashes between civil and military concerns that once again brought the two men towards confrontation. With the example of events during the First Sikh War, such clashes can appear worse than they actually were. In others words it can seem as if previous experience had caused the confrontations, when such confrontations would have occurred regardless of who was Commander-in-Chief and who was governor general. In short, it was simply a clash between the civil and military powers regardless of personalities.

The first major clash after the war was regards to the size of the army. It will be recalled that before the war Hardinge had desired to reduce the size of the army as a way of reducing the expenditure of the government of India. However due to the Sikh threat Hardinge had been unable to do that. Now with the Sikhs defeated he returned to the idea. The opposition he faced from Gough was not simply the commander-in-chief defending his army and his power, but a much wider concern over the future use of the army. Hardinge believed that the Army would be required far less in the years that lay ahead. Gough felt differently, already anticipated a further conflict with the Sikhs, and urged against large-scale reductions in the size of the army.

Hardinge, again ignoring the advice of his commander-in-chief, proceeded to reduce the size of the army. Hardinge felt that the new arrangements had secured a lasting peace and that the positioning of British brigades in Sikh territory would be sufficient to deal with any trouble that did break out. More than this, he was concerned with the state of the exchequer in India which had been in a poor state before the war and had been exacerbated by it. He therefore reduced the native army by 50,000 troops. This was done not by disbanding regiments but by reducing the establishment of every unit, with infantry battalions reduced from 1,000 to 800 men and cavalry regiments from 500 to 420 men. At the same time as the reductions eight new regiments of cavalry were recruited, yet this still meant that there was an overall reduction of 50,000 men.

After initially counselling against such a reduction, Gough's subsequent protest was rather weak. Perhaps tired of dealing with Hardinge he simply wrote that "I deeply regret the financial difficulties, and the consequent reductions rendered indispensable thereby, particularly until time shall have tested the feelings which the late arrangements with the Lahore Government may produce."[5] It was a warning, an expression of concern, but not really a strong protest. In reality any protest from Gough would have had little effect. He did make representations for specific battalions to be kept at current strength, most notably the Sirmoor Regiment, in recognition of the important part they had played in the recent conflict. He also attempted to communicate not only his concerns to Hardinge but also what he believed to be the consequences of what the latter intended to do. His first concern was that Hardinge was actually undertaking a far greater reduction than he realised. The majority of native infantry regiments, particularly those near the border, were already over their established levels, often by as many as 100 men. Thus reduction to 800 men was more like the release of 300 men rather than 200. The release of so many trained men was a concern to Gough, mainly for fear of whose employ they might join. The reduction in numbers was also to see a reduction in the number of NCOs, and whilst this might seem a sensible measure Gough voiced his concerns stating that "the non-commissioned grades are the mainstay of the discipline of our Native army, affording the Sepoy a motive for loyalty and good conduct."[6]

Gough remained concerned about the possibility of a further action in the Sikh state. To this end he managed to persuade Hardinge to increase the number of men along the Punjab frontier to 50,000 with a force of 60 guns. Gough felt that whilst this would be insufficient to put down any major revolt by the Sikhs it would at least be sufficient to contain it until reinforcements could arrive. This was perhaps a little ambitious, but under the circumstances of the demand for reductions of the army in the name of economy he had done well to achieve even that. What was to prove a major problem, and something that Gough was unable to prevent, was the loss of the transport organisation that had been built up during the war. Gough had hoped that a permanent arrangement could be maintained. However, in the face of demands for economy and Hardinge's believe that a major military action would not be necessary again, he was unable to prevent this being broken up. Thus when war broke out for a second time such an organisation had to be built up again with inevitable delays that this produced. Given that Hardinge had complained during the war about Gough's inability to understand that supplies had to be transported a great distance to reinforce him, it is rather strange that it was now Gough who was urging a permanent transport system to facilitate this and Hardinge who opposed it.[7]

5   Rait, *Gough*, Vol. II, p. 117.
6   Rait, *Gough*, Vol. II, p. 118.
7   Rait, *Gough*, Vol. II, pp. 118–119.

With regards to artillery Gough did have some success. Due to his representations, the number of guns was not reduced, however the number of horses was reduced from 130 to 90 per battery. Gough managed to ensure that this was confined to the light batteries. He also ensured that the amount of ammunition carried by the batteries was increased, no doubt influenced by his experiences during the recent conflict. However there was no attempt to increase the calibre of guns or provide a heavy siege train for deployment. To an extent the circumstances in the Sikh state, where many of the heaviest guns had been handed over to the British or destroyed, negated the requirement. Perhaps given his experience Gough would have been wise to attempt something along these lines, yet given the urge for economy and the great cost involved in such an arrangement he would have been unlikely to succeed.[8] His actions in increasing the amount of ammunition each gun had available was sensible and showed that he had learnt at least one lesson from the First Sikh War. It perhaps also points out that Gough had been as frustrated as anyone that the guns ran out of ammunition so quickly.

Gough had attempted to make the most of the situation. Aware that the need for economy was inevitable he tried to negate the worst of it and even to gain some improvements. Yet he failed in his attempt to get serious amounts of stores placed on the frontier for the possibility of a second round of hostilities. His attitude to the measures in the name of economy is best summed up by Sir Robert Rait: "The whole responsibility for the reduction of the army in 1847 lies with the Governor-General; Lord Gough accepted it only as a necessity which he deplored."[9]

Hardinge left India in late 1847. To his credit he had done much to improve the administrative position of the government in India. He had also started to do something about the massive hole that existed in the finances of India. His actions in the build up to the Sikh War had been honourable if somewhat unfortunate. Yet, however honourable and well intentioned his actions during the conflict had been, they were unfortunate in their consequences. As one historian put it, "A Governor-General's place is not with the army in the field and he should have left his Commander-in-Chief to carry on, or replaced him if he had no confidence in him."[10] Hardinge had instead created a situation whereby Gough was nominally independent but where Hardinge could interfere and second-guess him. It was not a good situation and certainly not conducive to effective command. Hardinge did prove useful during the conflict and indeed, had he truly been prepared to serve under Gough, could have been very useful to him in the capacity of Chief of Staff. This was a position the Army desperately needed throughout the conflict, although Major Patrick Grant as assistant adjutant general did the best he could. It is hard to be critical of Grant. He was not a great staff officer but considering he was trying to act as adjutant general, assistant adjutant general, and chief of staff, he did the best he could in a difficult situation. The fact that no permanent replacement was found for the invalid Adjutant General, and that Grant had to carry on in both roles, points to the general malaise over staff work that permeated throughout the British army for so long.

The departure of Hardinge brought James Andrew Broun-Ramsay, 10th Earl of Dalhousie, out to India as the new governor general in January 1848. Dalhousie, at only 36 years of age, was the youngest ever governor general or viceroy of India. Although not a soldier himself his father had served with distinction under Wellington. The latter was also something of a protector and mentor to young Dalhousie. Given his recent experiences with Wellington, Gough could have been forgiven for feeling anxious about the new appointment. It is interesting to note that despite

---

8   Gough would have had influence over Presidency artillery, but Royal Artillery would have been the responsibility of the Ordnance Board in London.
9   Rait, *Gough*, Vol. II, p. 119.
10   Cook, *The Sikh Wars*, p. 101.

his differences with Hardinge, and indeed discussions that had bordered on violent arguments, he remained an admirer of Hardinge. Indeed a friendship was maintained which despite what had occurred between them remained until Hardinge's death. It is interesting to note that Gough was a pallbearer at Hardinge's funeral in 1856. Gough stood by the coffin throughout the service, despite being nearly 80 years of age.

One gets the impression that Dalhousie, on the other hand, was a man that Gough never really warmed to. It is difficult to point to much in their correspondence that directly supports this. Perhaps it is more the absence of such positive comments, as one finds about Hardinge, that lead to this conclusion. It is certainly clear that Dalhousie was an 'operator' and to paraphrase the old saying he was 'a young man in a hurry'. He had been President of the Board of Trade under Sir Robert Peel. When Peel's Government fell, his successor Lord Russell offered Dalhousie the governor generalship of India.

Perhaps relations between Gough and Dalhousie were not helped by the age difference. The 32 years that separated them also meant that they were in a very real sense of a different generation. Gough was of the Georgian era whilst Dalhousie can certainly be classed as an early Victorian. If Gough resented being told what to do by such a young man, indeed one who was only a couple of years older than his own son, he never made any mention of this. Whilst age no doubt played a part in their difficult relationship, there was certainly more to it than that. It was as a much a clash of styles. Dalhousie was certainly ambitious. Hardinge shared this characteristic but with Hardinge there was a sense of honour that one never feels with Dalhousie. Whilst Hardinge was a soldier playing politics, Dalhousie was an out-and-out political animal.

At the same time as the change of governor general, there was also a change of leadership within the Sikh state. Henry Lawrence, who had worked tirelessly as British agent and resident to the regency council, was forced to take sick leave and was replaced by Sir Frederick Currie. It was a poor time for a double change of leadership. Sikh discontent with British influence, and indeed with many of their own leaders, was on the rise. Several minor campaigns had been necessary during the period between the two wars. They were generally small and localised and were dealt with relatively easily, sometimes even without fighting. Yet it was a worrying trend. In consequence Gough increased the garrison at Lahore, most notably with an additional British regiment, the 53rd Foot, and also sent Major General William Whish to take command. The latter was highly thought of by Gough, who had confidence in him that many later felt was misplaced. Whish was in his 60s and whilst it might be felt that a younger man was more suited to the position there were few, if any, of sufficiently high rank to take on such a command. The slow movement of advancement in rank was a problem that plagued both the East India Company Army and the British Army.

Dalhousie's tenure began in comfortable enough manner. To begin with at least, he seems to have won over Gough. The former had assured Gough that as the son of a former commander-in-chief in India he had the best interests of the army at heart.[11] Dalhousie had barely been in his position for four months when an incident occurred that would start the Second Sikh War. Whereas at the outbreak of the first war Gough had been blocked in his preparations, at the commencement of the second, war came so suddenly that there was little time for preparation. Whilst Gough, like many others, had thought that a second war was inevitable there had been little sign of a major insurrection and at first glance the unfolding events appeared to be another minor skirmish that could be put down. At the same time preparations were hampered by having to start from scratch in many regards. The transport system, as previously mentioned, had been totally dismantled. Gough

---

11 NAM: 8303–105, Gough Papers, Dalhousie to Gough, 19 July 1848. His father, General George Ramsay, 9th Earl of Dalhousie, had served as Commander-in-Chief, India from January 1830 to January 1832.

had also been unable to obtain permission to increase storage and depot facilities near the border and lay in stores ready for such a necessity. The reductions in the name of economy clearly had an effect on Gough's ability to quickly respond to the coming conflict, one which would place an even greater strain on his abilities and powers that the first war. In many ways this was to be both the toughest test and some of the darkest days of Gough's long military career and a time that would push him to the brink.

57

Outbreak at Multan and the Start of the Second Sikh War

To many, the events of 1848 and the subsequent military engagements came as something of a surprise. To those with only a cursory knowledge of the Sikhs or the actions of the first conflict, it had appeared that the First Sikh War had resolved the situation for good. The Sikhs, whilst not being annexed to British India, would be controlled and guided as a good many other princely states already were. Yet this was an underestimation of the Sikhs as a people and the way in which the First Sikh War had been resolved.

The former territory of the Sikhs and the Sikh state itself had experienced momentary occurrences of violence since the ending of the First Sikh War. To a large degree these had been easily contained, being put down by small forces of British and native troops, never more than 5,000 strong. To the politicians such as Hardinge and Dalhousie this had been interpreted as a reaction to the new order rather than the precursor to a large-scale uprising that would precipitate another major conflict.

Gough seems to have been more in tune with the reality of the situation and to have been convinced that another conflict would be likely. His main reason for believing this was simply because although the Khalsa had been broken and greatly reduced in numbers it had not been disbanded or taken under British control. While the Sikhs still had the means there was always the potential for another war. What would lead to war had initially seemed like just another outbreak of resistance to British influence, yet it soon developed into a major conflict.[1]

Henry Lawrence, whatever his failings might have been, had a good understanding of India, and particularly the north of the subcontinent. He was certainly an intriguer and perhaps was entrusted by Hardinge with greater responsibility than was appropriate. However, he had proved an effective tool of British control in the north and over the Sikh state. His departure due to ill health was unfortunately timed. It meant that there was simultaneously a new governor general and new political agent and resident at Lahore.[2] The choice of successor was also unfortunate. There had been a natural assumption that John Lawrence, experienced in the north, would be appointed to succeed his brother. Lord Dalhousie however had other ideas. Whether he wanted to move away from the Lawrence family dominance, or whether he simply wanted a more official presence is

---

1   An overview of Gough's correspondence shows that whilst Gough believed that a second conflict with the Sikhs was inevitable, he was slightly surprised at the timing, and, more to the point, the locality, of the outbreak of the second war. NAM 8303–105, Gough Papers, Gough to George Gough, 8 May 1848. The letter includes the line 'with much surprise' talking of events at Multan. This should not however be interpreted as an indication that Gough was surprised that a second conflict would be necessary, at merely the timing and location of the event that triggered it.

2   Allen, Charles, *Soldier Sahibs: The Men who made the North-West Frontier* (London: John Murray, 2000), pp. 73–76. Although the specific pages are mention the majority of the book deals with Lawrence. Allen gives a good account of Lawrence's many talents and skills, although perhaps overlooks some of his less creditable character traits and behaviour. A modern reassessment of Lawrence and his career is required.

unclear. Whatever the motivation, it was Sir Frederick Currie, and not John Lawrence, who was chosen to be the new resident at Lahore.[3]

Currie had been Hardinge's Political Secretary for many years and had accompanied him during the First Sikh War. Hardinge had thought very highly of Currie, appreciating his advice during the conflict, and Currie had played an important part in the drafting of the political settlement with the Sikhs. In that sense one can see the logic in his appointment. He was certainly not without experience or knowledge of the area, but he lacked the detailed local knowledge that the Lawrences had and was perhaps the wrong fit for the position. It would be difficult for him to break the Lawrence family dominance of the region. However he did not help himself by his attitude. He had insisted that the residency building in Lahore, which up to now had been shared by all the officers, was reserved only for him. He also refused to meet local petitioners, people bringing complaints and pleas, in the way that Lawrence had. He thus alienated himself both from his staff and the local populace so early on in his appointment.[4]

Local circumstances were also difficult for Currie, as he arrived in the middle of a developing situation with Dewan Mulraj the governor of the important town of Multan. Mulraj was not himself a Sikh but a Hindu whose father had served under Ranjit Singh and from whom Mulraj had inherited the governance of Multan. Under Ranjit Singh he had been given great autonomy in return for the payment of revenues from the land. He had for many years since the death of Ranjit Singh withheld such payments. Under British influence there was now an attempt to recommence the collection of such revenues for the court at Lahore. At first, Dewan Mulraj attempted to stall by asking to step down in favour of his son. As this was during the change of political leadership he was asked to remain in place until Currie arrived. Upon arrival in Lahore, Currie accepted his resignation but chose to replace him not with his son but with the Sikh, Sirdar Khan Singh. This was obviously not going to be a popular decision. Although writing a couple of months after the appointment and subsequent events, Gough told his son that he had feared for the consequences of the decision writing that, "This policy of such interference may be very questionable, as any attack upon our people must involve us; and such [an] attack becomes not only possible but probable, when the object is unpopular and those ordered to carry it out wholly unprotected."[5]

Gough's words were not entirely prophetic, as they were written after the events in question, but were an accurate description of what would happen. Khan Singh, accompanied by Patrick Vans Agnew as political agent and a small escort consisting of Lieutenant William Anderson and 500 Gurkha infantrymen in Sikh service, a troop of irregular cavalry, and some artillerymen set off for Multan.[6] Anderson had served under Charles Napier in the Scinde campaign. Napier considered him a very able officer. Anderson was also the brother in law of the future Lieutenant

3   Charles Allen in his book *Soldier Sahib* credits, or perhaps that should be discredits, Gough with Currie's appointment but gives no evidence to support this (the book is entirely without footnotes or endnotes). It is unlikely that Gough had any say or influence in this appointment. This was in effect a political appointment, and as we have seen from previous comments by Hardinge, Gough tended to steer clear of such matters. Allen also calls Currie 'an inexperienced office-wallah from Calcutta' completely ignoring that he had been Hardinge's political secretary for many years, had accompanied him throughout the First Sikh War, and had been largely responsible for the settlement at the end of the conflict. Hardinge said of Currie that he 'has been a long time in the country and is an able man', a somewhat different opinion to that of Charles Allen. See Singh, *The Letters of Viscount Hardinge*, pp. 144, 146, 150, all indicated the high level of respect Harding had for Currie's council, his ability, and his knowledge.
4   For more detail on Currie's early period as resident at Lahore see Allen, *Soldier Sahibs*, pp. 145–154.
5   NAM: 8303–105, Gough Papers, Gough to George Gough, 8 May 1848.
6   It will be recalled that it has been stated previously that such troops were not 'Gurkhas' in the traditional sense, and were often Kashmiris rather than Nepalese. The force was destined to garrison Multan and thus explained the fact that it was larger than a traditional escort.

General Sir James Outram. Whilst Khan Singh and the troops marched to Multan, Vans Agnew and Anderson preferred to sail in comfort along the many rivers of the area to the destination. The obvious problem was that when they arrived in Multan to take command they were completely unknown to the men of their 'escorting force' who they were now to command and who were the only protection for them and the new governor. Yet such was feeling of security that this very probably never crossed the mind of either Vans Agnew or Anderson.

It appears that the main source of concern amongst the locals was not so much Vans Agnew but the presence of Anderson in his military uniform. The clear association of this with the British meant that the arrival of such men appeared to the local population as the beginning of a British occupation. That said, Mulraj was obviously either a popular local figure or had successfully portrayed himself as the victim of British interference. There is a slightly unusual fact in that the attempt was to replace a Hindu with a Sikh that aroused the city in revolt. Yet clearly the fact that Khan Singh appeared with British officials led those to believe that he was little more than a stooge of the British.

Khan Singh, Vans Agnew, Anderson and their escort arrived on 18 April 1848. They were greeted cordially by Mulraj and it was agreed that the following morning the keys of the town and the fort would be formally handed over to Khan Singh in the presence of Vans Agnew. This took place. Exactly what happened next has always been subject to conjecture. Gough gave a detailed account in a letter to his son describing the situation.

> When they proceeded outside the Fort to mount their horses, Anderson appears to have preceded Agnew in company with Mulraj. The latter, Agnew, in mounting, was cut down by two of the garrison who had followed him, and, but for Khan Singh, who dismounted and stood over him, would have been killed. An elephant was obtained, on which he was removed; and, on their way to the Mosque, in which they had taken up their quarters, they found poor Anderson lying by the roadside with four severe sabre cuts, which had been given by men of the escort of Mulraj.[7]

Vans Agnew sent one letter to Lieutenant Edwardes another political officer at Derajat, and one to General Van Cortlandt commanding Sikh troops in the Bannu area. Given that Gough would ultimately receive one of the letters Vans Agnew wrote that evening warning of the danger, it is possible that Gough's account is accurate in its detail. The attack might have happened in a slightly different way, but it is sufficient to say that both Vans Agnew and Anderson suffered several sword wounds.

The three men and their detachment of infantry managed to reach their lodgings. Agnew despatched two letters warning of the uprising and requesting support. On the following day an angry mob of both locals and Mulraj's garrison broke into their lodgings and both Vans Agnew and Anderson were murdered. Their escort, rather than defending them, simply joined the rebels. Gough states that the bodies were mutilated and 'exposed on the walls of Multan'. Whilst mutilation is often reported, and indeed almost certainly took place, Gough is one of the few sources to claim the bodies were displayed on the walls.[8] Khan Singh was not killed but imprisoned in the fortress of which he was nominally governor.

---

7   NAM: 8303–105, Gough Papers, Gough to George Gough, 8 May 1848.
8   NAM: 8303–105, Gough Papers, Gough to George Gough, 8 May 1848.

Lieutenant Herbert Edwardes, a political agent in the Bannu district who had raised his own troop of Pathan horse around 300 strong, received one of Vans Agnew's letters on 22 April.[9] Gathering all the soldiers he could, about 330 men and two guns, he marched towards Multan. A message was also despatched to Henry Van Cortlandt, the son of a former British officer who was serving as a general in the Sikh Army. Edwardes advised him to move quickly with as many men as he could. Whilst some have seen Edwardes' desire to move promptly as an indication that he understood the seriousness of the rebellion and wanted to put it down before it could spread, it should be added that Edwardes acted as he did largely due to the fact that he saw it as a rescue mission. From what the letter told him, Vans Agnew and Anderson were still alive and their escort was still loyal. Edwardes therefore sought to come to their aid and relief. Edwardes was ably supported by his loyal Pathans, who had no time for the Sikhs and with whom Edwardes had built up a relationship of trust and respect. The Pathans or more correctly Pashtuns are a northern Indian people. They are the largest ethnic group in modern day Afghanistan and there are over 30 million Pashtuns living in Pakistan. Their dislike of the Sikhs made them great allies of the British at this stage. Edwardes' Pathans also provided him with excellent advice.[10]

Edwardes first task was to secure the boat bridge over the Indus. Once this was achieved, he secured the market town of Leia. It was on 24 April that Edwardes learnt of the murder of Vans Agnew and Anderson and the fact that their escort had joined the revolt. Edwardes' force was insufficient for the task of attempting to take Multan but he bravely, if perhaps inadvisably, decided to continue his advance towards Multan. He was now working with the theory that the revolt needed to be put down as quickly as possible. Under the belief that further British and allied forces were on the move he decided to act as something of an advanced guard for these forces. In a short action, his artillery and the prompt arrival of Van Cortlandt managed to force Mulraj's force back into Multan. However this was only a temporary setback. If Mulraj attempted to break out again there was every chance that Edwardes would be unable to stop him. As Edwardes himself characterised it he was "a scot terrier barking at a tiger."[11]

Edwardes had forwarded Vans Agnew's letter to Sir Frederick Currie. On receipt of the information, Currie had ordered Major General Whish to move to the rescue. At this stage speed was of the essence and Whish, at Lahore, took only what was ready to move at short notice. It was Currie who now informed Gough of the situation. Gough approved of Currie's decision to move Whish's force, and his only regret was that the whole force had not started to move. Yet on the news that Vans Agnew and Anderson had been murdered Currie stopped the movement of Whish. This decision, taken by Currie and not Gough as is sometimes intimated, was an understandable if regrettable choice. When the task was rescue, Whish's small force supported by Edwardes and other troops in the area was sufficient for the task. The prospect now was a siege and assault upon Multan. The latter was a strong well defended fortress that would require a sizeable force, and heavy artillery, to take. Thus Currie decided that it was best that proper preparations be made to allow a force large enough for the task to move. Currie was also concerned with the degree of restlessness in Lahore, which had been increased by events at Multan, and he was understandably reluctant to reduce the garrison at such a time. Currie in turn passed the matter over to Gough.[12]

Gough now found himself in a very difficult position. Immediate action to stop the spread of the revolt was the best course of action in the normal turn of events, yet in this situation it was not

---

9   Major General Sir Herbert Benjamin Edwardes (1819–1868) is a fascinating character whose varied and interesting career deserves, like so many who served in India during this period, a modern interpretation. Edwardes would later play an important role in the suppression of the 1857 Mutiny.

10   Cook, *The Sikh Wars*, pp. 115–118 & Bruce, *Six Battles for India*, pp. 207–213.

11   Allen, *Soldier Sahib*, p. 158.

12   Rait, *Gough*, Vol. II, p. 123, & Bruce, *Six Battles for India*, p. 205.

really practical. He could have despatched forces to the area quickly but they would be unable to undertake a proper siege of Multan. All they could do was bottle up the garrison. Yet the longer that native troops, many of them former soldiers of the Sikh state, were kept outside the fortress the greater the chance that they might go over to the enemy. Gough realised that a larger force was needed to operate in the Punjab. The problem was this would take time to organise. In the border area he had around 10,000 men who could be spared and around 48 guns of which few were of any great calibre. Gough estimated that for a major operation he would require 24,000 men and 50 heavy guns. He also declared that such a force needed to be created without including any soldiers at present in the Sikh state. This opinion was formed after correspondence with Major Robert Napier, chief engineer to Major General Whish, as regards the strength of Multan. Gough argued that the men at present in the Sikh state would be needed both to take Multan and to maintain order in the rest of the country. When this is considered, one can see that the total manpower requirements for operations during this period were actually far higher than the 24,000 force that Gough would directly command.[13]

To gather such a force together would take time, and the folly of Hardinge's decision to break up the transport arrangements was now shown as Gough had to start from scratch. Also the time of year was against him: mid summer, the worst possible time to attempt to move an army. A long march to the frontier and then pursuit of the enemy would create a situation whereby any British force entering the field of battle would already be reduced in numbers due to the difficulties of the movement. Thus Gough's reticence was understandable, but the longer before the revolt at Multan was put down, the greater the possibility of a more substantial uprising elsewhere. This was certainly Currie's concern and the reason why he was reluctant to denude Lahore of British troops.

Gough and Currie's difficulties were not sympathetically received by many. Herbert Edwardes launched into a tirade against the two men in a letter to William Hodson. Over the delay of several months Edwardes exclaimed:

> Postpone a rebellion! Was ever such a thing heard of in any government? Postpone avenging the blood of two British officers! Should such a thing be ever heard of in British Asia! I read in the papers of enormous military preparations. Editors puff the advancing columns. You tell me of a future 25,000 men, fifty siege guns, etc., etc., and all for what? Forsooth, to do nothing for five months! It is a burlesque upon politics, war, and government. Give me two of all these prophesied brigades, and Bahawal Khan and I will fight the campaign for you while you are perspiring behind tatties (sun screens) in Lahore and bottling up you British "indignation" at the slaughter of our countrymen. Action, action, action! Promptitude![14]

Edwardes reaction is understandable. As the man on the ground being shot at, and in imminent danger, he can be forgiven for not being able to appreciate the full picture. Currie and Gough had other concerns. Currie's initial reaction was the same as Edwardes, and it was Currie who despatched a relief force. Yet on learning of the death of Vans Agnew and Anderson, Currie appreciated that the nature of the mission had changed. He was advised that Multan was a strong fortress that could only be taken by a strong force and a lengthy siege. He was unwilling, and quite possibly unable, to undertake this with the forces at his disposal. Unlike Edwardes, concerned only with what lay before him, Currie had to consider wider issues. Currie had to consider the safety of the rest of the Punjab, particularly Lahore.

13   Rait, *Gough*, Vol. II, p. 126.
14   Allen, *Soldier Sahibs*, p. 153.

Gough, on the other hand, had to consider the safety of any force he despatched. Given his experiences in the first war one can appreciate his caution. Many problems had occurred during the First Sikh War because his troops arrived in dribs and drags rather than as a united force. The problems of transport and supplies were a grave concern. Largely due to political interference this had to be commenced from scratch. To Dalhousie Gough gave the following warning: "There is no carriage whatever for these troops, the whole having been discharged; and to move without camp equipage, Doolies, and ample Commissariat arrangements, through the hottest locality in India, at the worst season of the year would be certain annihilation."[15] Given his previous experiences, one can understand Gough's apprehension that if he had to enter war with the Sikhs again he wished to be better prepared and organised than before, and one can understand that he felt that to go without a strong force was to court danger.

Gough and Dalhousie were both unsure as to what exactly they were dealing with, and they both considered it likely that the revolt might die away from lack of support. This would leave Multan isolated and the fortress could then be besieged and taken. This was a somewhat naïve interpretation. Robert Needham Cust, deputy commissioner of Hoshiarpur, had despatched 'spies' after the outbreak at Multan to try and discover the reaction within his own district. He found that the majority of Sikhs, particularly those who had lost power authority and money since the change of control, felt that they had nothing to lose in supporting the outbreak if the opportunity arose.[16]

Dalhousie also had the political dimension to consider. Mulraj had technically rebelled against the Lahore government rather than the British. To intervene with military force was to give credence to those who believed that the British were controlling the Lahore Government and were really the rulers of the Sikh state. There was also the problem regarding the remainder of the Sikh Army who at this time showed no obvious sign of joining the revolt, but could possible join with Mulraj if the British were seen to be acting as an occupying power. Indeed the very nature of the revolt was something that was difficult to define. There has always been a question mark over how much involvement Dewan Mulraj had in the revolt. It has never been established that he was complicit in the attack and subsequent murder of Vans Agnew and Anderson. In the aftermath of the event he had little choice but to go along with those who had committed the act. This is perhaps to give him the benefit of the doubt without any evidence to either support his guilt or innocence. It is clear that afterwards he took full advantage of the revolt, but the nature of his endgame is difficult to establish.

Gough was also mindful of the fact that any action would certainly be his last command. His retirement as commander-in-chief was imminent. As Sir Robert Rait put it, Gough "was determined that, when that war broke out, there must be no question of insufficient resources. If, urgent and immediate action was now to be taken, it would probably provoke the final contest, and for that final contest the British forces were in no respect prepared."[17] Gough understood that any major British expedition into Sikh territory was likely to bring about further uprisings. Here we see the difficulty of his choice to wait until he was ready. To move in force was both prudent and necessary if, as he suspected, the presence of a large British army in Sikh territory was likely to arouse the feelings of resentment and hatred that lay just below the surface. To move quickly had the potential to contain the revolt to Multan. Yet there was no guarantee that, even if Mulraj and his followers were bottled up in Multan, there would not be further outbreaks elsewhere that would require further British troops.

15   NAM: 8303–105, Gough Papers, Gough to Dalhousie, 30 April 1848.
16   British Library: Add Ms 45392, 64: Diary of Robert Needham Cust, Vol. III.
17   Rait, *Gough*, Vol. II, p. 124.

If, as Gough feared, the presence of British troops led to further uprisings then it was better to have a substantial force ready for action. One can argue that in his belief that a field force of 25,000 men would be sufficient Gough was being somewhat overoptimistic. If the Sikh army revolted then, when supported by former soldiers of the Sikh Army, they were likely to be able to field a force larger than Gough's. Gough on the other hand had considerable manpower problems to cope with. Firstly there was the reduction in the army that Hardinge had undertaken. Secondly there was also the fact that the summer months were when most Europeans were apt to take leave. This was standard practice given the unlikelihood of having to fight a major operation during the summer months. From late May through to early October, high humidity, and then the monsoon season, made it very difficult to undertake military operations. It was also the time when many of the native troops were allowed to take leave and it has been estimated that as much as 25 percent of the native army could have been on leave at the time of the events in Multan. Even if this figure is not entirely accurate, it gives us an indication that raising the 25,000 men felt necessary for the operations was not going to be easily or speedily accomplished.[18]

That Gough preferred caution is understandable given the criticism he had for his actions in the First Sikh War that were often portrayed as reckless. Indeed Rait, without giving evidence to support his claim, writes that Gough, "was prepared for the attacks of the Indian Press; it would be a pleasant change, he thought, to be abused for inaction, instead of for overaction."[19] It is easy to understand why Edwardes felt the way he did but far harder to appreciate the pressure that Gough was actually under and even harder to understand the additional pressure that he thought he was under due to the perception of his performance in the First Sikh War. Gough also questioned the purpose of any major conflict, writing to his old friend from the First China War Lieutenant Colonel Mountain, "Are we to undertake movements of this magnitude, merely to support a Child [the underage Maharajah Dulleep Singh] without an Army, or means to maintain that which we at such considerable outlay will have to achieve?"[20] Indeed one can understand the confusion. After all this was a non-Sikh, Dewan Mulraj, rebelling against the Sikh authority at Lahore. This on the face of it did not constitute a Sikh uprising. Thus Gough's questioning of the purpose of any such campaign was apposite.

Dalhousie clearly hoped that the revolt might be put down without British support. Indeed he seems to have been of the opinion that as the revolt was technically against the Sikh government at Lahore it was they who should attempt to supress it. This was indeed correct in theory, but ignored many of the problems and conspiracies that were occurring with the Sikh court. There have also been suggestions, largely made from the Sikh side, that the British intentionally allowed the revolt to spread. The theory runs that, believing that a second conflict with the Sikhs was inevitable, the British wanted to provoke a general uprising. This would also provide the justification of greater British control, perhaps even annexation, and allow the abolition of the divisive and duplicitous regency council which was becoming increasingly difficult. This is perhaps where Dalhousie's lack of experience on the ground in India was a telling factor. It is also further evidence that there was little in the way of support for the Governor General in terms of counsel. Hardinge had claimed that only Currie gave him any useful advice and Dalhousie did not even have that luxury at close hand. Gough's questioning of the purpose of any movement at this stage, and the difficulty of accomplishing it for several months, probably took on greater significance than it would had a more experienced governor general been in office. We have already seen that Hardinge had no hesitation in overruling and overriding Gough's decisions and advice. That is not to say that Dalhousie had

18   Bruce, *The Sikh Wars*, p. 117.
19   Rait, *Gough*, Vol. II, p. 125.
20   Rait, *Gough*, Vol. II, p. 125.

any compunction about overruling his commander-in-chief, but that he did not have the experience to feel capable of doing it at this time.

There was also a slight problem in terms of the relationship between Dalhousie and Gough. Exactly when they met for the first time is unclear, but as late as the end of June 1848 Dalhousie was writing of his regret of not "having the honour of making your acquaintance in person."[21] This cannot have aided their relationship. Although they had been in communication a great deal the written word is not the same as the spoken word. Dalhousie would certainly have based much of what he knew of Gough on reports in the press at home, many of which were unfavourable. The fact that the first face-to-face meeting was so delayed did not help the relationship between the two. Dalhousie's comments on the army, whilst no doubt intended to be helpful, might also have concerned Gough as to exactly how the new governor general would act. Dalhousie wrote to Gough in late June 1848:

> As the son of a soldier, and coming of a soldier's family, I need hardly tell you how true and deep an interest I feel in all that concern a British army and you will readily believe that my interest in the army in India is quickened by the recollection that my father was once honoured with the command of it.[22]

Whilst part of the statement was clearly intended to show that Dalhousie had the best interests of the army at heart, it does say far more than that. It points to the possibility of his interfering with the army. It is also clearly a statement that the Governor General wanted to make it clear that he understood military matters, and the referencing of his father's time as commander-in-chief was clearly there to demonstrate that by association he understood the pressures, problems and difficulties of the position. Given the somewhat ambiguous nature of this letter, it is unfortunate that the two men had not met and developed a personal relationship before the trials of the revolt at Multan came upon them. Once again we see that the timing of the revolt was unfortunate due to a new governor general and to the fact that the man who had previously been the most capable advisor was now not directly at hand. Currie could of course give his advice, but the problems of communication meant that this could not have been as quick or immediate as it had been to his predecessor. Currie was also somewhat detached from information and was not so well acquainted with the problems of gathering a sufficient force that Gough faced.

The Sikh government at Lahore did initially attempt to put down the revolt and despatched three different columns of Sikh troops which converged on Multan from three different directions. Yet the real motives of many of the Sikh leaders were still open to question. In May, for example, Kahan Singh, a Sikh general, was tried and subsequently hanged for supposedly attempting to induce British sepoys to defect and as part of a general conspiracy against the Sikh council. In the aftermath of this, the suggestion was made that Kahan Singh's actions had been part of a wider plot in which the Maharani Jind Kaur (Rani Jindan), the mother of the underage Maharajah, had been implicated. Currie decided that the Maharani had to be removed from the Punjab and she was exiled, and she eventually settled in Kathmandu. Although this removed a possible rallying point against British influence, it also had the effect of creating a martyr. Currie had faced a difficult decision. Had he allowed her to remain it is unlikely that she would have ceased her plotting. The fact that she was removed helps to further combat the suggestion that the British were actually looking for a wider revolt, for if they had been then she would surely have been allowed to remain.

21   NAM: 8303–105, Gough Papers, Dalhousie to Gough, 19 June 1848. The date might be incorrect as the writing is very hard to read on this letter.
22   NAM: 8303–105, Gough Papers, Dalhousie to Gough, 19 June 1848.

The problem was that removing her was seen as yet further evidence of British interference and a further example to the Sikhs of where the power really lay. It also elicited much sympathy for the Maharani, both as a patriot but also as a mother separated from her son.[23]

For a time the revolt at Multan seemed to be the only major outbreak. There were however minor uprisings and the British forces in the Punjab were very much on guard. It was in early June that Edwardes, now with discretionary powers to act as he thought best against Multan, crossed the Indus.[24] Edwardes now commanded around 5,000 irregular Pathans and was supported by 1,500 regular Sikh soldiers under the command of Van Cortlandt and around 30 light swivel type guns, with heavier artillery still making its way to the battlefield. By careful planning beforehand and swift movement, Edwardes managed to cross the river uncontested. On the other side he faced a force from Multan about 9,000. Edwardes fought the almost forgotten Battle of Kineyri (Kineyree) on 18 June. The battle lasted over six hours and the decisive factor was the arrival during the battle of Van Cortlandt's 6 pdrs. They redressed the balance in artillery and proved the key to victory. The rebels from Multan lost over 500 dead and eight of the 10 guns they had brought to the field. Figures as high as 1,000 can be found for the estimate of total Sikh casualties, so the figure of 500 dead seems a reasonably accurate one. Edwardes had lost 58 dead and 89 wounded, mostly to artillery fire. The fact that a lieutenant commanding a force largely made up of irregulars was able to deal with the rebels tells us much about the nature of the revolt at this time. Although Van Cortlandt was a general in the Sikh service, he was junior to Edwardes. Edwardes of course held political authority.

That they were so easily beaten back tells us much of the quality of the rebels. It also helps to make Edwardes point that the revolt could be put down without the large-scale preparations Gough envisaged. However, as we have already seen, Gough's concerns were far wider than simply the taking of Multan. The problem was the wider implications of any major movement of British troops. Edwardes followed the retreating enemy back to Multan but was in no position to contemplate an attack or siege of the fortress. In the days that followed he was reinforced by the official forces of the Sikh government. He now had around 18,000 men under his command, yet he was still unable to undertake a major siege due to the lack of heavy guns. As of yet he still had no European troops. On 2 July he fought another action four miles from Multan itself. Again the decisive factor was Edwardes' superiority in artillery. The morale of Edwardes' men was growing whilst that of the Multan force was declining to the extent that there were even defections to the British. Edwardes' success also did much to prevent the outbreak of further revolts, as the news quickly spread throughout the Punjab.

The problem was there were not the means to finish off the rebels at Multan. This is why one can understand the frustration directed towards Gough at the length of time that preparations were taking. Yet to attempt to move large numbers of British troops, even if they had been available, during the month of June would have been near suicidal. The effect would have been that any British force that reached the Punjab would be greatly reduced in numbers due to sickness and illness and in no fit condition to fight a major battle. It interesting to look at the difficulties from the heat and the subsequent disease that Whish's force sustained in early July when they started

---

23   Although at the time the latter point was not much emphasised it has been as years have passed by. Indeed this appear, from reviews, to very much be the angle taken by the 2010 film *Rebel Queen* based upon her life.

24   A very useful source in examining the events during the operations and sieges of Multan can be found in the journal kept by the then Lieutenant, later Lieutenant General, George Godfrey Pearse of the Bengal Artillery. See BL: Mss Eur B115: Journal kept during the Siege of Multan by Lieutenant George Godfrey Pearse. This also includes some interesting sketches and drawing of the siege.

to move. From this it becomes clear that there is certainly some strength to Gough's case for not moving during the hottest period of the year.[25]

The problem of communication again rears its head. Had Gough and Dalhousie been able to better coordinate and communicate with Edwardes, a situation might have occurred where a small force of Europeans, and in particular heavy artillery, could have been despatched to give Edwardes the means to besiege and take Multan. Edwardes did great things with his force of irregular native troops, and all he really lacked was heavy guns. One can understand why Gough believed, based on his experiences in the first war, that European infantry would be essential to victory. Yet had he, and Dalhousie, been better and more immediately aquatinted with the results Edwardes had achieved they might have been prepared to act differently.

It can be argued that there had been the potential to prevent the spread of the revolt by dealing with the revolt at Multan quicker. The likelihood is that had this happened it would merely have succeeded in delaying the outbreak of a wider Sikh revolt, perhaps by a year or two, rather than preventing it completely. Yet to claim that the revolt in Multan could have been stopped from spreading is to ignore the practicalities of the British position and in particular the situation which Gough found himself in. It can also be argued that this is to misunderstand the episode at Multan, which although aimed at British influence was a revolt against the Lahore government rather than the British themselves. This developed into a wider Sikh movement to reassert their independence; however it did not start off as such.

Whilst the British authorities certainly should have been alive to the fact that events in the Punjab might encompass a much wider revolt, they had no way of knowing that this was how events would play out. Indeed the early actions of Edwardes suggested the contrary point of view. The resentment amongst many Sikhs over British interference was largely that the settlement at the end of the first war had in effect settled nothing. They were nominally independent but subject to large-scale British interference. Had they been annexed it is possible, however unusual that it might sound, that there would have been less trouble in the long term. When annexation finally did take place the Sikhs, largely through their military prowess, became an established and trusted part of British India. There was little trouble, and during the Mutiny of 1857 Sikh loyalty and willingness to fight for the British cause was a vital part of the ultimate suppression of the rebellion. It is therefore difficult to believe that had the revolt not spread from Multan that in the long term there would not have been a further round of fighting until either the Sikhs were annexed or their independence was recognised.

From this, it can be seen that the position Gough found himself in was far from simple, with many complex political considerations that were over his head. Gough saw it simply from the military perspective. He had expected a second war, so he had urged that economy not be taken too far and that plans for the possible deployment of British troops against the Sikhs be undertaken. At one point Gough made it clear to Dalhousie where his frustration lay: "All these delays, attending the movements of troops would have been obviated, had not the repeated assurance been given that the Sikhs were so well disposed as to render the large outlay of retaining carriage uncalled for."[26] Gough clearly had a point. Hardinge had indeed said in the aftermath of the first war with the Sikhs that, "it would not be necessary to fire a gun in India for seven years to come."[27] This was a bizarre statement, even if one presumes that Hardinge was referring to the necessity to fight a major

---

25   Bruce, *Six Battles for India*, pp. 229–230.
26   NAM: 8303–105, Gough Papers, Gough to Dalhousie, 30 April 1848.
27   Rait, *Gough*, Vol. II, p. 124. Bosworth-Smith, Reginald, *Life of Lawrence*, Vol. I (London: Smith, Elder, & Co, 1901), p. 214. The exact origin of this remark is unclear. It is often attributed to Hardinge, but may have originated with Henry Lawrence. It depends upon how one reads page 124 of Bosworth-Smith's work. It is not entirely clear whether he is referring to Lawrence or Hardinge when he gives the quote.

campaign. Even before the outbreak at Multan there had been numerous other minor uprisings, and the majority had been put down by the movement of British troops, but on occasions shots had to be fired. That Hardinge was attempting to justify the financially 'necessary' reduction of the army is clear.

Gough however now had to deal with the consequences of this decision. Despite his personal belief that a second conflict with the Sikhs was inevitable, he had seen his forces and his means of preparation reduced, and had been powerless to prevent it. A more political man than Gough might have attempted to fight a campaign in the press and British Parliament in this regard. Yet Gough had few friends in the press and had no desire to cultivate such relationships, still feeling a degree of bitterness towards them over the reaction to his conduct in the first war. He had few friends in Parliament, whereas Hardinge was so well connected in that regard. Gough had done all he could short of resigning. The latter would have done little good. What he had done was to place on record his objection and his concern particularly regarding the laying in of stores and transport for a future operation.

One can understand why Gough acted cautiously. The arguments were sound; Europeans would suffer terribly from the heat if they attempted to march and fight in the summer months; a major British presence in the Sikh state was likely to cause more trouble than it resolved; and to fight any major conflict a large force, properly supplied and with sufficient transport, was required, and this would take time to assemble. There was to be much criticism of Gough in the Indian press and many contemporary and future historians have criticised him for his delay. Gough felt much of the criticism was based on unsound judgement.

The main criticism in the press was that not to immediately avenge the deaths of Vans Agnew and Anderson was a stain on national pride. To his son Gough wrote that his critics, most notably in the press, were saying that,

> [I]f we do not immediately advance, our honour will be tarnished, that sun and inundation are mere shadows, that we have the boats of the four rivers at our command, and, if we can't get at the Fort by land, we can by water – the first time in my life I ever heard of an inland fortress invested by water! So laughable are some of the ideas promulgated, that I was almost tempted to answer them by saying that nothing can be done without the horse marines to man those boats![28]

Gough was very much in a position of being dammed if he did, and dammed if he didn't. He chose, somewhat against what was perceived to be his nature, to display caution and prepare. The fact that this was his decision illustrates that he was a more complex character than is generally believed. It demonstrates an understanding of the problems, if not necessarily an ability to deal with them. It is hard to blame Gough for his decisions during the early stages of the conflict, given the information available to him at the time. Only with the benefit of hindsight does it become easy to condemn Gough for what were on the face of it sound judgements made at the time.

---

28   NAM: 8303–105, Gough Papers, Gough to George Gough, 25 May 1848.

58

Planning for Operations in the Punjab

The revolt at Multan had not initially caused a region wide series of revolts. Indeed to a large extent it had been contained to Multan. With the efforts of Edwardes and his irregulars, Dewan Mulraj and his followers had been confined in Multan. Yet there remained the possibility that the revolt could spread and there was certainly a body of thought that felt the despatch of large numbers of British troops to the area might cause this. Thus there was, as we have seen, reluctance on the part of Gough to move until he was ready for a major campaign. Preparations for transportation and supplies needed to be readied, as due to the economic policies of Hardinge such arrangements that had existed during the first war had been cancelled. Gough also had other concerns such as the problem of moving troops during the summer months, gathering a large enough force together, and, due to delays in communication, knowing exactly what was going on. Gough took an understandably cautious approach to responding to events in the Punjab. However such an approach did not help the men on the ground, such as Currie and Edwardes, who had to deal with the situation that was developing before them and meet the emergency with the limited resources at their disposal. If, as a consequence, they failed to appreciate the difficulties under which Gough was operating they should not be judged too harshly. Both Currie and Edwardes were under extreme pressure, and it is with this in mind that any criticism they made of Gough, or each other for that matter, should be judged.

Sir Frederick Currie, although clearly not an admirer of Edwardes, was pleased with his success and sensed that there was an opportunity to end the revolt at Multan and perhaps prevent its spread. Exercising his political power to act in an emergency, Currie gave the order on 10 July for Major General Whish to move from Ferozepore to support Edwardes. Currie appreciated that Edwardes' main problem was his lack of guns, without which he could not undertake siege operations. Whish did not have a full siege train available at Ferozepore but it was felt there were sufficient guns to reduce Multan. Currie seems to have been influenced by the reports of the failing morale and desertions at Multan. He clearly hoped that the presence of heavy guns and the commencement of a siege might induce surrender. Gough was concerned about the deployment for several reasons. Prior to Currie's decision he had written to Dalhousie regarding moving troops from Ferozepore or Lahore:

> [N]o force could be assembled on the Sutlej, and reach Multan before the middle, if not the end, of June by which [time], from all accounts, the investment of the Fort would be impracticable, in consequence of the impossibility of carrying on siege operations in an inundated country. Remaining inactive before Multan would not only cause a fearful loss of life, but its moral effect would be most prejudicial to future operations, as the inaction would most assuredly be misrepresented.[1]

---

1   NAM: 8303–105, Gough Papers, Gough to Dalhousie, 30 April 1848.

It is likely that what Gough meant by this was that not even a small force could arrive before Multan until the end of June. Whish decided to move in force and therefore did not arrive until the middle of August. Gough's concern regarding the health of the troops given the time of year was not far from the surface. It was now not just a question of heat but also of entering the rainy season. The latter was bound to have a great impact of the ability to move any force but also to bring up supplies. Gough's words were also prophetic in regards to the dangers of being inactive before Multan. Although he did not specifically mention it, he must also have been concerned that with so many Sikhs and soldiers of the Sikh army present there was a real danger that the trials and tribulations of a lengthy siege might induce them to go over to the enemy. In this decision to delay operations he was supported by Dalhousie:

> The question you had to determine was a very painful and difficult one, and the responsibility heavy. I am very confident that your Excellency has exercised a most sound discretion in counselling the postponement of operations until after the rains. You will perceive from my letter to Sir Frederick Currie that I am alive to all the disadvantages – to all the dangers – arising from this delay. But I am satisfied the dangers created by following an opposite course would have been greater still.[2]

Dalhousie's letter further supported Gough's decision to delay until the sizeable force that he proposed was ready. Having communicated Gough's concerns to London, Dalhousie was able to inform Gough that the British Government, presumably through the person of the President of the Board of Control Sir John Hobhouse, the Duke of Wellington, and the Secret Committee of the Directors of the East India Company, "cordially approve of the resolution not to move till October."[3] So it can be seen that whatever views were taken about Gough's decision in later years, at the time it was generally supported by the authorities. To them it no doubt appeared to be justifiable caution.

Of the fact that it would be a long siege Gough had little doubt. Whilst Edwardes and Currie believed that the morale of the soldiers in Multan was low, Gough believed that the fortress would be hard to take. This opinion was no doubt partly based upon his own experience of siege warfare both in Spain and China, but also on the opinion of Colonel H. Jones in regards the operation of a siege, a man whom Gough described as "one of our best engineers."[4] Gough recorded Jones' opinion as being, "No policy at a siege can be worse than beginning the operations with a small quantity of material, and making the attack keep pace with the supply. It has the appearance of gaining time, but in fact it is otherwise."[5] Armed with the opinion of a leading engineer, Gough had a strong case. The earliest possible action against Multan would be mid July, once the forces had gathered and prepared for an assault. Gough was still concerned about deploying British troops during the hot months, and feared for the consequences.

Although Gough was armed with the words of a leading engineer in Colonel Jones, Currie and Edwardes' contrary point of view was supported by one of the most promising engineers in

---

2   Rait, *Gough*, Vol. II, p. 129.
3   Rait, *Gough*, Vol. II, p. 130.
4   It is presumed that this is the future Lieutenant General Sir Harry D. Jones, although Gough gives no more details than the rather unhelpful name of 'Colonel Jones'. At the time Harry Jones was only a lieutenant colonel but it would not be the first time that someone commissioned thus had been referred to simply as 'Colonel'. Jones had a good reputation as a military engineer and played an important part in the defence of Cadiz. Given this it is more than likely that Gough knew him personally. Jones would later play an important part in the Crimean War.
5   Rait, *Gough*, Vol. II, p. 128.

India; Major Robert Napier. He had determined that if the force under Edwardes command was strengthened with a British infantry brigade and a force of 8 inch howitzers, 8 inch mortars and 18 pdrs, even if only 20 guns in number, Multan could be taken. We will return to look at Napier's plan to take Multan in a little more detail momentarily, but for now it is sufficient to say that Gough felt this force was insufficient. Writing to Currie, Gough declared, "The Force now proposed by Major Napier and apparently assented to by you, I consider quite inadequate. I never could consent to recommend an insufficient force, such as a Brigade of any strength, being sent."[6] Gough's argument carried on, and it becomes clear that it is not simply the size of the force he objected to. He was also concerned as to the loyalty of the Sikh force, particularly that commanded by Sher Singh that was cooperating with Edwardes, and the wider position in the country stating that,

> I have always understood from you that both the Sikh Army and the Sikh population are disaffected and should be guarded against. I take it that these objections to weakening our force at Lahore and on the Frontier still exist. The movement of a siege train under these contingencies, with so insufficient an escort as a Brigade, would in my mind be a most hazardous measure.[7]

Gough also warned that as the means of supply and transportation for such a force would have to come from Lahore, and largely be supplied by the locals, the danger of their joining in the revolt rendered the movement of such a force not only difficult but dangerous. It was quite possible that they could become stranded without supply outside Multan.

There was also a problem in regards to Edwardes' account of what was going on at Multan. Before Whish's force arrived, Edwardes had written that Multan was 'invested'. By that Currie, Gough and Dalhousie assumed that Multan was cut off and unable to receive reinforcements or supplies. However this was clearly not the case. Whether Edwardes had been deliberately misleading his superiors is a debate that is beyond the scope of what we are dealing with here. However this different interpretation of the word 'invested' and indeed the true understanding of the word 'siege' did influence the thinking of Gough. Gough was under the impression from the correspondence he received that all Edwardes really needed was engineers, artillery and some European infantry to steady his native troops in action and to cooperate with the force already under his command. Even if there had not been doubts over Sher Singh's loyalty, Gough should perhaps have appreciated that this was overly ambitious on Edwardes' part. However in fairness it must be added that Gough was a long way from Multan and he understandably trusted the opinion of the man on the ground.

Eventually Gough began to realise that he had been given an overly optimistic view of the arrangements around Multan. In early September he wrote to Dalhousie that, "the besiegers were in reality the besieged." Exactly what Gough meant by this is unclear. It is possible he was referring to the fact that the British force was in a country that was becoming increasingly hostile, and were thus surrounded by the enemy. Gough also realised that it was not a siege in the traditional sense in that Mulraj could receive 'whatever reinforcements the disaffected choose to throw into the place'. Gough later stated that had he been aware of the true nature of the 'siege' at Multan he would have insisted that when Whish's force moved it had taken a larger force of cavalry with it, even if they had been sent further reinforcements from British India. With such a mobile force perhaps a true investment and cutting off of Multan would have been possible.[8]

Gough also suggested that both Edwardes and Napier were being overambitious with regard to Multan. Gough noted that Napier, now asking for 20 or 30 guns, had altered his opinion from

---

6   Rait, *Gough*, Vol. II, p. 142.
7   Rait, *Gough*, Vol. II, p. 142.
8   Rait, *Gough*, Vol. II, p. 165.

when Gough had first consulted him. Then, Napier had claimed that 50 guns were needed, and even then Gough had doubted that they were sufficient. In fairness to Napier it must be mentioned that as a practical officer he was attempting to suggest a means of taking Multan and was now certainly proposing a much smaller force than he ideally wanted. In later years Napier would accept that he had been overoptimistic in his statements and largely supported the more cautious approach that Gough had taken.[9] Gough suggested that taking Multan might not be as easily done as anticipated. To Dalhousie he used the example of the siege of Bhurtpore (Bharatpur) in 1826. The situation at Bhurtpore had not been dissimilar to that at Multan. Lord Combermere had commanded 25,000 men during the siege including one cavalry division, two infantry divisions and over 112 guns, of which the vast majority were siege guns. Even this sizeable force had taken over a month to take Bhurtpore, held by a little over 6,000 men. What impact this lesson from history had on Dalhousie we do not know. Gough however continued with the view that Multan would not fall easily. On 15 August Gough had written to Dalhousie, "I am not quite as sanguine as to the time it will take in its [Multan's] reduction as my friends at Lahore."[10] It was clear that Gough was using his knowledge of India and his experience of siege warfare to strengthen his case. It would also be understandable if Gough, given that he was the commander-in-chief and an experienced soldier, resented being lectured to on siege warfare by a young lieutenant and a major of engineers.

Edwardes was clearly a talented man, and Napier was a first rate engineer who would prove in the years to come to be one of the Empire's greatest generals, but at the time they were both junior officers. Edwardes was only 28 and although Napier was a little older at 37 he was largely experienced only as an engineer at this stage. It should also be remembered that Edwardes had been an ADC on Gough's staff during the First Sikh War and it was therefore hard for Gough to take such lessons from someone who only a short time ago had been a junior staff officer of his. So one can understand if Gough acted somewhat defensively at having his opinion questioned by two such junior officers. That said, Gough had a strong case. Multan would not be easy to take.

The situation gives us an interesting insight into Gough's understanding of the situation. He seems to have understood that they were on the verge of a major Sikh uprising. Yet rather than rushing into the Punjab with what men he had available he was planning for a major campaign. In this Gough was to be proved correct. Whilst the argument can be made that Gough's indecision created the necessity for a major campaign, this is perhaps a little unfair. As his statement makes clear, the Sikhs were on the verge of rebellion not only against their own government at Lahore but against British influence, and it was unlikely that even if Multan fell that this would be prevented. At the same time he made some very interesting remarks regarding Gulab Singh, the first maharajah of Jammu and Kashmir a princely state created in the aftermath of the First Sikh War. Gulab was a Hindu, who had been appointed governor of the area by the Sikh leader Ranjit Singh, and governed a predominantly Muslim area. His support for the British, or perhaps more importantly his lack of support for the Sikhs, during the First Sikh War had been important. As a reward he had been granted 'independence' as a princely state. In the years since the end of the First Sikh War there had been some issues between Gulab Singh and the British, and there was now a fear amongst the government in India that he might join the revolt. Gough seems to have understood Gulab Singh better than those advising Dalhousie. In October 1848 Gough remarked in a private letter:

Goolab [sic] Singh is, as he always was, a scoundrel. The politicians now begin to see that which I told them six months back, but the devil is never so black as he is painted. Notwithstanding,

---

9   Rait, *Gough*, Vol. II, p. 144.
10   NAM: 8303–105, Gough Papers, Gough to Dalhousie, 15 August 1848.

they now think Goolab will immediately take a post against us. I am confident he is too cunning a fox to do so. England's adversity will be Goolab's prosperity.[11]

In this he was to prove correct; Gulab did not join the revolt. The worst that can be said is that he allowed his troops to desert and join in the revolt, but this is perhaps a little harsh as there was probably little he could have done to prevent this. Gough's ability to make a sound judgement over this matter does perhaps allow us to question Hardinge's belief that in political matters Gough was unable to provide any advice.

Whilst believing that Gulab Singh was unlikely to join the revolt any time soon, Gough did not doubt the very real possibility that the revolt would spread. He believed that the arrival before Multan of British troops, as opposed to the irregulars commanded by British officers, would increase disaffection with regards to British interference and cause the revolt to widen. Gough also questioned the need to hurry with regards to Multan, stating that "I cannot see anything in the altered position of affairs which would justify me in taking upon myself the siege of Multan, at the present moment. On the contrary, the success of Lieut. Edwardes renders it less necessary in my opinion, to risk the lives of the European soldiers at this season."[12] This is an interesting point as Gough was clearly saying that he could, in an emergency, 'rush' troops to the area, regardless of the climatic conditions. However the situation at present did not warrant this risk in his opinion.

Also, this piecemeal deployment of troops would have made it harder for Gough to gather together the 24,000 men and guns, supplies, and transport that he needed to undertake a major operation. The requirement of supporting Sir Frederick Currie's scheme removed from his command a brigade of cavalry, two brigades of infantry, and two troops of horse artillery. This force would otherwise have formed the beginning of his army. Yet for political reasons he was deprived of this important cadre of troops. Gough was not unrealistic in his concerns or his insistence upon the size of the force required. As we have seen there were those who felt he was being over cautious and that a smaller force might be sufficient. Dalhousie aired these concerns with Gough. Gough seemed to believe that they were a further example of political interference with his military arrangements, and that the cause of economy was not part of the concern. This is perhaps to do Dalhousie a disservice. If one reads the correspondence, one can argue that all Dalhousie was doing was placing the concerns before Gough: in effect playing devil's advocate. His letter stated that whilst he had approved the preparation of the force he had been counselled that it was, 'larger than will be necessary'. He argued that a force of 20,000 men, largely made up of troops already in the Punjab or on the frontier, and supported by what he called a second class siege train, would be "a force greater than can be required by any combination of enemies' in the Punjab." It was a bold, if not reckless, statement given how little was known about the extent of the revolt. This was written in June before Sher Singh's defection dramatically altered events, but we will look at that in more detail in a few moments.[13]

Accordingly, Gough gave a detailed account of the proposed force, not simply the number of men, in correspondence with Dalhousie. He planned to place in the field a force consisting of seven batteries of horse artillery, six of field artillery, and seven reserve companies of artillery. The purpose of the latter was presumably to cover the gaps created by active service, both in terms of men and guns, and was no doubt influenced by his experiences during the first war. In terms of cavalry he planned for three British cavalry regiments, five native regiments, and five irregular regiments. For infantry he proposed to have five European battalions and 18 native battalions. No

11   NAM: 8303–105, Gough Papers, Gough to Archibald Galloway, 1 October 1848.
12   NAM: 8303–105, Gough Papers, Gough to Currie, 1 July 1848.
13   NAM: 8303–105, Gough Papers, Dalhousie to Gough, 10 June 1848.

doubt he wished he had more European infantry in his army, but they were in short supply. There was the hope that some of the European regiments already in the Punjab, such as those under Whish's command, could be attached to the force at a later date.

With regards to the native infantry, Gough urged that there establishment be returned, even if only for the duration, to 1,000 men in a battalion. He also proposed that the cavalry be returned to an established strength of 500 men. Gough had two reasons for suggesting this. The first was very obviously that it would increase the size of his force. If a battalion entered the campaign with 1,000 men then during the campaign it would likely be reduced through death and disease to around 750. If entered the field with 800 men then it could easily be reduced to 550. The second reason he spelled out in a private letter to Dalhousie: "There are from 12,000 to 15,000 drilled soldiers out of employment, ready to take service wherever they may get it. If we do not enlist them, those opposed to us assuredly will exert every nerve to get them."[14] Many of these were the men who had been removed from the army when the established strengths had been lowered. It would therefore be relatively easy to return them to units with which they would already be familiar. Gough's request was refused as the Governor General felt that the Board of Directors of the East India Company would not reverse the policy that Lord Hardinge had introduced as a means of economy. Gough's reply was that he was not asking for a permanent reversal of the decision merely a temporary one to meet the present emergency. He continued that he believed that Hardinge would not have introduced the scheme if he could, "have anticipated that the army of the Power we have engaged to uphold were ready, to a man, to turn against the present Government."[15]

The force that Gough proposed was to be completed by the headquarters staff and six companies of sappers and pioneers. Gough was also planning the transport situation and gave very detailed instructions for the amount of ammunition he wished to be gathered at Ferozepore. Whilst clearly recalling the ammunition supply problems of the first war, it was only a partial solution. To bring ammunition from Ferozepore to Multan or any other area in which the enemy forces might move would not be an easy task. It would require a large amount of transport, largely separate from that which accompanied Gough's force, and a force to protect its movement. One final preparation was a hospital unit that could accompany the army and also one that could remain at Ferozepore, or wherever the main depot was to be based, to receive casualties sent back from the front.

The detailed plans show that Gough was clearly planning for a major campaign and not simply attempting to put down a minor revolt at Multan. In a sense he was proved correct in this course of action. There will always be those who suggest that had he moved quicker he could have defeated the revolt at Multan before it spread. The likelihood of this being successful is small, and the argument ignores the situation at large in the Sikh state. However such arguments became irrelevant when in September further revolts took place in the Punjab, but most importantly amongst the troops commanded by Sher Singh before Multan.

14   NAM: 8303–105, Gough Papers, Dalhousie to Gough, 12 May 1848.
15   NAM: 8303–105, Gough Papers, Gough to Dalhousie, 9 June 1848.

59

The Conflict Grows

Given that Sir Frederick Currie, British resident at Lahore and head of the regency council for the Sikh state, had used his own authority to support Edwardes by deploying Whish's command, Gough felt he had a responsibility to support this action, yet he maintained his doubts. It was therefore with a rather limited blessing from the Commander-in-Chief that Whish's column started to move. The sickness and disease suffered by Whish's troops can be seen as justification of Gough's decision not to move during this period of the year. Corporal John Ryder of the 32nd Foot recalled that on the march to Multan on one day alone the 32nd lost 14 dead and 175 sick, mostly through malaria, which was exacerbated by the heat being around 130 degrees.[1] Whish's force consisted of a brigade of cavalry, two brigades of infantry, engineers and a small siege train consisting of 8 inch howitzers, 8 inch mortars and some 18 pdrs. At the same time the three Sikh columns sent by the Government at Lahore to put down the revolt were nearing Multan. This presented problems for Edwardes, who was unsure where to place them, largely due to his concerns over their loyalty. He placed them in such a position that they could not directly communicate with Multan for fear they would join Mulraj. This was not his only 'positioning' problem. Amongst the many Pathans he had raised were some who had long-time family feuds. Edwardes took such precautions as basing them at separate ends of his camp and of making sure they were always on opposite sides of the room during any meetings. Of particular concern to Edwardes was the force commanded by Sher Singh. Sher Singh's loyalty to the Lahore government was questioned not only by Edwardes but also it appears by Dewan Mulraj. On both 20 and 26 July Mulraj attempted to sally out of the town. On each occasion it appears his primary aim was the hope that many of the Sikh soldiery would join him and switch their allegiance. Given the fact that the longer events at Multan took the greater the chance that many of his troops might change their allegiance, one can understand Edwardes frustration at the delay to despatch British troops.[2]

The problem was that moving such a force as Whish intended to bring was not an easy task. Although the force moved together it used separate means of transportation. The British, or European, part of the force moved by boat along the River Ravi towards Multan whereas the native contingent moved along the river bank. On the plus side this reduced the problem of land transport, on the negative side it slowed down the movement. At first not all the force moved together with some leaving on 24 July and others two days later, save for the 32nd Foot which was not able to leave until 11 August. Whilst their movement was not exactly slow, Whish's himself did not reach the outskirts of Multan until 12 August, and much of his force did not arrive until the 19th. On 17 August the forward units of Whish's force were attacked by a force from Multan

---

1   Bruce, *Six Battles for India*, pp. 229–230.
2   There were some who did defect to the Sikh cause during the siege, but they were described as a trickle rather than the flood that Mulraj hoped for. For further information see BL: Mss Eur B115, 85d: Pearse's Journal.

and after a somewhat confused fight the rebels returned to Multan. They had 40 killed along with an unknown number of wounded and prisoners. Whish's force did not lose a man and had only six wounded.

By now the delay was starting to have an effect on the morale of the Sikh troops nominally loyal to the Lahore government. As Whish deployed his forces there were already signs that further defections might occur. On 4 September Whish called on Multan to surrender, issuing a proclamation that rather unwisely called on them to surrender in the name of 'the Supreme Government of India', naming both Queen Victoria and Maharajah Duleep Singh.[3] That and the presence of so many British and East India Company troops surely did a lot to convince any doubters that this was now a fight between British India and the rebels. Some of the Sikhs might still have been loyal to the Lahore Government at this point, but events were surely now convincing them that they were being asked to fight for the British rather than any sort of Sikh authority.

When surrender was not forthcoming, Whish held a Council of War on 6 September to determine how to take the city. Two plans were put forward by Robert Napier, acting in his more appropriate role as chief engineer. By this stage Napier had developed a reputation for himself both as a civil and military engineer. Although junior in rank to many at the council of war, one would have hoped that his position and his experience would have leant weight to his opinions. This does not appear to be the case. Napier proposed to concentrate all available firepower on one particular part of the wall, create a breach and then launch a general attack with all available manpower and carry Multan by weight of numbers. The plan lacked subtlety, but it was in many ways the most practical.[4]

The plan had the advantage that it would end the siege quickly. Given that Edwardes had often talked of the need to end the revolt at Multan quickly, one might have imagined he would support such an idea. Yet he did not, and declared that the political situation did not necessitate such a move. The second plan was a more traditional piece of siege warfare and required the army to move to the north of Multan and attack from that direction by regular approaches until it could be stormed and taken. The problem with this was not only time but also the fact that such a manoeuvre might be construed as weakness by both the rebels and the soldiers of the Sikh army. Indeed it was this final point that decided the council of war against this plan.

After rejecting both of Napier's options, a new plan, put forward by Lieutenant Edward Lake, was ultimately accepted.[5] It required the digging of a trench of over a mile from a point in the camp to an area of raised ground at Ramtirat. At the latter point heavy guns would be placed, two 8 inch howitzers, three 8 inch mortars and four 18 pdrs. From here they would force the enemy to retire to the fortress itself which would then come under heavy fire. The new gun emplacement gave support to an attack launched on 10 September. However the position to be attacked proved far stronger than anticipated and the attack failed for the cost of 15 dead and 127 wounded. On 12 September the attack was renewed, this time an attempt was made to turn the enemy position, and despite stern resistance the position was taken as were the suburbs of Multan. The enemy withdrew about half a mile further into Multan itself, having lost over 500 dead. Losses on the British side amounted to 39 dead and 216 wounded. At this point it looked as is Multan would shortly be induced to fall.

However the problems in the rest of the country were starting to increase. Chatar Singh, the father of Sher Singh, had already risen in revolt in Hazara. It has been suggested that Sher Singh might have been acting as a calming influence on Chatar Singh and had attempted to dissuade him

3   Bruce, *Six Battles for India*, p. 235.
4   Napier, H. D, *Field Marshal Lord Napier of Magdala: A Memoir* (London: Edward Arnold & Co, 1927), pp. 60–64.
5   Lieutenant Edward John Lake, was an officer of the Bengal Engineers who was attached to the Department of Public works and had partial responsibility for roads between Delhi and Multan.

402 Brave as a Lion

from taking to arms. Sher Singh was however under pressure not only from his family but also from many of his officers and men to follow suit. The revolt in Multan was now spreading and taking on a distinctly Sikh nature. On 12 September Sher Singh opened private communication with Mulraj. On that same day it has also been suggested that rather than openly move to join Mulraj he had attempted to kidnap Edwardes and take control of the entire force, although he would obviously have faced opposition from the British troops under Whish's command. This attempted abduction was prevented by the prompt actions of Van Cortlandt. Edwardes was in the habit of regularly dinning with his officers in his tent. A not uncommon visitor was Sher Singh. On the night of 12 September Sher Singh arrived with a large number of his men, far more than a normal personal guard. Vans Cortlandt, who was also present at the dinner, appears to have guessed that something was afoot. Excusing himself temporarily from the table he gathered a number of Pathan soldiers whose loyalty he could rely on to gather around the tent as protection. When Vans Cortlandt returned he contrived a reason to inform Sher Singh of what he had just done. Vans Cortlandt recorded that Sher Singh looked embarrassed. Vans Cortlandt's experience of dealing with the Sikhs no doubt saved both he and Edwardes from at best captivity and at worst death.[6]

On 14 September, Sher Singh marched off with his force to join the rebels at Multan. Sher Singh's defection altered the whole nature of the revolt. This was now a Sikh uprising and revolt against British interference. Sher Singh made this abundantly clear as he marched at the head of his army of over 10,000 men into Multan to the sound of Sikh religious drums. This not only signified that the revolt was now certainly a Sikh rising, but also it acted as a rallying cry to other Sikhs: in effect a call to arms. With their force reduced and the enemy's number almost doubled, it was impossible for Edwardes and Whish to maintain the siege. Indeed such was the position that they felt it necessary, after a council of war held in the tent of the wounded Major Napier, to withdraw from Multan itself. This was done on the 14th, save for a force that continued to hold the strong position at Ramtirat mentioned previously. On 15 September the main force moved to Soorujkund where they would remain despite a series of attacks over the months, culminating in what would become known as the Battle of Soorujkund on 5 November.

What had started as a revolt by a non-Sikh against the Sikh authority at Lahore had now developed into a Sikh uprising against British influence and interference. It is easy to look back with the benefit of hindsight and say that such a renewal of hostilities was inevitable given the unsatisfactory settlement at the end of the first conflict. Yet there were those, most notably Gough, who saw that a second war would occur. It could be argued that had Edwardes and Whish been able to move quicker and take Multan that it might have bought time for Gough to prepare his army and move it into position. To this one has to consider whether, with the fall of Multan, the authority for such a force to be moved and the expense it would have incurred would have been allowed. Given the politically driven need for economy one can wonder whether the fall of Multan would have given Dalhousie the justification to cancel Gough's preparations. If, subsequently, a wider Sikh uprising had occurred Gough would, likely as not, have found himself in the same position of having to improvise not only a force but its means of supply and transportation.

The widening of the revolt made the need for his intervention more likely, but, as Gough pointed out, the decision to move was not his. As he wrote in a personal letter, "The papers are crying out at my not at once pushing on troops, forgetting that I am not the government, to make war, or peace."[7] It is worth remembering that whilst Gough had been allowed to prepare a force to move into the

---

6   Cook, *The Sikh Wars*, p. 134.
7   NAM: 8303–105, Gough Papers, Gough to Archibald Arbuthnot, 13 October 1848. Mr Archibald Arbuthnot was Gough's son-in-law by marriage to his daughter Gertrude. Such letters were usually opened "Dear Archy".

Punjab, he was not allowed to form the force on the frontier. Permission to gather on the frontier did not come until early September, in the aftermath of the widening of the revolt. It is therefore unfair to criticise Gough, as military commander, for not moving without similarly criticising the political authorities who had not firmly decided upon military action.

This again raises the question of to what purpose was Gough supposed to move. For the papers it was largely to avenge the deaths of Vans Agnew and Anderson and restore honour. The question was how was this to be achieved? To take Multan and to deal with Dewan Mulraj was not likely to be the end of any revolt. Gough saw this, whereas those in the press could not or chose not to. Gough was certain that any intervention by a large British force was likely to create further revolts rather than supress them. Indeed one can make the argument that Sher Singh's revolt became easier to justify when Whish's British force arrived to attack Multan.

It must also be made clear that whilst Gough felt that his caution had been necessary, he regretted that it was. In a letter written in October 1848 Gough had said, "We have delayed the formation of an army until the eleventh hour, the disinclination of the government to upset all the political arrangements of the late Governor-General, has been a very great advantage to the rebel Sikhs."[8] It is interesting that Gough's criticism of the political arrangements that had placed him in difficulty were made in private. Whilst the criticism of his supposed 'inactivity' – supposed for we have seen that he was far from inactive – had largely been made public, Gough kept his council and did not respond in public. One can make the argument that Gough's caution actually saved the army from a potential disaster. Had he attempted to move sooner it was inevitable that British forces would have arrived in the Punjab at different times rather than in large numbers. When Sher Singh defected, and the revolt took on the nature of a far more general rising, they would have been in peril. Small contingents, largely without the means of supply or transportation, would have been spread throughout the area. Even if they had been able to gather together, with a combined strength of about 20,000 men, they were not an army. There was no headquarters staff, no commissariat, no transport, limited means of supply: in short no organisation. A mass of men does not make an army. Also, there was a lack of artillery support.

The last point perhaps needs clarification. Whilst there were a number of guns, indeed a second class siege train, using them would be a different matter. Firstly there was the problem of securing the guns. There would be little problem with the guns at Ferozepore, but the guns at Lahore would be a different matter if the revolt spread there. It would also be difficult to transport them. Bullocks, or possibly elephants, would be the only way to move them, and these would have to be acquired from local sources. There was also the problem of ammunition. Exactly what amounts were available is unclear, but we do that Gough was concerned that even at Ferozepore, the major depot, there was estimated to be only a week's supply of general material for the army, and it is hard to imagine that the ammunition situation was much better. Again we are faced with the fact that Gough had not been allowed, due to Hardinge's demands for economy, to increase the size of the storage facilities at Ferozepore.[9]

It was not always possible for Gough to make others understand the importance of preparation. This seems at odds with Hardinge's opinion of his organisational abilities, and perhaps points us towards the conclusion that Gough was not as inept in this regard as might be believed. Perhaps it is more to the point to say that Gough lacked the ability to make things happen. He understood the concerns, and even attempted to meet them, but was unable to drive thing through. This is illustrated in a private letter where he referred to Dalhousie as being "a young man his blood is very

---

8   NAM: 8303–105, Gough Papers, Gough to Archibald Arbuthnot, 13 October 1848.
9   NAM: 8303–105, Gough Papers, Gough to Archibald Arbuthnot, 13 October 1848.

hot, and he speaks of walking over everything. But to walk we must eat!"[10] It appears clear that Gough was aware of the importance of the need to store in supplies for what could potentially be a long campaign. The problem was putting his concerns into practice.

Whether Gough was over cautious is only part of the situation. There were also wider political concerns over what sort of campaign was to be fought. Had he not shown the caution he did, had he not ignored the complaints in the press and the representations from Edwardes and Currie, the situation had the potential for disaster. Had such an event befallen the British it was not Edwardes or Currie who would have been blamed, but Gough. Even Dalhousie would have been able to defend himself from accusations due to his relatively recent arrival and blame would have passed largely onto the commander-in-chief. Thus if Gough stood to be blamed either way, he chose to prepare a large force. This was no doubt influenced by his past experiences. One can imagine that the memory of the First Sikh War played a large part in convincing him that if he had to enter into another campaign in the region against the Sikhs he wanted a large force moving as one. In this light and given all the problems and concerns that he faced it is difficult to condemn the man for the course of action he took.

10   NAM: 8303–105, Gough Papers, Gough to Archibald Arbuthnot, 13 October 1848.

60

The British Response

With the defection of Sher Singh on 14 September the revolt changed in complexion. It now had a distinctly Sikh feel to it and a growing religious element. However Sikh religion and sense of nationhood were so intrinsically linked as to make such a rising appear nationalistic. It was now a rebellion against British interference and influence. What the endgame of the Sikhs who now joined the rebellion was has been debated for many years. Certainly the aim was to remove British influence and assert independence, but what form that would take has never been fully explained. However to a degree it was academic at that stage. What was required was a campaign to defeat the British and remove them from Sikh territory. Once that had been achieved other matters could then be considered.

To this end, many of the former soldiers of the Khalsa now re-joined the army that had been reduced and reorganised in line with the Treaty of Lahore. The Sikh forces of the Second Sikh War were different to that of the previous encounter. They lacked the strong cadre of elite regiments that the Khalsa of the First Sikh War had; those units that had been trained organised and developed along European lines. That said, there were still a number of strong professional regiments that commanded the respect of the British. More to the point there was no shortage of professional trained soldiers. Although there had been a large number of irregular units present during the first war, they now formed a far greater percentage of the Sikh army. The artillery, whilst still far stronger than would have been expected in an Indian campaign, was a shadow of the force which had equalled and in some ways bettered that of the British during the first conflict. What the Sikh army of this war did have was great mobility. They still presented a significant challenge to the British, and whilst not the force it was before the Sikh army should not in any way be underestimated.

Before moving on to look at the British response, and in particular the decisions taken by Gough, it is necessary to understand the growth of the revolt. The defection of Sher Singh had forced Currie to take further action. At Lahore he had ordered the 53rd Foot to take command of the palace and the treasury. The fort at Govindgarh near Amritsar was secured by the British with the use of subterfuge by the loyal Rasul Khan and William Hodson, of Hodson's Horse fame. There were now numerous outbreaks of revolt. Ram Singh led a revolt in Bari Doab which threatened the security of British territory acquired under the Treaty of Lahore and threatened to cause further problems for the movement of Gough's Army. This was dealt with by Brigadier Wheeler, who commanded a small column that was able to secure the forts at Pathankot, Shapur, Morari, and was able to blockade a fort at Rangar Nagal. His movement continued throughout the region and he did much to reduce the level of revolt. The Sikh troops at Peshawar and Hazara were in open revolt. The outbreak at Peshawar was potentially the most serious. Chatar Singh had promised Peshawar to the Afghans if they joined them in battle against the British. In October, such was the movement of the Afghans into the Peshawar region, that Captain James Abbott and Lieutenant Herbert, who had been attempting to prevent the revolt from spreading, were forced to abandon the region.

Whish and Edwardes, the latter now holding the local rank of major, had withdrawn only a few miles from Multan. This was still the largest force, despite the defections, that was operating in the field. Reinforcements were on the way and it was hoped that this would enable them to recommence the siege of Multan. The battle of Soorujkund on 7 November did much to stop the progress of the rebels from Multan. Although largely forgotten today this was an important action. The attempt had been made by Dewan Mulraj to force Whish away from the area around Multan. Although the siege had been lifted with the defection of Sher Singh, the British force had only moved a few miles away and still threatened Multan. Mulraj had sent a force, largely consisting of cavalry, to induce Whish to withdraw further. However Whish and Edwardes did not wait for the anticipated attack and moved forward to dislodge the rebels from their position. Van Cortlandt still had two loyal regiments of Sikhs who proved their worth in the battle that followed. Although the 10th and 32nd Foot led the way they were ably supported by the loyal Sikh regiments, three regiments of Bengal native infantry and Edwardes' Pathan irregulars.

The confused nature of the conflict was illustrated by an unfortunate incident in which men of the 32nd were unable to tell friend from foe and fired upon loyal Pathan irregular horse who had charged forward to attack the enemy and were on the wrong side of the battlefield when the 32nd advanced. The situation was saved by a certain Private Howell of the 32nd who, understanding a little Urdu, was able to recognise that the shouts of the men they were firing on were informing them that they were on their side. Private Howell ran to the front of his regiment urging them to stop. Fortunately they took notice of him and as a reward for his prompt action he was given 50 rupees by Edwardes.[1]

The battle had been a great success, so much so that on 7 December the siege commenced once more. On 21 December reinforcements from the Bombay Army, who had marched from Sindh, arrived to swell the numbers. Indeed the force had increased considerably since the battle of 7 November. At first they attempted to undertake Lieutenant Lake's aforementioned plan for reducing Multan. Colonel John Cheape, of the Bengal Engineers, now arrived with the army and assumed the role of senior engineer. He now proposed the same plan of attack that Napier had put forward four months earlier. It can be argued that now, with a region-wide rebellion, speed was now of the essence and Multan needed to be taken quickly so as to free the number of troops engaged in the siege for operations elsewhere. This justified such a bold frontal attack in a way which perhaps the circumstances had not four months earlier. However by this time Sher Singh had marched from Multan, on 10 October, to gather an army on the banks of the Chenab River. There has been some criticism of Sher Singh for not moving on Lahore. Whilst taking the seat of government of the Sikh state had many advantages it was probably not the wisest move and Sher Singh probably took the correct course of action. His concerns were similar to Gough's in many ways: he did not want to move until he had his force gathered together.

Sher Singh was anxious to create a camp where all those who had risen in revolt could join together. Lahore had a sizeable British garrison, and Sher Singh was reluctant to take action before he could gather in strength. He was also faced with the problem that the area he was in was not one that was naturally in support of him, as it was largely a Muslim area. Gough's view was that Sher Singh would not move on Lahore at this stage and in a letter to Dalhousie remarked that "As for Sher Singh's moving upon Lahore, it is all a farce." His view was that, even if Sher Singh expected the city to rise in support of him on his arrival, he was attacking a strong British garrison in a reasonably strong defensive position. It would also mean that Sher Singh would be turning his back on Gough's force that could move against him and pin him between his force and the garrison at Lahore. In the same letter to Dalhousie, Gough expressed his fear that the number of

---

1   Cook, *The Sikh Wars*, pp. 137–138.

British troops engaged in operations already throughout the Punjab was problematic. Obviously it made it harder for Gough to gather the size of force he required but there was also a concern that the troops could be frittered away in minor operations. Indeed Gough used that very phrase when he stated that, "By the 15th of November, I shall have a sufficient force assembled at, and in front of, Ferozepore, to effect this [to engage in a major battle with the Sikhs], if Sir Frederick does not fritter away the troops in little and useless operations." At the same time, Gough also expressed concern about the independent operations of Brigadier Wheeler. Whilst Wheeler had done good work in supressing further revolt, it did not help Gough directly. This demonstrates yet another difficulty Gough had in planning his operations and points to a wider problem of strategy. With so many troops spread throughout the Punjab, the fact that no permanent transportation system had been retained appears increasingly foolhardy. In effect there was no permanent means of supporting such troops in time of crisis quickly and efficiently.[2]

Whilst British forces had some success in preventing the revolt from becoming a much larger outbreak there was still great concern. We now need to go back in our narrative to the decisions Gough and Dalhousie had, and had not taken, in the months leading up to this point to gain an understanding of the British response to the revolt in the Punjab. It was clear that Gough's army would need to be able to move by October. Yet he had been delayed in his preparations by political interference. Many essential arrangements had been prevented due to the cost that would be incurred.

Even by the middle of July, the full equipping of the army was still being prevented by the refusal of Dalhousie to give the go ahead for such preparations. In a letter to Gough dated 12 July, Dalhousie informed him that,

> I am well aware of the necessity of not deferring preparations too long; but the state and prospects of our finances which are before my eyes for ever, although they are not forced on you, create a necessity at least equally strong for not incurring expense in preparation until it can no longer be possibly avoided.[3]

One must remember that this was at the time when Whish's force was moving towards Multan, so there was still the hope that he could prevent the spread of the revolt, take Multan, and avoid a major conflict with the Sikhs. This was perhaps a false hope, but one can understand Dalhousie's reasons for believing in it and indeed for wanting it. The pointed remark that Dalhousie had the finances of India, 'before my eyes for ever', was clearly a gentle reminder towards Gough that there were considerations beyond the commander-in-chief's responsibility. It was also a suggestion by Dalhousie that Gough clearly did not understand such things.

Whilst there was perhaps some truth in Dalhousie's implication, Gough could equally have turned around and said that there were military considerations that Dalhousie, for all his talk of understanding the army, did not appreciate. Whilst Gough wanted to delay movement of a force until October of that year, he did not want to delay its preparation. Indeed that was the point: it would take him until about October to gather his force and prepare it, if he started preparations in June or July. If he was prevented from preparing the most essential elements, such as the means of transportation, because of the expense, then he would be in no condition to move even in October. Here lay the major problem in Dalhousie's reticence to countenance the expenditure. The decision was needed in July if the army was to be ready for late September or early October. It would take

---

2   NAM: 8303–105, Gough Papers, Gough to Dalhousie, 23 October 1848.
3   NAM: 8303–105, Gough Papers, Dalhousie to Gough, 12 July 1848. See also Baird, J. G. A., *Private Letters of the Marquis of Dalhousie* (London: William Blackwood & Sons, 1910), pp. 28–29.

that long to find sufficient animals, carts, harness, saddles, and native bearers, and to build up the necessary supplies at a point near the frontier where they could support an army in the field. Such things took time, and once again we see the folly of not maintaining a permanent transport system sufficient to support an army in the field. Perhaps there was partly a failure on Gough's part to make Dalhousie really understand this. One gets the impression that by this point in his career Gough had had enough of arguing with politicians. Indeed, he seems not to have pressed the matter with Dalhousie any further. However he continued to write in his private communication with others, most notably his son, of the necessity for permission to make the necessary preparations. No doubt his experiences dealing with Hardinge had given him the view that such arguing was a pointless exercise.

By late August Dalhousie was starting to see that consent for the preparations might be necessary and on the 22nd had asked Gough to give him details of the size of force he would require. Yet even now he continued to argue that economy was paramount, stating that "financial considerations must weigh greatly in the determination the Government may form on this deeply important matter. It is upon the military part that I beg now to request the benefit of your counsel and experience. No decision, I need hardly say, has yet been formed." Again there seems to have been an attempt to put Gough in his place, particular when Dalhousie mentioned that it was the military part of the decision making process upon which he wished to have Gough's council. Dalhousie did not end the sentence "It is upon the military part that I beg now to request the benefit of your counsel and experience" with the word 'only' but one gets the impression that it was what he meant.[4] Once again this must have been frustrating for Gough. Firstly, he had already given such advice back in May, and now he simply repeated the same force requirements. Secondly, it was now late August and he had not been able to do anything other than general preparations of troop numbers. He had started to gather what he could, but he was still prevented from gathering the force on the frontier, and from making the expenditure necessary to transport and maintain such a force. Indeed, even these preparations had been complicated by the need to send reinforcements to the Punjab to support Currie and Whish.

The point was now coming where a decision was essential. At about the same time as Dalhousie's letter of 22 August, Gough had received further concerns from Currie as to the safety of Lahore and the spread of the revolt. Gough decided to act, and without waiting for the permission of Dalhousie, ordered the strengthening of the garrison at Lahore. On 9 September he also ordered that a cavalry force, not quite a full brigade at this stage, should move towards Multan. The aim was twofold, as it would both support Whish and Edwardes but also give a force that could move quickly towards Lahore should any danger occur. On the same day Gough ordered that an infantry brigade consisting of the 29th Foot and two native infantry battalions should move to Bahawalpur. Gough did all this without the permission of the Governor General, and whether he was within his rights as commander-in-chief to do so is a technical debate. As it was, Dalhousie supported his decision and indeed went further allowing Gough to organise a 10,000 strong force at Ferozepore. Gough intended this force to have two purposes. Firstly it would be the basis of any army to conqueror the Punjab, and secondly it would be sufficient to support Lahore should it come under attack.

In his letter to Dalhousie Gough made it clear that such a force would be gathered under the cover story of being preparation for the annual relief of the garrison at Lahore. Whether such a story would be believed by the Sikhs is certainly questionable. However it did give Gough and Dalhousie a defence against any accusation of sabre-rattling and of having brought on the coming conflict. Gough was anxious to act as he was concerned that when British troops arrived in the Punjab that

---

4   NAM: 8303–105, Gough Papers, Dalhousie to Gough, 22 August 1848.

it would be the signal for a wholesale rebellion against British influence. Indeed Dalhousie had softened his position somewhat since 22 August. Only two days later he had written to Gough that the latter may, "issue such orders as you may think necessary for ensuring a sufficient support to the force now at Mooltan [*sic*], in case it should need it, and for providing a defence against any outbreak at any time or anywhere upon the frontier."[5] Perhaps a different commander might have taken this as carte blanche to act as he wished. Yet Gough chose to follow the letter of the instruction. The communication reached Gough in early September.

Perhaps sensing how his previous communication might have been interpreted, on 13 September Dalhousie sent another letter. Although this might have had the intention of attempting to clarify the position it is likely that it achieved quite the reverse. In the letter of the 13th, Dalhousie asked that Gough should only gather on the frontier those units destined to create a force of 10,000 men at Ferozepore. The problem with this was that it was simply insufficient and did not address the wider problem of supply and transportation. It also appears that Dalhousie seems to have believed that this force of 10,000 men, supporting the troops already in the area, would be sufficient to the task at hand. Perhaps here the problem was that Dalhousie was looking at the total strength of British troops in the Punjab and considered that the 35,000-plus soldiery in the area should be sufficient. It is difficult to say for certain how many troops were in the area serving under British colours. It might have been over 40,000 at one stage. Yet with defections and only general figures for the number of irregulars raised it is difficult to be accurate.

On 6 September Gough had urged, as he had in June, that native infantry battalions be returned to 1,000 men from the 800 they had been reduced to and that cavalry regiments be returned to 500 men. In response on the 13th, the day before Sher Singh's defection, Dalhousie stated that he doubted whether a full scale war would be necessary, and refused this request. However Gough was now given permission to gather his force on the frontier. By the time this letter reached Gough, news of Sher Singh's defection had reached him and it was now clear that a major operation was inevitable and far more than the 10,000 men he had been given permission to gather on the frontier would be necessary.[6] At about the same time, Gough had moved further troops to the border, ordering the 3rd Light Dragoons to join the cavalry force already on its way to the frontier and sending the 98th Foot to Ferozepore. Whilst Gough had been limited in what he could do, he had at least been able to make sure that there were a considerable number of European regiments in or around the Punjab. As they were considered the pick of his troops, this had a reassuring effect upon those in the Punjab, such as Currie, who felt it showed a level of precaution and had a similar effect on Dalhousie.

When Gough began to hear of the defection of Sher Singh, at first rumoured and later confirmed, he was frustrated that he was not in a position to move. The delays in preparations that had been forced on him by political considerations were expressed by Gough in a letter to Sir Frederick Currie written on 15 September.

> Had the Army I proposed been formed, I should now, or shortly after this, have had a force of from 12,000 to 15,000 men ready to move upon Woozeerabad [Wazirabad] or to its neighbourhood, the point I always considered advisable, which would have kept all – Goolab [Gulab] Singh, the Maharajah, and Peshawur [Peshawar] – in check, and effectually have protected Lahore and repressed insurrection in the Mangha Doab.

5   NAM: 8303–105, Gough Papers, Dalhousie to Gough, 24 August 1848.
6   NAM: 8303–105, Gough Papers, Gough to Dalhousie, 6 September 1848 & NAM: 8303–105, Gough Papers, Dalhousie to Gough, 13 September 1848.

The point was well made and the frustration can clearly be heard in what he wrote. In the same letter Gough continued that:

> Troops are now on their march to Ferozepore, which I cannot but repeat I consider the proper base of operations, imperatively called for to check open revolt at this side [of] the Sutlej. I will take good care that Lahore shall not be threatened, without giving it effectual support; but, for a general Punjab War, I am not prepared. Such preparation must rest with the Government, which is, in simple truth, the immediate augmentation of the army.[7]

The words were hardly reassuring to Currie, but were a relatively accurate assessment of the situation in which the army now found itself. It is interesting to note that Gough was also concerned about revolt 'at this side [of] the Sutlej'. The possibility of a wider revolt against the British throughout India is one that some on the Sikh side, such as Sher Singh, called for but which few on the British side seem to have considered. The possibility of a rising south of the Sutlej is also a point which few historians of the war have fully considered. It is also worth noting that Gough is clearly considering his responsibilities as commander-in-chief rather than simply as the designated commander of the field force to be used against the Sikhs. He was therefore charged with security on both sides of the Sutlej. Given that to place the army in the field he had been forced to denude much of India of soldiery, one can appreciate the concern. One must remember that some of the spirit that would cause the Mutiny of 1857 was already at large in British India.

---

7   NAM:8303–105, Gough Papers, Gough to Currie, 15 September 1848.

61

Gough and Dalhousie

Although we have already looked at the relationship between Gough and Dalhousie to some extent, it is perhaps now appropriate to make some further comments in this regard before moving on to look at the conduct of the war. As has been previously mentioned, the fact that they had rarely met in person did not help the development of their relationship. The difficulty in their relationship largely stemmed from the fact that Gough again felt his preparations were being blocked for political and financial considerations rather than military reasons. The failure to prepare transport and to prepare sufficient stores in advance was a particular concern for Gough.

Gough was perhaps too optimistic about what he would have been able to achieve had the preparations been made when he had wanted. Exactly when Gough first heard of Sher Singh's defection is unclear, but it was certainly a few days after the event. By 20 September Gough was writing to Dalhousie that "I earnestly beg to press upon your Lordship the indispensable necessity of increasing the army, without the delay of a day." This shows Gough's concern at the fact that only 10,000 men had been gathered, despite his constant insistence that he required an army of 24,000 men for extensive operations against the Sikhs. Gough's letter also showed that he understood the pressure Dalhousie was under with regards to taking the decision over the great expenditure that this would require, stating, "I am ready to take upon myself all the odium of having pressed it upon the Government." In short he was giving Dalhousie the ability to say that he, Gough, had been placed in a difficult position where he had had to make a decision.[1]

Finally, although one can argue it was already too late, Dalhousie gave the necessary orders in early October. He allowed for the native army to be increased to its former level, in line with Gough's request. He also allowed troops of the Bombay Army to march to increase Gough's force and thus hopefully raise the army to somewhere near the levels Gough had asked for. Although Gough held the title of commander-in-chief in India he had only limited control over the Bombay Army, which was controlled by the governor general of Bombay and the commander-in-chief of the Bombay Army. The movement of troops from the Bombay Army and from Sindh, now garrisoned by the Bombay Army, was a much welcomed move. This would be particularly helpful if troops moved from Afghanistan to support the Sikhs.

The problem was that the British were now responding to a crisis rather than anticipating it. The level of dissent in the Sikh state was well known and the fact that the revolt at Multan spread should not have come as a surprise to anyone. One can perhaps forgive Dalhousie for not sanctioning the expenditure on preparing an army with transportation and supply, or the expenditure associated with gathering a force on the frontier, at the time at which Multan alone was in revolt. However, by the time there were other outbreaks of revolt in late July and early August, more identifiably Sikh in nature, and Dalhousie should have been aware of the implications and at this time have given his assent to the expenditure.

---

1   NAM: 8303–105, Gough Papers, Gough to Dalhousie, 20 September 1848.

Dalhousie would, in later years, lay the blame for delay at the feet of Gough. At the time, however, he was in full support of the decision to delay movement until October, and, as we have seen, was supported in this view by the home government and the Duke of Wellington. Dalhousie did rather take advantage of the poor opinion of Gough towards the end of the campaign to defend his own actions. Yet if Dalhousie had been dissatisfied at the time with the speed of Gough's arrangements, there is nothing in his surviving correspondence with Gough to support this view. Indeed, one can say quite the reverse. Through reading the correspondence between the two men at this time one gets the impression that it was the commander-in-chief trying to push along the governor general rather than the other way around. One of Dalhousie's biographers, Sir William Hunter, states that Dalhousie ordered troops to the Punjab, "with swift resolution", but as Gough's previous biographer Sir Robert Rait concludes, "his swift resolution ordered on the 5th of October what Lord Gough had pressed upon him on the 11th of May, and had repeatedly urged in August and September."[2]

Edwin Arnold, in his biographical study of Dalhousie's governorship of India, is particularly critical of Gough and places the delay for the blame squarely at his feet. He was perhaps unfair when writing of Gough's refusal to move earlier, before preparations had been completed, when he wrote that "Not a line of Lord Gough's refusal seemed reasonable then; read now, it appears unhappy in the last degree."[3] This is based upon the theory that a swift movement by Gough, with whatever troops he could manage, would have been sufficient to end the revolt at Multan before it spread. As we have already seen this is a rather flawed hypothesis. Indeed Arnold's book was, through no fault of his own, a rather flawed book. Published in 1862, he had access to official documents, but not to Dalhousie's private papers. Arnold therefore failed to appreciate that in his private correspondence Dalhousie continued to delay Gough in his preparations due to a failure to provide permission for the necessary expenditure for preparations. This infighting amongst biographers comes down to this: when Dalhousie did act he did so swiftly and with resolution, yet he delayed action far longer than was prudent. Had Dalhousie approved Gough's memorandum of 11 May when he had called for an army of the Punjab to be created, some 24,000 men strong, that all furlough be cancelled, and that the size of the battalions be returned to their previous levels, then by mid September an army would have been ready to intervene in the Punjab just at the moment of Sher Singh's defection and the widening of the revolt.

Dalhousie's decision not to give the approval for this was understandable. One can appreciate that he had to consider the financial impact of the creation of such an army for a contingency that might not occur. However to lay the blame for any delay upon Gough was incorrect. Gough had not wanted to move until late August or early September when the worst of the summer was coming to an end. Whilst there have been people who have questioned this decision, it was taken out of concern for his men and previous experience of the suffering extreme heat could do. He had experienced this not only in India, but also in China. One must also recall the situation that Gough had inherited in China, where the severe climate conditions had reduced his army dramatically before he arrived. Gough was in effect asking for three months to prepare an army for what he envisaged as a major campaign. One can understand Gough's frustration, as once again political considerations were overriding military necessity. Yet in line his character he did not air his frustrations in public. Even in his private correspondence it was only really to his son that he is critical.

2   Hunter, Sir William *The Marquis of Dalhousie: And the Final Development of the Company's Rule* (Oxford: Clarendon Press, 1895), p. 76 & Rait, *Gough*, Vol. II, p. 161.

3   Arnold, Edwin, *The Marquis of Dalhousie's Administration of British India*, Vol. I (London, Saunders, Otley and Co, 1862).

One other interesting point that should be mentioned at this time was the fact that Gough's appointment was up, and under normal circumstances he should have handed over command having served his term in office. It is interesting in the light of events towards the end of the First Sikh War, and with the later worsening of relations with Dalhousie, that at this time there seemed to be little suggestion that his replacement should take place as planned. The decision to reappoint Gough, at least on a temporary basis, came from the Government in London. John Hobhouse, President of the Board of Control stated that the Duke of Wellington as commander-in-chief of the British Army had also been consulted. From whom the idea originated is unknown. The news was announced in early September 1848. Yet the decision must surely have been taken some weeks before that. It was not unusual for such things to be worked out six months if not a year before hand. If there remained a doubt over Gough's ability amongst the contemporary audience, surely here was an ideal opportunity to replace him. At the very least it would have been a reason for him not to command the army in the field but to remain at headquarters to oversee the operations and await his replacement.[4]

One can understand the desire not to replace the commander-in-chief at that time due to the coming emergency, yet it raises questions. The decision to reappoint him must have been taken before Sher Singh's defection, indeed quite possibly even before the outbreak of revolt at Multan. Thus if the decision not to replace him was due to the fact that the government could see the coming crisis, one has to ask why at this stage permission was not given for the army to gather on the frontier and for proper preparations in terms of transportation and supplies to be made ready. If it was an emergency that meant a change of command was not considered prudent, then it must make Dalhousie's decision not to give the necessary permission a questionable one. It also raises the question of who would have replaced him. Whilst there were many ambitious men who wanted the position there was a dearth of experienced senior commanders who were felt to be up to the job. Although it is to get a little ahead of ourselves, when it came to talk of replacing Gough during the Second Sikh War there were only two men in the whole of the British Army considered up to the task, and as we shall see there was a question mark against each of them. It is all well and good to criticise Gough, and in some cases rightly so, for his ability and limitations as a commander but it is not so easy to see who would have been capable of doing a better job.

The problem of higher command ability has been a perennial one for the British Army throughout its history. Gough perhaps had a better claim than many to his high position, given that it was a reward for a successful campaign in China. Whilst one can question the quality of the alternatives, it meant that Gough could claim to have recent experience of commanding an expedition and an army in the field. Added to which he had defeated the Gwalior state, and perhaps more importantly had beaten the Sikhs before. There therefore seemed to be little desire to replace the Commander-in-Chief at this stage.

Gough now commenced to form an army on the frontier: the Army of the Punjab as it would become known. It was to consist of one cavalry and three infantry divisions. Whilst Dalhousie had been reluctant to change the command system and remove Gough as commander-in-chief before the start of the campaign, Gough himself had no such compunction with regards to his subordinate commanders. One decision regarding change of command that has been criticised was that to remove Colonel, acting Brigadier General, Sir Charles Robert Cureton as adjutant general and give him command of the Cavalry Division. Cureton was a fascinating character. He had originally been a militia officer who had got into debt and had faked his own death to avoid his creditors.

---

4   Lee-Warner, *The Life of Dalhousie*, Vol. I, pp. 159–160. Lee-Warner quotes a letter dated 6 July 1848 from John Hobhouse, the President of the Board of Control, stating that the Government, after consultation with the Duke of Wellington, had decided to reappoint Gough until further notice.

He had then joined the 14th Light Dragoons as a private under the name of Charles Robert. Eventually his true identity was uncovered and he was commissioned for bravery in the Peninsular War. Whilst there was no doubting Cureton's skill as a cavalry leader, there was no one adequate to fill his role as adjutant general.[5]

There was no doubt that Cureton was qualified for his new position. He was one of the finest cavalry commanders in the army, and had performed heroically during the First Sikh War. Gough's reasons for removing his adjutant general and giving him a divisional command are not recorded. It is possible that Cureton asked for it, and as an experienced commander Gough would have been open to such a request. It might also have been Gough's initiative, given that cavalry had played an important part in the first war, and that Cureton himself had been instrumental in that. Perhaps it is also an example of Gough's thinking in that he would sooner have a good divisional commander for his cavalry than a good adjutant general. It is possible to look at this decision and use it to support the theory that Gough did not appreciate the importance of good staff work. On the face of it, it does seem strange that Gough would remove such an important staff officer from his work just as a major campaign was about to begin. It was, however, the way things were done at this time: officers were happy to fill administrative positions in time of peace but when war came they wanted an active command. Either way it was a little unfair on Thackwell, who had led the cavalry during the first war with some success and was now replaced by an officer junior to him. Thackwell was given an infantry division instead. Perhaps this illustrates the point that Gough sort to use his best and most experienced commander in divisional positions rather than administrative ones.

In September Gough had discussed with Dalhousie how the force he was now organising should best be used. He put forward two plans of operation. The first was to abandon any attempt at taking Multan at this stage. This would thereby free the men around Multan to join Gough's main army. The manpower problem was a significant difficulty in gathering the size of army that Gough felt necessary. At Multan there were already 7,000 soldiers who could join Gough's army, over 3,000 reinforcements that would soon reach them, and at least another 7,000 who had already been committed to move towards Multan and were at various stages of their advance. Exact figures are difficult to find, and the above rough calculations might count some units twice. This is because when Gough came to gather his 10,000 men on the frontier he used some of the 7,000 reinforcements who were in various stages of their advance on Multan. Even so, the decision to abandon the area around Multan would have given Gough over 17,000 men which, when added to the 10,000 he was gathering on the frontier, would have culminated in a force at the level Gough had proposed. This would then allow Gough to move with this force throughout Sikh territory dealing with the revolts one by one before ultimately besieging and taking Multan and dealing with those who began the revolt.

Yet the problem with this plan was how such a withdrawal would be seen by the Sikhs and those within British territory. Whilst Gough liked this plan, stating in a letter to Dalhousie that "This, most decidedly, would be the more likely plan to command success", he appreciated that there were negative implications to such a decision. It was feared that it would give those in revolt the feeling of triumph, and induce many who at present were considering joining the revolt to do so. Gough also considered that the decision to abandon Multan, "may also create feelings, at our side of the water, adverse to our supremacy, and this is a subject of such vital importance to the stability of our rule in India that although I see the advantage of it in a military point of view, I cannot feel satisfied in recommending it."[6] Again Gough was considering the wider implication for the security of British India in a way that clearly shows an understanding and thoughtfulness away from the

5   Bruce, *The Sikh Wars*, p. 142.
6   NAM: 8303–105, Gough Papers, Gough to Dalhousie, 22 September 1848.

simple military operations being proposed. Dalhousie's response almost seems to ignore Gough's final sentence in which he says that "I cannot feel satisfied in recommending it", as the Governor General strongly asserted that "As long as there is a shot or a shell in the Indian arsenals, or a finger left that can pull a trigger, I will never desist from operations at Mooltan [Multan], until the place is taken, and the leader and his force ground if possible into powders."[7]

Although a dramatic statement, Dalhousie's declaration did rather miss the point of what Gough was saying. Given the tone of the letter one wonders if Dalhousie had been led to believe that this was what Gough believed he wanted to do. It is also perhaps an attempt to illustrate his resolution for the fight, despite his reluctance to allow full preparations for an army to be made ready. Indeed Dalhousie might have been slightly upset by Gough's pointed remark in the same letter that it, "would have been very different indeed had all our preparations been matured." It might be this phrase used by Gough was what elicited such a dramatic statement of defiance from Dalhousie.[8] Yet it would be wrong to conclude that this was the Governor General rejecting the Commander-in-Chief's plan. Indeed, Gough had gone on to comment that he felt that as there was a necessity for taking Multan he should proceed there as soon as possible and take command of the siege in person. The idea Gough now proposed was to take with him what reinforcements he could, which, when added to the troops already engaged and those on their way, would give him a force getting on for 20,000 strong. He could then take Multan before moving on to deal with the other revolts. Yet this did not meet fully with Dalhousie's approval. In response Dalhousie wrote that, "I am in hopes that troops may be forthcoming in sufficient quantities, when all our arrangements are completed, to enable us to undertake military operations in other quarters of the Punjab also, simultaneously with those directed against Mooltan [Multan]."[9] This, however, was more complicated than Dalhousie's letter suggested. Keeping two forces of such a size as would be required for both tasks would be difficult. If raising and maintaining one force of 24,000 was considered an expense that the Indian exchequer could not afford, then at the same time supporting a second force of over 17,000 men would be liable to bankrupt the government of India. Perhaps the simplest answer would have been to direct Whish and his additional forces to recommence the siege and take Multan as soon as possible. In a sense this was what they attempted, but Multan did not fall until 21 January 1849, and even then it surrendered rather than being taken by storming.

However Gough's dilemma over what to do was partly solved by the actions of Sher Singh, who on 9 October left Multan and moved to make a junction with his father Chatar Singh. Necessity now forced Gough to leave Whish and the supporting force from the Bombay Army to take Multan. He would now have to lead an army to watch the junction of father and son and to guard against their movement. This meant that Gough would not be able to gather the force of 24,000 that he had consistently urged was necessary. Yet even this smaller force would be hard to maintain. As he wrote in a letter dated 13 October, "Our commissariat is in a fearful backward state, not a week's supplies at Ferozepore, although since last May I have been both publicly and privately urging the subject." Gough felt forced to move to prevent actions by Sher Singh's combined force, and there had also been a revolt in the Dejarat that meant the situation was threatening to spiral out of control. Despite his having urged preparations they had not been undertaken and it was with an unprepared and insufficiently supported army that Gough would now be forced to move.[10]

7   Rait, *Gough*, Vol. II, p. 169.
8   NAM: 8303–105, Gough Papers, Gough to Dalhousie, 22 September 1848.
9   Rait, *Gough*, Vol. II, p. 169.
10 NAM: 8303–105, Gough Papers, Gough to Archibald Arbuthnot, 13 October 1848.

62

Early Movements: Ramnagar and Sadelupour

The delay in preparations for the coming campaign meant that when finally Gough was given political approval on 5 October he was still at best a month away from taking the field with an army anywhere near the level he had felt was appropriate. Even when he was able to take the field, supply problems were a great difficulty. It can be debated whether these problem were exacerbated by the poor preparations and staff work of Gough and his officers. Gough really had more important strategic matters to contend with, and he should have been able to leave such arrangements as supply and transportation to his staff to deal with. However there is no doubt that the main source of the problems with supply and transportation was the prolonged delay in permission being given for such preparations to be made.

Again it is worth recalling that it was only on 5 October that permission was finally given at a political level.[1] Up to that point Gough had been operating with one hand tied behind his back. This was where the folly of the delay in preparing an army was to really have an impact. Gough, who had urged its creation since May, now had to attempt to create in a month what he had hoped to be able to do in four or five. He still had the problem that many of the troops in the Punjab were not under his direct command. This was altered on 23 October when Gough decided that he needed to exercise authority over all the forces in the Punjab. This presented a slight problem in that he had been instructed by the Governor General to do all he could to facilitate any demands from Currie in Lahore for troops to protect and secure the area. This partly explains the unfortunate decision to leave some of the heavy guns at Lahore for protection of the city. Once again we see political considerations and limitations being imposed upon the commander-in-chief.

We have already seen that, due to the reluctance of the government to commit to the necessary expenditure, there were limited supplies held at Ferozepore the main depot on the frontier. One could turn around and say that preparation of the depot at Ferozepore should have taken place in the intervening years between the two Sikh wars. To an extent this is an appropriate criticism, and the old maxim that one should prepare in peace for what one needs in war rings true in this instance. Yet there were problems in attempting to do this. Firstly, it was widely believed in the Indian government that there would be no need for any such future conflict. In this, the words of Lord Hardinge that there would be no need to raise a gun in anger for a six years, were considered to be accurate. Whilst now appearing absurd, this view was well respected at the time and formed the common opinion. However this had not been Gough's opinion and he had seen a second war coming. Secondly, and the reason the Gough, despite anticipating a second conflict had been unable to do little in preparation, was the great desire for military economy. This was a major problem to any military preparation. The government of India was in a severe financial state. The military was an easy target, particular if one accepted the aforementioned idea that further conflict was unlikely in the near future.

---

1   NAM: 8303–105, Gough Papers, Dalhousie to Gough, 8 October 1848.

In the short term Gough sent Cureton with part of his Cavalry Division, consisting of the 3rd Light Dragoons, the 8th Bengal Native Light Cavalry and the 12th Bengal Irregular Cavalry, supported by three troops of horse artillery, across the Sutlej to keep a watch on the movements of Sher Singh. Initially he was supported by a brigade of infantry commanded by Brigadier Godby and consisting of the 2nd Bengal Europeans, and the 31st and 70th Native Infantry. Two further Native Infantry battalions joined him before long as did the 14th Light Dragoons. Brigadier Colin Campbell, later Lord Clyde, was despatched from Lahore to join Cureton but, due to a combination of insufficient transport and the nervousness that existed at Lahore, he left his European battalion, the 53rd Foot, at Lahore and marched with just two native battalions. Cureton would also be joined by one light field battery. By despatching Cureton, Gough had placed a force in the vicinity that would prevent Sher Singh from moving as he pleased. Yet at the same time he had made it clear that he hoped that they would not engage with the enemy until a stronger force had been established.[2]

This hope for a delay can be interpreted either as Gough's desire to be in command personally when battle was joined, thus ensuring that the credit for any victory fell to him, or as caution born of his previous battles with the Sikhs. The latter is perhaps the more accurate reading, particularly as Gough had been urging since May that he would only countenance fighting the Sikhs with a strong force. This caution would have implications for the early engagements with the Sikh fought by his subordinates. There were however still voices calling for immediate action. Much of this came from people either within the army or the press who were unaware, or unable to appreciate the full magnitude, of the difficulties that Gough was working under. The press had a fairly poor opinion of Gough anyway and thus their criticism at Gough's inaction was hardly surprising. It is perhaps the criticism from within the army that is more interesting.

One such example is found in the correspondence of Lieutenant, later Colonel, Daniel George Robinson of the Bengal Engineers. Robinson was a rather irascible character, whose correspondence contains continual references to Daniel O'Connell, the lawyer and Irish Nationalist. On his better days Robinson carelessly says of him, "What a pity Dan O'Connell was not hung whilst they were about it." On his more irascible days "Why don't some of the Tipperary Gentry shoot O'Connell as their greatest pest instead of some of their good landlords." Whilst the view might have been commonly held by many, it is symptomatic of the way in which Robinson wrote of people in general. It also points to a strong dislike of the Irish, and perhaps as a consequence of Gough. Robinson was not reticent in making his opinion of senior officers known. For example he described Robert Napier, arguably one of the finest soldiers in the Indian Army and already a rising star as, "wanting in dash and so amiable that he always gives into the advice of others."[3]

There is therefore something of a question mark over Robinson's judgement, yet his comments on Gough are interesting. With respect to Gough's decision to delay action until he arrived personally, Robinson comments that:

About the 8th of this month [November] one of the best officers in the Queen's service Brigadier Cureton arrived within one march of Ramnuggar on the Chenab with 6 regiments of Cavalry two of which were H.M, 1 H.M infantry, 3 N.I infantry and 24 guns. Opposed to them Chutter Singh's son Shere Singh with 10 guns and 6,000 or say 10,000 rabble. Cureton was for immediately smashing him but he received orders from 'bate 'em and pound 'em'

---

2   Rait, *Gough*, Vol. II, p. 177. Rait quotes from a letter in the Gough Papers, which appears to now be missing, to Brigadier General Colin Campbell dated 11 November 1848.

3   Thomas, R. N. W. (ed.) 'Daniel George Robinson: Letters from India 1845–1849'in Guy, Alan (ed.) *Military Miscellany I : Manuscripts from the Seven Years War, the First and Second Sikh Wars, and the First World War* (Stroud: Sutton Publishing for the Army Records Society, 1996), pp. 75 and 174.

[Gough] one of the least scientific officers of H.M. service not to attack him until he, Lord Gough, should arrive, 14 or 15 days later. In India people are governed by appearances and appearances are that we are afraid and so people think. The fact being that Gough was afraid that anyone else should have the honour of bating and pounding the 'Saikhs' as he calls them. [...] However the C in C seems determined to have a good fight of it and so gives the enemy lots of time and has assembled a most overwhelming army for the purpose.[4]

Robinson's comments, although wide of the mark in some respects, are an interesting interpretation of Gough's actions. Robinson cannot have been alone in his opinions, although he does perhaps overestimate Cureton's strength and underestimates the quality of Sher Singh's force. Robinson was of course interpreting events as they happened rather than looking back with the benefit of hindsight. The use of the nickname 'bate 'em and pound 'em' appears to be of Robinson's own creation. Yet, given the way in which it is phrased, one gets the impression that it is something he has heard Gough say. It is true that Gough had given orders to both Cureton and Campbell's force, moving separately for a time, not to engage the enemy unless they had no choice. Whilst one might suspect ulterior motives there was also a degree of sense. With so many British detachments spread throughout the Punjab, Gough did not want to risk them being defeated one by one before he could arrive.

Any British defeat, no matter the numbers involved, was likely to lead to further uprisings. It has also been argued that Gough hoped he could entice Sher Singh to cross the Chenab and then engage him in combat when his back was against the river. This was no doubt motivated by his memories of Sobraon. If Gough personally felt the need for a sort of redemption by decisively beating the Sikhs, it would be understandable. However it is unlikely that he was motivated by such thoughts. It was caution born of experience that was likely the reason for his order, not an attempt at personal aggrandisement. Later on in his account, Robinson turned his fire towards Dalhousie and the latter's direction to Gough that he was not to advance until he received the direct permission of the governor general:

It seems the fashion nowadays for the Governor-General be he a military man or not to control the movements of the army when a daily increasing enemy is in the field. In consequence of these instructions, repeated instructions I should say, the whole of the Punjab is now in rebellion and the opposing army has more than trebled in numbers and guns.[5]

Dalhousie, like Hardinge before him, was in a difficult position. There was a fine line between being ultimately responsible for the actions of the military and interference with the command of the army.

It is also worth noting that Dalhousie's interference went as far as preventing Gough from crossing the Chenab River without Dalhousie's approval. The only caveat to this was that Gough had the authority to attack Sher Singh in his position just across the Chenab at Ramnagar. This was unfortunate in that it meant that if Gough felt the necessity to attack the enemy he had only one point at which he could do it without waiting for further authority from the governor general. This again tied Gough's hands, and the action at Ramnagar can be viewed as Gough's attempt to do something to prevent disillusion amongst both his own men and also the local population. Inactivity in the face of the enemy was particularly dangerous in India. The fact that the British did not move could readily be interpreted as fear or weakness, with obvious consequences for British

---

4   Thomas, 'Daniel George Robinson', p. 182.
5   Thomas, 'Daniel George Robinson', p. 189.

support amongst the local population. Dalhousie had by this time moved to Amballa, but this was still over 200 miles from where Gough was forming his army. It made communication easier than had he been in Calcutta or Delhi, but at best, communications were still going to take several days. Thus Gough's movement was almost impossible until 17 December when Gough received new orders which freed him from reference to the governor generall.

Any frustration that Gough felt at this time can be easily understood. He was, not for the first time, being asked to conduct operations in the face of the enemy with one hand tied behind his back. The lack of preparation was down to political interference, and now the same political interference was preventing him from fighting the conflict the way he wished. The current situation was perhaps in many ways worse than that which he had to endure during the first conflict. At least then the governor general, Hardinge, had been present with the army most of the time, and had been doing his best to help prepare the army in a practical manner. Dalhousie was now physically detached but attempting to control the course of events. It was a position that was untenable, and the decision of 17 December to free Gough's hands was an inevitable, but unfortunately delayed, decision.

Yet before the decision of 17 December Gough had already exercised the authority he had to attack Sher Singh in the position that he held just across the Chenab River. Gough wanted to move his men across the river to attack Sher Singh and to force him to withdraw to the north, thus enabling Gough to more securely build up his army, secure his lines of communication, and to be active whilst awaiting the fall of Multan and the expected reinforcements that would bring to his army. Gough reached Ferozepore on 6 November and had crossed the Sutlej on his way into the Punjab on 9 November. On his arrival at Ferozepore he received the disappointing news from Peshawar that a force of over 7,000 men had deserted to the Sikh cause. From Gough's own account, the six regiments of Sikh infantry that this included were some of the best and most disciplined the army had. The men had remained loyal for as long as they had due to the influence of Major George Lawrence who was now taken prisoner. This force joined with Chatar Singh.

Although Lawrence is widely considered to have done good work, and was later thanked by both Houses of Parliament and the Governor General for his efforts, Gough had a slightly less charitable, and perhaps more accurate view of what Lawrence had done.

> That force consisted of six regiments of well-disciplined Sikh Infantry, about 1,000 Cavalry, and thirty guns, which, although in Major Lawrence's possession for months (all which time he must have known what would be the finale) he never attempted to render unserviceable. Such is the infatuation of every man who gets into the Political Department, but which I have thrown overboard, so much so as to order my officers in advance to send those attached to them, in irons, back to Lahore, if they interfere with my military operations. I had enough of interference before and felt the ill effects of it.[6]

This was perhaps a wider representation of his frustration with political interference, and of his low opinion of the political officers in general. There is however a legitimate point in terms of now such operations were conducted. Gough was no doubt expressing a fair point when he wrote of the almost inevitable defection of such troops. One can appreciate Gough's disappointment that the guns had not been put out of action but allowed to fall into the hands of the enemy who would now use them against him.

Although Gough did not mention it in the letter, one wonders if he was in his own mind comparing the actions of Lawrence with those of an American officer in Sikh service, Colonel

---

6   NAM: 8303–105, Gough Papers, Gough to George Gough, 16 November 1848.

Canora, in August of that year.[7] When Chatar Singh rebelled Canora, who had been commanding the horse artillery, refused to hand over the guns to him, stating that his loyalty was to Duleep Singh and the official government. Canora had died in the act of attempting to prevent the guns from being captured. Gough no doubt felt that Lawrence should have acted similarly. This was unfair on Lawrence but it is easy to understand Gough's frustration with the influence that others – Dalhousie, Currie, Edwardes, Lawrence and all the other 'political officers' – were having upon his effort to prepare an army and fight the Sikhs. By 13 November Gough had reached Lahore where he had picked up further reinforcements. However he found a still very nervous Sir Frederick Currie who was reluctant to allow much of the garrison to move. As previously mentioned, Gough had been requested by the Governor General to comply with all Currie's request for troops. One unfortunate consequence of this was that Gough decided to allow Currie to retain at Lahore a number of heavy guns. These would have proved very useful to Gough in a major battle with the Sikhs, but he allowed himself to be persuaded by Currie that they were vital to the defence of Lahore.

It was partly due to the news from Peshawar in early November that Gough decided to cross the river and attack Sher Singh. Yet even now he was showing caution, firstly due to the fact that his army was incomplete, secondly because he wanted to wait for the reinforcements from Multan, and thirdly because he was concerned as to whether or not he was overstepping his authority from the governor general. In regards to the last point, he had largely decided that he would if necessary ignore Dalhousie's order and later claim military necessity if the decision was criticised.[8]

Gough moved from Ferozepore with six battalions of infantry, two of which were European; a light field battery; six heavy siege guns, pulled by elephants; a reserve company of artillery, and a pontoon company to facilitate the crossing of the river. This would combine with Cureton's force and would also be joined by another infantry brigade, a brigade of irregular cavalry, two additional regiments of irregular cavalry, and a siege train of heavy guns. It would mean that whilst the force he would bring together would not reach the numbers he had previously hoped for he would be getting close to the 20,000 mark that he had envisaged. Movement of troops through the country was difficult. Not only were there the logistical problem but there were any number robbers, bandits, and disaffected individuals sometimes called Badmashes (which freely translates as scoundrel) who would attack any vulnerable looking unit. Baggage units were particularly targeted and as a consequence the poor state of supply deteriorated further. Often the target of the bandits was the pack animals themselves rather than what they were carrying. Such groups had no affiliation to those in revolt, nor were they an outpouring of anti-British sentiment. They were simply criminal gangs. Although they made things difficult for the British as they moved forward they were not supporting the Sikh revolt. The main enemy lay ahead of the British.

Gough's plan was to catch Sher Singh with his back to the river, hopefully forcing him to lose or abandon his guns. Gough then planned a flanking movement by Cuerton's cavalry and Campbell's infantry to cut the route to Wazirabad. Here he would be able to force a final confrontation, and would also be able to cut off any further support from the north or from Afghanistan. The plan was sound in theory. It would ask a lot of his cavalry, however they were the only force he had capable of doing what he planned. Also, given the supply situation, they were the best suited to the task. His problem would be that the rest of his army moving in support would only be able to move slowly

---

7   Little is known of Colonel Canora, and historians differ over their opinions of him. Bobby Singh Bansal in his book *Remnants of the Sikh Empire: Historical Monuments in India and Pakistan* (New Delhi: Hay House Publishers India, 2015) even questions if he was actually American and refers to him as an Irish man. His tomb can be found at Haripur in modern day Pakistan. The small monument of stones erected by Major James Abbott lists his name as John Francis Canora.

8   NAM: 8303–105, Gough Papers, Gough to Campbell, 15 November 1848.

due to the poor transportation situation. In this he was perhaps being overly optimistic. The Sikh force command by Sher Singh demonstrated great mobility, and whilst Cureton's cavalry would no doubt have been able to undertake their part of the plan, Gough's force might have been too slow to catch up.

However the plan was dependent upon no further wasting of resources, manpower, or indeed time. Unfortunately Gough could only control these factors to a very limited extent. To the acting Brigadier General Colin Campbell, Gough explained his plan in a little more detail. There were still some Sikhs on the wrong side of the Chenab and Gough hoped that Campbell would be able to clear them and score an easy victory. He was now of the opinion that Sher Singh had no intention of crossing the Chenab and that a crossing would have to be forced. Campbell was then told, "When you effect this, if you think you can without risk, I would then wish you to make a flank movement, without hurrying the men, upon Wuzzeerabad [Wazirabad]."[9]

Due to the fact that he hoped to engage with the enemy, Gough left Lahore after only three days, crossing the River Ravi on that same day, 16 November. Yet Gough was still unsure exactly what purpose he was acting for. Indeed he was still unsure whether a full war had now been declared by Dalhousie. On 15 November in his letter to Colin Campbell Gough confessed that, "I do not know whether we are at peace or war, or who it is we are fighting for." This was unlikely to have filled Campbell with much confidence: even the Commander-in-Chief did not know what was happening. However it was a reflection of the confusion and lack of political decisiveness on the part of Dalhousie that illustrate the difficulty under which Gough was operating.[10] In fairness, Dalhousie was in a difficult positon but it can be argued that he took too long in sanctioning the preparation for action, and in giving his commander-in-chief clear guidance as to the aims of the conflict. Dalhousie, some days after Gough had left Lahore, finally sent through the decision that the war was now against the Durbar, the Sikh Government, and the rebels and not, as it had been considered up until now, in support of the former against the latter.

---

9   NAM: 8303–105, Gough Papers, Gough to Campbell, 15 November 1848.
10   NAM: 8303–105, Gough Papers, Gough to Campbell, 15 November 1848.

63

The Action at Ramnagar

Gough made good progress in his push forward and by 21 November had joined the army on the banks of the Chenab less than eight miles from where Sher Singh was believed to be camped. Gough now had a considerable force under his command. It still lacked the majority of its heavy artillery, which was slowly making its way up country, but he had a full cavalry division commanded by Cureton. Cureton was considered one of the finest cavalry commanders in the British army and was probably the most able of Gough's subordinate commanders. Despite Lieutenant Robinson's aforementioned criticism of Gough's handling of Cureton, he had in fact placed great confidence in him and given Cureton the most difficult part of his battle plan to undertake. Gough had confidence in both Cureton and his division.

The Cavalry Division consisted of the 1st Brigade commanded by Brigadier White formed of the 3rd and 14th Light Dragoons and the 5th and 8th Native Light Cavalry, and the 2nd Brigade commanded by Brigadier Pope formed of the 9th Lancers and the 1st and 6th Native Light Cavalry. Gough had two infantry divisions one consisting of two brigades the other of three. Major General Gilbert's division consisted of the 1st Brigade commanded by Brigadier Armine Mountain containing the 29th Foot and the 30th and 56th Native Infantry and the 2nd Brigade commanded by Brigadier Godby and containing the 2nd Bengal European Regiment and the 31st and 70th Native Infantry. The other division was commanded by Major General Thackwell, who had commanded the cavalry in the first war but had been given an infantry command to accommodate the previously mentioned 'desire' to have Cureton command the cavalry. Thackwell's division consisted of the 1st Brigade commanded by Brigadier Pennycuick contained the 24th Foot and the 25th and 45th Native Infantry, the 2nd Brigade commanded by Brigadier Hoggan containing the 51st Foot and the 6th and 36th Native infantry, and finally the 3rd Brigade commanded by Brigadier Penny comprised entirely of native infantry, namely the 15th, 20th, and 69th. The artillery commanded by Brigadier Tennant consisted of six troops of horse artillery, three field batteries and two batteries of heavy artillery.

Although the majority of the Sikhs had crossed back over the Chenab there were still some outposts on Gough's side of the river. Gough's plan was to take these outposts and then cross the Chenab and form a camp on the banks of the river. To enable this he ordered Cureton to advance on the night of 21 November with a force consisting of the Cavalry Division and horse artillery, and a brigade of infantry and one field artillery battery commanded by Campbell. The intention was to attack the outposts and then take the village of Ramnagar which was about two miles from the river.

Early on in the movement, the difficult nature of the terrain became apparent with many of the guns having to be manhandled through the soft sand. This understandably became more of a problem the closer they got to the river bank. In attempting to attack the enemy, a gun was lost as it became stuck in the soft sand. Those who tried to rescue it came under fire and had to spike the gun and abandon it. Brigadier White's cavalry brigade initiated a charge which forced many

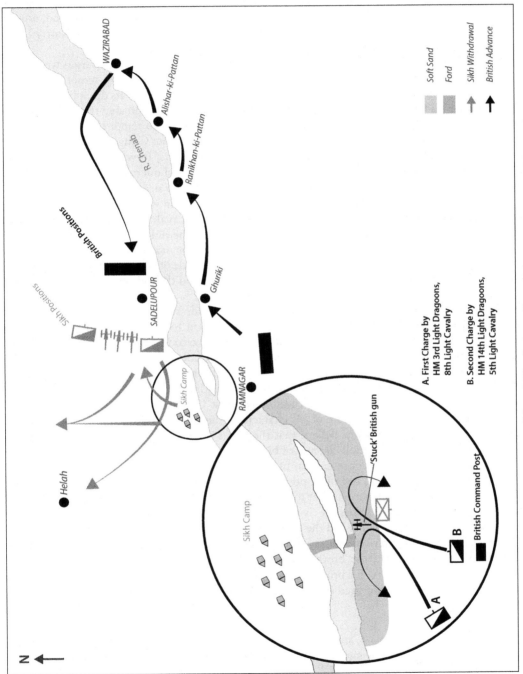

Map 13 The Action at Ramnagar.

of the Sikhs to withdraw. The problem was that they continued to fire from concealed positions. The 3rd Light Dragoons, for example, had success in driving away the Sikhs and managed to clear them from their camp. However they came under heavy fire. Although the fire did little damage it did force the cavalry to withdraw. What had been a greater problem was the soft sand, almost like quicksand, in which they had lost 17 horses. Although now supported by the 8th Native Light Cavalry, it was clear that remaining in the position they were was of little value.

Once the cavalry withdrew the Sikhs started to advance again. Two further charges were made and each time the Sikhs withdrew. It was clear that the Sikhs were trying to tempt the cavalry into an indiscretion and to charge too far. At this time the cavalry retained its discipline and good order. However on the left of the British position some Sikh cavalry had crossed the river and were threatening the British position. Again this was clearly an attempt to tempt the British into an injudicious and uncontrolled charge. To a degree it worked this time. Gough ordered Lieutenant Colonel William Havelock, commanding the 14th Light Dragoons, forward to clear the enemy from the left. Exactly what happened next has been questioned and queried for many years since. Before going any further in an attempt to say what did happen it is necessary to clarify what had not happened up to this point. Gough had not, as Colonel Malleson would write some years later, "joined and placed himself at the head of the advanced party of cavalry, unknown to the majority of his staff."[1] Gough was present and certainly gave orders yet he did not assume command and certainly he left command of the cavalry to Cureton. Indeed for much of the battle Gough was either observing from a house some distance from the field of battle or was on the right flank trying to help extricate the guns that had become stuck in the sand. So the notion of him taking direct command of the cavalry is false.[2]

Malleson also made the statement that the Sikhs were withdrawing and that there was no need to engage them in combat. Malleson argues that the decision to engage the Sikhs was due to Gough's fiery temper and his desire to 'charge at every enemy he could see'. This is not only a rather unfair stereotype of Gough but also ignores the fact that the enemy had indeed moved across the river to threaten Gough's left. One can argue the fact that this might have occurred simply because of Gough's attempts to clear the Sikh position. However it did happen and Gough needed to do something about it.[3] Many of the later accusations against Gough for the debacle that followed were based upon the perceived nature of his character rather than his actual actions. Gough did briefly, and indeed understandably, believe that the Sikhs might be attempting to cross in force. Given that Gough only had a small element of his army at his direct disposal, one can understand why this might have been an ever present fear in Gough's mind and why momentarily it came to the surface. Indeed had Sher Singh been in a position to launch such a movement it would have been an effective counter to Gough actions. Yet to what end could it have been used? Sher Singh had no desire to launch a major strike across the river at that time. He, in many ways similar to Gough, was waiting for further reinforcements and the opportunity to collect together a large army.

If there was impetuosity in what happened next it was unlikely that it was that of the Commander-in-Chief. William Havelock, the brother of Henry Havelock, had a reputation as a brave but impetuous leader of cavalry. As his brother later pointed out, "It was natural that an old peninsular officer, who had not seen a shot fired since Waterloo, should desire to blood the noses of his young

1   Malleson, Bruce, *Decisive Battles of India*, (London: W. H. Allen & Co, 1883), p. 357. Malleson seems to have taken the story from Captain John Henry Lawrence-Archer's *Commentaries on the Punjab, 1848–9*, (London: W. H. Allen & Co, 1878), p. 9. Neither was present at the time and neither gives any source for the story.

2   Rait, *Gough*, Vol. II, pp. 184–185. Both Sir Frederick Haines and Sir Charles Gough, both of whom were present, denied the claim and gave signed statements to Rait to that end.

3   Malleson, *Decisive Battles of India*, p. 358.

dragoons."[4] To such a man the orders given by Gough were unfortunate. Gough had told him to clear the enemy from the left and "If you see a favourable opportunity of charging, charge." In and of themselves the orders were neither impetuous nor foolish. Indeed they were an attempt to allow Havelock to exploit any opportunity he felt there was. Gough was no doubt recalling the excellent work done by his European cavalry, particularly the 3rd Light Dragoons, during the first war. The problem was not the orders but the way in which Havelock enacted them. He not only cleared the left, but carried on charging. Indeed he continued to charge across the river into a line of Sikh infantry, cavalry and artillery. In later correspondence Gough would somewhat charitably claim that this was because Havelock had lost the direction of the enemy. It is perhaps more accurate to say that the cavalry had the 'scent of blood' in their nostrils and continued to charge at anything they could see.

Cureton, seeing what was unfolding, charged forward with his escort of 5th Native Light Cavalry, to warn Havelock and call him back. However Cureton had barely moved forward when he was shot through the heart and killed. Gough was still some distance from the incident, on the other side of the battlefield where the guns of the horse artillery had become stuck in the soft sand, but also observed what was going on. He ordered Major Tucker to ride forward at all speed to recall Havelock. However such was the distance that Tucker could not reach him in time.[5]

The 14th Light Dragoons were finally extricated from their precarious position, with the support of the 5th Native Light Cavalry. The result was 50 dead including Havelock himself. It had been an unnecessary loss and credit has to go to Gough for not compounding the error by committing further troops. Indeed during the engagement he received a request from Campbell to be allowed to bring his infantry brigade to support the cavalry. Such a move whilst an understandable reaction would likely have resulted in more casualties in an uncontrolled battle. Gough, and Robert Rait on his behalf, would later claim that Gough had found out what he wanted to know and that in actual fact the entire movement had been a reconnaissance in force. To some degree this was correct but it does rather gloss over the fact that Gough, not for the first or last time, had not exercised effective control of the situation. Again this comes down to poor staff work, a lack of defined and precise written orders, and a lack of an overall plan. If the expedition was a reconnaissance in force it was not handled particularly well and the cavalry should have been employed along a far wider front. The horse artillery should have been better organised against the Sikh outposts, and should have been made aware of the nature of the terrain. Exactly what part Campbell's infantry were meant to play in such a reconnaissance is also unclear. Presumably rather than taking part in the reconnaissance they were there to provide infantry support if required, but this point is not entirely clear.

Gough had initially tried to take a hands-off approach and had acted merely as an observer, allowing Cureton to take the lead. To his son he wrote, "I intended having as little to do with the reconnaissance at Ramnuggur [Ramnagar] as you. I was upon a high summer house of Runjit Singh, which overlooked the plains and the river banks, three miles from the latter. Cureton went on with a portion of the Cavalry." Gough then went on to explain that he had left this position and become involved when he had heard that the guns had become stuck in the soft sand, on the right of his position. "It was then and not till then that I went down to see if it could be extricated."[6] It was only later that he met Cureton and according to Gough's account he was with him when the Sikh cavalry appeared on the left. Also according to Gough's account it was Havelock who asked Cureton, not Gough, for permission to charge. This is slightly at variance with other accounts

---

4   Marsham, John Clark, *The Memoirs of Major General Sir Henry Havelock* (London: Longman, Green, Longman & Roberts, 1860), p. 176.
5   NAM: 8303–105, Gough Papers, Gough to George Gough, 18 March 1849.
6   NAM: 8303–105, Gough Papers, Gough to George Gough, 18 March 1848.

which state that Gough ordered Havelock to attack on becoming aware of this Sikh force. The difference is minor but it does suggest that in his new position Gough might not have been as aware of what was going on across the field of battle as he would have been had he remained in his previous vantage point. For what followed Gough said that he was 'astonished':

> Why Havelock charged where he did, no human being can now tell. I myself believe he considered the Guns at this side of the river, and was determined to try and take them. I knew the greater portion were on the other side, because I actually went within 200 yards of the river, making my staff stay behind, not to draw the Enemy's fire upon me – or on them.[7]

Given that Gough had previously talked of his desire to take as many Sikh guns as he could before a major battle, this might have been Gough making an attempt to excuse Havelock with a logic that was likely missing from the cavalry commander thinking.

It is far more likely that it was simply a reckless charge that had fatal consequences. It was not the first time British cavalry had acted in such a way and would not be the last. This might also have been an attempt by Gough to 'save' the reputations of both Havelock and Cureton. Of the latter Gough remarked "I am sure Cureton was as much surprised as I was to have seen the career of the 14th, and it must have puzzled him to guess what object was aimed at."[8] Indeed Robert Rait has argued that the glowing references to both of the deceased soldiers that Gough made in his despatches was interpreted by his critics, most notably Malleson, as an admission of responsibility. Of Cureton Gough remarked, "A better or a braver soldier never fell in his country's service." His praise of Havelock was somewhat muted, saying that "he charged into a gole [narrow valley] of the enemy, and has not since been seen, regretted by every soldier who witnessed his noble daring."[9]

The losses were not particularly high in the great scheme of things. For all units involved the deaths totalled 26 and the wounded 59. This total of 85 is not particularly high and when one considers that around 50 of the casualties were as a consequence of the foolhardy charge led by Havelock, the operation could be argued to have otherwise been successful. Exact numbers of Sikh casualties are unclear but they were likely similar in number to those suffered by the British. The fact that the Sikhs had been driven from the south side of the river can often be lost in the controversy that surrounds the conduct of the battle. Perhaps a greater loss in terms of the future conduct of the campaign was the death of Cureton. Gough had lost perhaps the best of his commanders in a rather needless action. He was replaced as commander of the cavalry division by Thackwell. This was a more than adequate replacement, which also allowed Colin Campbell to assume the command of Thackwell's old division. Yet it had robbed Gough of one of a handful of experienced and reliable senior officers present with the army.

Yet in one sense Gough had achieved what he wanted. The Sikhs were cleared from the south side of the river, and he had now established a forward camp near the river and could arrange to bring up his army and cross the river in force. The aim now was to bring up the rest of the army and then cross the Chenab. The latter was easier said than done and Gough perhaps did not fully appreciate the difficult of such a move. Perhaps it would be fairer to say that given his lack of ability, and one might even say interest, in logistical matters, Gough could not grasp the difficulties involved in crossing such a river, even if appropriate places to ford could be found. He could understand the basic requirements of a river crossing but was unable to understand the full implications of putting this into practice. It would be too extreme to say that Gough was a general who pointed to

---

7   NAM: 8303–105, Gough Papers, Gough to George Gough, 18 March 1848.
8   NAM: 8303–105, Gough Papers, Gough to George Gough, 18 March 1848.
9   Rait, *Gough*, Vol. II, p. 188.

something and expected it done, but there is certainly an element of this tendency. It is because of this inability or unwillingness to deal with the minutia of logistical arrangements that it was all the more unfortunate that Gough was not better served by his staff. A good staff system would have freed Gough from such responsibilities.

The army suffered from the shortcoming not only of staff work but from the delayed preparations for the conflict. As the army gathered near the Chenab there were found to be many shortages that ranged from a lack of blankets, greatcoats, and ammunition, to more basic requirements for food for men and horses. The latter could be partially solved by scavenging from the local area. However Gough was reluctant to do this. As the inhabitants were largely Muslim they had no great love for the Sikhs and indeed needed little prompting to be openly hostile to them. By default they looked favourably upon the British if only because they would rid them of the Sikhs. Yet this favourable inclination would not last long if they were robbed of their animals and livelihoods by a hungry army.

One can make mitigation in terms of the poor state of supply due to the failure of Dalhousie to allow Gough to take proper preparations. Also, one must question whether it was really the job of the commander-in-chief of an army in the field to be undertaking such logistical matters himself. The fact was that this should have been organised by his staff officers. It was not for the Commander-in-Chief to personally order up supplies and make sure they were in position. This was the responsibility of the adjutant general, who acted almost as a chief of staff, and the quarter-master general. In short, Gough's responsibility was to make sure that the preparations were made, not to make them himself.

64

The Action at Sadelupour

On 26 November Gough wrote that:

> I am now making my combinations for a flank movement, passing the river several miles above the enemy's position, and turning it; but the river is so difficult and my information so defective, whilst the Enemy with his numerous Irregulars, both Cavalry and Infantry, watch everything like a Ford, that I shall have to await the arrival of some heavy guns (which I expect the day after to-morrow), in order to clear the opposite bank where the detached Force is to cross.[1]

The strategy was sound, indeed one may even say adventurous by Gough's standards. If put into practice and correctly supported, it had the ability to place the Sikhs in a very poor position and enable Gough to attack them from a strong position. The problem was that crossing the river and coordinating such an attack was not the simple task that the above statement may make one believe.[2]

It can also be argued that Gough made the wrong decision in deciding to cross the Chenab at this stage and that he would have been better served by remaining where he was for the time being. This would have allowed him to maintain a watch over Sher Singh's movements, whilst supporting the siege of Multan. In short if Sher Singh was to move Gough should move. His main purpose was to keep Sher Singh away from the siege of Multan. Once Multan fell, Gough would receive considerable reinforcements for his field army and a major blow would have been dealt to the Sikh cause. Thus when Multan fell Gough would have been in a better state of preparation with a force stronger and in better shape to tackle the main Sikh army. This was sound in theory but it ignored the circumstances under which Gough was now acting. By crossing the Chenab he would reduce the possibility of the Sikhs raiding into the relatively wealthy territory south of the river. Gough was also anxious to act before Chatar Singh joined with Sher Singh and created a more formidable army. If Gough could prevent this by crossing the Chenab and defeating Sher Singh he would shorten the war, for Sher Singh's force was more formidable than that of his father. If Gough could beat Sher Singh then even if Chatar Singh continued the fight he would be in a far weaker position from which to do so. There was also the fear that Sher Singh would move across country to join his father who was at present besieging Attock. This would require Gough to move further from his main source of supply than would be convenient. It would also require greater preparations and take far longer to achieve. Crossing the river would also interfere with Sikh preparations and in particular their supply system.

---

1   NAM: 8303–105, Gough Papers, Gough to Fitzroy Somerset, 26 November 1848.
2   A contemporary critic of Gough's actions was Henry Marion Durand, later a major general and Knight of the realm. Durand submitted articles for the *Calcutta Review*, and called the movement across the Chenab, "untimely, objectless, and fruitless". See also Malleson, *Decisive Battles of India*, p. 359.

Ever the critic of Gough, Malleson claimed that Gough's desire was simply "to seek the enemy wherever he could be found, attack him and beat him [...] larger aims than this lay outside the range of his mental vision."[3] It is easy to believe this in that it fits the presumed character of Gough. It is rather amusing that the same author who criticises Gough for delaying in his movement to the frontier now criticises him for moving too quickly. Yet Gough's decision to cross the Chenab was motivated by larger aims, as mentioned above. If Gough had stayed where he was and the rebellion had spread, or the two Sikh armies had joined together, supported by Afghan forces crossing into Sikh territory, Gough would have been criticised for not moving sooner. Gough could not win either way. If he stayed where he was he would be accused of inactivity and neglect, accusations which had already been made against him since the start of the conflict. By instead crossing the Chenab as he did, he was accused of recklessness. Malleson went further and said that "A really great commander would have been content that they should remain there, eating up their scanty supplies." In making this comment Malleson was guilty of doing what he accused Gough of in not appreciating the 'larger aims'. To have remained where he was could well have worked out as Malleson hoped, but Gough could not be sure of this. If Sher Singh attempted further action, if Chatar Singh moved quickly, or if further outbreaks of revolt occurred, Gough would be forced to react to events rather than being proactive.[4]

Gough's decision to cross the river was not in and of itself a poor decision. In fact it had much to commend itself. Gough was anxious to get at the enemy, partly in the hope of ending the war quickly but also in the light of the possibility of further revolts, possibly in British territory, if he were perceived to be delaying out of fear. The problem was the way in which he tried to cross the river. It was sound in theory but in practice there was too much that could go wrong. The most natural movement, directly across the Chenab, was out of the question. As had already been seen, the river bank with its very soft sand would make crossing extremely difficult if not to say dangerous. The difficulty of the crossing was added to by the positioning of entrenched Sikh guns on the other side of the river. Thus any attempt to cross the river would be slow due to the nature of the terrain and would have to be undertaken under heavy fire.

The way in which Gough reached his decision to cross the river can in one sense be criticised because he did so without a full consultation with his officers. As he wrote in a letter to his son, "I have no councils of war, but, having made up my mind, I clearly explain my views, and ask each if he understands them, giving each then a written statement."[5] It would be understandable if Gough had become disillusioned with councils of war from his experiences in the first conflict, but it would perhaps have been wise to seek the opinions of his senior commanders. It was perhaps this lack of consultation that caused some of the future resentment from his subordinates. The problem was that there were so many wider considerations that went into the Commander-in-Chief's decision to cross the Chenab that it would not have been possible or prudent for him to inform his officers of. It was therefore necessary for Gough to make a decision and present his officers with that decision.

There were known to be several crossing points further up the river from Ramnagar. The nearest at Ghuriki, roughly eight miles away, was not considered practical as it was believed to be well defended. At the next crossing after that, some 13 miles at Runiki, there were two possible crossing points close together. After that the nearest was at Wazirabad about 20 miles from Gough's present position. After the war the brother of Joseph Thackwell, Mr Edward Thackwell, wrote an account of the river crossing that sought to defend his brother.[6] In so doing he claimed that Gough had

3   Malleson, *Decisive Battles of India*, p. 360.
4   Malleson, *Decisive Battles of India*, p. 359.
5   NAM: 8303–105, Gough Papers, Gough to George Gough, 30 November 1848.
6   Thackwell, Edward, J *Narrative of the Second Seikh War*, in 1848–49 (London: Richard Bentley, 1851).

not undertaken a reconnaissance of the various river crossings before making his plan. This point was later used by Malleson and others to lay the blame at Gough's door. This is erroneous as on 18 November Gough ordered Colin Campbell to prepare a report on the various river crossings. This was undertaken by Lieutenant William Hodson, better known as Hodson of Hodson's Horse. On his arrival Gough ordered that a further report and reconnaissance be undertaken by the Quartermaster General, Lieutenant Colonel William Garden. Before a flanking column was eventually despatched on 30 November, there had therefore been two detailed investigations of the crossing points and any suggestions that Gough had failed to consider the nature of these points is incorrect.[7]

There was, however, a problem with the nature of the Chenab River itself that does not seem to have been picked up on. The Chenab was in this area very broad. As we have already seen, the sand around the banks of the river was very soft and this was exactly the same for the sand at the bottom of the river. Therefore the river bed was a mixture of shifting sand. Where one day the river might be comfortably fordable at one point, a week or so later it could become all put impractical for that purpose due to the shifting nature of the river bed. This was something that Gough does not seem to have been aware of, and the two reports he had commissioned into the plausibly of using the various crossing points do not appear to have highlighted this problem. Even if it had been known it would not, in and of itself, have been cause to abandon the flanking movement. It would simply have required a reconnaissance immediately before the crossing to ascertain the depth of the river at that time.

Gough gave command of the flanking movement to Major General Joseph Thackwell. Although an experienced commander it was rather a baptism of fire given that he had just moved from commanding an infantry division to commanding the cavalry. That said Thackwell had experience as a cavalry commander having commanding the cavalry during the Afghan campaign of 1838–39 and at Sobraon during the First Anglo-Sikh War. Thackwell's appointment again demonstrates the unfortunate consequences of Ramnagar and the death of Cureton. Thackwell's force consisted of the 3rd Light Dragoons, the 5th and 8th Bengal Light Cavalry, and the 3rd and 12th Bengal Irregular Cavalry. Added to this were Thackwell's old infantry division, now commanded by Campbell, consisting of the 24th Foot and five battalions of native infantry. There were also three horse artillery batteries and two light field batteries accompanying the force and a pontoon train of sappers to support the proposed crossing. To enable the force to move quickly they travelled with only two days' worth of supplies.

The first crossing at Ghuriki was considered impractical not only because it was so well defended but also because investigations had found that the crossing was too narrow to allow a quick crossing. It was also considered to be too close to the camp of Sher Singh, and would therefore not really act as a flanking movement. The two crossing points near Runiki were found to be plausible but both had problems due to the fast flowing nature of the river at that point and the high banks either side of the river that made movement to the river difficult. The depth of the water is recorded as being about four feet deep. The best point for crossing was found to be Wazirabad. Here the water was reported to be only four feet at the deepest point and that this was only for some 20 or 30 yards of the total crossing. The river bed was also said to be hard and firm. This was reported from the point

---

7   Hodson, William, S. R. & Hodson, George, H. *Hodson of Hodson Horse: Twelve Years of a Soldier's Life in India* (London: Kegan Paul, Trench & Co, 1889), pp. 52–53. Hodson also alludes in June 1848, to previous knowledge of the rivers which no doubt assisted him in his survey. A copy of the survey was at the time of Robert Rait's biography of Gough to be found amongst his private papers. It has not survived with the present collection of Gough papers at the National Army Museum. However Rait quotes from this report from Major Tucker to the Quartermaster General (Colonel John Bloomfield Gough) dated 26 November 1848.

of view of allowing men, animals, guns and waggons to cross without worrying about getting stuck in soft sand. However it also meant that the river bed was unlikely to shift and that therefore four feet, about waist or chest height on the average man, was the worst point of the crossing. Indeed Major Tucker's report concluded that Wazirabad was a point that allowed for "crossing without risk of any sort."[8]

It was clear that Wazirabad offered the best possible crossing point. The only problem was that it was over 20 miles from the present British position. Gough ordered that Thackwell's force would march at midnight on 30 November in the direction of Wazirabad. Gough's instructions were to move with the intention of crossing at Wazirabad, but that if when he reached Runiki Thackwell felt that a crossing was possible he was to attempt it. Although issuing him with what Gough called a written statement rather than instructions, he also gave Thackwell discretion to use his own judgement to cross where he thought it would be safest and easiest. This was sensible as Thackwell would be detached from the force and out of communication with Gough, and therefore a certain degree of discretion was appropriate.

Also on 30 November Gough received his heavy artillery. This was a timely arrival and Gough decided to use this to aid his subterfuge by launching an artillery bombardment of the Sikh positions across the river from Ramnagar. This he hoped would engage the Sikhs and convince them of his intention to force his way across the river at Ramnagar. Given their previous encounter with Havelock's force at Ramnagar, it was reasonable to believe that this might aid in convincing the Sikhs. Also the Sikhs' understanding of Gough's character and his previous penchant for frontal attack might help in convincing them that this was his intention. Whether Gough deliberately intended this, or was even aware that this was the reputation he had amongst the Sikhs, is not clear. It was perhaps a happy accident.

Gough then hoped that if Thackwell had managed to make his crossing and was able to descend upon the Sikh base from their side of the river, that Gough would be able to develop the façade of an attack into reality in support of Thackwell. The scheme was sound, although it was perhaps an overly ambitious one. Yet it had every chance of success if properly coordinated and carried out. Here, once again, the problems of staff coordination would be tested. On the eve of Thackwell's march Gough wrote the following letter to his son.

> I attack tomorrow, if my flank will be successful; that is, if it can get across, everything will go well; if, on the contrary, they find the ford impracticable, they will have to go on to Wazirabad and force a passage. If my friends opposite me move in any numbers, one way or the other I shall punish them; but with a treacherous river in my front I cannot prevent their running away. They have all the boats, and, by keeping eight or ten guns at the only ford here, and sending off the rest a couple of days' march ahead, they may say "Catch me who can". For a Sikh Army will march three miles for two any other army can march. However, if they fly, and fly they must, the moral effect will be good, – and the numbers now moving to take service will be likely to return to their homes.[9]

Gough was clearly in positive mood. The weariness of some of his letters in the build up to the campaign and the early movements appears to be gone. Although he had earlier written of a reluctance to go back to war, it was clear, now he was within touching distance of the enemy, that his warrior spirit had been roused. This letter also demonstrated a healthy respect for the Sikhs and suggests that he was fully aware of the potential of the army before him. In particular Gough was

8   Rait, *Gough*, Vol. II, p. 193.
9   NAM: 8303–105, Gough Papers, Gough to George Gough, 30 November 1848.

concerned over the mobility which was a key strength of the Sikhs in the second war. The letter also exhibited his belief, or perhaps hope, that an early defeat of the Sikh army commanded by Sher Singh would shorten the war, return many rebels to their homes, and prevent others from joining the cause.

Thackwell's march was delayed by several hours and did therefore not take place until the early hours of the following day. The problem appears to have been that in the dark Campbell's division was not able to find the rendezvous point. It was about two hours after midnight that the flanking force finally began to march. Whilst Thackwell's cavalry appears to have moved undetected, the level of noise created by Campbell's men, and in particular the camp followers, meant that the movement of the flanking force was known. Whether the Sikhs understood its intention is unclear, and indeed there were many possible reasons for the movement of such a force, given that troop movements were common at this time as the army was being assembled.

The delay caused by Campbell's men being unable to find the rendezvous point meant that it was not until 1100 on 1 December that the flanking force arrived at Runiki. The two crossings nearby were studied for around three hours whilst it was considered whether crossing the river at either point was feasible. At the first crossing there appeared to be some Sikh infantry, but it was doubted that they would be able to oppose the crossing to any great extent. The real problem was that at both points it was considered that the sand was too soft to allow wheeled vehicles to get across. At around 1400 it was decided that they would have to press on towards Wazirabad. At this time Campbell suggested that they returned to Ramnagar concerned as he was about the supply situation, communication with the rear, and the dangers of pressing on towards Wazirabad. Whilst Thackwell listened and appreciated Campbell's concerns, he decided to march on to Wazirabad. Shortly before they had left the main army, Thackwell had received instructions from Patrick Grant, the Adjutant General, that if they could not get across the river and be ready for action at 0100 on 2 December they were to take the extra day. This shows us that Gough and Grant appreciated the difficulty of the crossing, and that they were prepared to allow Thackwell to exercise caution rather than risk a hurried crossing and an army in poor order for the coming battle. It also meant that Thackwell was not overly concerned about the need to press on towards Wazirabad.[10]

The flanking force arrived at Wazirabad at 1700 on 1 December. Boats, about 20 in number, had been seized by the advanced guard and before the end of the day the two fording points had been prepared for the crossing and a ferry had been rigged up about three quarters of a mile from the ford to allow the crossing of the heavier vehicles. Some of the men were crossed that night, and spent an unpleasant evening unsupplied, cold and hungry, and on constant watch against a Sikh attack. The remainder of the force followed on the morning of 2 December, and it was not until 1400 that Thackwell's whole force was across the Chenab. The delay was unfortunate, but perhaps inevitable. It is easy to say with the benefit of hindsight that Thackwell would have been better served by heading straight for Wazirabad. Perhaps it can also be argued that Gough should have made this clearer to Thackwell and not allowed him the choice. Yet at the same time Gough had wisely ordered that Thackwell was not to hurry unduly or take any chances. Gough had, with the benefit of his own experience, warned Thackwell against attacking the Sikhs late in the day. It does appear that if Gough learnt no other lesson from the first war it was not to attack in the failing light unless there was no choice.[11]

Once across the river, Thackwell advanced to within nine miles of where the Sikhs were believed to be camped without encountering any opposition. Thackwell had contacted Gough informing him that they were safety across the river and moving on the Sikh position. In return Gough

10   Rait, *Gough*, Vol. II, pp. 196–197.
11   Rait, *Gough*, Vol. II, p. 197.

replied that "I shall make as great a fuss as possible here to-day, by a cannonade, to keep their guns here, and […] I hope to throw a body to cooperate with your left. Do not hurry your men; bring them and your guns well up in hand, and we are sure of success."[12] One gets the impression that Gough was so far pleased with the way things were going. Although it had taken a little longer than initially expected, Thackwell was safety across the river and moving on the enemy. Gough could now cooperate with him as he moved forward on 3 December and had every hope that they could inflict a serious reverse upon the Sikh army.

For a time Gough's actions seemed to have convinced the enemy that he intended to force the crossing at Ramnagar. All seems to have been going to plan until the first reports of Thackwell's advance started to come in. It does appear that whilst the Sikhs knew that Gough had been moving elements of his force away from Ramnagar, they were not aware of where they had gone. Now realising what was happening, Sher Singh moved his army away from the river to meet Thackwell. Here was the potential for disaster for the British. Although Gough had given Thackwell a sizeable force it was not ideally suited for taking on the main Sikh army. Sher Singh had sent 10,000 men to engage Thackwell. Whilst Thackwell's force was not numerically much weaker there was a strong reliance on cavalry and on native infantry. Indeed Thackwell had only one European battalion, the 24th Foot. Thackwell had by this time reached and secured the ford at Ghuriki and it was here that Gough sent reinforcements, the 9th Lancers, the 14th Light Dragoons, and a brigade of infantry commanded by Brigadier Godby consisting of the 2nd Bengal European Regiment and the 45th and 70th Native Infantry. Gough sent word that Thackwell was to wait the arrival of Godby's reinforcements before attacking. The problem was that the crossing at Ghuriki proved a most difficult one. Indeed it appeared impractical to ford, and boats needed to be secured to enable Godby's men to get across. This inevitably led to further delays and is recorded as being a source of great frustration to Gough.

Thackwell had moved about a mile from Ghuriki to Sadelupour. This was open country and ahead lay three villages. Thackwell sent Campbell forward to secure the villages with his infantry. Thackwell had interpreted Gough's order to await Godby's brigade as a check on his earlier discretionary powers to engage the enemy. He had sent the infantry forward to take the villages as a precaution, and to give advanced notice of any coming Sikh attack. However as Campbell's men advanced, at around 1400 on 3 December, they came under sustained fire from Sikh artillery. The fact that the enemy were so close without being noticed speaks ill of the reconnaissance and intelligence-gathering of Thackwell's force. This is particularly worrying given the large number of mounted men that made up Thackwell's command. Yet they were surprised, and Thackwell took the decision to recall his infantry. This was understandable as a field of sugarcane obscured their line of fire; however it was a source of encouragement to the Sikhs. Seeing the British infantry retreating, the Sikhs advanced as to attack. Sikh cavalry appeared on each flank of the army, and for a moment it appeared that they were attempting to turn the British position. The situation was saved by the excellent deployment of the horse artillery that stopped the Sikh advance. At the same time Thackwell deployed his cavalry on both flanks which checked the Sikh advance. There appears to have been no great desire on the part of the Sikhs to press the attack, although their artillery continued to fire on the British infantry. However, Thackwell ordered the men to lie down and thus they were saved from the worst of the Sikh artillery fire.

Thackwell was now unsure what to do. About an hour after the Sikhs had opened fire on Campbell's men, around 1500, Thackwell received another message from Gough. Gough seems to have realised, after sending his previous message to Thackwell regarding Godby's reserves, that this could be interpreted as overruling his previous discretionary power to him to act on the offensive if he felt a good opportunity arose. Gough had not intended this to be the case, and he wanted Thackwell, an experienced commander, to use his initiative if he felt a good opportunity presented itself. Thus Gough sent a second message telling Thackwell to use his own initiative if he felt it was best. Thackwell had many problems. Firstly, his men had been on the move with little rest or food for almost three days. Secondly, he was unsure of the exact numbers of the enemy ahead of him. He had so far only seen a small portion of what Sher Singh had sent to confront him, although whether Thackwell realised this is open to interpretation. Thirdly, there appears to have been divided opinion amongst his officers as to whether he should attack. The last point has been the subject of much debate and differing accounts have emerged. Thackwell later claimed that whilst he favoured an attack he was only supported in this by Brigadier Pennycuick, commanding officer of the 24th Foot and commanding an infantry brigade as part of Campbell's division. Campbell for his part would later claim that he had twice urged upon Thackwell the need to attack the Sikhs during this time, but that Thackwell rejected his proposals.

Thackwell ultimately decided that an attack was too risky. He would later state that he believed that such an attack went against the spirit of Gough's instructions. To an extent he was correct in this belief. Gough's instructions were somewhat unfortunately delivered. One can understand how Gough, some miles distant from Thackwell and engaged in his own operations, wishing to give Thackwell discretionary powers. Thackwell for his part seemed reluctant to use them, despite his later claims that he wished to attack. He was probably wise to take the course of action he did, as he would have been attacking into the unknown. Whilst the terrain was largely open country his manoeuvring would have been limited by the field of sugar cane. It was also unfortunate that Godby was delayed in getting across with his reinforcements. Had he arrived earlier Thackwell would likely have felt confident in launching an attack.

Gough, however, felt that Thackwell should have attacked and many historians have taken the same view.[13] To launch an attack would have been a great risk, and whilst wars are not won without such risks being taken this was perhaps an unnecessary one. Gough, as usual, refused to criticise Thackwell in public, and in his despatch defended his decision. In private however he was angry that Thackwell had not taken the opportunity to attack, and made his often quoted remark that "I placed the ball at Thackwell's feet, and he would not kick it." Gough's lack of clarity in his orders can also be used as mitigation for Thackwell's indecision. Once again this seems to be an example of poor staff work in that the original communication from Gough, via the Adjutant General, did not express Gough's viewpoint fully.[14]

Gough artillery bombardment at Ramnagar had shown the limitations of his artillery, particularly when the Sikhs were in a strong defensive position. Gough launched a heavy bombardment including nine 24 pdrs, but they were able to do little damage. Sikh guns fired from a position that gave them good cover and the best the British could see were the barrels of their guns. They kept Gough's gunners fully employed in an artillery duel, despite withdrawing many of their guns and leaving just six to keep up the battle. At around 2200 on 3 December the Sikhs withdrew under cover of darkness. At dawn this was discovered by the British and Gough immediately sent his cavalry across to pursue them, but it was too late.

13   Thackwell and Colin Campbell would in later years enter into a debate in print over exactly what happened. Campbell, in his correspondence quoted by Shadwell, Lawrence, *The Life of Colin Campbell, Lord Clyde*, Vol. I (London: William Blackwood & Sons, 1881), p. 194, asserts that he twice urged Thackwell to attack. Thackwell would deny this in a letter to the historian William Napier. Criticism of Thackwell can be found in most accounts of the conflict. Cook, *The Sikh Wars*, p. 151, whilst more understanding of Thackwell's position, still considers that he should have pressed on.
14   Rait, *Gough*, Vol. II, p. 200.

Thus the battle of Sadelupour, if it can be called such, and the exchanges across the Chenab merely petered out after some opening artillery and cavalry exchanges. That an opportunity had been missed to defeat the enemy was only a minor point in regards to the operation as a whole. The most important factor was that the army was now across the Chenab and the Sikhs had withdrawn from the river. What could have proved a very difficult and costly operation had been achieved with relative ease and few casualties, amounting to around 20 killed and 50 wounded. Sikh casualties are unknown but were likely around the same number as the British. The Sikhs had also lost eight guns, around 60 boats, and a large quantity of ammunition, the latter being intentionally blown up before they withdrew. Gough had entered into the operations simply with the intention of getting across the river. That he had also wanted to inflict a defeat upon the Sikhs was a secondary consideration caught up in his desire, for reasons we have already explained, to bring the conflict to a speedy conclusion. Yet, for all that, Sadelupour was like Ramnagar an abortive battle that did damage more to the morale of the army and the reputation of its officers than it did in terms of the course of the war. Sadelupour was perhaps a missed opportunity, but it could equalled be argued that it was a potential disaster averted.

The failure was partly Gough's. What was often seen as his lack of organisation was more accurately a lack of good staff work. For this Gough is partly to blame. Indeed as commander-in-chief the buck stopped with him. It was his responsibility to make sure that his staff was up to the task at hand. At Sadelupour there was possibly a missed opportunity and if one believes that this was so then the reason for it was poor staff work and in particular poor communication between the commander-in-chief and his subordinate commander. Yet casualties had been relatively light. Gough in his despatch written on 5 December called the action a great success. The Chenab had been crossed, casualties were far lighter than would normally be expected for such an operation, the enemy had withdrawn, and Gough now had the opportunity to advance against Sher Singh and hopefully force a decisive battle. He could now reunite his force and be in a much stronger position to attempt this. Yet despite the military advantage being Gough's, political considerations would prevent him from making the most of his opportunity.

65

Across the Chenab River

Gough had the opportunity, after crossing the River Chenab, to follow quickly on the heels of Sher Singh's withdrawal. Given the speed with which the Sikh army could move he might not have been able to catch up with him. However, in pursuing Gough might have forced Sher Singh into an indiscretion that would have given Gough an opportunity to give battle under favourable conditions. Had been able to do this he would likely have been able to prevent the junction of the forces of Sher Singh and his father Chatar Singh. He might well have been able to force battle in a more promising position or at the very least have harassed Sher Singh's army and prevented an orderly withdrawal.

However once again political interference prevented military operations from being directed as the Commander-in-Chief wished. Whether this was for good or ill is difficult to say. On the one hand, one could say that political interference placed a brake on Gough's reckless nature. On the other hand, it can be argued that Gough was being asked to fight a campaign with one hand tied behind his back. Before looking at the first great battle of the Second Sikh War, it is first necessary to return to the political constraints under which Gough was acting, and the concerns that Dalhousie had over the campaign. This will help us to understand the process that brought Gough to the field of battle at Chillianwala. Gough was under instruction from Dalhousie not to follow Sher Singh. Indeed his operations were to be limited to crossing the Chenab and forming of a base of operations on that side of the river. Dalhousie, however, was not at the scene of operations. In that sense, his political interference was far worse than that of Hardinge during the first war with the Sikhs. At least Hardinge had been present with the army and had been able to see with his own eyes what was going on, even if often what he saw was not the same as the vision of his commander-in-chief.

Yet Dalhousie, away from the scene of operations, had on 27 November ordered Gough, "that on no consideration shall Your Excellency advance into the Doab beyond the Chenab, except for the purpose of attacking Shere [sic] Singh in his present position, without further communication with me, and my consent obtained."[1] Gough therefore felt able to cross the river but not to go further. This restriction placed on him by the political authorities is often overlooked when assessing the actions around the Chenab River. Gough desperately wanted to pursue the enemy after crossing the river, and, indeed, sensed a real opportunity to prevent the joining of the armies of Sher Singh and Chatar Singh.[2] There was, however, another limitation on Gough's ability to pursue Sher Singh and move further into Sikh territory. The supply situation was in a poor state. Again this had much to do with the failure to prepare during the previous months. The organisation at a staff level within the army does not seem to have been very efficient. However it easy to make this appear

---

1   Rait, *Gough*, Vol. II, p. 204. Rait quotes a letter from Dalhousie to Gough dated 27 November 1848.
2   NAM: 8303–105 Gough Papers, Gough to Dalhousie, 22 December 1848. At this date Gough was still unsure of what authority he had to advance, stating that, "I did feel I was restricted from promptly acting without reference to your Lordship."

to be the main cause and thereby obscure the fact that there had been a serious failure on the part of Dalhousie in not allowing preparations to be carried through earlier and for a forward base to be prepared and the correct expenditure made to create a supply base correctly provisioned for the army.

In a sense, it depends upon how one views this situation. Was Dalhousie's decision not to allow Gough to pursue Sher Singh due to the poor state of the supply system or was it a wider policy decision? It does appear that the latter is the case: if Dalhousie was concerned about the supply situation, this was a secondary consideration. His main concern, certainly in light of his surviving correspondence, was the desire, if not necessarily need, to await the fall of Multan and the arrival of the reinforcements that would join Gough's army because of this. However, if one takes the poor state of the commissariat and supply situation as being the main cause of Dalhousie's orders that Gough was not to move deeper into enemy territory then the Governor General has to shoulder a greater share of responsibility in this regard.

However Dalhousie's argument was that, with the presumably imminent fall of Multan, Gough should wait until the fortress had been captured. Once completed, "The arrival of reinforcements at Multan, and the surrender of that fortress, will shortly place such an additional force at your disposal as will admit of the army advancing without exposing our present position to the imminent risk in which it would otherwise be placed."[3] This argument lost something when translated into the reality of the situation. Whilst it would give Gough a larger army, the delay would mean that it would not be possible to stop the coming together of the two large Sikhs forces commanded by Sher Singh and Chatar Singh. Ultimately Gough would still be fighting an enemy who could equal him in number and likely exceed his strength.

Dalhousie was now at Amballa but still a great distance from Gough's position. Even when advised of the present situation and Gough's successful crossing of the Chenab, Dalhousie did not change his stance. On 8 December he wrote, "I cannot, as at present advised, consent to your advancing from the line of the position I mentioned, in order to attack them, until the fall of Mooltan [Multan]. The cursed delay which has been permitted renders it uncertain when this event may come to pass."[4] This letter only serves to reinforce the folly of Dalhousie's position. Even now that he had admitted that the fall of Multan would likely be delayed, he still refused to contemplate Gough using the force at his disposal to attack the Sikhs. For his part, Gough did not envisage a large-scale movement too far forward from his present position. In this he was still mindful of the limitations of his commissariat. In short, he feared for the ability to supply and maintain his army much further from his lines of communication. However, had he been able to pursue Sher Singh it is a distinct possibility that he would have been able to force a confrontation before it was necessary to advance too far from the river. The fact that he did not was partly due to the failure to prepare sufficient stores in advance of the campaign, largely a political failing; partly due to the poor state of the commissariat, which was both a military and a political failure; and partly due to the constrains of movement placed upon him by the Governor General.

This also leads one to question Dalhousie's earlier remarks that Gough was asking for too large a force. Indeed, the force that Gough had with him after just crossing the Chenab was around the size that Dalhousie had earlier written was sufficient for the task at hand. One cannot help but feel that there was something else behind Dalhousie's delay. If it was a lack of belief in Gough's ability, then one wonders whether the addition of the extra force from Multan was really the solution. One would also have to question why Dalhousie agreed to the extension of Gough's service if he had a lack of confidence in him as a military commander. It could be that it was an attempt by the

---

3   Rait, *Gough*, Vol. II, p. 204.
4   Rait, *Gough*, Vol. II, p. 205.

Governor General to reign in the perceived reckless nature of Gough. By restricting his movement Dalhousie may have hoped that he would restrain a wild an ill-conceived attack. This is perhaps to give too much credit to Dalhousie. The Governor General was perhaps attempting to consider the bigger picture. If reinforcements from Afghanistan attempted to move to support the Sikhs in larger numbers than they already had, then Multan needed to be in British hands. If large numbers of Afghan troops crossed in the direction of Multan, not only would the siege once more become untenable, but it would also threaten the route into India, and give the potential for Gough to be outflanked and even attacked from two directions at once.

Such political considerations were not the province of Gough, yet Dalhousie had to consider them. There was also the potential for civil unrest within the newly claimed British territory ceded under the Treaty of Lahore, but also within British India itself. Such concerns were political in nature and therefore beyond the concern of Gough. Dalhousie also wanted to be able to say that the deaths of Vans Agnew and Anderson had been avenged and that Dewan Mulraj had been dealt with. Again this was largely a political concern motivated by the outrage in the press and wider European society in India that this offence had so far gone unpunished. Whilst understandable, these were not necessary views that contributed towards the military decision-making process. Indeed, in some way it could be argued that they had superseded military necessity. Dalhousie was no more ignorant of the military necessity of certain actions than Gough was ignorant of the political difficulties. Yet it was impossible for Gough to become involved in such matters. This was both from a legitimate constitutional point of view but also from the intellectual point of view that he was not suited to such political concerns and intrigues. As has already been mentioned he was by this time thoroughly sick of political games. One cannot help going back to the comment made by Hardinge towards the end of the First Sikh War that Gough was in this sense a 'mere soldier'.

It would be wrong not to appreciate the difficult position Dalhousie was in. He had inherited a crisis in the making. His position both within India and at home, whilst secure, was somewhat difficult after following such a distinguished man as Hardinge. One can appreciate that Dalhousie did not wish to be seen to openly contradict the policy of his predecessor or to suggest that he had acted incorrectly. Yet Hardinge's assertion that there would be no need to fight another campaign against the Sikhs, or even in India itself, for a number of years was clearly an inaccurate assessment of the situation. Dalhousie now had to live with the consequences of that whilst trying to keep a lid on expenditure in general. In the latter regard the army had been an easy target and it was understandably attractive to accept Hardinge's assessment and justify cuts in the army using this hypothesis. The expense was also the reason why no preparations for bases on the frontier had really been made between the two wars and why there was such a delay in agreeing to the preparations that Gough had desired. Political considerations concerning the best use of resources and the army that had also led to the limitations placed upon Gough.

In the days that followed the crossing of the river, Gough pushed the limits of his authority. Indeed in a letter of 22 December Gough wrote to Dalhousie that whilst he recognised that his instructions prevented him from "promptly acting without reference to your Lordship, at a moment when prompt measures might be beneficial and might bring to a termination a rebellion that time might strengthen", only those being "upon the spot can alone judge of the feelings and the false movements of an opposing army." So one can see from this the indication that, whilst he would be reluctant to do so, Gough was prepared to disobey Dalhousie's instructions if he felt it militarily expedient to so do.[5]

---

5   NAM: 8303–105, Gough Papers, Gough to Dalhousie, 22 December 1848. Rait, *Gough*, Vol. II, p. 207. Rait unfortunately misquotes this passage, and gives the impression that Gough had more blatantly said he would defy Dalhousie. This was not the case if one reads the original letter.

Gough had already pushed his instructions to remain by the river and not advance too far inland by allowing the cavalry commanded by Thackwell's to follow Sher Singh's force. At times they were within touching distance of each other, but no major combat took place. The reason for this was not so much Dalhousie's instructions as the practicalities of the situation. The country in which the two armies moved did not allow for such action to take place. In many places the jungle was too thick to allow the cavalry, or the horse artillery that had accompanied it, to engage the enemy. Intelligence was also difficult to come by as the British were now entering an area that was largely loyal to the Sikh cause.

Gough decided to move on to Wazirabad and concentrate his force there. At the same time he would hold Gujerat as a forward position and here await the fall of Multan. It was a decision he took reluctantly but one in which he had little alternative given the limitations under which he was forced to act. Wazirabad would make a better base of operations than his present location just across the river. It also had better facilities for gathering a large army. It did mean that the force marching from Multan after the fall of the fortress would have slightly further to march, but this was not a major problem. The danger with such a movement was that it opened the possibility that the Sikh army might cross the Chenab and place itself between Gough and Lahore. However Gough was not concerned about this and, indeed, his comments suggest that he would have welcomed such a move. In a letter to Dalhousie he remarked that, "If the Sikhs, joined by the Peshawur [Peshawar] force, move to get between me and Lahore, it is just what I want."[6] By this Gough meant that in this situation the Sikhs would be between two British armies; Gough's main army and the still quite considerable number of troops retained at Lahore. Cut off from their retreat as they would be, any battle against the Sikhs would be decisive and a British victory under such circumstances would destroy the Sikh army and virtually end the conflict.

Yet his plans changed due to reports of the movement of the Sikh army. Gough decided not to advance towards Wazirabad and use that as his main base of operations. Leaving a small force at Ramnagar, mainly to care for the wounded but also to watch the crossing, Gough moved on 29 December to a new camp at Janukee (modern day Jokalian). This was to watch the movement of Sher Singh who had been threatening the village of Dinghi (modern day Dinga). If Sher Singh took that place it was feared that he would then use this to attack Ramnagar and cross the Chenab. However, on Gough's movement to Janukee the Sikhs moved part of their force from Moong (Mong) to a village called Tupai near Russool (Rasool). At the same time they began constructing a boat bridge across the Jhelum River near Russool to facilitate the movement of reinforcements across the Jhelum to join Sher Singh's army. Gough's movement had forced Sher Singh's forces away from Dinghi.

On 9 January Gough moved his force to within three miles of Dinghi. His decision not to take Dinghi was from fear that it might induce the Sikhs to retreat over the Jhelum River. This would have placed a far greater distance between the enemy and Gough and created not only further supply problems but also the need for a further river crossing. On that same day Gough became aware, via a letter from Dalhousie, that a successful assault had been made upon Multan and whilst at the time of writing the letter did not confirm that the fortress had fallen, it seemed inevitable. This letter from Dalhousie dated 7 January also included one other remarkable piece of news. In effect it freed Gough from the restrictions on action placed on him by Dalhousie. In a letter that shows Dalhousie's obvious relief and joy at the imminent fall of Multan, he granted Gough permission to move as far as the Jhelum River, and indeed it could be inferred that he gave him permission to cross it if appropriate.[7]

6   NAM: 8303–105, Gough Papers, Gough to Dalhousie, 7 December 1848.
7   NAM: 8303–105, Gough Papers, Dalhousie to Gough, 7 January 1849.

Ever the politician, Dalhousie did cover himself by emphasising that he was "in ignorance as to the details of the position taken up by the Sikhs, and as to your own views of the means at your disposal for assaulting it, as well as of your plans." Although the letter gave Gough the freedom to move, such movement was clearly at his own peril so far as the consequences were concerned. Dalhousie's letter gave him the ability to say that if 'disaster' fell upon Gough's movement that he was not aware of the exact position. The letter makes it clear that as far as Dalhousie was concerned Gough had not consulted him with his plan of operation, and this gave him the ability to say that had he known Gough intentions he would have counselled caution. The letter does inform Gough that Dalhousie would "be heartily glad to hear of your having felt yourself in a condition to attack Shere Singh with success."[8]

This was quite a turnaround from Dalhousie's previous position that it was essential for Gough to wait for the reinforcements from Multan. At first glance it is difficult to understand why there was this sudden change of view. Many reasons have been but forward. There was the fact that inactivity and the handling of the war was being criticised. Public opinion was now focussed against the Governor General as much as the Commander-in-Chief. The fall of Multan and a follow-up victory on the Jhelum would end this. Dalhousie was also aware that Attock had fallen and of the consequences this would have in terms of Sikh reinforcements for Sher Singh. Dalhousie did not mention the fall of Attock in his 7 January letter to Gough. The reason might be that although he had received reports to that affect they had not yet been confirmed. There had also been reports that the Sikhs had been attempting to undermine the loyalty of the native troops in British employ and that Dalhousie considered this would only become more tempting the longer that Gough's force remained inactive.

Perhaps the granting of permission also demonstrates Dalhousie's appreciation that reinforcements would be needed at some stage for Gough's army, rather than being essential to Gough's ability to engage the enemy. Now with the fall of Multan and arrival of such reinforcements likely before too long, Dalhousie was prepared to let Gough take offensive action, with the guarantee that considerable reinforcements were on the way. Sir Robert Rait however took a slightly different view and stated that, "This permission to attack before the arrival of the Multan forces was an admission of the wisdom of the policy which Lord Gough had pursued in spite of the suggestions of the Governor-General."[9] Yet it was perhaps more than that. It was in one sense an illustration of the nature of Dalhousie's thinking, rather than the suggestion that he was wrong and Gough was right. It shows that Dalhousie operated under a cautious approach, for whatever accusations of caution were laid at the door of Gough the same was true of Dalhousie. He had been in support of Gough's cautious approach, but, more than that, he had encouraged it. At the same time he had pressed for action against minor outposts, so as to be seen to be active. However when Gough had objected to this dilution of his forces, Dalhousie had made no major objection to this.

The new instructions gave Gough clear permission to move against Sher Singh and engage him in battle. The delay was unfortunate and had the permission come a week or two earlier Gough may have been able to pursue a somewhat disorganised Sikh force. That was not now the case but one can understand, given the frustration of the previous instructions, Gough's great desire to press on. Perhaps this was not the wisest move but it was understandable.

Just as important as the fall of Multan to the possible course of the war was the fall of Attock in early January to Chatar Singh's forces. The most likely date for the fall of Attock 2 January 1849 but there does appear to be some dispute over this. Lieutenant Herbert had held out at this outpost near the Afghan border, but had finally been forced to surrender. Gough did not receive confirmation

---

8   NAM: 8303–105, Gough Papers, Dalhousie to Gough, 7 January 1849.
9   Rait, *Gough*, Vol. II p. 210.

of this until 10 January. This meant that somewhere around 12,000 men would be moving to join Sher Singh's army which was already at least 26,000 strong. Indeed, as it stood, Gough was already outnumbered not only in terms of men but just as importantly in number of guns. The situation would not alter much with the arrival of Major General Whish and the reinforcements from Multan, as Sher Singh would now shortly be joined by his reinforcements from Attock and the army of his father. Gough could see the need for speed of movement and having received the Governor General's letter on the 9th and the news of the fall of Attock on the 10th he was by the morning of 11 January 1849 ready to move against Sher Singh's position near the River Jhelum. Rait concluded that this demonstrated that, "So advanced were his preparations that on the 11th he was ready to march to Dinghi."[10] Yet this description of his preparations might be to stretch matters too far. The commissariat was still not as advanced as it should have been, little reconnaissance of the area into which they marched was undertaken, and the movement and direction was necessitated by the need to find fresh water. It can therefore be argued that Gough was once again moving into the unknown.

---

10   Rait, *Gough*, Vol. II p. 210.

66

Movements to Chillianwala

Although Gough was marching into the unknown in many respects, he did know the position of the enemy. Sher Singh had dug in not far from the Jhelum River in an outward crescent formation: or as one author has put it in the shape of a Tulwar.[1] To his left was the village of Russool. To the front of the Sikh position was the village of Chillianwala. Gough decided to advance on Chillianwala and occupy the village. From here he could rest and prepare for battle. The key factor in deciding his move on Chillianwala was that he knew that it was a source of fresh water. This movement would be criticised in the light of what was to follow, however it was in many ways logical.

It has been claimed, by the ubiquitous Colonel Malleson among others, that a far better movement would have been to attempt to turn the Sikh position on the right and attack Russool directly. In this Malleson claims that Major, later Major General Sir, Henry Durand, an officer on the staff of Colin Campbell, approached Gough at a council of war with the idea of doing this and that Gough initially warmly accepted it saying it was a scheme worthy of Frederick the Great.[2] The problem is that there is not a source for this assertion by Malleson. Indeed whilst Durand would claim in the *Calcutta Review* that he did approach Gough, he only mentioned an attack on Russool as a 'feasible plan of attack' in that article. Also, the biography of Durand prepared by his son makes no mention of this scheme. In fact it does not even recall him attending the council of war. Indeed, given the nature of the engagement that would follow it is unlikely that a formal council of war ever took place. Whilst this in and of itself is lamentable, it does call Malleson's statement into question. Even if this was Malleson's accurate recollection of a private conversation with Durand, it is not verifiable.[3]

Yet despite Malleson's assertions, attacking Russool would be difficult if not impossible. It would mean a turning movement in front of the enemy, and in difficult terrain. Russool was at the top of some hills and there were many deep and treacherous ravines on the movement towards it. Russool was also defended by two battalions of infantry, five guns and a body of irregular horse. Due to the terrain and the enemy, an attack on Russool would not be easy. It was perhaps as Durand recorded, 'feasible', but that is a long way from being either desirable or advisable. However in any event Chillianwala, with its fresh water, would have to be taken first. There is therefore the question as to whether Gough ever intended to attack at Russool. There is no evidence from his own hand that this was what he intended.

---

1   Cook, *The Sikh Wars*, p. 165.
2   Malleson, *Decisive Battles of India*, p. 371.
3   Durand, Henry Mortimer, *The Life of Major-General Sir Henry Marion Durand* (London: W. H. Allen & Co, 1883), pp. 113–115, Malleson, *Decisive Battles of India*, p. 371.

Whilst taking Russool had much to commend it in a purely tactical sense, in a practical sense it can be categorised as an unnecessary risk. It was too hard a position to take. Colin Campbell wrote in the aftermath of the battle, and after having examined the position at Russool that:

> I never saw a stronger position, nor did I ever see one so well improved by works so admirably arranged, and so well adapted for the purposes of defence. It was indeed most fortunate that we had not to storm this place, for most probably we should have failed, and even had we been successful our loss must have been frightful.[4]

This lends strength to the idea that attacking Russool was not the bright idea that some have suggested. It was certainly not the solution to taking the Sikh position.

Had Gough wished to attempt to turn the flank of the Sikhs he would have been much better served by attempting it on the right of their position. Here the terrain, whilst far from comfortable, was easier. It was also further away from the river. That it was a more vulnerable position is illustrated by the fact that Sher Singh positioned four regiments of infantry, 17 guns and one regiment of cavalry to protect this flank. Thus to attempt a flanking movement here would have necessitated a large portion of Gough's army being detached for the purpose. It was also risky as it would mean moving near the river, and any force diverted such a distance could easily find itself cut off by Sikh irregular cavalry and in a very difficult position. It was a possible option, but hardly an ideal solution. However from a letter written to Dalhousie on 11 January it is clear that Gough did not intend to attempt to turn either flank. His intention was to attack the Sikh centre. Whilst this might sound like a poor decision, and is certainly one that can be used to enforce the notion that Gough had a predisposition towards the frontal attack, there was a sort of logic to it. In his letter to Dalhousie he stated that "It is my intention to penetrate the centre of their line, cutting off the regular from the irregular portion of their army."[5] The unusual positioning of the army by Sher Singh had indeed made this a possibility. Over half the Sikh infantry that would be deployed in the battle were newly raised units, untried and untested. If Gough could isolate them from the tried and tested battle-hardened veterans of the Khalsa, he had the chance of a great victory.

We have already seen that turning either flank of the army would not be an easy prospect. Furthermore, regardless of any action on the flanks Gough would still have to move on Chillianwala village to secure water, and in theory from this position the easiest point of attack was the centre. His intention was however a little more sophisticated than simply attacking the centre. If, as he hoped, he was able to split the Sikh Army in half he could then deal with each force separately. This was a good way to overcome the fact that he was outnumbered by the enemy. It would also, hopefully, negate the Sikh superiority in artillery. There were also detachments of Sikhs at Russool, Moong, and Lucknawalla that could be dealt with after the main army had been split and defeated. It was ambitious, and perhaps over-optimistic.

However, even with the argument mentioned above, attacking the centre was a decision open to question. As it was the issue was somewhat forced upon Gough. On the morning of 13 January the army moved from just outside Dinghi, towards Chillianwala. At first the movement took them along the road in the direction of Russool and this might add further credence to the idea that Gough intended to try and turn the enemy flank there. However Gough explained that, "I made a considerable detour to my right, partly in order to distract the enemy's attention, but principally to get as clear as I could of the jungle."[6] Before turning towards Chillianwala, Gough halted the army

---

4   Shadwell, *Life of Colin Campbell*, p. 216.
5   NAM: 8303–105, Gough Papers, Gough to Dalhousie, 11 January 1849.
6   Rait, *Gough*, Vol. II, p. 216.

and sent forward a party for reconnaissance. The whole issue of reconnaissance is one that we will return to a little later on, but it was not an easy task under the circumstances. Gough's intelligence staff had provided a little information from scouting and it was known that there was a small Sikh outpost on a mound overlooking the village of Chillianwala. Gough decided that this would have to be taken. Whilst a sensible precaution, given that the outpost would have been able to fire into his proposed camp at Chillianwala, it alerted the Sikhs not only to his presence, which they likely as not were already aware of, but it also seemed to confirm the view that Gough intended to attack the centre of the Sikh line using Chillianwala village as a starting point.

Gough also remarked that the driving off of the outpost allowed his officers to scout ahead. The problem of the dense jungle had prevented much in the way of reconnaissance from being carried out until now. From the slightly raised positon in front of Chillianwala they were now able to see the battlefield more clearly. By now it was midday and Gough had walked to the top of the tallest building in the village to survey the Sikh positions to his front. He could now see that from his position at Chillianwala any attempt to turn the Sikh right was impossible, given the density of the jungle. This extended for many miles and any force attempting to outflank the Sikh right would have to make a major detour to undertake this attack. Coordinating such an attack would have been difficult to say the least. Perhaps a more imaginative commander might have feigned an attack on the Sikh right, maybe by despatching some of his native cavalry in an attempt to convince the Sikhs that this was his intention. The likelihood of this deception succeeding was negligible. Yet had it been attempted it would have demonstrated imagination. It would also have protected him from the accusation that he merely thought of the frontal attack and his usual 'Tipperary Tactics'. Yet Gough's mind did not think that way and would not have considered how his actions would be perceived. In this sense the political side of command remained completely alien to him.

As Gough observed the battlefield at midday on 13 January he was tempted to attack almost immediately. His main reason for considering this was that the Sikhs had partly left their entrenched positions. In particular their guns had been moved forward and were more vulnerable should he launch an attack. If he could take the Sikh guns out of action then he would most certainly have the advantage. Yet there were several problems. From his position Gough could not ascertain the true position of the Sikh line, and in particular their guns still in position, as the Sikhs had used the cover well. Gough was also hesitant about launching an attack for fear of the fading daylight. There was another factor in his decision making process that warrants further discussion. This is particular because it has often been misinterpreted or misunderstood. It concerns the nature of the jungle that lay ahead of him, which is often referred to as being very dense and thick. Whilst this was the case it was not accurate for the whole of the battlefield. Over to the left of Gough's position, on the Sikh right, it appears to have been particularly dense and difficult, if not impossible, to manoeuvre through. However to the front there were clear sections of the jungle that were passable. Indeed Gough remarked that in parts it was not as bad as the terrain, in that case forest, that he had to move through at Talavera or in other places during the Peninsular War.[7] Indeed it has also been stated that the worst of the jungle was before one reached Chillianwala village.[8] The problem was not so much the thickness on the jungle that lay ahead but the difficulty in finding a way through it. The Sikhs, obviously with the benefit of local knowledge, managed to find their way through it. Yet the inability to reconnoitre the paths through the jungle by the British before the battle commenced was to be a costly error.

The jungle would prove a problem, but there was no real alternative open to Gough than to try and move through it. We have already seen that a turning movement on the left or right flank was

---

7   NAM: 8303–105, Gough Papers, Gough to George Gough, 11 May 1848.
8   Lawrence-Archer, *Commentaries on the Punjab Campaign 1848–49*, p. 39.

impossible. The only alternative would have been to attempt to move behind the Sikh entrenchment with a wide sweeping march. Firstly, Gough's army was not really suited for this and did not have the speed to do this. Secondly, they knew little of the terrain in which they had to move. Thirdly, such a move was impossible on the Sikh left due to the proximity of the flank to the Jhelum River. The only way this could have been done would have involved a crossing and recrossing of the river, and this was far too much of a gamble even if it had been practical. On the Sikh right such a movement would have to move far beyond the flank at Lucknawalla. Indeed it would have almost necessitated moving around the flank and attacking Moong and the Sikh entrenchments from behind. This might have been possible, but it would have been a difficult manoeuvre. It might have been worth attempting simply from the point of view that it might have forced the Sikhs to abandon their position. This would therefore have given Gough the possibility of fighting them on a position more in his favour. One imagines that this is what Wellington in his prime, with his keen eye for terrain, would have attempted.

Yet Gough was not Wellington and we have no evidence that he even contemplated this. Such a course of action would likely have had the knock-on effect of encouraging the Sikhs to cross the Jhelum. As Gough, and indeed Dalhousie, wanted to deliver a major reverse to the enemy it can be questioned if this was desirable. It would also have meant that Gough would be unable to prevent the junction of Sher Singh and his father. In the end the frontal attack seemed the most likely to succeed. In many ways it was the one that carried the least risk. Although casualties would be high, attempting any of the alternatives mentioned above had the potential for disaster and could have seen Gough's army decimated, and indeed cut off from the route back to British territory. However the decisions Gough made and the course of the battle that followed would prove to be the most controversial part of his entire career.

67

The Decision to Fight at Chillianwala

Gough chose to hold his position at Chillianwala overnight rather than attack in the afternoon of 13 January. The hope was also that a thorough reconnaissance of the area could be conducted during the afternoon and early evening so that preparation for an attack the following morning could be prepared. He ordered that a camp be made around the village of Chillianwala so that he could make best use of its fresh water supply. It was perhaps the wisest move. During the process of making camp it was brought to the attention of Gough that the Sikhs had sent forward some horse artillery which was now firing on the outposts of the British camp. What happened next, and indeed how the battle of Chillianwala came about, has been widely disputed. Once again much of the criticism of Gough stems from Malleson's book. This has often been the basis for historians' subsequent criticism of Gough's handling of the battle. The anti-Gough bias of Malleson is as clear as the bias of Rait in attempting to defend Gough. Malleson's interpretation was that this attack by the Sikh horse artillery was a deliberate gambit made by Sher Singh to entice a reaction by Gough.

Malleson's interpretation is that:

> Sher Singh was determined to force on a battle that afternoon. Knowing the temperament of the British commander, that the fire of artillery was the music which would make him dance, he despatched to the front a few light guns and opened fire on the British position. The fire was distant and the effect innocuous, but the insult roused the hot Irish blood of the leader of the English army. It "drew" him, in fact, precisely in the manner designed by Sher Singh. He at once directed his heavy guns to respond, from their position in front of Chillianwala, to the fire of the enemy. The distance from the enemy's advanced guns was from fifteen to seventeen hundred yards. Yet the density of the jungle prevented the English gunners from getting any sight of the Sikhs, and they had to judge their distance by timing the seconds between the report and the flash of the hostile guns. Their fire failed to silence that of the enemy, for Sher Singh, determined to complete the drawing operation he had so well begun, sent the whole of his field artillery to the front, and, the Sikhs, excellent gunners, maintained an equal contest with their foe. This was more than Gough could stand. A thorough believer in the bayonet, and looking upon guns as instruments which it was perhaps necessary to use but which inter-fered with real fighting, he, wild with excitement, ordered his infantry to advance and charge the enemy's batteries.[1]

This very negative exposition of Gough's actions is based largely on hearsay and Malleson's own interpretation not only of events but of Gough's temperament. Rait on the other hand places a rather different interpretation on the events that led up to the commencement of the battle:

---

1   Malleson, *Decisive Battles of India*, pp. 374–375.

Lord Gough's attention was called to the fact that the enemy had advanced some horse artillery, and had opened fire upon his outposts. To silence these, he ordered the heavy guns to proceed in front of the village of Chillianwala, and to reply to the Sikh fire. His artillery was answered by a response from the whole Sikh line, the position of which was thus revealed—'their whole line evidently thrown out much in front of their different positions'. This fact altered the whole complexion of affairs. The Sikhs, in the first place, had completely abandoned their entrenched position; if the attack were delayed till next day, they would have time to throw up entrenchments. In the second place, they would be able to open a cannonade at any time in the night. Retreat was impossible and to encamp was unsafe. In these circumstances, the Commander-in-Chief resolved upon an immediate attack.[2]

Each historian places their own interpretation on the events. Whilst Malleson makes some clear mistakes in his interpretation, Rait is perhaps too passive in his account. Malleson was incorrect in some of what he said, as Rait took great delight in pointing out. This is particularly the case when it comes to the 'drawing' on of Gough. Malleson accepts the battlefield rumour that this provoked Gough into attack, but chooses to ignore the similar rumour that the Sikh commander of the horse artillery opened fire without permission and in error. This theory suggests that the intention of Sher Singh was to use his entire artillery, now pushed forward of their entrenched position, to attack the British camp as it was being prepared. The horse artillery had been pushed further forward, due to its shorter range, but it had been intended that it should wait until the whole line of artillery was ready to fire.[3]

It can be suggested that Sher Singh had intended to draw Gough into a trap, but not the one that Malleson claims. Sher Singh had rightly assumed that Gough would make camp at Chillianwala, with its supply of fresh water. He had therefore allowed Gough to reach the camp without harassment and planned for an artillery attack with all the guns he could muster whilst the British were making camp to create the greatest amount of confusion. The idea that Sher Singh then expected Gough to launch a full-scale attack is based on at best a battlefield rumour. What he wished to do was inflict damage on Gough's force and perhaps force him to withdraw. Rait for his part points to the fact that Gough was aware of the full line advance of the Sikh artillery, and was therefore not duped by the attack of the horse artillery into an artillery duel which prompted the entire Sikh artillery line to attack. Gough's own account does suggest that his own reconnaissance, previously mentioned, had identified that the Sikh guns were forward of their entrenchments.[4]

Gough's actual response to the horse artillery firing on his position had been to bring up his two batteries of heavy guns. This would have been overkill to deal with the Sikh horse artillery alone and suggests that he was anticipating the rest of the Sikh artillery to join in the bombardment, which they did. Malleson's claim that Gough in fact provoked the remainder of the Sikh artillery into opening fire appears to be a misrepresentation of events. By this stage one gets the impression that Gough could not have won either way as far as Malleson was concerned. Had he not returned fire he would have been criticised for leaving his men and the mercy of the Sikh guns, for returning fire he was accused of provoking an even heavier bombardment.[5]

Yet it would be wrong to believe that Gough had not been caught in a trap of one kind. Indeed it is easy to be critical of Gough's decision to attack, but he had placed himself in a position where

2   Rait, *Gough*, Vol. II, p. 218.
3   Rait, Gough, Vol. II, pp. 218–219, Cook, *The Sikh Wars*, p. 166 & Bruce, *Six Battles for India*, p. 287.
4   Rait, *Gough*, Vol. II, pp. 218–219. Rait quotes a 'Diary' kept by Gough during the Second Anglo-Sikh War. This appears to have disappeared and has not been available to present author. The 'Diary' includes the line, "their whole line [of artillery] evidently thrown out much in front of their different positions."
5   Malleson, *Decisive Battles of India*, pp. 374–375.

he had little choice. His plan relied upon the village of Chillianwala, as a source of fresh water. Once that decision had been made the potential for the trap was there. Sher Singh had appreciated this, but it was hardly a startling insight. Sher Singh had been in the area for a little while and was no doubt aware of the supply and water situation. His own water supply was secured by the river to his back, and he was therefore denying this to the enemy. So with possession of Chillianwala a necessity, Gough had little option but to advance upon it if he intended to engage the enemy in battle. His desire to engage the Sikhs was not simply his own natural instinct; he also wanted to move against Sher Singh before his father reinforced him. Gough also felt a duty to attack after his recent communication with Dalhousie. Whilst Dalhousie had meant his words largely as a recommendation Gough had taken it as akin to an order.

Once at Chillianwala, Gough had sensibly decided not to attack that afternoon, but to make camp and await reinforcements. A battle was not intended that afternoon and it was in effect forced upon Gough. Once the Sikh artillery opened fire on him he had little option but to attack. To remain in his camp was not an option as he had little protection from the enemy guns. Also his own artillery, whilst putting up a good show, was inferior both in terms of numbers but also in terms of position. Although forward of their line, the Sikh gunners had made good use of natural cover and were thus not obvious targets for their British counterparts. In fact it has been said that the only way the British were able to return fire was by aiming for the flash of the enemy cannon as they fired.[6]

As he could not remain where he was Gough had only two options: to withdraw or attack. The former was difficult for two separate reasons. Firstly, it would clearly be seen as a retreat in the face of the enemy. The Sikhs guns, having inflicted casualties on the British, would have been seen to have driven Gough from the field. Also, withdrawal left open the question of what his next option was. Secondly, any such withdrawal would be done with the enemy in close pursuit. It would have been messy, disorganised, and certainly have cost a great number of his men their lives. None of the options open to Gough was particularly appealing. To attack was perhaps the lesser of three evils: hold, withdraw or attack. Even though such an attack was likely to be costly, if it were successful he would still be able to achieve his campaign strategy. Indeed it was the only option that would allow him to continue with this strategy to divide the enemy force in front of him and defeat them in detail. The Indian Army officer and historian Lieutenant Colonel R. G. Burton was far from a supporter of Gough's, yet in his 1911 narrative of the Sikh Wars the often critical Burton sums up Gough's position just prior to the battle: "It was now evident that the enemy intended to fight, and would advance his guns, so as to reach the encampment during the night. To encamp was, therefore, manifestly impossible. Retreat was out of the question, and a battle was inevitable."[7]

To question Gough's decision to attack at Chillianwala is to misunderstand the situation. Under the circumstances he had little option but to attack. The problem lay with his strategy on moving on Chillianwala in the first place. There was clearly a failure on Gough's part because he was unable to control the situation. He was also let down by his reconnaissance, and one has to question the leadership and handling of the cavalry. Gough's failure was the fact that he did not insist upon this and compel his cavalry commanders to undertake such work. Intelligence on the area around Chillianwala had been difficult to come by before movement to the area. In his defence it must be remembered that Gough had intended to spend the remainder of the day reconnoitring the battlefield and the Sikh positions before attacking the following morning. Yet Sher Singh did not allow him to do this and by launching an artillery bombardment he had placed his opponent in a position

6   Crawford, 'The Sikh Wars, 1845–9', pp. 61–62 and Malleson, *Decisive Battles of India*, p. 374.
7   Burton, Reginald George, *The First and Second Sikh Wars: An Official British Army History* (Reprinted paperback of 1911 original, Yardley, Pennsylvania: Westholme Publishing, 2007), p. 94.

whereby he must either attack or withdraw. The latter was unthinkable, and would certainly have been construed as a defeat. It would also have been difficult to achieve. The former therefore was Gough's only option now he was at Chillianwala.

In retrospect, Gough might have been better served by heading for an unguarded part of the Jhelum River, to the left of the Sikh position at Chillianwala. Here he would have found his source of fresh water. He could also have threatened the rear and flank of the Sikh entrenchments. The terrain might have made a fight difficult, but there was a real possibility that Sher Singh would have crossed the river and Gough's opportunity to deliver a knockout blow would have been lost. Indeed had Sher Singh crossed the river such an occurrence would also have been interpreted as a failure on Gough's part. It is also to use the benefit of hindsight to criticise Gough's decisions, knowing as we do the outcome of the battle that would follow at Chillianwala.

68

The Battle of Chillianwala

The Sikhs had somewhere in the region of 30,000 men and 62 guns at Chillianwala on the day of the battle.[1] Exactly how many were engaged in the battle is unclear, and there were certainly other detachments of Sikh soldiers in the area defending certain points. Ram Singh commanded the Sikh right with one regiment of cavalry, four infantry regiments and 17 guns. In the centre were the troops of Lal Singh and Atar Singh, consisting of two cavalry regiments, 10 infantry regiments and a further 17 guns. The centre was perhaps the strongest part of the army as of its 10 infantry regiments six were units of the old Khalsa army. Although not of the same quality as the Khalsa regiments of the First Sikh War, they were still a well-disciplined body of men trained in European tactics and more than a match for any but the best of the British forces they faced. The left wing of the army was personally commanded by Sher Singh and consisted of a cavalry regiment, nine regiments of infantry and 20 guns. There were also various irregular units under Sher Singh's command. Of his nine regiments of infantry four were of the old Khalsa.

As mentioned previously, Russool was also defended. The forces here consisted of an unknown number of irregular horse, two infantry regiments and five guns. There were also numerous irregular units between the main line and the village of Moong. The quality of the Sikh army should not be underestimated. Whilst it is true that many of the units were newly raised, there was a strong cadre of old regiments to provide a backbone to the army. Also, many of the new regiments, whilst new in terms of organisation, had many experienced and battle-hardened veterans in them. The artillery was as usual a mixture of calibres. Although not the fearsome artillery train of the first conflict it was very well served by some experienced and skilled gunners. Indeed the early bombardment at Chillianwala was a testament to the way in which the Sikh guns were handled.

The British force numbered 12,000 men and around 66 guns.[2] Although this gave the British a slight numerical superiority in guns the majority were lighter guns and horse artillery: Gough had but few heavy guns. They were also firing from inferior positions. Gough deployed his army in the order in which it had marched. However, perhaps learning from previous experience, the army had been organised on the march so that it could quickly deploy for battle.

Thus deployed, the army consisted of White's cavalry brigade on the left, consisting of the 3rd Light Dragoons, and the 5th and 8th Native Cavalry, supported by a battery of horse artillery. The six batteries of horse artillery had been divided equally between Campbell's and Gilbert's divisions.

---

1   Burton, *The First and Second Sikh Wars*, p. 92. As ever exact numbers for the Sikhs are unknown. Occasionally the figure is inflated to 35,000 Sikhs. However some historians, particularly from the Sikh perspective have questioned whether it could have been as high as 30,000. Malleson, *Decisive Battles of India*, p. 373, claims only 20,000–25,000 Sikhs.

2   Again figures vary, but the above is a reasonable estimate. Allen, *Soldier Sahibs*, p. 190, claims that Gough had 92 guns, but gives no source for this claim. This seems an extraordinary high number and may possibly relate to a total number under Gough's overall command, but it seems almost impossible that he had many more than 60 able to take part in the battle.

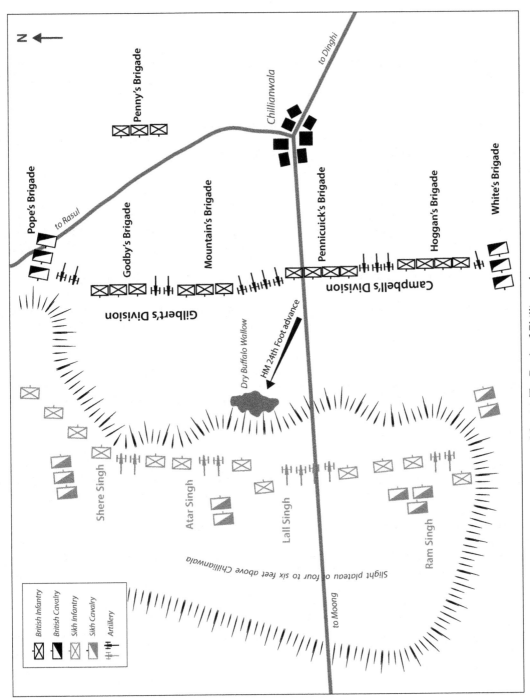

Map 14 The Battle of Chillianwala.

In turn each division attached one battery of horse artillery to the cavalry brigade on its flank. Next to White's brigade, just behind Chillianwala village, was Campbell's infantry division, and it was therefore one of the three horse artillery batteries attached to Campbell's division that supported White. Campbell's division consisted of three infantry brigades. Hoggan's brigade on the left, consisting of the 61st Foot and the 36th and 46th Native Infantry, and on the right Pennycuick's brigade, consisting of the 24th Foot and the 25th and 45th Native Infantry. The third brigade, commanded by Penny and consisting of the 15th, 20th and 69th Native Infantry, was held in reserve. The intention was that Penny's brigade would be used to exploit any breakthrough made by the other two. This was a sensible deployment that allowed fresh troops to be ready to exploit such an opening, and given that in the First Sikh War Gough had often lacked such an advantage it is likely that this was done in light of that experience. Campbell's division was supported by a battery of field artillery to the left of Hoggan's brigade and another between the two brigades.

As we move across the British line, next were the two heavy batteries of artillery, now pushed in front of Chillianwala village. Next was Gilbert's division of two brigades. Mountain's brigade, consisting of the 29th Foot and the 30th and 56th Native Infantry, was to the right of Pennycuick's brigade. Next to Mountain's brigade was a battery of field artillery and next to that was Godby's brigade consisting of the 2nd Bengal Europeans and the 31st and 70th Native Infantry. To the right of Godby's brigade was a battery of horse artillery. This latter battery had the combined task of supporting the infantry and Pope's cavalry brigade, consisting of the 9th Lancers and the 1st and 6th Native Light Cavalry. Although the 14th Light Dragoons were still attached to White's brigade during the march, for the battle itself they joined Pope's brigade.

Once formed up, Gough ordered the army forward from Chillianwala, parallel to the position of the heavy guns. Here the jungle was not as dense, and Gough intended to wait here for his opportunity to attack. Allowing his heavy guns to bombard the enemy position, he awaited the end of the artillery duel. At times during this period Gough ordered various lighter batteries of artillery to support the heavy guns. The artillery duel lasted for over an hour before Gough committed his infantry to the attack. However, before looking at the advance of the infantry it is necessary to look at the way the army was handled up to that point. There had been any number of errors, most of which had their root in the recurring problem of poor staff work.

A good example of this, and one that has mystified historians, is the movement of Robertson's battery of field artillery during the early part of the battle. It will be recalled that this was positioned to the left of Campbell's division and was there to support the infantry as it advanced. In the early stage of the advance Robertson endeavoured to do this, but was then ordered to move to the left. The need of his support of the left was very real. Warner's battery of horse artillery had found itself outgunned in a duel with a Sikh battery that had been pushed forward. The aforementioned Sikh battery was in an excellent position to do real damage, firing across Campbell's division as it advanced. Robertson received, and subsequently followed, the order to move to support the horse artillery and engage the Sikh battery in good faith. Yet exactly where the staff officer who gave this order came from remains a mystery. The orders had certainly not come from Gough. Thackwell, commanding the cavalry division and on the left flank, denied that the staff officer had come from him. Campbell was also unaware of this and indeed sent one of his officers off to try and find the 'missing' battery as he started his advance.[3]

Whilst it appears that Robertson had achieved his task in silencing the Sikh battery, he was unable to undertake the task for which he had been designated in Gough's plan of attack. Robertson, for his part, continued to hold to the fact that the staff officer had indeed given such an order, something which his junior officers vouched for. Yet the problem was that because he received no

3   Cook, *The Sikh Wars*, p. 168.

order to the contrary he remained where he was until he himself saw the advance of Campbell's division. It was at this point that Robertson, using his own initiative, realised that he must move his battery forward to support Campbell's advance. The problem was that by now it was too late. Robertson does not deserve the blame for what happened; indeed he had acted both honourably and sensibly. There is every reason to believe that he did receive orders from this mysterious staff officer. There are echoes of occasions in the First Sikh War when staff officers gave orders that came from unknown sources. Officers commanding fighting units had little option but to obey such an order that appeared to all intents and purposes to come from a bona fide source. Whether the order actually came from a commander of any sort seems unlikely. Indeed the most likely answer is that a staff officer issued the order on his own initiative seeing the potential for the Sikh artillery to attack Campbell's advancing division. The problem was that this was contrary to the plans of the Commander-in-Chief and the said staff officer did not send the battery back to its original duty once the danger from the Sikh artillery was averted.

Yet what this speaks of is the generally poor standard of staff work within the army. Partly this was Gough's responsibility. Whilst he could not be expected to oversee every order, there was a general slackness in the work of his own staff which seemed to filter down throughout the army. Whilst Grant, in effect his Chief of Staff, possessed many great qualities he was rather lackadaisical in his approach to staff work. Nothing illustrates this as well as Grant's failure to keep copies of the orders issued.[4] Gough was partly to blame for this, as he was an intuitive general rather than a detailed pre-planner. He should perhaps have kept a tighter ship, but it would be wrong to believe that as commander-in-chief he should be concerned with the minutia of staff work: indeed this was what his staff officers were for. Perhaps again this illustrates the point that he was a 'Blucher who never found his Gneisenau'. Lacking in such skills himself, he needed a great organiser, an administrator, who could relieve him of this burden. Not only this incident, but perhaps the whole Battle of Chillianwala, illustrates this clearly.

After the artillery duel, which as usual had proved indecisive, the army advanced towards the Sikh position. The time was now just after 1500. On the left White's cavalry brigade advanced and, despite the difficult of the terrain and other problems, were able to clear the Sikh irregular cavalry as the infantry continued their advance. There has been the suggestion that the 5th Bengal Light Cavalry failed to support the charge of the 3rd Light Dragoons. Whether this was reluctance or defiance is unclear.

Given the nature of the terrain, in particular the density of the jungle, Campbell concluded that he could not possibly command his entire division, and instead decided to ride with Hoggan's brigade. This was perhaps a mistake. Brigadier, later Major General, John Hoggan was an experienced officer with many years' service in India. He could have been safely left to command. Indeed in the aftermath of the battle Campbell would praise Hoggan for his leadership. Campbell's other brigadier, John Pennycuick, was a different case. He was an experienced officer, having seen service in the First Anglo-Burma War and the First Anglo-Afghan War, but he had only recently assumed command of the 24th Foot having transferred to it from the 17th Foot. He had officially transferred in April 1847, but had only recently taken up an active command with the 24th. His command of the brigade was due to him being the senior officer of the regiments attached to it, and he had little experience of brigade command. At least Hoggan could point to some periods in which he had held brigade command, even if only temporarily. Perhaps this helps to explain why in the action that followed Hoggan would be praised for his control of the brigade, whilst Pennycuick seems to have lost control of his.

---

4   Wylly, H. C., *The Military Memoirs of Lieutenant-General Sir Joseph Thackwell* (London: John Murray, 1908), p. 267.

Campbell's would perhaps have been better served by following Pennycuick's brigade. They had by far the harder route and would no doubt have benefited from the presence of the divisional commander. It was certainly going to be this brigade, largely due to the terrain and jungle, that was going to be the harder to control, and thus the added presence of the divisional commander and his staff would have helped in this direction. One can understand that Campbell was worried about his flank and chose to accompany that part of his division. He had been right in assuming that it would be impossible to command the division as a whole. Once the advance had begun the two brigades quickly lost sight of one another and as Gough later remarked, they, "never saw one another after the order to advance was given."[5]

This was perhaps the pivotal part of the battle. Campbell had advanced without the level of artillery support he had expected, due to the aforementioned error, but he did give a less than helpful order to his division before they advanced. History records him as saying to the 24th Foot that, "There must be no firing, the bayonet must do the work."[6] As a consequence of this it has been suggested that the 24th did not even bother to load their muskets. Accounts differ in this regard, even amongst those present at the time as to whether or not the 24th Foot loaded their muskets before battle. It has been suggested that this might have been done early in the morning, and thus when the rest of the army was loading before the battle the lack of need for the 24th to so do was interpreted as failure to load before battle. The simple fact is we cannot know for sure. Gough had already told the 24th earlier in the day, 'Give them the cold steel, boys'. The latter and the former whilst sounding similar are in contrast to one another. The former is an order not to fire, given to the 24th by their divisional commander. The latter is a message of encouragement given by the commander-in-chief in passing, not an order to use the bayonet alone. The key motivation in Gough's remarks was to maintain momentum in the attack, something that would be essential if such a strong position was to be taken.[7]

The two brigades of Campbell's division were now separated and unable to support each other. Pennycuick was on his own in command of a brigade consisting of one European and two native battalions. The pace of his advance was so rapid as to outstrip the guns of the artillery that was supposed to support him. Indeed the whole pace of his attack was something of a problem. Not only was his artillery support unable to keep up, but he was also attacking ahead of the rest of the army. It would be Campbell's division who would be the first into action and bear the brunt of it. As Campbell later reported, the jungle, and a number of large trees, broke the line of the advance. It was not surprising that under such circumstances the line became broken and the lead battalion, the 24th Foot, somewhat disjointed. Because there were only certain paths through the jungle these naturally became crowded, and as they emerged from the jungle these bunched groups of men made easy targets for the waiting Sikh gunners.

It was this artillery fire that killed Brigadier Pennycuick. Indeed, it killed not only Pennycuick but Captain Charles Harris, his brigade major, and Major Henry Harris of the 24th Foot. Indeed such was the loss amongst the 24th Foot as they sought to press on that they lost Lieutenant Colonel Robert Brookes (sometimes recorded as Brooks), Major Harris, Captains Lee, Shore, and Travers, Lieutenants Phillips, Payne, Woodgate, Phillips, and Collis, all killed. Added to which was young Ensign Alexander Pennycuick, the 17-year-old son of the Brigadier, who was shot when

5   NAM: 8303–105, Gough papers, Gough to George Gough, 18 March 1849.
6   Forrest, G. W. *The Life of Field Marshal Sir Neville Chamberlain* (London: Blackwood & Sons, 1909), p. 212.
7   Atkinson, C. T. *The South Wales Borders, 24th Foot 1689–1937* (Cambridge: Regimental History Committee, University of Cambridge, 1937), p. 295.

going to the aid of his fallen father. Amongst the wounded were a further major, two captains and seven lieutenants.[8]

The 24th suffered terribly from this bombardment, but continued to attack. The attack was somewhat sporadic and disjointed given the poor order into which the battalion had fallen during its movement through the jungle. Coming out of the jungle there is confusion as what actually happened. The 24th Foot rushed at the enemy in an uncoordinated attack. It is easy to say with the benefit of hindsight that Pennycuick should have formed his brigade up and attacked *en masse*. However this would certainly have been easier said than done. The 24th charged almost without word of command. In one sense, it was a natural response to coming under fire. Gough later tried to explain away the lone charge of the 24th as a misinterpretation by the men, in the noise and heat of battle, to Pennycuick and Lieutenant Colonel Brookes waving their swords above their heads encouraging them. Gough claimed that the battalion mistook this as an instruction to move in double-time and as a consequence outstripped the rest of the brigade in their advance against the Sikh guns.[9] This interpretation was contradicted by officers who were present at the event. It is likely that this interpretation was Gough's attempt to defend the honour and reputation of the fallen commanders. This was not the first time that Gough had failed to criticise the actions of the fallen. One gets the impression that Pennycuick did not have good control of the brigade. Under the circumstances this might have been understandable. There is a question as to whether if Campbell had been present he might have been able to handle things in a better way. Yet this might be to underestimate the difficulty of the situation. Charles Napier later remarked of the event that, "there was nothing for a brave and able commander to do but what Colonel Pennycuick did – dash forward, cheering on his men, and by his example supporting the impulse he could not check and ought not to check."[10]

That the 24th Foot reached the guns and indeed took the gun line is to the eternal credit of the men and the regiment. Campbell claimed later on that, "The batteries were carried without a shot being fired by the regiment or a musket taken from the shoulder." There is a question as to whether or not this was true. Indeed there are reports of men of the 24th firing, and indeed even reloading and firing again. Yet what Campbell described heroically, Gough called 'an act of madness'.[11] Malleson, amongst others, would later claim that the decision to attack without firing was a reckless order given by Gough. This is simply not the case. Gough's original orders were that the guns should be taken with bayonet and musket, and supported by artillery fire. The failure of the guns and infantry to combine was, as we have seen, not due to Gough's failure.[12]

The native infantry battalions within Pennycuick's brigade had pressed on and suffered large casualties, albeit not at the same level as the 24th, but were not able to support the 24th as they came under attack from Sikh infantry. It has been said that the problem lay in the fact that they delayed pressing on in order to spike the Sikh guns. Whilst this obviously halted the momentum of their attack, it was a decision no doubt born of the First Sikh War, when a failure to spike Sikh guns when the gun line had been captured had serious effect upon the advancing British infantry. Often it required the taking of the gun line twice. Indeed on Gough's orders, or at least the orders

8   The calculation of officers killed and wounded is sometimes recorded differently. Lieutenant Archer is sometimes not recorded amongst the wounded as he was an officer of the 96th Foot attached to the 24th. Also, Brigadier Pennycuick and Captain Charles Harris are included separately as brigade staff despite the fact that they were both officers of the 24th Foot.
9   Burton, *The First and Second Sikh Wars*, p. 97, quotes the despatch of Lord Gough.
10 Atkinson, *The South Wales Borderers*, p. 295.
11 Rait, *Gough*, Vol. II, p. 224–225, NAM 8303–105, Gough Papers, Gough to George Gough, 11 May 1849.
12 Malleson, *Decisive Battles of India*, p. 375, Rait, *Gough*, Vol. II, pp. 224–225.

of his staff, each company marched with two spikes for the Sikh guns. Yet this delay meant that when the Sikh infantry launched its counterattack, what remained of the 24th Foot was unready to meet the attack and was forced into withdrawal. Indeed they withdrew back to Chillianwala itself, with Sikh Ghorchara irregular cavalry following them all the way and inflicting further casualties on an already mauled battalion. The 24th Foot lost 231 killed and 236 wounded. Exactly what strength it was on the day of the battle is unclear. It is likely that they went into battle with under 1,000 men and 27 officers. Twenty-three of those officers were casualties, 13 of whom were killed. In short the battalion had lost around half its strength and the majority of its officers. It had also lost one of its colours. Whilst the regimental colour was saved what happened to the Queen's colour has never been established. It was lost but it was not taken by the Sikhs. One theory is that it was saved by a soldier who wrapped the colour around himself to save it from falling into Sikh hands. It is possible that when this man was killed the colour, still wrapped around him, was buried with him.

The two native infantry battalions were criticised for not 'coming on' in support of the 24th Foot. This seems to be unfair criticism. Firstly, the 24th was moving at such speed it was difficult to keep up with them. This was not only due to the better discipline of the 24th but also the fact that they were naturally the lead battalion of the brigade. Secondly, the casualty returns for the two native battalions, whilst not as severe as those of the 24th, tell a somewhat different story. The 25th Bengal Native Infantry lost one officer and 98 men killed and two officers and 90 wounded. There were also 12 missing and the battalion lost both its colours. The 45th Bengal Native Infantry lost 17 killed and three officers and 55 men wounded. They had only three missing and lost two colours out of the three they carried in the field that day.[13] The problem was not so much a lack of courage on the part of the native infantry but a lack of coordination with the 24th Foot. Had the brigade moved as one, and reached the gun line at roughly the same time, the story would have been quite different. The three battalions together, even in their weakened state, would have had a far better chance of seeing off the Sikh counter-attack.

To the left of them Hoggan's brigade also attacked. Their route was slightly easier as the jungle was not as thick. The failure of the artillery to protect them had caused some problems. Yet when the Sikh artillery opened up at a range of around 400 yards, its aim was off and much of the fire went over the heads of the brigade. The 61st Foot were the first to attack. Although confronted by cavalry their volley fire was enough to drive them off, before they successfully captured the Sikh guns. The 36th Native Infantry were confronted by Sikh infantry and were beaten back, retreating in confusion and losing both their colours. The 46th Native Infantry fared better and despite being confronted by cavalry were able to drive them off. However, with the withdrawal of the 36th Native Infantry the right flank of the 61st was now unprotected. They came under attack from this direction, but Campbell, taking personal command, wheeled around the two companies nearest the right flank to meet the attack and the Sikhs were repelled. This also had the added effect of defeating the infantry that were pursuing the retreating native infantry. The 61st and 46th resisted further attacks from Sikh infantry and cavalry, and eventually swept along the line of the Sikh defences to the point where Pennycuik's brigade had been defeated. In the process they captured 13 guns, although only three were able to be taken from the field.

Eventually they joined up with Brigadier Mountain's brigade. They were joined by batteries of horse artillery and a squadron of the 8th Bengal Light Cavalry who had been acting as escort for the guns. The latter was a wise precaution put in place on the initiative of Thackwell. However, before leaving the battle on the left flank it is important to note that the cavalry of White's brigade, commanded by Thackwell in person, achieved little during the battle. This was largely due to

---

13   Burton, *The First and Second Sikh Wars*, pp. 146–147.

the nature of the terrain. If the jungle was difficult for the infantryman to navigate it was almost impossible for the cavalryman. Although offensively they achieved little, they did keep most of the Sikh cavalry away from the infantry and artillery on that side of the battlefield. Seeing that there was little opportunity to attack Thackwell wisely used his cavalry to support and cover the attack led by Campbell.

Gilbert's division on the right on the British position had also met its fair share of resistance. The left hand brigade was that of Brigadier Mountain, and we have already mentioned how they eventually joined Campbell's division on the Sikh line. Rather than the tradition of placing the European regiment between the two native infantry battalion, Mountain had positioned the 30th Native Infantry on the left, the 56th Native Infantry in the centre and the 29th Foot on the right. In an interesting moment, when the 29th Foot cleared the jungle, they halted, regained their order, fired a volley and then advanced. This perhaps points to the fact that the orders not to fire and to clear the Sikh line with the bayonet only were more the attitude of individual commanders, be that at regimental or divisional level, than a general order given by Gough. The 29th's volley did cause some damage to the Sikh line. Fierce hand-to-hand fighting then ensued with Sikh infantry and the gunners, who as usual defended their guns manfully. The Sikhs withdrew and the battalion captured 12 guns. However the two native infantry battalions did not fare as well. The 56th lost order with what turned out to be the mortal wounding of their commander, Major Daniel Bamfield, and a number of officers, and were driven back by Sikh cavalry. The Grenadier Company made a stand, but to little effect. The 30th eventually managed to join up with the 29th Foot.

Meanwhile the 29th had been under continued attack. From their right they were attacked by Sikh infantry. The battalion was wheeled to the right and managed to see off the attack. However almost immediately they were attacked in the rear by Sikh cavalry. Seeing off this new threat they joined up with the 30th and the Grenadier Company of the 56th Native Infantry. The brigade had suffered large-scale casualties. The 29th lost 31 killed and four officers and 203 wounded. Given the severity of the battle they had faced, the casualties were hardly severe, and point to the good way in which the regiment was handled. The 56th Native Infantry had two officers and 43 men killed and six officers and 227 wounded. One of the officers wounded, the aforementioned Major Bamfield, subsequently died of his wounds and this accounts for the occasional discrepancy in the number of officers killed.[14] The 30th Native Infantry lost two officers and 65 men killed and 10 officers 209 wounded. The remainder of the 56th eventually rallied and joined up with Godby's brigade. At the same time the 31st native infantry, attached to Godby's brigade, had become detached from this formation and found their way to Mountain's brigade. All serves to illustrate the rather confused nature of events. Partly the poor control of the army, from the top down, can be blamed for this. However the terrain and in particular the thickness of the jungle added to the usual confusion and disjointed nature of a battlefield, all played a part.

To complete the narrative of the battle we turn to the right flank where the other brigade of Gilberts' division, commanded by Brigadier Godby, and Pope's cavalry brigade were to be found. In a bizarre incident that has never been fully explained, Pope's cavalry suffered a severe setback and were virtually taken out of the battle. Exactly what happened is uncertain, and it is yet another piece of a generally confused battle. Pope had no experience of commanding such a large formation, and this has sometimes been used as a reason for the poor performance of the cavalry on this flank. As we have already seen from the other flank, the terrain and jungle did not help the deployment and use of the cavalry. Pope's biggest mistake was to organise his cavalry in one long line. This meant that he had no reserve or support for any part of his brigade. In theory, Pope was supported by a battery of horse artillery, but the brigade seems to have advanced ahead of them. When this

---

14   Burton, *The First and Second Sikh Wars*, pp. 146–147.

battery was eventually able to come up in support, it was unable to fire for fear of hitting the cavalry in front of it. Seeing some Sikh cavalry in front of them Pope ordered 'threes right' to deal with the threat. However it has been argued, and it was certainly the opinion of Major James Hope Grant, later a general and a knight but this day commanding the 9th Lancers, that the horse sighted might not even have been Sikh at all. Grant felt it was in fact some of their own irregular horse who were on the right of the battlefield to watch the Sikh forces at Russool.[15]

Exactly what happened next has never been established. Some officers of the Bengal Light Cavalry came charging back with news of the Sikh cavalry. Somewhere or somehow the order 'threes about' was heard. Whether this was a mishearing of 'threes right', a response to the somewhat frantic movement of the officers of the Bengal Light Cavalry, or whether the order was actually given, has never been established and will likely never be known. Thus in the face of the enemy the entire brigade turned about and started to move to the rear. The Sikhs, doubtless hardly able to believe their luck, charged the rear of the brigade and it was soon in full flight. The horse artillery were unable to withdraw their guns quickly enough and four guns were lost to the Sikhs, with their commander also falling as he tried to defend his guns. The two native light cavalry regiments, the 1st and the 6th, seem to have left the field entirely. The 9th Lancers and the 14th Light Dragoons were eventually rallied, but took no further part in the battle.

Thus through a misunderstood order, or perhaps such a command being given by someone without the authority to do so, the entire cavalry force on the right side of the field had been sent flying from the field. It is hard not to lay the blame at the feet of Pope. In fairness it must be added that in the early part of the incident he was wounded and unable to give much command, however it again speaks ill of the staff arrangements that no one could stop this ridiculous incident. It was only when they had fled to their starting point that any sense of order was restored. Much credit in this regard has been given to the Rev Walter Whiting, who stopped many troopers, even going so far as to threaten some at gunpoint to turn around.[16] The legend has grown that he had assured the men that God would not allow a Christian army to be routed by heathens. Much of his role has perhaps been exaggerated, largely due to its somewhat unusual nature. It must be pointed out that Captain Frederick Haines, Gough's military secretary, Lieutenant Colonel John Bloomfield Gough, quartermaster general, and even Lieutenant Colonel Patrick Grant, adjutant general, were equally active in helping to stem the flow of retreating troopers and bring some order to proceedings.

Brigadier Alexander Pope clearly has to take his fair share of the blame. Once a fine and dashing cavalry officer, he was now nearing 60 years of age, in ill health, and vastly overweight to the point where he could not mount his horse without assistance. He was also without experience of commanding such a large body of cavalry. His position as brigadier was owed to the fact that he was the senior officer, and again illustrates the problems associated with promotion. One must question Gough's decision to keep such a man, based upon the state of his weight and physical condition alone, in such a position. Yet it is easy for the modern reader to criticise something which seems anachronistic to us but would not have created the same reaction in the time we are speaking of. Gough, in one sense, was obliged to use the officers he had. Pope had committed a tactical error in lining his men up in one continuous line without supporting units. His main problem was his lack of control. Whether he gave the order to turn around in the face of the enemy is only part of the question. The major problem was his failure to exercise control, or to regain control, after this had

---

15   Cook, *The Sikh Wars*, pp. 176–177. Burton, *The First and Second Sikh Wars*, pp. 101–102.
16   The Rev Walter J. Whiting, MA was an assistant was an assistant chaplin in the Bengal presidency station at Umballa (Amballa). He died in 1885 and is buried in Arnos Vale Cemetery in Bristol.

been given. In fairness it must be pointed out that he was wounded in the skirmish and would later die of his wounds on 20 April 1849.

Thackwell certainly felt that the failure lay with the actions or inaction of Pope and later wished that:

> Could I have anticipated such an untoward circumstance I should have been on the spot to have given the benefit of my experience to an officer deemed fully competent to have the command of a Brigade of Cavalry, and I feel assured, from what I have heard of Brigadier Pope and the conduct of the cavalry of the right, that their retrograde movement originated more from mistake than a fear of encountering an insignificant enemy.[17]

Indeed perhaps Thackwell would have been better served by accompanying Pope's rather than White's brigade. That he did not was probably due to the faith he had in the two British regiments attached to Pope's Brigade rather than Pope himself.

This bizarre incident had robbed Gilbert's division, and in particular Godby's brigade, not only of its cavalry protection but also much of its artillery support. This brigade had deployed in the more traditional formation with the 2nd Bengal Europeans in the centre flanked by the 31st Native Infantry on its left and the 70th Native Infantry on its right. The brigade suffered far less from Sikh artillery than the other brigades. However Gilbert was particularly concerned that with the defeat of the cavalry his right was unprotected. To guard against this he ordered Godby to place the 70th in square formation to guard against any cavalry attack from that direction. The 2nd Bengal Europeans made the Sikh defences and cleared the Sikhs. However shortly after that they started to come under fire from the rear. It appears that some Sikh infantry had manoeuvred behind Godby's brigade. At the same time Sikh cavalry prepared to attack. Whilst the European Regiment wheeled around to meet the infantry threat, the cavalry were dispersed by artillery fire from a field battery that had come up in support of the assault. Gilbert now ordered the 2nd Bengal Europeans to charge the enemy and they managed to clear the Sikh infantry directly behind them. The battalion then continued to lay down volley fire to clear other Sikh infantry that threatened to attack. They had performed bravely despite being largely unsupported, save for the battery of field artillery, as the 70th held the right flank in square formation and the 31st Native Infantry had become lost and joined up with Brigadier Mountain's brigade. The 70th Native Infantry suffered only slight casualties, five killed and 20 wounded, and this reflected the fact that their main effort had been to cover the right flank left exposed by the cavalry brigade's exit from the battlefield. The 31st had also suffered few casualties due to getting lost, suffering only three killed and 14 wounded. Yet despite the fact that they had been quite heavily engaged, and unsupported, for much of the action the 2nd Bengal Europeans only had six killed and 61 wounded. The relatively low number speaks to the way in which they were handled by their battalion commander Major James Steel.[18]

The only major part of the army that we have not mentioned is the reserve brigade commanded by Brigadier Penny that consisted entirely of native infantry. When Gough became aware of the problems being experienced by Pennycuick's brigade, he ordered Penny's brigade forward. However, like many other units on the battlefield, it became lost and when it eventually found its way to the front it met up with Godby's brigade. On arrival, Penny usefully filled the gap that had emerged between Godby's and Mountain's brigades.

---

17   Rait, *Gough*, Vol. II, p. 235.
18   Burton, *The First and Second Sikh Wars*, pp. 146–147. Although he appears on the 'India List' as Major James Steel, Burton refers to him as 'Major Steele'.

The battle was to all intents and purposes at an end. Night was falling and, despite a desire to pursue the Sikhs as they withdrew towards the Jhelum, Gough prudently decided that this was a risk too far. It was also the case that he had a tired army. The problems with his cavalry may also have had a bearing on his decision not to pursue. His first intention was to hold the position that his men had taken. Yet he was prevailed upon by many of his officers, most notably Campbell, to fall back on Chillianwala village, with its supply of fresh water, as a better place to camp the night. It was also where most of the baggage was to be found, as Gough had ordered up the remainder of it to Chillianwala village. Although reluctant to lose the ground that he had gained Gough felt it necessary to withdraw. However he would not leave his wounded behind and refused to leave until all the wounded had been withdrawn. Gough is often quoted as saying, "I'll be damned if I move till my wounded all are safe." Gough later recorded that only one wounded soldier was left behind that night, and in the morning even that solitary soldier was successfully withdrawn.[19]

The case of the wounded needs some further explanation. During the battle many wounded are recorded as being killed by the Sikhs, something which later in the battle the British reciprocated. This may have influenced further Gough's natural inclination to withdraw all his wounded. It was later recorded that some wounded that were missed in the darkness and thickness of the jungle were later murdered. However whether this was the action of the Sikhs or the local villagers is open to conjecture. Many of the bodies were stripped, and this might suggest that the villagers were the more likely suspects. Also, a number of British prisoners in the hands of the Sikhs were well treated and two men of the 9th Lancers were returned after the battle. It also goes somewhat against the Sikh character to have committed such cold-blooded murder after the battle, although that is not to say that it did not happen.

Sadly the inevitable happened during the night, and the Sikhs returned to the battlefield, retrieved many of the guns they had lost, and were able to remove anything they wanted from the battlefield. After spending the night at Chillianwala, Gough had intended to continue the battle the following day. However the weather had turned and for the next four days heavy rains prevented a renewal of action and, indeed, prevented any major movement. There is every reason to believe that had the weather been better that Gough would have continued his pursuit of the enemy with success.

Perhaps Gough's luck ran out at Chillianwala. There was no quirk of fate or fortune to act in his favour this time. It is certainly true that not all that went wrong was his fault, and others do deserve their share of blame. Yet one can question the decision to give battle. In a letter to Dalhousie, written the day after Chillianwala, Gough lamented the high casualties but questioned if it could have been otherwise.

> I before said our loss has been great, but when it is taken into account the determined struggle of the Sikhs, their mostly superior force and the strength of their position which could not be turned, as by attempting the [Sikh] right I would have thrown the army into infinitely a more dense jungle, whilst their left was upon a precipitous hill intersected with deep ravines and almost resting on the river, that loss, although it is deeply to be regretted, could hardly be avoided.[20]

Gough's statement makes a strong case in his defence but it does raise questions. Given that the Sikhs occupied a strong positon, that his artillery had been unable to do much damage, and that he

---

19   Forest, *Life of Chamberlain*, p. 222.
20   NAM: 8303–105, Gough Papers, Gough to Dalhousie, 14 January 1848.

was unable to turn either the left or right flank, the question has to be asked in regards to whether or not he should have given battle.

Perhaps a more astute commander would have continued to march his army, hoping, or indeed trying, to engineer a better situation in which to give battle, although given his limited options this would have been easier said than done. Yet one cannot believe that not giving battle ever crossed Gough's mind. Partly this was due to practicalities. To move to his right or left would require a major river crossing, and given the debacle at Ramnagar one can understand him not wanting to attempt this. As a consequence the direction of his movement would be known.

It was also unlikely that he could move quickly, unlike the Sikhs, so he was unable to outmanoeuvre them. There was also the very real question of morale. Gough took this incredibly seriously and the idea of withdrawing before the face of the enemy, even if for sound tactical reasons, was akin to a defeat. Just an importantly he feared that it would be construed as such, firstly by his army and in particular his native contingent, but also by the press and by the politicians. It is interesting that in a long letter to Dalhousie, written after the battle, Gough made no hint that he considered anything other than giving battle. Indeed he was sure that to have waited could have brought about an even harder battle, giving the Sikhs time to improve their defences and bring more men to the field.

It is easy for anyone to sit at home in Britain or India, months or years after the event, and condemn Gough for giving battle. The casualties were high, but as he himself pointed out, how could they be otherwise under the circumstances? Total British losses were 602 killed, 1,651 wounded and a further 104 unaccounted for. This total 2,357 was large and quite unexpected for a campaign against native opposition, yet that would be to both underestimate the Sikhs, their equipment, and their training. Perhaps more troubling were the lost colours and guns. This gave the battle the air of an inconclusive action or even worse a defeat. It was the mention of lost guns and colours and the high casualty returns for a battle against natives that led to an outcry in the press. Yet Chillianwala was not a defeat by any stretch of the imagination. It was at worst a draw. If one calls it a victory it was to a degree a pyrrhic one. In 1862, the historian Edwin Arnold called the battle of Chillianwala a 'disastrous success'.[21] Sikh losses have never been established accurately. Whilst some have sought over the years to reduce the likely number it is hard to believe given the actions fought in the battle that they were much if at all less than British losses. A figure of around 3,000 Sikh casualties seems entirely reasonable.

The future Field Marshal Neville Chamberlain, who was present at the battle, considered that it was a draw but that it broke the Sikhs ability to continue the war for much longer.[22] Whilst Chamberlain perhaps went a little too far in his comments, there was some justification. The Sikhs had lost men and ammunition that they would have great difficulty in replacing, whereas Gough already had reinforcements coming from Multan and had the possibility of supplies from British India. Even the addition of Chatar Singh and reinforcements from Afghanistan would not adequately replace the stores, guns and men lost by the Sikhs at Chillianwala. There was even a source from within the Sikh camp that stated that it was fortunate for them that Gough was not able to follow up his attack the following day, as the Sikhs had been badly shaken by Chillianwala and were vulnerable. Indeed the same source noted that had there been an attack it is likely that the Sikhs would have been driven into the Jhelum, and the war could have been all but ended.[23] Yet the

---

21   Arnold, *The Marquis of Dalhousie's Administration of British India*, Vol. I, p. 176.
22   Forrest, *Life of Chamberlain*, pp. 225–227.
23   Cook, *The Sikh Wars*, p. 179, quotes a Sikh 'General' by the name of Elihu Baksh as the source for information about the state of the Sikh army after Chillianwala. Forrest, *Life of Chamberlain*, pp. 225–227, has Chamberlain also supporting this view but does not name Elihu Baksh.

circumstances, and in particular the elements, did not allow Gough to follow up his attack on the morrow. It is in this sense that perhaps Gough's luck ran out.

There is also a sense in which Gough was partly let down by the mistakes of his subordinates. Indeed it would be wrong to lay all the blame on Gough. Pennycuick should perhaps have kept better order of his brigade. The mysterious movement of Robertson's horse artillery on the orders of an unknown staff officer was also something over which Gough could have little control. The failure of the artillery to keep up with the advancing infantry, or perhaps the failure of the infantry to wait for its artillery support, was a problem of coordination over which he could have little control. It is worth remembering that it was Gough's plan in the first place to coordinate the attack in this way.

The poor performance of Brigadier Pope has already been considered, and he justly deserves a share of the blame. The performance of Campbell is also one that was mixed. His leadership of Hoggan's brigade was excellent. In this he was helped by Thackwell not only covering his advance and supporting his attack but also by his decision to give an escort to his artillery support. Yet his decision not to attach himself to the brigade that had the more difficult route, and was therefore likely to need the benefit of extra officers, was questionable. Exactly what role he played in the 'bayonet only' saga has been debated by historians for years, and is to an extent beyond our remit. Rait, in his defence of Gough's performance at Chillianwala became rather bogged down with it, and as we have already discussed there was a wider debate about the effectiveness of firing before a final charge which was prevalent at the time. It was felt in many quarters that the decision to halt and give a volley before the final charge only served to slow momentum. Yet in reality this was only a minor point in regards to the battle. There were far more serious problem on the day than that.

Yet whoever else deserves a share of the blame, the responsibility ultimately lay with Gough. It is to his credit that whatever he said in private he never publicly blamed any of his subordinates. The problem was that a perception either rightly or wrongly had grown of Gough as a 'cold steel' general much favouring the 'Tipperary Rush' or 'Tipperary Tactics'. To an extent this was justified. He was a largely unimaginative general who believed that the power of the British Army lay in the steady and determined nature of its infantry. However there were few imaginative British generals of this age, and few who would have believed in different tactics to those he used. It should be recalled that Gough had before the battle considered the turning of either flank yet this was infeasible. However, mitigation was not what the press, politicians or the public wanted to consider. The performance of the army had been below their expectations, the loss of colours and guns, high casualties, and a failure to hold the gains taken during the battle, smacked of a defeat. An explanation, if not a scapegoat, for this occurrence was wanted. It was found in the commander-in-chief. Whatever difficulties Gough had faced in the campaign up to now were nothing to the storm of criticism that would come his way in the aftermath of the battle.

69

The Aftermath of Chillianwala: The Press Reaction

News of the battle of Chillianwala took its time to reach Britain. Indeed by the time it did the war was all but over, and Gough had won the final victory of Gujrat. When news broke in early March 1849 regarding the battle of Chillianwala, news of Gujrat was still far behind. Indeed, such was the usual pace of bureaucracy that private accounts of the battle arrived long before Gough's official despatch. This delay in correspondence and communication between India and London needs to be appreciated. It is why in our consideration of the aftermath of the Battle of Chillianwala we look at events, many of which took place after the war had been ended but before that information reached the authorities in London.

The Times summed up the sentiments of the press in general in its edition of 5 March 1849. It declared that:

> Awful is the responsibility of those who have for so long maintained in command a General whose incompetence they have never hesitated to confess, and who have tendered the feelings of an obstinate old man at the expense of a carnage which has filled so many households with mourning, and deprived the British Army of hundreds of its choicest soldiers.[1]

Although the above quotation from *The Times* called Gough incompetent, it did suggest that the blame lay more with the politicians who had kept him in place rather than Gough himself. However the same article continually attacked both the character and ability of Gough. Indeed, the article began with criticism both of Gough and the politicians for the way in which the 'victory' had been received

> The Intelligence from India, though heralded by Royal salutes and announced in terms of official gratulation (sic), will only be received in this country with universal sentiments of regret and dismay. The field of Ferozeshah has been fought over again, with the simple difference that the carnage was on this occasion purely gratuitous, and the result wholly unproductive.[2]

The article went on to criticise Gough's 'protracted inaction' in the campaign thus far, his failure at reconnaissance, the undefined nature of his artillery bombardment, and his unusual decision to attack the main defences at Chillianwala head on. All were legitimate questions, yet there was no attempt to examine either the reason or mitigation. Indeed no attempt was made to understand the build up to the battle or the circumstances in which it was undertaken. There was no mention of Dalhousie's 'instructions' to attack. No mention of Dalhousie's delays in preparing the army that

---

1   *The Times*, 5 March 1849.
2   *The Times*, 5 March 1849.

led to the inaction of the early campaign. Indeed the article was simply an attack on Gough and those seen to be responsible for him still being in power.

The Times followed up its attack by printing extracts of letters it claimed were from people present at the camp of the Army of the Punjab. *The Times* was careful never to actually say that the letters were from people who had been present at the battle itself, but that was certainly what the reader was expected to conclude. They included such comments as, "It indeed has been a sad business, and it is impossible to predict when our mishaps, and such fearful butchery and wanton sacrifice of life, will end or stop, under such a Commander-in-Chief."[3] The identity of the individual who had written this was not disclosed. Although, given the critical nature of his letter, this is understandable, it gives us no idea of exactly what role or rank he held in the army. Indeed we do not even know that he was a soldier or that he was even at the battle, just that he was in the camp of the Army of the Punjab on 19 January.

The authenticity of such letters must be questioned. There are some errors in the letter, such as a letter written on the 19 January declaring that Brigadier Alexander Pope had died of his wounds, something that could not have been known at the time, as indeed on 19 January Pope was still alive. It claims the British lost six guns, as opposed to only four. The letter also makes the statement that "His Lordship [Gough] fancied himself at Donnybrook Fair, and was in the thick of it, in the melee, and lost to sight!"[4] This was not true, and it will be recalled that when Pope's cavalry brigade had made their way back they were eventually stopped by officers of Gough's staff, with whom he was present throughout. It is likely that Gough went forward to better judge for himself the precise nature of the events, but that was later in the battle. Such behaviour as riding forward to get a better feel for the battle was not unusual, and indeed Wellington did it often, perhaps most notably at Waterloo. Such letters in *The Times* had a powerful effect, but as has already been mentioned they were only half the story. They had more of an effect upon politicians than they might, had Gough's own report of the battle been received before *The Times* made such statements.

The Times also stretched the truth in concluding that the failure of Pope's cavalry was down to a lack of confidence in Gough's leadership and an example of the rock-bottom morale in the Army and extreme lack of confidence in Gough. Such a statement was so far removed from the truth as to be amusing in another context. There was no lack of morale at this stage. Yet when opinions such as this were being expressed without an alternative point of view, it was extremely dangerous.[5]

It would also be dangerous to take the opinion of one or indeed several unnamed individuals as being the prevailing opinion in the army. Perhaps here is a problem in discerning the views of the army. Those officers who felt bitterly about the way in which the army had been led were likely to vent their frustration in their correspondence. However those who were indifferent or indeed even supportive of the Commander-in-Chief did not have the same motivation to express such an opinion. Indeed on the evening of the battle as his weary men lay resting they cheered Gough profusely as he made a tour of his camp at Chillianwala.[6]

The problem with *The Times* was that it clearly had an agenda, and that agenda was to blame the perceived failure of the army squarely on leadership rather than the state of the army. We will examine later the motivation behind such an agenda, but for now it is sufficient to say that the newspapers were largely devoid of any contrary opinion. As previously mentioned it was not only those who felt aggrieved who felt the need to express their opinions. Many officers might have gained completely the wrong impression of the battle from their vantage point. Such critical

3   *The Times*, 5 March 1849. The letter from the anonymous 'correspondent' is dated 19 January 1849. Yet no place is given from where the letter was written.
4   *The Times*, 5 March 1849.
5   *The Times*, 5 March 1849.
6   Bruce, *Six Battles for India*, p. 296.

letters were likely to be written by officers who had seen the worst of the battle. The problem was that there was no attempt at balance by placing both critical and non-critical letters in the public domain. Indeed there were many scores being settled and much partial criticism. This was a view supported by Edward Joseph Thackwell, son of Gough's cavalry commander Joseph Thackwell. The younger Thackwell was no fan of Gough and indeed was deeply critical of him in his book on the Sikh wars. Yet even he felt that the criticism of Gough was dubious in nature:

> The letters which appeared in the Indian newspapers during the progress of the campaign, containing animadversions on Lord Gough, were often based on false statements, and dictated by the most paltry malice. Men, who had been unsuccessful in their application for staff appointments, vented their spite in elaborate articles, casting the most unwarrantable aspersions on the character of that illustrious soldier. Thus they were able to gratify their vindictive feelings without any fear of detection, for the papers to which their dastardly libels were sent did not previously insist on their authentication.[7]

It was, however, only the critical letters that saw the light of day in the press at this time. Yet the alternative point of view did exist and was expressed. Lieutenant George Galloway was an officer on the staff of Major General Gilbert and was present at the battle. Lieutenant Galloway was the son of Major General Sir Archibald Galloway, formerly an officer in the East India Company Army, a noted writer on Indian and military tactics in general, and a Director of the East India Company. In 1849 he would become its Chairman, and one can understand that his son would be aware that any criticism of Gough could easily rebound on his father. Whilst it could be argued that he had a vested interest in supporting Gough, his opinions are worth hearing if only for the sake of contrast.

> It is so easy to condemn in generalities. What will be thought of the battle of Chillianwala is easily surmised [sic] from the abuse heaped upon Lord Gough for the affair of Cavalry before Ramnuggur. His Lordship had quite as much to say to what went wrong in the one as to the reckless bravery which alone caused the great loss we sustained in the other. [...] Until some proof is given that it was wrong to attack Shere Sing [Sher Singh] at Chillianwala, Lord G. is no more blameable for what occurred than I am.[8]

Galloway also makes an interesting point regarding the way in which the battle was perceived. He argues that but for the failure of two individuals, Pennycuick and Pope, the battle would, in his words, "have rivalled any Victory yet won against this brave and formidable Enemy." In one sense this is a valid point.[9]

The achievements of the army at Chillianwala should not be lost in the face of the high casualties. They had taken a well defended Sikh position. The casualties were at their highest where mistakes had been made either by Campbell, Pennycuick or Pope. The loss sustained by the 24th Foot did unbalance the casualty returns: of the 601 killed at Chillianwala, 204 were sustained by that regiment. In other words about 34 percent of the fatalities sustained at Chillianwala were men of the 24th Foot. Indeed if one goes further and calculates the casualties sustained by Pennycuick's brigade it accounts for 53 percent of those killed in the battle. It is therefore tempting to blame Pennycuick and attach to him the reason for the high casualty returns at Chillianwala. This would

---

7   Thackwell, *Narrative of the Second Seikh War*, p. 192.
8   Rait, *Gough*, Vol. II, pp. 242–243.
9   Rait, *Gough*, Vol. II, p. 243.

be unfair. Pennycuick was trying to do the best he could in a bad situation. He was slightly let down by his divisional commander, but, as Charles Napier later pointed out, what else could Pennycuick have done. Yet there is clearly a case to answer in regards to the handling of this brigade, an action made harder by the high casualties amongst its officers.

This does not exonerate Gough from blame, but it does illustrate the fact that there was more to the story than appeared in the press at the time. Indeed there was something akin to hysteria around the whole issue. Gough was also being judged on his past record, or, perhaps more accurately, the perception of his past record. It also did not help that men who did not know all, or indeed even half, of the facts, spoke on the matter with 'authority'. This was particularly unhelpful when they were distinguished gentleman such as Lord Hardinge who publicly claimed that Gough had with him an army of over 60,000. What Hardinge might have meant was that the total forces commanded by Gough were around this number, although 50,000 was really the most he had to hand. Yet such forces were spread over a wide area. However, Hardinge's figure was subsequently quoted as being an accurate total for Gough's forces at Chillianwala, when in actuality he had around 24,000 men. Yet of this total, only around 13, 000 were engaged in the battle. Even this figure was misinterpreted when in late April the President of the Board of Control, John Hobhouse, stated in the House of Commons that Gough had commanded 18,000 men at Chillianwala. The inability of the politician responsible to Parliament for India to give an accurate figure gives us an idea of how partial the knowledge of events was even by this time.[10]

Yet in one sense this was part of a wider campaign against Gough that had existed before Chillianwala became known. In an interesting editorial on 2 February 1849 *The Times* had questioned not so much Gough's ability for command as his suitability.

> There is, to speak the truth, a resemblance between Lord Gough and his troops far closer than is desirable in the compound which should result from a Commander-in-Chief and his army. What is required with British soldiers is such a guidance as shall rather control than excite them, as shall rather economize than expend their superabundant valour, and as shall substitute the tactics of a saving for costly appeals to personal daring. Lord Gough directs a forlorn hope as naturally as he would lead one, and confines his reliance to that physical valour which has so often stood him in stead.[11]

These comments by the newspaper, before any detail of Chillianwala had arrived before them, illustrate a wider dislike of Gough's style. This is not so much a tactical criticism as a personal one. The suggestion is that Gough was a brave and determined leader but not the right sort of man to command an army. In short he was 'as brave as a lion, but he has no head piece'. To an extent there is some truth in this view put forward by the newspaper. Gough was a brave and determined leader who led from the front, and was able to motivate and encourage his men to almost suicidal bravery. His tactics were not as simplistic as are often portrayed but were far from sophisticated. That said, there were few within the British Army of that age who had a sophisticated approach to battle. Let us not forget that it was Charles Napier, the man thought most appropriate to replace Gough, who had written that 'Firing is a weapon of defence not of attack'.

Although there had been minor changes, this was still the army and the tactics of the Napoleonic Age. Gough's greatest failure, and the way in which the above quote from *The Times* is correct, is in that Gough was not a typical commander-in-chief in the strategic sense. He had only limited administrative ability, but more importantly he had a lack of interest in such work. In one sense

---

10   Rait, *Gough*, Vol. II, p. 287, *Hansard*, House of Commons Debate, 24 April 1849, Vol. 104, cc734–57.
11   *The Times*, 2 February 1849.

this is what a staff should have been able to do for Gough. That he was let down by staff officers is unquestionable. Gough had complicated matters by having his nephew and his son in law on his staff, and thus he perhaps failed to see their failings because of this. Patrick Grant, who as adjutant general acted as chief of staff in all but name, was not really the right man for the job in terms of ability. Yet he was loyal and devoted to Gough, something that the latter valued highly.

The *Times* was far from the only newspaper to take aim at Gough during this period. *The Morning Herald* gives another good example of the 'authoritative' but ill-informed nature of press coverage and reaction. The *Morning Herald* stated that, "Lord Gough, in spite of the protest of wiser men than himself, in spite of his own promise, threw himself upon the enemy's position without a thought of reconnoitring it." Exactly who the 'wiser men than himself' were is hard to define. Indeed there is no record of any one of his officers appealing for an alternative plan of campaign before the battle. A great many claimed to be wise after the event and wrote of turning flanks that were all but impossible to turn. Indeed it is slightly strange that when Gough was criticised for not reconnoitring the ground before him properly, that the press and numerous authors presented schemes that showed a complete ignorance of the topography and geography of the area, not to mention the deployment of Sikh forces.[12]

If the British newspapers seemed to have an agenda against Gough, more than purely in terms of the results of Chillianwala, then the Indian newspapers were little different. Indeed Gough had a poor relationship with the Indian press. This probably stemmed from a public comment when he had referred to them as the 'curse of India'. Chillianwala gave them an opening and the Indian press could, in the words of Sir Robert Rait, 'enjoy its revenge'. Indeed much of what emerged in the British press was based on reports from Indian newspapers or journalists in India.[13]

Yet Gough retained, in public at least, a dignified silence. His only public comment was to issue a signed statement repudiating the aforementioned passage in the *Morning Herald*, stating that its accusations were "all gratuitous falsehoods, without a shadow of truth in any one of them."[14] It would have been difficult for Gough to have fought back any other way. He had few friends in the press to present his side of events. He was also still, when the first stories broke, on campaign and thus had more important things on his mind. Gough actually cared little for what the press wrote. He accepted it as an almost inevitable fact of life. Whilst others would in later times spring to his defence, he felt no need to do so himself against the comments of the press.

12   Rait, *Gough*, Vol. II, p. 289.
13   Rait, *Gough*, Vol. II, p. 288.
14   Rait, *Gough*, Vol. II, p. 289.

70

The Aftermath of Chillianwala: The Political Reaction

Exactly how much the government's decision to take action, and supersede Gough, was motivated by press clamour is difficult to ascertain. It is inconceivable that it did not play a factor. Yet there was perhaps a deeper concern. To some it no doubt felt as if they had been here before, and there are obviously analogies to the discussions that took place during the First Sikh War, although it was of course now a different government that considered the matter. Perhaps of greater concern to those in power were not the words of the press but those of the Governor General. It is perhaps to Dalhousie's comment on Gough that the greatest burden for the eventual decision to replace Gough laid. Sir Robert Rait concluded that "Lord Dalhousie, more than any other man, was responsible for the action taken by the Government." Rait would go on to claim that, because of Dalhousie's previous appointment as a member of the cabinet of Sir Robert Peel during the First Sikh War and his familiarity with the discussions and comments made by Hardinge to the government, Dalhousie "therefore, commenced his career in India with a prejudice against Lord Gough, a prejudice which he believed to be known to the Government of Lord John Russell." Whilst perhaps a little unfair, there was some truth to Sir Robert's belief.[1]

It would be wrong not to appreciate that Dalhousie was in a difficult position. He only knew part of the story regarding Chillianwala. He had inherited something of a poisoned chalice from Hardinge when he succeeded him as governor general. Arrangements regarding the new territory, the relationship with the Sikh state, and the reductions in the army, had already been established before he arrived. There was also a clash of personalities between him and Gough but perhaps also a generational clash. Gough after all was now 69 years old and a product of the old order whereas Dalhousie was nearing his 37th birthday. Dalhousie was also something of a modern figure whereas Gough could with some justification be said to belong to an era that was fast dying out. Dalhousie was a young man in a hurry anxious to advance. He was a clever man, with great self-confidence, but also a rather overbearing nature. He did rather presume to talk to Gough as an equal on military matters, which did surely not go down well with the older man. This was particularly true when in the aftermath of Chillianwala, Dalhousie wrote a letter to Gough in which he lectured him about the importance of artillery. Gough took this letter with remarkable good grace, and did not respond in anything other than a positive way. Gough would most certainly have been forgiven for reacting angrily to such presumption on the part of Dalhousie. Yet Gough's opinion of Dalhousie is somewhat harder to define. Regardless of what Dalhousie's biographer states, Gough did sometimes find Dalhousie's 'suggestions' and 'advice' in his letters somewhat objectionable and did at times resent his presumption.[2]

Yet, as we have already seen in an earlier chapter, despite these concerns regarding Gough Dalhousie had not seriously objected to the renewal of Gough's period of command shortly before

---

1   Rait, *Gough*, Vol. II, p. 290.
2   Lee-Warner, *The Life of Dalhousie*, p. 217.

the Second Sikh War commenced. There was any number of plausible and legitimate reasons under the guise of which Dalhousie could have objected to this. As governor general, his opinion was asked for and had he stated clearly that he felt a new, perhaps younger, man was necessary such an opinion would have been listened to. Yet he did not and why has never been firmly established. Whether it was a case of 'better the devil you know' is uncertain. Robert Rait certainly believed that it was Dalhousie's chivalrous nature that prevented him from objecting to Gough's period of command being extended. That seems too easy an explanation, and such a chivalrous nature, if it existed, did not prevent Dalhousie from launching a very strong attack on Gough in his private correspondence in the aftermath of Chillianwala.

Dalhousie's positioning was somewhat unhelpful. He had placed himself at Ferozepore, which whilst still a great distance from the seat of war was near enough that he was wont to panic about his proximity to events, but also to receive somewhat dubious information from the front. Rumours reached him in Ferozepore that would have taken far longer to reach Delhi and which might never have reached Calcutta at all. So Dalhousie was both too close for comfort and too far away to be effective. He was around 100 miles from the Chenab River and roughly another 50 from the scene of the action at Chillianwala. Even before that battle, Dalhousie seems to have convinced himself that Gough would be unable to bring the campaign to a successful conclusion. Whether this was based upon the information he was receiving, the frustration at Gough's slow pace and the failure of Multan to fall sooner, or simply from people 'whispering in his ear', it is hard to ascertain. The truth is that it was probably a combination of all of these things.

Dalhousie's correspondence was also a little hasty, as it was written in the immediate aftermath of Chillianwala. His initial reading of the situation was that the battle had confirmed his opinions regarding Gough. Had he waited, he might have written differently as reports of the action at Chillianwala filtered through. However had he waited at best his report would have been less harsh rather than favourable to Gough. For example his comment that, "the conduct of the battle was beneath the contempt even of a militiaman like myself", was largely based upon gossip rather than fact.[3] Whilst he would not defend Gough's conduct, Dalhousie would in time realise that he was unfair in such a damming indictment of his commander-in-chief. His letter of 22 January to the Duke of Wellington did much damage. It presented the battle in a way which was unfair. It also demonstrates that Dalhousie was relying largely on gossip for his account of the battle rather than fact.

Of the artillery duel before the battle Dalhousie informed Wellington that, "The practice was splendid, and was silencing the enemies batteries and committing tremendous havoc, when he [Gough] ordered the whole army to advance in line, stopping the guns. He had no support or reserve, except two regiments Native Infantry."[4] The idea that the British guns were silencing their Sikh opponent or causing great havoc is incorrect. It will be recalled that the British guns could not see their counterparts and were simply firing at the smoke. Any damage they were doing to the Sikhs was purely due to good fortune. There is also a mistake in that there were in fact three reserve regiments of native infantry, and indeed the cavalry should also have been acting as a reserve. It also ignores the fact that Gough's plan of advance called for the artillery to support the infantry and accompany their attack. It has commonly been asserted that Gough had a vast superiority in guns. He did not. Reports suggest a numerical parity, but, other than his eight heavy guns, Gough had little in the way of artillery that was greatly superior to the Sikhs in terms of size. Yet this story that Gough had overwhelming superiority in guns persists to this day.

3   Lee-Warner, *Life of Dalhousie*, p. 208. Cook, *The Sikh Wars*, p. 180.
4   Lee-Warner, *Life of Dalhousie*, p. 207.

Dalhousie's letter also claims that Gough, "would listen to nothing."[5] Again we have this statement that Gough was being advised against giving battle and was obstinately ignoring such calls. There is little evidence that any officer spoke to him in such a way before the battle. Indeed Gough had already decided to wait until the morrow. It was only when he came under attack that he was forced into action. Dalhousie seems to ignore the point regarding what alternative was there for Gough. He was under fire from Sikh heavy guns, in an undefended position. To stay in position was not an option. To withdraw was not acceptable, and surely would not have been taken kindly by Dalhousie.

Later in the same letter Dalhousie returned to this point regarding his failure to take advice, writing, "Had the Commander-in-Chief acted on the advice universally given, he would have been able to follow up his success, and have driven every man of them before him, taking all their guns."[6] Again, what advice Dalhousie is referring to is unclear. Was this advice not to give battle when fired upon? To withdraw in the face of the enemy? Or not to have advanced upon Chillianwala in the first place? There were a good many people who were wise after the event and talked about turning flanks that could not be turned, or not engaging until the following day, but who were clearly not aware of the actual situation.

Dalhousie again seems to rely upon gossip rather than fact when he stated that,

> In the hands of the Commander-in-Chief I do not now consider that force safe, or free from the risk of disaster. There is not a man in that army from his Generals of Division to the Sepoys who does not proclaim the same thing and write it to his friends. They do not feel themselves safe in his hands, and I grieve to say that much gloom prevails in his camp.[7]

The final point about the mood in the camp is open to debate. It clearly raises the question of how Dalhousie knew this given that he was not himself present in the camp. At best he was getting second-hand information, presumably from officers who owed their allegiance to him rather than Gough.

There were certainly dissenting voices within the camp, as there are in any army, but the circumstances of the Battle at Chillianwala meant that their opinions were being listened to and taken notice of. Exactly who these officers were is never established. Gough did not receive such advice from his senior commanders once the Sikh artillery had opened fire. Before that point anyone who advised Gough to wait until the following day before attacking would have found the Commander-in-Chief in full agreement with them. One such officer was possibly Colonel Frederick Mackeson. He certainly fell into the category of those who had a grudge due to being overlooked for appointments, although ironically in Mackeson's case it probably had more to do with the governor general than the Commander-in-Chief. Mackeson was a political officer and in effect the representative of Dalhousie as governor general rather than Gough as commander-in-chief. Whatever opinion Mackeson had of Gough it was not reciprocated, and Gough had actively sought the appointment of Mackeson to his staff.[8]

Mackeson later claimed that he had advised Gough not to attack, urging greater use of artillery, and that the route of attack was almost impossible for the men to take. Mackeson recorded that Gough rather arrogantly responded that, "I am the Commander-in-Chief and I desire you to be silent."[9] If true, and there is a doubt to its veracity, one can understand Gough's reluctance to

5   Lee-Warner, *Life of Dalhousie*, p. 207.
6   Lee-Warner, *Life of Dalhousie*, p. 208.
7   Lee-Warner, *Life of Dalhousie*, p. 209.
8   NAM: 8303–105, Gough Papers, Gough to Dalhousie, 24 November 1848.
9   Allen, *Soldier Sahibs*, p. 190.

listen to what he would no doubt have interpreted as political interference. Mackeson's role was largely political and Gough would have been understandably reluctant, maybe even resentful, of the presumption in Mackeson's comments. Yet even if this story was true it was not the same as if Gough had been advised by his senior staff or divisional commanders.

Mackeson's version of events was clearly relayed to Dalhousie, and indeed had a great influence upon him. So did the account of an officer called Gifford who informed Dalhousie that he had overheard Gough in conversation with one of his brigadiers comment that, 'Indeed, I had not intended to attack to-day, but the impudent rascals fired on me. They put my Irish blood up, and I attacked them'.[10] The language used in Gifford's statement is clearly not that which Gough would have used and does not really fit into the style of the man. Such a derogatory statement about the supposed temperament of the 'Irish' is one that Gough, a man proud of his Irish heritage, is unlikely to have used. It is therefore likely that at best Gifford was paraphrasing. Indeed an overheard conversation is hardly a reliable source, and it is remarkable that such a comment so often finds its way into accounts of the campaign, given its unreliable source. Part of the reason for this is that the conversation appears to fit the perception of Gough as a short-tempered, aggressive, commander. There are also wider issues regarding the low opinion of the Irish character during this period that also mean that Gough's supposed actions fit into a wider stereotype.

Perhaps Dalhousie should have taken his time and taken wider soundings before he wrote home. One can understand that Dalhousie, whilst not necessarily panicking, was deeply concerned about the future. So much of the British military machine was now committed against the Sikhs that the potential for disaster was huge. Once again the shadow of Afghanistan loomed large over proceedings. Dalhousie, based on the progress of the campaign thus far, convinced himself that Gough was either incapable or unable to bring the campaign to a successful conclusion. It was in this vein that he wrote to the government expressing his concern. It is important to note that in his correspondence with the Government he never directly recommended that Gough be removed. However it was obvious that this was the likely consequences of his comments, particularly on, as he thought, the entire lack of confidence in Gough's ability that existed within his Army.

The closest Dalhousie came to actually saying that Gough had to go was in a letter to Sir John Hobhouse, President of the Board of Control, in which he stated; "If he [Gough] disregards in his obstinacy these means again [the use of his artillery], if he fights an incomplete action with terrible carnage as before, you must expect to hear of my taking a strong step; he shall not remain in command of that army in the field." Dalhousie did not necessarily say that Gough would be removed as commander-in-chief, simply that he would not command the army in the field, and it is clear that for some time Dalhousie had been looking for a way to remove Gough from command of the army without having to take the dramatic step of removing him as commander-in-chief.[11]

Dalhousie's statement is ironic for two reasons. Firstly, because it was written on the very same day, 21 February 1849, that Gough won the battle of Gujrat that effectively ended the war. Secondly, because when news that Gough was to be superseded by Sir Charles Napier reached Dalhousie he was angry that it had been done without reference to him. It is clear from the work of Dalhousie's biographer that he clearly felt that it should have been his decision to make. Perhaps here we see a glimpse of the power politics in which this whole scenario was being played. Not only was it over the war with the Sikhs, and the command and even control of the army, it was also a part of a wider battle over the authority of the British government and the government of India, the latter being

---

10   Lee-Warner, *Life of Dalhousie*, p. 210. Lee-Warner simply calls him Gifford. It is likely that this was Captain James Gifford of the 2nd Bengal Native Infantry, who was attached to the Adjutant General's office.
11   Lee-Warner, *Life of Dalhousie*, pp. 211–212.

embodied in Dalhousie as governor general.[12] That this was part of the power politics between London and India is perhaps illustrated by the change in attitude of Dalhousie after the victory at Gujrat. Whilst one can point to the obvious fact that Gough's success at Gujrat had changed the whole nature of their relationship, and that any immediate danger both in a political and military sense now seemed to have passed, it is also clear that Dalhousie felt a degree of fear as to how his actions would be interpreted. It must be recalled that at this stage the full extent of the outcry in the British press was not fully realised.

Dalhousie's change in tone was illustrated in a letter to Colonel Mountain, who had served under Gough's command in China and the Second Sikh War, when he wrote "If I had made any suggestion to the people at home unfavourable to him [Gough], he should have been himself the first person informed of it." This was a somewhat disingenuous comment and was to an extent an attempt by Dalhousie to place a positive spin on his previous letters home. Indeed Sir John Hobhouse, the President of the Board of Control was greatly annoyed at Dalhousie's repudiation of responsibility with regards to the replacement of Gough. Hobhouse informed Dalhousie that, "The first care of a public functionary should not be for his own reputation."[13]

Dalhousie's biographer, Sir William Lee-Warner, took a similar view and expressed the opinion that:

> There can be little doubt that the anxiety which Lord Dalhousie felt during the earlier stages of the war, and the criticism he had expressed as to its conduct, had, whatever his intention, contributed directly towards the sudden termination of Lord Gough's career in India.[14]

Again, one has to question this statement. Dalhousie can surely have been under no illusions as to the likely consequence of writing home in such a negative tone about Gough. Let us not forget that Dalhousie knew through his political connections how close the government had been to replacing Gough during the First Sikh War, thus he surely cannot have expected that his correspondence would have done anything other than start a repeat of that. One also has to question the wording of Lee-Warner's comments. Replacement as commander-in-chief was not so much an early termination of Gough's career in India than a termination of his prolonged career. It must be remembered that Gough had already served his time and had been granted, by the same government and governor general who had conspired at his removal, an extension to his term of command.

Yet Dalhousie never directly expressed the opinion that Gough should be removed or replaced. In that sense Lee-Warner is correct when he asserts that Dalhousie "had certainly not recommended Lord Gough's recall, nor had he expected such a step without further action on his part. His expressions of regret were therefore honest and sincere, and Lord Gough accepted them as such." Dalhousie was indeed disappointed that the decision to replace Gough had been taken without his approval, yet it is not possible that he did not envisage such a possibility. It is more a case that he felt his authority' was such that no decision would be taken without further consolation with him.[15] There was however a legitimate problem in this regard. The length of delay in communication with India would have caused a potentially severe delay whilst consultation took place. Indeed, had it been attempted, it is unlikely that any decision could have been reached before July at the earliest, and this was unacceptable for a number of reasons. The perception of the situation as a crisis in need of immediate action was one that prevailed in England. It was therefore understandable that

12   Lee-Warner, *Life of Dalhousie*, pp. 226–227 & 248–249.
13   Rait, *Gough* Vol. II, p. 292–293 & Lee-Warner, *Life of Dalhousie*, p. 250.
14   Lee-Warner, *Life of Dalhousie*, p. 250.
15   Lee-Warner, *Life of Dalhousie*, p. 250.

the decision was taken largely without reference to the Governor General. It would also have been interpreted through his correspondence that whilst he did not specifically advocated Gough's removal, he would not have been violently opposed to it.

Whether Gough accepted Dalhousie's expressions of regret as being sincere depends upon how much Gough actually knew of his correspondence with the home government. It does appear that Gough knew little of what had been written home by Dalhousie. He certainly knew there had been correspondence with the home government, but he knew not the nature or content of such correspondence. Gough in fact became convinced that the conspiracy against him emanated from the Duke of Wellington, and not necessarily Dalhousie. Given his knowledge of the close relationship between Dalhousie and the Duke, Gough would have been aware that correspondence passed between them on such matters. If Dalhousie expressed his anxiety and displeasure with the way Gough was running the war this was to be expected. Indeed, he had written as much to Gough in his correspondence with him, so he would hardly have expected him not to have mentioned it to Wellington. Thus Gough's acceptance of Dalhousie's sincere expression of regret was because Gough knew little of his involvement in the affair. He certainly did not know that he had threatened to remove him on his own recourse on the very day of the Battle of Gujrat.

71

Plans to Supersede Gough

Gough certainly saw Wellington's hand behind the move to replace him. The first correspondence from Wellington to Gough concerning matters of this nature was dated 5 March.[1] It is certainly no coincidence that this was the same day that the aforementioned condemnation of both Gough and those who had, in the words of *The Times*, 'maintained' Gough in command was published. It points to the fact that manoeuvring to replace Gough had been going on behind the scenes before the attack by *The Times*. Yet this article in the press must have played a role in Wellington's decision to write that same day. It no doubt prompted Wellington to write to Gough on the matter. In the letter, Wellington started by saying that news of the fall of Multan and the battle of Chillianwala had now reached London and he continued that, "upon which I sincerely congratulate you." However the positive tone of the letter then took an unusual turn. Wellington stated that:

> Her Majesty's servants being sensible that the term of your command was approaching, and that it was probable that you would wish to return to England upon the termination of the campaign had been for some time anxious that a successor to you should be [gap in original letter] and even nominated and different officers had been thought of and Her Majesty's pleasure had been taken on the subject.

Had this been all the letter said Gough might have been forgiven for wondering exactly what was going on. In a letter that was rather rambling Wellington then went on to say that:

> [W]hen the accounts of recent military events in India reached London on Saturday, and the opinions of those in India and also the public opinion was so strongly manifested here of the necessity of talking immediate measures to secure the advantage of having on the spot an officer in whom confidence could be placed in the exercise of the command of the army when you shall come away that I was requested without loss of time to submit to Her Majesty the name of Lt-General Sir Charles Napier as the one most likely by his local experience and the

---

1   It is important to note the debates over superseding Gough did not take place until March 1849, and therefore after Gough had fought the Battle of Gujrat on the 21 February 1849. There is therefore no way that Gough could have known about the decision to replace him with Napier when he fought the Battle of Gujrat. It can therefore be seen that Charles Allen is in error when on page 196 of his book *Soldier Sahibs*, he theorises that Gough knew by this stage that he was to be replaced by Napier and that, "the prospect of being sent home in disgrace concentrated his mind". Napier had on 29 January 1849 been sounded out about, and rejected, the possibility of replacing Gough, but it is important to note that this is before news of Chillianwala had reached London and was therefore not in response to the actions of that battle. It should be recalled that Gough was of course already past his term of office. It was not until the first few days of March 1849 that Napier was pressed to take over from Gough by the Duke of Wellington. NAM: 8303–105, Gough Papers, Wellington to Gough, 5 March 1849.

qualities which he had manifested in his former service in that country to fulfil the expectations of the country, and to carry into execution the views and plans of the government.[2]

The letter was somewhat ambiguous, and Gough can be forgiven for his failure to understand what was meant. Gough was unclear form the letter whether Napier, who was junior to Gough on the Army List, was being sent to support him, to replace him when he retired, or to supersede him with immediate effect. The latter genuinely seemed unlikely to Gough, and it is possible from the tone of some of his correspondence that he did not at first realise that this was even a possibility. Indeed Wellington had referred to his successor being appointed at the 'termination of the campaign'. Gough seems to have convinced himself, to begin with at any rate, that this was merely the military machine preparing for his retirement from command. The timing might have seemed strange but it must be recalled that Gough was technically overdue to leave India and had received an extension to his command.

Wellington would later state after reading Gough's report that, "The loss in the battle is certainly severe, and the details are not satisfactory, but the loss is not half of what must have occurred if it had been necessary to take the citadel of Multan by storm after opening breaches in the walls." Indeed Wellington here places Chillianwala in perspective. The loss was indeed severe, but as Gough pointed out given the nature of the task they could be little else. It perhaps also shows that Wellington, just like everyone else in Britain, did not have the full story of what occurred by March of 1849.[3]

Wellington's role in the affair is somewhat ambiguous. He seems to have been tasked with breaking the news to Gough that he was to be replaced by Napier. However he did it in such a roundabout and poorly written letter that Gough was unaware of its true intention until he started to become aware of the full-scale reaction to the outcry in the press. At first Gough had thought such press coverage was the usual type of overreaction and had not taken it very seriously. It is quite likely that he had not even bothered to read it himself, merely obtaining the gist of what had been written from what others told him. Indeed, on 19 March, still unaware of the contents of Wellington's letter of the 5th of that month, Gough had written of the press outcry that, "I hardly however think the Duke will be swayed by newspaper reports from which he himself suffered."[4] Yet in May of 1849 it became clear to Gough that the Duke had indeed been swayed by press reports, as it must be said in fairness had the rest of the government. Napier arrived in India with orders to 'at once assume command'.[5] It now dawned on Gough that Wellington's letter had been intended to relieve him of command. This was not the way he had read it, and based on the parts of the letter quoted above, one can understand why. Gough later wrote that, "How his Grace the Duke of Wellington will get over his observation in his letter to me, that Sir C Napier came out to be present to relieve me when I went away, time must show."[6]

Despite Wellington's letter, it was clear from the way in which the announcement of Napier's appointment was made that he was to supersede Gough. The official announcement came in the House of Commons in answer to a question raised by the Mr Joseph Hume, MP for Montrose Burghs. Hume, although technically a Tory, is often described as a radical. He was rather independent in his voting and ideas, advocating economic retrenchment and radical social reform. He was a great supporter for the rights of trade unions, a strong advocate of the abolition of flogging, both in the army and society at large, and the abolition of the press gang. He also advocated prison

2   NAM: 8303–105, Gough Papers, Wellington to Gough, 5 March 1849.
3   Lee-Warner, *Life of Dalhousie*, pp. 209–210.
4   NAM: 8303–105, Gough Papers, Gough to Unknown, 19 March 1849.
5   NAM: 8303–105, Gough Papers, Gough to George Gough, 26 May 1849.
6   NAM: 8303–105, Gough Papers, Gough to Unknown, 30 July 1849.

reform. He was in short a champion of civil liberties. This also took place on 5 March, and was again no doubt motivated by the comments in the press, most notably *The Times*, of that morning. Hume rose in the House of Commons and asked the Prime Minister, Lord John Russell:

> relative to the affairs of India, the state of that country can no longer be a matter of indifference to every man who looks to the future. I should be sorry needlessly to prejudge any man, and particularly one who is not present to answer any statements that might be made; but certain facts which are developed in the despatches which were received three or four weeks ago, without any relation to the late melancholy transactions that have taken place, authorise me in inquiring whether Her Majesty's Ministers have taken any measures to place the army in India under such command as shall obtain the confidence of the men, and secure all those advantages of art and science which we, as a civilised nation, possess for the purposes of warfare? It appears from the despatches, that in recent events those advantages were not used; and I do hope, therefore, that Her Majesty's Government will state what measures they have taken to ensure better success for the future.[7]

Hume's comments give us a good understanding of how events in far off India were being perceived based on the accounts of Gough's despatch, but also wider speculation and correspondence from officers in India. Hume was clearly a man of intelligence and did his best to be fair in his comments. It is interesting to note that he mentions a perceived lack of confidence in Gough, but also talks of the failure to use 'the advantages of art and science' no doubt a criticism of the perceived lack of artillery.

Russell's reply came in two parts. In answer to Hume on 5 March he declared that:

> There can be no doubt that the state of our military operations in India must be a matter, not certainly of indifference, but of the deepest interest, to every Member of this House. I can, however, only state at present, that Her Majesty's Government, after considering the intelligence which has been received, have humbly offered to Her Majesty that advice which they think best calculated to meet the emergency which at present exists in that part of Her dominions. But I have not as yet received Her Majesty's reply to the advice which I have humbly tendered to Her Majesty; but as soon as that answer is received, and can be with propriety communicated to this House, I will lose no time in laying it before it.[8]

The following day the Prime Minister returned to the House of Commons and gave the second part of his answer to Mr Hume's question. Russell explained that he had been unable to reply in full yesterday and that:

> until I had received a reply from Her Majesty, I could not answer the question of the hon. Gentleman. I have now to state, that the advice which was by us humbly tendered to Her Majesty was, that Sir Charles James Napier should be appointed Commander-in-Chief of the troops in India. Sir, Her Majesty was pleased most graciously and fully to approve of that appointment; and both the Duke of Wellington, the Commander-in-Chief, and I, have seen Sir Charles James Napier to-day; and I have the satisfaction to state that he is ready to obey Her Majesty's wishes, and to proceed to India in the capacity to which Her Majesty has appointed him.[9]

7   *Hansard*, House of Commons Debate, 5 March 1849, Vol. 103, cc167–8.
8   *Hansard*, House of Commons Debate, 5 March 1849, Vol. 103, cc167–8.
9   *Hansard*, House of Commons Debate, 6 March 1849, Vol. 103, cc252–3.

As the previous day's statement had stated that they were looking to appoint someone 'to meet the emergency that at present exists' it becomes quite clear that the intention was that Napier would replace Gough and continue the war and bring it to a successful conclusion. Yet this was not the way in which Wellington explained the situation to Gough.

It was only really in May of 1849, after the Second Sikh War had been concluded, that the true nature of events that had taken place at home and within government circles in India became clear to Gough. He became quite bitter for a time, and one can understand why. The situation is perhaps best summed up by Sir William Napier, a man who had a series of run-ins with Gough over the years and was not usually to be found amongst his defenders, in his biography of his brother Charles Napier.

> It was wrong and unbecoming to accompany that cry for Sir Charles Napier with a manic one against Lord Gough, who would have been stoned to death in the streets if he had appeared. And the foremost instigators would probably have been the ministers.[10]

The comments regarding Gough do appear to represent the view that press hysteria had helped to developed.

The idea that Gough might have been lynched by the mob is not as fanciful as one might imagine. This was a volatile time in English history and indeed in the development of British India. Passions were roused with consummate ease by a press that was able to publish with increasing readership. Let us not forget that even the one-time national hero Wellington had at times received similar threats of violence, and equally sort out by the mob for retribution, for his role in championing Catholic emancipation and then his refusal to agree to the Reform Act. Yet in Gough's case one wonders exactly what such outrage was in regards to. As William Napier also stated:

> Lord Gough was a noble soldier of fifty years' service, and had always been victorious, whether obeying or commanding; no man heard, because no man dared to say, that personal comfort, or idleness, or fear, had induced him to shrink from danger or responsibility, or labour. What then was his crime? He had fought a drawn battle, the enemy was not crushed! For that only Lord Gough's destruction was called for![11]

There was clearly an overreaction to events. It is, however, easier to say that with the benefit of hindsight and knowledge of the victory at Gujrat and a successful conclusion to the war, than it was for contemporaries to take such a calm approach.

The press had played their part in creating and indeed developing the outcry against Gough and the handling of the war, but they were in fairness only playing on existing concerns. On the one hand there were concerns around Gough's ability, or perhaps more accurately suitability, for high command. Much of this dated back to the first Sikh War and many stories and opinions that had lain dormant since then were now to recur. Any number of people in the press, the army, and politics now expressed concerns which they had apparently held for many years. Much of this was due to people running for cover to defend themselves or simply taking great delight in saying, in effect, 'I told you so'.

There was also a wider fear over the safety and future of British India that press reports played upon. The ghost of Afghanistan, various minor uprisings, and a general fear over the security of

10   Napier, William, *The Life and Opinions of General Sir Charles James Napier*, Vol. IV (London: John Murray, 1857), p. 151.
11   Napier, *Life and Opinions of Charles Napier*, p. 151.

India all played on the collective mind of the British populace when the press reports were made. The high casualty figures, the loss of colours and guns, and the perception that firepower and technological advantages had been negated on the whim of the officer commanding, all added to the perceived peril of the situation. In such circumstances, the panic and violent outpouring against Gough is to be appreciated. It is under such circumstances, and with such emotions and fears to the fore, that the decision to supersede Gough with Napier must be viewed.

Napier was very much Wellington's man in a way which Gough never was. It has been argued that Wellington took advantage of the situation to, "force Sir Charles Napier upon the Director of the East India Company."[12] Napier was for his part reluctant to return to India. He later recalled that, "When the Duke of Wellington first told me of my appointment, I objected that my enemies in India would mar all usefulness; he laughed, pressed the matter home, and concluded thus 'If you don't go I must'."[13] This was a most extraordinary statement and recalls something of the panic that prevailed. It also says little for the officer corps of the British Army, if indeed the only two men considered fit were firstly a controversial, unusual, and widely hated man, at least in India, and secondly a man who would be 80 in May of that year. Indeed the idea that Wellington could even consider in his own mind, yet be seriously considered by others, as suitable for command is almost unbelievable. Whether Wellington seriously meant what Napier records him as saying, or was simply using it to drive home the point of how serious he perceived the situation to be, is unclear. It is likely that it was Wellington's way of persuading Napier but also highlighting the danger of the situation. However if Wellington thought he was up to another command he was deluded. Whilst it is unlikely that he was seriously taking command it should be recalled that only nine years previously when sounded out by the King of Prussia about the possibility of commanding Prussian and German troops against the French if war broke out, Wellington had indicated that he would, provided his sovereign agreed.[14] Yet that was nine years ago and his health had changed since then, but perhaps in his own mind Wellington still clung to a notion, perhaps even a hope, that he had one last campaign left in him. One last triumph in the profession that had been his life's work. However this was impractical. Not only his age but his general health and physical wellbeing make this unthinkable. Indeed it is unlikely that he would even have survived the journey to India.

All this does also raise the wider point of the fact that Wellington was still in a position of authority. Based on a meeting about a year later, Henry Havelock described Wellington as "a spectacle of mouldering greatness", and describes his profound deafness, his inarticulate speech, and that, "He begins, but rarely concludes a sentence, and where he breaks off in a period the spectator doubts from his manner whether he will commence another, or fall down apoplectic in the next effort to begin one."[15] It was nearing 44 years since he had last been to war. Whilst he had once been arguably the finest commander of the day, and indeed Gough had once called Wellington "the first General of the age", this day was long gone. He had not held a serious active military command for over 30 years. Wellington was not a serious option for command. This left Napier in effect as the only man considered fit for the task, and made his appointment almost inevitable. Yet for so many reasons it was hardly an ideal appointment for either Napier personally or the state.

That Napier had enemies in India was no exaggeration. They had made his previous appointment there all put impossible for him to continue in. This combination of politicians, civil servants, and the press in India had put about some very unpleasant lies about him, so much so that an official report was sent to the Council of the Governor-General and to the Court of Directors. If the

12   Rait, *Gough*, Vol. II, pp. 294–295.
13   Napier, *Life and Opinions of Charles Napier*, p. 152.
14   Guedalla, Phillip, *The Duke* (London: Hodder and Stoughton, 1974), pp. 457–458.
15   Cooper, Leonard, *Havelock* (London: The Bodley Head, 1957), p. 75.

Indian press disliked Gough, they positively hated Napier. In March 1846 Napier had said of the Indian press that, "There is no falsehood that the Indian press –with one exception or two – does not proclaim against me! One mass of spite, jealousy, malice, hatred, fury, is poured out upon me and all I do."[16] His time as governor of Scinde had led to many scurrilous claims being made against him. William Napier quoted headlines from various India newspapers that referred to Charles Napier as 'The sordid and shameless leader of the Scinde', 'the autocrat of the Scinde', 'The Scinde Czar', 'The unscrupulous murderer of the soldiers of the 78th and 28th Regiment', and 'The liar at the Head of the Scinde Government'. If Napier was perhaps the people's choice, or even the politicians' choice, to be the saviour of British India, he was never likely to be that of the India press.[17]

It was not just the press in India that was against Napier. He had many enemies within the political establishment. Indeed during his previous appointment they had even secretly registered a false complaint against him. This was officially recorded by the Bombay Government and passed to the Court of Directors of the East India Company. The complaint ran than Napier had artificially raised grain prices and kept them there so as to benefit not only his own purse but so that grain prices to the army were at an inflated price causing the government to bear the burden of this. The allegations were false, and only came to Napier's attention due to the 'error' of a civil servant. Napier later stated that, "Had the clerk not made this mistake, I should have had, in both the Bombay and Calcutta archives, a heinous crime registered against me by my bitter enemies, which hereafter might be brought to light and given to the world when I am no more, as an indefatigable proof of my bad conduct."[18] Napier placed on record an official rebuttal. However the affair had further soured relations and created further bad blood. There are two interesting points to add to this tale. Firstly, Charles and William Napier both questioned whether the civil servant did make an 'error' or was in fact an honourable man who felt guilt at his part in the affair. Secondly, should it be felt that Napier was paranoid over this matter it is worth pointing out that in 1857, four years after Charles Napier's death, this matter did in fact come to light. Accusations were made in the House of Commons based on the original report of complaint placed on file. It appears that Napier's official rebuttal which was to have been placed alongside this had been 'lost'. Fortunately he was defended and the record was set straight by Mr Henry Bruce, MP for Merthyr Tydfil, and a future Home Secretary in Gladstone's first ministry.

It can, therefore, hopefully be seen that whatever qualities and merits there were to Napier's appointment from a military point of view, from a political point of view it was an accident waiting to happen. Too much had passed between Napier and the government in India, and the press, for him to be able to undertake his task for any length of time. He was at best a short term solution to hopefully end the conflict. The fact that by the time Napier arrived, in late May, the war was long since finished was only a minor embarrassment for all concerned. The government looked at worst as though they had overreacted, which was better than having been perceived to have failed to act. The problem was that they were reacting to press and public outrage, to misguided reports from India, and from a governor general, who although based in India was distant from the seat of war. The Duke of Wellington's roundabout letter had not helped as it never stated clearly that Gough was to have been replaced.

Wellington would later contradict himself in public. On 17 March at the farewell dinner for Sir Charles Napier, he gave a speech in which he declared that there was no great emergency and tried to paint a picture that the despatch of Napier was simply a natural decision.

16   Napier, William, *General Sir Charles Napier and the Directors of the East India Company* (London: C. Westerton, 1857), p. 5.
17   Napier, *Napier and the Directors of the East India Company*, p. 6.
18   Napier, *Napier and the Directors of the East India Company*, pp. 6–7.

If we are to fight great battles, if great risks are to be run, we must expect to incur losses in the attainment of great ends. [...] As the period of service of the noble Lord who now commands in India will soon expire, and he will be desirous of returning to this country, it is desirable that an officer of such distinguished services and abilities as my honourable and gallant friend should be on the spot to take command of the army.[19]

In fairness, Wellington had always defended the heavy losses sustained when fighting the Sikhs and had not overly condemned Gough for that. Yet he persisted with this idea that Napier was to replace Gough when the latter choose to stand down, which was contrary to Napier's orders to proceed and take immediate command. Attempting to defend the despatch of Napier in the House of Commons, Lord John Russell continued along the same lines as Wellington.

We are of opinion that sending Sir Charles Napier to India was a step calculated to maintain the credit of the British Army. Everybody knows that Lord Gough's usual service had expired, and that we might at any moment expect to receive such an announcement from him [...] begging that a successor might be appointed in his place.[20]

Russell's statement was even less convincing than Wellington's. Even if it were believed, it does not explain the urgency on receipt of the reports of Chillianwala. The situation that both Wellington and Russell described had been the case for many months. It was indeed these two men who had agreed to Gough's extension. If their account is to be believed then surely such preparations should have been considered some months previously. The fact that they were so last-minute is shown by the fact that the Prime Minister could not give a full reply in the House of Commons to a question on the possible replacement of Gough until the day after he was asked a direct question. The question had been asked on 5 March and that date is significant in that it was the day in which *The Times* so vehemently attacked both Gough and those responsible for him being in place, and was also the day on which Wellington had written to Gough.

The final twist was that Gough had actually saved them all the trouble and had, on the conclusion of the war, written to Wellington asking to be replaced. Yet of course the delay in communication meant that this was unknown in England until late April. This was not, as has sometimes been suggested, a reaction to the actions of the government and the decision to send Napier. In fact Gough did not know of it at the time. It was simply the action of a man who would turn 70 later that year, who had been 12 years in India, had a wife in ill health, and had ended his career on a high winning the Battle of Gujrat. There was also a sense in which he was relieved that he had reached the end of his career. Although a little melodramatic, Gough was now, put simply, a tired old man anxious for retirement.

---

19   Rait, *Gough*, Vol. II, p. 296.
20   *Hansard*, House of Commons Debate, 24 April 1849, Vol. 104, cc734–57.

72

Movements towards Gujrat

Having now examined the press and political reaction to Chillianwala and the decisions made as a consequence, we now return to the battlefield. Chillianwala clearly had an effect on Gough, but the main feeling he had in its aftermath was one of frustration rather than regret. His frustration lay not only in the fact that the battle had not gone according to plan, but also that the weather in the following days had not allowed for pursuit of the Sikhs. He was largely unaware at this stage of the controversy that the battle had caused and instead was concentrating on the next battle and the defeat of the enemy.

In the aftermath of Chillianwala there was a general air of frustration that would last for over a month. This was not confined to the army, and the growing frustration of the governor general at Ferozepore was the cause of many of the critical letters home that were written by him during this period. Yet the growing criticism and frustration does not seem to have been of great concern to Gough; indeed he was largely unaware of it. This is perhaps why when Gough finally heard of the disquiet at home and of his supersession by Sir Charles Napier he was deeply offended. Although initially frustrated that he was not able to follow up his attack in the days after Chillianwala, Gough soon settled down to play a waiting game.

Whatever frustrations others had with events in the immediate aftermath of Chillianwala, they were nothing compared to those experienced by Gough. The morning after Chillianwala he awoke early, determined to renew the contest. At dawn he was ready to continue the battle. Yet the dark and stormy early hours of the morning were a prelude to the heavy rains that would fall a few hours after dawn as the army was being prepared. The rains continued solidly for three days, by the end of which the ground had turned to mud and any attempt at an attack would have been disastrous. The frustration that Gough felt was not simply based on his inability to follow up on his attack of 13 January. His main aim in attacking Sher Singh had been to defeat him before he was able to join with his father and the force of Sikhs and Afghans he was bringing to the field. The junction of the two forces was now inevitable and there was nothing Gough could do to prevent it. Yet after this initial frustration Gough settled down to await reinforcements from Multan and elsewhere, and to prepare his army for what he hoped would be a decisive battle.

During this time there were defections from both sides. Although few in number, some Sepoys did join the Sikhs. Yet this was far from one-way traffic. On 19 January several Sikh artillerymen surrendered to the British. Although serving on the Sikh side they were Muslims, or to use the language of the time 'Mohammedans', and perhaps their loyalty to the Sikh cause was from the start questionable. This incident in particular has been used to support the idea that Chillianwala had shaken the morale of the Sikh forces. There was no doubt some truth to this but it would be wrong to place too much trust in the theory based upon the defections of a few Muslim artillerymen. Equally, it would be wrong to claim the same for British morale based upon the defection of a few sepoys.[1]

---

1   Cook, *The Sikh Wars*, p. 181.

When the weather cleared Gough was now reluctant to launch another attack. He had many factors playing on his mind. Not least of which was the heavy loss in Europeans, the backbone of his infantry, at Chillianwala. It was one thing to renew a battle from the day previous when both sides would have been reduced in number, but another to commence a fresh operation after several days' rest. By 19 January Gough considered that attacking again was too risky until he was reinforced. In a letter to Dalhousie written on that day he remarked that, "I do not feel justified in attacking him [Sher Singh] in a position, to carry which, however shaken as he undoubtedly is, would cause a loss far greater than we can afford with our present list of wounded."[2] One could, as Dalhousie certainly did, interpret this as an admission of failure at Chillianwala. Gough certainly did not mean it as such. That would be too simplistic and would, as we have already seen, be to discount the mistakes made by others, most notably Pennycuick and Pope, which had been the cause of the largest casualties. Gough had never been under any illusion that attacking at Chillianwala would mean high casualties. Yet as we have already seen he had been left with little choice.

One can however see why Dalhousie grew angry over this matter. It would have appeared to him that Gough was now exercising caution too late. Indeed there were all manner of stories regarding Gough that were emanating from those said to be with the army. It was said that Gough's inaction was down to stubbornness, or that he had lost his nerve after Chillianwala. Indeed Rait states that it was said that, "his old blood was cool, and he dared not seize his opportunity." The suggestion was that Gough's inaction was not only due to his failure to appreciate the opportunity, but also to a failing of his nerve after Chillianwala.[3]

Although Gough had not lost his nerve, he was concerned about giving battle at this stage before the reinforcements arrived. However had he seen an opportunity, or been forced into it, he would certainly have given battle. In this sense the casualties of Chillianwala did influence him and it would be wrong to ignore the effect high casualties had on him. Again we see that whilst he was not hesitant about taking action that he thought would cause high casualties, he did regret them and felt deeply for his men. His concern was both strategic and humanitarian. To this Dalhousie argued that, had Gough been this concerned about casualties before Chillianwala, the British position might not be as precarious as it now appeared. Yet Gough saw a different picture, and decided that the best course of action was to await the arrival of the reinforcements that would come with the imminent fall of Multan, which eventually took place on 22 January 1849. In the meantime he simply took precautions against the Sikhs crossing the Jhelum River. There is a slight irony in the fact that Dalhousie had previously insisted that Gough wait for the fall of Multan and the reinforcements that Major General Whish would be able to bring with him. Yet now Dalhousie, through his political agent Major Mackeson, counselled a policy of immediate action.[4]

Gough received all manner of advice during this period. It varied from one extreme to the other. Some counselled withdrawal back towards the Chenab River. The main reason for such concern was the thought that the Sikhs could get behind the British and threaten the Chenab crossing. There were however several problems with this theory. Firstly it credited the Sikhs with greater strength and resources than they had. To move such a force to the Chenab would be difficult to achieve. It would be one thing for irregular cavalry to raid British movements, but this was not the same as a wholescale movement of a force to block any serious British attack. It would also place such a force between Gough, the force moving from Multan and further reinforcements from the

2   NAM: 8303–105, Gough Papers, Gough to Dalhousie, 19 January 1849.
3   Rait, *Gough*, Vol. II, p. 263.
4   Arnold, *Dalhousie Administration of India*, p. 176.

direction of Ferozepore. The Sikhs were short on supplies and the barren landscape would provide little in the way of support.[5]

The period of inaction after Chillianwala was actually of great advantage to the British. Although in matters of morale, and the wider effect of the 'defeat' of Chillianwala on British India, inaction might have caused concern, to the army this was a chance to grow stronger. Not only did it give Whish a chance to move with reinforcements but it also allowed for supplies to finally reach the army, for extra guns to make their slow journey from Delhi to join Gough, and for a general period of reorganisation. Whish brought with him not only extra European troops but also extra guns which gave Gough a superiority not only in terms of guns but the amount of metal they could fire at the enemy for the first time in either of the Sikh Wars. At the same time, whilst the Sikh numbers opposing Gough were likely to grow this was a two-edged sword. Many of the troops were irregulars and whilst there was little doubt of their fighting ability there was good reason to doubt their discipline. Whilst these reinforcements gave Sher Singh a larger force they also presented a logistical problem. Having been forced from the rich and fertile land north of the Chenab River, he was already finding it difficult to keep his army fed and supplied from the area around the Jhelum River. Gough, on the other hand, could have his supplies transported, and although they might have to cover greater distances they were more readily available than any were for Sher Singh and his ever-increasing army.

Dalhousie, after months of urging against reinforcements, now altered course completely and proposed sending troops from wherever he could to reinforce Gough. To some of these suggestions Gough responded positively, such as the movement of the 53rd Foot and a body of irregular cavalry to reinforce him. However there were other suggested reinforcements that Gough rejected for fear of the effect it might have elsewhere. The key example of this was Dalhousie's proposed movement of the Sirmoor Battalion of Gurkhas and the 98th Foot to reinforce him. Gough felt that it was unwise to remove two such reliable regiments from the Sirhind Division where there was, as he put it, "assuredly a large body of men who served in the Seik [Sikh] Army within the protected states."[6] This incident is important for several things that it shows us. Firstly, it emphasises the rather unnerved state that Dalhousie was in and his desire to send any troops he possible could. Secondly that Gough was confident in his preparations and considered the existing reinforcements adequate. Thirdly, that even in the midst of the campaign Gough's strategic mind was considering the wider picture. The final point is perhaps most interesting. Given the circumstances, one would have forgiven Gough for thinking purely of the enemy in front of him. Yet here is a demonstration that he was aware of the wider considerations, the dangers posed by the local Sikhs and former soldiers.

It is interesting, too, that in this period of inactivity Gough's mind was already turning to the endgame. Gough was now clearly working on the strategy that he would fight a large-scale battle against the Sikhs and thereby bring to an end the ability of the Sikhs to continue the war for any length of time. This was clearly his intention as is seen in the correspondence with Dalhousie of this period. He was, however, also considering what would happen after this battle. At one point he annoyed Dalhousie by stating that he felt he would not be in a position to prevent the Sikhs from retreating with part of their army and maybe even a few guns after such a battle. Dalhousie was unable to understand that the geography of the area and indeed the close proximity of the Sikh army to Jhelum River meant that Gough was unlikely to be able to prevent at least a handful of guns escaping across the river.[7] To Dalhousie in his already agitated state of mind this was an admission of failure if not incompetence. To him it appeared that Gough was actually saying that

5   Rait, *Gough*, Vol. II, p. 263, Cook, *The Sikh Wars*, pp. 181–182.
6   Rait, *Gough*, Vol. II, pp. 260–261.
7   NAM: 8303–105, Gough Papers, Gough to Dalhousie, 13 January 1849 & 30 January 1849.

he could not completely defeat the Sikhs in battle. What he was in fact saying was that in their current position he could not prevent at least a partial retreat. To an extent this was correct, but the difference was that whilst Dalhousie interpreted this as an indication that there might be further considerable conflict, Gough interpreted it as the need for mopping up operations to be taken in an expedition across the Jhelum River. As it was, the situation altered when the Sikhs moved away from their present strong defensive position.

It is interesting to note that for the proposed mopping-up operations across the Jhelum, Gough did not propose himself for command. Whether this was Gough's own appreciation, or inkling, of how his performance had been judged is difficult to know. There is a possibility that he felt he would not be allowed to continue in command much longer. However in one sense this was not the sort of operation that required the presence of the commander-in-chief. Gough proposed that the command of the expedition across the Jhelum be given to Major General Walter Gilbert.[8] Whatever others thought of Gilbert, and there was some legitimate ground for concern in his ability, Gough had confidence in him. One could question Gilbert's suitability given his age, as he would be 64 in early March, yet that did not necessarily preclude him from the appointment. Indeed the age of senior officers was a concern throughout the campaign and 64 was not overly old for a major general. Whatever the wisdom of Gough's recommendation might have been, it is interesting to note that Dalhousie agreed to it. It may be, however, that this was motivated more by a desire to rid himself of Gough than any vote of confidence in the abilities of Gilbert.

Robert Rait has suggested that Gough's caution was justified during this period, if for no other reason than an immediate attack was what the Sikhs desired. In one sense this is understandable. The waiting game was indeed in Gough's favour as the circumstances existed at that time. Yet by not taking the initiative he allowed the possibility that fortune might turn against the British. This might have taken the form of further unrest elsewhere in India or an unfortunate mishap to part of the army. At the same time the Sikhs continued to attempt to force Gough into action and some act of indiscretion that would change their fortune and turn the circumstances against the British.[9] In late January Sher Singh had threatened an attack against the British position in the hope that they would withdraw rather than fight. It is clear that the Sikhs were aware of Gough's intention to await the reinforcements from Multan and not to undertake any operation before then if at all possible. They therefore hoped that if they feinted an attack that Gough would withdraw, thus allowing them to gain a morale boosting victory. Whatever Gough's true intentions might have been, he was not so easily manipulated.

Whether he intended to defend his position or not, Gough led the Sikhs to believe he would and built a large earthwork just in front of his positon. This led Sher Singh to believe that Gough intended to defend his position and in such circumstances he was reluctant to attack. Although the Sikhs were able to inflict great casualties on the British when acting on the defensive, it would be foolish to believe that if the positions were reversed that Sikh casualties would be any less than those sustained by their opponents. Indeed, there was the potential for greater losses due to the greater fire discipline of British infantry. Given that Gough was not going to be moved from his position by any such strategy, Sher Singh decided to withdraw. He moved his army to the Khoree Pass, save for 10,000–12,000 men and 22 guns which remained in position at Russool.

On 11 February 1849, Sher Singh tried one final attempt to force Gough into what would have been an injudicious attack upon the Sikh position at Russool, the difficulty of assaulting which has been discussed in a previous chapter. Sher Singh sough to lure Gough away from his position.

---

8   Rait, *Gough*, Vol. II pp. 261–262.
9   Rait, *Gough*, Vol. II pp. 263–267.

The situation and Gough's response are perhaps best explained by the man himself. In a letter to Dalhousie written on 12 February, Gough remarked that

> The enemy yesterday came forward, apparently with the whole of the force he had at, and in the neighbourhood of, Khoree, with the evident view of drawing me out of this encampment, in order that a strong force he had concealed amongst the jungle towards Mong might have an opportunity of attacking my camp. My Cavalry Patrols, consisting of only four squadrons, kept the whole of the enemy's cavalry at bay. This proved that they had no intention of bringing on an action at the point they advanced to, but to draw me on to attack them in the thick jungle in their rear, in which they were ready to fall back.[10]

This incident is important for several reasons. It shows us that Gough did have a strategic brain if perhaps not a tactical one. If in the past he had been accused of falling into the trap laid by the enemy, on this occasion he most certainly did not. He saw the movement made by Sher Singh for what it was and refused to act. It could be argued that his caution was a reaction to Chillianwala, and to an extent there must be some truth to this. He had, partly because of the losses at Chillianwala, decided to remain on the defensive until the reinforcements from Multan arrived. However that is not the same as saying he would not have attacked had circumstances been different. It is clear from the statement made to Dalhousie that he envisaged the difficulty of fighting in the 'thick jungle'. That his cavalry was able to keep the enemy at bay was also testament to the fact that this was a feint rather than a real attack. If the intention had been to launch a full-scale attack, the enemy would have pressed on against his cavalry patrols. Yet the Sikhs did not do this.

Gough followed up the strategic success of having rebuffed Sher Singh's lure with a tactical success when the future Field Marshal Neville Chamberlain, then a lieutenant with the 9th Irregular Cavalry, led his men in a raid on the exposed Sikh rear in which around 80 camels where captured. As has already been mentioned, the Sikhs were having supply problems and the loss of so many camels would have had a real effect. This demonstrates that Gough was willing to take action on a limited scale if he saw an opportunity. Chamberlain had also been part of a cavalry action on the 30th January when a cavalry patrol had encountered a greatly superior force of Sikh cavalry. The British irregular cavalry had killed 16 of the enemy and driven off the rest.[11]

Sher Singh had failed in his attempt to tempt Gough into an injudicious attack. It was now his turn to act injudiciously. Having failed to force an attack, Sher Singh decided to withdraw from the area. Whether this was a sensible decision or not is rather beyond the scope of this work. It could be argued that he might have been better staying roughly where he was for the time being. However Sher Singh was obviously aware of the fall of Multan, and his intelligence on other matters was so good that he must have been aware that there were considerable reinforcements, supplies and artillery moving from Ferozepore to strengthen Gough yet further. Thus his attempting to move, and perhaps force a battle in another position, before the reinforcements arrived was understandable. Yet he had left a very strong defensive position with good prepared defences. This was attested to by Gough when following their abandonment he toured the Sikh lines and was impressed at their strength. Indeed if the defences the British faced had been better understood, the criticism of the casualties at Chillianwala might have taken on a different light.

Sher Singh sent a party of 4,000 horsemen to secure Gujrat, still technically loyal to the official Sikh government. However no resistance was made and subsequently, on 14 February, Sher Singh marched his entire army to Gujrat. He took up a position between Gujrat and the crossing at

10   NAM: 8303–105, Gough Papers, Gough to Dalhousie, 12 February 1849.
11   Cook, *The Sikh Wars*, p. 181–182. Forrest, *Life of Chamberlain*, pp. 227–229.

Wazirabad. The intention was clearly to make Gough attack him, by threatening not only Gough's rear but also the crossing on the Chenab. Yet in so doing Sher Singh was now going to give battle in a position that was not as strong as the one he had just left. This was, in a sense, the price he had to pay for bringing Gough to battle when it became clear that Gough was not going to attack him again in the strong position he held. The problem was not that Gough would never have attacked Sher Singh's previous defensive position again, but that he would only have done so after his reinforcements had arrived. Given how close to a considerable defeat the Sikhs had been at Chillianwala, it was understandable that Sher Singh did not relish a repeat attack with fresh troops and most importantly extra European battalions. So whilst Sher Singh's decision to move from a strong defensive position might seem strange, there was a strategy behind it. Perhaps it also helps to illustrate the difficult position the Sikhs were in, a factor that too often gets ignored in the concentration on the fault and failures of Gough and his strategy.

Gough had, on hearing of the movement of Sher Singh, sent a force of irregular cavalry to secure the crossing at Wazirabad on the Chenab River. This precipitated any Sikh attempt to secure the crossing, but also protected the advance of the force from Multan and the reinforcements from elsewhere. By this stage Major General Whish had arrived at the crossing at Ramnuggar with his staff and the advanced element of his army and secured the crossing. There were roughly 6,000 Sikh troops, mostly irregulars, in the area around Wazirabad and although they positioned themselves on the northern side of the crossing they made no attempt to engage the British force. By the morning of 16 Februray the crossing at Wazirabad, as well as that five miles above at Sudra, had been secured by Whish's men. Whish had apparently had the same idea as Gough and had also sent a party of cavalry forward to secure the crossing and protect his advance.

Robert Rait attempts to suggest that Gough had planned and hoped that the Sikhs would move to Gujrat. Indeed he goes so far as to say that by moving to Gujrat the Sikhs had, "thus carried out, to a nicety, Lord Gough's wishes."[12] This might be to give too much strategic credit to Gough. However it is clear that his determination to wait placed the ball in Sher Singh's court and forced him into a decision. Rait supports his argument with a conversation between Gough and Mackeson witnessed by Captain Frederick Haines, an officer on Gough's staff who also served as his military secretary. On news of the movement of the Sikhs, Mackeson, as he had before, urged that Gough should move with alacrity to engage the Sikhs. Gough refused. Haines recorded that the conversation then went as follows: "'But they (the Sikhs) may go to Dinghi', said Mackeson. 'Why shouldn't they go to Dinghi?' was the reply. 'But they may go to Gujerat', persisted the Political Agent. 'That is exactly where I hope to find them' said the Commander-in-Chief."[13]

It is difficult to know exactly how to interpret the aforementioned conversation. In the first place we do not know how accurate it is in terms of exact language. Rait interviewed the by then over 80-year-old Field Marshal Frederick Haines in the early years on the 20th century as part of his research for his 1903 book, so the accuracy of Haines' recollection must be considered. Yet it does to an extent fit what we know. Mackeson had been urging Gough to take the offensive. It is understandable that he saw the movement of the Sikh army as an opportunity. Whether Gough specifically wanted then to move to Gujrat, in that he already planned to fight a battle there, is open to debate. Perhaps the point Gough was trying to make was that Gujrat is a position which served his purpose of wishing to attack the Sikhs in an open position. Mackeson was further annoyed by the fact that in the days that followed Gough moved so slowly in the direction of Gujrat. There were many reasons why Gough wanted to move at such a speed. The most important was clearly that he wanted to give time for the force from Multan to reach him and be absorbed into his command.

---

12   Rait, *Gough*, Vol. II p. 267.
13   Rait, *Gough*, Vol. II pp. 267–268.

This point was alluded to by Colin Campbell when Gough's army reached a position to threaten Gujrat that, "the political officers [such as Mackeson] wanted to move some days ago, and which, most likely, would have brought on a general action before the Mooltan [Multan] force had joined us."[14]

Gough's slow movement also placed less strain on his troops and allowed for more careful preparation. It had also become clear, through intelligence reports, but also from the course that the war was now taking, that the Sikhs did not intend to move from Gujrat. This series of short marches, some covering barely five miles a day, were important for the health, discipline and order of Gough's army. They were mostly undertaken in battle formation, so as to avoid any unwanted surprises from the enemy. This meant that the army became used to the formations it would fight in and became accustomed to forming them. The short marches had also presented little time for the Sikhs to attempt any operations against the British whilst they were on the march. Had this been attempted they might have been able to precipitate an action before Gough was ready.

Whatever one might think of Gough's strategic ability or intellectual capacity, it is clear that he was able to learn from previous errors. In the past he had been caught on the march and forced into a conflict before he was ready. This time he was not running that risk. Cynically, one could say that it was about time that he learnt such a lesson; however this could be countered with the old saying 'better late than never'. One can argue whether it was circumstances or a change in attitude that led to this new style of operation before the engagement at Gujrat. One can also argue that Gough was now able to undertake such an operation because of the strategic position. In short the Sikhs had now largely confined themselves to the defensive and were allowing Gough to operate in this way.

On 18 February Gough finally arrived at a place called Tricca about 10 miles from where the Sikhs were positioned. Here he was joined on the same day by Major General Whish and elements of the Multan force. The next day the remainder of the Multan force arrived and Gough was now at full strength. The two elements of the army combined. Both were in good heart. Gough's main army had enjoyed the rest after Chillianwala. They were also starting to be re-equipped and resupplied. The army Gough commanded was now a strong force. His careful movements and patience in the aftermath of Chillianwala were now to pay dividends as he sought to confront the Sikh army at Gujrat.

14   Shadwell, *Life of Colin Campbell* Vol. I, p. 218.

73

The Battle of Gujrat

Despite the events of Chillianwala there was by now a great deal of confidence within the army as it gathered at Gujrat. Also, the movement towards Gujrat had brought them into an area where supply was plentiful. The rather barren landscape of Chillianwala and the area around the Jhelum River had given way to fields of corn and other sources of food in the fertile land near the Chenab River. Although the force from Multan had undertaken a gruelling march, covering 235 miles in 18 days, they were also in good spirits. The fall of Multan had not only been an occasion of great pride, but also great relief from the tedium and hardship of a siege. To be now moving freely through the countryside, for they experienced little of the expected resistance during the march, was a more appealing prospect that the prolonged effort they had just endured in the siege lines.

Yet there was clearly something more to this spirit of confidence. Whatever might have been said about his ability or his decision making by individuals it is difficult to deny the confidence that the army, and specifically the rank and file, had in Gough. Whilst stories of officers writing home in disgust at the way in which he had handled the army were given a great deal of attention, the attitude of the men who were at the sharp end of the engagements is often overlooked. A story from an unnamed officer tells of the reaction Gough received before the battle of Gujrat:

> While we were waiting, our attention was drawn to a curious sound in the far distance on the right. The noise grew louder and nearer, and we saw the Regiments, one after another, in a most excited state, cheering like mad. It was Lord Gough, at the head of his Staff, riding along the front. When he passed us, our men were not behindhand with their acclamations. He soon passed out of sight, but we heard the cheering till it died away in the distance. It was the same the day after Chillianwala. It was the most fervid demonstration of affection I ever saw in my life, and it made a great impression on me.[1]

Whilst such acclamations for a commander-in-chief were not uncommon they were not guaranteed, and the fervour with which Gough was greeted should not be quickly dismissed. The men, for whatever reason, loved Gough. Partly it was his genuine concern for their welfare, as shown by his constant refusal throughout both wars to abandon his wounded or to move until they had been cared for. Yet there was something more than that this. It was his personality, undoubtedly his great personal courage, his willingness to suffer hardships with his men, and just as importantly his willingness to place himself in harm's way during the battle. His very appearance in his white fighting coat was an example of this that made him easily identifiable to friend and foe alike. There could never be any suggestion that Gough personally hid away from the enemy. Indeed, quite the reverse: he made himself a target and would, as we have seen, use this to draw the fire from his men.

---

1   Rait, *Gough*, Vol. II, p. 274

In the build up to Gujrat careful preparations were made. The use of reconnaissance was at its best, the ground was, and indeed already had been, examined fully, and the army was moving at a steady speed and to its own timetable. The great difference between this and any other battle during the Sikh Wars was that the Sikhs were now allowing Gough the freedom to act. Yet it would be wrong not to acknowledge the fact that Gough had learned a thing or two in his previous battles with the Sikhs. There was a determination on Gough's part to bring the war to a conclusion with a devastating defeat of the enemy. In the past he had always attempted such a thing but had not been concerned if it necessitated another battle. On this occasion he intended to destroy the enemy force at Gujrat and then pursue the remainder to destruction. The fact that he had already prepared Major General Gilbert to undertake such a pursuit across the Jhelum River is testament to that.

The Sikh army at Gujrat had positioned itself 3,000 yards from the city of Gujrat between two *nullahs*. The formation has often been described as being in a crescent shape, but it does appear that the Sikh infantry in the centre was at an angle and thus the shape was not a natural crescent. There appears to have been little attempt on the part of the infantry to dig in and prepare adequate defences. The *nullah* on the Sikh left was 'wet' – that is boggy, rather than flowing water – and ran down to the Chenab River. This made it difficult to cross. That on the Sikh right was dry and presented only a minor obstacle. The Sikh left was held by cavalry who were positioned behind the boggy *nullah*, although there were also two units of cavalry the other side of the *nullah* joining with the infantry in the centre. The infantry in the centre of the formation were in two lines and the front line had been interspersed with guns. At a slight angle one unit of Sikh infantry and some guns held the dry *nullah* on the Sikh right. On the other side of the dry *nullah* was a large formation of Sikh cavalry. The Sikhs also held two villages that lay forward of their main position: Bara Kalra and Chota Kalra. Both were defended by a combination of artillery and infantry. Indeed at Bara Kalra the Sikhs had placed two batteries of their heaviest guns. Exact numbers of for the Sikh army are as ever unknown. The figure of 60,000 men and 59 guns is often used, although this might be a little on the high side in terms of men. However let us not forget that this was not only Sher Singh's force, but also that of Chatar Singh and the Afghan contingent. The actual number might be a little lower, but not by much. A figure of between 45,000 and 50,000 is a more reasonable assumption.[2]

Against this combined Sikh force, Gough now had a combined army of around 24,000 men and 96 guns. However with the need to protect communications and his baggage this was slightly reduced to a force of 20,000 men, and possibly only 88 guns, actually deployed in battle. On the right was the cavalry brigade that had formerly been commanded by Pope and was now under the command of Colonel Lockwood, containing the 14th Light Dragoons, the 1st Bengal Light Cavalry, and the 11th and 14th Irregular Cavalry. The second cavalry brigade on the right was commanded by Colonel Hearsey and made up of the 3rd and 9th Irregular Cavalry. The two brigades of cavalry were also supported by a troop of horse artillery.

Next to the right wing cavalry were the two brigades of Major General Whish's division. Brigadier Hervey's brigade consisted of the 10th Foot and the 8th and 52nd Native Infantry supported by a company of pioneers. Behind Hervey's brigade was Brigadier Markham's brigade consisting of the 32nd Foot and the 51st and 72nd Native Infantry. Markham's job was to follow behind Hervey, support him if necessary, to exploit any success he achieved. Hervey was supported by one troop of horse artillery, and two further troops of horse artillery accompanied Markham. They were also supported by a light field battery.

---

2   Burton, *The First and Second Sikh Wars*, p. 125, estimates the Sikhs at 60,000 men and 59 guns. Bruce, *Six Battles for India*, p. 306, estimates the Sikhs at 40,000–50,000 strong and with 59 guns.

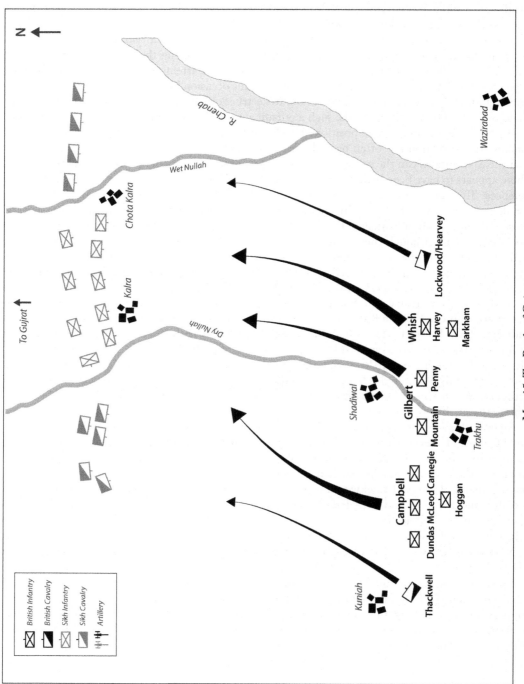

Map 15 The Battle of Gujrat.

Next in line was Major General Gilbert's division of two brigades. Brigadier Godby was no longer in command of his brigade, having been sent to command at Lahore. He had been replaced by Brigadier Penny who had moved from Campbell's division to assume command. This Brigade now consisted of the 2nd Bengal Europeans and the 31st and 70th Native Infantry. Next to them was the second brigade of Gilbert's division commanded by Brigadier Mountain and consisting of the 29th Foot and the 30th and 56th Native Infantry. On the left of Gilbert's division, next to the dry *nullah*, was a heavy battery of 18 guns. This consisted of ten 18 pdrs and eight 8 inch howitzers.

The British force was then separated by the dry *nullah*. On the other side of this was Brigadier General Campbell's division. Nearest the *nullah* was Brigadier Carnegie's (sometimes spelt Carnegy) brigade containing the 24th Foot and the 25th Native Infantry. Next to this was Brigadier Mcleod's brigade containing the 61st Foot and the 36th and 46th native infantry and supported by two light field batteries. In reserve behind these two brigades were the 5th and 6th Bengal Light Cavalry and the Brigade of native infantry commanded by Brigadier Hoggan containing the 45th and 69th Native Infantry and a battery of Bombay light field artillery. To the right of Campbell's division was the contingent from the Bombay Army commanded by Brigadier Dundas containing the 60th Rifles, the 1st Bombay European Fusiliers, and the 3rd and 19th Bombay Native Infantry. This was supported by a light field battery from the Bombay Army. The left flank was then completed by the cavalry, under the overall command of Lieutenant General Thackwell, of Brigadier White's brigade consisting of the 3rd Light Dragoons, 9th Lancers and 8th Bengal Light Cavalry, along with the 1st and 2nd Scinde Irregular Horse from the Bombay Army. They were supported by two troops of horse artillery.

Although the Sikh defensive position was nowhere near as strong as the one they had held at Chillianwala, it had as usual been well chosen for the natural cover that it afforded the army. On the morning of 21 February Gough's army was ready to attack. The morning was clear and dry, and given that both armies had been largely in place the night before there were no large clouds of dust created by large-scale movement of columns to create poor visibility. This was to prove extremely valuable to the artillery. At 0730 Gough moved the entire army forward two miles towards the Sikh position. At 0900 they were within range of the Sikh artillery. The Sikhs opened fire and the battle had begun. Gough halted his army and engaged in what would be a three hour artillery battle.

The length of this artillery engagement is pointed out in terms of the fact that Gough was finally allowing his guns time to do their work. It must firstly be pointed out that for the first time he had superiority not only in terms of number of guns but also in size. However even more importantly than this or the length of the artillery duel, was the fact that he pushed his guns forward. By so doing he was able to get the most out of their ability. For many years the tactical doctrine of the British Army would be, even until the end of the 19th century, to push the guns as far forward as possible to get maximum effect from them. This doctrine of pushing guns forward was partly responsible for the debacle at the Battle of Colenso on 15 December 1899.

Gough's failure to push his guns forward in his earlier battles had been a criticism levelled against him in the past. Indeed, as far back as Sobraon, the Duke of Wellington had noted Gough's failure to do this and had told Dalhousie that this is what he would have done.[3] Yet there was something else that was different about the artillery that morning and that was the way in which it was handled. Many remarked that the British gunners served their weapons better at Gujrat than they had at any other time during either of the Sikh Wars. In similar vein to Gough's handling of the artillery the point should be made that his gunners did for once enter a battle with superiority

---

3   Lee-Warner, *The Life of Dalhousie*, p. 92.

in artillery and the confidence that came from that. In his own despatch Gough recognised the effectiveness of the 'cannonade' against the Sikhs.

> The cannonade now opened upon the enemy was the most terrible I ever witnessed, and as terrible in its effect. The Sikh guns were served with their accustomed rapidity, and the enemy well and resolutely maintained his position; but the terrific force of our fire obliged them, after an obstinate resistance, to fall back.[4]

This obviously shows that Gough had an appreciation of what artillery could do and raises further questions about his inability to use it in the past.

Rait was in no doubt as to what Gujrat told us about Gough's military understanding:

> The result of this artillery duel somewhat surprised the Sikhs, who thought that the British did not sufficiently understand the use of their guns. They had formed this opinion partly in ignorance of the weakness of the British ordnance, but it was partly the natural effect of the wild rush of Pennycuick's Brigade at Chillianwala. Our weakness in artillery had long been deplored by Lord Gough, and when, for the only time throughout the Sikh wars, he excelled in that important arm, he made full use of the opportunity.[5]

There is undoubtedly some truth in this. Gujrat was indeed the first time that Gough had true superiority in terms of guns, and it is easy simply to leave the matter at that. Yet further examination shows that there was indeed better use of the guns, both by the gunners themselves and the commander-in-chief. The pushing forward of the guns was part of this. Another was the better selection of targets.

However in this both Gough and his artillerymen were helped by the fact that the Sikhs had occupied perhaps their weakest position during either war, with the possible exception of Aliwal. This meant the Sikhs were firing from largely undefended positions. This had often been the other way around during the conflict, with the British firing from exposed positions. At Gujrat the topography of the battlefield offered the British more protection that the Sikhs. Yet perhaps the biggest difference was that the Sikhs were allowing Gough to act without attempts to interfere with his plans. The Sikhs had exposed their guns and made no attempt to reinforce them, withdraw them, or divert fire away from them, during this early stage of the battle.

Yet to some this effective use of artillery seemed out of character. So much so, that a story developed that Gough, who had been observing the battle from a windmill, was 'imprisoned' there by his staff who took the ladder away and would not let him down until the artillery battle had taken place. The story is without truth and no officer on the staff that day makes any mention of the story other than to deny it. Indeed the idea that staff officers would undertake this course of action is hard to believe, given that it was a court martial offence.[6] Yet to those who had taken the public misconception of Gough's disdain for artillery seriously, it fitted. Indeed, Colonel Malleson in his usually uncharitable manner said of the story 'Se non e vero, e ben trovato' – if it is not true, it is well conceived. The idea that the story is well-conceived would be based upon a too simplistic understanding of Gough's character.[7]

---

4   Rait, *Gough*, Vol. II, p. 274.
5   Rait, *Gough*, Vol. II, pp. 274–275.
6   Rait, *Gough*, Vol. II, p. 275–276.
7   Malleson, *Decisive Battles of India*, p. 389.

In a similar vein credit for the successful use of artillery at Gujrat is sometimes erroneously given to Dalhousie. Indeed, Rait suggests that Dalhousie's correspondence to the home authorities confirms the fact that Dalhousie was claiming this to be the case. This is perhaps unfair on Dalhousie, as the comments made by him to Gough regarding artillery were at most a gentle reminder in the benefits of firepower against native opposition. It is also perhaps unfair to suggest that Dalhousie actually attempted to claim his part in the success of the artillery at Gujrat. Gough had resented Dalhousie's original letter, and indeed reminded the Governor General of the danger of relying on battlefield gossip.[8]

Yet whatever the truth about the use of artillery, there was no doubt that on that day at Gujrat British artillery was used well and proved an important factor in victory. However, it should not be believed that this was a one sided contest. Sikh artillery had matched the British in the early stages of the bombardment, but then gun after gun of the Sikh artillery was steadily silenced as the superiority of British guns started to tell. The Sikh artillery had been able to inflict some casualties on the British, but not to any great effect. Their main success was against British gunners and it is interesting to note that at Gurjat the proportion of artillery casualties was higher than that suffered by the infantry.

Before leaving the matter of artillery there are two further points to be made. The first is to state that the artillery not only silenced the enemy's guns but also covered the advance of the British infantry when the time came. This point is important and meant that the remaining Sikh artillery and infantry were unable to deliver serious fire upon the advancing infantry. This was as important a tactical use of artillery as had been the pushing forward of the guns. Both tactics meant that Gough was not only enjoying the advantage of superior numbers of artillery but also making the fullest use of that advantage. Gough therefore not only enjoyed a numerical superiority but also a tactical superiority. That the guns were well used and served on the day gives credit not only to Gough but to Brigadier General James Tennant in overall command of the artillery and to the officers and men who manned the guns on that day. The other point with regards to artillery is that despite a bombardment of over two and a half hours there were still those who criticised Gough and felt he should have allowed the duel to go on longer before ordering his infantry forward. Unsurprisingly chief amongst these critics was Colonel Malleson. He paints a picture of a Gough who, "had been anxiously waiting for the moment when he could use his infantry", and thus committed his infantry far earlier than was wise.[9]

The whole debate around this supposedly premature advance of the artillery has already been thoroughly examined by Sir Robert Rait and does not require repeating here. It is arguable that Gough did perhaps act earlier than he ought and another commander might have allowed his artillery to continue to pound the Sikh lines and positions. Malleson certainly thought that had Gough, having largely silenced the Sikh Artillery, turned his heavy guns on the two fortified villages of Chota Kalra and Bara Kalra he may have been able to force the two villages to be abandoned rather than requiring assault.[10] It was during the assault on the two villages that many of the British infantry casualties of the battle were sustained, so one can see the logic in what Malleson was saying. However, reading Malleson's comments one finds it hard not to agree with Rait's analysis that Malleson was simply looking for any excuse to criticise Gough.

Gough claimed that the reason he had committed the infantry was to protect the batteries of horse artillery that were being fired upon from Bara Kalra.[11] Whilst it might have been wise to

8   Rait, *Gough*, Vol. II, pp. 275–276.
9   Malleson, *Decisive Battles of India*, pp. 389–391.
10   Rait, *Gough*, Vol. II, pp. 274–278.
11   Rait, *Gough*, Vol. II, pp. 277–278.

continue the bombardment, Gough was also mindful of the time. It was gone noon and Gough was already anxious about the hours of light left for him to not only complete the battle but also the rout which he hoped would follow it. He wanted to leave sufficient time for his cavalry to pursue the Sikhs and bring about the total destruction of their army. Perhaps the fact that he was conscious of this was not only testament to his learning from past experience, but also his nervousness about completing a conclusive and decisive battle. Thus Gough was anxious to get his infantry involved as they alone could bring the battle to a conclusive result.

Whilst the artillery battle had been going on there had been some cavalry skirmishing on the British right. Sikh cavalry, on either side of the 'wet' *nullah* moved in an attempt to turn the flank of the British army. Although Lockwood's brigade of cavalry moved to intercept, it was in fact the horse artillery on that flank that caused the major damage to the Sikhs, holding them at bay and prevented their attack from developing fully. They were finally forced away by the cavalry before they could threaten the infantry of Hervey's brigade on the right flank. At one stage they had been near enough so that the infantry could fire upon them, but it had never been a serious threat as the flank was well covered by horse artillery and cavalry, and the nearest native infantry battalion had formed into square. The only exception to this was a band of about 30 Afghan horsemen who charged through the line and threatened the position from where Gough was watching the battle. Although the Commander-in-Chief was momentarily in danger the Afghans were dealt with by a troop of the 5th Bengal Light Cavalry assigned as bodyguard to Gough. It was said that none of the Afghan horse escaped the British line. The fact that they had been able to get that close to the commander-in-chief is attributed to them being misidentified by an unnamed staff officer who mistook them for some of Nicholson's Pathan horse.[12]

When the infantry moved forward the first targets were the two fortified villages on the right-hand side of the battlefield. Hervey's brigade that had earlier on been threatened by the Sikh cavalry was now sent to attack the village of Chota Kalra. Their advance was supported by artillery that continued to push forward in support of the infantry. The 10th Foot led the attack, supported by the 8th Native Infantry. The 52nd Native Infantry were held back to guard against any Sikh counter-attack. This was because the advance upon the other village of Bara Kalra by Penny's brigade had advanced ahead of Hervey's brigade and a gap had developed between the two. It was feared that The Sikhs might advance into this opening, and thus the 52nd were held back in case this should be attempted.

At Bara Kalra, Penny's brigade had taken the village. Penny had placed himself at the head of the 2nd Bengal Europeans as they led the advance, supported by the 70th Native Infantry. The other battalion of the brigade, the 31st Native Infantry, had been ordered to hold in reserve until the village had been taken. Thus, once taken, fresh troops could be brought in to face any counter-attack. The only problem with this had been that they were exposed to Sikh artillery fire as they waited. Eventually they were used to take the battery that had caused them so much trouble. The 31st suffered 140 casualties during this part of the battle, about the same as 2nd Bengal Europeans. Some might say this was needless, and perhaps there was a slightly careless handling of the troops, but this can hardly be laid at the feet of the commander-in-chief. The fight at Bara Kalra was hard fought. The Sikhs in some cases literally fought to the last man.[13] At Chota Kalra, similar resistance was put up but the casualties were far less. Indeed for the whole battle the 10th Foot only lost seven killed and 53 wounded. The gap between Hervey's and Penny's brigades was threatened by

---

12   Rait, *Gough*, Vol. II, pp. 280–281 & Cook, *The Sikh Wars*, pp. 187–188. Cook suggests the danger was greater than Rait suggests. It may be that Rait had the insight of Frederick Haines into this matter.

13   This and all subsequent casualty figures for the battle are taken from Burton, *The First and Second Sikh Wars*, pp. 147–148. This in turn is taken from the official returns of the army.

a body of Sikh infantry and cavalry. However with the movement forward of Markham's brigade the gap was closed. Chota Kalra was taken and the two batteries of artillery that supported the attack undertook sterling work, but suffered accordingly; indeed men from the 10th Foot had to be detached to help work the guns.

On the other side of the battlefield the advance went far more easily. The three infantry brigades of Campbell division advanced under artillery support. This was so effective as to clear any resistance from their path. Only as they reached the Sikh line did a threat emerge, as a large body of Sikh horse supported by infantry attempted to attack the British line. Their main target was the Bombay Brigade on the furthest flank of the infantry. This attempted counter-attack was halted by the horse artillery on that flank, and then turned into a rout by the cavalry charges of White's Brigade which was led in personal by Lieutenant General Thackwell. This had the effect of turning the enemy's right flank.

It is interesting to note, given previous criticism in this regard, that only a handful of the men in Campbell's division fired their muskets at all during the battle. The only notable incident of infantry under Campbell's command firing their weapons is when a few men in the 24th Foot fired at some Afghan cavalry who attempted to break through. However this was only a minor use of the musket. When the battle had turned into a rout the 60th Rifles did fire at a unit of Sikh cavalry. The cavalry had been escorting six guns when the 3rd Light Dragoons came into view. The Sikhs charged at the British cavalry, who retreated in a deliberate attempt to draw them onto the 60th Rifles. The cavalry were either killed or forced to withdraw. The Sikh gunners were killed defending their guns, and all six guns were captured.

The advance made by the British had been remarkable. In barely an hour since the infantry had been committed they had taken the two villages, the Sikh lines, the Sikh camp and the town of Gujrat itself. The Sikhs had shown the usual courage and tenacity, but their determination and their ability to resist had been greatly reduced by the artillery bombardment. Thackwell and White's cavalry now followed the retreating Sikhs to the Jhelum River, preventing many from crossing and capturing a number of guns. On the British right, Lockwood and Hearsey also advanced and at around 1600 both wings of the cavalry joined up. Any Sikhs that had not already escaped were now unlikely to be able to.

The cavalry continued to be in action until around 2200, but this was merely mopping up. The British victory had turned into a rout, and Sher Singh's army was totally defeated. British casualties were slight by the standard of the battles fought against the Sikhs. There were 96 killed and 706 wounded. Of the killed 27 were from the artillery, which gives us a good idea of the nature of the battle. The 11 soldiers killed from the 31st Native Infantry was the highest number from any individual infantry unit. Indeed the 31st also suffered the second highest number of wounded with 131, as opposed to the 135 of the 2nd Bengal Europeans. The British captured 53 of the 59 Sikh guns they had brought to the field of battle – 42 guns in the battle itself and a further 11 during the pursuit of the enemy. Alongside this, the Sikhs had lost a great many colours, all their supplies, baggage and ammunition stored in the camp at Gujrat. Exact Sikh casualty figures are as always difficult to calculate accurately. Somewhere over 2,000 seems a reasonably estimate. Given the overwhelming victory the Sikh casualties do not on the face of it seem that high. Indeed they were over 1,500 less than at Chillianwala. In one sense this points to the crushing victory the British had inflicted. It had not simply been a case of killing large numbers of Sikhs; the spirit of the army had been broken and the Sikhs had turned and run.

The importance of this last point should not be lost. In previous battles the Sikhs had fought tenaciously and had not yielded willingly. At Gujrat for the large part they broke and ran. To anyone who knows the Sikh spirit and determination this is proof of the crushing nature of defeat. One of the greatest minds of the British Army in the latter half of the 19th century once wrote that "It is better to kill fifty men in an enemy battalion, if that makes the rest run away, than to kill a hundred men if the rest stand firm."[14] This was particularly true at Gujrat where the artillery bombardment weakened the morale and steadfastness of the Sikh Army.

Rait in his defence of Gough claimed that:

> The most obvious comment on the battle of Gujerat is the similarity of its plan to that of the action of Chillianwala. [...] The formation of the British line was precisely similar; the same orders were issued to Divisional Commanders and Brigadiers; the disposition of the artillery at Gujerat was a reproduction of the arrangements made at Chillianwala.[15]

Rait then quoted Gough as saying:

> When I knew the error committed in one [battle], I gave positive directions that the whole should touch the centre, and upon no account separate—to soldiers such a prohibition should never be considered necessary. At Goojerat, I saw it fulfilled myself, at Chillianwallah I could not; but I scout the idea of the jungle being so formidable; in many parts it was sufficiently open for all arms to act, in none was it as dense as that in which I was attacked on the 27th [June] at Talavera.[16]

Whilst the plan was ostensibly the same there was one obvious tactical difference in his deployment that allowed him to carry through his plan at Gujrat and that was the use of reserve brigades to support the front line. One thinks particularly of the occasion when there became a gap in the line between Penny and Hervey's brigades. When the Sikhs threatened to throw troops into this gap Major General Whish was able to close the gap with Markham's brigade. This made the difference. On the other flank Brigadier Hoggan's brigade would have provided similar support. One also gets the sense from Gough's comments, that he had a more hands on approach. Although he did not criticise his subordinates in public, he had clearly been let down at Chillianwala by their failure to follow his instructions. At Gujrat he paid closer attention to this and in his own words 'saw it fulfilled' himself.

Whilst there is credence to Rait's claims, and there was a great similarity between the plans for the two battles, something feels different about the two battles. Comments have already been made about the fall in Sikh morale, and the rise in British morale since Chillianwala is equally important. The reinforcement of the army that had fought at Chillianwala was also an important boost in confidence. Beyond that, however, the battle at Gujrat just seems better organised. Part of this may be due to the fact that Gough had been given time to deploy his men and prepare for the assault. At Chillianwala the conflict was rather forced upon him, and therefore the organisation of that battle must always compare badly with Gujrat where Gough had the time to prepare correctly. The other great difference in this regard was that the Sikhs allowed Gough the time at Gujrat, which they had not at Chillianwala. This may also have been due to the change in Sikh morale.

One can argue that Sikh morale had been greatly reduced by the battle of Chillianwala, and an argument could be made that without Chillianwala there could have been no Gujrat. This is perhaps a little inaccurate, but the effect upon Sikh morale of the carnage at Chillianwala had taken its toll. There were wider factors with regards to the rebellion which had somewhat lost steam

---

14   Brice, Christopher *The Thinking Man's Soldier: The Life and Career of General Sir Henry Brackenbury, 1837–1914* (Solihull: Helion & Co, 2012), p. 49. This is a quote from Brackenbury's 1873 lecture 'The Tactics of the Three Arms as Modified to meet the Requirements of the Present Day'.
15   Rait, *Gough*, Vol. II, pp. 282–283.
16   Rait, *Gough*, Vol. II, p. 283. This quotes NAM: 8303–105, Gough Papers, Gough to George Gough, 11 May 1849.

and direction, and this also effected Sikh morale. Also having a negative effect was the poor supply situation for the army, and the difficulty of surviving near the Jhelum River on limited supplies, whilst the British could not only convoy in supplies from British India but also supplement this with local produce from the fertile lands near the Chenab River.

Yet based upon the experience of previous encounters with the Sikhs during both wars, Gujrat justifiably appeared to be an overwhelming success. The Sikh Army was broken. In the days that followed much of the army deserted Sher Singh. The Afghan troops retreated towards their own border. Many of the Sikh infantry deserted the cause, and although Sher Singh still had an army of around 20,000 it was largely made up of irregular cavalry and had barely 10 guns to support it. It could still have fought a guerrilla style campaign, and delayed the conclusion of the war. However serious resistance was difficult unless time could be bought to raise another army and to prepare it, and this seemed unlikely. Such time was not given because of pursuit by a force under Gilbert's command and a separate one made up of Campbell's infantry division.

Although there was little to criticise in the preparation of or course of the battle itself, there were those who criticised the aftermath.[17] After moving two miles beyond Gujrat, Gough ordered that his infantry should halt rather than continue the pursuit. Whilst it could be argued that Gough should have pressed on, it was wise to rest his men and wait until the following day. The light would fail before too long and he wanted his men altogether in one camp rather than strung out in pursuit. If he had followed the latter course, given the large quantity of enemy cavalry still around, his men might have suffered loss through twilight cavalry attacks. However whilst the infantry halted the cavalry did not and continued the pursuit until around 2200.

---

17   Malleson, *Decisive Battles of India*, pp. 394–395. Bruce, *Six Battles for India*, p. 317.

Part 8

Retirement, Memorial and Conclusion

Part 3

Victory with Bitterness

Gujrat had been an overwhelming success. It had signalled not only the end of the Sikhs' ability to continue the war for much longer, but it had also signalled the end of Gough's long military career. Whilst it might not have been the textbook battle that Aliwal has been described as, it was a near thing. In fact it was the first time that everything went to plan, and proved to an extent that Gough had always been correct in his tactics, just not his execution. At Gujrat the two had been combined and allowed Gough to complete his career as a victorious commander.

The war did not end at Gujrat, but Gough's role in it was limited after that. The main burden fell upon Major General Gilbert, who continued the pursuit of the remaining Sikh formations. On 12 March he received the surrender of Sher Singh and his father Chatar Singh, and on the 14th, at Rawalpindi, he received the surrender of the remaining Sikh army. This ended Sikh resistance, but there was still the Afghan force commanded by Dost Mohammed that had to be pursued over the border back into Afghan territory. By 21 March the Afghans had gone and the war was over. This time the Sikh state was annexed by British India as of 30 March 1849. The Maharaja Duleep Singh was awarded a pension of £50,000 (almost £3 million in modern money) a year for life on the condition that he left the Punjab. For a time he resided in India but in 1854 he went to Britain. The Punjab would instead be ruled by a Board of Control whose first President would be Henry Lawrence, previously British resident to the Lahore Government before the war.

Whilst Gujrat had not been the end of the war, it had been the decisive victory Gough had been looking for. Gough took great delight in the victory, particularly given the strong criticism he had previously received from the press. There was however a degree of bitterness, at least at first, that overshadowed his happiness at having brought the war to a successful conclusion. Partly because of this, Gough also took delight in the fact that it was the cause of some little embarrassment to those who had on receipt of the news from Chillianwala despaired of his ability to conclude the campaign, and had appointed another officer to supersede him. Several politicians, including the Prime Minister, now attempted to 'clarify' remarks they had made previously regarding Gough. In fact, many of them had simply jumped on the bandwagon, and pandered to public outcry.

Men who had painted the whole affair in India as an emergency were now made to look rather foolish. Questions were how raised in Parliament as to the reasons for the panic and the advisability of sending "a general from this country, a distance of 15,000 miles, to lead the army to victory."[1] The MP who asked the question was Ross Donnelly Mangles, representing the Guilford constituency from 1841–1857. A former civil servant of the East India Company in Bengal, he had since 1847 been a Director of the East India Company and in 1856 he would be appointed Deputy Chairman of the East India Company, and the following year he became its Chairman (the second-to-last man to hold that distinction). In the atmosphere of the House of Commons, many members attempted to expose those who it appeared had panicked, whilst those who had possibly been

---

1   *Hansard*, House of Commons Debate, 24 April 1849, Vol. 104, cc734–57.

guilty of panicking or joining in with public outcry did their best to explain away their position. This was most notable in the House of Commons on 24 April 1849 during the vote of thanks to the army, the governor general and the commander-in-chief. The Prime Minister, Lord John Russell, was amongst those who had to defend his actions of 5 and 6 March. Hansard records that when an MP remarked that Russell had previously said that the state of affairs was an emergency and that despondency prevailed throughout India, Russell, somewhat angrily one imagines, replied, "I did not say anything of the kind." Whilst it is true that he did not actually say those words, as we have seen in a previous chapter this was certainly the tone in which his remarks to the House of Commons on 5 and 6 March were made.[2]

Whereas in the past criticism had been made of Gough's performance, now praise was to be found although in the case of Sir John Hobhouse, President of the Board of Control, one gets the impression that it was reluctantly done. Only at the end of his statement of general thanks did he finally mention the commander-in-chief. The exact words are worth studying.

> It is not for me to presume to say anything of the Commander-in-Chief, who's good fortune it has been to close a long and honourable career with this great and decisive victory. He, Sir, has received from a gracious Sovereign and from a grateful Parliament rewards which will hold him up, and deservedly, to his country, as one of its bravest soldiers. And I am sure. Sir, that amongst all those honours and all those distinctions, there is none which he will more prize than the thanks of the representatives of that people too whose military glory he has added so much, and to whose dominions he has contributed additional security.[3]

It should be remembered that Hobhouse had been in close communication with Dalhousie, and that it was to Hobhouse that Dalhousie had threatened to remove Gough from command on his own authority. Hobhouse's comments, whilst generally positive, were hardly a glowing tribute. The words 'good fortune' seem to have been carefully chosen. They do rather give the idea that the President of the Board of Control felt that victory had been achieved more by luck, or divine intervention, rather than judgment.

The second speaker after Hobhouse was Sir Robert Peel, the former Prime Minister. Peel appeared more genuine in his praise. He started by stating that he had on four previous occasions taken part in debates that had noted Gough achievements: for China, Ferozeshah, Sobraon, and the vote of thanks at the end of the First Sikh War. In a statesman like speech Peel added that:

> It was with the utmost satisfaction that I heard that that noble soldier had closed a long career of victory and of glory by an achievement worthy of his former exploits. He has now, I believe, for fifty-four years served the Crown as a soldier. If at the earlier period of the recent campaign in the Punjab, doubts were entertained by some as to the ultimate result of that campaign, in those doubts I never shared. I felt the utmost confidence that the final issue of it would redound to the honour of Lord Gough, and would give new security to the British dominion in India.[4]

This has the feel of a genuine tribute. However it is a statement on Gough that could not have been made a little over a month earlier without the speaker, even one as distinguished as Peel, being subject to derision and hate.

2   *Hansard,* House of Commons Debate, 24 April 1849, Vol. 104, cc734–57.
3   *Hansard,* House of Commons Debate, 24 April 1849, Vol. 104, cc734–57.
4   *Hansard,* House of Commons Debate, 24 April 1849, Vol. 104, cc734–57.

Peel concluded his remarks by adding "I trust the House will excuse me for bearing this superfluous testimony to the services of Lord Gough; but I could not permit his military career in India to close, without taking advantage of a fifth occasion to take a part in proceedings which do honour to his name." Later in the proceedings, Peel also made an interesting resolution on how the thanks should be given. He suggested that the thanks to Dalhousie and the thanks to the Gough and the army should be separate. This was approved. Whilst on the one hand this meant that Dalhousie received an individual thanks "for the zeal and ability with which the resources of the British empire in the East Indies have been applied to the support of the Military Operations in the Punjab", he was not included as part of the military operation. The credit for this rested solely with Gough and the army. Peel achieved this by praising Dalhousie, something which the House was keen to do.[5]

However the effect that it had, and surely one that Peel was striving for, was to ensure that Gough received individual praise for having won the war. The final vote of thanks concluded that,

> The Thanks of this House be given to General the Right hon. Lord Gough, Knight Grand Cross of the Most Honourable Order of the Bath, Commander-in-Chief of the Forces in India, for the conspicuous intrepidity displayed by him during the recent Operations in the Punjab, and, especially, for his conduct, on the 21st of February, 1849, in the Battle of Goojerat, when the British Army obtained a brilliant and decisive Victory.[6]

The word intrepidity is fitting. If one takes it to mean undaunted courage, as some dictionaries do, then Gough had certainly demonstrated that. In one of his more angry letters, and one in which the bitterness over how he had been treated is all too apparent, Gough threatened to break his silence.

> If anything should be done, I am prepared to act so as to uphold my own character from whatever quarter it may come. If from the Court [of Directors] by throwing in their face their pension. If from the Horse Guards, publishing ever letter that has happened between me and the Governor-General. I am sick of what either may think. Were I inclined I have a tale to unfold which would be very unpalatable to my honourable masters.[7]

Had Gough ever published his correspondence with Dalhousie he could have ruined him. The letters would have shown the deep resistance of Dalhousie to preparations for war, the counter-manding of Gough's orders, the failure to allow proper transportation arrangements to be made, the failure to allow for the army to be returned to its previous establishment, and a general lack of understanding of the situation under which the army operated. Had such documents been made public at the very least Dalhousie would have been forced from his position as governor general.

Sir James Hogg, MP for Honiton and a Director of the East India Company, spoke in the same debate not only praising Gough but quoting from what he said was a private letter about the Battle of Gujrat written to a friend. This friend may well have been Major General Sir Archibald Galloway, a Director of the East India Company who in 1849 became its chairman. Galloway, or Archie as he is often styled in Gough's letters, had been a supporter of Gough's since the First Sikh War and was clearly a friend. Hogg read the following quotation from the letter:

---

5   *Hansard*, House of Commons Debate, 24 April 1849, Vol. 104, cc734–57.
6   *Hansard*, House of Commons Debate, 24 April 1849, Vol. 104, cc734–57.
7   NAM: 8303–105, Gough Papers, Gough to George Gough, 19 March 1849. At this stage all Gough knew was that the press, both in India and England had been very hostile towards him. As of the date of this letter he knew nothing of the moves to replace him.

I send you a rough sketch (but a very true one) of my last and best action—I say my last, as I have this day applied to his Grace to recommend a successor to Her Majesty for the proud position I have so long occupied. I say best, because both for the action itself, and its annihilating effects, I feel it well and justly merits that observation. The Sikhs have successively evacuated all the strong passes in the hilly country towards Rawull Pindee [Rawalpindi]. The few guns they have are scattered in twos and threes. Several Sirdars have surrendered, or are about to surrender, themselves.[8]

Hogg, according to Hansard, followed with the remark that "A more complete victory, he believed, had never been won. It was not only complete as a victory, but final and complete in its results."

Similar praise was echoed throughout the debate. Indeed it was remarkable how quickly the public, politicians, and press, opinion had changed. When *The Times* printed the news of this debate the tone had changed completely. Lord Hardinge, who felt that Gough had been unfairly treated, particularly by the press, sent Gough a copy of the paper. It was no doubt meant as a kindly act intended to make Gough feel better. However at that time Gough was in no mood for such kind thoughts. In a letter to Dalhousie dated 2 June 1849, Gough displayed the bitterness he clearly felt over the way he had been treated by both the press and the politicians. He began by referring to the issue of *The Times* that Dalhousie had also sent him a copy of, stating that it was, "As Lord Hardinge in his letters to me calls it 'a rascally paper'." However his criticism soon passed on to the politicians. Referring to the debate in the House of Commons and the vote of thanks Gough wrote that:

> When the same Houses of Parliament a few weeks previously vociferously cheered the appointment of an officer to supersede me, for supersession it undoubtedly was, notwithstanding the public denial of an untruthful minister, at a time when such supersession might have brought my grey hairs with sorrow to the grave, and plunged my family into immedicable grief, I can hardly be expected to feel either pride or pleasure in the approval of what they are as little capable of estimating as they were of judging faithfully of my military arrangements for Chillianwalla, which were precisely the same I made at Goojrat.[9]

The anger and bitterness can be felt in this letter. From whom Gough received the information that the House of Commons 'vociferously cheered the appointment' of Napier is unknown. That the decision was welcomed by the House is certain, but whether it was treated in the way Gough claimed is uncertain. The public denial of his supersession likely refers to Hobhouse, but could equally have applied to Russell or Wellington, although the latter was not technically now a minister.

Gough made a very pertinent point when he stated that "I can hardly be expected to feel either pride or pleasure in the approval of what they are as little capable of estimating as they were of judging faithfully of my military arrangements for Chillianwalla." This once again highlights the lack of reliable information in Britain on matters taking place thousands of miles away. They did not know what was going on and even when they received information from India, such as the letters from the governor general, they were written by someone who was over 150 miles from the seat of battle and was at best relying on second-hand information from junior officers not from the senior commander who understood the whole plan and could see the bigger picture.

There is one other interesting contribution from the debate in the House of Commons that is worthy of mention. It points to perhaps an underlying factor in the strong criticism of Gough

---

8   *Hansard*, House of Commons Debate, 24 April 1849, Vol. 104, cc734–57.
9   NAM: 8303–105, Gough Papers, Gough to Dalhousie, 2 June 1849.

that we could be forgiven for ignoring. The comment comes from Henry Grattan, MP for Meath. Grattan was a follower of Daniel O'Connell's campaign to repeal the Act of Union of 1801 and to re-establish the Irish Parliament; in effect, of devolution for Ireland. He stated that:

> the laudations that had been poured out on the gallant Commander-in-Chief in India would be responded to not the least warmly by the country to which Lord Gough belonged. It was the misfortune of that part of the empire to which he had just alluded, to have incurred the indignation of the vehicles of public news, and, he would add, of private slander, in this country; and it happened that when the career of Lord Gough was a little obscured, they opened their batteries upon him, and not the least serious of the charges against him was, that he happened to belong to his (Mr. Grattan's) unfortunate country. It was said that he was an old man, that he had not (the) head, and that he never would gain a victory, though he might suffer a defeat. A great deal was said about his Tipperary tactics; but, unfortunately for *The Times*, there was a letter extant, from the pen of Sir Charles Napier, his successor, praising these very Tipperary boys that were abused so much. He believed that Lord Gough happened to be a true Irishman, and he only hoped that the country would have many Lord Gough's, many Sir Charles Napier's, and many such bad Tipperary gentlemen.[10]

Whilst it would be wrong to read too much into Grattan's comments there was clearly some truth behind it. Gough was indeed a proud Irishman, and would never attempt to deny his birthright. He spoke, we are told, with a strong Irish brogue, and would proudly talk of being Irish.

Grattan alludes to the suggestion that many of the character and command defects that were perceived in Gough were seen as being on account of him being Irish. There was an extent to which Gough was seen to fit into the stereotype of being strong and brave but with little intelligence, a stereotype of the Irish which continued for many years. Indeed one of the most dangerous rumours to come out of the battle of Chillianwala was this supposedly overheard conversation in which Gough was said to have remarked that he had not intended to attack but that the enemy had put his 'Irish Blood up'. We only have a third-hand account of this supposed conversation – a junior officer told Gifford, who subsequently told Dalhousie – and have no idea of the context in which the remark might have been made. Yet that this very quotation has been so often used in subsequent histories does in a sense support the view that it conveniently fitted the explanation of Gough's Irish heritage being the cause of his rash behaviour, and supports Grattan's view that there was an anti-Irish agenda behind the criticism of Gough. We must remember that Grattan himself had an agenda and was attempting to expose what he believed to be anti-Irish sentiment. Gough publicly claiming his Irish heritage would have been rather unpopular in that era of Anglo-Irish relations. This does not mean that there was a negative campaign against Gough based upon anti-Irish feeling, but it would also be wrong to dismiss such a notion of prejudice entirely.

For a time Gough continued in bitter mood. Even as praise came from within India it did not mollify him. One gets the impression that at the end of the Second Sikh War Gough was a bitter and exhausted man. He longed only to be with his family and to return with them to England and then to Ireland. His military career was effectively over and he now longed for the peace of retirement. In the years that followed, Gough would lose much of his bitterness towards his treatment. However there is no doubt that he had been unfairly treated. The press had created an exaggerated outcry which captured the public imagination. It was in many ways this, rather than the correspondence of Dalhousie, to which the politicians reacted, or one might say overreacted.

---

10   *Hansard*, House of Commons Debate, 24 April 1849, Vol. 104, cc734–57.

75

Farewell to India

In late May of 1849 Gough wrote to his son that, "I am glad to get rid of the office, the government and the responsibility."[1] It had been a task to which he had never truly been suited. Gough was a brave and courageous leader and a good commander of troops. He was an excellent battalion commander, a good brigade or even divisional commander, yet he was only an average commander-in-chief. That might sound strange when one thinks that he had in his own words, "conquered the Punjab twice by hard fighting."[2] That his achievements in this regard deserve recognition goes without saying. He had at times been extremely fortunate, and luck had been on his side more often than not. He had also suffered from political intrigue from political penny-pinching and decisions made with political interests rather than military ones to the fore.

As has already been mentioned, when Sir Charles Napier arrived in India it was discovered that his commission as commander-in-chief called on him to take over command immediately. The exact words were 'without loss of time'. This, as Rait put it, placed Gough in 'a false position'. It is clear from Napier's correspondence that he felt uncomfortable with the situation. In fairness he had felt uneasy about being asked to replace Gough from the very beginning and it was only the insistence of the Duke of Wellington that had convinced him.[3] To a very real extent Napier did not want to be there. He was even more unpopular with the press and politicians in India than Gough had become. Indeed Rait stated that Napier, "was more obnoxious to them than any other living man, and it must be admitted that the Directors' appeal to Sir Charles Napier, to save India, was a personal triumph for the Duke, as well as for Napier himself."[4] Indeed on another occasion Rait went further and suggested that Wellington took advantage of the situation to 'force' Napier upon the East India Company.[5]

Certainly Napier was not thrilled by the prospect of returning to India. Whilst part of Napier might have wished to settle some old scores from his last spell in India, it was unlikely that he would get the opportunity. Instead he found himself despatched to fight a war which by the time he arrived in Calcutta, 6 May 1849, had already been over for a couple of months. The fact that he felt uncomfortable is seen in his account of his first meeting with Gough upon landing in India. By this stage Dalhousie had informed Gough of the wording of Napier's commission and that he was to assume immediate command. Despite what Dalhousie had said of Gough in the past, he took no delight in informing him of this and was said to have done so in a considerate and sympathetic manner. Indeed it appears that Dalhousie now thought that Gough had been rather hard done by.

1   NAM: 8303–105, Gough Papers, Gough to George Gough, 26 May 1849.
2   NAM: 8303–105, Gough Papers, Gough to unknown, 19 March 1849.
3   NAM: 8303–105, Gough Papers, Gough to George Gough, 26 May 1849. Rait, *Gough*, Vol. II, p. 298.
4   Rait, *Gough*, Vol. II, p. 295.
5   Rait, *Gough*, Vol. II, pp. 294–295.

This view was shared by Napier, who seems in part to have had genuine pleasure in the fact that his services were not needed to bring the campaign to a conclusion. Writing home Napier remarked that "You will have heard that the war is over in India, and Lord Gough has come off with flying colours. Both these things rejoice me much."[6] Napier did not seem to have simply been trying to make the most of the situation, and was genuinely pleased that Gough had successfully ended the conflict without him. Gough later heard from Admiral Sir William Parker, his colleague from the campaign in China, who had spoken with Napier as he passed through Alexandria and where Napier had expressed his hope that his services would not be required.[7]

There is of course the possibility that Napier, had he arrived before the end of the war, might not have exercised his right to command and may have served under Gough. Of their first meeting Napier wrote, "I told him that my wish was that he would order me home; it would be a kindness, and so saying I told him the truth."[8] With this obvious example of Napier's reluctance to command, one wonders whether or not had the circumstances been different as to whether he would have exercised his rights. Yet even if he had only been present for the final battle much of the credit would naturally have gone to him rather than Gough, even if the latter had still been in ultimate command.

There seems to have been no animosity from Gough towards Napier. Gough was clearly of the view that Wellington and the politicians at home, influenced by the press, were behind his supersession. To Napier he showed nothing but kindness, clearly believing that Napier was simply following orders. Napier recorded that "Again let me express my delight with old Gough; he is so good, so honest, so noble-minded."[9] Gough's generosity, at a time when he was clearly feeling very hurt by the actions that had been taken against him, was a credit to the man. It would have been entirely understandable if, under the circumstances, Gough had acted angrily towards both Dalhousie and Napier. The fact that he did not demonstrates a calmness and almost relief at the culmination of events. In his last letter to Napier written in India, Gough, after discussing promotions and rewards for those who had served during the recent war with the Sikhs, ends with the words, "Wishing you once more health, success, and happiness."[10]

Gough was indeed relieved that it was all over. Unbeknown to most people he had been experiencing great anxiety in his personal life since taking the field for the Second Sikh War. His wife had been ill before he left her for the commencement of operations, and by January it looked as if Lady Gough was dying. Theirs had been a true love match and the added burden of the ill health of his wife is one that it would be all too easy to dismiss. It is often overlooked that even a commander-in-chief has feelings and emotions and personal concerns that surely affect them. Exactly what was wrong with Lady Gough is not certain. Although she had suffered from the extremely painful condition of trigeminal neuralgia for many years, there was clearly more to her ill health than this. The climatic conditions of the subcontinent had not helped her general health. It was as much for his wife's health as his own that Gough so quickly asked to be relieved of command once the war had been concluded.

Whilst Gough was away Lady Gough stayed with her daughter Frances at Meerut. This obviously placed a great burden on Frances. What we know of Lady Gough's illness comes from the letters between Frances and her husband Lieutenant Colonel, later Field Marshal Sir, Patrick

6   Bruce, William Napier, *Life of General Sir Charles Napier* (London: John Murray, 1885), p. 364.
7   Phillimore, Augustus *The Life of Admiral of the Fleet Sir William Parker* Vol. II, p. 504. This is an extract from Parker's letter to Gough dated 13 April 1849.
8   Bruce, *Life of General Sir Charles Napier*, p. 364.
9   Bruce, *Life of General Sir Charles Napier*, p. 364.
10   Rait, *Gough*, Vol. II, p. 309.

Grant.[11] Grant was Adjutant General to the army commanded by Gough. Although she obviously had servants, Frances was tasked with looking after her invalid mother and her own three children, all under the age of four. In some ways her letters to her husband were something of a safety valve in which she was able to unburden herself of her fears and concerns. It therefore has to be considered in this light when we look at the health issues effecting Lady Gough. It was clear that Lady Gough was seriously ill, but the exact nature of her illness is also unknown. She did in the later years of her life suffer from a serious throat infection, which modern medicine might have diagnosed as throat cancer. Whether it was this or some other illness we do not know. Yet it was clearly serious. Gough was obviously aware of his wife's ill health and that it was serious. It maybe that he did not know the full extent, and one wonders if Grant dared show him the letters or discuss the details of their contents. As a staff officer, Grant would have been well aware of the responsibilities and problems that weighed heavily upon Gough and might not have wished to add to them by disclosing the full extent of Lady Gough's illness, and in particular the fact that her daughter thought she was dying.

One wonders if Gough's comments in his letter to Dalhousie regarding press reports of Chillianwala, when he refers to them and his possible supersession, are also indicative of the personal concerns. His comment that such supersession might have "brought my grey hairs with sorrow to the grave, and plunged my family into irremediable grief", may allude to the personal trials he was also undergoing alongside those connected with his military career.[12] We have already seen that the Goughs were a devoted couple, and the state of his beloved's health cannot have been far from his mind. Yet one thinks that Gough would not have worried about it in the sense that we might expect. Although he was surely concerned and would mourn the loss of his wife, his deep Christian faith would have seen it as God's will.

The ill health suffered by Lady Gough was still a problem by the time the war had been concluded. This presented difficulties. With Charles Napier's arrival, Gough had officially been relieved and was therefore no longer officially able to use the residency of the commander-in-chief. Although Gough was no doubt eager to leave India as soon as possible, the problem of Lady Gough's health was a difficulty in this regard. The time of year meant that the long journey would be ruinous to her health, and indeed would be difficult for Gough himself. The Goughs therefore decided to remain in India until the winter months would allow a more conducive journey. Charles Napier extended to the Goughs the continued use of Bentinck Castle, the official residence of the Commander-in-Chief, which was situated in the hill station of Simla where the climate was more conducive to good health. It was yet another act of kindness of the part of Sir Charles towards Lord Gough. Simla, or Shimla, was to become the summer capital of British India due to the more favourable climate. Bentinck Castle had been built as the residence of Lord Bentinck governor general of India 1828–1835. His successor as governor general did not use it and it was taken over by the commander-in-chief. The original building burned down in 1922.

Gough gave his farewell order to the army on 19 March and then proceeded to Simla. He joined his wife at Bentinck Castle on 19 April. At some point they moved from the castle to a cottage in Simla where they remained until November 1849. Lady Gough's health during this period was not helped by a nasty fall when she fell backwards off a veranda, on 31 May, estimated to be 10 or 12 feet off the ground. Amazingly no bones were broken, however there was severe bruising and

---

11   Grant, Isabel Frances *Extracts from the Army Quarterly: Everyday Letters Written During the First and Second Sikh War* Vol. X, No. 2, July 1825 (London: Army Quarterly, 1925), pp. 347–351. Isabel Frances Grant was the granddaughter of Patrick and Frances Grant, and therefore the great-granddaughter of Lord Gough.

12   NAM: 8303–105, Gough Papers, Gough to Dalhousie, 2 June 1849.

the shock to the already delicate health of a 61-year-old lady can be imagined.[13] There was further bad news in late July of that year when Gough heard of the death of Margaret Gough, wife of his nephew Colonel Sir John Bloomfield Gough who it will be recalled had previously served on his staff and played an important part during both Sikh Wars. Margaret was the daughter of Sir John McCaskill who had been killed at Mudki. Gough was fond of John Bloomfield Gough and also of his wife and felt the news of her death dearly.[14]

In late October 1849, as the Goughs were preparing to leave India, there was happier news. Firstly there was the relief at leaving India, but also the news that the Goughs had another grandson, who bore the names of his grandfather and father as Hugh George Gough. The baby Hugh was actually born in August 1849 but it took some time for the news to reach the Goughs in India. He would become the 3rd Viscount Gough in 1895. On 3 November 1849 Hugh Gough celebrated his 70th birthday. A week later, on 10 November the Goughs began their journey back to the British Isles.

On the journey from Simla to Calcutta Gough had, on the orders of Dalhousie, been given and treated with all the military honours that were due to a commander-in-chief. He was, however, a little reticent at some of the adulation. Perhaps still feeling rather hurt by the gossip and insinuations after Chillianwala, he refused all offers to attend the many dinners given in his honour.

All that is, bar one. On arrival at Allahabad on 1 December he found that part of the 87th Foot, the regiment he had led with such distinction in the Peninsular and of which he was now colonel, was in garrison there.[15] He broke his own rule and attended the dinner given in his honour. The Goughs stayed in Allahabad for five or six days and spent much of it with the 87th. On the 6th, Gough returned the favour and gave a dinner for the officers of the 87th at the hotel he was staying at.

Again the warm welcome was not just for the colonel of the regiment but for the role he had played in the regimental history of the 87th. Lieutenant James Baille, who was certainly far too young to recall the days in the Peninsular, told the story of Lady Gough showing him a piece of the old regimental colour from Barrosa and a gold leaf from the eagle captured that day. Baille later recorded that "Lady Gough put them both into my hand, and I really felt it an honour to touch such relics."[16]

The Goughs reached Calcutta on 29 December 1849. There they were given an enthusiastic welcome both by the public and the government. On the following evening a ball was given at Government House in Calcutta in his honour. After a few days in Calcutta it was on 8 January 1850 that Gough left India for the last time aboard the P&O passenger ship *Haddington*. The ending of his time in India had fittingly been marked with official recognition and acknowledgement at Government House. Yet to an extent Gough was still too hurt to really appreciate the honour given to him. It was only when he returned to England and entered into a prolonged period of official and unofficial recognition of his accomplishments that he started to appreciate such honours.

13 Rait, *Gough*, Vol. II, p. 307.
14 Rait, *Gough*, Vol. II, pp. 307–308.
15 Cunliffe, *Royal Irish Fusiliers*, p. 216. Lieutenant Colonel Campbell and four companies had moved up to Berhampore, and the rest of the regiment remained in Allahabad. The regimental history records that Gough arrived in Allahabad on 1 December. However Rait, *Gough*, Vol. II, p. 308, records that he arrived on 30 November.
16 Cunliffe, *Royal Irish Fusiliers*, p. 216.

76

Return To England

The single-screw steam-powered ship *Haddington*, which would transport the Goughs to England, was a relatively modern vessel having made her maiden voyage in December 1846. At top speed she could do over 10 knots, a relatively fast speed for the era. After a brief stop in Madras, to acknowledge Gough's previous appointment in that area and allow a formal farewell to be made, the journey continued. *Haddington* transported the Goughs from Calcutta to Suez. As this was in the days before the canal, a journey overland was then made to Cairo. From there they moved to Alexandria where they boarded another P&O liner, *Indus*, on which they would complete the journey. On boarding the *Indus*, *The Times* records, a 15-gun salute was fired whilst the band of the ship played 'See the Conquering Hero Comes'.[1] This tune originates from George Frideric Handel's oratorio *Judas Maccabaeus* and was originally composed as a compliment to the Duke of Cumberland to acknowledge his victory at Culloden in 1746. Since that time it had regularly been used to welcome military heroes. The playing of it for Gough was perhaps more of an honour than the modern reader will appreciate. The ship called at Malta and Gibraltar along the way. Lord and Lady Gough had sailed accompanied by their daughter Frances Grant, and Lord Gough's nephew Colonel John Bloomfield Gough. At some point during the journey they were joined by their son George Gough. George did not sail with them from India, but we know that he disembarked with them from Southampton. It is unclear whether he joined the ship at Alexandria, Malta or Gibraltar.

On Sunday 24 February 1850, at around 1600, the *Indus* arrived at Southampton. In the two days prior to Gough's arrival, the authorities in Southampton had been preparing. On the Friday the military officers in Southampton, numbering over 40 and representing both services, had held a meeting to organise a reception committee. Major General Arnold and Vice Admiral Dick organised the following reception for Gough. When the ship docked they went aboard to ask the Goughs to remain in Southampton overnight so that an official presentation could be made the following day.[2]

Unfortunately the civil powers did not support these preparations. On Saturday 23 February the Mayor of Southampton had organised a similar meeting for the civil power to organise the civic side of such a reception. However being a Saturday the council chamber was largely empty and it was later calculated that as many as 21 councillors were absent. The Mayor, Mr Andrews, proposed that a civic reception and address be prepared to recognised Lord Gough's arrival. The motion was strongly opposed by Councillor Clarke, of the Society of Friends, who organised opposition to the motion. His argument was that it was wrong to 'hero-worship' military leaders, and felt that the civil power should have no part of this. The much reduced council was tied at nine votes each. The deadlock was broken by the Mayor. Bizarrely, given that he had originated the proposal, he joined

---

1   *The Times*, Monday 25 February 1850.
2   *The Times*, Monday 25 February 1850.

Councillor Clarke's opposition and the motion was rejected. Clearly local politics played a part in the Mayor's change of heart.[3]

As it was, this caused more embarrassment to the civil powers of Southampton than it did Lord Gough. The embarrassment and accusations against the Mayor of Southampton were such that at a dinner given in late August in Southampton where the guest was the Lord Mayor of London, the Mayor of Southampton felt it necessary to publicly state that he had not "done dishonour to a noble, valiant and gallant soldier."[4] The council was made to look rather foolish as the local military, clergy, magistrates and many prominent local citizens and councillors ignored the official decision and cooperated with the military preparations. The result was that, apart from the absence of the mayor, one would not have realised that there had ever been any issue around an official welcome for Gough. When the *Indus* tied up a large crowd of dock workers and local people thronged the dockside to welcome home Lord Gough. Numbers are unknown, but *The Times* described it as a great crowd. Gough and the other passengers disembarked to thunderous applause.

Further to the original story, an update sent by 'electric telegraph' was added sent at 2100hrs. There were 114 passengers on board the *Indus*. Apart from Lord and Lady Gough this included their daughter Frances Grant, although not her husband, Colonel John Bloomfield Gough, Major General Campbell and his wife, and Major Herbert Edwardes. Apart from Gough the crowd also gave a great welcome to Herbert Edwardes, whose reputation had increased due to his exploits around Multan. According to the report from *The Times* it appears that the presence of Colin Campbell, in many ways the outstanding general of the recent war, was largely unnoticed. Perhaps this further illustrates how little was truly known of the details of the campaign itself.[5]

That same evening, it being Sunday, the Gough family attended the evening service at All Saints Church in Southampton. The Goughs remained in Southampton at the request of the organising committee so that an official address could be made the following day. At noon the following day the Goughs were welcomed at the Royal Victoria Archery Rooms by a great number of the local military, magistrates, clergy, and prominent local residents. The official address declared that:

> We, the undersigned residents of Southampton and its neighbourhood, beg leave to respectfully offer your Lordship our sincere congratulations on your return to your native country, and to express our unfeigned admiration of the many splendid victories gained by the British arms under your Lordship's command. We are not unmindful that your Lordship has been engaged upwards of 50 years in the service of your country, leading our soldiers to victory in the Peninsular, in China, and India, more particularly in the Punjab where the splendid achievements of the army under your Lordship's command have placed your name in the proud position of one of the most distinguished soldiers of this or any country.

Lord Gough responded by saying that:

> I thank you very sincerely for this flattering mark of attention towards one, a perfect stranger to many of you, without other pretention than that to which so many naval and military men may justly lay claim, an anxious wish to fulfil to the utmost of their power and ability their duty to their Queen and Country, and to uphold that which has been so justly acquired by the Anglo-Indian army, the supremacy of British power in India, contributing as it does so largely to the proud position England now holds, proud from her military achievements, but

3   *The Times*, Monday 25 February 1850.
4   *The Times*, Wednesday 28 August 1850.
5   *The Times*, Monday 25 February 1850.

much more proud from the loyalty of her sons. An absence of 13 years has not lessened my nationality. […] Again, my dear countrymen, allow me, on the part of lady Gough and myself, to return you my best acknowledgments , my warmest thanks, for this to me the most valuable testimony of your approval.[6]

No sooner had he finished speaking than the assembled crowd broke forth into loud cheers. The welcome in Southampton had been gratifying to Gough for two of reasons. Firstly because it was a place with which he had no connection, and secondly because it alleviated any lingering doubts he had about how he would be received. Any past dissatisfaction was largely gone. Indeed a feeling now existed that Gough had in fact been somewhat hard done by and that there had been a reaction to Chillianwala which events at Gujrat had largely proved was not justified.

Indeed, he was to find a similarly positive and lively reception as he continued his journey. At 1400 on the 25th the Goughs left Southampton by train. The railways were anxious to show Gough the proper respect and honour and thus a private train was to have been organised. However Gough, with usual humility, kindly rejected the honour and travelled by the regular train.[7] When the train reached Waterloo, at around 1700, a great crowd had gathered to great his arrival. Gough acknowledged the crowd, which led to further cheering. Major Edwardes had also been on that same train, and as the two men shook hands as they took their leave of each other the noise of the crowd increased further. *The Times*, with its usual flair for accuracy, reported on 26 February that Herbert Edwardes was accompanied by his wife and two children. He had neither. The two 'children' were the daughters of John Lawrence, who Edwardes escorted to England, and the 'wife' was his aunt Lady Edwardes. Herbert Edwardes wrote to *The Times* to clarify the situation and they subsequently published his letter 27 February 1850. Lord Gough would suffer from similarly inaccurate reporting of events when 27 October 1854 *The Times* reported that the Major Gough who had been wounded at the Battle of Alma was his son. In fact, his only surviving son, George, had retired from the army with the rank of captain many years before.

From Waterloo Station, the Goughs returned with their son George to his residence at Upper Brook Street. The following day Gough left the house early to travel into the city to visit East India House for the purpose of reporting to Sir Archibald Galloway the Chairman of the Company. Again this illustrates the humility of the man that he felt it incumbent upon him to make the journey. As it happened, his journey crossed that of Sir Archibald, who arrived at George Gough's residence at around 1000 to present his compliments to Lord Gough and discuss with him a banquet that the Company planned to hold in his honour to mark his return. Galloway was not the only visitor that morning, and just as he was about to leave to return to East India House to meet Gough, Lord Hardinge arrived. Hardinge had also come to see Gough, and it appears that his was a personal visit rather than any sort of official business. This again leads credence to the belief that whatever difficulties they had in the past in India, Gough and Hardinge remained friends for many years. Galloway and Hardinge then travelled back to East India House together. *The Times* recorded that Gough greeted Hardinge, "with all the sincerity of the heartiest friendship." After this Gough and Galloway, who it will be recalled had been one of Gough's few defenders during the dark hours after news of Chillianwala reached England, had a long meeting. One imagines that the meeting was largely a pleasant discussion between friends rather than a serious business meeting.[8]

---

6   *The Times*, Tuesday 26 February 1850.
7   *The Times*, Tuesday 26 February 1850.
8   *The Times*, Wednesday 27 February 1850.

The fact that Gough had bypassed both Galloway and Hardinge when they came to call on him is further illustration of the sense of humility and duty that Gough continued to demonstrate. It is also showed his underestimation of how important he had now become. Given his long 13 year absence from Britain, he had never before experienced the rise in status that he had achieved since last he had been in England. He had never before been in England as the hero of China, the conqueror of the Gwalior, and the man who had defeated the Sikhs in two separate campaigns. The importance he now held no doubt started to dawn on him as the day continued.

During the 26th, many notable people came to call on Gough at his son's house. If *The Times* is to be believed, over 47 different people, varying from officers of both services to members of the aristocracy, called on the Goughs on that first day in London. This list does not appear to include any members of the Gough family, and there must have been other family members who called at some point during that day. Over the days that followed, many other notable people presented themselves at the house of George Gough to pay their respects to Lord Gough. This was a strange mixture of the recognition of his celebrity status, social convention, and the status of being able to say they had visited Lord Gough. To some it may also have been out of a sense of unease at how he had been treated.[9]

On following day, 27 February, the visitors to Lord Gough included the former Prime Minister Sir Robert Peel and the current Prime Minister Lord John Russell. Presumably Gough welcomed the visit of the former far more than the latter. Also calling on him that day was the Adjutant General, Sir John Macdonald. That morning Gough, accompanied by his son, had called at Horse Guards. Interestingly they were met by Lord Fitzroy Somerset, the military secretary to the commander-in-chief, rather than Wellington himself. Perhaps this speaks more of the fact that the now 80-year-old Wellington was less frequently at Horse Guards than of any deliberate slight of Lord Gough. Indeed Gough probably found it more congenial to talk with Somerset, whom he liked, than to have had a rather uneasy meeting with Wellington.[10]

Gough then called on the President of the Board of Control Sir John Hobhouse. Although we know no details of this meeting, it cannot have been an easy one. It was Hobhouse who had urged Gough's supersession, and Gough was no doubt fully aware of it. Hobhouse does not appear to have had any feelings of remorse about what he had done, and indeed stated in the House of Commons at a later date that he and the Government had acted correctly and in the best interests of the Empire. It would be fascinating to know what Gough said to Hobhouse.

On the return journey Gough and his son called at Buckingham Palace, where Lord Gough signed the visitor's book and left his card. That same evening, the 27th, Lord and Lady Gough left London at 1700 to travel to Bath to visit their eldest daughter Letitia, now Mrs Supple. Lady Gough remained there some days but the following morning Lord Gough journeyed back to London and arrived in the early afternoon. That evening he dined with the Marquis of Londonderry. In the meantime the Palace had been in contact and Gough was given an audience with Prince Albert on 1 March 1850. That same evening he dined with Her Majesty. On that same day Gough was privileged to receive a visit from Ernest II, Duke of Saxe-Coburg and Gotha, the brother of Prince Albert. The presence of the Duke in London at this time is interesting as it is during the First Schleswig-Holstein War. The Duke, as a corps commander, had played an important part in the German victory over the Danes at Eckernforde. As both men had recently come from the experience of active service, this would also have been an interesting conversation to have overheard.

1 March was also the day he finally met with Wellington, the latter calling at George Gough's residence. According to *The Times*, Wellington had 'a long interview with the noble Lord'. Again

9   *The Times*, Wednesday 27 February 1850.
10 *The Times*, Thursday 28 February 1850.

no record of what must have been a very interesting discussion survives. It would be intriguing to have read what Gough made of Wellington, for it was around this time that Havelock referred to him as 'a spectacle of mouldering greatness'. Havelock also stated that Wellington's mind was said to wander and that he would often start sentences but be unable to finish them. This might explain the long meeting, for there was no business for them to discuss. Perhaps Wellington tried to clarify what he had meant by his letter about Charles Napier.[11]

On Saturday 2 March, Gough paid a visit to Lord Hardinge, before dinning with Lord Palmerston in the evening. Palmerston held a high opinion of Gough from his time in China, and both men held a fairly low opinion of Lord John Russell, so they no doubt found much to talk about. It might be that a friendship developed as the following Saturday Lord Gough, this time accompanied by Lady Gough, visited Palmerston again. However this might have had more to do with the fact that Gough was at this time the 'fashionable' guest to have. On the second occasion Gough dressed formally in his full uniform as a general of the British Army.[12]

On Monday 4 March, Gough was visited by Lieutenant General Sir James Lushington, the Chairman of the Oriental Club and former Chairman of the Court of Directors of the Honourable East India Company, who brought with him a deputation to ascertain a suitable date for a dinner to be given in Lord Gough's honour. It was decided that Tuesday 9 April would be a suitable date and arrangements were made accordingly.[13] On 7 March Lord and Lady Gough were guests of the Prime Minister and his wife at 10 Downing Street. The party commenced at 2200 and guests were still said to be arriving at midnight. Although the party continued into the early hours of the morning one imagines that the Goughs left before that time. Also present were Sir Robert and Lady Peel, the Duke of Wellington, and many foreign dignitaries.[14]

Perhaps only now Gough started to appreciate the importance that was attached to his name. If he bothered to read *The Times*, which, given his history with that paper, he would be forgiven for not doing, he would have noticed the very different manner in which his name was mentioned. Certainly its reporting of his triumphant return to England was one part of this, however even before his return there was a different feel. In an article 3 January 1850, discussing the possibility of his son George Gough standing for the Parliamentary constituency of Limerick City, Lord Gough was referred to as, "the gallant Lord Gough."[15] This was a very noticeable difference to what that same newspaper expressed the previous year. By April even the Battle of Chillianwala was being referred to as a, "hard fought and fiercely contested" battle, a far more positive interpretation than that which had been placed upon it the previous year.[16]

There is a wonderful quote from *Punch* regarding Lord Gough, which deserves repeating here, as it illustrates the change in the way in which Gough was represented in the press. *Punch* had been highly critical of Gough. In particular a poem by William Makepeace Thackeray had attacked Gough and praised Napier. Thackeray had penned a poem entitled 'The Story of Koompanee Jehan', in which Gough was thinly disguised as 'Goof Bahawder'. Thackeray had a rather low opinion of Gough that would find its way into other parts of his work. It is however interesting to note that Thackeray's cousin was Major Richmond Campbell Shakespear, who had served as Gough's ADC at Mahrajapore and then had commanded a battery of six heavy guns at Chillianwala and Gujrat. Whether Shakespear was Thackeray's 'source' for his opinions on Gough is unclear. It would appear

---

11   *The Times*, Saturday 2 March 1850. Cooper, *Havelock*, p. 75.
12   *The Times*, Monday 4 March 1850 & Monday 11 March 1850.
13   *The Times*, Tuesday 5 March 1850.
14   *The Times*, Thursday 7 March 1850.
15   *The Times*, Thursday 3 January 1850.
16   *The Times*, Monday 1 April 1850.

unlikely. Shakespear seems to have had a high opinion of Gough, despite attempts by Malleson to use comments made by Shakespear out of context to attack Lord Gough.

This had not been the only 'joke' at Gough's expense. Earlier in the year the following had appeared in Punch. "Lord Gough is the greatest military economist of the age, for by his operations in India he has carried into practice the principle of reducing the Army to an extent almost without precedent."[17] This unkind, not to mention rather macabre interpretation of Gough's conduct would probably have hurt him far more than Thackeray's parody. The comments in *Punch* brought with it a suggestion of a lack of concern with regards to the lives of his men. As we have already seen Gough cared deeply for his men, and such accusations would have hurt him deeply.

With Gough's success at Gujrat *Punch* like all the other members of the press found itself in a somewhat embarrassing position. However, unlike other periodicals, *Punch* at least had the good grace to admit to its error. The following appeared in *Punch* shortly before Gough returned to England.

> *Punch* hereby begs to present his thanks to Lord Gough, and the officers and soldiers of the British Army in India for the brilliant victory which they had the good fortune to gain the other day at Goojerat; and *Punch* by these presents, extols his Lordship and his troops to the skies. A few weeks ago *Punch* sent Lord Gough his dismissal, which *Mr. Punch* is now glad did not arrive in time to prevent the triumph for which he is thus thankful. Having violently abused Lord Gough for losing the day at Chillianwallah, *Punch* outrageously glorifies him for winning the fight at Goojerat. When Lord Gough met with a reverse, *Punch* set him down for an incompetent octogenarian; now that he has been fortunate, *Punch* believes him to be a gallant veteran; for *Mr. Punch*, like many other people, of course looks merely to results; and takes as his only criterion of merit, success.[18]

There are several comments that need to be made by way of correction. Gough was not an octogenarian. At the time of Chillianwala he was yet to have even his 70th birthday. Also, the term 'good fortune' might sound like damning with faint praise to the modern reader to whom it no doubt draws the parallel with the term luck. However in the era in which it was written the term would be better described as 'providence' and it did bring with it a degree of religious undertone suggesting the providential guiding hand of God. This was in effect the position that the majority of the press, and indeed one could argue wider society, had taken. However, only *Punch* boldly admitted its change of stance. Indeed the commentary was correct in the sense that a 'good' general is a 'winning' general. Now that Gough was once again the 'winning' general the press lauded him.

17   *Punch*, Vol. XVI, January to June 1849 (London: Bradbury & Evans) p. 177.
18   *Punch*, Vol. XVI January to June 1849, (London: Bradbury & Evans), p. 177.

77

'The Conquering Hero'

For a time Gough became the national hero. Wherever he went, celebrations were made to honour the man who less than a year ago would, in the words of William Napier "have been stoned to death in the streets if he had then appeared."[1] Yet now everyone wanted to pay their respects. Now it was 'dinners' and not 'stones' that were to be thrown in his honour.

The East India Company was not the only organisation that announced a dinner in Gough's honour. The United Service Club announced that they would be giving a diner at which Lord Gough would be the guest of honour. On 27 February it was announced that the dinner was now full and that no further places were available. The Worshipful Goldsmith's Company also honoured Gough by giving him the freedom of the guild and announcing an event in his honour to be held at the Goldsmith's Hall. He was also to be awarded the Freedom of the City of London, Londonderry and Edinburgh and the town of Clonmel. Oxford University also conferred upon Gough an honorary Doctorate of Civil Law which was presented to him in a ceremony on 12 June 1850.

The United Service Club held its dinner in honour of Lord Gough on 20 March 1850. At 1900, over 200 guests started to arrive at the Club in Pall Mall. At 1945 they started to make their way from the drawing room to the dining room. General Sir James Macdonell acted as President with Lord Gough on his right and the Duke of Wellington on his left. After the toast to the Queen and the Prince Consort, the health of Lord Gough was proposed and loudly received and Gough then gave a short speech in response. As with all his speeches during this period there was, in the words of Robert Rait, no 'self-laudation' or 'self-defence'. Indeed, during it Gough paid tribute to Lord Hardinge and the assistance he had given him during the First Sikh War. The more cynical mind might think this was a veiled attack upon Dalhousie, but it is unlikely that such a thought ever occurred to Gough.[2]

The Duke of Wellington then rose to give a speech honouring Lord Gough. What detail we have of this speech comes from the report in *The Times*. This account gives a little hint of it, but some who were there recorded it as being a somewhat rambling speech. Indeed so obsessed did the Duke become at one point with praising Hardinge that it is to be wondered as to whether Wellington had become confused as to who the dinner was in honour of. The fact that Hardinge was sat next to him, whilst the Chairman sat between Wellington and Gough, obviously did not help matters. However it is unusual that in a speech about Lord Gough, almost half of it should be devoted to praising Hardinge. Obviously Gough's mentioning of Hardinge meant that it was understandable that Wellington should also acknowledge his contribution, but one could become slightly paranoid about this and suggest that this was because Hardinge was one of the Wellington's 'set' in a way in

---

1   Napier, *The Life and Opinions of General Sir Charles James Napier*, Vol. IV, p. 151.
2   *The Times*, Thursday 21 March 1849. Rait, *Gough*, Vol. II p. 312.

which Gough never was. There might be some truth it that. Yet Wellington was an old man, not in the best of health, who had already entered into what was to be the last three years of his life.

However, despite this, it should not be thought that Wellington did not give praise to Gough. Indeed, this speech was a vast improvement upon his speech in the House of Lords. Towards the end of it he remarked that:

> We have seen that, throughout the services carried on under the direction of my noble friend, Lord Gough, he has himself afforded the brightest example of the highest qualities of the British soldier in the attainment of the glorious successes which have attended the British army under his command.[3]

After Wellington's speech further tributes were paid by fellow senior officers of the army. The Marquis of Anglesey, the Master General of the Ordnance, remarked that the 'gallant and distinguished' Lord Gough had, "surmounted every difficulty, and accomplished successfully a campaign which – I speak advisedly – is one of the most memorable on record." Anglesey also remarked upon the presence of Hardinge, but largely to praise Gough for having recognised his important contribution. There was also a rather barbed remark by Anglesey, which was no doubt directed at Dalhousie, alluding to the lack of support Gough had received in the Second War as opposed to the First. Sir Archibald Galloway, Chairman of the Court of Directors of the Honourable East India Company, remarked that Lord Gough had been "a faithful servant of the East India Company, and in the command of the noble army of India had added lustre to British arms and a kingdom to the British Crown."[4]

That same evening both Wellington and Gough attended a party at 10 Downing Street given by Lady Russell. Having come straight from the United Service Club they arrived at around 2300. This round of parties and dinners was no doubt tiring for Lord Gough, but at the same time no doubt a great source of pride to him. There was to be one further great dinner in his honour that same week. On Saturday 23 March the East India Company organised a dinner at the London Tavern, which had been especially decorated with trophies and works of art supplied by the Company. Apparently a large crowd gathered outside and as the guests arrived there was cheering, especially for the arrival of Sir Robert Peel but also for the guests of honour Lord and Lady Gough accompanied by various members of the family. Lady Gough and her daughters were present as the guests arrived, around 1900, but retired once the dinner commenced, returning later for the speeches. The meal, the menu of which was printed in *The Times* on 25 March, was made up of eight courses and *The Times* correspondent recorded that 'The wines and deserts were excellent'. It appears that no expense had been spared and the Company had not been miserly in paying tribute to Lord Gough. One could argue that given the great increase in the size of its territory which he had achieved, a first rate meal was the very least Gough deserved from the Company.

The band of the Coldstream Guards provided a musical programme during dinner, and after the royal toast accompanied the singing of the National Anthem. Following this the Chairman, Sir Archibald Galloway, addressed the gathering:

> My Lords and Gentlemen we are assembled here this evening to do honour to one of the bravest and most distinguished soldiers of the British Army. A soldier who has commanded, has fought, and has conquered, in more battles than any general who has ever been in Asia. Battles, the results of which, in importance to the British nation, have only been second to

---

3   *The Times*, Thursday 21 March 1850.
4   *The Times*, Thursday 21 March 1850.

those of that illustrious chief whose achievements have never been equalled ... it is unnecessary in this assembly for me to detail to you the services of Lord Gough; they are identified with the imperishable records of the British Army. Full 30 times and more has Lord Gough fought for his country in many of our bravest battles.[5]

Galloway then went on to briefly detail the actions of Gough and the 87th in the Peninsular War, before turning to his service for the East India Company.

My Lord Gough has been a faithful servant to the East India Company. He has served the Government of India as Commander-in-Chief of our armies with his full heart, with entire devotion – with that singleness of mind which is so peculiar to him, with that faith, and that success, that demand from them the deepest acknowledgment. My Lords and Gentlemen, we see China – the vast Empire of China – submitting to his victorious arms; in India he gained a magnificent kingdom for the British Crown.

In summing up Galloway turned to address a visibly moved Gough directly and remarked that:

My Lord Gough, in the name of the East India Company I have the highest gratification in expressing to you their cordial acknowledgements of the eminent services which you have rendered to them. In their name I welcome you heartily to your native land, and I am sure there is no individual present in this great assemblage who will not unite with me in the fervent prayer that you may long live to enjoy the honours and the rewards which have been conferred upon you by a gracious Sovereign and a grateful country. My Lords and Gentlemen, I beg to propose to you "the Health of Lord Viscount Gough with all the Honours".

After the toast the band of the Coldstream Guards played 'See the Conquering Hero Comes', the playing of which was said to have been 'almost drowned by the loud and hearty "hurrahs" of all present'.

Gough's response was given with great emotion. He thanked the chairman and the East India Company for the honour they had given him but also for the privilege of serving them over the years. As at the United Service dinner he paid his respects to Lord Hardinge, and yet again there was no mention of Dalhousie. One gets the sense that despite their differences when Hardinge was governor general that Gough had a deep respect for him. It may also be that his experiences in the Second Sikh War had given him a greater appreciation of the role Hardinge had played during the earlier conflict, and how valuable to him those services had been. Given that Galloway had mentioned China, Gough also paid tribute to Admiral Sir William Parker, who had been so helpful during the China War. Gough referred to him as

an individual I cordially recognise as my friend, and am happy in such recognition. Who, when he found he had performed all the duties incumbent upon him as Commander-in-Chief of the Navy on the coast of China, was ever at my side when operations were going on on shore, leading his gallant men to honour and to glory, and nobly supporting the person who addresses you.

5   *The Times*, Monday 25 March 1850.

Given the expression of thanks to Parker, who had advised and supported him in a similar role to Hardinge, for Parker was in overall command until the men were ashore, gives further support to the theory that Gough had missed that sort of senior assistance during the recent conflict.[6]

It is interesting that of the officers that had served with him during the Sikh Wars the only one he mentioned by name, and indeed later proposed a toast to, was Sir Walter Gilbert. Perhaps this had much to do with the fact that Gilbert had led the pursuit across the Jhelum after Gujrat. He had, after all, played an important part in concluding the conflict. It could also be construed as Gough defending his decision to give Gilbert the command, which as we have already seen was not a popular decision. Yet the fact that Gough gave Gilbert the command, and the fact that he was the only officer who had served under him during the Sikh Wars who he mentioned in his speech, tells us something of the confidence that Gough had in him.

There followed expressions of gratitude from representatives of both services, before the Prime Minister rose to speak. Given the events of the previous year, the words of Lord John Russell do rather smack of the opportunist political art, rather than any expression of sincerity. Indeed Russell early on remarked that now was not the time for 'political questions', no doubt hoping to move past the fact that he had played an important role in the supersession of Lord Gough by Sir Charles Napier.[7] After comments from representatives of the House of Lords and the Board of Control, for neither the Lord Chancellor nor the President of the Board of Control were present, Sir Robert Peel was asked to speak. *The Times* recorded that the cheering for Peel was greater than that for his successor as Prime Minister had been. He stated that:

> I cannot witness without satisfaction the tribute of cordial esteem and gratitude which has been paid to the services of Lord Gough. It has been my good fortune on many occasions either to propose or concur in public testimonies of respect offered to him by the House of Commons, and I must say that at no period of his career did I ever despair of his ultimate success. I had that just confidence in his early victories, in his known valour, in his known skill, constancy, and perseverance, that I felt, whatever might be the temporary difficulties by which he was embarrassed, they would be overcome by the skill and valour of himself and his glorious comrades in arms, and by the constancy, resolution and discipline of the army which he commanded.[8]

Peel's tribute is interesting. It is, if one reads between the lines, a political speech. Peel had expressed confidence in Gough, when no one else did. Rather than naivety this was possibly the voice of experience. Indeed Peel had been here before. No doubt the situation in the Second Sikh War reminded him of the First Sikh War when he had been the Prime Minister. Despite doubts being expressed about Gough he had brought the war to a successful conclusion. It was with this experience that Peel had greater confidence in Gough, and perhaps less confidence in rumours, than many of his contemporaries. This was after all the voice of one of the most experienced politicians in the country. In short it was a criticism of Russell for having overreacted, whilst Peel was able to legitimately say that he had not joined in with the 'panic'.

The dinner had been a great occasion for Gough, and one gets the impression that he valued this more than the dinner given by the United Service Club. In one sense this is understandable, in that the East India Company had in effect been his employers, and recognition from them was all the more important because of that. It might also be that Gough felt kindlier towards the East India

---

6   *The Times*, Monday 25 March 1850.
7   *The Times*, Monday 25 March 1850.
8   *The Times*, Monday 25 March 1850.

Company, as they had to a large degree stood by him. The presence of Sir Archibald Galloway as Chairmen was also a pleasing thing for Gough as he had a high opinion of Galloway and the two men got on well. Sadly, this was the last time Gough would see Galloway. Two weeks later, on 6 April, Sir Archibald Galloway died.

In early April the Goughs went down to Bath for an extended stay with their daughter. The local community organised a banquet in his honour held at the Guildhall in Bath. He returned to London of 9 April to a dinner in his honour at the Oriental Club. There were over 100 guests and *The Times* reported that "The dinner offered every delicacy of the season, and the tables and sideboards glittered with plate, assisting to compose a scene which would dazzle, and, at first sight, almost bewilder, a person introduced suddenly to the festivity." Lieutenant General Sir James Lushington presided over an event whose guests included Hardinge, and most the directors of the East India Company. Although there is no recorded mention of it, one wonders if the death two days earlier of Sir Archibald Galloway cast a shadow over proceedings. Lushington gave the type of speech which Gough must have become accustomed to by now. He commenced by welcoming him home and thanking him for his service. He then, as so many speakers did, proceeded to state that there was no need to detail his career, before going on to do just that. The only interesting detail was that he credited Chillianwala as a victory albeit, "after a hard fought and most bloody battle." In responding to the toast Gough once again paid tribute to Hardinge, but gave perhaps his most glowing tribute to the native army: "To them the praise is due. I, as their leader, have only to say that I have been most gallantly and devotedly supported by that army."[9] It is presumed that Gough returned to Bath the day after the dinner at the Oriental Club. However he returned to London again at some point later in the month to attend a dinner given in his honour by the Junior United Service Club. This was held on Wednesday 17 April, 'at the Club-house, in Charles Street, St James'. The president was Captain Henry Boldero MP, and guests included the Marquis of Anglesey and Lord Hardinge. It was according to *The Times* an evening that passed off with "much good feeling and conviviality."[10]

The celebration of Lord Gough was not simply in the form of dinners. A number of works of art were prepared with him as the subject. The noted portrait painter Lowes Dickinson was commissioned to paint a portrait of Lord Gough. An engraving of this portrait was undertaken by Mr Samuel Cousins and sold by Messrs Dickinson Brothers, of Bond Street. There was certainly a degree of prestige in having perhaps the finest portrait artist and one of the finest engravers of the age prepare works in one's honour, and this was added to further by the sculpting of a bust of Lord Gough by George Gammon Adams. *The Times* reported on 2 May that "It had been submitted to the notice of His Royal Highness Prince Albert, who expressed his approbation of the likeness to the original, and the artistic skill of the sculptor. Lord Gough has acknowledged the justice done to him in this representation of his features." Adams was much in demand for his work, and notable busts he produced included Wellington, Havelock, Cambridge, Harry Smith, and Palmerston. His most lasting legacy is perhaps the two statues of Charles Napier, one in Trafalgar Square the other in St Paul's Cathedral, which he produced. They were however greatly criticised at the time and one critic even went so far as to call it 'the worst piece of sculpture in England'. Later in May, a lithographic portrait of Gough by Mr J. Harwood was produced for sale and for a time became very popular.[11]

9   *The Times*, 10 April 1850.
10   *The Times*, 18 April 1850. Captain Henry Boldero was MP for Chippenham from 1831–32 and then from 1835 to 1859. From 1841 to 1845 he was Clerk of the Ordnance. Boldero was a Tory and it is said that in 1842 a political disagreement with Craven Berkeley, MP for Cheltenham and a Whig, led to a duel being fought between the two men.
11   *The Times*, 2 May 1850.

78

Return to Ireland and Settling Down

Given the amount of territory that Gough had added to the British Empire, the material wealth he had brought to the country, and the growth in British prestige achieved by his victories, such rewards that he had received would seem to pale into insignificance. Yet not for Gough, who was grateful to his sovereign and the state for the honours he had been awarded. The bitterness that followed his reading of the reports of Chillianwala had now gone. Whilst there was still some celebrations given in his honour to go through, his main attention was now turning towards settling down. Chief in this was purchasing property.

On 26 April 1850 Lord Gough left London for Dublin. The evening before, he had been the guest of the Goldsmiths' Company, at a banquet given in his honour.[1] On his return to Ireland he came both as a visitor and as a returning son and was treated as such. The crowds cheered and honours continued to be showered upon him. Behind the scenes, however, there were other motives at work. In late March it was being suggested in the press that Gough was being considered as Commander-in-Chief, Ireland. The idea was that a stronger personality than Lieutenant General Sir Edward Blakeney, who had held the position since 1836, was required. The names of Gough, Hardinge and Prince George of Cambridge – later Duke of Cambridge and commander-in-chief of the British Army from 1856–1895 – were, according to the press, all being considered for the job. Gough made no mention of this in his correspondence. It might be that it was simply press speculation. It could also be that the government were fully aware of his desire to retire from public life. That said one wonders if he might have been tempted by the Irish command had it ever been offered, which to the best of our knowledge it never was.[2]

He arrived in Dublin on the evening of 27 April. Although not accompanied by Lady Gough, his son George and his nephew Colonel John Bloomfield Gough were present. *The Times* recorded that:

> Long before the steamer entered the harbour a crowd of persons had assembled on the pier, and when the gallant veteran set foot on his native soil his presence was hailed with a loud and protracted cheer – a genuine *caide mille failthe* [or more correctly *cead mile failte*] – such as Irishmen, of all other nations, can best bestow upon the latest object of public enthusiasm[3]

As further evidence of the changing attitude of the Times towards Gough it is interesting to note that they called him 'The Indian Hero'.

---

1   *The Times*, Thursday 25 April 1850.
2   *The Times*, Tuesday 26 March 1850.
3   *The Times*, Monday 29 April 1850. *Cead mile failte* is an Irish welcome that freely translates as 'a hundred thousand welcomes'.

That evening Gough dined with the United Service Club in Dublin. Sir Edward Blakeney presided over the evening, which was attended by over 100 guests. The room was adorned with several captured Sikh standards taken by regiments stationed in Ireland, including the 31st Foot. Both Blakeney and Gough spoke of their friendship and many years of association. Gough then went on to speak warmly about his pleasure at being back in Ireland. He spoke of his fondness for his native soil and his delight at seeing so many old soldiers who shared with him the decorations "they had won by so many years toil and danger."[4]

On Wednesday 1 May 1850 Gough reviewed the garrison in Dublin, although not in uniform himself. The fact that he had not worn his uniform meant that he was not immediately recognised by the large crowd that had gathered to watch the events. Gough reviewed the troops accompanied by the Lord Lieutenant, the Earl of Clarendon, and the garrison commander, the future Duke of Cambridge. At one point the review was delayed by an event which was typical of Gough as a man. Gough had spied a pensioner with a medal and number of bars. The man was clearly a veteran of many battles, most probably from the Peninsular War, and Gough spent much time in conversation with him. We know little more than that. It is possible that the medal bars told Gough that the man had served at many of the same battles as himself, indeed it is even possible that the man was a veteran of the 87th Foot and a face that Gough remembered after all this time.[5] It might also simply be that this was a case of two old veterans becoming involved in conversation over their many years of service. It would be fascinating to know what was said, but we have no record. However it is typical of Gough that he took time to speak to this veteran soldier and thought nothing of delaying the events or the protocol involved. The crowd delighted in the scene and we are told that their cheering became 'somewhat boisterous'. A more cynical man might have been accused of playing to the crowd, but in Gough's case this was just typical of the paternalistic care he had always had for 'his' soldiers.[6]

The review commenced at 1100 and did not finish until after 1400. Perhaps Gough's conversation did delay proceeding but there were plenty of troops to review as the garrison consisted of three regiments of cavalry, five of infantry, a troop of horse artillery and several batteries of field artillery. It is therefore not surprising that the review took three hours to complete. Later that day Gough left Dublin for Tipperary. *The Times* records that he was accompanied by members of his staff and the Very Rev. the Dean of Derry. The staff mentioned, were in fact his son George and his nephew John Bloomfield Gough.[7] The paper seems to have missed the fact that the Dean of Derry was Thomas Bunbury Gough, the brother of Hugh Gough and the father of John Bloomfield Gough. As he travelled through the area, he received a warm welcome and was loudly cheered at all points. In this instance Gough's 'Irishness' was an advantage. This was a difficult time in Anglo-Irish relations and the Great Famine was causing wide spread suffering throughout Ireland. Whilst the immediate cause of the famine was the failure of the potato harvest and could not therefore be blamed on the British, the famine was exacerbated by the policies of British rule and the careless, almost callous, attitude taken by British authorities.

Under these circumstances one would not have been surprised if the arrival of a British general had been met with antipathy if not necessarily hostility. Yet Gough's Irish character meant that there was something positively Irish that could be celebrated. Perhaps that is an oversimplification, but it is part of the explanation to the positive response he received upon his return. The other part was perhaps alluded to in the House of Commons by Henry Grattan. In a speech calling for money

---

4   *The Times*, Tuesday 30 April 1850.
5   *The Times*, Thursday 2 May 1850.
6   *The Times*, Thursday 2 May 1850.
7   The Times, Monday 6 May 1850.

to be made available for famine relief, Grattan said the following: "Ireland had given you her blood and treasure; her sons had reaped your harvests, had built you palaces and ornamented your cities; she had given you a Gough and a Wellington; and she had immortalised your name."[8] This identification of Gough as a son of Ireland was significant. However the very great difference between Gough and the other general mentioned in that speech, in this respect, was that the former 'owned' his Irish nationality whilst the latter disowned it.

Gough was back in England by 30 May when, in the morning, he received the Freedom of the City of London. In the evening he attended a banquet given in his honour by the Lord Mayor of London that was held at the Mansion House. It was reported that "nearly 300 of the most distinguished inhabitants of the metropolis were invited." An unnamed military band was in attendance and a number of vocalists also added to the entertainment. After the loyal toast the next to be proposed was to the Duke of Cambridge, as protocol demanded.[9] The Duke responded and in so doing referred to Gough as his 'noble and gallant friend'. Amongst those to acknowledge Gough during the toasts were two slightly unusual speakers. One was the Bishop of Oxford, Samuel Wilberforce, who gave an interesting address. Acknowledging the fact that it might appear strange for a man of peace to be lauding a soldier returned from war, Wilberforce spoke about the need for that peace to be honourable. He then went on to praise Gough for the fact that "in the heat of battle and in the pride of victory he had dared to acknowledge his gratitude to the God of battles."[10]

The second slightly unusual speaker was Abbott Lawrence, the American Minister to the Court of St James: in other words the Ambassador. Mr Lawrence alluded to Gough's past in China when he said that, "his Lordship had laid the United States also under great obligations for the distinguished manner in which he had received the citizens of that country on all occasions." It will be recalled that on various occasions during the First China War Gough was protecting American citizens as well as British subjects. Lawrence continued that "On this occasion he did more than admire – he could truly and clearly offer his respects to Lord Gough, not only for his military prowess, but for his high moral sentiments, founded on his religious character." The Minister went on to speak further about the shared blood of their two countries and the admiration for Britain.[11] It was a remarkable speech for an American Minister to make in this era as the great rapprochement between the two powers had not yet really taken hold.

After the majority of the celebrations on his return had died away, the Goughs turned to the more pressing matter of where they would settle down permanently to live out their remaining years. For a time this had been left in abeyance as they enjoyed the triumphant return. As they toured the country looking at prospective property they found that they were greeted with similar honours as they had been when they first returned. In July they were in Devon and in Barnstaple a great celebration was prepared in their honour. As a mark of honour the horses of their carriage were removed and the coach was brought into Barnstaple by being pulled by local men as crowds cheered their arrival. Indeed this was not just a celebration for the people of Barnstaple and many came from miles around, including a band from Torrington to provide a proper welcome. The now quite common tune of 'See the Conquering Hero' was played yet again. This sort of scene was repeated at they continued their movement through the West Country.[12]

8   *Hansard*, House of Commons Debate, 17 May 1850, Vol. 111, cc171–232.
9   The Duke of Cambridge in question is Prince Adolphus, the 7th son of King George III. He would die in July 1850 and be succeeded in the title by his only son Prince George, perhaps best known for being commander-in-chief of the British Army from 1856–1895.
10   *The Times*, 31 May 1850.
11   *The Times*, 31 May 1849.
12   Rait, *Gough*, Vol. II, p. 318. *The Times*, Thursday 8 August 1850.

In August they travelled to Scotland. This was part sight-seeing, part property hunting, and part official duties. In Edinburgh on 5 August, Gough was finally awarded the Freedom of the City which had been announced some months previously. The Lord Provost's speech suggests that there was a sense in which they wished that Scotland should be seen to be honouring Lord Gough in the same way that England and Ireland had. It was as much about the prestige of Edinburgh as a major city as it was their respect for Lord Gough. In response, Gough reminded them that he had actually started his regular military service in a Scottish regiment. He also spoke warmly of the Scottish officers he had served under including Sir Ralph Abercromby and Sir Thomas Graham.[13]

On 9 August the Goughs were involved in a strange but potentially fatal incident whilst travelling to Oban. They had boarded the steamer *Shandon* for the journey from Crinan Canal to Oban. Exactly what happened is unknown but it was reported that part of a lady's gown became entangled with the chain that moved the rudder of the ship. This jammed the ship's steering and caused it to go off course where it hit a sunken rock. The *Shandon* remained fast on the rock and could not be moved. Also the heavy swell meant that the ship now rolled violently from side to side and it was said to be difficult for even the sailors, no doubt used to the swell, to maintain their footing. Fortunately there were a number of other boats in the vicinity and they were able to help take off the women and children. Gough played an important role in the evacuation, largely by keeping things calm. *The Times* later reported that

> Truth compels us to state that several of the gentlemen passengers, some of them valiant looking men, with a large breadth of moustache, exhibited symptoms of most painful trepidation, and the veteran Lord Gough distinguished himself by urging, if not commanding, these timid gentlemen to give precedence to the ladies and children in the boats.[14]

One imagines that Gough's language was more in the mode of 'commanding' rather than 'urging'. As it was, there were no casualties and the evacuation of the women and children had the effect of lightening the load sufficiently to allow the *Shandon* to free herself from the rock and return under her own power. Lord Gough's own account, with typical modesty, made no mention of his own part in the event. However contrary to the opinion expressed in *The Times* that "The officers of the Shandon behaved themselves admirably on the occasion", Gough declared that after running aground the ship had been "very badly managed by the Captain."[15]

From Oban the Goughs moved on to Inverness where they remained until November 1850, apart from a period in late September when Lord Gough was a guest of Sir John Hay Williams at the Royal Eisteddfod at Rhyddlan Castle in Denbighshire. At this time serious consideration was given to buying a property in Scotland. At some point in their considerations a property in Warwickshire had also been looked at seriously.[16] However on each occasion the desire to return to Ireland was strong. They did already own a property in Rathronan, County Limerick, Ireland, but were unable to stay there at the present. Their old house in Rathronan had been let during their stay in India but was soon to become available again with the termination of the lease. Hugh Gough decided that rather than moving back there he would sign the house over to his son George and look for another property himself.

In Ireland there were numerous reports of properties he was supposedly interested in buying. In May 1850 *The Times* reported that Gough was negotiating for the purchase of the Killymoon

13   Rait, *Gough*, Vol. II, p. 319. *The Times*, Thursday 8 August 1850.
14   *The Times*, Thursday 15 August 1850. *The Times* referred to Gough as, "the hero of Goojerat"
15   *The Times*, Thursday 15 August 1850. Rait, *Gough*, Vol. II, p. 319.
16   Rait, *Gough*, Vol. II, pp. 319–320.

estates in county Tyrone. This report was republished in September of the same year. The main reason seems to be that the paper believed that as this property was on the market and that as Lord Gough was known to be looking for a property that this would obviously suite him. That said Gough did have some interest in it.[17] The property at Killymoon was on the market as the previous owner, Colonel James Stewart, had died with large debts. In April the following year the *Limerick Chronicle* reported that Gough had offered £91,000 (about £5,327,000 in modern money) for the property.[18] Startlingly the creditors believed this sum to be too small to pay off the late Colonel Stewart's debts and urged that the property be put up for public auction where it was hoped a far greater price might be received. Their calculation was that the property and estates were worth at least £120,000.[19] At around this time Gough's personal wealth suffered a decline likely due to the failure of the Tipperary Bank in which he had invested.[20] He was not short of money, but it did perhaps mean that the large-scale property investment of somewhere like Killymoon was no longer viable.

In late 1851 Lord Gough purchased a large house called St Helen's in Booterstown, County Dublin. The property was a little over four miles from Dublin itself. Booterstown had been a very wealthy area. Before the Act of Union it had been a popular area with the rich and powerful of Ireland. However with the closing of the Irish Parliament after the Act of Union, many such people had moved to England, or at the very least did not require such large properties in Ireland. There were therefore a great number of large estates in the area.[21] St Helen's was already an impressive property before Gough purchased it. It came with 53 acres of land. In the years that followed, the Goughs extended the house and undertook a largescale refurbishment of the interior. The house had been built in the early 1750s and originally been called Seamount. The name was changed by Colonel Henry White, later 1st Baron Annaly, a distinguished Peninsular War veteran who had been an MP and was currently Lord Lieutenant of County Longford, to St Helen's. Originally the firm of architects of Carmichael and Jones were employed on the refurbishment of St Helen's. However the relationship ended unsatisfactorily and Gough took legal action against the firm for negligence. In 1863 the Goughs extended the house, using the well-known Dublin architect John McCurdy. Amongst McCurdy's other achievements, he was the official architect of Trinity College Dublin. He was also president of the Royal Institute of Architects of Ireland for 10 years.

The gardens were also extensively redesigned. Indeed Gough seems to have taken great interest in the gardens. The noted gardener and landscape architect Ninian Niven was employed to oversee the work. Niven was much in demand and it would have been something of a coup to obtain his services. The sloping grounds of the gardens, facing towards the sea, were laid out in terraces. It is said that Gough had each terrace named after one of his battles. The garden had thousands of plants and was said to rival any garden in the Dublin area. In later years the gardens were open to the public.[22]

This was not the end of their property purchases. In 1854 Gough purchased Lough Cutra Castle in County Galway. The estates had been the property of the Viscounts Gort and amounted to some

17 *The Times*, Friday 24 May 1850 & Monday 8 September 1850.
18 *The Times*, Tuesday 1 April 1851.
19 *The Times*, Wednesday 23 April 1851.
20 The Tipperary Bank or Sadlier's bank as it was also known, would finally collapse in 1856. Charles Dickens novel *Little Dorrit* features the character of Mr Merdle, who it is said was a parody of the Bank of Tipperary's Mr John Sadlier.
21 For further information on Booterstown and the surrounding area see, Smyth, Hazel P. *The Town on the Road: The Story of Booterstown* (Bray, Ireland: Pale Publishing, 1994).
22 Smyth, *The Town on the Road*, p. 103. There are conflicting statements as to whether the gardens were opened to the public by the 1st or 2nd Viscount.

12,000 acres. Indeed it was the 2nd Viscount Gort, Colonel Charles Vereker, who commissioned the building of the castle at Lough Cutra. On a visit to the Isle of Wight he had been impressed by East Cowes Castle which had been built, and indeed was the residence of, the noted Regency architect John Nash.[23] The story goes that on a visit to East Cowes Vereker had said that he wished he could transplant the castle to his estate in Galway. Nash is said to have responded, "Give me fifty thousand pounds and I'll do it for you." In the end the Castle at Lough Cutra cost £70,000 (roughly £3,000,000 in modern money). The project was overseen by James Pain, a former apprentice of Nash, and his brother George Pain.[24] However for various reasons the Gorts suffered financial problems and in 1851 the 3rd Viscount Gort was obliged to put the estate up for sale. At this stage the estate was portioned up to make it easier to sell. The castle was sold to the Religious Order of Lorreto for £17,000, who proceeded to turn it into a convent school. In 1854 it is said that Lord Gough in person approached the Superior of the convent with an offer to buy the castle. The fact that Gough went in person speaks not only to the direct nature of his character, but also a belief in the personal touch. Given his previous experience over Killymoon, which had been handled through intermediaries, Gough understandably wanted to try the hands on approach.[25]

Robert Rait states that Gough had admired the property before his departure to India. His return had not only given him the means but also the motivation to purchase the property. He subsequently bought the house for between £20,000–24,000 (between £1.1 and £1.4 million), giving the Order of Lorretto a profit of £3,000–7,000 on the original purchase.[26] At the same time it is reported that Gough was buying the surrounding land and restoring the estate to roughly its former size. The next four years were spent improving the castle and its grounds.

After this period, Lord Gough decided that the move from St Helen's to Lough Cutra would be too much for himself and Lady Gough, settled as they now were. Indeed although Lady Gough's health was still far from good she enjoyed far more 'better days' once they were settled into St Helen's than she had for many years. Under such circumstances one can understand their reluctance to do anything that might alter this. The project had always been under the control of his son George, and so Lough Cutra Castle was made over to him for his use. Lord Gough continued to visit Lough Cutra but never really lived there for any extended period of time, and it was his son who undertook most of the work.[27]

Indeed after one such visit to Lough Cutra an incident took place that showed that Gough never forgot his years as a soldier, and that he was still greatly liked by the soldiers of the army. On 9 October 1854 Gough was returning from Lough Cutra to St Helen's and passed through the town of Gort. Having heard that Gough was passing through the area, the 40th Foot made a slight detour on their journey from Clare Castle to Galway to welcome the man who had been their commander-in-chief in India. With fife and drum and cheering they greeted Gough. Gough was moved by their behaviour and in a gesture that no doubt lifted their opinion of him even higher

---

23   Interestingly, East Cowes Castle later came into the possession of the Gort family. John Nash's notable work includes the development of Regent Street in London, the redevelopment of St James Park, the Royal Pavilion at Brighton (although the original design was by Henry Holland), the remodelling of Buckingham Palace, the Royal Mews and Marble Arch. Amongst his lesser known works is the beautiful All Souls Church, Langham Place, London.

24   Rait, *Gough*, Vol. II, pp. 320–321. See also, *Restored Ireland: Documenting our Heritage, Lough Cutra Castle, Co. Galway*, <http://www.abandonedireland.com/LoughCutra>.

25   *Restored Ireland.*

26   Rait, Gough, Vol. II, p. 320. There is some confusion over prices, but this may just be inaccurate reporting by *The Times*. The newspaper declared that Gough paid only £20,000. It also declared he won it at auction after 'spiritless bidding'. *The Times*, Monday 14 August 1854.

27   Rait, *Gough*, Vol. II, p. 320–321.

he left £5 with which the battalion could drink his health.[28] It will be recalled that the 40th Foot had served under Gough during the Gwalior campaign in 1843. There may have been some who had served under his command, but it is also another demonstration of the collective memory of a regiment.

As with St Helen's, refurbishments and improvements were made by the Goughs at Lough Cutra. A clock tower was built at the south west quarter of the castle and an 'American Garden' was also constructed. For the interior refurbishment George Gough obtained the service of Frederick Crace & Son the leading interior decorators of the day. Frederick Crace had designed the interiors of Buckingham Palace and Brighton Pavilion and thus had experience at working with the architecture of John Nash. It is however likely that much of the work at Lough Cutra was actually the inspiration of his son John Gregory Crace, who would later work on Buckingham Palace, Windsor Castle and design the interiors of the rebuilt Houses of Parliament. Many of the trophies from China and the Sikh wars were kept at Lough Cutra, including the guns captured at Ferozeshah and Sobraon that had been presented to Gough.[29]

The purchase of property, and the people who were paid to redesign and decorate them, tells us that whilst Lord Gough might have suffered some financial misfortune he was still a very wealthy man. Also, property prices were generally lower in Ireland and so he obtained far more for his money than he would have done in Britain. The property that he purchased came from the money he had received in recognition of his military career. A cynic might state that his purchases were the spoils of imperial aggrandisement, yet really they were simply the recognition of a lifetime of devotion to the Crown. He had served those who had created the wars, rather than start conflict through his own actions. He had always considered himself to be a loyal servant of his sovereign and before he retired from public life he had one last service to perform in her name.

28   *The Times*, Saturday 14 October 1854.
29   *Restored Ireland.*

79

Mission to the Crimea

In June 1854, although largely retired, Lord Gough was promoted to the rank of full general. Although between March 1843 and the resignation of his command in India he had held the temporary/local rank of general, he only held the rank of lieutenant general and had reverted to that rank after leaving India. In February 1854 he had been appointed colonel in chief of the 60th (King's Royal Rifle Corps). In June the following year he was also given the honour of being appointed colonel of the Royal Horse Guards. He was the first officer ever to be appointed a colonel of the Royal Horse Guards without any prior cavalry service.[1] His promotion, and the two colonelcies, were all marks of social status and recognition of his years of service rather than any expectation of practical military service. A similar ceremonial honour was that of being appointed Gold Stick in Waiting to the Queen. In times gone by the Gold Stick and Silver Stick had been in effect bodyguards for the monarch on state occasions. However this had long since passed and the role was largely a mark of respect to colonels of the Royal Horse Guards. At state occasions one Gold Stick in Waiting had to be present. Obviously as years went on Gough found it increasingly difficult to perform this duty due to age, but also the length of journey from Ireland to London.

Gough had also taken his seat in the House of Lords since his return, although this was more in a figurative than a practical sense. His residence in Ireland meant that he physically took his seat in the Lords rarely. Indeed throughout his entire career as a member of the House of Lords he is only recorded as having spoken twice. On each occasion it was on a motion of thanks to the army.

The first was to Fitzroy Somerset, now Lord Raglan, and Army in the Crimea on 15 December 1854.

> I rise, under circumstances of considerable difficulty, to claim the indulgence of your Lordships, but I quite conceive that I should not be justified in preserving silence upon the motion now before your lordships. I am proud, my lords, to say that the position I now hold is attributable, and solely attributable, to the deeds of the Army of England; and I cannot therefore pass by without remark a vote of thanks to that army, now serving in the Crimea, many of whom assisted -nobly assisted- me in another part of the globe. It is for this reason that I join – most cordially join – in the vote of thanks to the noble individual who now happily hold the command of that army, as well as to the officers and soldiers of that noble army.[2]

---

1   To the best of the author's knowledge there has only been one other purely infantry officer appointed a colonel of the Royal Horse Guards and that is Field Marshal Sir Gerald Templar. It is interesting to note that Templar's first regiment had been the Royal Irish Fusiliers, the successor to Gough's old regiment the 87th Foot. Wellington is not included because although primarily an infantry officer he had served for three years as an officer of the 12th Regiment of Light Dragoons.
2   The text of his speech does vary slightly. It was reported in *The Times* on Saturday 16 December 1854 as stated above. However *Hansard* records it somewhat differently: 'I rise, my Lords, with a considerable degree of diffidence, to claim the indulgence of your Lordships; but I quite conceive that I should not be

The speech also makes mention of Gough having recently returned from a visit to France. We know little of why he went, but Gough mentioned in his speech in the House of Lords that "I had the pleasure of passing some time in association with officers of the French army, and with some of the officers who are now in command of that portion of that army which is serving with our own troops in the Crimea."[3] Whether this visit had anything to do with the task Gough was soon to be asked to perform can only be guessed at.

In early May 1856, with the war now at an end but much of the army still in place, Gough was approached by Lord Panmure, Secretary of State for War, to undertake a mission to the Crimea as the representative of Her Majesty.[4] The role was to be purely ceremonial and its purpose was to present the honours to various allied generals in recognition for their service in the war. As he would be representing Her Majesty, Lord Gough would be treated to many of the privileges and protocol normal given to the Monarch. Although Gough journeyed to the Crimea after peace had been concluded, there had been suggestions that he might be asked to make the journey of a somewhat different nature whilst the war was still on. There were those who suggested that Gough was the right man for command of the army in the Crimea. Amazingly amongst this number was *The Times*, no doubt suffering from a severe short-term memory loss. The same newspaper that six or seven years earlier had decried Gough's military ability, had claimed that he was frittering away the army, and who had in their opinion been unable to decisively beat a 'native' army, now suggested him as the man to face the Russians. The turnaround was extraordinary, but like so much press coverage was a knee-jerk reaction. Gough had been criticised beyond what he deserved and then similar praised and lauded beyond was he deserved by the press. Perhaps their view, and that of others, had been coloured by the great triumphant return Lord Gough had made after the Second Sikh War and the many dinners, banquets and honours that had been given in his name.

There is an interesting article from *The Times*' special correspondent in the Crimea when Gough was on his way there to present the awards. The following opinion was offered by *The Times* correspondent – no longer the famous William Howard Russell, who had left the Crimea in December 1855, but instead Frederick Hardman who during the war had been correspondent for *The Times* in Constantinople.

> It would be curious to ascertain what Lord Gough think of the Russian position, and it is to be hoped that he will examine it thoroughly. Perhaps the government may learn privately what are his Lordship's notions regarding the impregnability of the heights from the sea to Simpheropol. Often during the siege, when discontent ran high and men grumbled, "they knew not why," at the conduct of our commanders, old Indians might be heard sighing "Old Gough – he'd soon have a go at the place, and be done with it". It seemed indeed to be thought that his Lordship would not be content with a tolerably safe position during the assault, and that it was no improbable he would issue out of the advanced trenches and lead the attack on

---

justified in preserving silence upon the Motion now before your Lordships. I am proud, my Lords, to say that the position I now hold is attributable, and solely attributable, to the deeds of the army of England; and I cannot therefore pass by without remark, a Vote of Thanks to that army, now serving in the Crimea, many of whom assisted—nobly assisted—me in another part of the globe. It is for this reason that I join—most cordially join—in the Vote of Thanks to the noble individual who now happily holds the command of that army, as well as to the officers and soldiers of whom it is composed'. *The Times* version does not quite sound right for Gough. The language is certainly not his. Rait, *Gough*, Vol. II, pp. 333–334, has yet another version of this speech.

3   *Hansard*, House of Lords Debate, 15 December 1854, Vol. 136, cc313–37.
4   Fox Maule-Ramsey was known as Lord Panmure from 1852–1860. In 1860 he became 11th Earl of Dalhousie, succeeding his cousin, the Dalhousie we discussed earlier, in that title.

the Redan himself, if he held the position of Commander-in-Chief, and saw that matters were going badly.[5]

Whether this should be taken too seriously is difficult to discern. Often in such situations, calls to remove someone from command, whether in war, politics, business, or sport, concentrate on the desire to remove the individual in place rather than serious consideration of the proposed replacement's ability. In this way the proposed candidate's previous track record can become obscured. For an example of this we need look no further than when Lord Gough was to be superseded. The candidate for the job was Sir Charles Napier, a man who had been vilified in India by the press, was widely disliked by the government of India, and had been criticised for his command of operations in Scinde. In the same way any suggestion that Gough should replace the present commanders in the Crimea suffered from similar short sightedness. Perhaps rather than a call for Gough to take command, the statement is more a reflection on the quality of the leaders of yesteryear as the article also makes mention of the now-deceased Wellington. Indeed this was part of a wider problem with the Crimea that the army, press and society, were looking back to the golden age of the powerful British army of the Peninsular War and late Napoleonic era, rather than looking forward to the future and realising that although the British Army had changed little since Waterloo, warfare already had, and was on the cusp of changing yet further with new technology and innovation.

There is no reason to believe that Gough would have been any more successful than any other British commander had he been given the command in the Crimea. Indeed his temperament would not have suited the circumstances. Whilst his active nature would have been welcomed, his lack of organisational and logistic knowledge would have been a drawback. Had he been appointed, the position of chief of staff would have been key. If it had been someone who could finally have been 'the Gneisenau to match his Blucher' then there was the possibility that his appointment might have worked. Yet age, temperament, and outdated notions of war, would have made Gough a risky appointment to say the least. Indeed, whatever its motivation it was not a practical suggestion. Gough was not the man for the task. There appears to be little evidence to suggest that Gough had any desire for the command or recommended himself in any serious way. Indeed the idea that Gough might be offered command in the Crimea appears to be purely speculation. That said, his whole life he had been a loyal servant of the crown and had his sovereign asked him he would have gone willingly, whatever his better judgement might have said.

This was the same approach he had when asked to represent Her Majesty at the honours ceremony in the Crimea. The honour attached to such a duty no doubt appealed to Gough and he was anxious to undertake the task. However he had slight reservation about his own health. He was of course now 76 years of age and there was concern over the effect such a long journey may have on his health. Gough also had another health concern; not his but that of his wife. There was no question of Lady Gough accompanying him, but Lord Gough was concerned for her health in his absence. However Lady Gough urged that he should go and Lord Gough informed Panmure "that he had but to give the word 'march' and Lord Gough would start in the hour."[6]

The journey was a speedy one. Within a week of his task being confirmed he was in Paris on route to Marseilles. He sailed from Marseilles on the afternoon of 21 May aboard HMS *Caradoc*, an iron paddle gunboat that had seen service during the Crimea War. She was a fast ship for her day with a top speed of 16 knots. They reached Malta on 24 May. Gough's plan was to take the wise precaution of stopping at both Malta and Constantinople for a few days rest before journeying on to Sevastopol. Gough had left without the decorations that he was to present, but had been assured

---

5   *The Times*, Wednesday 18 June 1856.
6   Rait, *Gough*, Vol. II, p. 334.

they would be waiting for him at Malta.[7] However on his arrival the awards were not there. Gough decided after a few days rest to continue his journey hoping that the awards would be waiting for him either at Constantinople or army headquarters in Sevastopol. The rest of the journey was to be made in the steam powered wooden paddle frigate HMS *Terrible*. A somewhat slower ship, she was still able to do a respectable 11 knots which was reasonable for the era. She had played an important role in naval bombardments during the Crimea War. During his stay in Malta Gough inspected the garrison, but most of the time he rested. They departed for the Crimea on 27 May.

Gough arrived in Constantinople on 1 June. Despite his plan to rest in Constantinople for a day or two, he was obliged to leave the following day. His journey was now becoming urgent as the French Generals still in the Crimea were getting impatient and desired to leave as soon as possible. Travelling direct, Gough landed at Sevastopol on 4 June. As speed now seemed to be of the essence, the presentation of the honours to the French Generals was arranged for 6 June.

At around 1100 the ceremony took place outside the British headquarters. A large marquee had been raised for the occasion, and decorated with the colours of the two nations. On three sides, facing the marquee, were paraded British infantry and artillery. Gough, as representative of the Crown, sat on a throne at the end of the marque. He wore the dress uniform of the Royal Horse Guards. *The Times* described Gough as looking like "the beau ideal of an English soldier, standing erect beneath the canopy, in the uniform of a colonel of the Life Guards, was the centre figure in the picture, and his frank and graceful bearing was observed with pleasure and interest by all the spectators."[8] Gough read the official decree from Her Majesty before giving his own speech. His speech, according to Marshal Pelissier, was 'suitable to the occasion'.[9] It was said that the speech was of Gough's own composition, and whilst a reproduction of the entire speech is unnecessary it is interesting to look at part of it:

> As however I have commanded large portions of the British Army, and well know the anxieties and responsibilities attending such commands, I may be permitted to form a just estimate of and duly to appreciate gallant and distinguished services such as yours... The Army will have the proud satisfaction of knowing that to their exertions and self-devotion Europe is indebted for a peace honourable to all parties and therefore the more likely to be durable. The soldiers of England and France have fought side by side in this great contest, only emulous as to who should best fulfil his duty to his Sovereign and to his country. May the union and good fellowship which a reciprocal admiration of great military daring must engender and which has been cemented by a prodigal sacrifice of the best and noblest blood of the two nations, be long cherished by the two greatest military powers upon earth.[10]

It was a thoughtful and surprisingly diplomatic speech, being careful to praise both the British and French armies in equal measure.

---

7   *The Times*, Monday 2 June 1856.
8   *The Times*, Wednesday 25 June 1856. I am grateful to Andrew Bamford for pointing out an error in *The Times* report that did not occur to the present author. *The Times* says Gough wore the uniform of a colonel of the Life Guards when in fact he was colonel of the Royal Horse Guards. This was quite a mistake to make given that the former was a red tunic the latter a blue tunic.
9   *The Times*, Monday 23 June 1856. Whilst Pelissier recorded that Gough read the proclamation, another report states that it was actually done by Gough's ADC Captain Bates.
10   Rait, *Gough*, Vol. II, pp. 336–337. *The Times*, Monday 23 June 1856, has a slightly different account of the speech. Rait takes his account from the handwritten copy of the speech that Gough read from. The difference is probably due to *The Times* correspondence recording of the speech.

Gough then proceeded to decorated Marshal Pelissier, General de Salles and General MacMahon, with the Grand Cross of the Order of the Bath (GCB). The award of Knight Commander of the Order of the Bath (KCB) was made to five other French Generals. The award of Companion of the Order of the Bath (CB) was made to 20 French officers. Marshal Pelissier remarked that after each award was presented Gough 'addressed a flattering compliment' to the individual. In what was described as 'a short and energetic speech' Marshal Pelissier thanked Lord Gough and referred to him as '*le vainqueur du Punjab*'.[11] A friendship seems to have developed between the two men and in October of 1856 Pelissier was scheduled to be a guest of Lord Gough's at St Helen's when he attended the Crimea dinner given in Dublin. Unfortunately Pelissier's health ultimately did not allow him to attend.[12]

Although the awards to the French commanders are the part of his duty that is best remembered, it should also be recalled that Gough also presented awards to British officers. Four officers were presented with the KCB, and four with the CB. After the awards, there followed a review of the troops on parade, led by Gough, and then a gun salute fired by the Royal Artillery. After this Lieutenant General Sir William Codrington, senior British commander in the Crimea, gave a dinner at Army Headquarters. The Times correspondent mentioned previously would have been pleased to learn that during his visit Gough did extensively tour the lines around Sevastopol and the Redan itself. On the same day as he arrived in the Crimea, Gough rode around the positions of the previous operations in the company of Codrington and Major General Charles Windham, his chief of staff. Apparently Gough and Codrington spent a long time riding around and discussing the various points around Sevastopol.

The defences and situation there were so unusual that they had to be seen to be fully appreciated and understood. In the words of *The Times*' correspondent, "Sebastapol [*sic*] is to the military what the state of Ireland used to be to the political world – a matter not to be comprehended by strangers and outsiders."[13] However Gough's opinions of the defences around Sevastopol and any notion of how he would have handled such operations is unfortunately not recorded. The defences were in some ways similar to those he had faced at Chillianwala, and one cannot only wonder whether his experience there would have given him an idea of how to break the Russian position.

On 10 June Marshal Pelissier gave a dinner in Gough's honour at the French headquarters, prior to which he had reviewed the French troops in the company of Pelissier. The following day Gough departed the Crimea.[14] On the 16th they landed at Constantinople. On either the same day or the following day he was presented to the Sultan by the British Ambassador. It is presumed that this had been intended when he first past through Constantinople, but due to the desire to speed to the Crimea with all haste to presented the awards to the French generals who were impatient to return home, it was saved for the return visit. From here he boarded the despatch steamer *Banshee* which took him to Malta which was reached on 21 June, from whence it continued to Marseilles. On his journey through Paris Gough had a further duty to undertake in presenting awards to those French officers who had already left the Crimea before Gough had arrived.[15]

What was to be his last mission for the Crown had been a sterling success. In Paris he was received with all honours by the Emperor Napoleon III, which must have been rather unusual for someone who had fought so many battles against the previous incarnation of the Napoleonic Empire. However times had changed and Gough had played his part in helping to further

---

11   *The Times*, 23 June 1856. Although not a precise interpretation it was translated into English as 'The conqueror of the Punjab'.
12   Rait, *Gough*, Vol. II, p. 340.
13   *The Times*, Wednesday, 25 June 1856.
14   *The Times* records that Gough departed on the 11th. However Rait says that it was on the 12th.
15   Rait, *Gough*, Vol. II, p. 341.

strengthen relations between Britain and France. The role he had played in this was summed up by the French War Minister Jean-Baptiste Philibert Vaillant, himself a veteran of the invasion of Russia and of Waterloo. Vaillant informed Gough that, "You have made a common friend of the whole Army, and I can assure you the Emperor thinks so highly of your address to the French Officers, that he has ordered me to have it printed and published as a public record."[16]

16   Rait, *Gough*, Vol. II, p. 341.

80

Final Years

It was with great relief that Gough returned to St Helen's after his mission to the Crimea. Despite the success of his mission he had found it tiring and a strain upon his health. At home in Ireland he settled into the quite life of retirement. On 30 January 1857 Gough was made a Knight of the Order of St Patrick, in recognition for his work in the Crimea. Gough was the first non-Irish peer to be awarded the honour, outside of members of the Royal family. To explain, although Gough was an Irishman, his title was not part of the Peerage of Ireland. Only 22 knights plus the monarch were allowed at any one time, so it was an exclusive honour, and one that as an Irishman Gough was proud to receive. At the same time he was appointed to the Privy Council.

Although now largely divorced from the army he still remembered his old connections and from time to time came into contact with the army. In May 1861 the 87th Foot returned to Dublin, or more accurately Kingstown harbour (now known as Dun Laoghaire). Despite no longer having an official connection to the regiment, having ceased to be its colonel in late June 1855, Gough retained an emotional connection to the regiment he had led during the Peninsular War. Indeed it is likely that in retirement his memories and nostalgia for the 87th Foot increased. The 87th had been serving in China as part of the Second Anglo-China War, and had sailed from China in December 1860. The long six month voyage had been a trying time for the 87th and they were therefore understandably delighted to sail into Kingstown harbour. The delighted was added to by the appearance of the 81-year-old Lord Gough waiting for them on the quayside accompanied by one of his grown up granddaughters. The word went around the ship that it was Lord Gough, and once again the collective memory of the regiment came into effect and "every man on the ship took off his hat or his forage cap and sent up a ringing cheer."[1]

The band was ordered on deck as the gangway was lowered. The colonel and his staff accompanied Lord Gough and his granddaughter on board as the band appropriately played 'The Battle of Barrosa'. Gough was then invited to review the troops. As an officer who was present recorded, as Lord Gough passed through the ranks "I am sure that the tears were running down both from his lordship's and his grand-daughters eyes." Gough then insisted on shaking the hand of every man present as the band played 'The Battle of Barrosa' again along with 'The Rocky Road to Dublin', 'St Patrick's Day', 'Garryowen to Glory' and other Irish airs. When Gough finally left them it was to three rousing cheers, which was then repeated twice.[2]

This final contact with his beloved 87th Foot reinforces many of the opinions of Gough that we have already highlighted during this work. He was clearly an emotional man, and not simply

---

1   Cunliffe, *The Royal Irish Fusiliers*, p. 222. It has not been possible to identify the granddaughter in question. We are given to believe that she is young but not a child. It is unlikely to be one of the Gough, Grant or Haines granddaughters. The likelihood is that it was one of the Arbuthnot or Supple/Collis girls.
2   Cunliffe, *The Royal Irish Fusiliers*, p. 222.

because of the report of tears running down his face. The fact that he would travel to meet them at the age of 81 speaks of emotion, or at least emotional attachment, to the regiment. Yet there is clearly more than this. The fact that they had returned from fighting in China increased the personal attachment to Gough. There is also something of the common-touch about his determination to shake the hand of ever man of the regiment before he left. This is also another indication of the paternalistic care he had for soldiers in general but the men of the 87th in particular. It also spoke to the high regard in which he was held by the ordinary soldier. This love, respect, and admiration had been important to him as a field commander and had enabled him to ask and receive from the men more than they might have given to other leaders. It might sound slightly romanticised, but this respect and admiration for the man as much as the general was key to Gough's leadership. As one historian put it, "he inspired men to face death", and this ability was largely based on the respect and affection they had for him.[3] This might be a strange concept to the modern reader, yet in the social and military systems of the day it was both important and powerful.

The honours would continue to come his way even in retirement. On 18 June 1861 he received a letter from Sir Charles Wood, the Secretary of State for India, dated 5 June. The letter started by stating that Her Majesty had in February of that year approved the new award of the Order of the Star of India. It then continued that, "I have great pleasure in apprising you, that Her Majesty has been graciously pleased to name you one of the Knights of the Order."[4] The list of the original Knights is an incredibly select group. Twenty were named, two were members of the British Royal Family, 10 were Indian Royalty, one was the present governor general and two more the governor generals of Madras and Bombay. The remaining appointments were Gough, Colin Campbell (now Lord Clyde), Sir John Lawrence, Sir James Outram and Sir Hugh Rose. The day after Gough received the letter he wrote to his nephew John Bloomfield Gough to tell him the good news. "I yesterday received the accompanying letter from Sir Charles Wood. It took me quite by surprise, but I wrote a very complimentary answer. I am sure my friends in County Tipperary will be glad to find that Her Majesty does not forget old Irishmen."[5]

The following year in November 1862 he received the ultimate honour for a British officer and was promoted to the rank of Field Marshal. At the age of 83 it was clear that the promotion was honorific rather than practical, as promotion to Field Marshal often was, but that did not lessen the pride that Gough felt in the promotion. As we have already seen, Lady Gough's health had been bad for many years, and she had reportedly been close to death many times. Yet when death came on 15 March 1863 it was still a shock to Lord Gough, particularly as the beginning of 1863 had seen general improvement in her health.[6] They had been married for 55 years. The role that Frances Gough played in the life of her husband has been rather brushed over in this study. Yet it would be wrong not to acknowledge the importance of her role. She was genuinely the love of his life, but also his support, his confidante, and his leading advocate.

At times there were suggestions that her defence of Hugh Gough rather overstepped the mark. As a consequence some, most notably Hardinge, saw her as rather a manipulative and interfering influence. On occasion this view point is clearly understandable. However whatever Frances Gough's actions, her intentions were always motivated by the desire to support her husband. For the most part she demonstrated great tact, which her husband generally lacked. However, such was her devotion that she occasionally went too far in defence of the man she loved.[7]

3 Farwell, *Eminent Victorian Soldiers*, p. 61.
4 NAM: 8303–105, Gough Papers, Sir Charles Wood to Gough, 5 June 1861.
5 NAM: 8303–105, Gough Papers, Gough to John Bloomfield Gough, 19 June 1861.
6 Rait, *Gough*, Vol. II, p. 331.
7 Singh, *The Letters of Viscount Hardinge*, p. 13. This quotes from a letter Henry Hardinge wrote to his wife Emily dated 4 March 1847.

Yet at the same time she was an important support, particularly in areas where Gough's skill was lacking. As Rait remarked:

> It was no mere reliance on wifely duty and womanly devotion. His confidence in her tact and wisdom was as absolute as his faith in her love and loyalty. He felt himself, above all else, a soldier, with all the defects of a soldier's qualities, and in the difficulties of ordinary life he looked to her for guidance and for help. No man ever fought for his native land with more real love of country or single-minded zeal in her service; but love of country was second to one other source of inspiration in moments of difficulty and danger. All his successes were tried by the test of his wife's approbation; if he had satisfied her, he had found a satisfaction against which the resources of calumny were powerless. Over and over again, he had been brave to 'fear not slander, censure rash,' strong in a mind conscious of rectitude and in a perfect love that was also a perfect trust.[8]

In other words, she was the barometer for his actions. If he had her approval little else mattered, and such approval was not given unreservedly or unthinkingly. The only major part of their correspondence that survives concerns the Peninsular War, although some does survive from the Sikh Wars. From this we see that she was not uncritical in her advice. However, in short, her greatest attribute in this regard was that she had his full confidence. The only other person whom Gough had a similar level of trust and faith in was his son George. Yet there appears to have been no attempt to influence her husband: there were no Machiavellian machinations behind the scenes, despite Hardinge's opinion. There was another aspect to this in that Frances was also a calming influence upon him. We have seen in some of his correspondence the anger than he could demonstrate when he felt he had been treated unfairly. In that regard Frances was able to calm her husband and soothe him. Partly this was done by her devoted confidence in him, and further supports the idea that Hugh Gough valued the opinion of his wife above virtually all others.

The years of marriage had not been easy for Frances Gough. Much of the early period was blighted by separation due to the absence of her husband during the Napoleonic Wars. A particularly dark time must have been in 1813 when their son Edward died shortly before his third birthday. Their separation due to the war must have been particularly acutely felt at this time. Yet such was the strength of their union that they overcame all obstacles. This included Frances Gough's health, which seems to have been a problem for many years. The full extent of her illness is unknown. The throat problems of later years do perhaps suggest that there was some form of throat cancer developing, but there is not enough evidence to state this categorically. Modern medicine may well have diagnosed this, but we cannot know for sure. Yet the problem with her throat was only part of her health problems. A problem that she had experience for many years was tic-douloureux or trigeminal neuralgia. The intense pain in the face caused by this illness is excruciating and it is said that this is one of the most painful conditions known to mankind. Rait suggested that this was linked to the throat problems she later suffered, and it is certainly possible. The modern treatment includes anticonvulsant medication, yet this was largely unknown at the time: the earliest anticonvulsant medication was potassium bromide that came on the market in 1857, and it is possible that Lady Gough used this in later years. The alternative was pain management, normally in the form of morphine, which had been marketed commercially since 1827.

The constant pain had obvious wider affects for her general health. She became quite frail physically, although there appears to have been no reduction in her mental capacity. She did her very best not to let it interfere with her official duties as the wife of Hugh Gough. There are reports that she

---

8   Rait, *Gough*, Vol. II, p. 322.

would often attend official dinners and balls whilst suffering greatly from the pain of her condition. Rarely did this prevent her from attending any event alongside her husband. However the sheer scale of the events honouring Lord Gough after his return from India meant that it became too much for her. On a number of occasions Lord Gough is described as being accompanied by one of his daughters, usually Mrs Grant. Of one such occasion Frances had said she could not have attended even 'for a 1,000 guineas'.[9]

Frances Gough was acutely aware that the life style she was expected to maintain was not helping her health. In a letter written to one of her daughters whilst still in India, she was quite candid about this:

> I am sure I should suffer far less leading a quiet regular life, but this cannot be done without leaving your Father, which remedy I consider far worse than the disease. I wish, however, some of us could persuade him not to like fixing his camp for the length of time he does, in those horrid large stations, where he invites so many that we are never alone even with our own large Staff. [...] I do wish he would take us away, but he is so delighted reviewing troops and inspecting hospitals and barracks, and looking at new marching inventions, that we are in the greatest fear he will remain a month. [...] I see very little of your dear Father, except when we are both working officially, up to the eyes, but I often flatter myself (perhaps it is vanity) that I can be useful to him, and my little help enables him to get out an hour sooner than he otherwise could, which hour is invaluable to his health.[10]

One of the interesting things that we get from the letters of Lady Gough is this level of complaint about Lord Gough's actions that she would never have said to him in person. It is rather intriguing that for the large part she suffered in silence, and this gave her correspondence the character of a safety valve in which she could let off steam without either effecting or influencing her husband's choices or career path.

Lord Gough obviously knew she was ill and in pain, but one imagines that had he known to what extent and that it was pushing her nearer to an early grave he would not have hesitated to take action. Had it been a choice between his career and his wife, there would only have been one winner. Such was his devotion for his wife that it would even have trumped his loyalty to the Crown, of whom he was immensely proud to serve. Yet Frances Gough was the love of his life and for him he would have given up anything: even soldiering. There is no evidence, but it would be interesting to know if Frances Gough urged retirement on her husband after the conclusion of the First Sikh War. It will be remembered that his term of service was almost up, and indeed would officially conclude before the start of the Second Sikh War. It would have helped Frances Gough immensely if they could have returned to Europe at that time. Her health had not been helped by the anxiety of the war. Although she made no mention to her husband, in a letter to her daughter Gertrude, by then Mrs Arbuthnot, Frances Gough confesses her wish that they would soon depart India:

> The last mail was of great importance to me. I had hoped it would have brought out the appointment of a successor to your dear Father [...] Putting myself out of the question, I really thought the dear Father had been long enough in India. However, as everything has been, all my life, through the goodness of God, "for the best", I am sure this is too. This itself pleased

9   Rait, *Gough*, Vol. II, pp. 324–325.
10   Rait, *Gough*, Vol. II, p. 324.

him, but the delight expressed by all the General Staff at having "Got your Lordship for another year at all events" has greatly gratified him.[11]

Whilst obviously the letter does point to her own desire to leave India it is interesting that she also thinks this would be in the best interest of Lord Gough. Between the two conflicts Gough had aged considerably in appearance. An officer who had known him in the first conflict but had not seen him since, remarked upon meeting him during the second war that he was "much altered since I saw him three years since looking very old, very seedy and it seemed to me that his mind was apt to wander at times."[12] It might well be that this alteration in health since, and in part due to, the First Sikh War was what Lady Gough alluded to. In reality it might simply have been the case that a long stay in India was demanding for any couple, not least of all one in their sixties. The peace and tranquillity of retirement may well have been calling to Lady Gough more than her husband.

It will be appreciated that during both wars with the Sikhs, Frances Gough was "within reach of the baseless rumours which alarmed British India."[13] This was particularly acute during the First Sikh War when after Ferozeshah rumours reached then that the army had been massacred. In such a case Frances also had to comfort her daughter, who had recently given birth and whose husband Patrick Grant was with the army, and assure her that the rumours were just that. Indeed it appears that it was at this stage of the First Sikh War that Frances Gough felt most concerned. This is understandable as in this instance the rumours were coming from people who claimed to have been at Ferozeshah and escaped before the final destruction, whereas in the Second Sikh War the attacks on her husband came from an already hostile press, of whom Frances Gough shared the low opinion that her husband held in this regard.

Her feelings were best described in a letter written at the conclusion of the First Sikh War:

> The last few months have committed great havoc, and no wonder, for amidst all my trials of the Peninsula, China, or 'Captain Rock', I never knew so fully the depth of misery and anxiety these months occasioned. [...] As to anxiety, never can you have any idea of the intensity of Fanny's [Mrs Grant] and mine the twelve days before the 31st December. Never, never shall I forget it. In anxiety to keep her up, on account of her babe, I strove to disguise a part of mine, but the cord had nearly cracked, and I was getting nearly crazed when on the 31st we had the blessing of seeing his (Hugh Gough's) handwriting once more. Daily, twice a day, we heard different reports. One day we heard they were defeated and the Sikhs were coming down in force to these lower stations. Another day that Ferozepore and Loodianah were taken – in short, we got up but to be miserable, and lay down but for sleep disturbed and full of dreadful dreams.[14]

It is interesting to note that such was the anxiety at this time, largely through not knowing, that even the very loyal and devoted Frances Gough started to doubt, and as she said had become 'nearly crazed'. Yet even at this time of immense personal anxiety Frances Gough did not forget her duty as the wife of the commander-in-chief and could often be found visiting and consoling the families of officers who had been severely wounded or killed. Partly this was a sense of duty and responsibility but it was also her natural caring nature.

---

11   Rait, *Gough*, Vol. II, p. 326. Rait tells us that this letter was written in the summer of 1848.
12   Thomas, 'Daniel George Robinson', p. 189.
13   Rait, *Gough*, Vol. II, p. 325.
14   Rait, *Gough*, Vol. II, pp. 325–326.

There was certainly relief when they finally left India. After the rather tiring round of official receptions and banquets given in the Gough's honour after their return from India, there was a great enjoyment at being able to settle down at St Helens. Both of them enjoyed improved health, for there is no doubt that in the finally years in India the strain of command told on the health of Lord Gough. Whilst Lord Gough would make fairly regular journeys across the Irish Sea to carry out his official duties, and make similarly regular journeys to Lough Cutra, Lady Gough rarely ventured beyond St Helen's. By so doing she improved the state of her general health and probably helped to prolong her life. In fact we know of only one trip she made away from St Helen's, when she ventured to see the property at Lough Cutra for the one and only time.[15]

St Helen's became not only a haven for Lord and Lady Gough but a playground for many of their grandchildren. Most of the family was now at home, apart from Patrick Grant's time in India as commander-in-chief of the Madras Army and later taking part in the suppression of the Mutiny. Thus the children of the Arbuthnots, the Grants, the Haineses, and George Gough's grandchildren were all regular guests at St Helen's. Lord Gough delighted in his grandchildren and he was happiest when engaging in games with them. A story exists of a game of musical chairs played by the grandchildren, Lord Gough, and George Howard, 7th Earl of Carlisle and Her Majesty's Lord Lieutenant of Ireland.[16] As a consequence the last years of their married life were pleasant family filled years. Given the amount of separation they had experienced through their marriage, and the strain of the final years of active life, this was no doubt a great comfort and relief to them.

Amongst the many letters of condolence Gough received from friends and family after Frances' death, there was no single letter that gave him as much pride or as much comfort as that which he received from Her Majesty. In a letter dated 23 March Queen Victoria wrote:

> The Queen has heard with much concern of the sad affliction which has befallen Lord Gough, and is anxious to express personally her sincere sympathy with him. She recollects having met his lamented wife at the Phoenix Park, ten years ago, and how kind and amiable she was. Irreparable as his loss is, how blessed to have lived on together till the evening of their lives, with the comfort and hope of the separation being but a short one. To the poor Queen, this blessing, so needful to her, has been denied, and she can only hope never to live to see old age, but to be allowed to rejoin her beloved great and good husband, ere many years elapse. The Queen sincerely hopes that Lord Gough's health may not have suffered, and asks him to express her sincere sympathy to his family.[17]

It was as personal and sympathetic a letter as protocol would ever have allowed. Indeed the expression of her own personal grief at the loss of Prince Albert, only a little over a year ago, was perhaps a little unusual. However the grief that Queen Victoria felt over the loss of Prince Albert has been well documented. Yet the expression of the desire for an early death so that she can be reunited with her beloved in the afterlife is rather an unusual statement from such an individual, even given her confident Christian belief in heaven.

Gough's reply to Queen Victoria is also interesting to read:

> Your Majesty's most gracious sympathy is a solace to a wounded heart. May the God of Mercy and Grace bless Your Majesty and restore you to that peace which He reserves for, and freely bestows on, all who love and serve Him. Your Majesty's sympathy is a balm to the stricken of

---

15   Rait, *Gough*, Vol. II, p. 328.
16   Rait, *Gough*, Vol. II, p. 329.
17   Rait, *Gough*, Vol. II, p. 331.

this family. They bless Your Majesty for this sympathy, and devotedly pray that the God of all Mercy and Grace may vouchsafe to our honoured Sovereign His choicest Blessings here below, and when re-united to one so deservedly beloved, pronounce that joyful summons: 'Come, ye beloved Children of My Father, receive the Kingdom prepared for you from the beginning of the world'.[18]

Both letters confirm not only the Christian faith of both correspondents, but also the great comfort that it provides them at this time of need. If anything Gough's letter is more positive and hopeful than the slightly negative letter from the Queen. Perhaps this was due to the fact that despite the separation that had periodically come during their marriage the Goughs had enjoyed a 'lifetime' together whereas the marriage of Queen Victoria and Prince Albert had been all too short.

Lord Gough lived on for another seven years. He was increasingly to be found staying with his family. The Grants were often to be found staying at St Helen's, and when Patrick Grant was appointed as Governor of Malta in 1867, Gough's daughter Jane, Mrs Haines, came to stay with him at St Helens. At other times Gough would stay with the Grants. Obviously there was a family connection with Patrick Grant but also the fact that he was an old comrade in arms no doubt helped Gough. However one such stay with the Grants at their home in Scotland, in January 1865, nearly ended in disaster. The house caught fire and burnt to the ground. All were safely evacuated. Yet the trauma of having to escape a burning house on a now 85-year-old man can be imagined. On a lesser individual the shock, not to mention the exposure to the elements after the evacuation could have had serious implication on their general health. On Lord Gough however there was no impact. Indeed the most unfortunate consequence of the fire has been to historians who have unfortunately been robbed of nearly all the official and private papers of Patrick Grant. This is especially unfortunate for all historians concerning the Sikh Wars, and it is a great shame that the evidence of the Adjutant General of the Army in both wars was lost in such a manner.[19]

Yet despite his advanced age it appears that Gough still travelled from time to time. He would visit Lough Cutra, Scotland, England, and even occasional trips to the Continent. Even in the last couple of years of his life there were occasional trips to London to fulfil his duties as Gold Stick in Waiting. However towards the end of 1868 Gough became seriously ill and he was confined to St Helen's, and indeed mostly to his bed. In January 1869 he seemed near to death yet with the typical fight to which his life had been testament he hung on until Tuesday 2 March 1869. On that day he died at St Helen's. In his last moments he had been surrounded by his children and grandchildren and by all accounts he passed peacefully. He was now into the 90th year of his life in an era when such an age was uncommon. Yet it had only really been in the last two years that he had become noticeably frail and ill.

A week later, on 9 March 1869 Hugh Gough was laid to rest in the churchyard of St Brigid's, next to Lady Gough. Although both the Goughs were buried at St Brigid's Church in Stillorgan, they had not been regular attenders at that church. Indeed their church was St Phillip and St James in Booterstown, not far from St Helen's. The reason they were not buried there was quite simple: St Phillip and St James did not have a graveyard. Also at the time of their deaths extensive building work was taking place at St Philip and St James and a funeral service might not have been practical.[20]

---

18 Rait, *Gough*, Vol. II, pp. 331–332. The verse quoted from scripture is found in Matthew chapter 25 and verse 34. Gough probably quoted this from memory as the actual reading in the Authorised Bible is "Come ye blessed of my Father, inherit the kingdom prepared for you from the foundation of the world".
19 Rait, *Gough*, Vol. II, p. 343–344.
20 I am grateful to Karen D'Alton of St Brigid's Church for her assistance in this matter.

On his instructions it was not a martial funeral as would have been fitting for a Field Marshal. Exactly why Gough did not wish a martial funeral is unclear. It might simply be that in the small village of Stillorgan it was felt that this would be either impractical or inappropriate. It might have been considered inappropriate for other reasons. This was of course the time just after the Great Famine and just before the land war of the 1870–80s. Thus a martial funeral might not have been entirely welcomed. It is unlikely that Gough's expressed wish that it not be a martial funeral was motivated by any ill feeling towards either the state or the Army. Without directly stating why, *The Irish Times* agreed with the choice but also added the sentiment that such a martial funeral would have been deserved, if not necessarily appropriate to the situation.[21]

The funeral was due to take place at 0900 and an hour before this the funeral party had been prepared. Lord Gough was taken from St Helen's, where he had been lying in state, to a hearse drawn by six horses. His suite of coffins was said to be of relatively simple and plain design. On the lid it simply said, 'Field Marshal Hugh, 1st Viscount, Gough: born November 3, 1779; died March 2, 1869'. Indeed the ceremony would be a simple affair. *The Times* correspondent later reported that Gough "was borne to his last resting place without any of the pomp and splendour of a public funeral, but with a ceremonial more impressive in its simplicity."[22] Whilst Gough's desired for such a ceremony might have expressed an awareness of the political and social climate in Ireland, it was in many ways fitting for the man. As *The Times* reported, "It accorded with the unobtrusive character of the veteran warrior."[23] *The Irish Times* went further in its praise and referred to Gough as "one of the most gallant and distinguished soldiers that ever reflected honour on the bravery of Irishmen."[24]

Behind the hearse were six mourning coaches. The first contained his son and his grandsons, then two coaches containing his nephews, including John Bloomfield Gough. The fourth coach contained his cousins, the fifth the clergy and family friends, and the six included the estate steward and his household steward. Behind this followed on the private and state coaches of Lord Gough, containing various family members. Then came the coaches of the numerous dignitaries, nobility, and gentry.

Amongst those in attendance were Her Majesty's Lord Lieutenant, the 5th Earl Spencer in the first of his two stints in that office, and Lord Strathnairn, Commander-in-Chief, Ireland who had also been a successor of Gough's as commander-in-chief in India. Interestingly Strathnairn would succeed Gough in another area, replacing him as a colonel of the Royal Horse Guards. Also present were Lieutenant General Hall, former Lord Chief Justice Lefroy, and former Lord Chancellor Brewster. There were also numerous military officers, but given Gough's advanced age when he died there were of course none of his contemporaries present. Both Hardinge and Dalhousie preceded him, as had many of the generals who had served under him such as Campbell, Smith, Havelock, and Gilbert.

The funeral cortege proceeded along the Stillorgan Road to St Brigid's Church. There the procession was met by the church wardens, and the coffin was carried into the church draped in black. The service was led by the Rev. S. Gray, assisted by the Rev. I. Burkitt and the Rev. E. Gough, the latter the nephew of the deceased. After the service the coffin was laid in the family vault next to that of Lady Gough. The simple limestone structure survives to this day. The writing is worn but it does not appear to be written in 'Irish' as *The Times* reported. The vault is however surmounted with a large shamrock, and even in death Gough continued to affirm his Irish identity.

---

21   *The Irish Times*, Wednesday 10 March 1869.
22   *The Times*, Thursday 11 March 1869.
23   *The Times*, Thursday 11 March 1869.
24   *The Irish Times*, Wednesday 10 March 1869.

The funeral was well attended and many of the local population turned out to pay their last respects along the route. Somewhat unusually, an armed guard was placed over his tomb for three nights. Exactly why this was is uncertain. It is easy to presume that it was to protect it from vandalism or desecration but this might be to jump to the wrong conclusion. It may have been done as a mark of respect. Although it had not been a martial funeral an armed guard, if indeed it was a soldier as seems likely, might have been a mark of respect to the late field marshal. However, given the political situation in Ireland at this time it is easier to believe that someone was expecting trouble. If so the question is was any possible vandalism of the tomb because of who Gough was or what he represented? Was it Gough the man or Gough the British soldier who was felt likely to provoke an attack?

If it was Gough the man it would be unfortunate, and to a large extent go against what we know of him. He was firstly a proud Irishman, albeit of the Anglo-Irish clan. Yet it would be strange if Irish nationalist sentiment rose against him because of this. Secondly, Gough had by the limited account we have regarding it, been quite a liberal landowner and landlord. He had not been harsh and had shown the same discipline but paternalistic care to his tenants as he had his soldiers. Perhaps the former did not love him for it as much as the latter, but it would seem unlikely that he had upset the general populace to any great extent. It might be that the authorities had one particular tenant or former tenant in mind that bore a grudge against the Goughs for whatever reason.[25] If not this, though, then we come to the most likely conclusion, which is that the authorities feared there might be an attack on his tomb because of what he represented rather than who he had been. One can easily imagine that the tomb of a field marshal of the British Army would be a tempting target for Irish nationalists. As we shall see, despite his Irishness Gough would later become a target for Irish nationalists, largely based on what he represented, rather than any understanding of the man himself.

On 22 April Gough's will was proved in London, having already been proved in Dublin shortly before this. Gough's wealth in Ireland was slightly in excess of £11,000 (about £503,000 in modern money) and his wealth in England £27,000 (about £1,234,000 in modern money). This tells us that despite his residence in Ireland he still kept much of his money and investments controlled from London rather than Dublin. As the total did not exceed £40,000 the probate duty was paid to the tune of £525 and not at the considerably higher amount had it exceeded that rate.[26] After having made a good report of Gough's funeral, *The Times* usual flair for 'accuracy' returned when it reported the proving of his will. It stated that he had died at the age of 80, not 90. It also stated that his wife was still alive and that she had been left the house for her lifetime and £2,000 a year. Obviously the passing of Lady Gough in 1863 had passed *The Times* by.[27] Gough's pension of £2,000 a year from the East India Company stopped, but the pension granted by Parliament for his service during the Sikh Wars continued for his next two heirs in accordance with the terms of its awarding. His son George, now the 2nd Viscount Gough, was the sole executor. A generous provision was made for Hugh Gough's daughters, but the vast majority of his wealth was inherited by his son.

There was a nostalgia looking back at the time of Gough's death. This largely came about because he was one of the last Peninsular War veterans, and certainly one of the last officers to command a regiment during that period. Indeed there was slightly more concentration on this in the newspapers than on his other campaigns. The Sikh Wars had largely been forgotten in the wake of the Mutiny and the First Anglo-China War had been replaced in the public consciousness by

25 *The Times*, Thursday 11 March 1869.
26 *The Times*, Saturday 8 May 1869. I am grateful to Turtle Bunbury for allowing me to view a digital copy of the will.
27 *The Times*, Saturday 8 May 1869.

the Second Anglo-China War. Indeed, it was 20 years since Gough had last taken the field. The army and indeed the Empire had moved on from that point. Although an early Victorian military commander, the era in which he served had changed little from the Georgian era. By 1869 the Victorian era had seen a considerable change in society. In a sense even by 1869 Gough had become a distant memory from an era now dead, and this is supported by the fact that *The Times* lamented him as one of the last field officers to have served under Wellington in Spain.[28]

28   *The Times*, Wednesday 3 March 1869.

81

The Gough Statue

There is one final area to look at before we turn to our concluding remarks on the life and career of Lord Gough. The story actually occurs after his death. On 21 May 1869 the Mayor of Dublin, William Carroll, convened a public meeting at which it was desired to erect a statue in memorial of the recently decease Viscount Gough. The motion was seconded by Sir Maziere Brady and Abraham Brewster, both lawyers and judges who had retired as Lord Chancellor of Ireland. It will also be recalled that Brewster had attended Gough's funeral. Exactly what the nature of their relationship was is unknown. It was then moved that "the eminent services rendered to his country by the late Field Marshal Viscount Gough, KP, GCB, GCSI, deserve to be suitably acknowledged and commemorated by all classes of his countrymen." Thus a public fund was established to pay for an equestrian statue, with Lord Strathnairn, Maziere Brady, Abraham Brewster and Sir Joseph Napier, a future Lord Chancellor of Ireland, as trustees.[1]

The task of completing the statue was offered to John Henry Foley. J. H. Foley, as he is better known, was one of the leading sculptors of the age. Born in Dublin in 1818, Foley moved to London in 1835 to study at the Royal Academy. Indeed his reputation was worldwide and an argument could be made for him being the greatest sculptor of the Victorian era. Foley's reputation has suffered from being seen as a sculptor of Empire and as a consequence a great many of his sculptures have either been destroyed or are today neglected. Thankfully a reassessment of his career has taken place in recent years due to a biography published in 1999 and a 2008 documentary film of his life and career. Despite his work for Empire, some of his sculpture survives in Dublin to this day, most famously the statue of Daniel O'Connell on the street named in his honour. O'Connell, Edmund Burke, Oliver Goldsmith and a few others are all that survives of his architecture in Dublin. The fact that they are non-Imperial figures is the main reason they have survived.[2] Foley's work has caused significant problems for the authorities in Ireland. Whilst his sculptures are generally recognised as great works of art, the subject matter often meant that they sat uncomfortably with Irish nationalism and Republicanism. Gough's statute certainly fell into this category and had a rather chequered history. Although in one sense this is beyond the scope of our biography, it is interesting to note that a man who had been a controversial figure in life remained so in death. In both cases one can argue that the controversy was somewhat undeserved.

In approaching Foley, the Dublin committee had taken a very positive step. Not only was he the foremost sculptor in the land and in great demand, but he also enjoyed Royal patronage. Prince Albert had been impressed by his work and his patronage had helped advance Foley. The Royal

---

1   NLI: Gough Memorial, Collection of proceedings from Gough Memorial Committee (Dublin: 1879). See also articles from *The Irish Builder*, Vol. XIV, no. 299. 1 June 1872, Vol. XXI, no. 472. 15 August 1879 & Vol. XXI, no. 478. 15 November 1879.

2   Sheehan, Ronan, *Foley's Asia: A Sketchbook*, (Dublin: The Lilliput Press, 1999). The 2008 documentary film, directed by Se Merry Doyle, was entitled *John Henry Foley: Sculptor of the Empire*.

connection did not end with Albert's death. Indeed when a replacement sculptor was needed for the Albert Memorial due to the death of Carlo Marochetti, Queen Victoria, knowing of Albert's love of Foley's work, insisted that he be given the job. There is a sense in which by continuing royal patronage towards Foley Queen Victoria believed she was honouring and remembering her late husband. Other notable works by Foley had included the equestrian statues of Lord Hardinge and Sir James Outram. The latter was considered to be one of the finest equestrian statues ever made due to the magnificent detail involved. Indeed, Foley excelled at sculpting horses and there is a detail and accuracy to his work that is almost unsurpassed. It therefore was understandable that the suggestion of the Gough statue as an equestrian one seems to have originated from Foley.

After being approached by the council Foley wrote to them stating his interest in the project. Indeed he stated that he 'would gladly undertake' the commission. The problem was money. The committee quibbled about Foley's fee. Foley took great delight in pointing out to the committee that: "I need scarcely repeat how gratifying the task would be to me, and how willing I am to forego my usual consideration of profit in my desire to engage myself upon it. This may be best proved by the fact that double the amount has been my charge for similar works." That Foley was prepared to do the work for the amount they offered, despite the fact that it was half what he was normally paid, demonstrates that he clearly had a desire to do the work. This was not simple to honour Lord Gough. As he further explained in his letter: "I feel that the time has arrived for our native country to add to the memorials of her illustrious dead an equestrian statue, and that Lord Gough at once presents a worthy subject for such a memorial." One can appreciate how a man renowned for his equestrian statues jumped at the chance to produce one for the city of his birth.[3]

Yet even with this greatly reduced fee the committee were struggling to fund the project. To that end Foley assisted by asking the committee to approach the War Office to provide gun metal for the sculptor thus saving on the cost. This was supplied to the tune of 15 tonnes of gun metal from captured guns. It is suggested that the gun metal used was fittingly taken from guns captured from the Sikhs. Although the accuracy of this cannot be verified, this was certainly what the Dublin committee believed. Rait suggests that whilst some of the metal might have come from this source other parts of it came from captured Mahratta and Chinese guns. At the very least it is thought the gun metal came from cannon captured during Gough's campaigns.[4] In a further attempt to save money, rather than use a new design of horse a copy of the one used for Lord Hardinge's statue was substituted. This might also have had another reason behind it, as before the statue was completed John Henry Foley died. His student completed the work to his specifications. Yet despite these problems the resulting statue was a fine piece of sculpture. The statue showed a proud and erect Gough astride his charger and was a heroic and patriotic masterpiece whilst also being aesthetically pleasing. Unfortunately the statue was about to find itself in a storm of controversy that would last a century.

Whilst everyone in the Dublin Committee was pleased with the new statue they now faced a very real problem. Where was it to be placed? The original idea had been for Foster Place in Dublin, but Foley and others felt that this was unsuitable. The location was left in abeyance until the sculpture was completed. The end of what would become O'Connell Street, but was then still known as Sackville Street, was considered and indeed was in many ways a suitable place. However this met with objections from Nationalists on the Dublin Council. The reason was that it was already proposed to have a statue of Daniel O'Connell in the middle of the street that would later bear his

3   NLI: Gough Memorial, J. H. Foley to David M'Birney, 25 August 1869.
4   NLI: Gough Memorial, Collection of proceedings from Gough Memorial Committee (Dublin: 1879). Rait, *Gough*, Vol. II, p. 347.

name. If, as suggested, the Gough statue was placed at the other end of the street facing O'Connell it would appears as if Gough, mounted on his horse, was preparing to charge at O'Connell![5]

This objection was overcome slightly by the intention of placing Gough's statue at the bottom of Sackville Street by the proposed new Carlisle Bridge, now known as the O'Connell Bridge, over the River Liffey. It would not be facing the proposed O'Connell statue but would still be in a prominent position by the side of the new bridge. This seemed an acceptable position. The problem was that the existing Carlisle Bridge was undergoing significant rebuilding work that was scheduled to continue until 1880. However a much bigger problem than the placing of the statue arose in August 1874 when J. H. Foley died unexpectedly. He left several pieces of work uncompleted including the Gough statue. Amongst the others there were two that were considered of far greater importance when it came to completing them. One was the statue of Prince Albert for the Albert Memorial, and the other was that of Daniel O'Connell. Priority was given to Prince Albert, but there was also a desire to see O'Connell finished as soon as possible. The task of completing his sculptures was given to Foley's former pupil Thomas Brock, who would become a noted sculptor in his own right based on his completion of Foley's work.

The Gough statue appears to have been completed sometime in 1878. In January 1878 a committee meeting agreed that the statue should be placed on the other side of the Carlisle Bridge, by the entrance to Westmoreland Street. This was agreed and the plan seems to have been that when the new bridge was completed the statue would be placed there. However in November 1878 the committee received a report from Mr Neville, the city engineer, who reported that the Carlisle Bridge would not be ready for at least 18 months and that until that time no work could be done to prepare for the placing of the statue. This meant that even once the bridge was completed there would be a further delay as the plinth for the statue was prepared.[6] With a now-completed statue the delays were not only annoying but also costly as storage had to be found for the statue whilst a site was located. By July 1879 the situation deteriorated yet further when a report from the City of Dublin Paving and Cleansing Committee stated that, "in view of the present condition of the adjoining bridge and its approaches, the committee decline to recommend the council to grant a site there for any statue whatever at present." This report was received by the Dublin Committee on 3 July. At a meeting on 23 July a note of caution was raised as to the need to settle a site and get the statue out of storage as soon as possible. If not it was likely that a site would have to be sought in London and as the committee reported, "thereby the city and the citizens of Dublin will permanently lose this fine work of art."[7]

It was eventually decided that the delays at the Carlisle Bridge and the intersection with Westmoreland Street, which was also being developed, meant that although in many ways the location was very appropriate it was no longer practical. Eventually the committee decided to seek a spot in Phoenix Park as an alternative. Phoenix Park suited the equestrian nature of the statue and should in theory have been an end to all controversy. The statue itself was over 13 feet high and rested on a plinth that was itself seven feet tall. In early February 1880 the construction of the statue in Phoenix Park commenced. Exactly when it was completed was unclear, but it was decided that the unveiling ceremony would be on 21 February 1880, marking as it did the 31st anniversary of the Battle of Gujrat.

The ceremonial unveiling of the statue in 1880 was a large-scale event. Whether it was due to security concerns or because it was felt appropriate for a field marshal, the number of troops formed up was recorded to be one of the largest ever in Dublin's history in time of peace. There were also a

5   NLI: Gough Memorial, Collection of proceedings from Gough Memorial Committee (Dublin: 1879).
6   NLI: Gough Memorial, Collection of proceedings from Gough Memorial Committee (Dublin: 1879).
7   NLI: Gough Memorial, Collection of proceedings from Gough Memorial Committee (Dublin: 1879).

considerable number of honoured guests, including the Lord Lieutenant, John Winston Spencer-Churchill 7th Duke of Marlborough. Amongst the audience was his five-year-old grandson, Winston Churchill, whose own father was the Duke's Private Secretary. In his book *My Early Life 1874–1904*, Churchill recorded it as one of his earliest memories:

> A great black crowd, scarlet soldiers on horse-back, strings pulling away a brown shiny sheet, the Old Duke, the formidable grandpa, talking loudly to the crowd. I recall even a phrase he used: 'And with a withering volley he shattered the enemy's line.' I quite understood that he was speaking about war and fighting and that a volley meant what the black-coated soldiers (riflemen) used to do with loud bangs so often in the Phoenix Park where I was taken for morning walks.[8]

No doubt the line he could remember his grandfather reciting described one of Gough's battles. Given the date of the unveiling it could be a description of Gujrat, but one cannot help but think that the line might better apply to the Battle of Barrosa and the capture of the Eagle by the 87th. That Churchill could remember the event so many years on speaks not only of the grandeur of the event but also of the imposing nature of the statue. Altogether the statue was over 20 feet high and one can imagine that such a huge structure would make a lasting impact on a five-year-old when it was unveiled.

The position it took in Phoenix Park was on the high road through the park, not far from either the Wellington Testimonial or the statue of Lord Carlisle.[9] Such was the crowd that gathered for the unveiling that two temporary stands were constructed for the more distinguished guests to sit in. The Duke of Marlborough gave what *The Times* described as an 'eloquent speech' that had 'traced the brilliant career of the late Field Marshal'. As Marlborough pulled the strings to unveil the statue a trumpet fanfare was sounded, after which the bands played 'See the Conquering Hero Comes'. General Sir John Michel, Commander-in-Chief, Ireland, then ordered a salute to be fired before the massed bands played the tune 'St Patrick's Day'.[10]

The inscription on the statue read:

> In Honour of Field-Marshal Viscount Gough, KP, GCB., KG, an Illustrious Irishman, whose achievements in the Peninsular War, in China and India, have added to the lustre of the military glory of the country which he faithfully served for 75 years, this Statue, cast from cannon taken by Troops under his command, and granted by Parliament for the purpose, was erected by his Friends and Admirers

The words of Sir John Michel at the unveiling are worth repeating:

> Honoured I have been by the temporary deposit in my hands of this memorial of glory. I now surrender it to the safeguard of Ireland's sons. Keep it, Irishmen, as an everlasting memento of your glory. Treasure it as a sacred deposit. Glory in it as the statue of one who was an honour to your country, one whose whole life, whether civil or military, was one continued career of kindness, honour, honesty of purpose, nobility of heart, combined with the purest loyalty, and

---

8   Churchill, Winston. S., *A Roving Commission: My Early Life*, (New York: Charles Scribner's Sons, 1930), p. 1. Churchill mistakenly recollects the year as 1878, however given the passage of time one can forgive this slight lapse.
9   Often called the Wellington Monument it should more correctly be referred to as a testimonial as its work was proposed and commenced whilst Wellington was still alive.
10 *The Times*, Monday 23rd February 1880.

the most enthusiastic patriotism. He was loved and honoured by his countrymen. He was *par excellence* our Irish chevalier, *sans peur et sans reproche*, and to wind up all, he was heart and soul an Irishman.[11]

This glowing tribute does in some ways foreshadow the problems that the statue would experience in later years. Although it points correctly to his Irish heart and soul, the glory it speaks of would largely be considered the glory of Empire. To the Nationalist in Ireland this was anathema. Indeed it is somewhat surprising that the statue enjoyed as much peace as it did. During the 1920s many such statues of Empire were destroyed during the Civil War and the creation of the Irish Free State. During this period Gough's statue survived largely unscathed.

Indeed it was not until 1944 that the first major nationalist attack upon the statue took place. On Christmas Eve 1944 the statue was beheaded. The attack was largely ignored by the local population, who thought little of it. The general indifference was summed up by Brian O'Nolan's column in *The Irish Times* in early January 1945. "Few people will sympathize with this activity; some think it is simply wrong, others do not understand how anybody could think of getting up in the middle of a frosty night in order to saw the head of a metal statue!"[12] Some time later the head was found. It had been dumped in the River Liffey and came ashore at Islandbridge. The head was screwed back on and the statue was left in peace for a short time.

Further attacks took the form of vandalism, and on one occasion white paint was thrown over it. At some point the sword was stolen. In 1950's there was a spate of nationalist attacks on monuments in Ireland. Although often attributed to the IRA they were actually the work of a splinter group. In November 1956 an attempt to blow up the statue succeeded in blowing off the horse's hind leg. However in July 1957 a follow up attack succeeded in blowing both horse and rider from the plinth. Again there was a general disinterest amongst most of the citizens of Dublin, and it was hardly a major blow for 'Irish Independence' or 'anti-Imperialism'. Its main result was to inspire the creation of a rather bawdy, if not downright rude, poem about the attack that generally mocked those who had undertaken this rather bizarre attack. The poem, by Vincent Capriani, an Irishman of Italian heritage, referred to the 1956 attack.

There are strange things done from twelve to one in the Hollow at Phaynix Park, There's maidens mobbed and gentlemen robbed In the bushes after dark; But the strangest of all within human recall concerns the statue of Gough, 'twas a terrible fact, and a most wicked act, for his bollix they tried to blow off! 'Neath the horse's big prick a dynamite stick some gallant 'hayro' did place, for the cause of our land, with a match in his hand bravely the foe he did face; Then without showing fear – and standing well clear – he expected to blow up the pair but he nearly went crackers, all he got was the knackers and he made the poor stallion a mare! For his tactics were wrong, and the prick was too long, the horse being more than a foal, it would answer him better, this dynamite setter, the stick to shove up his own hole! For this is the way our 'haroes' today are challenging England's might, with a stab in the back and a midnight attack on a statue that can't even shite.

These attacks placed the Irish Government in a difficult position. The continued attacks on the statue meant they did not feel it was appropriate to restore and return it to its position in Phoenix Park. Indeed there did not appear to be anywhere in Ireland that would be appropriate. Yet at the same time the government was mindful of it as a piece of art and indeed as one of the last statues

11   *The Times*, Monday 23rd February 1880; Rait, *Gough*, Vol. II, pp. 347–348.
12   Brian O'Nolan wrote as Myles na gCopaleen in *The Irish Times*. *The Irish Times*, 4 January 1945.

of J. H. Foley. For many years it remained in storage with the authorities too nervous to restore and replace it, but at the same time unwilling to destroy or dispose of a notable work of art. There is one final irony with regards to the vandalism and attacks upon the Gough statue given its proximity to the Wellington Testimonial. It remains somewhat bizarre that a statue of Gough, a man who publicly declared his Irish identity should be so vandalised and destroyed, whereas the Wellington Testimonial, to a man who despised the country of his birth, has escaped large-scale attack.[13]

The Gough statue remained in storage until 1986 when it was sold to Robert Guinness, of the famous Irish family. This was supposedly on the condition that the statue was removed from Ireland. It now stands in the grounds of Chillingham Castle in Northumberland having been restored in the late 1980s and early 90s. Whilst England does seem a more fitting place for the statue, despite Gough never having lived in England for any period of time, it does seem a shame that a man born in Limerick, who lived most of his life in Ireland, and indeed who died just outside Dublin, should not have his statue in his native land. In recent years there have been suggestions that his statue might return to Phoenix Park as part of the attempt to obtain World Heritage status for the Park from UNESCO. However, the desire for it to return is largely due to the fact that it is one of the last statues of J. H. Foley rather than anything to do with Gough. Indeed, the fact of who the statue is seems to make little difference to most people in Dublin. What is more important is the connection to Foley as part of an ongoing reappreciation of his work. Whether Gough's statue will ever return to Ireland cannot be known, but it would be a positive move if it were to ever happen.

If the statue ever returns to Ireland, as has been suggested in recent times, it will be done to honour Foley rather than Gough. In one sense it is regrettable that Gough is not better remembered and appreciated in the country of his birth. Yet given the course of Anglo-Irish relations it is entirely understandable, particularly when one considers that even in Britain, the country in whose army Gough served for so many years, he is largely forgotten and what is remembered tends to be the negative aspects of his career and character. Yet hopefully there will come a day in both Ireland and Britain when the positive side of Gough's career will also be considered.

---

13 There has been vandalism of the Wellington Testimonial, yet this seems largely to have been criminal rather than political. Metal from it has been stolen from it, presumably for scrap value rather than political motives.

82

A Case Study – Gough: Military Incompetence?

Of all the accusations levelled against Gough, the worst is that he was incompetent. The incompetent general is a danger to, but also an insult to, the men whose lives are in his hands. Whilst the present author would not agree with the accusation, it does perhaps merit further discussion. The most important work on military incompetence was written by Professor Norman Dixon. His book *On the Psychology of Military Incompetence* is an excellent insight into this subject. It benefits from the fact that Dixon was a Professor of Psychology. His professional knowledge of the psychology is therefore very strong. At the same time the fact that he served for ten years as an officer in the Royal Engineers and saw active service means that he understands the military world. The book is therefore not simply a psychologist theorising on a subject he has no practical experience of. Legitimate criticism of the book can be made in that it is not written by a historian, and at times some of the historical analysis of battles, Generals and campaign is somewhat lacking. However in our instance that is not an issue as it is not the intention to use Dixon's book as a historical reference, but in terms of psychological analysis. We are therefore only using the criteria for judging military incompetence constructed by a senior Professor of Psychology, rather than relying on its historical content.[1]

Before the concluding chapter of this biography the author has determined to look at and analyse the case for military incompetence that has been levelled against Gough, using the criteria of Professor Dixon. It is hoped that it will prove useful to the reader to see an examination of this matter from a psychological as well as a historical point of view. It is all too easy to become transfixed by the historical outcomes of battles and campaigns as an analysis of leadership and competence rather than looking more fully at the motivations and psychology that went into making those decisions.

Dixon sets out 14 'tests' for military incompetence.[2] As an exercise, and in an attempt to better understand Gough's thinking, we will consider each in turn. Much of this concerns Gough's actions in the Sikh Wars, as it was from this period that such accusations of incompetence came. However the attempt to apply the test to his entire career is also made.

The first test is a serious wastage of human resources and a failure to observe the important military rule of economy of force. Gough was perhaps guilty of this, but as we have seen there was certainly mitigation. Whilst Gough's tactics would inevitably lead to a loss of life, Gough did indeed become anxious about economy of force, particularly as regards his European infantry.

The second point is a fundamental conservatism and clinging to outworn tradition and a failure to learn from mistakes. Again one can certainly see elements of this. However Gough did learn from his mistakes and altered his tactics as the conflicts against the Sikhs continued. Gough was not fundamentally conservative in outlook, although he was certainly the product of a bygone age.

---

1   One can argue that with the original book having been published in 1976 that the psychological analysis might be slightly out of date, but the fact is that Dixon's book remains the best of its kind available.

2   Dixon, Norman, *On the Psychology of Military Incompetence* (London: Pimlico Press, 1994), pp. 152–153.

One can however argue that conservatism or outworn tradition was the reason for his lack of use with regards to artillery. Yet as we have seen this would be to misunderstand the circumstances that Gough acted under.

The third point is a tendency to reject or ignore information, either because it is unpalatable or because it conflicts with preconceptions. Gough certainly liked to see things at first hand himself, rather than rely on the information of others. Certainly his reliance on cold steel meant that he had a preconceived notion of how a battle should be fought. Yet examples of him refusing to believe information because it did not fit in with his beliefs are rare.

The fourth point is a tendency to underestimate the enemy and overestimate the strength of one's own side. Gough did not really at any point underestimate the enemy in the traditional understanding of the term. He recognised their strength, particularly in the Sikh Wars. In China if anything he overestimated the strength of the Chinese, and the fact that they did not appear in the strength he suspected caused him to doubt whether he was being led into a trap. One can say that there is an overestimation of his own strength in the sense that he believed in the innate superiority of British infantry and cold steel.

The fifth point is indecisiveness and a tendency to abdicate the role of decision maker. Of the many charges that could be levelled against Gough this does not, on the face of it, appear to be one of them. He was a decisive leader, although this was sometimes construed as recklessness. Far from abdicating responsibility Gough was sometimes felt to have clung to it too much and to have greatly resented others interfering with the decision making process, no matter now well intentioned that interference might have been.

The sixth test is an obstinate persistence in a given task despite strong contrary evidence. This is certain something that many of Gough's critics would have accused him of. The constant reliance on the frontal attack would be used in evidence in this regard. Yet as we have seen, Gough was often presented with little alternative to the frontal attack. It would be wrong to characterise Gough as not being able to adapt, even if such a process came slowly to him. Gough certainly liked to do what he was used to, preferring the tried and tested to ingenuity and guile.

The seventh test is a failure to exploit a situation and a tendency to pull punches rather than push home an attack. One could criticise Gough for this failing. It would appear strange to accuse Gough of ever pulling his punches, yet it could be argued that he sometimes failed to push home an attack. This would certainly be a criticism levelled against him in the wake of Chillianwala where it was felt he delayed too much. Yet as we have seen there were reasons, most notably the weather, behind this decision. In his career overall one could not accuse Gough of failing to exploit a situation. Indeed it was one of his strengths. Indeed Richard Holmes commented that, 'Whatever Gough's limitations, he has an acute sense for the balance of a battle'.[3]

The eighth point regards a failure to make adequate reconnaissance. This is a somewhat difficult one to judge. In China Gough would often undertake such work himself to be assured of his information. He also attempted to do this with varying degrees of success during the Gwalior campaign and the Sikh Wars. At certain points in his career one could certainly accuse Gough of poor reconnaissance; however, undertaking adequate reconnaissance was often easier said than done during the Sikh Wars. The terrain made this difficult to undertake, and the large number of enemy irregular cavalry meant that such reconnaissance was best undertaken by Gough's own cavalry. Gough's desire was always to see for himself. This was a drawback, and not really what a commander-in-chief should be doing.

The ninth point is perhaps the most obviously characteristic as applied to Gough, and that is a predilection for the frontal assault. Even when Gough attempted flanking movements, they were

3   Holmes, *Sahib*, p. 15.

often only in support of a main frontal attack. There is no doubt that Gough favoured this tactic and had a firm belief in its effectiveness. At the same time it must be made clear that, particularly in the Sikh Wars, there was often little alternative. The Sikhs chose their ground well, had a superiority in artillery and would generally manoeuvre a situation where there was little alternative to the frontal attack. Gough did not have either the material, or for that matter the intellectual, means to undertake a grand turning strategy of the enemy position.

The 10th point is linked to the former in that it is a belief in brute force rather than the use of a clever ruse. Gough clearly believed in brute force. The idea of overwhelming the enemy was key to his military thinking. Gough did at times attempt to deceive his enemy with the use of a ruse, but did not succeed. It was not really his style and was dependent upon a level of organisation and planning that he did not possess himself, nor did he have the 'Gneisenau' to plan this for him.

The 11th point is a failure to make use of surprise or deception. Gough certainly failed in this regard. Such attempts at deception that were made whilst he was in command were half-hearted or badly coordinated. In China he perhaps had limited success in this regard, but this can largely be put down to the half-hearted way in which the Chinese fought the war. In India, he rarely attempted such actions. At Ramnagar the attempt to deceive the enemy as to his true intentions was a woeful failure.

The 12th characteristic is an undue readiness to find scapegoats. Such a characteristic certainly does not apply to Gough. There were many times during his career when he could have legitimately pointed to the failures of others. Yet, in public, Gough refused to criticise those who served under him. In private he might express such concerns, but even then he was careful to whom he disclosed such criticisms. There were really only two people in whom he had sufficient confidence to make such statements: his son George Gough, and occasionally his nephew John Bloomfield Gough. So there was not in Gough's case any real attempt to find scapegoats to account for military setbacks.

The 13th point is the suppression, or distortion, of news from the front, usually in the name of maintaining morale or security. It is hard to find this characteristic present in Gough. One could perhaps argue that his total insistence that Chillianwala be treated as a victory, partly for the benefit of morale, fits this to an extent. However it would be wrong to suggest that this was a usual trait in Gough's character. In reality Gough cared little for what was written. His rather dismissive remark about the newspapers, and the fact that he by in large did not read them, is recorded as "I can afford abuse, but I cannot afford to pay for it."[4] Had he cared he would surely have attempted to do something about the numerous critical letters from junior officers, in breach of military discipline, which often found their way into the newspapers.

The 14th and final point is a belief in mystical forces such as fate or bad luck. Dixon makes no mention of religion in this regard, and that might be the only way in which one could attribute this characteristic to Gough. Gough clearly had a profound faith in God and a belief in His ever-present care and protection for him. Whilst there was perhaps a belief in fate or destiny on the part of Gough, this was only really manifested as part of his faith in God as his guardian and protector.

Whilst it can be seen that Gough did, on first glance, share many of the characteristics of military incompetence that Professor Dixon outlines, it would be wrong to conclude that there is sufficient evidence based upon this analysis to conclude that Gough was guilty of military incompetence. Even if one did conclude that he was guilty, it would only really cover the period of the two wars against the Sikhs. As has already been pointed out there is much in the way of mitigation, given the strength and ability of the Sikhs as an enemy and the difficult circumstances under which Gough had to take the field during each conflict. There are certainly some of the aforementioned characteristics that can be seen in the career of Gough. However with regards to the wastage of

---

4   Rait, *Gough*, p. 340.

human life a clear point has to be made. As Dixon points out, the main failing with regards to military incompetence is a lack of care and attention. There is an acceptance that, in battle, casualties are inevitable. Whilst high casualties in battle can be a sign of military incompetence it does not necessarily follow that they always are. At times, such is the difficulty of the position to be taken that heavy casualties are inevitable and have to be accepted if the target is to be obtained. However sometimes this can be used as a justification to excuse poor planning and leadership that has necessitated the attacking and taking of such a difficult position. In this regard each individual battle must be judged on its merit.

When talking of wastage of human life the main concern is that which is needless due to poor logistical and medical arrangements. Throughout his career Gough did his best to care for the needs of his men. The difficulties of the medical services during the Sikh Wars was largely due to the failure of the political leadership to sign off on the expenditure soon enough for them to be ready for the initial engagements. From that point on they were consequently playing catch up. As for Gough himself he would always make sure that his wounded were taken care of. On numerous occasions he refused to move until the wounded had been gathered in.

There will always be those who characterise Gough as being incompetent. In many ways it is easier to make the case for the failings of the Sikh Wars as being due to the actions of one man. It is far harder to stand back and appreciate that there were many other factors that contributed to the aforementioned failings. It is far harder to appreciate the failings in the army, subordinate commanders, staff work, political interference, and numerous other contributing factors. To blame one man, to in effect find a scapegoat, has always been far easier for politicians, the press, and the general public to accept, rather than to deal with the fact that long held ideals might be wrong. In that sense Gough was a scapegoat.

That said, Gough was clearly not without his faults. He did have a devotion to the bayonet, or more accurately the British infantryman's use of it, as the decisive weapon of war. As has been said numerous times, this was understandable when one looked at Gough past military experiences, and was not an attribute unique to Gough within the British Army of that era. He also had a rather lackadaisical approach to staff work. Whilst this was not as bad as some, notably Hardinge, suggested, he did have a detached role in staff work. This would have been alright had he had an able staff to do the work for him. The fact that he did not was partly down to Gough as he did have a degree of control over who was appointed to his staff. However it would be wrong to single out Gough for criticism with regards to poor staff work as this was a perennial problem of the British army throughout much of its history.

Conclusion

Attempting to write a concluding chapter for a biography of a life and career such as that of Field Marshal Gough is not an easy task. That is why to an extent an attempt has been made to analyse his career throughout the previous chapters of this work. In this sense much of our conclusion has already been written. It would be all too easy to become bogged down in an analysis of Gough's career during the two Sikh Wars. Indeed his command during the two Sikh Wars could fill a book by itself. Yet as we have attempted to demonstrate there was far more to the story of Gough's life than that. Indeed to understand his leadership during the Sikh Wars one has to understand his background and experience. It is impossible to divorce from the story of his role in the Sikh Wars his part in previous conflicts in China or the Peninsular War, or for that matter his entire military career.

However we cannot ignore this period and must return to the Sikh Wars for part of our conclusion. This is necessary because it is the major blot on the copybook that was Gough's military career. Although there has perhaps been an over-concentration on this part of his career at the exclusion of all else, it would be wrong not to recognise the importance of the two conflicts upon Gough and his subsequent reputation. To an extent the Sikh Wars were a defining moment for Gough, but, perhaps just as importantly, this was also a defining moment for the British Empire in India. It is very difficult to separate the two.

The Sikh Wars came at a difficult time for the British in India, a crossroads at which the whole future of British power in India was open to debate. It was Gough's misfortune to be asked to command an army during this period against the strongest enemy the British had ever faced in India. The British had hitherto enjoyed great success in India. Although there had been occasional setbacks the empire in India had continued to expand. The military, both East India Company and British Army, had been key in this. Although continually outnumbered, their professionalism, discipline, and technological and tactical advantages had secured them success time and time again. One by one, native armies had fallen to British arms. The Sikh Empire was the last impediment to British dominance in the subcontinent.

At the time of the conflict against the Sikhs, however, the aura of British military superiority had taken a blow as a consequence of the disaster of the First Anglo-Afghan War. The massacre of an Anglo-Indian force on the retreat from Kabul in 1842 had been a bitter blow to British prestige. Indeed the Afghan campaign would cast a shadow over the Sikh Wars and in turn place extra pressure upon Gough. After the First Anglo-Afghan War, the morale of the Bengal Army in particularly had been greatly reduced. Indeed the mutinies that followed can be linked, to an extent, to this. The aura of invincibility was also gone, and Indians lost a great deal of their respect or fear for the British. The Afghans had beaten the British using similar tactics to those which the Sikhs had employed in the late 18th century against Punjabi Muslims and the Afghans themselves. The Sikhs were quite capable of fighting a conventional battle, and had good disciplined and organised infantry and artillery with which to do this. However they were equally adept at fighting a hit and run style of campaign where their irregular cavalry would be a match for any enemy. In short they were even better at the style of warfare that had defeated the British in Afghanistan than the Afghans themselves.

The First Anglo-Afghan War also placed extra pressure on Gough's shoulders in terms of how his leadership would be viewed. Much of the blame for the failure in Afghanistan was placed, rightly or wrongly, on the shoulders of Major General William Elphinstone. Elphinstone has been described as elderly, weak, indecisive, and incompetent.[1] Certainly throughout the war he was extremely ill and this had obviously not helped matters. He was also seen as lacking imagination and ability. One cannot help but wonder when reports of such traits being demonstrated by Gough were being circulated how much this was due to the fact of the recent experience with Elphinstone. No doubt the memory of Elphinstone loomed large and fear of a repeat failure against a native enemy, not due to the poor state of the army but the poor state of its leadership, was feared. A cursory reading of the career of the two men would suggest a great deal of similarity. Elphinstone was only a couple of years younger than Gough and had also led a regiment during the Napoleonic Wars, although without the distinction Gough had achieved. Yet Elphinstone did not have the command experience that Gough did. Elphinstone had been promoted largely through the patronage of his father, who had been a director of the East India Company. Gough's advance through the army had been due to his reputation on the battlefield.

Indeed it is easy to lose sight of the standing of Gough's reputation before the Sikh Wars. Gough's reputation as a good battalion commander during the most significant military operations in British memory had been added to by his achievements in China. After China there was no serious question mark over Gough's ability. Indeed his handling of the troops and his leadership during the conflict saw him marked as one of the best officers of the army. Had Gough retired after China, as he had been prepared to do, how differently would history remember him? The problem was that the Sikhs were not the Chinese. This might sound blatantly obvious, but there is a serious point. The Chinese were overconfident and deluded, at least as far as their military might was concerned, as to the strength of their position. The Sikhs were a strong people and rightly confident in their military prowess. Indeed, the Sikhs could not even be described as usual Indian opposition: they were superior to that. In military strength, training, discipline, and organisation, they were far closer to a European than an Indian power. Whilst the Sikh army that Gough faced in the First Sikh War was not quite the same efficient military machine that it had been under Ranjit Singh, it was still a considerable force to be reckoned with.

In an era when, as the Duke of Wellington intimated, the British public had 'forgotten that Indians could fight' it was all too easy to underestimate them. Indeed even Wellington's cautionary comments do still have something of underestimation about them, in that he is comparing the Sikhs as a military force to other Indian armies, such as the Mahrattas. The Sikhs as a military force were without equal in India. The martial spirit of the race had naturally developed good fighting men, but there was far more to it than this. The organisation that Ranjit Singh had developed made the best use of the raw material. The Sikhs became organised, disciplined, well-trained, and equipped. Indeed the use of European mercenaries as leaders, teachers and advisers had developed a European style military. That this was not appreciated in Victorian England, or most of British India for that matter, was partly ignorance and partly arrogance.

The underestimation of the Sikhs and the failure to appreciate fully their military prowess made by contemporary commentators was clearly a reason for the excessive criticism Gough received. The question as to whether or not Gough himself underestimated the Sikhs is slightly more complex. He certainly appreciated their military prowess, discipline, and organisational order. Indeed his correspondence before the First Sikh War illustrates this. The problem is that at the same time there is something of an underestimation in the fact that Gough was clearly of the opinion that, despite this, the Sikhs would not be able to stand up to the old cold steel of his European infantry.

---

1   Haythornthwaite, *Colonial Wars Source Book*, p. 134. Mason, *A Matter of Honour*, p. 119.

To an extent this assumption was correct. The problem was that Gough does appear to have become somewhat fixated upon this as his main tactic. It would be wrong to suggest that Gough did not appreciate his artillery or cavalry, but he did clearly think that his infantry would win the day. This was of course partly true. The over emphasis on this arm of his force is understandable given Gough's experience and background. He had seen the Chinese off with the bayonet, he had even seen off Napoleon's front line infantry with the bayonet, so one can understand why he felt this way. It was not so much that he did not appreciate the fighting quality of the Sikhs or respect their army, it was more that he had a belief that no infantry in the world could withstand a British bayonet charge.

There is also a case to be made for Gough being a 'scapegoat' so that Parliament, the press, and the wider public, could avoid some rather unpleasant alternatives. It was far easier to blame one man for a failure than to examine wider problems with the governance of India. Far easier to blame one man than to acknowledge and deal with deficiencies in the British Army and admit to weakness in such an organisation. Far easier to blame one man than to accept that a 'native' army could equal the prowess of the 'European' with all the consequences for the perception of racial supremacy that this would entail. In short, it was easier to blame Gough than to fully examine and analyse the wider problems that the Sikh Wars exposed. That is not to say for one minute that Gough did not make mistakes or to suggest that his leadership was faultless. It is perhaps however to allow for the fact that there was more to the matter than simply the actions and attitudes of one man, however important he may have been.

In the introduction, we referred to the opinion of Professor Sir Hew Strachan that compared Gough to the Prussian commander Blucher but lamented the fact that he never found his 'Gneisenau'. Gough had the same level of determination and tenacity as the great Prussian field marshal. Yet the problem was that he had no chief of staff who could handle the administration, planning, and general business of the army. This important role was for far too long neglected within the British military community. There was a need for a good administrator and coordinator to work with the fighting general. Although widely considered one of the greatest generals of all time, it is important to recall that even Napoleon relied upon Louis-Alexandre Berthier in this regard. Even the greatest military commander needs a reliable organiser behind him. Gough was not the greatest of military commanders and thus the need was in his case even greater.

Gough was in general let down by the quality of his staff officers during his career but particularly during the two wars with the Sikhs. As we have seen, there were several incidents in the conflicts where orders were issued by staff officers that caused great difficulties and did not come from the commander-in-chief. There was also the incident in China where an officer had not passed on the order to withdraw and a company had not withdrawn with the rest of the army. All this points to the general problem of staff work in the British military at this time. However, during the Sikh wars this problem was particularly acute. One can turn around and say that Gough is partly to blame because he did not exercise greater control over his staff and issue specific orders on a regular basis. This is where a chief of staff of quality would have been invaluable. Patrick Grant, Gough's son-in-law, did his best to act in this capacity, yet he was both out of his depth and unsure of his position. The fact that the Deputy Adjutant General, and a man quite junior in rank, was taking on so much responsibility does not speak well of the general staff arrangements.

Hardinge complained that this staff work often fell upon him during the First Sikh War, and, allowing for his natural exaggeration, there was no doubt some validity in what he said. Indeed, had Hardinge agreed to serve as chief of staff rather than as an ill-defined second in command, he would have done greater service. Had he fully taken on this organisation and logistical side then a great burden would have been lifted from Gough's shoulders. In China Rear Admiral Parker had undertaken much of this work due to the fact that many of attacks were largely amphibious in nature.

In fairness to his staff, it must be noted that Gough was not always the easiest person to work with. The comments made by Robert Napier of some of his conversations with the commander-in-chief illustrate this.[2] Gough also had the ability to fall out with people, such as Havelock, if he felt that there was in anyway an attack upon him. In this way he was particularly sensitive. It was not quite a persecution complex but it was certainly heading in that direction. One sees an example of this when, after the First Sikh War, he felt there was a conspiracy against him involving Hardinge, the Duke of Wellington, Lord Ripon, and even the Prime Minister Sir Robert Peel.

Leaving aside the issue of administration, and admitting freely that it was not Gough's forte, there is a wider question about his tactical and indeed strategic ability. As has already been established, Gough was very much an infantry man and believed deeply in the strength of the British infantryman and the 'old cold steel'. This was to be expected. Not only was the power of the bayonet the widely held doctrine of the British army at this time, it was also based upon experience. Gough had seen at first hand during the Peninsular War the power of British infantry and the bayonet. When one thinks back to the battles discussed earlier in this book and considers how the British infantry had stood up to, received, and repelled, countless attacks from a French army that had conquered all before it throughout Europe, it is easy to understand why Gough held such a belief. Yet there was clearly more to it than that. On one hand there is something of a notion of arrogance, or even racial superiority, over non-Europeans that created a belief that they could not resist the superior British infantry. On the other hand, whilst artillery and cavalry were useful tools in victory it was almost unheard of for them to win battles in their own right during this era. At some point the infantry had to advance on the enemy.

It is interesting to recall the evidence mentioned earlier that during the Napoleonic era the majority of attacks by infantry never actually engaged with the enemy. Usually the enemy would flee in the face of the advancing infantry if volley fire did not stop such an advance. This was also true of the vast majority of native opponents Britain would face during the era of empire. However on most occasions this did not apply to the Sikhs. Their discipline and bravery meant that they would often receive a British infantry charge face on. Under such circumstances British casualties were bound to be higher.

Although there was a theme of condemnation of Gough's tactics throughout the Sikh Wars, the particularly damaging battle was that of Chillianwala. Given the history of Gough against the Sikhs, it was perhaps given harsher treatment than it deserved. The battle was of course a mess. Gough had not intended to give battle but had found himself under fire and, unable to withdraw, and had little choice but to attack. The battle was badly handled not only by Gough and his staff but also by many of the subordinate commanders. Pope and Pennycuick often take the lion's share of the blame, but even the usually reliable Colin Campbell had a questionable day. To reiterate, the battle was a mess. If it was a victory it was pyrrhic in nature. Yet at the same time it was not a defeat. It was put simply an inconclusive or drawn battle.

Gough thought it a victory, but as someone who had been at Talavera this was understandable. Mention has already been made of that battle, in which Gough fought and the future Duke of Wellington commanded. There were those in the press and parliament who questioned the nature of the victory at Talavera, were outraged by the losses, and questioned the commander of the British force. Then, as at Chillianwala, there was a failure to understand the situation. In both battles, the commander was not only concerned about the enemy in front of him but also another force of the enemy who was moving in support but whose exact whereabouts were unknown. What, however, was the significant difference between the two was the perception of the quality and ability of the enemy. Few at this stage doubted the quality or ability of the French army, yet there

2   Napier, *Personal Narrative*, pp. 4, 6 & 15.

was a lack of appreciation of the Sikhs. Whilst by Chillianwala it was not the well-disciplined and drilled Khalsa of years gone by, it was still a formidable enemy for the Anglo-Indian army that Gough commanded.

Again, we are in danger of becoming somewhat obsessed with the wars against the Sikhs, although we have tried to look more generally at the tactical limitations of Gough. This is mainly due to the criticism that Gough's tactical and strategic choices drew: particularly, the idea that he shunned the use of his artillery, and did not make best use of his cavalry. Yet if we turn to China we see a different story. Here Gough did make great use of his artillery. To an extent this was out of his hands as much of his firepower came from the ships of the supporting fleet commanded by Admiral Parker. Yet it would be wrong to ignore the part that his land-based artillery played. One could be forgiven for believing that it was a different Gough that fought the Chinese to the one that fought the Sikhs. This was not simply the way in which he used his artillery. It also included his use of skirmishers, so much so that he raised a special company for the purpose. There was good reconnaissance throughout. Also the organisation of his campaign was far superior. There was good administration and well organised logistics. This was again partly due to the fact that the Royal Navy took care of most of this, and in this regard Parker played the part of 'Gneisenau'. However the role that Major Armine Mountain played as deputy adjutant general should not be underestimated.

There are many factors that account for this difference, from the quality of the opposition to logistics, terrain, technology, and any number of differences in the nature of the two campaigns. Yet there is something deeper than this. Gough used his artillery effectively and efficiently in China. The answer to why he did not appear to effectively use this arm against the Sikhs can be found in the quality of the opposition's artillery. For every battle of the First Sikh War he was either outnumbered or outclassed in terms of artillery. It was not just the number of guns that made the difference, but the fact that they were of larger calibre, firing heavy shot, and were well designed and built. In that regard the usefulness of European, mostly French, mercenaries was important. They allowed the Sikhs to design and build their own guns to the standards of European artillery. Such mercenaries were also important in terms of organisation and training of the Sikh artillery corps. Whereas in China Gough had an overwhelming superiority in artillery both in terms of quality and the way in which the guns were handled, in the Sikh wars he never enjoyed this advantage until Gujrat.

The quality of Sikh artillery is only something that started to become appreciated years after the wars. At the time there was hardly a mention of it, although the quality of the Sikh artillerymen was often praised. It is hard to know what Gough really thought of the use of artillery. The oft quoted line about the artillery ammunition running out during the battle of Sobraon and Gough responding 'Thank God, Then I'll be at them with the bayonet!' can be misconstrued. It could be seen as Gough having distain for this arm of the army, or as him wanting to keep up the morale of his staff and men. If, as appears likely, the message that the ammunition was running out was delivered in rather a panicked manner, then Gough response can certain be seen as giving confidence to his men.

Yet Gough's tactical limitations were only partly attributed to his lack of understanding and use of artillery. There was a wider feeling that he lacked subtlety and guile. In a very real sense this was accurate. Yet the aforementioned character traits were in short supply amongst the officer corps of the British Army of this age, and it would be wrong to unfairly single out Gough for criticism in this regard. Grand sweeping manoeuvres were not his forte, nor were they in truth within his ability to conduct. It is interesting to note the words of Napoleon Bonaparte in regards to the simplicity of war.

The art of war does not need complicated manoeuvre; the simplest are the best, and common sense is fundamental. From which one might wonder why generals make blunders; it is because they try to be clever. The most difficult thing is to guess the enemy's plan, to find the truth from all the reports. The rest merely requires common sense; it is like a boxing match, the more you punch the better it is.[3]

There would be much in the above statement that would chime with the tactical approach of Lord Gough. Yet it would be wrong not to appreciate the subtle nuances of the statement by Napoleon. Perhaps this quote tells us that it takes a genius to call such matters 'simple'. The key point is that it confirms the opinion mentioned previously that Gough was better trusting to what he knew rather than attempting something complicated that might well prove beyond his grasp.

Perhaps a more serious character or leadership fault was the perception that Gough was a reckless commander. There is perhaps a thin line between reckless and courageous. Gough was certainly not afraid to chance his arm. The view that he had expressed when an officer in Spain that, "if a man does not venture, he will never win", was almost the mantra by which he led his military life.[4] At Mudki Gough had followed on so closely behind the infantry advance that only two of his and the governor general's staff were not either killed or wounded. Whilst one historian has referred to this as 'reckless', another could equally describe it as 'courageous'.[5] The point should be made that whilst this was appropriate behaviour for a commander of a battalion, a brigade, or perhaps even a division, it was not what one would expect of a commander-in-chief. Whilst a commander-in-chief of this era would be closer to the action than one of the more modern era, Gough did perhaps take it to the extreme. His courage could never be questioned, but perhaps his prudence can.

Yet to have commanded from afar was not Gough's way. He needed to be near the action both for his own peace of mind, but also because a great deal of his tactical ability relied upon encouragement and confidence. The fact that Gough shared in the hardship and dangers faced by his men is rather glibly mentioned at times. The influence that this had upon the morale and confidence of his men should not be underestimated. Men stood more defiantly, attacked more courageously, because of Gough's presence. It sounds clichéd, but in Gough's case it was also reality. The sight of him, even of just his famous white fighting coat, was a huge boost to morale and encouraged men to acts of bravery above and beyond. As has been alluded to previously, simply the fact that he wore such a distinctive coat was an act of courage. There could be little doubt who the commander-in-chief was and that made him a clear target. In an act of great courage, Gough even used this to his own advantage deliberately drawing the fire of the enemy away from his men and directly onto himself. With such acts and such clear courage it was no wonder that the vast majority of his men loved him and were devoted to him, and fought all the harder because of it.

Whilst we have considered Gough as the military commander we also have to consider the man. Hugh Gough had many fine qualities. He was kind, caring by the standards of the day, brave, determined, resolute, forgiving, and loyal. Yet at the same time he could display great temper, although it often quickly passed, and could be vindictive towards those who he thought had wronged him. He could be vitriolic in his condemnation, yet had the good sense to confide most of this to private correspondence with trusted confidants. Despite this one would not say he had an abundance of tact. Diplomacy was certainly not his calling. Neither had he the mind to play the political game. That is not necessarily to condemn his intelligence but to explain that he had not the gifts or desire

3   Cornwell, Bernard *Waterloo* (London: William Collins, 2014), p. 29.
4   Rait, *Gough*, Vol. I, p. 73. Quoting a letter written by Gough to his wife dated 23 November 1811.
5   Allen, *Soldier Sahibs*, p. 63. Allen believes it to be the former rather than the latter.

to play such a game. It was said of several occasions that he had a soldier's outlook, and thus he was unwilling to get too involved in politics. Like many soldiers he found such matters distasteful.

Gough's kindness was well known, as was his generosity. His failures relating to soldiers pay and pensions in the early day of his career, when he had allowed them too much, should be viewed as acts of misguided kindness rather than neglect or incompetence. Early on in our narrative we mentioned the story of the soldier who Gough had released from the army for bad behaviour, but out of such misguided kindness he had seen that the man had a second chance by incorrectly giving him an honourable rather than a dishonourable discharge. Such acts of kindness were the mark of the man. Such kindness was also to be found in his family life. He had married for love in an age where that was still rare. The Goughs were a devoted couple who remained deeply in love throughout their lives. The family life was also one of love in which the children were cared for and nurtured. Even in later years Gough delighted in the company of his grandchildren and took time to play with them and to continue the nurturing process. Behind the gruff exterior he sometimes portrayed, there was clearly a very caring and compassionate man.

Having read this narrative of Hugh Gough's life and career it is unlikely that any readers will have concluded that Gough was a military genius or even a great commander in chief. The author has not reached that conclusion either. Yet Gough clearly had some talent as a soldier and commander. He was an excellent battalion commander, quite arguably the best in the Peninsular War. That combination of discipline, paternalistic care, determination, and great personal bravery, mean that he stands out in this regard. At this level his administrative ability was good, and his battalion was often in better order than the majority of the army. He was a good brigade commander, and as his time in Ireland shows he was both adaptable and able to combine the different arms of the army. In China he commanded what roughly amounted in size to a division. Whilst commander of the land forces Gough was in fact joint commander of the military operation, with Admiral Parker giving admirable support and experience.

Had Gough risen no higher than divisional command, and seen further service in that capacity, historians might talk of Gough as a good divisional or corps commander who never got the opportunity to test his ability at a higher level. The problem is that Gough did get that opportunity and in many ways was found wanting. Gough was not really the type to be commander-in-chief. He needed to be where the action was. His command style depended upon personal encouragement to his men to overcome the obstacle before them rather than relying on tactical skill, subtlety, or guile to confound an enemy. Although it is easy to condemn such a command style, Gough was far from unique in relying on such a method of command and control, particularly for the era in question and particularly for the British Army.

Part of the problem was that Gough was the product of a bygone age as Britain moved towards the modernity of the late 19th century. His lack of imagination, a presumed reluctance to embrace modern technology and tactics, caused many to be critical of him in a way that would have been less likely 50 years before. Gough was rightly questioned, at times, for high casualties. However those who made such remarks often failed to appreciate the circumstances. Gough's supposed lack of logistical skill and poor staff work does not feature very highly in contemporaneous criticism of Gough's leadership, perhaps demonstrating the continued failure to appreciate the importance of such matters. It is only in later years that this became a major source of criticism.

Gough had been a loyal servant of the British Crown and Empire. Although occasionally feeling that he had been treated unfairly, he never displayed anything but loyalty to his sovereign. As part of the Anglo-Irish community he perhaps felt this loyalty stronger than most. At the same there was his strong identification as an Irishman that would have been rather unfortunate at times during the era in question. Yet Gough never denied his nationality and would proudly proclaim his Irish identity. As a servant of the British Empire this makes him rather anathema in the modern day country of his birth. The unfortunate controversy surrounding the Gough memorial statue had little to do with Gough the man and a great deal to do with Gough the British general. It seems apt, if not entirely fitting, that such a fuss should be made specifically regarding Gough. It seems unfortunate that whilst his statue was desecrated and ultimately had to be removed, the Wellington memorial, which one would feel was a far more fitting target for Irish nationalists, has escaped largely unharmed.

In modern day Britain his reputation fares no better. Like the vast majority of Victorian generals he has largely been forgotten. His Imperial connections, his role in subjugating thousands more to the British Empire, is something that modern British society struggles with and, for the vast majority, it is something that they would rather forget. Gough also struggles because what little is known of him refers to the First Anglo-China War, which retains its link with opium and is often called the Opium War, and to supposed failures during the two Anglo-Sikh Wars. None of this is likely to endear Gough to contemporary audiences.

Gough had served the British Crown to the best of his abilities. He had never held back from sacrifice or danger, he had committed the vast majority of his life to the Army. It is perhaps hard to criticise Gough too strongly for his actions. He was to an extent out of his depth in higher command. Had he been better supported he may well have fared better. Yet his career should certainly not be viewed as having been disastrous or a failure. The only major criticism one can find of his career is in his handling of the two wars against the Sikhs. Although some of the criticism is justified it should not detract from a remarkable career, if only in its longevity, and a life of devoted service to his nation and his monarch.

Bibliography

Archives

Bodleian Library, Oxford
Lord John Russell Letter-Book MS Eng Letters d. 307.
Napier (William) Papers MS Eng Letters c. 251.
Colonel John Sidney North Ms North b. 9, c. 18, d. 29, d.33, e.1, e. 4.[1]

British Library
Allowances of General Sir Hugh Gough during period of service in connection with the China
     Expedition IOR/F/4/2019/90485.
Broadfoot Papers Add MS 40/217.
China Expedition Papers IOR/F/4/2003/89448, IOR/F/4/2027/91544, & IOR/F/4/2055/94009.
Correspondence of Successive Presidents of the Board of Control Add MS 40867, Add Ms 40872,
     Add MS 40874, Add MS 40875, Add MS 40876 & Add MS 40877.[2]
Diary of Robert Needham Cust, Vol III, Add Ms 45392, 64.
Duties in the Garrison of Fort St George by Sir Hugh Gough, Mss Eur F133/58.
Gough Papers MSS Eur A176, Mss Eur C754, and Mss Eur D648.
Hardinge Papers Mss Eur B299 & Mss Eur C655.
India and Bengal Despatches, Correspondence of the Commander-in-Chief IOR/Z/E/4/18.
India and Bengal Despatches, Correspondence of the Commander-in-Chief IOR/Z/E/4/19.
India and Bengal Despatches, Correspondence of the Commander-in-Chief IOR/Z/E/4/20.
Journal kept during the Siege of Multan by Lieutenant George Godfrey Pearse, Mss Eur B115.
Napier (Charles) Papers Add MS 49169.
Thomas Pierce Papers Mss Eur A106, 5.

National Army Museum
Gough Papers 8303–105.
Napier (Charles) Papers 2000–05, 2005–06.
Nicholls Papers 6210–168.

National Archives
China War Correspondence FO 682/1975/2

---

1   Colonel John Sidney North was born John Doyle and was the son of Lt-Gen Sir Charles Doyle, nephew
     of Sir John Doyle founder of the 87th Foot. John Sidney Doyle changed his name to North by Royal
     licence in 1838 to assist in his wife's inheritance of the North Barony.
2   Although technically the papers of President of the Board of Control this collection holds copies of
     Wellington's Peel and Hardinge's correspondence with Gough, most of which is duplicated in the Gough
     papers held at the NAM.

Letter from Chinese representatives FO 682/1975/2.
Parker correspondence with Pottinger FO/705.
Pottinger Papers FO 705/62, FO 705/63.
Earl Granville Papers PRO 30/29/23/11

National Archives of Ireland
State of the Country Papers (SCOP) 1 2512/5, 2516/25, 2614/11, 2614/37.

National Library of Ireland
Gough Correspondence Ms 15, 759.
Gough letter to the Vereker (Gort) Family Ms 21, 967, MS 21, 968.
Gough letters and despatches from the China War Ms 638.
Gough Memorial, Collection of proceedings from Gough Memorial Committee (Dublin: 1879).
National Records of Scotland
RH2/8/69: Folio 26 W.M. Stewart to the Lindesay Family
Private Collection
Correspondence between Hugh and Frances Gough during the Peninsular War in the possession
    of the 5th Viscount Gough.

Newspaper and periodicals

British Parliamentary Papers
Hansard
The Illustrated London News
The Irish Times
The Times

Contemporary Books, Autobiographies, Biographies, and Edited Diaries and Papers

Anglesey, The Marquis of (ed.) *Sergeant Pearman's Memories* (London: Jonathan Cape, 1968).
Anonymous, *India and Lord Ellenborough*, (London: W. H. Dalton, 1844).
Arnold, Edwin, *The Marquis of Dalhousie's Administration of British India*, Vol I (London, Saunders,
    Otley and Co, 1862).
Baird, J. G. A. (ed.), *Private Letters of the Marquis of Dalhousie* (London: William Blackwood &
    Sons, 1910).
Boulger, Demetrius Charles, *History of China* Vol II, (London: W. H. Allen & Co, 1882).
Broadfoot, William, *The Career of George Broadfoot in Afghanistan and the Punjab* (London: John
    Murray, 1888).
Bruce, William Napier, *Life of General Sir Charles Napier* (London: John Murray, 1885).
Bunbury, Major Thomas, *Reminiscences of a Veteran* (London: C. J. Skeet, 1861).
Burton, Reginald George, *The First and Second Sikh Wars: An Official British Army History* (Reprinted
    paperback of 1911 original, Yardley, Pennsylvania: Westholme Publishing, 2007).
Cannon, Richard, *Historical Record of the 22nd Foot*, (London: Parker, Furnivall and Parker, 1849).
——— *Historical Record of the Eighty-Seventh Regiment*, (London: Eyre & Spottiswoode, 1853).
Coley, Rev. J., *Journal of the Sutlej Campaign 1845–6* (London: Smith, Elder, 1856).
Cooper, Leonard, *Havelock*, (London: The Bodley Head, 1957).
Durand, Henry Mortimer, *The Life of Major-General Sir Henry Marion Durand* (London: W. H.
    Allen & Co, 1883).

Edwardes, Herbert, *A Year on the Punjab Frontier in 1848–49*, Vol II (London: Richard Bentley, 1851).

Ellenborough, Lord & Colchester, Lord (editor)*History of the India Administration of Lord Ellenborough in his correspondence with the Duke of Wellington*, (London: Richard Bentley and Son, 1874).

Forrest, G. W. *The Life of Field Marshal Sir Neville Chamberlain* (London: Blackwood & Sons, 1909).

Gough, Charles, & Innes, Arthur. D., *The Sikhs and the Sikh Wars* (London: A. D. Innes & Co, 1897).

Grant, Isabel Frances *Extracts from the Army Quarterly: Everyday Letters Written During the First and Second Sikh War* Vol X, No. 2, July 1825 (London: Army Quarterly, 1925).

Hall, W. H. & Bernard, W. D., *Narrative of the voyages and services of the Nemesis*, (London: Henry Colburn, 1845).

Hardinge, Charles, *Rulers of India: Viscount Hardinge*, (Oxford: Clarendon Press, 1891).

——*Viscount Hardinge and the advance of the British dominions into the Punjab* (Oxford: Clarendon Press, 1900).

Hodson, William, S. R. & Hodson, George, H. *Hodson of Hodson Horse: Twelve Years of a Soldier's Life in India* (London: Kegan Paul, Trench & Co, 1889).

Humphries, James, *The Hero of Aliwal: The Campaigns of Sir Harry Smith in India 1843–1846* (York, Leonaur Ltd, 2007).

Hunter, Sir William *The Marquis of Dalhousie: And the Final Development of the Company's Rule* (Oxford: Clarendon Press, 1895).

James, William *Naval History of Great Britain* Vol I (London: Harding, Lepard & Co, 1826).

Law, Edward, 1st Earl of Ellenborough, *History of the Indian Administration of Lord Ellenborough, in his correspondence with the Duke of Wellington*, (London: R. Bentley & Son, 1874).

Lawrence, George, *Forty-Three Years in India* (London: John Murray, 1874).

Lawrence, Rosamond, *Charles Napier: Friend and Fighter 1782–1853* (London: John Murray, 1952).

Lawrence-Archer, Captain John Henry, *Commentaries on the Punjab Campaign, 1848–9* (London: W. H. Allen & Co, 1878).

Lee-Warner, William, *The Life of the Marquis of Dalhousie* Vol I (London: Macmillan & Co Ltd, 1904).

Lehmann, Joseph H. *Remember you are an Englishman: A Biography of Sir Harry Smith 1787–1860* (London, Jonathan Cape, 1977).

Malleson, Bruce, *Decisive Battles of India*, (London: W. H. Allen & Co, 1883).

Marsham, John Clark, *The Memoirs of Major General Sir Henry Havelock* (London: Longman, Green, Longman & Roberts, 1860).

Mountain, Mrs Armine (editor), *The Memoirs and Letters of the late Colonel Armine S.H. Mountain* (London: Longman, Brown, Green, Longmans & Roberts, 1858).

Napier, H. D., *Field Marshal Lord Napier of Magdala: A Memoir* (London: Edward Arnold & Co, 1927).

Napier, Robert, *Personal Narrative written shortly after the Actions of Moodkee and Feroze-shuhur by Captain R. Napier, Bengal Engineers*, (Hertford: Printed for private information only, 1873).

Napier, William, *General Sir Charles Napier and the Directors of the East India Company* (London: C. Westerton, 1857).

——*The History of the War In the Peninsular* VI Volumes(London: G Routledge, 1828–1840).

——*The Life and Opinions of General Sir Charles James Napier*, Vol IV (London: John Murray, 1857).

Peel, Sir Robert, *Speeches of Sir Robert Peel, delivered in the House of Commons*, Vol IV, (London: George Routledge & Co, 1853).

Phillimore, Augustus, *The Life of Admiral of the Fleet Sir William Parker, Vol II*, (London: Harrison, 1879).

Rait, Robert, *The Life and Campaigns of Hugh First Viscount Gough Field-Marshal* Vol I & II (London: Archibald Constable & Co, 1903).

—— *The Life of Field Marshal Sir Frederick Paul Haines*, (London: Constable & Co, 1911).

Shadwell, Lawrence, *The Life of Colin Campbell, Lord Clyde*, Vol I (London: William Blackwood & Sons, 1881).

Singh, Bawa Satinder (ed.), *The Letters of the First Viscount Hardinge of Lahore to Lady Hardinge and Sir Walter and Lady James, 1844–1847* (London: Office of the Royal Historical Society, University College London, 1986).

Smith, Sir Harry & Moore Smith, G. C. (ed.), *The Autobiography of Lieutenant-General Sir Harry Smith* Vol II (London: John Murray, 1902).

Thackwell, Edward, J *Narrative of the Second Seikh War*, in 1848–49 (London: Richard Bentley, 1851).

Thomas, R. N. W. (ed.), 'Daniel George Robinson: Letters from India 1845–1849'in Guy, Alan (ed.), *Military Miscellany I : Manuscripts from the Seven Years war, the First and Second Sikh Wars, and the First World War* (Stroud: Sutton Publishing for the Army Records Society, 1996).

Trotter, L. J., *The Life of Hodson of Hodson's Horse* (London: J. M. Dent & Sons, 1912).

Unknown, *The War in India: The Despatches of Viscount Hardinge, Lord Gough & Sir Harry Smith* (London; John Ollivier and Ackermann & Co, 1846).

Wilson, William John, *History of the Madras Army* Five Volumes (Madras, Government Press, 1882–1889).

Wylly, H. C., *The Military Memoirs of Lieutenant-General Sir Joseph Thackwell* (London: John Murray, 1908).

Later Published Sources – Books

Allen, Charles, *Soldier Sahibs: The Men who made the North-West Frontier* (London: John Murray, 2000).

Atkinson, C. T., *The South Wales Borders, 24th Foot 1689–1937* (Cambridge: Regimental History Committee, University of Cambridge, 1937).

Bajwa, Fauja Singh, *Military System of the Sikhs during the period 1799–1849* (Delhi: Motilal Banarasidas, 1964).

Bamford, Andrew *Sickness, Suffering, and the Sword: The British Regiment on Campaign 1805–1815* (Norman, Oklahoma: University of Oklahoma Press, 2013).

Barthorp, Michael, *The British Army on Campaign 1816–1853*, (London: Osprey Publishing, 1987).

Bartlett, Thomas & Jeffrey, Keith, *A Military History of Ireland* (Cambridge: Cambridge University Press, 1996).

Beeching, Jack, *The Chinese Opium Wars* (London: Hutchinson & Co, 1975).

Beckett, Ian, *The Victorians at War* (London: Hambeldon & London, 2003).

Bond, Brian (ed), *Victorian Military Campaigns* (London: Hutchinson & Co, Ltd, 1967).

Bosworth-Smith, Reginald, *Life of Lawrence*, Vol I, (London: Smith, Elder, & Co, 1901).

Brereton, J. M., *A History of the Royal Regiment of Wales (24th/41st Foot) 1689–1989* (Cardiff, Published by the Regiment, 1989).

Bruce, George *Six Battles for India* (Calcutta: Rupa & Co, 1969).

Cardew, Lieutenant F. G., *A Sketch of the Services of the Bengal Native Army to the Year 1895* (Calcutta: Office of the Superintendent of the Government of India, 1903).

Chandler, David, *Dictionary of the Napoleonic Wars* (New York: Simon & Schuster, 1993).

Churchill, Winston. S, *A Roving Commission: My Early Life*, (New York: Charles Scribner's Sons, 1930).

Cook, H. C. B., *The Sikh Wars 1845–6 & 1848–9* (London: Leo Cooper, 1975).

Cunliffe, Marcus, *The Royal Irish Fusiliers 1793–1950* (London: Oxford University Press, 1952).

David, Saul, *Victoria's Wars: The Rise of Empire* (London: Viking, 2006).

Dixon, Norman, *On the Psychology of Military Incompetence*, (London: Jonathan Cape, 1976).

Donnelley, James S. *Captain Rock: The Irish Agrarian Rebellion 1821–1824* (Cork: The Collins Press, 2009).

Edwards, Peter, *Talavera: Wellington's Early Peninsular Victories 1808–9* (Ramsbury, Wilts.: The Crowood Press Ltd, 2005).

Esdaile, Charles, *The Peninsular War: A New History* (London: Allen Lane, 2002).

Farwell, Byron, *Eminent Victorian Generals: Seekers of Glory*, (New York, W, W. Norton & Co, 1985).

—— *Queen Victoria's Little Wars* (London: Allen Lane, 1973).

Featherstone, Donald, *At them with the Bayonet! : The First Sikh War* (London: Jarrolds, 1968).

—— *Colonial Small Wars, 1837–1901*, (Newton Abbott: David & Charles, 1973).

—— *Weapons & Equipment of the Victorian Soldier* (Poole: Blandford Press, 1978)

Fedorak, Charles John, *Henry Addington, Prime Minister, 1801–1804: Peace, War and Parliamentary Politics* (Akron, Ohio: University of Akron Press, 2002).

Field, Andrew. W., *Talavera: Wellington's First Victory in Spain* (Barnsley: Pen & Sword, 2006).

Fletcher, Ian, *Peninsular War: Aspects of the struggle for the Iberian Peninsula* (Staplehurst: Spellmount, 1998).

Fortescue, Sir John, *History of the British Army*, Vol II (London: Macmillan & Co, 1899).

Gates, David, *The Spanish Ulcer: A History of the Peninsular War* (London: Pimlico, 2002).

Gaunt, Richard A., *Sir Robert Peel: The Life and Legacy* (London: I.B. Tauris, 2010).

Gash, Norman, *Sir Robert Peel: The life of Sir Robert Peel after 1830* (London: Longman Group Ltd, 1972).

Gelber, Harry G., *Opium, Soldiers, and Evangelists: Britain's 1840–42 War with China* (New York: Palgrave Macmillan, 2004)

Glover, Michael, *The Peninsular War, 1807–1914* (Newton Abbot: David and Charles, 1974).

—— *Wellington As Military Commander*, (London: Penguin Books, 2001).

Guedalla, Phillip, The Duke (London: Hodder and Stoughton, 1931).

Harfield, Alan, *British and Indian Armies on the China Coast 1785–1985* (Farnham: A and J Partnership, 1990).

Haythornthwaite, Phillip, *The Armies of Wellington* (London: Arms and Armour Press, 1994).

—— *The Colonial Wars Source Book* (London: Arms and Armour Press, 1995).

—— *The Napoleonic Source Book* (London: Arms and Armour Press, 1990).

—— *The Peninsular War: The Complete Companion to the Iberian Campaigns 1807–14*, (London: Brassey's, 2004)

Heath, Ian, *The Sikh Army 1799–1849* (Oxford: Osprey Publishing, 2005).

Heathcote, T. A., *The Military in British India: The Development of British Land Force in South Asia 1600–1947* (Manchester: Manchester University Press, 1995).

Hoe, Susanna & Roebuck, Derek, *The Taking of Hong Kong* (London: Curzon Press, 1999).

Holmes, Richard, *Sahib: The British Soldier in India, 1750–1914*, (London: Harper Collins, 2005).

Holt, Edgar, *The Opium Wars in China* (London: Putnam & Co Ltd, 1964).

Hurd, Douglas, *Robert Peel: A Biography* (London: Weidenfeld & Nicholson, 2007).

Inglis, Bryan, *The Opium War* (London, Hodder & Stoughton 1976).

James, Lawrence, *Raj: The Making and Unmaking of British India* (London: Abacus Books, 1998).

Jourdain, Lt-Col H. F. N., *The Connaught Rangers* Vol I (London, Royal United Service Institution, 1924).

Judd, Denis, Empire: *The British Imperial Experience from 1765 to the present* (London: Harper Collins, 1996).

—— *The Lion and the Tiger: The Rise and Fall of the British Raj, 1600–1947* (Oxford: Oxford University Press, 2004)

Keay, John, *The Honourable Company: A History of the English East India Company* (London: Harper Collins, 1991)

Kingston, W. H. G., *Blow the Bugle Draw the Sword: The Wars, Campaigns, Regiments and Soldiers of the British & Indian Armies during the Victorian Era, 1839–1898* (York: Leonaur Ltd, 2007).

Knight, Ian, *Go to Your God Like a Soldier: The British Soldier Fighting for Empire 1837–1902* (London: Greenhill Book, 1996).

Kumar, Virendra, *India Under Lord Hardinge* (New Delhi: Rjesh Publishing, 1978).

Lawson, Phillip, *The East India Company: A History 1600–1857* (London: Longman, 1993).

Lloyd, T. O., *The British Empire 1558–1983* (Oxford: Oxford University Press, 1984).

Lovell, Julia, *The Opium War: Drugs, Dreams, and the making of China* (London: Picador, 2011).

Mason, Phillip, *A Matter of Honour: an Account of the Indian Army its Officers and Men*, (London: Macmillan Publishers Ltd, 1986).

—— *The Men Who Ruled India* (London: Pan Books, 1987).

Oman, Charles *History of the Peninsular War* VII Volumes (Oxford: Clarendon Press, 1911).

Peers, Douglas. M, *Between Mars and Mammon: Colonial armies and the garrison state in early nineteenth century India* (London: Tauris academic Studies, 1995).

—— *India Under Colonial Rule: 1700 to 1885* (Harlow: Pearson Longman, 2006).

Pollock, John, *Way to Glory: The Life of Havelock of Lucknow* (London: John Murry, 1957).

Pottinger, George, *Sir Henry Pottinger: First Governor of Hong Kong* (Stroud: Sutton Publishing, 1997).

Ralston, David, *Importing the European Army: The introduction of European military techniques and institutions in the Extra-European world, 1600–1914* (Chicago: University of Chicago Press, 1990).

Robins, Nick, *The Corporation that Changed the World: How the East India Company shaped the modern multinational* (London: Pluto Press, 2012)

Robinson, C. W., *Wellington's Campaigns: Peninsular to Waterloo 1808–15*, Part III (London: Hugh Rees Ltd, 1905).

Rogers, H. C. B., *Artillery Through the Ages* (London: Military Book Society, 1971).

—— *The British Army of the Eighteenth Century* (London: Allen & Unwin, 1977).

Rosen, Stephen, *Societies and military Power: India and its Armies* (New York: Cornell University Press, 1996).

Roy, Kaushik, *Military Manpower, Armies and Warfare in South Asia* (London: Taylor & Francis, 2013).

—— *War and Society in Colonial India, 1807–1945* (Oxford: Oxford University Press, 2006).

—— *War Culture and Society in Early Modern South Asia, 1740–1849* (Abingdon: Routledge, 2011).

Selby, John, *The Paper Dragon: An Account of the China Wars* (London: Arthur Baker Ltd, 1968).

Sidhu, Amarpal, *The First Anglo-Sikh War* (Stroud: Amberley Publishing, 2010).

Singh, Fauja, *The Military System of the Sikhs 1799–1849* (Delhi: Motilal Banarsidass, 1964).

Singh, Khushwant, *A History of the Sikhs: 1469–1838*, Vol I (London: Oxford University Press, 2004).

Singh Madra, Amandeep & Singh, Parmjit, *Warrior Saints: Four Centuries of Sikh Military History*, Vol I (London; Kashi House, 2013).

Singh, Patwant & Rai, Jyoti, *Empire of the Sikhs: The Life and Times of Mahraja Ranjit Singh* (London: Peter Owen Publishers, 2008).

Singh Bansal, Bobby, *Remnants of the Sikh Empire: Historical Monuments in India and Pakistan* (New Delhi: Hay House Publishers India, 2015).

Smyth, Hazel P., *The Town on the Road: The Story of Booterstown* (Bray, Ireland: Pale Publishing, 1994).

Strachan, Hew, *From Waterloo to Balaclava: Tactics, Technology, and the British Army 1815–1854* (Cambridge: Cambridge University Press, 1985).

—— *The Reform of the British Army 1830–54* (Manchester: Manchester University Press, 1984).

Streets, Heather, *Martial races: The military, race and masculinity in British Imperial culture, 1857–1914* (Manchester: Manchester University Press, 2004).

Sweetman, John, *Raglan: From the Peninsular to the Crimea* (London: Arms and Armour Press, 1993).

Later Published Sources – Articles

Bowers, Rick, 'Lieutenant Charles Cameron's Opium War Diary', *Journal of the Royal Asiatic Society Hong Kong Branch*, 1 January 2012, Vol.52, pp. 29–61.

Crowell, Lorenzo, 'Military Professionalism in a Colonial Context: The Madras Army', *Modern Asian Studies*, 24, 1990, pp. 249–273.

Hao, Gao 'Prelude to the Opium War? British Reactions to the 'Napier Fizzle' and attitudes towards China in the mid-eighteen thirties', *Historical Research*, August 2014, Vol.87(237), pp. 491–509.

Hill, Katrina, 'Collecting on Campaign: British Soldiers in China during the Opium Wars', *Journal of the History of Collections*, 2013, Vol.25(2), pp. 227–252.

Mclean, David, 'Surgeons of the Opium War: The Navy on the China Coast', *The English Historical Review*, 2006, Vol. CXXI(491), pp. 487–504.

Melancon, Glenn, 'Honour in Opium? The British Declaration of War on China, 1839–1840' *The International History Review*, 01 December 1999, Vol.21(4), pp. 855–874.

Nicholls, Mark, 'A Surgeon in the Second Sikh War: Ludovick Stewarts Account of the Battle of Chillianwala', *Journal of the Society for Army Historical Research* LXXI, 1993, pp. 216–225.

Peers, Douglas, 'Between Mars and Mammon: The East India Company and Efforts to Reform its Army, 1796–1832', *Historical Journal*, 33, 1990, pp. 385–401.

—— 'Colonial Knowledge and the Military in India, 1780–1816', *Journal of Imperial and Commonwealth History*, 33, 2005, pp. 157–180.

—— ' "The Habitual Nobility of Being": British Officers and the Social Construction of the Bengal Army in the Early Nineteenth Century', *Modern Asian Studies*, 25, 1991, pp. 545–569.

Sheringham, Michael, 'The Opium War: Drugs, Dreams and the Making of China', Asian Affairs, 1 November 2012, Vol.43 (3), pp. 521–523.

Singh, Bawa Satinder, 'Raja Gulab Singh's Role in the First Anglo-Sikh War', *Modern Asian Studies*, 1971, Vol 5, pp. 35–59.

Index

Index of People

Index of Places

Index of Military Formations & Units

Index of Ships

Index of General & Miscellaneous Terms

Lightning Source UK Ltd.
Milton Keynes UK
UKOW07n1649090917
308882UK00004B/15/P